Networked Sociability and Individualism:

Technology for Personal and Professional Relationships

Francesca Comunello
Sapienza University of Rome, Italy

Information Science
REFERENCE

Managing Director:	Lindsay Johnston
Senior Editorial Director:	Heather Probst
Book Production Manager:	Sean Woznicki
Development Manager:	Joel Gamon
Development Editor:	Myla Harty
Acquisitions Editor:	Erika Gallagher
Typesetters:	Chris Shearer, Mackenzie Snader
Print Coordinator:	Jamie Snavely
Cover Design:	Nick Newcomer

Published in the United States of America by
Information Science Reference (an imprint of IGI Global)
701 E. Chocolate Avenue
Hershey PA 17033
Tel: 717-533-8845
Fax: 717-533-8661
E-mail: cust@igi-global.com
Web site: http://www.igi-global.com

Library of Congress Cataloging-in-Publication Data

Networked sociability and individualism: technology for personal and professional relationships / Francesca Comunello, editor.
p. cm.
Includes bibliographical references and index.
ISBN 978-1-61350-338-6 (hardcover) -- ISBN 978-1-61350-339-3 (ebook) -- ISBN 978-1-61350-340-9 (print & perpetual access) 1. Internet--Social aspects. 2. Social media. 3. Interpersonal relations. I. Comunello, Francesca.
HM851.N4767 2012
303.48'33--dc22
2011014352

British Cataloguing in Publication Data
A Cataloguing in Publication record for this book is available from the British Library.

All work contributed to this book is new, previously-unpublished material. The views expressed in this book are those of the authors, but not necessarily of the publisher.

Table of Contents

Section 2
SNS, Relational Patterns, and Identity Performances: New Research Trends

Section 3
Social Media and Institutions: New Research Trends

Detailed Table of Contents

The chapter discusses the emergence of social media, especially wiki environments, as collaborative knowledge tools that function within a given set of individualistic and community-oriented cultural and functional constraints. The chapter provides the reader with an understanding of wiki social functions and technical capabilities and of the main value and cultural promises associated with them. It also examines the social and knowledge production challenges they create and their likely impact on knowledge production in an individual and community setting. One main conclusion of the chapter is that wiki technologies need to be understood not as an overcoming of the tension between individualism and community, but as a product of their conflict, which they epitomize.

This chapter argues for the rigid dichotomies between online and offline in current discourse on social interactions to be reconsidered. By identifying that space is produced by the intersection of interactions it can be said that online and offline narratives are situated relationally rather than dichotomously. Drawing on the concept of affordances (Gibson, 1977, 1986; Norman, 1988; Hogan, 2009) and the work of Doreen Massey (1994, 2005, 2009), it can be shown that subjects act on perceived affordances in narratives of online and offline relations which intersect to produce the spaces in which social interactions are situated. This chapter proposes the concept of 'networked spaces' as a strategy for resolving the problematic binary of online and offline. Networked spaces are dynamic, the contexts or narratives within them relational. It is through the lived experiences of interactions in these spaces that the contexts of social interactions are suggested to be best examined.

Preface

Networked individualism is a social pattern, not a collection of isolated individuals. (Castells, 2001, p. 131)

The younger sister of a close friend of mine recently returned to Rome after a period spent abroad (on the Erasmus exchange program). As is fairly normal among Erasmus students, she fell in love with a young man living abroad. When she was providing me with some of the details of her romance, face-to-face and mediated interactions between the couple were given the same importance: she mentioned hour-long conversations that took place on Skype, Facebook messages that were exchanged throughout the day, and an extensive use of the mobile phone (both for coordinating their meetings and negotiating their meanings).

Over dinner, I heard myself saying: "When I was on my Erasmus program, 12 years ago, I did not have a mobile phone, while Facebook and Skype simply didn't exist." We did have emails, but we had to be at home or at university to check them. Some of my fellow students already had a cell phone (it was mainly a matter of who could afford them), and only a small minority of us were using instant messaging platforms.

Even if some major applications (such as Facebook or Skype) were conceived later on, communication technology already existed. What has changed completely, over the past 10 or 15 years, is the way in which common people use technology: the way it is integrated in our everyday lives, especially with regard to personal communication. Portable devices and wireless connectivity offer new environments in which people can manage their personal relationships, allowing people to maintain long distance ties more easily, by staying in touch throughout the day. Moreover, *multitasking* practices allow people to experiment with multiple relationship patterns, both on and offline, by offering them forms of *social presence* that do not necessarily imply exclusivity (I can be chatting with more than one friend, while at the same time talking at the phone and/or sending emails; moreover, we can experience lighter forms of social presence at a distance, where our presence often only consists of having an open channel for communication, and we may not even be continuously talking to our contacts).

By the time I was on my Erasmus program, scholars had already begun to explore the characteristics of the "network society" (Castells, 1996) and the transformation of social patterns that has led to "networked individualism" (Wellman, 1999). In the subsequent years, digital technology has become increasingly integrated in common people's everyday lives, becoming an even more important tool for the management of personal relationships. This book explores some of the main characteristics of digitally-mediated sociability.

INTRODUCING NETWORKED SOCIABILITY AND INDIVIDUALISM

The aim of this introductory chapter is to offer a brief overview of the main conceptual perspectives that are shared by all of the chapters in this volume. I will therefore briefly introduce Wellman and Castells' understanding of networked individualism and networked sociability, describing the shift from communities to networks and underlining that networked individualism does not lead to isolation, but instead gives rise to new patterns of sociability. I will then focus on the "online vs. offline" dichotomy, which is still widely adopted, both by scholars and by mainstream media: as digital media are embedded in our everyday lives, the "online vs. offline" dichotomy is quite useless, both from a theoretical and an empirical point of view. Even if they can primarily be observed in online environments, the processes that are described in this book are not *determined* by technology. Technology, instead, offers powerful environments that *enable* people to manage their identity performances and their relationships. Each digitally-mediated platform offers specific *affordances* that contribute to the construction of unique communication environments. Social network sites (SNS), for instance, are powerful playgrounds, both for the user and for the researcher. After a brief overview of the international literature on SNS, I will focus on some of the recent research trends surrounding this topic. In the age of the *convergence culture,* however, the phenomena which need to be addressed are wider than SNS, and include the wide variety of ways in which people are linked to each other. In the final part of this introductory chapter, I will briefly present each chapter of this book, also mentioning the theoretical and methodological options that have guided this choice of chapters.

From Communities to Networks: A Brief Overview of Networked Individualism and Networked Sociability

In late modern societies (Giddens, 1991), identity performances and social relations are increasingly being understood through the frameworks of *networked individualism* and *networked sociability.* Far from being immersed in densely-knit groups or *communities*, people are instead leaving the "little boxes" they used to live in (Wellman uses the term "little boxes" to refer to the group-based societies in which people's homes, neighborhoods and workgroups used to play a major role; Wellman, 1999, p. 1) and are moving towards a "network society."

The concept of "community" has a long theoretical history. According to Bauman, the very concept of community, based on early formulations by classic sociologists such as Toennies, evokes "everything we miss and what we lack to be secure, confident and trusting" (2001, p. 3). Many definitions can be found for "community," both in sociological literature and in public discourse (Baym, 2010, p. 74). Although urban sociologists have argued, from the late 1970s onwards, that community should be understood independently of the physical neighborhood (Wellman, 1979), the "community question" arises periodically in scientific literature (for a recent reconceptualization, see Hennig, 2007).

In contemporary societies, community has to be understood in a "weak" sense, as referring to a culture and a set of ideas, rather than a physical place (see Parks, 2011, p. 107), as intended by Anderson (1991) when he proposed the idea of an "imagined community." Following on from this perspective, the widespread debate on "virtual communities" arose in the early 1990s, following Rheingold's (1993) proposals.

While intriguing, and able to capture the zeitgeist of the emerging online world (Parks, 2011, p. 105), the term "virtual community" can be somewhat misleading, if it is understood as the main pattern of sociability to be found online, both because of the term "community" and because of the term "virtual" (I will elaborate on the opposition between virtual and real later in this chapter). Both on and offline, communities can arise as specific patterns, but are not to be understood as the dominant form of sociability (Parks, 2011; Baym, 2010). Most of the time, and in most contexts, people are immersed in sparsely-knit self-centred networks, rather than in densely-knit communities (Wellman, 2001); nevertheless, personal networks can also include densely-knit groups (Boase & Wellman, 2006).

Moving from *place-to-place* towards *person-to-person* and *role-to-role* connectivity, "the person becomes the portal" (Wellman, 2001). Such a shift in the nature of social relationships has been facilitated by both mass transit and telecommunication systems. According to Boase and Wellman (2006), these social relationships have at least three important attributes: "(1) Relationships are both local and long distance; (2) Personal networks are sparsely-knit but include densely-knit groups; (3) Relationships are more easily formed and abandoned" (Boase & Wellman, 2006, p. 718).

These three elements have been used by Wellman over the past decade to define networked individualism. Boase and Wellman (2006) have further elaborated on this model by adding two more characteristics: "(4) While homophily still exists, many relationships are with people from different social backgrounds; (5) Some social ties are strong, but many more are weak" (Boase & Wellman, 2006, p. 718).

In a context where networks are becoming increasingly personal (Wellman, 2007), it is the individual's responsibility to activate and manage his or her own relational networks, thereby continuously switching between the different roles he or she plays in everyday life (with family, and in his or her personal or professional life, etc.). The individual has become "the primary unit of connectivity [...]. Each person is a switchboard, between ties and networks. People remain connected, but as individuals rather than being rooted in the home bases of work units and households" (Wellman & Haythornthwaite, 2002, p. 34).

Our societies have experienced an overall shift toward individualism. In this context, the following are the three main elements that have contributed to the rise of networked individualism: the personalization of communication flows (facilitated by increasingly personal and ubiquitous digital technology), ranging from one-to-one communication to what Castells defines as *mass self-communication* (Castells, 2009); the privatization of sociability; and role-to-role connectivity.

According to this perspective, however, individualism does not lead to social isolation, nor to the atomization of individuals. Through their personal networks, people negotiate and obtain support, information and a sense of belonging (Wellman & Haythornthwaite, 2002, p. 34). In other words, they also experiment with new forms of sociability, but they are more likely to experience them as individuals, rather than as part of a broader group.

The culture of individualism does not lead to isolation, but it changes the patterns of sociability in terms of increasingly selective and self directed contacts. [...] The critical matter is not technology, but the development of networks of sociability based on choice and affinity, breaking the organizational and spatial boundaries of relationships [...]. Networked sociability leads both to an individual-centered network, specific to the individual, and to peer-group formation, when the network becomes the context of behavior for its participants. (Castells et al., 2007, pp. 143-144)

While sociability and sociality may appear to be synonymous, sociability can be defined as "the ability to perform the social behaviors that lead to sociality" (Papacharissi, 2011, p. 316). Networked sociability emerges as a specific social pattern, both leading to ego-centred networks and to the formation of peer groups. It is enabled by multiple sets of environments, both digitally-mediated and not; digital media, and so-called social media in particular, however, appear to have a central role in enhancing this particular type of sociability. Their affordances "permit persons to maintain the individuality of their private sphere as they traverse to sociality" (Papacharissi, 2011, p. 317).

A deeper understanding of networked individualism and sociability requires a knowledge of the multifaceted concept of *identity*. As many scholars have pointed out (Goffman, 1959; Giddens, 1991; Thompson, 1995; Buckingham, 2008), contemporary identity has to be seen as a process, or as a performance. In this tension between a process-based understanding of identity and the opposing viewpoint, according to which an individual identity is consistent and stable over time, resides what Buckingham (2008) defines as "the paradox of identity." While the Latin root of the word "identity" (*idem*) means "the same," "the term nevertheless both implies similarity and difference" (Buckingham, 2008, p. 1). The self can be described as a "reflexively organized symbolic project" (Thompson, 1995, p. 233), or, in Buckingham's words: "identity is something we do rather than simply something we *are*" (Buckingham, 2008, p. 8).

Following this framework, the individual side of identity cannot be separated from the social aspect: identity is a social process (R. Jenkins, 2008). In accordance with this belief, while observing the self in so-called social media, Papacharissi has pointed out that "individual and collective identities are simultaneously presented and promoted" in such environments (Papacharissi, 2011, p. 305). Baym underlines the role of both individual and social identity in the self-presentation processes that people perform in digital media (Baym, 2010, pp. 105, 111).

Even before digital technology became widespread, scholars had underlined the central role of the media in identity formation processes (Thompson, 1995; Meyrowitz, 1983), as the (mass) media provide "mediated experience," to be incorporated "reflexively into the process of self formation" (Thompson, 1995, p. 233). As we will see in the following paragraph, social media develop this process even further, contributing a great deal to the process of self-formation, together with "older" media and "lived experience" (Thompson, 1995).

BEYOND THE ONLINE VS. OFFLINE DICHOTOMY

When faced with each new communication technology, from writing to the Internet, people have always tended to react in a polarized fashion. Some of them express fears and concerns about the consequences that the new communication tool may have on personal relations, culture and society as a whole, young people and learning processes, while others tend to draw an enthusiastic picture of the "new world" that could be achieved through the adoption of new technologies. As people become more familiar with new technologies, such polarities become weaker, and "we come to see [new communication media] in more nuanced ways. Eventually they become so taken for granted they are all but invisible" (Baym, 2010, p. 1).

The same is happening with regard to the Internet, and especially to those digital environments that can be used as tools for personal communication. Through the work of Wellman (2004; 2011), we can identify three ages of Internet studies. In the first age of Internet studies (1995-1998), which was strongly affected by *presentism* and *parochialism*, *utopians* saw the Internet as a "bright light shining above everyday concerns. It was a technological marvel, thought to be bringing a new Enlightenment to transform the world" (Wellman, 2011, p. 18). On the other hand, *dystopians* worried that the Internet could "disconnect [...] us from each other" (Wellman, 2011, p. 19). In this first age, opinions were rarely based on social science knowledge. Moreover, it was commonly believed that what happened on the Internet (in terms of identity performances and social relations) could be explained in terms of the online world alone, without paying attention to the broader context in which people lived.

While the digital divide still constitutes a major issue, especially for non-Western countries (for a comprehensive analysis of the digital divide, see Warschauer, 2003; Wilson, 2004; van Dijk, 2005; Ferro et al., 2010), in subsequent years, the Internet was rapidly adopted, and digital technology progressively became a part of the everyday life of a growing number of the global population (Wellman & Haythornthwaite, 2002; Bakardjieva, 2005; Bakardjieva, 2011). At the same time, scholars started to carry out systematic research, recognising that "neither the utopian hopes [...] nor the dystopian fears [...] have been borne out" (Wellman, 2011, p. 20). Technology is not disconnecting us from each other, as early dystopians feared; nor is it creating world-wide democracy and wealth, as predicted in many utopian visions. We are now living in the third age of Internet studies (2004 to the present day), in a "world of ordinary people routinely using the Internet" (Wellman, 2011, p. 20). Social researchers are now focusing on the relations between online and offline sociability, in an attempt to understand the specific affordances of each digital environment that help people to become "a communication and information switchboard, between persons, networks, and institutions" (Wellman, 2011, p. 22). Nevertheless, echoes of both utopian and dystopian claims are still to be found in public opinion, and mainly in broadcast media.

Both early utopians and dystopians based their opinions on the assumption that online and offline environments should be considered as completely separate worlds, moving from a "deep confusion about what is virtual – that which seems real but is ultimately a mere simulation – and what is real" (Baym, 2011, p. 5). In theoretical terms, as proposed by Lévy (1995), "virtual" is not the opposite of "real," but of "actual." Moreover, the degree of "reality" of any communicative act, in terms of emotional or cognitive value, cannot be determined by assessing the delivery system which it adopts. It depends, mainly, on the subjective perceptions of the people involved, and on the value which they attribute to any specific communicative act.

Furthermore, both utopian and dystopian critics implicitly adopted a technologically deterministic perspective, focusing on the consequences of Internet adoption and use, and failing to consider, instead, "what people do with mediated communication" (Baym, 2010, p. 59), what contexts they are living in, what purposes they are pursuing and the mixture of media which they adopt in personal communication.

The processes described above (the shift from communities to networks, the rise of networked individualism and of networked sociability) are not determined by technology. Technology, instead, *enables* each person to build and manage their own social networks, both on and offline. Technology facilitates such processes by providing tools that are increasingly personalized, portable, and ubiquitous; these transformations, however, are clearly rooted in broader social phenomena.

As Jensen points out, in the early years of Internet studies, the divide between online and offline practices "may have been a necessary step for theory development" (Jensen, 2011, p. 43). As the Internet has become a part of our everyday lives, however, it "has become increasingly counter-productive in methodological terms" (Jensen, 2011, p. 43). Even if we still experience the "popular mythology of the digital boom, promising a placeless, raceless, bodyless future," Rybas and Gajjala have shown that, when interacting with others online, people cannot "escape real world identity completely," as each of us is shaped by the ways in which race and other characteristics affect us offline (Rybas & Gajjala, 2007).

Therefore, we need to abandon our dichotomous vision, and adopt a more nuanced one: "we cannot really separate our being online from being offline, because online and offline are not discrete entities" (Gajjala, 2009, p. 61; for a broader debate on this topic, see Orgad, 2009 or Bakardjieva, 2009).

Moreover, as technology becomes increasingly ubiquitous and portable, the practices of multitasking lead us to experience both an online and an offline presence simultaneously. This happens explicitly when we use geosocial networks (digital environments aimed at integrating the physical location of the user with his or her online activity), but also each time we use a digital device while situated in an offline context.

Moreover, in the age of the *convergence culture* (Jenkins, 2006), we cannot separate what we do with one medium from what we do with another. Nor can we strictly separate so-called "old" media from "new" ones. People are continuously – and seamlessly – shifting from offline contexts to online ones, from mediated to non-mediated experiences, and from one platform to another.

When it comes to personal relationships, there are two main elements to be considered in order to overcome the online vs. offline dichotomy: (a) first, with regard to the kinds of relationships which people maintain using the Internet, empirical research has shown that people mainly use digital technology in order to communicate with people they also know in the so-called real world; (b) second, with regard to specific relationships between pairs of people, these subjects use a wide variety of platforms in order to communicate with each other, and adopt a wider variety of media when in closer relationships (a phenomenon that has been defined as "media multiplexity" by Haythorntwhaite, 2005, pp. 130-134).

The same applies to identity processes: as Turkle points out, when we engage with digital media, we do not create "second selves," as suggested in her earlier works (Turkle, 1985); instead, we are facing "a new state of the self, itself" (Turkle, 2006, p. 121) that is *tethered* to "always-on" devices and is able to continuously switch from one role to another.

Furthermore, if we were to consider this topic analytically, the overall distinction between online and offline communication is far too generic, as every environment offers distinct and specific affordances to the user, in terms of forms of expression (text-only or multimedia; the communicative styles supported; one-to-one, few-to-many, many-to-many communication) and the social norms and habits that are shared by the users. For example, wording turn management not only depends on whether or not the platform mainly supports synchronous or asynchronous (or almost-synchronous/almost asynchronous) communication, but is also deeply influenced by the social and cultural norms that are intersubjectively negotiated by their users. Moreover, external contexts also deeply influence the way in which people communicate online (the strength of the ties between them, their socio-cultural backgrounds, etc.).

Digital platforms, in fact, can be analyzed though the lens of *architecture*: they build environments that offer specific affordances (as happens in the case of traditional architecture, which shapes the affordances of our physical environment). People build their communication strategies, both by taking advantage of such affordances and by further shaping this architecture (boyd, 2011).

WHAT IS A NETWORK?

As the term 'network' is widely used throughout this book, it is worth clarifying its meaning. In fact, its very definition is that a network is a set of interconnected nodes (a network is formed of nodes and links). Communication networks can be defined as "the patterns of contact that are created by the flow of messages among communicators through time and space" (Monge & Contractor, 2003, p. 3). The scientific investigation of networks is rooted in "graph theory," as previously discussed by Euler and further elaborated on by the mathematicians Erdős and Renyi (for information on graphs and graph theory, see Easley & Kleinberg, 2010).

Networks are not only technological tools; they are also social patterns. When he first proposed the theory that our societies were experimenting with a shift from communities to networks, Wellman (1979) was certainly not referring to the Internet. Although telecommunication networks played an important role in his model, he was primarily referring to a shift in social patterns. Over recent decades, social network analysis has examined social relations and social structures, starting from "the assumption of the importance of relationships among interacting units" (Wasserman & Faust, 1994, p. 4). More recently, physicians and mathematicians have started to study numerous different networks, giving birth to what has been (somewhat emphatically) defined as "the new science of networks." The two approaches share not only an interest in similar objects (network patterns), but also some important concepts (such as the "small world" theory, proposed by Milgram, 1967), which constitutes a core element of the contemporary understanding of network structures, and the "strength of weak ties," proposed by Granovetter, 1973). Nevertheless, the first attempts at a convergence between the two approaches have only been observed in the last few years (Easley & Kleinberg, 2010; Watts, 2004; Barabási, 2011; for an analytical reconstruction of "network science," including both approaches, see Lewis, 2009; for an insightful perspective on network theory, see Galloway & Thacker).

In fact, this "(new) science of networks" appears to be primarily oriented towards the identification of recurrent network patterns, such as "scale-free networks," which are structures that are dominated by a small number of highly interconnected hubs, while large numbers of nodes have only a few connections between them (Barabási, 2002). These have been found in a wide variety of different networks, ranging from the World Wide Web to the professional relationships between actors (the so-called Kevin Bacon number), and from the power grid to metabolic processes. While insightful and fascinating, some of these assumptions seem not to be fully integrated with a knowledge of social science, which is absolutely necessary when studying social relationships, which are intrinsically reliant on the "subjective responses of subjects" (Newman, Barabási, & Watts, 2006, p. 5). On the other hand, social research would benefit a great deal from a deeper integration of network scientists' research methods.

Some scholars have criticized network sciences, and specifically the related social models, by arguing that they are proposing a deterministic approach (see, for example, Musso, 2003, who critiques Castells' work). On the contrary, when he first proposed the idea of a "network society," Castells (1996) was fully aware that it was not a technology-driven phenomenon. In fact, as he argues, networks have always represented effective organizational structures in human history, due to "their strength in their flexibility, adaptability, and self-reconfiguring capacity." Nevertheless, "beyond a certain threshold of size, complexity, and volume of exchange, they become less efficient than vertically organized command and control structures, *under the conditions of pre-electronic communication technology*" (Castells, 2004, p. 5).

In accordance with this perspective (and the significant amount of research produced by social network scholars), we can therefore surmise that social networks have always existed (or, to be more precise, that social structures could always be analyzed in terms of network patterns), even before the spread of information and communication technology. However, digital technology offers a wide variety of affordances that enable specific relational patterns, making it easier, among other features, to manage large amounts of relationships, long-distance ties and long-distance feedback. The Internet, in fact, offers "appropriate material support for the diffusion of networked individualism as the dominant form of sociability" (Castells, 2001, p. 131).

SOCIAL NETWORK SITES: A POWERFUL PLAYGROUND FOR SOCIAL RESEARCH

The recent popularity of SNS such as Facebook, Linkedin, and MySpace, as well as microblogging sites such as Twitter, shows that there is a growing interest in articulating, making visible and managing personal or professional relationships through technology-enabled environments. The phenomenon addressed is wider than SNS, and includes the wide variety of ways in which people are linked to each other. For a better understanding of identity performances and relational patterns, this book will not only examine SNS, but rather consider the wider context, including the variety of ways in which people are linked to each other: a context in which old and new media collide, and where mediated and face-to-face social relations are becoming increasingly integrated.

Nevertheless, SNS are powerful playgrounds, both for the user and for the researcher. From a sociological point of view, one of the main points of interest of SNS, besides their ever-growing popularity among Internet users worldwide, is that they represent powerful environments in which to observe "publicly articulated" (Boyd, 2004) self-presentation and identity performances. SNS make such processes visible, trackable, and, therefore, easier to study. Far from constituting an alternative or "virtual" world, social media are embedded in everyday life: using SNS, people connect to one another in ways which they perceive as seamlessly connected to their face-to-face relationships. Nevertheless, this aforementioned "trackability" has increased people's awareness (we are now more consciously engaged in the management of our personal networks than ever before).

According to the work of Boyd and Ellison, we can define SNS as web-based services that allow individuals to:

1. Construct a public or semi-public profile within a bounded system;
2. Articulate a list of other users with whom they share a connection;
3. View and traverse their list of connections and those made by others within the system.

The nature and nomenclature of these connections may vary from site to site. (Boyd & Ellison, 2007)

As these two authors underline, in SNS, the emphasis is not on "relationship initiation, often between strangers" (so-called "social networking"), but on "articulating and making visible" the user's pre-existing social networks. More recently, during a broad discussion on the Association of Internet Researchers (AoIR) list, boyd (2009) further clarified this definition, distinguishing between "social networks" ("ties between people, regardless of mediating infrastructure"); "online social networks" (ties between people that are mediated by online technology); "social networking" and "online social networking" (the practice of creating new ties, regardless of mediating infrastructure or with the mediation of online technology) and "social network sites" (see definition by Boyd & Ellison, 2007).

The definition outlined above suggests that the main elements of SNS are *profiles* and *contact (friend) lists*. Consistently, early SNS research has mainly focused on self-presentation and identity performances, social relations and "friending" strategies. Another important research topic, from the inception of SNS research, has been concerns about privacy. Sonia Livingstone (2008) studied the way in which teens articulate their identity performances in SNS, and proposed two different models: *identity as display* and *identity as connection*. Of course, we are not faced with a rigid dichotomy between identity as display and identity as connection; we could see it instead as a *continuum*, in which each user positions himself or herself, often changing his or her strategies as time goes by.

Identity performances in SNS have mainly been conceptualized in terms of personal profile shaping, underlying people's awareness in self-presentation practices (Pearson, 2009; Mallan & Giardina, 2009; Livingstone, 2008; Rybas & Gajjala, 2007; boyd, 2008a; Zhao, Grasmuck, & Martin, 2008; Walther, Van Der Heide, Kim, Westerman, & Tong, 2008; Pearson, 2009) and *impression management* processes (Ellison, Heino, & Gibbs, 2006).

The most popular SNS (such as Facebook, MySpace, Friendster, etc.), although they have different emphases, share some of the categories which users can fill out in order to shape their own profile: personal *tastes* (referring to music, films, television shows, books etc.) appear to be powerful tools for impression management, leading to what has been defined as *taste performances* (Lizardo, 2006; Liu, 2007; Liu, Maes, & Davenport, 2008; Lewis, Kaufman, Gonzalez, Wimmer, & Christakis, 2008; Baym & Ledbetter, 2009). These practices appear to be consistent with the aforementioned assumptions regarding the central role of cultural consumption in identity processes (Thompson, 1995; Meyrowitz, 1983).

In most SNS, these processes can mostly be described as "writing identity and community into being" (Boyd, 2007), thereby underlining the role of "typing" in self-production strategies (Rybas & Gajjala, 2007, p. 5). It is important, however, to focus on the specific affordances of each platform, as each platform "structures [...] identity work according to the site's own internal logic" (Mallan & Giardina, 2009).[1] Profile pictures and personal photographs also play a major role in self-presentation processes, as has been underlined by several authors (see, among others, Sessions, 2009; Mallan & Giardina, 2009; Ellison, Heino, & Gibbs, 2006).

In accordance with the idea of an evolving and process-based identity, most users seem to be engaged in continuous profile redefinition and re-shaping activities. They modify, for example, their profile pictures, their status updates, their taste statements and even their friends list, engaging in what has been defined as a "continuous revision of the self" (Livingstone, 2008, p. 403).

Early research on SNS has also focused on social relations and "friending" strategies. Some scholars focus on the strength of the ties which we create online (Boase, Horrigan Wellman, & Rainie, 2006), while others argue that even *weak ties* can serve as the foundation of social capital (Ellison, Steinfield, & Lampe, 2006). Research has been carried out on "friending" strategies and on the relevant negotiation practices, especially among teenagers: in some cases, acceptance/refusal decisions, as well as inclusion/exclusion from "top friends" lists, can lead to authentic "social dramas" (boyd, 2010, p. 15; on this topic, see also boyd & Heer, 2006). Some scholars focus on the consequences of SNS use on the overall structure of social relations (Andon, 2007; Ito et al., 2008; Tong et al., 2008; Lee, 2009; boyd, 2008c; Lewis & West, 2009), while others underline that the public display of a friends list contextualises each user's identity (boyd & Donath, 2004), while *friending* activities represent an explicit identity performance (Tong et al., 2008).

Even if "friendship" has received relatively little systematic attention from sociologists, important distinctions have to be drawn between "friending" strategies in SNS and our understanding of the overall concept of friendship (regardless of the mediating infrastructure, as defined by, among others, Spencer & Pahl, 2006; Adams & Allan, 1998). In general terms, we can observe a mismatch between the friending practices supported by SNS and the common methods of friendship management which people experience offline, following at least three directions: (a) first of all, SNS require friendship *formalisation*, through the public articulation of social connections; generally, people receive (or send) a friend request which they have to respond to (in a context in which ignoring it has a similar value to refusing it), and their friends list is shown on their personal profile. On the contrary, in everyday life, friendships are seldom formalised or explicitly established and verified; (b) moreover, as argued by boyd

(2010), constant negotiations are underway regarding friending practices, which can have consequences in the offline world (Fono & Raynes-Goldie, 2006; Donath, 2007). The decision of whether to include acquaintances, parents, workmates and people you do not know offline appears to be subject to social norms that are still developing (Lewis & West, 2009); (c) furthermore, SNS generally support a binary and dichotomous definition of "friendship" (friend vs. not a friend), which is far from the nuanced definitions which users adopt in their offline lives.

Finally, early research on SNS has also focused on issues of privacy, claiming that a "privacy paradox" exists (Barnes, 2006), as while users generally appear to be concerned about their privacy in digital environments, they are (paradoxically) often ready to disclose large amounts of personal information (Gross & Acquisti, 2005; Acquisti & Gross, 2006).

Most early researchers looking at SNS adopted a mono-platform approach and limited their observations to online activity. Cross-platform comparisons were missing, as well as more in-depth contextualizations of online activity among the wider (identity-based and relational) contexts in which people live.

In recent years, SNS have become understood according to the framework of "networked publics" (Ito, 2008; Varnelis, 2008; Boyd, 2008a; 2008b). According to Boyd, networked publics "are publics that are restructured by networked technologies; they are simultaneously a space and a collection of people" (Boyd, 2011, p. 41). They offer specific affordances, four of which appear to play a major role: *persistence; replicability; scalability and searchability* (Boyd, 2011, p. 46).

More recently, we have witnessed what could be defined as a *normalization* of SNS use. Their ever-increasing popularity among Internet users worldwide has transformed SNS into "mainstream sites of relational maintenance" (Baym, 2010, p. 134; for information on the *democratization* of SNS see Lenhart, 2009). This means that SNS are becoming increasingly integrated in people's everyday lives: recent research has started focusing on the relationship between SNS use and the wider contexts in which people live, referring to both relational patterns and identity performances (Lewis & West, 2009, for instance, also focused on the means through which people stay in touch with their close friends; see also Baym, 2010). This also means that cross-platform comparisons are needed in order to identify the specific affordances offered by each platform. From a broader cross-platform analysis, SNS-user typologies may also emerge, as seen in Hargittai and Hsieh (2011).

When it comes to concerns regarding privacy, for instance, the need for a deeper understanding of the wider context in which people live implies that we should adopt a *social privacy* perspective (Raynes-Goldie, 2010), focusing on *context collision* and on the ability to control "who knows what about me" (Livingstone, 2008, p. 404), rather than adopting a traditional definition of privacy, based mainly on the disclosure of information. Moreover, recent research has also underlined that people generally have a high level of awareness when it comes to the revelation of information on SNS (Patchin & Hinduja, 2010). For an up-to-date bibliography on privacy and SNS, see Raynes-Goldie (2011).

As SNS have become *mainstream*, the associated research needs to become more specialized. While relational and identity-based topics are still an important part of SNS scholarship, a growing amount of research is being devoted to the practices of applying SNS to more specialized fields, such as civic engagement, political participation, public administration, branding and consumption, etc.

Moreover, a deeper level of integration between social research and information science has started to offer powerful insight into volumes of data that are unprecedentedly large in the field of social science.

Finally, as new platforms emerge, the research turns to focus on them. Geo-social networks constitute an interesting and emerging trend, as platforms that provide a high level of integration between the online and offline dimensions.

THE BOOK

While SNS certainly appear to be one of the most powerful environments for networked sociability-related research, a wider range of phenomena need to be addressed, including blogs, other websites and, in more general terms, the wide variety of digital environments that enable the practices of a *participatory culture* (Jenkins et al., 2009). The theoretical chapters of this book, while addressing specific aspects of networked sociability and individualism, include in their analyses a wide variety of environments; the majority of research chapters, on the other hand, specifically address SNS, as such environments offer powerful resources for social research.

The first section of this book ("Networked Sociability and Individualism: Emerging Conceptual Patterns") focuses on specific theoretical and conceptual concerns, ranging from collaborative practices in wiki environments to a reconsideration of the online vs. offline dichotomy in networked spaces; from online surveillance and registry culture to a reflection on audience research on web 2.0.

More specifically, the opening chapter (Matei & Bruno) focuses on the emergence of social media as collaborative tools functioning within a set of individualistic and community-oriented patterns. By focusing specifically on wiki environments (and Wikipedia in particular), the authors analyze and provide insight into collaborative practices, which are understood to be one of the core elements in contemporary social media. Far from emerging as a means to overcome the tension between individualism and community, collaborative practices appear instead "as a product of their conflict, which they epitomize."

Kennedy analyses social interactions in digital environments, reconsidering the rigid dichotomy between online and offline interactions and proposing the concept of "networked spaces" as a tool for overcoming this dichotomy. Drawing on the concept of affordances, the author focuses on everyday practices in networked spaces, arguing that "the social is spatial."

Zavala focuses on new models of online surveillance. This chapter aims to question the predominance of the organizational perspective in "surveillance studies" by reclaiming a "social" dimension, thereby contextualizing "surveillance" within a "networked sociability" framework. The author deliberately uses terms such as "register," "record" and "trackability," instead of those associated with unidirectional relations (such as "surveillance" or "privacy").

Andò focuses on audience research on Web 2.0, reflecting on the newly emerging trend of "sentiment analysis" (the analysis of the views and opinions that individuals express in the social media web). The author reflects on the opportunity to apply such methods to media audiences, considering the context of the research, and the critical issues relating to this quantitative approach.

The second section of the book ("SNS, Relational Patterns, and Identity Performances: New Research Trends") consists of nine chapters which each propose empirical research on networked sociability and individualism, mainly (but not exclusively) focusing on SNS. SNS have become *mainstream* tools for relational behaviour, and are therefore becoming increasingly integrated into people's everyday lives. As a result, new research trends have emerged, regarding both the relational and identity-related implications of SNS, as well as more specialized social media usage practices, which mainly refer to institutions. Section 2 offers innovative research perspectives on relational patterns and identity performances on SNS, by filling some conceptual gaps that are to be found in the previous research. The chapters range from a study of *latent social interactions* through an analysis of a large social graph, to proposing comparisons over time and platforms; from analysing social behavioural patterns in non-English speaking countries, to considering the dynamics of "brand appropriation" in the identity performances that take place on Facebook, and analyzing the use of emerging locative technologies, such as Gowalla and Foursquare.

More specifically, the opening chapter of the research section (Metzger, Wilson, Pure, & Zhao) provides an unprecedented insight into *latent social interactions* (which involve passive activities such as "profile browsing") through an analysis of Renren, the largest SNS in China. The data presented in this chapter are based on a social graph with 42 million users and 1.66 billion explicit social links. The authors have compared the structural properties of the latent social interaction graph with those of both visible interaction graphs and social graphs, offering new insights into the current debates surrounding both relational online behaviour and identity management in SNS.

Utz adopts a cross-platform approach, documenting Dutch students' migration from Hyves (formerly the most popular Dutch SNS) to Facebook. Self-centered and other-centered SNS use is explored, as well as the relations between personality and SNS adoption. This chapter fills a major conceptual gap (the lack of comparisons across time and platforms) and addresses, from this perspective, the main theoretical debates surrounding SNS (relational patterns, identity processes, privacy concerns). The data presented show that SNS have become an important tool for many Dutch students, and that they are mainly used for interaction between close friends.

Kneidinger focuses on social behavioral patterns by discussing data that are based on an online survey of Facebook users from German-speaking countries (Austria, Germany, and Switzerland) and on qualitative interviews. The motives for using Facebook, the role of status updates as a tool for self-presentation, and positive and negative social feedback on SNS are also addressed in this chapter.

Roberti and Marinelli focus on the relations between individuals and brands in the process of identity construction. For this purpose, they have carried out a qualitative explorative study, monitoring the *buzz* generated on Facebook by four popular brands. This chapter focuses on identity construction and on the social dimensions of consumption, showing the extent to which Facebook can constitute a powerful environment for "talking about ourselves through brands."

Berg proposes an analysis of the "spatial turn" in Internet research, focusing on locative technology. Applications such as Foursquare and Gowalla are understood to be examples of the increasing degree of integration between the online and offline dimensions, the boundaries of which are collapsing. Through an analysis of qualitative interviews carried out with Swedish Foursquare and Gowalla users, the author underlines the relations between what he defines as "electronic flâneurs" and digital geographies.

Section 3 ("Social Media and Institutions: New Research Trends") focuses on more specialised social media usage practices, which address – to varying extents – different institutional contexts. The chapters include an analysis of our reliance on digital media and SNS for political information (analyzing selective exposure both to blogs and to SNS), a study of public communication strategies on Facebook and an analysis of Church blogging in Australia.

Johnson, Bichard, and Zhang focus on political information-seeking on blogs and political websites, underlining the role of "selective exposure" (purposefully seeking out agreeable political information) and "selective avoidance" (purposely dodging disagreeable political information). The data presented are based on an online panel of Internet users, and this study aims to investigate, among others, the following dimensions: motivations for using the Internet to gather political information (information needs, entertainment needs and communication needs); reliance on online sources for political information; selective exposure to blogs; and selective exposure to political websites. As the authors argue, "the question of whether people practice selective exposure to information has important implications for the democratic system."

Kaye and Johnson propose an analysis of selective exposure to SNS for political information in the US. By analyzing the responses of 1530 politically interested SNS users, they have provided insight into: selective exposure and selective avoidance; reliance on SNS for political information; motivations for using SNS for political information; and the respondents' political attributes and demographics.

Lovari and Parisi focus on how SNS influence public communication strategies and online users' interactions. They propose an exploratory analysis of the Facebook activity of the capital cities of four Italian provinces, comparing their web pages and carrying out a content analysis in order to identify the prevalent types of messages on their Facebook walls. Although representing a recent tool in the public communication media-mix, Facebook seems to offer important opportunities for communication to municipalities, especially regarding direct interaction with citizens.

Emerson Teusner focuses on Church blogging, showing how the use of blogging technology can fuel networked individualism's impact on religious identity and community. By carrying out an exploratory content analysis of 30 blogs created by Australians involved in the "emerging Church movement," the author shows that "the creation of fluid, decentred, and global networks plays an important role in the development of religious identity."

By sharing the conceptual framework of networked sociability and individualism, these chapters offer new perspectives on both theoretical concerns and research practices. The theoretical chapters explore emerging conceptual patterns that are crucial for a deeper understanding of relational practices in a networked world, while the research chapters explore emerging trends by adopting innovative and multidisciplinary approaches. Moreover, while existing research on these topics mainly (although not exclusively) focuses on the Northern American context, chapters in this book analyse various international contexts (from the US to Italy, from Australia to the Netherlands, from China to Sweden, etc.).

As digital technology is becoming increasingly integrated in our everyday lives, it is widely recognised that a deeper understanding of the relational and identity-based patterns it enables is crucial, both with regards to theory and to the broader social context. We hope that the multidisciplinary and cross-national approach proposed by this book will make a significant contribution to advancing our knowledge of such topics.

Francesca Comunello
Sapienza University of Rome, Italy

REFERENCES

Acquisti, A., & Gross, R. (2006). *Imagined communities: Awareness, information sharing, and privacy on the Facebook. Proceedings of the 6th Workshop on Privacy Enhancing Technologies, Cambridge, UK.* Retrieved March 12, 2011, from http://privacy.cs.cmu.edu/dataprivacy/projects/facebook/facebook2.pdf

Adams, R. G., & Allan, G. (Eds.). (1998). *Placing friendship in context*. Cambridge, UK: Cambridge University Press.

Anderson, B. (1991). *Imagined communities* (2nd ed.). London, UK: Verso.

Andon, S. (2007). *Evaluating computer-mediated communication on the university campus: The impact of Facebook.com on the development of romantic relationships. Internet Research 8.0*. Retrieved January 10, 2011, from http://aoir.org/conferences/past/ir-8-2007

Bakardjieva, M. (2005). *Internet society. The Internet in everyday life*. London, UK: Sage.

Bakardjieva, M. (2011). The Internet in everyday life: Exploring the tenets and contributions of diverse approaches. In Consalvo, M., & Ess, C. (Eds.), *The handbook of Internet studies* (pp. 59–82). Chichester, UK: Wiley-Blackwell. doi:10.1002/9781444314861.ch4

Barabási, A. L. (2002). *Linked. The new science of networks*. Cambridge, MA: Perseus Publishing.

Barabási, A. L. (2011). Introduction and keynote to a networked self. In Papacharissi, Z. (Ed.), *A networked self. Identity, community, and culture on social network sites* (pp. 1–14). New York, NY: Routledge.

Barnes, S. (2006). A privacy paradox: Social networking in the United States. *First Monday*, *11*(9).

Bauman, Z. (2001). *Community: Seeking safety in an insecure world*. Cambridge, UK: Polity Press.

Baym, N. (2010). *Personal connections in the digital age*. Cambridge, UK: Polity Press.

Baym, N. K., & Ledbetter, A. (2009). Tunes that bind? Predicting friendship strength in a music-based social network. *Information Communication and Society*, *12*(3). doi:10.1080/13691180802635430

Boase, J., & Wellman, B. (2006). Personal relationships: On and off the Internet. In Vangelisti, A. L., & Perlman, D. (Eds.), *The Cambridge handbook of personal relationships* (pp. 709–723). Cambridge, UK: Cambridge University Press.

Boyd, D. (2004). *Friendster and publicly articulated social networks*. Conference on Human Factors and Computing Systems (CHI 2004) April 24-29. Vienna, Austria: ACM.

Boyd, D. (2008a). *Taken out of context: American teen sociality in networked publics* [PhD thesis]. University of California, Berkeley.

Boyd, D. (2008b). Why youth (heart) social network sites. In Buckingham, D. (Ed.), *Youth, identity, and digital media* (pp. 119–142). Cambridge, MA: MIT Press.

Boyd, D. (2009). *Social network sites nomenclature*. Retrieved February 10, 2011, from http://listserv.aoir.org/htdig.cgi/air-l-aoir.org/2009-May/018980.html

Boyd, D. (Ed.). (2010). Friendship. In M. Ito, et al. (Eds.), *Hanging out, messing around, geeking out. Kids living and learning with new media* (pp. 39-58). Cambridge, MA: MIT Press.

Boyd, D. (2011). Social network sites as networked publics. Affordances, dynamics, and implications. In Papacharissi, Z. (Ed.), *A networked self. Identity, community, and culture on social network sites* (pp. 39–58). New York, NY: Routledge.

Boyd, D., & Ellison, N. (2007). Social network sites: Definition, history, and scholarship. *Journal of Computer-Mediated Communication*, *13*(1), 210–230. doi:10.1111/j.1083-6101.2007.00393.x

Boyd, D., & Heer, J. (2006). Profiles as conversation: Networked identity performance on Friendster. *Proceedings of the Hawai'i International Conference on Social Systems*, *HICSS-39* (January), 4–7.

Buckingham, D. (2008). Introducing identity. In Buckingham, D. (Ed.), *Youth, identity, and digital media* (pp. 1–22). Cambridge, MA: The MIT Press.

Castells, M. (1996). *The rise of the network society*. Malden, MA: Blackwell.

Castells, M. (2001). *The Internet galaxy. Reflections on the Internet, business, and society*. Oxford, UK: Oxford University Press.

Castells, M. (Ed.). (2004). *The network society. A cross-cultural perspective*. Northampton, MA: Edward Elgar.

Castells, M. (2009). *Communication power*. Oxford, UK: Oxford University Press.

Castells, M., Fernández-Ardèvol, M., Linchuan Qiu, J., & Sey, A. (2007). *Mobile communication and society. A global perspective*. Cambridge, MA: MIT Press.

Donath, J. (2007). Signals in social supernets. *Journal of Computer-Mediated Communication, 13*(1), 231–251. doi:10.1111/j.1083-6101.2007.00394.x

Easley, D., & Kleinberg, J. (2010). *Networks, crowds, and markets. Reasoning about a highly connected world*. Cambridge, UK: Cambridge University Press.

Ellison, N., Heino, R., & Gibbs, J. (2006). Managing impressions online: Self-presentation processes in the online dating environment. *Journal of Computer-Mediated Communication, 11*(2), 415–441. doi:10.1111/j.1083-6101.2006.00020.x

Ellison, N., Steinfield, C., & Lampe, C. (2007). The benefits of Facebook 'friends': Social capital and college students' use of online social network sites. *Journal of Computer-Mediated Communication, 12*(4), 1143–1168. doi:10.1111/j.1083-6101.2007.00367.x

Ferro, E., Dwivedi, Y. W., Gil-Garcia, R., & Williams, M. D. (Eds.). (2010). *Overcoming digital divides: Constructing an equitable and competitive information society*. Hershey, PA: IGI Global.

Fono, D., & Raynes-Goldie, K. (2006). Hyperfriends and beyond: Friendship and social norms on Live-Journal. In M. Consalvo & C. Haythornthwaite (Eds.), *Internet research annual, volume 4: Selected papers from the association of Internet Researchers Conference* (pp. 91-103). New York, NY: Peter Lang.

Gajjala, R. (2009). Response to Shani Orgad. In Markham, A., & Baym, N. (Eds.), *Internet inquiry. Conversations about method* (pp. 61–67). Thousand Oaks, CA: Sage.

Galloway, A. R., & Thacker, E. (2007). *The exploit. A theory of networks*. Minneapolis, MN: University of Minnesota Press.

Giddens, A. (1991). *Modernity and self-identity*. Cambridge, UK: Polity Press.

Goffman, E. (1959). *The presentation of self in everyday life*. New York, NY: Anchor.

Granovetter, M. S. (1973). The strength of weak ties. *American Journal of Sociology, 78*(6), 1360–1380. doi:10.1086/225469

Gross, R., & Acquisti, A. (2005). *Information revelation and privacy in online social networks*. ACM Workshop on Privacy in the Electronic Society (WPES). Alexandria, VA.

Hargittai, E., & Hsieh, Y. P. (2011). From dabblers to omnivores: A typology of social network site usage. In Papacharissi, Z. (Ed.), *A networked self. Identity, community, and culture on social network sites* (pp. 146–168). New York, NY: Routledge.

Henning, M. (2007). Re-evaluating the community question from a German perspective. *Social Networks*, *29*, 375–390. doi:10.1016/j.socnet.2007.01.008

Ito, M. (2008). Introduction. In Varnelis, K. (Ed.), *Networked publics* (pp. 1–14). Cambridge, MA: MIT Press.

Ito, M. (Eds.). (2010). *Hanging out, messing around and geeking out: Kids living and learning with new media*. Cambridge, MA: MIT Press.

Jenkins, H. (2006). *Convergence culture*. New York, NY: New York University Press.

Jenkins, H., Purushotma, R., Clinton, K., Wiegel, M., & Robison, A. J. (2009). *Confronting the challenges of participatory culture: Media education for the 21st century*. Mac Arthur Foundation.

Jenkins, R. (2008). *Social identity* (3rd ed.). Abingdon, UK: Routledge.

Jensen, K. B. (2011). New media, old methods. Internet methodology and the online/offline divide. In Consalvo, M., & Ess, C. (Eds.), *The handbook of Internet studies* (pp. 43–57). Chichester, UK: Wiley-Blackwell. doi:10.1002/9781444314861.ch3

Lee, S. (2009). Online communication and adolescent social ties: Who benefits more from Internet use? *Journal of Computer-Mediated Communication*, *14*(3), 509–531. doi:10.1111/j.1083-6101.2009.01451.x

Lenhart, A. (2009). *The democratization of online social networks, IR10.0.* Retrieved December 11, 2010, from http://www.pewinternet.org/Presentations/2009/41--The-Democratization-of-Online-Social-Networks.aspx

Lévy, P. (1995). *Qu'est-ce que le virtuel?* Paris, France: La Découverte.

Lewis, J., & West, A. (2009). Friending: London-based undergraduate experience on Facebook. *New Media & Society*, *11*(7), 1209–1229. doi:10.1177/1461444809342058

Lewis, K., Kaufman, J., & Christakis, N. (2008). The taste for privacy: An analysis of college student privacy settings in an online social network. *Journal of Computer-Mediated Communication*, *14*(1), 79–100. doi:10.1111/j.1083-6101.2008.01432.x

Lewis, T. (2009). *Network science: Theory and applications*. Hoboken, NJ: Wiley.

Liu, H. (2007). Social network profiles as taste performances. *Journal of Computer-Mediated Communication*, *13*(1), 252–275. doi:10.1111/j.1083-6101.2007.00395.x

Liu, H., Maes, P., & Davenport, G. (2008). Unravelling the taste fabric of social networks. In Romm-Livermore, C., & Setzekorn, K. (Eds.), *Social networking communities and e-dating services: Concepts and implications* (pp. 256–282). Hershey, PA: Idea Group Inc.doi:10.4018/978-1-60566-104-9.ch002

Livingstone, S. (2008). Taking risky opportunities in youthful content creation: Teenagers' use of social networking sites for intimacy, privacy and self-expression. *New Media & Society*, *10*(3), 393–411. doi:10.1177/1461444808089415

Lizardo, O. (2006). How cultural tastes shape personal networks. *American Sociological Review*, *7*, 778–807. doi:10.1177/000312240607100504

Mallan, K., & Giardina, N. (2009). Wikidentities: Young people collaborating on virtual identities in social network sites. *First Monday*, *14*(6).

Mehdizadeh, S. (2010). Self-presentation 2.0: Narcissism and self-esteem on Facebook. *Cyberpsychology, Behavior, and Social Networking*, *13*(4), 357–364. doi:10.1089/cyber.2009.0257

Meyrowitz, J. (1983). *No sense of place*. New York, NY: Oxford University Press.

Milgram, S. (1967). The small world problem. *Psychology Today*, *2*, 61–67.

Monge, P., & Contractor, N. (2003). *Theories of communication networks*. New York, NY: Oxford University Press.

Musso, P. (2003). *Critique des réseaux*. Paris, France: Presses Universitaires de France.

Newman, M., Barabási, A., & Watts, D. (Eds.). (2006). *The structure and dynamics of networks*. Princeton, NJ: Princeton University Press.

Orgad, S. (2009). How can researchers make sense of the issues involved in collecting and interpreting online and offline data? In Markham, A., & Baym, N. (Eds.), *Internet inquiry. Conversations about method* (pp. 33–53). Thousand Oaks, CA: Sage.

Papacharissi, Z. (Ed.). (2011). *A networked self. Identity, community, and culture on social network sites*. New York, NY: Routledge.

Parks, R. (2011). Social network sites as virtual communities. In Papacharissi, Z. (Ed.), *A networked self. Identity, community, and culture on social network sites* (pp. 105–123). New York, NY: Routledge.

Patchins, J., & Hinduja, S. (2010). Trends in online social networking: Adolescent use of MySpace over time. *New Media & Society*, *12*(2), 197–216. doi:10.1177/1461444809341857

Pearson, E. (2009). All the World Wide Web's a stage: The performance of identity in online social networks. *First Monday*, *14*(3).

Raynes-Goldie, K. (2010). Aliases, creeping and wall clearing: Understanding privacy in the age of Facebook. *First Monday*, *15*(1).

Raynes-Goldie, K. (2011). *Annotated bibliography: Digitally mediated surveillance and social network sites. The cyber-surveillance in everyday life: An international workshop, Toronto, Canada.* Retrieved March 12, 2011, from http://www.k4t3.org/wp-content/uploads/2011/02/sns_and_privacy_raynesgoldie.pdf

Rheingold, H. (1993). *The virtual community: Homesteading on the electronic frontier*. Reading, MA: Addison-Wesley.

Rybas, N., & Gajjala, R. (2007). Developing cyberethnographic research methods for understanding digitally mediated identities. *Forum Qualitative Sozialforschung/Forum: Qualitative. Social Research, 8*(3), 35.

Sessions, L. (2009). You looked better on MySpace: Deception and authenticity on web 2.0. *First Monday, 14*(6).

Spencer, L., & Pahl, R. (2006). *Rethinking friendship: Hidden solidarities today*. Princeton, NJ: Princeton University Press.

Thompson, J. B. (1995). *The media and modernity. A social theory of the media*. Cambridge, UK: Polity Press.

Tong, S. T., Van Der Heide, B., Langwell, L., & Walther, J. B. (2008). Too much of a good thing? The relationship between number of friends and interpersonal impressions on Facebook. *Journal of Computer-Mediated Communication, 13*(3), 531–549. doi:10.1111/j.1083-6101.2008.00409.x

Turkle, S. (1985). *The second self. Computers and the human spirit*. New York, NY: Simon & Schuster.

Turkle, S. (2006). Always on/always on you: The tethered self. In Katz, J. (Ed.), *Handbook of mobile communication and social change* (pp. 121–137). Cambridge, MA: MIT Press.

Utz, S., & Krämer, N. (2009). The privacy paradox on social network sites revisited: The role of individual characteristics and group norms. *Cyberpsychology: Journal of Psychosocial Research on Cyberspace,* 3(2). Retrieved January 12, 2011, from http://cyberpsychology.eu/view.php?cisloclanku=2009111001&article=2

Van Dijk, J. (2005). *The deepening divide. Inequality in the information society*. Thousand Oaks, CA: Sage.

Varnelis, K. (Ed.). (2008). *Networked publics*. Cambridge, MA: MIT Press.

Walther, J. B., Van Der Heide, B., Kim, S.-Y., Westerman, D., & Tong, S. T. (2008). The role of friends' appearance and behavior on evaluations of individuals on Facebook: Are we known by the company we keep? *Human Communication Research, 34*(1), 28–49. doi:10.1111/j.1468-2958.2007.00312.x

Warschauer, M. (2003). *Technology and social inclusion. Rethinking the digital divide*. Cambridge, MA: MIT Press.

Wasserman, S., & Faust, K. (1994). *Social network analysis. Methods and applications*. Cambridge, UK: Cambridge University Press.

Watts, D. J. (2004). The new science of networks. *Annual Review of Sociology, 30*, 243–270. doi:10.1146/annurev.soc.30.020404.104342

Wellman, B. (1979). The community question. The intimate networks of East Yorkers. *American Journal of Sociology, 84*, 1201–1231. doi:10.1086/226906

Wellman, B. (1999). Living networked in a wired world. *IEEE Intelligent Systems, 14*(1), 15–17.

Wellman, B. (2001). Physical place and cyberplace: The rise of personalized networking. *International Journal of Urban and Regional Research, 25*(2), 227–252. doi:10.1111/1468-2427.00309

Wellman, B. (2004). The three ages of Internet studies. *New Media & Society*, *6*(1), 55–64. doi:10.1177/1461444804040633

Wellman, B. (2007). The network is personal: Introduction to a special issue. *Social Networks*. *Social Networks*, 29.

Wellman, B. (2011). Studying the Internet through the ages. In Consalvo, M., & Ess, C. (Eds.), *The handbook of Internet studies* (pp. 17–23). Chichester, UK: Wiley-Blackwell. doi:10.1002/9781444314861.ch1

Wellman, B., & Haythorntwhaite, C. (Eds.). (2002). *The Internet in everyday life*. Hoboken, NJ: Blackwell. doi:10.1002/9780470774298

Wilson, E. J. (2004). *The information revolution and developing countries*. Cambridge, MA: MIT Press.

Zhao, S., Grasmuck, S., & Martin, J. (2008). Identity construction on Facebook: Digital empowerment in anchored relationships. *Computers in Human Behavior*, *24*(5), 1816–1836. doi:10.1016/j.chb.2008.02.012

ENDNOTE

1 Due to the initial *bug*, for instance, MySpace allowed users to elaborately customise their personal pages, using html code to change the backgrounds and layouts of personal profiles and to embed multimedia content (mainly music and video) in sections of personal profiles originally intended to be filled by textual information.

Acknowledgment

An edited book is the result of the work of many people, and I wish to take this opportunity to thank those who have directly or indirectly contributed to the volume.

A special word of thanks goes to the members of the Editorial Advisory Board, for their continuous guidance and support. I am highly grateful to the reviewers, whose work has deeply contributed to the final versions of the chapters. This book gave me the opportunity to collaborate with scholars whose work I admire: I thank the authors of each of the chapters for their outstanding contributions. I am also thankful to the people at IGI Global, namely Emily Golesh and Erika Carter, for managing the book proposal, Jan Travers, for handling the contract, and Joel Gamon and Myla Harty, for managing the whole project.

I am also grateful to my colleagues and students for the stimulating intellectual community that I have been experiencing over the years at the Department of Communication and social research, Sapienza University of Rome.

Finally, I would like to thank my parents and my friends, for their constant presence (both face-to-face and online), and for forgiving my absences.

Francesca Comunello
Sapienza University of Rome, Italy

Section 1
Networked Sociability and Individualism:
Emerging Conceptual Patterns

Chapter 1
Individualist Motivators and Community Functional Constraints in Social Media:
The Case of Wikis and Wikipedia

Sorin Adam Matei
Purdue University, USA

Robert J. Bruno
Missouri Southern State University, USA

ABSTRACT

This chapter discusses the emergence of social media, especially wiki environments, as collaborative knowledge tools that function within a given set of individualistic and community-oriented cultural and functional constraints. The chapter provides the reader with an understanding of wiki social functions and technical capabilities and of the main value and cultural promises associated with them. It also examines the social and knowledge challenges they create and their likely impact on knowledge production in an individual and community setting. One main conclusion of the chapter is that wiki technologies need to be understood not as an overcoming of the tension between individualism and community, but as a product of their conflict, which they epitomize.

INTRODUCTION

Heralded by what some view as a paradigm shift, labeled by others as Web 2.0 (O'Reilly, 2005), a whole class of Internet-based applications has made its way into the world, with a profound impact on the manner in which we think about knowledge production, selection and dissemination (Shirky, 2008, 2010; Tapscott & Williams, 2006a; Williams & Tapscott, 2010). Emphasizing the direct involvement of ordinary consumers of knowledge in the process of production, social media such as wikis, blogs, social networking, or collective filtering of information (Digg, Slash-

DOI: 10.4018/978-1-61350-338-6.ch001

dot), have transformed our information and social habits (Reynolds, 2006; Weinberger, 2007). The most tangible signs of this transformation are the emergence and success, despite its prominent flaws, of Wikipedia as a universal reference tool, the rise of blogging as a public agenda-setting actor, the influence exercised by social bookmarking and filtering systems such as Digg and Slashdot in shaping PR campaigns, the role played by Facebook and My Space in structuring social interactions of the young and not-so-young, and the explosion of social publishing and networking sites such as Hi5, WordPress.com, YouTube and Flickr (Boyd & Ellison, 2007).

Less visible in the public consciousness, but increasingly influential, are marketing and for-profit publishing systems that harness the power of the multitudes to create and disseminate new products, such as CreateSpace, Lulu, Cafe Press or Amazon's Astore program, which collectively illustrate the idea of "peer production" in the field of e-commerce (Benkler, 2002, 2007; Raymond, 2001). Last but not least, software development has changed in a significant way under the influence of the collaborative, open source paradigm represented by projects such as Linux and Apache (Benkler, 2002; Fox, 2007).

Collaborative technologies enabled by Web 2.0 encompass myriad communication processes and interactions, including knowledge production, self-expression, collaborative learning, business-related projects, social-communicative acts/social networking, and community building. Also of interest with the coming of Web 2.0 are the cognitive impacts of these new media, their effects on organizational structures and decision making, and how traditional media institutional structures themselves have been transformed.

These electronic interaction platforms support both synchronous and asynchronous communication through a variety of devices and channels, allowing for textual, visual and aural elements. At the elementary level, emerging collaborative technologies can be conceived of as "Read-Write-Edit" systems, forums in which anyone, anywhere can contribute to and alter the discussion and/or other ongoing processes (Gillmor, 2006). These mechanisms, most recognizably embodied by tools such as wikis, are uncluttered in design and extremely easy-to-use. Nearly all are free, easy to sign up for, and simple to utilize. Furthermore, all interactions and communicative acts taking place within them are recorded and archived for further reference or use at a later point, offering an extra knowledge dimension to our information-rich world (Leuf & Cunningham, 2001).

At the same time, the Web 2.0 revolution brings with it not only promises, but also challenges. The most important is that of understanding the very nature of the basic social mechanisms, including those by which norms are created, roles enforced, and rewards assigned in online social media/collaborative environments. Equally important and still underdeveloped is the empirical literature that discusses the likely socio-psychological mechanisms responsible for the extraordinary growth of some Web 2.0 projects and the high failure rate of many others.

This chapter will discuss some of these problems, focusing on wiki environments. A first section of the chapter will provide the reader with an understanding of the nature and intended utility of wiki collaborative technologies and of the main promises associated with them. We will then examine the social and knowledge production challenges they create and their likely impact on our social interactions, both in individual and community settings. This discussion is divided into two sections. The first one discusses the current literature and the broader debate about the value, validity, and trustworthiness of content produced with support provided by wiki collaborative technologies and especially by Wikipedia. The second section proposes a new way of reconsidering this debate, focusing on the emerging tension between the individualistic values and community-oriented functional constraints of wiki technologies.

ONLINE COLLABORATION: FROM BULLETIN BOARDS TO WIKIS

Online collaborative knowledge platforms are not a new phenomenon. They are, in fact, as old as the online universe itself. They were part and parcel of the original vision of a "man-computer symbiosis" and of the computer envisioned as a communication device described by Robert Licklider, the influential administrator at ARPA, the agency responsible for the developing the first version of the Internet. In two seminal papers Licklider delineated the future of the yet-to-be invented Internet (Licklider, 1960; Licklider & Taylor, 1968). He emphasized that computers should be used not as simple message delivery mechanisms, but as social knowledge processing and modeling environments, not unlike contemporary social media. Through them, individuals who have partial knowledge of a problem would be able to interact with other users, who possess different knowledge sets and control a variety of areas of expertise.

The more direct predecessors of the computing networking and social interaction sites that we use today were the electronic bulletin boards of the late 1970s – early 1980s, whose facilities and intended utilities, at least in principle, presage more contemporary online wiki environments. For example, a specific class of bulletin board systems, including EIES, EMISARI, Plato, and Delphi, were intentionally designed to create methods for knowledge polling, brainstorming, forecasting, and group decisions (Belson, 1994; Hiltz & Turoff, 1978; Turoff, 1973). One of them, Turoff's Electronic Information Exchange System, supported as early as late 1970s utilities for synchronous and asynchronous conferencing, group editable documents, and user networking (Hiltz & Turoff, 1978).

In fact, most of the early electronic bulletin boards had far greater ambitions than their name suggests. Their designers aimed to create a seamless network whereby users could generate individual or collective knowledge employing a large array of information devices and techniques. For example, EIES was designed in part to support the Delphi forecasting method, which involved polling a panel of experts via computer conferencing (Hiltz & Turoff, 1978).

Most early methods of online collaboration via bulletin boards were, however, significantly limited by scope and facility of use and primitive interaction affordances. Research, business or governmental applications were their main intended use while the earlier adopters were high technology workers, researchers or technophile amateurs. Taking advantage of early collaborative system capabilities required knowledge of command line interfaces and even some low-level programming skills.

The emergence of the World Wide Web as a gateway for the Internet has changed the expectations, target audiences, and interaction affordances for collaborative technologies. The Web, initially deployed as a one-way publishing environment, has over time morphed into a many-to-many editable space (Gillmor, 2006). This trend, described by some as a shift from the World Wide Web to the Read-Write Web, has transformed the very notion of online interaction (O'Reilly, 2005). While previously online collaboration meant sending back and forth uneditable messages, with the transition to Web 2.0 services we have witnessed a shift toward deeper interaction and collaboration. This involves simultaneous work on a variety of textual, audio, video or even virtual 3D environments. Of these, wiki technologies have emerged as a powerful and widely utilized method of collaboration and communication.

Key Terms and Definitions

Wiki platforms are a central Web 2.0 technology. According to O'Reilly (2005) Web 2.0 is a method for creating and delivering computing tools, software applications, and content that uses the Web, as opposed to the classic desktop computer, as its main support. This idea can be better understood through the cognate term proposed by O'Reilly, "The Web as Platform." The term "platform" is borrowed from computer science parlance and it should be understood either as "operating system" (i.e., Windows, Mac, Linux) or as a combination of operating systems and afferent applications and hardware. The Web as a platform concept imagines a world where all major computing functions and applications (word processing, image manipulation, communication, file sharing, etc.) reside online, while the physical machine that is used for accessing them is reduced to a "thin client," preferably running only a browser. In addition, shifting applications to the network enables users to collaborate on any given task with other individuals and to instantaneously share the results of their work with third parties.

Wikis meet all of these characteristics. At heart they are nothing more than an online document editing and publishing system. Wikis emerged in the mid-1990s as an attempt to simplify the process of editing and creating web pages. The first wiki system, christened by computer programmer Ward Cunningham with the Hawaiian adjective for "fast" or "quick" (wiki), was meant to be a "quick Web" publishing tool (Leuf & Cunningham, 2001). Users with little time or interest to mess around with HTML code could directly make changes on a page by using very simple textual conventions. All editing could be done in the browser (the Web navigation tool) using text boxes and text input. In time, more sophisticated systems have been proposed. Many of them are complex database-driven applications, which very clearly separate content from the instructions for graphic representation and layout. Web pages are created on the fly by computer scripts triggered at each URL request for a page. The content itself can be easily and meaningfully tagged and exported to other platforms. In addition, wiki sites include tools for tracking content changes and user-to-user communication tools.

Wiki sites are powered by dedicated software packages, many of them licensed for public, free, or non-profit use (MediaWiki, TikiWiki, or DokuWiki). Software creators sometimes release just the code for the packages, their users having to manually install them on their own servers. In other situations software developers offer hosting solutions as well (e.g., MindTouch, Google Sites, or Wikia). As wikis have become more popular, their platforms have diversified. Among the most popular is MediaWiki (Rahman, 2007), one of the fastest-growing wiki technologies. MediaWiki is the central technology that powers Wikipedia, the free online encyclopedia, but it has also been adopted by organizations such as Intel, CIA (Majchrzak, Wagner, & Yates, 2006) or Wikileaks.

Wiki platforms are seen as great advances in the world of online collaboration and publishing. Among their most often mentioned advantages are: information can be edited instantaneously and collaboratively, a large network of individuals can be constantly updated about the progress made during the editorial process, content can be exported and imported instantaneously. A more specific expectation is that these platforms will perform better due to their non-hierarchical nature (Tapscott & Williams, 2006b). These capabilities, combined with the premise that all contributors are well intended and that the greater the number of actors, the more likely that mistakes will be weeded out, have led many observers and adopters to believe that wiki technologies can produce knowledge that is more accurate than the one generated via normal (centralized, hierarchical) editorial processes (Davies, 2004; Klobas & Beesley, 2006).

These potential promises have been vigorously debated in the public and scholarly arenas. The two core issues that have emerged through these debates are the motivators and the constraints that can be found on wikis. Motivators refer to the internal and external incentives that determine individuals to contribute content or managerial activities to a wiki site. Constraints refer to the socio-cultural norms, institutional boundaries, or functional requirements that moderate contributions or activity online.

In what follows we will focus more closely on the substantive discussions carried out around these two issues. We will direct our attention on the particular expectations and challenges implied by individualistic motivators and community constraints. Our aim is to propose an interpretive framework for their interplay, which emphasizes the tension between individualistic values and motivators and community functional constraints.

Current Debates about Collaborative Online Technologies

Much has been made about the potential revolutionary changes individuals, groups and organizations (both commercial and otherwise) will undergo upon adopting collaborative technologies in general and wikis in particular. The expectation is that these technologies will "level the playing field." Whether these egalitarian collaborative tools further democratize communication processes or change power structures (Reynolds, 2006; Sunstein, 2006) remains to be seen. Early evidence indicates, however, that at least in terms of outcomes, most social media projects are dominated by a few voices, an issue to which we will return later on (Kittur, Chi, Pendelton, Bongwon Suh, & Mytkowicz, 2007; Kittur, Lee, & Kraut, 2009; Ortega, Gonzalez-Barahona, & Robles, 2008). But some changes wrought by these collaborative technologies are already clear as demonstrated by how historic boundaries have been crossed, how new voices have joined the discourse, and how multitudes of other individuals have been empowered.

A number of recent popular books and intense press coverage have seeded and spread the idea of mass collaboration and peer-production having a great impact on the public imagination (Williams & Tapscott, 2010). Academic observers, such as Jenkins (Jenkins, Clinton, Purushotma, Robinson, & Weigel, 2006) have launched new interpretive frameworks for these developments, which herald the birth of a new "participatory culture." Such discursive themes create a vision in which social media in general and wikis in particular are meant to greatly improve if not supplant our current methods of communication. But what exactly is happening? The following list distills the major phenomena that seem to be occurring due to the dawning of these emerging technologies and the issues they raise:

- A convergence, blending, and juxtaposition of news producer and audience roles into a participatory form of content production/public discourse;
- A transformation of existing and traditional media structures, the older cross-pollinating with the cutting-edge into a new kind of hybrid form which takes into account the new interactive, participatory discourse;
- A morphing of information-knowledge itself into fresh shapes and aggregations, which can be accessed, exchanged (multi-dimensionally as opposed to one-way, uni-directionally) and utilized in different manners and more easily than before;
- New self-correcting systems, safeguards and protocols that have been intentionally instituted or have occurred naturally within the technological ecosystem that call on the power of numbers and the masses to ensure the value and accuracy in information and knowledge production, and which tend to manifest in a socially, structurally unequal manner;
- And, the predictable claims of information anarchy, loss of objectivity and cultural relativity native to this burgeoning information landscape.

In *Everything is Miscellaneous,* Weinberger (2007) discusses the effects of new media primarily from the perspective of how it is transforming traditional institutions – and forms of mediated communication – and creating new ones in their stead. Because they have upset traditional information dissemination processes these new forms of media threaten any person or institution that is part of the *old-line* establishment. From a pure publishing perspective this is so because collaborative technologies especially do away with traditional information producers, systems and gatekeepers, thereby turning historical publishing processes on their heads. Consumers no longer have to rely solely on the "mainstream" media or publishers or even on traditional sources of information, such as printed books or journals. Weinberger et al. theorize that collaborative technologies turn knowledge into "conversations" (Levine, Locke, Searls, & Weinberger, 2000), that any individual is able to enter unimpeded into the discussion, whereas in the past the lines of delineation between the haves (media institutions) and the have-nots (the general audience public) were clear and nearly impossible to cross.

These new media paradigms are causing, according to Weinberger, information itself to take new shapes and forms, and therefore be accessed and utilized differently. Wikis, for example, are altering traditional notions of information organization and structure, which has led to widespread negative outcry, especially related to their perceived lack of authority (McHenry, 2004) and intrinsic relativism (Matei & Dobrescu, 2011). Because the greatest achievement of wikis, Wikipedia, utilizes the power of the many, as opposed to the authority and expertise of the few – which is the traditional encyclopedia model – much concern has been expressed about the credibility and objectivity of the information it makes available. Weinberger, however, argues for the power of the rationality of the many over that of the few. Furthermore, he posits that this new information dynamic and its manifested structures may more closely reflect how the human mind itself works. His main contention is that information processing in the human mind takes place through rough, empirical approximations of any given situation and is liable to change at any point. Thus, his belief is that organizing of information according to deductive, a priori schemata is obsolete. Preordained, abstract taxonomies, such as the Dewey decimal system or old-line alphabetical sequencing are not at all intuitive, but instead completely arbitrary, believes Weinberger. They were needed only as long as access to information could not be operated using "random access" methods. With the birth of computers and their ability to sieve through large amounts of information very quickly, seekers of information no longer needed to labor through arbitrary organizational systems such as the alphabetical index. The Internet and its constitutive elements, including wikis and blogs, are not limited by real "space" in the same way that books, magazines and newspapers are or by real "air time" in the same way radio and television is and has always been. Thus, information can be organized in ad-hoc taxonomies, in which as he puts it, "everything is miscellaneous."

Weinberger also directly addresses the commonly-voiced concern that wikis or other social technologies are the domain of amateurs (Weinberger, 2007). He concludes pragmatically that the wisdom of amateur "crowds" that contribute to Wikipedia, if not actually more valuable than the academic voices of the few who are invited to contribute to Britannica, are at least worthwhile competitors as long as their products can be continuously improved and instantaneously checked against the plethora of information found just a click away from any wiki page. In other words, due to the sheer breadth and numbers of its users, the accuracy and credibility of Wikipedia articles could, at least theoretically, increase more and more over time. Also, discussion areas which are part and parcel to Wikipedia, or any wiki really, add a self-correcting and contextual dimension that traditional media will never offer. Finally,

Weinberger points out that traditional media are compromised by the fact that they are commercial operations, something that is not true of most online entities.

In *The Cult of the Amateur,* Keen (2007) provides a strong counterpoint to Weinberger. Echoing a broader issue, also voiced by other online activists and observers (Lanier, 2006), his position grows out of the concerns stirred up by incidents that pointed to the ambiguous if not misleading nature of information and personal reputations on Wikipedia (Hafner, 2006; Jaschik, 2007; Seigenthaler, 2005). Keen emphasizes the flawed nature of this medium, pointing to incidents such as the discovery that the Wikipedia entry for a former Robert Kennedy aide was spiked with slanderous allegations or that an important Wikipedia contributor profiled by the New Yorker as a tenured professor at a prestigious university turned out to be a 24 year-old paralegal with no college credentials (Cohen, 2007). Keen prefers things as they were before emerging technologies upset the cultural landscape and, contrary to Weinberger, strongly believes that as a result both truth and objectivity have been greatly victimized. The author mints new collaborative technologies such as wikis as "the blind leading the blind," and worse, founts of ignorance, misinformation and deception. Not buying into the notion of the power of numbers, Keen's main knock on new media is that it does not have the set system of checks and balances that hold traditional publishing operations to certain ideals and standards, thereby making them unaccountable. From this vantage point, civic contribution to online media naturally slants toward the provocative and controversial. Keen sees in this user-generated world a blurring of the lines that separate professionals from amateurs, reality from fiction, and objectivity from subjectivity.

Keen's book also highlights an intellectual position that has become more and more evident in the public debate. This focuses not only on the lack of criteria or credibility, but also on the fact that far from making the modern world a more participative place, new technologies have actually further separated the haves and have-nots. Web 2.0 technologies have created their own digital divides. Following Keen's angle of attack one can say that these gaps are to be defined not in terms of physical access, but in terms of actual contributions. Such concern is illustrated by findings of some recent empirical research, which highlights that social media projects such as Wikipedia are the product of a very uneven process of collaboration.

For example, Ortega (2008) used the Gini coefficient to measure equality of contributions on Wikipedia. The Gini index varies between 0 (perfect equality) and 1 (maximum inequality). Perfect equality is represented by a situation where the members of a group share equally the resources available to them or the burden of effort. For example, if 10 individuals contributed 10 words each to a 100-word long Wikipedia article, the Gini coefficient of this group of contributors would be 0, reflecting a situation a perfect equality. However, if one individual contributed 91 words, and the rest of the members only one word each, inequality would be very high, namely,.8. Ortega found that inequality on Wikipedia hovers between.8 and.9 for most of its versions (English, German, Spanish, French, etc). The magnitude of this level of inequality can become more apparent when compared to other contexts in which inequality is present and can be measured. For example, economists have been measuring income inequality at national level for many decades. According to the United Nations Development Program (http://hdrstats.undp.org/en/tables/default.html), maximum income inequality in a nation rarely goes over.6. The Gini coefficients of the nations with the widest gap between rich and poor are well under the.8 threshold that characterizes contribution inequality of online social environments. For example, the most unequal nation of the world, Sierra Leone, has a Gini coefficient of.63. The second most unequal country in the world is Brazil (.61), followed by Angola (.59). In contrast, the most egalitarian nations in the world, such as Sweden, Norway, or Finland are characterized by Gini coefficients that are significantly lower, varying around.25.

The extremely high contribution inequalities detected on Wikipedia are not unique to this medium. They were documented for other environments, such as the Linux development environment and the Flickr or YouTube content sharing sites (Bruno, 2010). From an ideological point of view they are quite problematic, because they indicate that an unseen elite of "power users" tends to dominate the public discourse. This is bound to generate confusion as to what the "social" and "egalitarian" attributes associated with new media really mean. From a more pragmatic point of view, the fact that wiki and social media spaces are divided into "power" and ordinary users might just illustrate a fact as old as human labor and social organizations: groups need leaders and greater effort generates unequal rewards. As we will discuss below, these phenomena need to be more carefully studied and understood in a more nuanced way before sweeping them aside or explaining them as exceptions or suboptimal results of imperfect social media designs.

Returning to Keen's arguments, the social discrepancies one can observe in social media suggest that instead of leveling the playing field, and arming each and every citizen with powerful knowledge, social media might in fact create a new type of order, which is not necessarily egalitarian. Furthermore, continuing Keen's proposition, one can speculate that large corporations or various forms of bureaucratic control could co-opt the power users, those 1% of users who generate 90% of the content, turn them into an emerging digital facilitator class and use them to promote their own commercial or political interests.

Yet, despite fears that the Internet might usher in a future anarchy and/or control instead of utopia, Keen does temper and balance his position by allowing that emerging technologies hold the potential to enhance our information futures. The Wikipedia project Citizendium.org is offered as an example of an effort that could undeniably combine the best of both the old and new media worlds. Citizendium.org is built upon a wiki foundation, but instead of being driven almost solely by amateurs it is controlled by experts in their respective fields. This seems a reasonable position within a debate that oftentimes becomes overly passionate and partisan.

Gillmor (2006), however, in *We the Media,* contends that the transformation of the consumer into a "prosumer" (i.e., producer and consumer at the same time) has already taken place and that the distinction between use and creation will only become more blurred as time goes on. Although certainly touching on the social-psychological impact of emerging, collaborative technologies, Gillmor, a journalist, takes a decidedly media-focused approach. Given the title of his tome, he sets out to demonstrate how, through blogs, wikis and other interactive media, the audience has already become part of the news generating process. This is because, in today's hyper-mediated world, many barriers to entry have indeed been eliminated – which was certainly never the case with the traditional media environment. Entering the newspaper or television reporting fields, or landing a job as a book editor, to say nothing of attaining higher-level management and decision-making positions at media institutions both large and small, has always required proper credentials, specific talents and a whole lot of luck. Yet, these days, anyone with a blog or simply with the passion to know and free time necessary to contribute to Wikipedia can publish and/or broadcast to the entire world.

The power of hypertext and the read-write Web has changed everything, dramatically altering the landscape – especially as the technical tools have become over the last several years easier and easier to use. What was once one-to-many or one-to-one communication can now be many-to-many, few-to-few, or any other kind of dynamic limited only by the technology and its users' imaginations. At their own peril, traditional media institutions at first ignored these developments; however, more recently mainstream publishers have decided to ride with the times and stake their own claim to this new frontier. Even Britannica nowadays allows ordinary users to contribute some content to its site, albeit such contributions are to be vetted and verified before being published (Van Buskirkr, 2008). The result has been a blend of the old and new, a symbiotic ecosystem that will inevitably morph as technological diffusion increases and more individuals join the participatory journalism movement. However, Gillmor believes that these shared newsgathering and dissemination processes may under certain conditions create a false sense of excitement in some segments of the populace, while leaving a good part of it cynical.

At the same time, and in contrast to Keen, Gillmor views modern technology as a correcting influence by directly refuting inaccurate and deceptive information with the help of a huge number of voluntary fact checkers. He sees wikis and social media not as uncontrolled, editorial anarchies, but "works in progress" that hue more closely to the truth over time. These new, user-generated technologies allow for real, unconstrained human voices to join the mediated discourse. In sum, this is what Gillmor terms "emergence," a not entirely new concept, which suggests that the knowledge whole is better and smarter than the sum of its parts.

In *Infotopia*, Sunstein (2006) continues in a similar vein. This is a much more optimistic volume, coming after a rather skeptical previous book, Republic.com (Sunstein, 2001), in which he excoriated the balkanization of knowledge and social affiliations induced by new media. Infotopia rediscovers the virtues of the Internet. It focuses especially on the ability of the medium to poll large amounts of opinions and to synthesize more truthful facts out of a myriad of partial opinions. Not lacking caveats, especially those derived from the jury theorem, which mainly affirms that a group will make the right *decisions if and only if* a majority of the members *know the facts* and are capable of making a good judgment *independently* of each other, he mostly revels in the potential rewards of collaborative online platforms, especially those powered by moderated wiki and expert opinion polling.

Sunstein conceives the world as a collection of individual human minds that emerging collaborative technologies draw together with dramatic and dynamic consequences. He sees a coalescence of these individual bits of information into cumulative knowledge as well as the actualization of latent creativities. Furthermore, the wiki is again viewed as a metaphor for human knowledge itself. The human mind is an amorphous environment that can shift and grow at a moment's notice, but also abides certain guidelines and norms. Wikipedia follows similar implicit and explicit rules both operative and social, namely in the form of what is called "wikiquette" and of its hierarchical structure. It is this concertive control that allows a kind of quality assurance to exist and prosper in new mediated realms. It follows then that this "immense range of voices unquestionably adds to the stock of perspectives and information in a way that can and does correct social errors." (Sunstein, 2006, p. 196)

Furthering the human mind/knowledge-building metaphor, Sunstein invokes in effect a convincing rationale for the very existence and primacy of the scientific method, which more recently seemed to have fallen in disfavor: that through these powerful new technologies, we "are standing on the shoulders of giants." Through tools such as wikis, prediction markets (INTRADE) or collaborative, filtered sites (Slashdot, etc.), we are continually building – and with a permanent account, no less – a vast store of human inquiry and knowledge that builds on the knowledge of others. After all, what is knowledge? A simple way to paraphrase Sunstein's position would be to say that he believes that what we do know is that which has been already known by countless other minds that are constantly adding to the existing universal body of information. We depend on those who came before, and we will depend on those who will come after. Wikis are the realization and manifestation of this process.

Sunstein effectively characterizes the brave new world of collaborative technology and human connection not as an inward, selfish kind of "media" but more an "us-dia," in its inclusivity and apparent spirit for the betterment of humankind. He certainly believes the good vastly outweighs the worthless in the world and that this manifests itself within Infotopia.

A similar stance is taken by Jenkins (2006), especially with regard to the impact of collaborative technologies on learning. Drawing on the observation that over half of American teens have created some form of online content, he believes that we are witnessing the emergence of a new "participatory culture," which he sees as one:

1. With relatively low barriers to artistic expression and civic engagement,
2. With strong support for creating and sharing one's creations with others,
3. With some type of informal mentorship whereby what is known by the most experienced is passed along to novices,
4. Where members believe that their contributions matter, and
5. Where members feel some degree of social connection with one another. (Jenkins et al., 2006, p. 7)

These cultural traits allude to the emergence of a dual process, which on the one hand is impelled by a sense of individual worth and on the other supported by social networks. Despite its "win-win" appearance, such a process of collaboration and production is not without drawbacks. Despite the fact that social support is present in collaborative environments, participation is a function of individual motivations and skills. These are necessary conditions for involvement in social media processes and they can be undermined by three factors. Jenkins identifies them as: (1) a participation gap, expressed as unequal access not only to technologies but also to experiences and skills, (2) a transparency problem, born out of the fact that young people do not always clearly see how media can shape the world and their choices, and (3) an ethics challenge, which consists in the breakdown of traditional forms of training and socialization. The later is particularly important since it might deny some potential actors proper exposure to new ideas and technologies and clear channels for exploiting their potential. As we will discuss below, these are important issues, especially in view of the fact that effective participation is at times uneven and distribution of benefits unequal. Jenkins advises educators and learners to pay more attention to preparing young learners for future encounters with social media. Media literacy and skill acquisition should be a central concern for all educators. Societal debate about social media and its purported beneficial effects should shift "from questions of technological access to those of opportunities to participate and to develop the cultural competencies and social skills needed for full involvement." (Jenkins et al., 2006, p. 4)

To conclude, the public discourse on social media or collaborative technologies as is defined by popular books such as Gillmor's, Sunstein's, or Weinberger's, despite their overall positive tone, raises a number of critical issues. One of them, and not always clearly seen or even identified, is the already mentioned fundamental inequality of contributions and benefits that characterize many social media/online collaborative environments. The second issue that needs to be discussed is the motivating factors and the cultural and normative constraints that moderate contributions to social media environments. In other words, the theoretical perspectives proposed by Sunstein, Weinberger or Keen invite us to offer more refined and deeper explanations of social media technologies work in the real world. In what follows we would like to propose a possible interpretive lens for understanding the cultural forces that undergird social media, emphasizing the interplay between individualistic tendencies and community-functional constraints, which together moderate the emergence and functioning of social media.

CULTURAL INDIVIDUALISTIC UNDERPINNINGS AND COMMUNITY FUNCTIONAL CONSTRAINTS IN WIKI SYSTEMS

The broader philosophical and sociological discussion about the deeper nature of Web 2.0 collaborative technologies should be considered in relation to the widely accepted fact that they have lowered the barriers to entry, both technical and social. A deliberate design decision for most social media sites, lowering the barriers to entry was premised on the expectation that openness is a strong motivation to contribution (Lih, 2010), which in addition fosters self-healing and self-improvement mechanisms for most social media platforms and especially for wiki sites (Bryant, Forte, & Bruckman, 2005). Openness creates virtuous feed-back loops and self-regulative processes by allowing a plurality of voices to talk to each other and to point to each other's strengths and weaknesses.

The idea of "self-regulation" sounds very appealing, yet the concrete mechanisms by which such a process takes root and functions in social media environments are yet to be discovered. At first blush, the self-regulation concept seems to suggest a harmonious interaction between users who are eager to cooperate by giving each other feedback or helping one another make the best decisions, use the best terms, or propose the most efficient policies.

Yet, several Wikipedia studies (Beschastnikh, Kriplean, & McDonald, 2008; Kittur, B. Suh, Pendleton, & Chi, 2007; Kittur et al., 2009; Kriplean, Beschastnikh, McDonald, & Golder, 2007) suggest that wiki social coordination and control is often more complex than expected and involve quite a bit of conflict and controversy (Matei & Dobrescu, 2011). This seems to be convergent with research conducted on other online or open-content social media. A number of early studies that go as far back as the early 1990s mention the role of conflict in shaping on-line environments (Kollock & M. Smith, 1996; Postmes, Spears, & Lea, 1998; A. D. Smith, 1999). More research on collaboration practices in open-source software (OSS) communities also revealed that conflict is at the heart of the OSS collaborative process (Elliott & Scacchi, 2003). Furthermore, research on Wikipedia's editorial process has revealed that one of the most frequent types of debate between Wikipedia contributors is about the meaning and significance of their definitions (Stvilia, Twidale, Gasser, & L. Smith, 2005). Eight of 22 salient issues identified by Stvilia et al. in the discussion pages that accompany Wikipedia entries referred to definitions and meaning. The issues included language misinterpretations/mistakes, stylistic choices (wording and semantics), subjective meanings, etc. This emphasis on disputation or subjective interpretation of meaning, which was also identified in more traditional virtual community interactions (Matei, 2005) and on Wikipedia (Matei & Dobrescu, 2011), suggests a social environment defined by conflict as a structural characteristic.

The prominent presence of conflict in online collaborative systems highlights not only that such environments might at times encounter difficulties, but that conflict and controversy could be central for their functioning. An argument can be made that if social media can be seen as akin to "demassification" technologies, whose aim is to recover the importance of individual and subjective meanings embedded in human experiences (Weinberger, 2002), then the plurality of meanings and perspectives they naturally attract might lead to conflict as a necessary modus vivendi for Web 2.0 spaces in general and for wikis in particular. In simpler and more specific terms, if Wikipedia is the "encyclopedia anyone can edit," as the moniker goes, it should be no wonder if the plurality of opinions it attracts violently clash for the right to leave their imprint on the most current version of an article.

Rephrasing this idea in a more rigorous manner, we can say that the goals of social media such as Wikipedia are many-fold. On the one hand, such collaborative sites focus on producing a specific type of content (knowledge or information). On the other hand, they are "political" (as in the policy of an online polity of sorts) and social projects. Their aim is to create a wider, more complex, and *different kind* of information universe. Through it a plurality of voices can be heard and integrated (Matei, 2005). Social media are, thus, not only about knowledge or content, but also about power production. Specifically, they are a means for producing empowerment for ordinary individuals, who are encouraged to abandon their passive consumer role and to become active content creators (Gillmor, 2006).

Turning individuals into creators is also a call for individualization and for affirming the autonomy of each individual, which is a characteristic long recognized for post-industrial societies (Bell, 1976; Bellah, Madsen, Sullivan, Swidler, & Tipton, 1996; Inglehart, 1997). Collaborative technologies should thus be seen as an extension of the contemporary yearning for individualization, for personal autonomy, and for a renewed sense of selfhood (Matei, 2005). Social media could therefore be viewed as a continuation of a decades-old attempt to reverse the regulation of everyday life by technological bureaucracies (Schuler & Day, 2004). Collaborative technologies should be integrated in the broader social movement inspired by the "meaning revolution" of the 1960s counterculture (Wuthnow, 1976), which also gave us Ted Nelson's Xanadu (Keep, McLaughlin, & Parmar, 2000), the techno-reversionary project (Roszak, 1994), the hacker culture (Levy, 1985), the free software movement (Feller, 2005), and the WELL's "virtual community" project (Rheingold, 2000). Wikipedia and other more recent social collaborative projects are natural continuations of these projects. Like their predecessors, the newer social media have created a socio-technical space that emphasizes the role of creative individuals in society and the necessity of reinventing community.

Yet, the attempt to create a social space in which power is decentralized, individual participation is high, group allegiance is multiplex, and social control is low is not devoid of contradictions. The most important is that generated by the ambivalent relationship between individualism, especially of the "expressive" kind (Bellah et al., 1996), and a specific understanding of "community," seen as a "virtual," "decentralized," "voluntary" organization (Fernback, 1997; Matei, 2005).

These contradictions can be most vividly captured by observing social groups aggregated around wiki projects. In such projects we see, on the one hand, an apparent erasure of identity and on the other acrimonious disputes over territory and meaning. The fact that articles are not individually signed does not dampen territoriality, but to the contrary, makes it even more heavily felt since the only way to make sure that your opinion counts is to make sure that your views, ideas, or words "stick" during the natural growth and evolution of a wiki article. This has a more philosophical implication. Being an individual on Wikipedia, an "I", is not the product of solipsistic regression and withdrawal from the world, but an affirmation of being an other-directed, expressive "me" (Mead, 1934). Yet, the social compact that emerges from this process is still an individualist one, albeit one characterized by a "networked individualism" (Wellman, 2001). This ethos satisfies the desire of being part of collective entities greater than the self by turning this collective environment into a "sounding board for the self" (Matei, 2005).

Collaborative technologies, such as wikis, are powered by the aggregated passion of myriad creative "I"s to produce a large amount of content, knowledge-wise or of another kind. Yet, as this content is produced to satisfy some inner need of self-expression it will retain its connection with its creator, who will try to defend his or her version of the knowledge that is developed collaboratively. A direct consequence of this lingering relationship of the creative "I" with the content it generated is, for example, the manner in which narrative and strategic meaning of Wikipedia entries and policies are continuously appropriated, discussed and contested.

Wikipedia editors themselves recognize this process of appropriation and contestation, especially when it comes to defining and enforcing rules. On Wikipedia rules are susceptible to interpretation and personal appropriation just like any other piece of content, since they are too the product of collaborative editing. For example, making what in mass communication research is known as a "framing" argument (Scheufele 1999), some active Wikipedians suggested that one of the core Wikipedia policies, Neutral Point of View (NPOV), which states that "representing fairly, proportionately, and as far as possible without bias, all significant views that have been published by reliable sources" ("Wikipedia:Neutral point of view - Wikipedia, the free encyclopedia," n.d.) is virtually unenforceable and that quite frequently contributors try to circumvent it or to interpret it in such a way as to defend their own point of view. According to the opinions expressed on a collection of Wikipedia pages dedicated to discussion regarding NPOV and its enforceability ("Wikipedia:Neutral point of view - Wikipedia, the free encyclopedia," n.d.), attempts to subvert the policy and insert specific points of view in the editorial process could be at times quite subtle. Even if individual articles might not biased content-wise, a preponderance of articles describing concepts or ideas aligned with a specific ideology would naturalize that ideology and impose a particular viewpoint. Another type of bias could emerge from focusing on the failings or negative aspects of a topic at the expense of its positive facets. These systemic biases appeared to some to emerge on Wikipedia not only statically, through the initial choices made by the early or active registered users who frequent certain topics, but also dynamically, through the process by which topics are pruned out or rewritten during editing by the editors that spend the most time and are invested the most in the articles.

This type of bias is quite insidious and it cuts across the political and ideological field. For example, a Wikipedian protested the alleged left-wing bias of the political articles posted on Wikipedia,

[...] Articles that are critical of the US are almost always kept. Articles critical of anti-American attitudes are as a rule deleted as "POV". Examples: Arab dictatorships – deleted Ameriphobia – deleted Islamophilia – deleted Islamophobia – kept 911 conspiracy theories – kept. So it seems that anything too critical of anti-American terorrism or bigotry is immediately deleted, because it is "POV", while POV articles whose very titles imply a position (Islamophobia, History of US Imperialism, etc) are rigorously defended. Even editing such articles brings a swarm of RVs [misspelled RW, revert wars] [...] The most important matter seems to be whether the admin agrees with the article or not politically, ie. fringe Leftwing ("Wikipedia talk:Neutral point of view/Archive 004 - Wikipedia, the free encyclopedia," 2005).

In counterpoint, a supporter of left-wing causes, whose personal Wikipedia page was at one point adorned with the Communist hammer and sickle and which carried as an extended motto the lyrics of the Communist anthem "L'Internationale," (Shorne, 2006) affirms on the NPOV discussion page that "pretensions to NPOV and accuracy notwithstanding, Wikipedia as currently managed is hopelessly slanted towards the right. No topic of political significance can be adequately discussed here; structural defects ensure that" (Shorne, 2006).

Subordination of NPOV policy to individual perspectives and its selective enforcement can be detected not only upon examining its enforcement through a framing lens, but also from an ethical angle. Some Wikipedia authors think that assessing the "neutrality" of an entry by how close it comes to what at a specific point in time is seen as "majority view," could be quite problematic since it prevents individual dissent. One Wikipedian raised the question "what if the number of people who hold a position is in dispute?" ("Wikipedia talk:Neutral point of view/Archive 003 - Wikipedia, the free encyclopedia," 2005). This opinion resonates with similar perspectives that can be found on the NPOV discussion page, such as this one, expressed by a supporter of the idea that aliens have visited Earth:

'Mainstream' isn't always right, is it? Therefore, in the interest of not excluding information that may potentially be proven correct at some point in the future, minority views have to be included. The worst offenders for the 'mainstream' bullshit are the pages about extra terrestrial intelligence. I've given up try to add views to THAT page. Unless you can PROVE there's aliens and UFO's any attempt to add such views gets immediately wiped ("Wikipedia talk:Neutral point of view/Archive 002 - Wikipedia, the free encyclopedia," 2005).

The most revealing intersection between the Neutral Point of View policy and the individualistic motivations of Wikipedia authors can be detected in the discussion about the moral judgment implied in NPOV's requirement to abstain from making a moral judgment even in cases that require such judgment. Some Wikipedia contributors feel that NPOV should not and cannot demand them to abstain from individual moral judgments when common sense and human decency demand that they should speak up. One contributor expressed this concern quite eloquently:

I have just been struck by a thought: – sometimes the nature of an article makes it a subjective issue, based on points of view. The fact that these points of view exist, in my view is factual in itself. Now POV [Note: "Point of View," biased view] goes against Wiki Policy, I know, but the exclusion of POV can mean the omission of facts, leading to an incomprehensive or incorrect dataset. Take World War II: neutral POV in its basic form would not make any destinction between who was right and wrong – after all Hitler was convinced he was right. [...] Unless the POVs are noted (and noted as such) then the reader will end up with, if you like, a "neutral bias ("Wikipedia talk:Neutral point of view/Archive 002 - Wikipedia, the free encyclopedia," 2005).

Such opinions about manipulation of "Neutral Point of View" on Wikipedia argue compellingly that open, non-moderated collaborative technologies naturally generate their own systemic constraints, which clash with the individualistic motivators that fuel contributions. Some debates require individual points of view. Expressing and more importantly "making them stick" often leads to personal conflict and continuous editing and re-editing, while rules and political processes verge on radical anarchy. Such processes create a social interaction universe full of contradictions and conflict and of individual attempts to sway articles in such way to reflect one's own beliefs and values.

According to some participant-observers, the system of peer-to-peer arbitration Wikipedia uses for solving such situations can be easily corrupted by political manipulations and top-down measures (expulsion or censorship). Truth and "neutrality" become whatever each user intends it to mean and is enforced not by intellectual consensus but by topic "squatting," which reflects that Wikipedia editors care profoundly about their own individual interpretation of the topic at hand. This behavior has not only individual but also group behavioral implications. Some Wikipedia editors form political alliances with other members or use bureaucratic manipulation and persistence to make sure that their own perspectives of certain issues are preserved. In effect, they become a type of beat cop who "patrols" (a recognized term in the Wikipedia lingo) specific entries. This process of personal appropriation of content and collective pacts is described by a former Wikipedia top administrator who left the project because of it:

Admins are supposed to be "just another editor with a few extra buttons", but too many admins today get drunk on that power. They insist that normal editors are "beneath" them, that they should be able to own articles and give their friends a hand up when content disputes arise. If you're friends with an admin, rest assured that your buddies will call someone a name, get one called back, and then ask you to punish the other guy for "incivility." And you'll do it, too, without a moment's hesitation, simply because you have the power to do it. (Peters, 2006)

This type of power dynamic highlights how far some collaborative technologies can veer from claims of self-regulation through "emergence," (Johnson, 2001; Kelly, 1995; Resnick, 1994) a term used sometimes to explain how Wikipedia "really works." Technically, "emergence" is described as the spontaneous process by which system-level rules and behaviors appear without any intentional activity on the part of the individual actors (Johnson, 2001). An example frequently mentioned in these conversations in support of the fact that Wikipedia is an "emergent" phenomenon is the speed with which random changes (designated on Wikipedia as "massive edits") are eliminated or, as Wikipedians call this process "reverted" (Viegas, Wattenberg, & van Ham, 2007). Yet, empirical data suggests that such "reverts" are more likely to occur where editing is closely controlled by a group of long term editors.

For example, an early study (Viegas, Wattenberg, & Kushal, 2004) observed that massive Wikipedia edits tend to be reverted after 3 minutes, compared to 90 minutes, in median, for regular edits. This can be explained by the fact that massive reverts are more likely to occur in more heavily "patrolled" articles, where one or more long-term members actively control the content and the editorial process. This proposition is directly supported by a study (Stvilia, Twidale, L. Smith, & Gasser, 2005) that compared a random sample of 834 entries to a subsample of "featured" (heavily edited and patrolled) articles. Stvilia et al. found that the median number of reverts for random articles was 0, compared to 12 for "featured" articles. In brief, Wikipedia entries seem to be more likely to be changed when they are in the center of the public discussion and controlled by specific groups of interested actors.

To summarize this discussion about Wikipedia's core values and functional constraints, one can draw the line by saying that like many other collaborative projects, Wikipedia attracts a fair number of individuals who are willing to spend their time and resources on editing Wikipedia articles in order to make a difference. This is an individualistic motivator. Contributions to Wikipedia are worthwhile not only because they represent a contribution to the world repository of knowledge, but also because they represent adding one's *own contribution* to that knowledge. Working for Wikipedia is an expression of the creative power and autonomy of the individual who performs the work. Since Wikipedia comes with the functional constraint of a policy that demands a "neutral point of view" and of speaking with one voice, editors create power mechanisms of inclusion and exclusion, of filtering content and of deciding what is "right" and "wrong." This leads to a number of biases, some of them subtle, that naturalize specific perspectives not as much in terms of what is said, but in terms how topics are prioritized or framed.

THE INEQUALITY OF ONLINE WIKI INTERACTION AT THE INTERSECTION BETWEEN SOCIAL VALUES AND FUNCTIONAL CONSTRAINTS

In the previous section we discussed the very particular way in which one can say that Wikipedia is an "open" collaborative system. Namely, we proposed that openness can lead to conflict and appropriation of work and policy making by a group of editors that have time, resources, and knowledge necessary to "patrol" and "squat" a specific article. Furthermore, such behaviors can shape Wikipedia's social structure in a definite way, namely, by making it quite top heavy, an issue that is empirically supported by the research cited above that revealed that Gini coefficients for Wikipedia are unusually high (Ortega et al., 2008). Wikipedia, as many other social media, is dominated by a small group of power users who are responsible for a large proportion of the social production of its content. Understanding this group, their motivations and constraints, is vital for understanding Wikipedia in particular, but also social media in general, since these are central functional characteristics for most collaborative technologies.

A possible explanation for the emergence of a hierarchal structure on Wikipedia and of a leading group of contributors can be found at the intersection of two functional factors. On the one hand there is the cultural imperative of individualistic and self-expressive cultural proclivities, mentioned above. Social media promises a fulfillment of and attracts those individuals that care more about deeply held ideas, passions, and convictions. Thus, some people would automatically contribute more. On the other hand, naturally-occurring participation inequalities are due to coordination costs and division of labor requirements, two dimensions of collaborative projects that Wikipedia shares with many other group endeavors. Recent studies have shown that the exponentially-increasing contribution rates among Wikipedia participants reflect decades-old research into small discussion groups working on tasks, which found similar relative rates of input by team members and which explained them in view of labor coordination and emergence of specialized roles.

Bales (1950; 1955; 1965) discovered that group members' differing participation levels were due to role differentiation, with each individual roughly assuming positions of leaders or followers who respectively either contribute to the success of the collaboration in a task or in a process-related manner. Role differentiation, relative rates of participation (Stephan & Mishler, 1952) and participation inequality are clearly occurring on the larger scale of Wikipedia as well and a number of analyses have confirmed this. Yet, this proof alone may not be what is truly notable about these primarily social self-organizing phenomena online – but the fact that these systems (which operate from a form of implicit coordination) appear to work *better* than their more equitable, unstructured counterparts. Empirical studies have in fact found a correlation between participation inequalities and Wikipedia article quality (Arazy & Nov, 2010; Kittur et al., 2009).

Extending the research agenda, optimal levels of structural inequality (Matei & Oh, 2005) in online collaboration has been proven (Bruno, 2010) to exist as well. Both Kuk (2006) and Bruno (2010) found a significant curvilinear relationship between participation inequality and a measureable performance outcome: the quality of open source software code and participator learning. These overt leader-follower dynamics would seem to argue for systems that simultaneously promote individualist and communal values.

If we are to return to some of the observations made in the earlier part of this chapter, especially to Jenkins' (2006), it is important to note that participation or "participative culture" can only partially and in a very qualified manner be substituted with "egalitarian" or "even" participation. Furthermore, Jenkins' call for "closing the transparency gap" by increasing our efforts to educate the next generation of media producers about the processes that take place "behind the scenes" becomes more germane than ever. Strong and meaningful participation in open social media projects such as Wikipedia needs to be supported by effective training and increased efforts to raise both the young and old social media users' level of media literacy.

Sensitivity to media literacy is particularly important in the context in which we hear more and more calls, such as those launched by Jimmy Wales, Wikipedia's leader an cofounder, for spreading the use and attracting more contributors to his project (Kopytoff, 2011; Wollman, 2011). Such calls need to be accompanied by concerted efforts at explaining and visualizing on the site itself the great contribution and participation inequalities that characterize this medium. Potential editors should also be trained and primed for the particular types of social interaction that take place on Wikipedia, which include negotiating numerous and subtle barriers to entry and a rather arcane system of power distribution.

Although some tools for visualizing social contributions to Wikipedia are available on the site, these are usually provided by third parties and hidden under obscure links that only advanced users can fully take advantage of. A whole new set of visualization tools has been created in the last several years that aim to support those interested in revealing the inner working of wikis and Wikipedia. They bring visualization to the very interface of Wikipedia, aiming to help users and editors better understand who is responsible for what part of the content. Projects such as Visible Effort – http://veffort.us (Matei, Bruno, & Morris, 2010) or WikiTrust – http://wikitrust.net (Adler & de Alfaro, 2007) are two such tools. They could be used in conjunction with any wiki project to visualize either the level of collaborative evenness that generated specific wiki articles (Visible Effort) or the degree to which content has been considered "valuable" by previous editors and left untouched (WikiTrust).

CONCLUSION AND FUTURE RESEARCH DIRECTIONS

Our chapter points to several advantages and challenges created by the emergence of a new generation of online collaborative environments, especially wikis. While complementary and productive in terms of gross output, more convenient and cheaper to implement than other, more traditional platforms, they raise a number of delicate issues. Poor understanding of motivations and social structures in open wiki systems has led to much early enthusiasm for their capacity to harness the power of the many to deal with what appeared to be intractable issues. Many "crowdsourcing" wikis have failed by not recognizing that wiki sites work better when there are clear leaders and dedicated users (Howe, 2009), who are willing to sink their time and energy into the project. And when successful, as is the case of Wikipedia, some observers have ignored or preferred to explain away (Lih, 2010) that their success is due to the fact that there is a hierarchy at work and that some individuals do take charge of the editorial process and do imprint the project with their individual or group preferences in overt or more subtle terms. In the present chapter we argue that successful wiki projects emerge at the intersection of specific individual cultural values with functional constraints. The meteoric success of Wikipedia, which has surpassed any known encyclopedic endeavor, illustrates these contradictory processes very well. Bringing them to light is important because Wikipedia content is affected by subjectivity and subtle framing and selection bias. These biases are in part generated by the individualistic expectations of many power users that their creative capabilities should be recognized and used. These biases cannot be simply cast aside as side effects or accidents, since they are in part the motivators that fuel editors' willingness to contribute and are responsible for Wikipedia's success.

In other words, social media such as Wikipedia have created a de facto digital hierarchy that seems to be just as interested as any hierarchy to impose its imprimatur on the content it is supposed to administer. Furthermore, it appears that a moderate amount of inequality might be a natural requirement of *any* efficient social interaction online.

To conclude, the advent of collaborative technologies such as Wikipedia has changed many information habits and certainly has distributed ordinary users' ability to collect, process and disseminate information. These new information environments require continued explicative efforts. We need to more address the issue of social motivation and social structure in collaborative technologies, such as wikis more carefully. We also need to create the tools for sieving through the masses of information these information repositories generate and disseminate and to assess their accuracy, validity and group biases. Finally, we need to study in what ways the social and cultural auspices under which these media emerge influence the nature of their content and of the consumption habits of their users. These are all extremely interesting topics, which promise a very promising research agenda for many years to come.

REFERENCES

Adler, B. T., & de Alfaro, L. (2007). A content-driven reputation system for the Wikipedia. In *Proceedings of the 16th International Conference on World Wide Web - WWW '07* (p. 261). doi:10.1145/1242572.1242608

Arazy, O., & Nov, O. (2010). Determinants of Wikipedia quality: The roles of global and local contribution inequality. In *Proceedings of the 2010 ACM Conference on Computer Supported Cooperative Work*, (pp. 233–236).

Bales, R. F. (1950). A set of categories for the analysis of small group interaction. *American Sociological Review*, *15*(2), 257–263. doi:10.2307/2086790

Bales, R. F. (1955). The equilibrium problem in small groups. In T. Parsons, R. Bales, & E. Shils, *Working papers in the theory of action*. Glencoe, IL: The Free Press.

Bales, R. F. (1965). Small group theory and research. In Merton, R., Broom, L., & Cottrell, L. (Eds.), *Sociology today*. New York, NY: Harper Torchbooks.

Bell, D. (1976). *The cultural contradictions of capitalism*. New York, NY: Basic Books.

Bellah, R. N., Madsen, R., Sullivan, W. M., Swidler, A., & Tipton, S. M. (1996). *Habits of the heart: Individualism and commitment in American life (Updated.)*. Berkeley, CA: University of California Press.

Belson, D. (1994). *The network nation revisited* (Bachelor). New Jersey Institute of Technology. Retrieved from http://sunsite.utk.edu/FINS/Periodicals_and_Newspapers/Fins-PaN-33.txt

Benkler, Y. (2002). Coase's Penguin, or, Linux and the nature of the firm. *The Yale Law Journal*, *112*(3), 369–446. Retrieved from http://www.yale.edu/yalelj/112/BenklerWEB.pdf. doi:10.2307/1562247

Benkler, Y. (2007). *The wealth of networks: How social production transforms markets and freedom*. Yale University Press.

Beschastnikh, I., Kriplean, T., & McDonald, D. W. (2008). Wikipedian self-governance in action: Motivating the policy lens. *Proc. ICWSM 2008*.

Boyd, D., & Ellison, N. (2007). Social network sites: Definition, history, and scholarship. *Journal of Computer-Mediated Communication, 13*(1), 11. Retrieved from http://jcmc.indiana.edu/vol13/issue1/boyd.ellison.html. doi:10.1111/j.1083-6101.2007.00393.x

Bruno, R. (2010). *A democracy of unequals* (Ph. D. Dissertation). West Lafayette, IN: Purdue University.

Bryant, S. L., Forte, A., & Bruckman, A. (2005). *Becoming Wikipedian: Transformation of participation in a collaborative online encyclopedia*. Sanibel Island, FL: ACM.

Cohen, N. (2007, March 5). A contributor to Wikipedia has his fictional side. *New York Times*. Retrieved from http://www.nytimes.com/2007/03/05/technology/05wikipedia.html?pagewanted=2&_r=1

Davies, J. (2004). *Wiki brainstorming and problems with wiki based collaboration.* (Master's thesis). University of York.

Elliott, M. S., & Scacchi, W. (2003). *Free software developers as an occupational community: Resolving conflicts and fostering collaboration*. Sanibel Island, FL: ACM.

Feller, J. (2005). *Perspectives on free and open source software*. Cambridge, MA: MIT Press.

Fernback, J. (1997). The individual within the collective: Virtual ideology and the realization of collective principles. In Jones, S. (Ed.), *Virtual culture* (pp. 36–54). Thousand Oaks, CA: Sage.

Fox, J. (2007). Getting rich off those who work for free. *Time*. Retrieved from http://vnweb.hwwilsonweb.com/hww/jumpstart.jhtml?recid=0bc05f7a67b1790e43f188a0944caaa997c3f03c1167820e090dc389e2346f69d2c219bb19f24143&fmt=C

Gillmor, D. (2006). *We the media: Grassroots journalism by the people, for the people*. Sebastopol, CA: O'Reilly.

Hafner, K. (2006). *Growing Wikipedia refines its "anyone can edit" policy*.

Hiltz, S. R., & Turoff, M. (1978). *The network nation: Human communication via computer*. Reading, MA: Addison-Wesley.

Howe, J. (2009). *Crowdsourcing: Why the power of the crowd is driving the future of business (unedited edition.)*. Crown Business.

Inglehart, R. (1997). *Modernization and postmodernization: Cultural, economic, and political change in 43 societies*. Princeton, NJ: Princeton University Press.

Jaschik, S. (2007, January 26). *A stand against Wikipedia*. Retrieved from http://www.insidehighered.com/news/2007/01/26/wiki

Jenkins, H., Clinton, K., Purushotma, R., Robinson, A. J., & Weigel, M. (2006). *Confronting the challenges of participatory culture: Media education for the 21st century*, (pp. 1–72). Chicago, IL. Retrieved from http://digitallearning.macfound.org/atf/cf/%7B7E45C7E0-A3E0-4B89-AC9C-E807E1B0AE4E%7D/JENKINS_WHITE_PAPER.PDF

Johnson, S. (2001). *Emergence: The connected lives of ants, brains, cities, and software*. New York, NY: Scribner.

Keen, A. (2007). *The cult of the amateur: How today's internet is killing our culture*. New York, NY: Doubleday/Currency.

Keep, C., McLaughlin, T., & Parmar, R. (2000). *The electronic labyrinth: Ted Nelson and Xanadu* (Vol. 2002). Keep, Christopher McLaughlin, Tim Parmar, Robin.

Kelly, K. (1995). *Out of control: The new biology of machines, social systems and the economic world*. Reading, MA: Addison-Wesley.

Kittur, A., Chi, E., Pendelton, B., Suh, B., & Mytkowicz, T. (2007). *Power of the few vs. wisdom of the crowd: Wikipedia and the rise of the bourgeoisie*. Presented at the CHI 2007, San Jose, California. Retrieved from http://www.parc.com/research/publications/files/5904.pdf

Kittur, A., Lee, B., & Kraut, R. E. (2009). Coordination in collective intelligence: The role of team structure and task interdependence. In *Proceedings of the 27th International Conference on Human Factors in Computing Systems* (pp. 1495-1504). Boston, MA: ACM. doi:10.1145/1518701.1518928

Kittur, A., Suh, B., Pendleton, B. A., & Chi, E. (2007). He says, she says: Conflict and coordination in Wikipedia. *Proceedings of the SIGCHI Conference on Human Factors in Computing Systems*, 453-462.

Klobas, J. E., & Beesley, A. (2006). *Wikis: Tools for information work and collaboration*. Oxford, UK: Chandos Information Professional Series.

Kollock, P., & Smith, M. (1996). Managing the virtual commons: Cooperation and conflict in computer communities. In Herring, S. (Ed.), *Computer-mediated communication: Linguistic, social, and cross-cultural perspectives* (pp. 109–128). Amsterdam, The Netherlands: John Benjamins.

Kopytoff, V. (2011, January 13). Wikipedia marks 10th anniversary - NYTimes.com. *New York Times Bits blog*. Retrieved February 21, 2011, from http://bits.blogs.nytimes.com/2011/01/13/wikipedia-marks-10-years-of-edit-it-yourself/

Kriplean, T., Beschastnikh, I., McDonald, D. W., & Golder, S. A. (2007). Community, consensus, coercion, control: CS* w or how policy mediates mass participation. In *Proceedings of the 2007 International ACM Conference on Supporting Group Work* (pp. 167–176).

Kuk, G. (2006). Strategic interaction and knowledge sharing in the KDE developer mailing list. *Management Science, 52*(7), 1031. doi:10.1287/mnsc.1060.0551

Lanier, J. (2006, May 30). Digital Maoism: The hazards of the new online collectivism. *Edge webzine*. Retrieved March 11, 2008, from http://www.edge.org/3rd_culture/lanier06/lanier06_index.html

Leuf, B., & Cunningham, W. (2001). *The Wiki way. Quick collaboration on the Web*. Boston, MA: Addison-Wesley.

Levine, R., Locke, C., Searls, D., & Weinberger, D. (2000). *The cluetrain manifesto*. Cambridge, MA: Perseus Books.

Levy, S. (1985). *Hackers: Heroes of the computer revolution*. New York, NY: Dell.

Licklider, J. C. R. (1960). Man-computer symbiosis. *IRE Transactions on Human Factors in Electronics, HFE-1*(March), 4–11. doi:10.1109/THFE2.1960.4503259

Licklider, J. C. R., & Taylor, R. W. (1968, April). The computer as a communication device. *Science and Technology*, 21-31.

Lih, A. (2010). *The Wikipedia revolution: How a bunch of nobodies created the world's greatest encyclopedia*. Aurum Press, Limited.

Majchrzak, A., Wagner, C., & Yates, D. (2006). Corporate wiki users: Results of a survey. *Proceedings of the 2006 International Symposium on Wikis*, (pp. 99-104).

Matei, S. A. (2005). A sounding board for the self: Virtual community as ideology. *The Journal of Technical Writing and Communication, 35*(4), 345–365. doi:10.2190/402T-KPLQ-V5QD-PCFX

Matei, S. A. (2005). From counterculture to cyberculture: Virtual community discourse and the dilemma of modernity. *Journal of Computer-Mediated Communication, 10*(3). Retrieved from http://jcmc.indiana.edu/vol10/issue3/matei.html.

Matei, S. A., Bruno, R., & Morris, P. (2010). Visible effort: A social entropy methodology for managing computer-mediated collaborative learning. In *Proceedings of the Fourth Global Communication Forum*. Presented at the Global Communication Forum, Shanghai: Jiao Tong University. Retrieved from http://matei.org/ithink/?p=22040

Matei, S. A., & Dobrescu, C. (2011). Wikipedia's "neutral point of view:"Settling conflict through ambiguity. *The Information Society, 27*, 1–12. doi:.doi:10.1080/01972243.2011.534368

Matei, S. A., & Oh, K. (2005). *Collaboration and communication in online environments: A social entropy approach*. Presented at the National Communication Association Annual Conference, Austin, TX.

McHenry, R. (2004). *The faith-based encyclopedia*.

Mead, G. H. (1934). *Mind, self, and society from the standpoint of a social behaviorist*. Chicago, IL: University of Chicago Press.

O'Reilly, T. (2005). *What Is Web 2.0?* O'Reilly Publication. Retrieved March 11, 2008, from http://www.oreilly.com/pub/a/oreilly/tim/news/2005/09/30/what-is-web-20.html

Ortega, F., Gonzalez-Barahona, J., & Robles, G. (2008). On the inequality of contributions to Wikipedia. In *Proceedings of the 41st Annual Hawaii International Conference on System Sciences,* (p. 304). doi:10.1109/HICSS.2008.333

Peters, P. (2006). *Quitting Wikipedia and wanted you to know why* (Vol. 2006).

Postmes, T., Spears, R., & Lea, M. (1998). Breaching or building social boundaries? *Communication Research, 25*, 689–715. doi:10.1177/009365098025006006

Raymond, E. S. (2001). *The cathedral and the bazaar: Musings on Linux and open source by an accidental revolutionary (Rev.)*. Cambridge, MA: O'Reilly.

Resnick, M. (1994). *Turtles, termites, and traffic jams: explorations in massively parallel micro-worlds. Complex adaptive systems*. Cambridge, MA: MIT Press.

Reynolds, G. (2006). *An army of Davids: How markets and technology empower ordinary people to beat big media, big government, and other Goliaths*. Thomas Nelson.

Rheingold, H. (2000). *The virtual community: Homesteading on the electronic frontier* (2nd ed.). Cambridge, MA: MIT Press.

Roszak, T. (1994). *The cult of information: A neo-Luddite treatise on high tech, artificial intelligence, and the true art of thinking* (2nd ed.). Berkley, CA: University of California Press.

Schuler, D., & Day, P. (2004). *Shaping the network society: The new role of civil society in cyberspace*. Cambridge, MA: MIT Press.

Seigenthaler, J. (2005, November 29). A false Wikipedia biography. *USA Today*. Retrieved from http://www.usatoday.com/news/opinion/editorials/2005-11-29-wikipedia-edit_x.htm

Shirky, C. (2008). *Here comes everybody: The power of organizing without organizations*. The Penguin Press.

Shirky, C. (2010). *Cognitive surplus: Creativity and generosity in a connected age*. The Penguin Press HC.

Shorne. (2006, August 2). *User: Shorne*. Retrieved December 13, 2010, from http://en.wikipedia.org/w/index.php?title=User:Shorne&oldid=67292482

Smith, A. D. (1999). Problems in conflict management in virtual communities. In M. Smith & P. Kollock (Eds.), *Communities in cyberspace*, 134-163. New York, NY: Routledge.

Stephan, F. F., & Mishler, E. G. (1952). The distribution of participation in small groups: An exponential approximation. *American Sociological Review*, *17*(5), 598–608. doi:10.2307/2088227

Stvilia, B., Twidale, M. B., Gasser, L., & Smith, L. (2005). Information quality discussions in Wikipedia. In S. Hawamdeh (Ed.), *Knowledge Management: Nurturing Culture, Innovation, and Technology - Proceedings of the 2005 International Conference on Knowledge Management*, (pp. 101-113). Charlotte, NC: World Scientific Publishing.

Stvilia, B., Twidale, M. B., Smith, L., & Gasser, L. (2005). Assessing information quality of a community-based encyclopedia (pp. 442-454). Cambridge, MA.

Sunstein, C. R. (2001). *Republic.com*. Princeton, NJ: Princeton University Press.

Sunstein, C. R. (2006). *Infotopia: How many minds produce knowledge*. Oxford, UK: Oxford University Press.

Tapscott, D., & Williams, A. D. (2006a). *Wikinomics*. New York, NY: Portfolio.

Tapscott, D., & Williams, A. D. (2006b). *Wikinomics: How mass collaboration changes everything*. New York, NY: Portfolio.

Turoff, M. (1973). Human communication via data networks. In Blanc, R., & Cotton, I. (Eds.), *Computer networking* (pp. 241–245). IEEE Press.

Van Buskirkr, E. (2008, June 9). Encyclopaedia Britannica to follow modified Wikipedia model. *Wired Magazine*. Retrieved December 13, 2010, from http://www.wired.com/epicenter/2008/06/ency/

Viegas, F., Wattenberg, M., & Kushal, D. (2004). Studying cooperation and conflict between authors with history flow visualizations. In *Proceedings of the SIGCHI Conference on Human Factors in Computing Systems* (pp. p. 575–582). Vienna, Austria: ACM. Retrieved from http://alumni.media.mit.edu/~fviegas/papers/history_flow.pdf

Viegas, F., Wattenberg, M., & van Ham, F. (2007, January 3). Talk before you type: Coordination in Wikipedia. *IBM Research*. Retrieved October 28, 2008, from http://www.research.ibm.com/visual/papers/wikipedia_coordination_final.pdf

Weinberger, D. (2002). *Small pieces, loosely joined: A unified theory of the web*. Cambridge, MA: Perseus Pub.

Weinberger, D. (2007). *Everything is miscellaneous: The power of the new digital disorder*. New York, NY: Times Books.

Wellman, B. (2001). Physical place and cyber place: The rise of personalized networks. *International Journal of Urban and Regional Research*, *25*(2), 227–252. doi:10.1111/1468-2427.00309

Wikipedia. the free encyclopedia. (2005, April 16). *Wikipedia talk: Neutral point of view/Archive 002*. Retrieved December 13, 2010, from http://en.wikipedia.org/wiki/Wikipedia_talk:Neutral_point_of_view/Archive_002

Wikipedia. the free encyclopedia. (2005, January 13). *Wikipedia talk: Neutral point of view/Archive 003*. Retrieved December 13, 2010, from http://en.wikipedia.org/wiki/Wikipedia_talk:Neutral_point_of_view/Archive_003

Wikipedia. the free encyclopedia. (2005, June 17). *Wikipedia talk: Neutral point of view/Archive 004.* Retrieved December 13, 2010, from http://en.wikipedia.org/wiki/Wikipedia_talk:Neutral_point_of_view/Archive_004

Wikipedia. the free encyclopedia. (n.d.). *Wikipedia: Neutral point of view.* Retrieved from http://en.wikipedia.org/w/index.php?title=Wikipedia:Neutral_point_of_view&oldid=248166492

Williams, A. D., & Tapscott, D. (2010). *Macrowikinomics: Rebooting business and the world.* Portfolio Hardcover.

Wollman, D. (2011, January 12). On 10th anniversary, Wikipedia aims for diversity. *MSNBC News.* Retrieved February 21, 2011, from http://www.msnbc.msn.com/id/41045439/ns/technology_and_science-tech_and_gadgets/

Wuthnow, R. (1976). *The consciousness reformation.* Berkeley, CA: University of California Press.

Chapter 2
Conceptualizing Social Interactions in Networked Spaces

Jenny Kennedy
Swinburne University of Technology, Australia

ABSTRACT

This chapter argues for the rigid dichotomies between online and offline in current discourse on social interactions to be reconsidered. By identifying that space is produced by the intersection of interactions, it can be said that online and offline narratives are situated relationally rather than dichotomously.

Drawing on the concept of affordances (Gibson, 1977, 1986; Norman, 1988; Hogan, 2009) and the work of Doreen Massey (1994, 2005, 2009), it can be shown that subjects act on perceived affordances in narratives of online and offline relations, which intersect to produce the spaces in which social interactions are situated.

This chapter proposes the concept of "networked spaces" as a strategy for resolving the problematic binary of online and offline. Networked spaces are dynamic, and the contexts or narratives within them, relational. It is through the lived experiences of interactions in these spaces that the contexts of social interactions are suggested to be best examined.

DOI: 10.4018/978-1-61350-338-6.ch002

INTRODUCTION

This chapter argues for a blurring of the hitherto rigid dichotomies between the terms online and offline. Early studies of the internet considered online phenomena to be separate to that occurring offline (Sveningsson, 2004; Wellman, 2004), a convention which has not yet been fully overcome given that many more recent studies continue to give little consideration to offline contexts in the studies of online practices (Beer, 2008; Orgad, 2009). By considering how space is produced in the intersection of relations it can be shown how online and offline, while remaining distinct, are not separate but work together to produce the space in which social interactions occur.

Drawing on the concept of affordances (Gibson, 1977, 1986; Norman, 1988; Hogan, 2009) and the work of Doreen Massey (1994, 2005, 2009) it can be demonstrated that subjects act on affordances in narratives of online and offline relations which intersect to produce the spaces in which social interactions are situated. These spaces are neither online or offline specific, but are produced in the intersection of multiple relations across digital and material domains.

BACKGROUND

Digital interactions cannot be considered in isolation from social frameworks (Parikka, 2007). In their study of Trinidadian internet users, Daniel Miller and Don Slater (2000) identify that the internet is in fact embedded within existing social practices (p. 2). They argue that: "we need to treat internet media as continuous with and embedded in other social spaces, that they happen within mundane social structures and relations that they may transform but that they cannot escape into a self-enclosed cyberian apartness" (p. 5).

Similarly Lori Kendall (1999) argues that awareness of the offline context of online social interactions is important to the analysis of such interactions (p.71). While this conclusion has been reached by researchers repeatedly over the past decade, it appears that there is still a continuing inclination to separate online activity to offline (Beer, 2009). There is a historical and disciplinary inclination for online/offline activities to be divided while a synergistic approach is what is required. Leah Lievrouw and Sonia Livingstone (2009) argue that the challenge to the discourse of online/offline division is still there to be had (p. 4).

Far from being distinct singular activities, interactions that occur online have synchronistic contexts offline. The relations between synchronistic activities produce the spaces in which social activity is situated. Increasingly then, new media scholars are questioning the strict binary of 'online' and 'offline'. Situating social interactions discursively as online or offline is problematic because people are always one and often both at the same time. I argue that there is a need to reconsider the spatial context and the embodiment of interactions in current discourse to account for this.

Although this chapter seeks to transgress the online/offline divide it does not dismiss or ignore that there is a distinction between online and offline. Taking into consideration existing literature on the internet in everyday life (Haythornwhaite & Wellman, 2002; Bakardjieva, 2005), it seeks to situate the everyday practices of subjects so that the relations between online and offline contexts can be identified. Taking a phenomenological approach enables actions or interactions to be examined in context with attention given to the embodied condition of all interactions. Examining in context means to identify the intersecting relations that also bear on interactions taking place and contribute to producing the space in which interactions are situated.

Space is produced socially (Lefebvre, 1991). Space is an on-going production of spatial relations. It has a symbiotic relation to that which it is produced through: "Social space is not a thing among other things, nor a product among other products: rather, it subsumes things produced and encompasses their interrelationships in their coexistence and simultaneity—their (relative) order and/or (relative) disorder" (Lefebvre, 1991, p.73). Spaces are situated by specific socio/cultural frameworks. These spaces are learned by those occupying them. Lefebvre explains this through a conceptual triad. Lefebvre refers to the (re) production of learned practices within spaces as *spatial practices* which provide continuity and consistency. "In terms of social space, and of each member of a given society's relationship to that space, this cohesion implies a guaranteed level of competence and a specific level of performance" (Lefebvre, 1991, p.33). An example of this is how subjects engage or act in particular spaces such as swimming at a swimming pool or commenting on a thread in a forum. Space is produced in the manifestation of the spatial practices which it is perceived to afford. *Representations of space* "are tied to the relations of production and to the 'order' which those relations impose, and hence to knowledge, to signs, to codes, and to 'frontal' relations" (Lefebvre, 1991, p.33), meaning that spaces are mediated by the properties of that space and the perceived affordances represented within those spaces. For example representations of space are constructed in maps of transport, shopping malls and websites indicating 'you can go *here'*. The final concept of the triad, *representational spaces* can be explained as they lived experience of spatial practices and representations of space (Lefebvre, 1991, p.39). Representational space is space as it is experienced through symbolic use of objects such as that of art, photography and film and in social movements such as the streets of London as experienced in the student riots over tuition fees in December 2010. Space is important in addressing the distinctions between online and offline for the contextualisation of social interactions. There is a need to identify and resolve the issue of online and offline division in the context of everyday practices (Beer, 2009, Kendall, 1999, Lievrouw & Livingstone, 2009, Miller & Slater, 2000). The context of an interaction should then situate it in the narrative of everyday practices for the individual or human subject in question and identify the spatial context of the interaction.

With the development of communication technologies the spatiality of interactions requires reconsideration of place-specific definitions (Meyrowitz, 1985; Thompson, 1995). I use Michel de Certeau's (1988) notion of "space as a practiced place" (p. 117) where place is tangible, fixed, locatable and finite, whilst space is abstract, learnt, and ambiguous as a starting point to argue that social interactions are located in what I term here as networked *space* rather than networked *place*. Importantly for the concept of networked spaces, a space can be occupied by more than one thing while place cannot. Space rather than place therefore affords a convergence of online and offline properties that can articulate the lived experience.

Convergence is both a technological process and a socio-cultural process where separate actions intersect or merge to produce new spaces and meanings (Jenkins, 2006; Rheingold, 2000). Communication technologies such as mobile phones and wireless connectivity are central to the process of convergence in a network society where individual or human subjects are multimodal, moving fluidly between interactions across different devices, sites and platforms. As the technologies in use become ever more mobile there is an increased convergence of mediated social interactions (Ito, Okabe & Matsuda, 2005; Jenkins, 2006).

Mediated Social Interactions

All interactions are mediated (Mantovani & Riva, 1999; Milne, 2010). Computer mediated communication and mediated communication are often assumed to be synonymous however computer mediated communication implies mediation through and with specific technologies whereas mediated communication allows for the mediating effects of greater societal structures – politics, economy, power. However, much discussion of mediation tends to focus on the technological mediation of interactions often at a particular site as evidenced in the discussions focusing on the specificities of social network sites over recent years (boyd & Ellison, 2007).

Topics of study on social network sites have amassed a great deal of data and have included issues of network strength (Baym & Ledbetter, 2009; Ellison, Steinfield, & Lampe, 2007), privacy (Acquisti & Gross, 2006; Barnes, 2006; Gross & Acquisti, 2005), representation of self (Back et al., 2010; boyd & Heer, 2006; Ellison, Heino & Gibbs, 2006), special interest groups (Baym, 2007; Mellins, 2008) and specific social network site activities such as blogging (Baker & Moore, 2008; Bruns & Jacobs, 2006) or prosumerism (Bruns, 2008; Lange, 2008). Many of the studies in this area have limited their focus to a particular demographic such as teens (boyd, 2008, 2008b; Lee, 2009; Livingstone, 2008; Patchins & Hinduja, 2010) or to a single social network site such as Facebook (Ellison, Steinfield & Lampe, 2007; Walther, Van Der Heide, Kim, Westerman, & Tong, 2008) or Twitter (Crawford, 2009; Java, Song, Finin & Tseng, 2007; Marwick & boyd, 2010).

While many studies consider (in varying depths) the technological mediation of social network sites, few fully account for the embodied mediated situation in which the subject is situated in their engagement on the social network site in question. Instead the technologically mediating relations take precedence over non-technical mediating relations though these also shape the interaction. This dichotomy of computer mediated over the non-computer mediated maps clearly onto the online/offline divide. As with the online/offline divide, there is certainly a difference between the two principles and as with the online/offline divide it is much more complex than a clearly definable dichotomy. When considering the context of social interactions it is necessary to consider the perceptual cues beyond those associated with technology that subjects act upon and which also mediate and shape interactions.

NETWORKED SPACES

Situated in the 'third age' of internet studies where descriptive documentation of the network society gives way to analysis (Wellman, 2004), emphasis in this chapter is given to the development of a theoretical concept of space which addresses both online and offline contexts. This chapter puts forth the author's own concept of 'networked spaces' as a synergistic approach to define spaces of social interactions. Networked spaces supersede the terms online and offline. If the interaction of subject to subject or subject to object can be viewed as a narrative, then a networked space is a space produced in converged narratives. I propose the concept of networked spaces as a strategy for resolving the problematic binary of online and offline. Put simply the term 'networked space' accounts for all sites both physical and digital in which interactions occur. Its use highlights the need for social interactions to be contextualized holistically. A networked space is a site of converged narratives. A networked space is not online or offline, but is produced in the convergence of multiple narratives of which there may be online and offline parts (Massey, 2009, p. 17). Networked spaces allows for what has been termed elsewhere the 'context collapse' of physical and digital materiality to be properly examined and show that it is not so much a context collapse as the intersection of more diverse narratives that create the social spaces subjects produce and operate in (Wesch, 2009).

The term 'networked spaces' signals a development of thought on relations and spatiality. Secondly, the term further develops thoughts found in existing literature. Network space is conceived as central to social structure (along with temporal variables) by Harrison White in *Identity and Control* (1992), his work influenced David Stark and Balázs Vedres (2006) in their work on the evolution of network spaces in the field of foreign investment. Stephen Graham and Simon Marvin (2001) consider the relational dynamic between social structure and network space which they refer to as 'secessionary networked spaces'. In *Splintering Urbanism: Networked Infrastructures, Technological Mobilities, and the Urban Condition* (2001) they argue that privileged access to networked spaces unevenly influences social structure, particularly the structure of networked infrastructure, an argument sustained by Roger Burrows and Nick Ellison (2004). Also from an urbanist framework, Joe Doak and Gavin Parker (2005) regard networked spaces as measures in urban planning to improve participatory practices.

Commonly, each of these theorists identifies networked spaces as being produced and grounded in social practice. The working definition of networked spaces offered here maintains these commonalities to show that networked spaces are the spaces of social interactions and are defined (and re-defined) in use.

Contextualised Actions in Networked Spaces

Networked spaces are spaces of converged contexts. Given this how can the cues for interactions be properly identified that allows for the relations between interaction-specific contexts? One such way might be to apply Miller and Johnson-Laird's concept of regions as de Certeau has done (Miller & Johnson-Laird, 1976, as cited in de Certeau, 1984, p. 126). Miller and Johnson-Laird refer to the space created by an interaction as a 'region'. The concept of regions identifies a boundary between interactions whilst still allowing for the relations between interactions to be examined. Each interaction-delineated region can be analysed for how it might shape or be shaped by the other interactions occurring within the same networked space thus acknowledging multi-modal behaviour, though breaking interactions into regions does little to breach the online/offline computer-mediated/non-computer mediated divide. There is some currency in Pierre Bourdieu's concept of fields where interactions are mediated by cultural, social and economic capital, and by which frameworks interactions are grounded, though this also does not sufficiently account for the relations between interactions (Bourdieu, 1984).

Consider the following scenario:

Clare is meeting a friend for mid-afternoon coffee. Clare arrives first at the coffee shop where they are meeting so she orders a coffee at the counter and takes a seat at one of the tables. While she waits she digs out her smart phone and starts to write a hurried email to a work colleague. Her phone beeps and she interrupts her email writing to check the message. It is from her friend who she is waiting for, to say that they have just left their office and will be five minutes later than planned. She texts back then resumes writing her email, now taking more time to consider the phrasing and include additional details. Having sent the email, Clare opens the Facebook app on her phone and 'checks in' to the coffee shop. She then checks the profile page of the friend she is waiting for then browses through the news feed looking at other status updates and posts. She comments on a photo and responds to two different conversations on people's walls, one of whom is a mutual friend of the person she is waiting for. Her friend arrives at the coffee shop, they great each other with a hug and a kiss on each cheek.

The unit of analysis here is the networked space produced in the intersection of the interactions described above. How best can the interaction(s) in the above scenario be contextualized?

Paul Dourish divides theories of contextualization into three groups: positivist, critical and phenomenological (Dourish, 2004). In a positivist framework context is informative, delineable and stable and is separate from activity (p.5). In the scenario described above where Clare is sitting in a coffee shop but is also on Facebook and engaging in asynchronous interactions by both SMS and email, a positivist contextualization might be that the setting is a public commercial place, the relationship between Clare and the person she is meeting with is friendship-based and the relationship between Clare and the person she is emailing is business-related. It might count how many profiles she views on Facebook or how many posts she reads and which networks those people are from in relation to Clare.

Critical definitions of context are somewhat broader and tend towards the view that context is produced socio-economically reflecting relations of power and control (Dourish, 2004). Critical definitions would include the relationship between Clare and the work colleague, such as whether one is in a superior position to the other, the reciprocity of the relationships between Clare and the contacts on Facebook as well at the reciprocity of the relationship between her and the person she is waiting for. That she is waiting might also be of significance to the critical context.

A phenomenological framework defines context as relational and dynamic. Context is particular to setting or occasion and arises from activity. An example of phenomenological definition based on the scenario above could relate to the reason Clare is meeting her friend, if it is to share news, to console or celebrate or if it is a routine that they act upon each week at the same time. This understanding of the meeting will be negotiated between Clare and her friend. Likewise, the setting is a place chosen and agreed upon by the subjects for subjective reasons, perhaps because of its proximity to another place, its ambience or the perceived privacy of its tables. Clare may write the email to her work colleague because it is an urgent matter or because she does not like to sit in a public place alone and unoccupied. Also a phenomenological contextualization of Clare's checking Facebook would consider her subjective interpretation of what she views there.

A phenomenological paradigm, rather than positivist or critical, best allows for the consideration of converged contexts and the dialogue that occurs as a result of such convergence. There are many distinct relations within the scenario described above which may each have bearing on the subject's experience of that space. Rather than consider each contextual element in singularity (and thereby potentially perpetuating the online and offline divide), the dynamic between contextual elements can be analyzed as intertwining narratives that produce social space (Massey, 2005). These spaces are referred to in this work as networked spaces. Networked spaces are dynamic, the contexts or narratives within them relational. It is through the lived experiences of interactions in these spaces that the contexts of social interactions are suggested to be best examined.

Applying a phenomenological framework considers the negotiations subjects make in social practices which enables their interactions to be examined in a way that is relational and dynamic. This approach to contextualization is most appropriate for networked spaces for it allows for the consideration of converged contexts that change over time and the dialogue that occurs as a result of these convergences.

Affordances

Meaning is negotiated not only across interactions but also within interactions. When negotiating meaning in interactions subjects act on cues. These cues are relational to the social structure in which the interaction occurs. Subjects perceive these cues as affordances that can be acted upon. Affordances are relational and can be seen as the perception of features that infer structure (Hogan, 2009). Perception of these features is relative to one's being-in-the world.

James Gibson defines affordances as available features that provide potential for action, perceived or not (Gibson, 1986). A less positivist definition is that affordances are perceived, actual or not and that affordances indicate properties of use which are dependent on a subject's positioning (Norman, 1988). Social affordances are the properties or features that are perceived as enabling social action. To give an example, if I am sitting at a bar with friends and we each have our mobile phones on the table in front of us we may each perceive a feature of those phones as enabling us to make calls (ignoring for the moment the many other features phones with smart capabilities may have). Though each subject may perceive the feature of a telephone, the type of interaction that the telephone affords may differ from subject to subject. While we may each perceive the feature of the phone as functioning to make or receive calls, we will each perceive the affordances of that feature differently depending on what numbers we have access to, who has access to our number that they might call us, whether it is a business phone used only for professional purposes, a personal phone used reluctantly under duress of a family member to remain contactable or whether we have sufficient credit to make a call. Though each of us may perceive the features of the phone similarly, the social affordances of those features to enable interactions may be experienced differently.

Hogan identifies informational, relational, temporal and spatial cues which mediate interactions by suggesting affordances of action to subjects (Hogan, 2009, pp. 30-40). Information cues are the content or context of interactions, they include gestures, expressions, language, text, symbols or objects coded with significance. Informational cues might be the name on the screen, indicating who is calling or being called or the sound, sight, vibration of the phone ringing. There is a distinction between potential information that may (not) be accessible and information that is available to the subject and that can be accessed or interpreted in a meaningful way (p. 32). Relational cues are similar to informational cues in that they are semiotic by nature though relational cues are based around the relationship between subjects rather than content or context. Relational cues are the relationship between subjects such as whether everyone knows each other or if there are people from different networks present. Temporal cues structure time and mark the occurrence of events. Temporal cues also provide information regarding access such as when someone might be available to contact or how an interaction might occur. From a socially-orientated perspective, spatial cues apply to place and distance (p. 38). Spatial cues suggest what relations are possible within a given setting. Temporal cues in the examples above might be indicated by the time of day. If it is evening then a phone call is likely to be personal whereas if the above scenario is set at lunch on a weekday, then it could be that we are all taking a break from work and may be interrupted at any moment by a business-related phone call. Spatial cues might be the placement of each phone to the subjects indicating probable ownership or spatial relations between subjects might indicate that should one subject's phone start to ring it is not likely to be another person sat at the same table who is calling them.

Affordances in the Rhetoric of Networked Individualism

The concept of social affordances has been most clearly articulated in discussions on networked individualism (Hogan, 2009, Wellman et al., 2003). From a networked individual framework social affordances are understood as the cues a subject perceives or accesses from their particular position within their network(s) according to specific temporal-spatiality, relativity and information (Hogan, 2009, pp. 30-40). Social affordances in this framework can be understood as who a subject may interact with in a given time and space, how they might be connected to another subject and what information is available to the primary subject regarding this interaction.

Networked individualism is used to explain perceived changes in social behavior and structures over the past few decades: "It is the move from densely-knit and tightly-bounded groups to sparsely-knit and loosely-bounded networks" (Wellman et al., 2003). For technology theorists such as Manuel Castells (1996), Barry Wellman (2002), Andreas Wittel (2001), networks are *the* defining social structure where technology provides social cohesion in networks "linking individuals with little regard to space" (Wellman, 2002, p.2). This is not to say that space does not play a role in the network society for it is clearly articulated in the 'space of flows' (Castells, 1996) where all expressions and materialities of culture and society 'flow' from node to node, or networked individual to networked individual.

As will be demonstrated in the latter parts of this chapter, space *is central* to social interactions in the network society. For this reason I argue that the networked individualism rubric is too frequently applied rhetorically. It is applied in emphasis of the mediation by technology (Cameron, 2001), the structure of social relations (Saffo, 2007) and the decline of community (Putnam, 2001). These claims are not entirely technological deterministic yet they do suggest that the developments of sophisticated communication technologies contribute to the rise of ego-centric networks and the atomization of subjects. Amit (2007), Hogan (2009) and Postill (2009) assert that such claims oversimplify what are complex social relations. Postill (2009) argues further that "personal media are contributing, together with other media, to the ongoing diversification of sociocentric formations around the globe ... not to the replacement of one single dominant pattern of sociability by another" (p. 3). These sociocentric formations include the increasingly complex converged contexts in which subjects find themselves.

I propose that one way to address this conflict is to make a subtle shift away from how the individual is situated in networks to look towards how interactions intersect in networked spaces. This may better allow for the operation of social affordances in diverse 'sociocentric formations' (Postill, 2009) to be understood. One of the key differences between networked individualism and networked spaces is the unit of analysis. For networked individualism the unit of analysis is the individual and the network(s) they interact in, for networked spaces the unit of analysis is the networked space produced in the intersection of interactions.

Networked individualism is an egocentric framework for it places the subject at the centre of analysis whilst the networked spaces model is interaction based. Because interactions are the focus of analysis in networked spaces, multiple interactions may be identified and the relations between them examined. Not only does this shift in focus allow for the intersection of multiple networked interactions but it may also account for the relation between interactions too.

As well as being egocentric, networked individualism is structural. Networked individualism is often (over)simplified in social network analysis where the structure of networks is the central point of focus (Amit, 2007), or in studies of tie strength – the duration, emotional intensity, intimacy and reciprocity of contact (Granovetter, 1973, p. 1361, Postill, 2009). Networked spaces as a strategy identifies the interrelated activities occurring within a space and the relations between them and how this relationality produces space. Because it allows for the relationship between activities to be identified, activity occurring across multiple platforms can be accounted for and the relations between these actions considered.

Networks in networked individualism are often portrayed as static, stable entities. Networked spaces are transient, they shift and evolve over time. Space is conquered (physically) in networked individualism (Wellman, 2002, p.2) whereas space is continually 'learnt' and produced in networked spaces. Here, social affordances are persistently perceived. While analysis of social affordances are in many instances interpretivist, social affordances from a networked spaces paradigm are better understood phenomenologically because the experience of these interactions within the perceived structure shapes and gives meaning to the interactions occurring there.

These differences are summarized in the following table, though it is stressed that the table is not intended to be read as situating networked spaces in diametric opposition to networked individualism, rather as one continuum to it. A table is used to emphasise differences and is intended as a provocation.

Social affordances are the cues one acts upon in social interactions, and without wishing to revert to strict structure/agency reductionism, are separate to the act(s). Social affordances then do little to circumvent the online/offline divide for they do not account for the potential relationship between interactions in which networked space is produced. To better understand the social affordances of networked spaces we must consider the lived experience of these spaces and how the relationality of interactions produce these spaces.

I turn now to the work of Doreen Massey (1994, 2005, 2009). Applying the concept of social affordances and Massey's concept of social space,

Table 1. Networked individualism vs. networked spaces

Social affordances + Networked Individualism	Social affordances + Networked Spaces
Individual focused	Interaction focused
Egocentric	Space-centric
Fixed, stable	Dynamic
Identifies structure	Identifies activity
Interpretivist approach	Phenomenological approach
Analysis of singular activity	Multi-layered analysis
Individual and networks as units of analysis	Networked space of interactions as units of analysis

I can show how these two frameworks together provide a means of understanding how networked spaces are produced and how a subject may act upon the affordances within a networked space. Space for Massey is the product of interrelations and is an inherent feature of social practices, one which is frequently overlooked. Massey (2005) conceptualizes space in three ways: it is produced through relations; it is potentially multiplex; and it is constantly in the process of being made. Space does not remain constant so it is experienced differently by subjects and across time. It is unbounded though not limitless meaning that it does not have set, fixed boundaries yet it cannot connect everything to everywhere simultaneously. Space is multidimensional and consists of or is constructed by many, shifting relations.

The Social is Spatial

The strategy of networked spaces applies Massey's social spaces concept to specifically address the false division of online/offline. All social activities or interactions have a spatial component (Massey, 1994: 265). The social is spatial. Massey's ongoing work demonstrates the centrality of space to social relations. Online and offline activities are many; there are many online and offline spaces that intersect or converge. At the point of convergence or intersection, each space is shaped and shapes those it is connected to. Space then, is made of these relational convergences, each relational tangent is dynamic which means that space is constantly being made.

Space is produced in the intersection of relations. Relations are the connections between subject to subject and subject to object. Network spaces applies Massey's social spaces concept specifically to the addressing of the on/offline divide. Networked space is the space produced by the intersection of interactions, building on Massey's idea of social spaces. Interactions occur subject to subject. Interactions are mediated by relations and affordances and are perceived differently by each subject. If space is created by multiple relations, networked spaces are produced by multiple social interactions which acknowledge both the relations between these interactions and that each interaction has multiple relations within it also.

Lefebvre (1991) identifies the perceived, conceived and lived aspects of social spaces. The experience of the lived is always in relation to the context in which it is both conceived and perceived. Phenomenology argues that the subject is constructed in relation to the culture in which they are situated (Merleau-Ponty, 1962). This relationship between subject and the social world is referred to as the lived experience. Networked spaces are learned, they function according to the socio/cultural frameworks in which they are situated and it is through this lived experience that subjects understand them as a networked space and act on the affordances they contain. Through the lived experience in networked spaces of social affordances subjects experience proximity to others. Presence is constructed in the cultural learning of a given networked space and is manifested by a subject acting upon the affordances of a space (Picciano, 2002: p. 24).

Presence perception varies by subject, spatiality and temporality. As with the perception of mediation and features of social affordances it may occur differently for different people, across different temporal-socio-cultural settings. Presence is a sense of proximity or of belonging, physically, emotionally and/or psychologically. Networked spaces afford presence but this does not mean that presence will or must be experienced, only that it is possible. In interactions that do occur, the experience of presence is dependent on the mediating properties in which interactions take place.

Everyday Practices in Networked Spaces

This chapter argues that the rigid dichotomies between online and offline in current discourse on social interactions need to be reconsidered. By identifying that space is produced in the relations between interactions, it can be said that online and offline narratives are situated relationally rather than dichotomously. It is revealed that online activities are as equally embedded in social practices as offline activities, and that this situational context of interactions ought to be reflected in current discourse. This chapter suggests the term networked space as a strategy to address the issue of the online/offline division of social activity. Networked spaces addresses this problematic binary by identifying the rich relationality of interconnecting narratives. These interconnecting narratives demonstrate the lived experience of social interactions, where no interaction occurs in isolation but shapes and is shaped by the interactions it intersects with. I argue that explorations of the everyday practices of subjects ought to account for this relationality. This chapter does not seek to eradicate the distinctions of online and offline, but does refrain from positioning them as opposites of each other so that the significance of each can be better accounted for in studies of everyday practices.

In order to make sense of how subjects experience networked spaces, consideration is given to how social interactions are mediated. The division of mediation between the technologically mediated and the non-technologically mediated has been demonstrated as mapping onto and intensifying the online/offline divide. All interactions are considered here in this writing to be mediated. Interactions are mediated by perceptual cues or affordances perceived by subjects. Hogan's typology of affordances consists of informational, relational, temporal and spatial cues (Hogan, 2009, p. 30-32). Affordances account for the perception of mediation within interactions but become problematic when considering the relationality of everyday practices in networked spaces. Networked spaces are produced by intersecting narratives of interactions between subjects and between subjects and objects. Interactions within a networked space may share mediating cues or may be mediated by cues exclusive to that particular interaction. Hogan's typology of affordances cannot account for the relationality of these intersections, nor for the spatiality their nexus produces. Both affordances and the lived experience of networked space are relational. Affordances are understood as features which subjects perceive in relation to their being in the world and which may be acted upon. Affordances are relational. The relationality of affordances is specific to subject and time. The interconnectivity of narratives is also specific to subject and time. Spatiality is perceived differently and acted upon differently by each subject and across different times. If conducting empirical analysis in this area we can only attempt to understand the subject's perception of a networked space at a particular moment in time (Massey, 1994, p. 4).

The lived experience gives meaning to interactions in networked spaces. The social practices of networked spaces are indentified phenomenologically and are defined relationally and dynamically. Social practices are learned. Networked spaces are learned and produced by subjects in their everyday practices. The perception and acting upon of affordances constitute multiple narratives. Networked spaces are produced in the intersections of these narratives by the relations between them. The dynamic intersection of narratives produce spaces networked by the relations between these narratives. As for Lefebvre and Massey, space is an ongoing production of relations. The dynamics of relations in networked space mean that these spaces are always in a state of production. They transition and evolve over time as networked spaces are re-produced.

FUTURE RESEARCH DIRECTIONS

The centrality of space to social interactions could be further developed with closer readings of the work by spatial theorists such as Massey (1994, 1999, 2005, 2007, 2009), Soja (1989) and Lefebrve (1991). This spatial turn in the social sciences and humanities is already underway as demonstrated by recent publications such as *The Spatial Humanities: GIS and the Future of Humanities Scholarship* (Bodenhamer, Corrigan & Harris, 2010) and *The Spatial Turn - Inter-disciplinary Perspectives* (Warf & Arias, 2008).

The idea put forth in this chapter are a work in progress and are likely to undergo refinement and revision by the author as the ideas are developed further. What is offered here then is a starting point from which the context of social interactions can be rethought in order to move beyond the on/offline divide. Emphasise is made that this is a theoretically grounding chapter which informs the empirical research to follow. The next step for this author is to conduct empirical research to provide detail rich case studies that identify the lived experiences of networked spaces which will assist in consolidating the ideas expressed here further.

A qualitative study of how individuals interact in networked spaces is currently underway. This study will address the role new media plays in the production of networked spaces and consider consciousness of distinct narratives and the intersection of public and private in networked spaces for individuals.

CONCLUSION

In this chapter I have explained how I have developed the term 'networked spaces', shown how it can be applied to the online/offline problem and given an indication of the empirical research that is underway to further test this theory.

The purpose of the chapter has been to outline the concept of networked spaces as a strategy for resolving the problematic binary of online and offline. This chapter has argued for the rigid dichotomies between online and offline in current discourse on social interactions to be reconsidered. By identifying that space is produced in the intersection of interactions it has been shown that online and offline narratives are situated relationally rather than dichotomously. A key contribution of this chapter has been the application of Massey's work to communication in the networked age.

REFERENCES

Acquisti, A., & Gross, R. (2006). Imagined communities: Awareness, information sharing, and privacy on the Facebook. In P. Golle & G. Danezis (Eds.), *Proceedings of 6th Workshop on Privacy Enhancing Technologies.* (pp. 36-58).Cambridge, UK: Robinson College.

Amit, V. (2007). Globalization through weak ties: A study of transnational networks among mobile professionals. In Amit, V. (Ed.), *Going first class* (pp. 53–71). Oxford, UK: Berghahn.

Back, M., Stopfer, J., Vazire, S., Gaddis, S., Schmukle, S., Egloff, B., & Gosling, S. D. (2010). Facebook profiles reflect actual personality, not self-idealization. *Psychological Science, 21*(3), 372–374. doi:10.1177/0956797609360756

Bakardjieva, M. (2005). *Internet society: The Internet in everyday life*. London, UK: Sage.

Baker, J., & Moore, S. (2008). Distress, coping, and blogging: Comparing new MySpace users by their intention to blog. *Cyberpsychology & Behavior, 11*(1), 81–85. doi:10.1089/cpb.2007.9930

Barnes, S. (2006). A privacy paradox: Social networking in the United States. *First Monday, 11*(9), 11–15.

Baym, N. (2007). The new shape of online community: The example of Swedish independent music fandom. *First Monday, 12*(8).

Baym, N. K., & Ledbetter, A. (2009). Tunes that bind? Predicting friendship strength in a music-based social network. *Information Communication and Society, 12*(3). doi:10.1080/13691180802635430

Beer, D. (2008). Social network (ing) sites... revisiting the story so far: A response to danah boyd & Nicole Ellison. *Journal of Computer-Mediated Communication, 13*(2), 516–529. doi:10.1111/j.1083-6101.2008.00408.x

Bodenhamer, D. J., Corrigan, J., & Harris, T. M. (Eds.). (2010). *The spatial humanities: GIS and the future of humanities scholarship*. Indianapolis, IN: Indiana University Press.

Bourdieu, P. (1984). *Distinctions. A social critique of the judgement of taste*. Cambridge, MA: Harvard University Press.

boyd, d., & Ellison, N. (2007). Social network sites: Definition, history, and scholarship. *Journal of Computer Mediated Communication, 13*(1), 210-230.

boyd, d., & Heer, J. (2006). Profiles as conversation: Networked identity performance on Friendster, *Proceedings of the Hawai'i International Conference on Social Systems – HICSS-39*, Kauai, Hawai'i, New York, NY: IEEE Computer Society.

boyd, d. (2008). *Taken out of context: American teen sociality in networked publics*. (Doctoral dissertation), University of California-Berkeley, California.

boyd, d. (2008b). Why youth hearth social network sites. In D. Buckingham (Ed.), *Youth, identity, and digital media*. Cambridge, MA: MIT Press.

Bruns, A. (2008). *Blogs, Wikipedia, Second Life, and beyond: From production to produsage*. New York, NY: Peter Lang.

Bruns, A., & Jacobs, J. (Eds.). (2006). *Uses of blogs*. New York, NY: Peter Lang.

Burrows, R., & Ellison, N. (2004). Sorting places out? Towards a social politics of neighbourhood informatization. *Information Communication and Society*, *7*(3), 321–336. doi:10.1080/1369118042000284588

Cameron, D. (2001). The rocket in your pocket: How mobile phones became the media by stealth. *Asia Pacific Media Educator*, *11*, 141–149.

Castells, M. (1996). *The Information Age: Economy, society and culture, Vol. 1: The rise of the network society*. Blackwell, UK: Oxford.

Crawford, K. (2009). Following you: Disciplines of listening in social media. *Journal of Media & Culture Studies*, *23*(4), 525–535. doi:10.1080/10304310903003270

de Certeau, M. (1984). *The practice of everyday life*. Berkeley, CA: University of California Press.

Doak, J., & Parker, G. (2005). Networked space? The challenge of meaningful participation and the new spatial planning in England. *Planning Practice and Research*, *20*(1), 23–40. doi:10.1080/02697450500261699

Dourish, P. (2004). What we talk about when we talk about context. *Personal and Ubiquitous Computing*, *8*(1), 19–30. doi:10.1007/s00779-003-0253-8

Ellison, N., Heino, R., & Gibbs, J. (2006). Managing impressions online: Self-presentation processes in the online dating environment. *Journal of Computer-Mediated Communication*, *11*(2). doi:10.1111/j.1083-6101.2006.00020.x

Ellison, N., Steinfield, C., & Lampe, C. (2007). The benefits of Facebook friends: Social capital and college students' use of online social network sites. *Journal of Computer-Mediated Communication*, *12*(4), 1143–1168. doi:10.1111/j.1083-6101.2007.00367.x

Gibson, J. (1977). The theory of affordances. In Shaw, R., & Bransford, J. (Eds.), *Perceiving, acting, and knowing: Towards an ecological psychology* (pp. 67–82). Hillsdale, NJ: Laurence Erlbaum.

Gibson, J. (1986). *The ecological approach to visual perception*. Hillsdale, NJ: Laurence Erlbaum.

Graham, S., & Marvin, S. (2001). *Splintering urbanism: Networked infrastructures, technological mobilities and the urban condition*. London, UK: Routledge. doi:10.4324/9780203452202

Granovetter, M. (1973). The strength of weak ties. *American Journal of Sociology*, *78*(6), 1360–1380. doi:10.1086/225469

Gross, R., & Acquisti, A. (2005). *Information revelation and privacy in online social networks*. Paper presented at the ACM, Alexandria, VA.

Hogan, B. (2009). *Networking in everyday life* (Doctoral dissertation). University of Toronto, Toronto.

Ito, M., Okabe, D., & Matsuda, M. (Eds.). (2005). *Personal, portable, pedestrian: Mobile phones in Japanese life*. Cambridge, MA: MIT Press.

Java, A., Song, X., Finin, T., & Tseng, B. (2007). *Why we Twitter: Understanding the microblogging effect in user intentions and communities*. Paper presented at WebKDD, San Jose, CA.

Jenkins, H. (2006). *Convergence culture: Where old and new media collide*. New York, NY: New York University Press.

Kendall, L. (1999). Recontextualizing cyberspace: Methodological considerations for on-line research. In Jones, S. G. (Ed.), *Doing Internet research: Critical issues and methods for examining the Net* (pp. 57–74). Thousand Oaks, CA: Sage.

Lange, P. (2008). Publicly private and privately public: Social networking on YouTube. *Journal of Computer-Mediated Communication, 13*(1), 361–380. doi:10.1111/j.1083-6101.2007.00400.x

Lee, S. (2009). Online communication and adolescent social ties: Who benefits more from internet use? *Journal of Computer-Mediated Communication*, 14.

Lefebvre, H. (1991). *The production of space*. Oxford, UK: Blackwell.

Lievrouw, L., & Livingstone, S. (2006). *The handbook of new media (updated student edition)*. London, UK: Sage.

Livingstone, S. (2008). Taking risky opportunities in youthful content creation: Teenagers' use of social networking sites for intimacy, privacy and self-expression. *New Media & Society, 10*(3). doi:10.1177/1461444808089415

Mantovani, G., & Riva, G. (1999). Real presence: How different ontologies generate different criteria for presence, telepresence, and virtual presence. *Presence (Cambridge, Mass.), 8*(5), 540–550. doi:10.1162/105474699566459

Marwick, A. & boyd, d. (2010). I Tweet honestly, I Tweet passionately: Twitter users, context collapse, and the imagined audience. *New Media & Society*. Online.

Massey, D. (1994). *Space, place, and gender*. Minneapolis, MN: University of Minnesota Press.

Massey, D. (1999). Spaces of politics. In Massey, D., Allen, J., & Sarre, P. (Eds.), *Human geography today* (pp. 279–294). Cambridge, UK: Polity Press.

Massey, D. (2005). *For space*. London, UK: Sage.

Massey, D. (2007). *Is the world getting larger or smaller?* Retrieved from http://www.opendemocracy.net/globalization-vision_reflections/world_small_4354.jsp

Massey, D. (2009). Concepts of space and power in theory and in political practice. *Documents d'Analisi Geografica, 55*(55), 15–26.

Mellins, M. (2008). The female vampire community and online social networks: Virtual celebrity and mini communities: Initial thoughts. *International Journal of Media and Cultural Politics, 4*(2), 254–258. doi:10.1386/macp.4.2.254_3

Merleau-Ponty, M. (1962). *Phenomenology of perception* (Smith, C., Trans.). London, UK: Routledge. (Original work published 1945)

Meyrowitz, J. (1985). *No sense of place: The impact of electronic media on social behaviour*. New York, NY: Oxford University Press.

Miller, D., & Slater, D. (2000). *The Internet: An ethnographic approach*. Oxford, UK: Berg.

Milne, E. (2010). *Letters, postcards, email: Technologies of presence*. New York, NY: Routledge.

Norman, D. (1988). *The psychology of everyday things*. New York, NY: Basic Books.

Orgad, S. (2009). How can researchers make sense of the issues involved in collecting and interpreting online and offline data? In Markham, A. N., & Baym, N. K. (Eds.), *Internet inquiry: Conversations about method* (pp. 33–53). Thousand Oaks, CA: Sage.

Parikka, J. (2007). *Digital contagions: A media archaeology of computer viruses*. New York, NY: Peter Lang.

Patchins, J., & Hinduja, S. (2010). Trends in online social networking: Adolescent use of MySpace over time. *New Media & Society, 12*(2), 197–216. doi:10.1177/1461444809341857

Picciano, A. (2002). Beyond student perceptions: Issues of interaction, presence, and performance in an online course. *Journal of Asynchronous Learning Networks, 6*(1), 21–40.

Postill, J. (2009). *The weakness of weak ties: Personal media and social leadership in a Kuala Lumpur suburb*. Paper presented to the Anthropology Department, University of Vienna.

Putnam, R. (2001). *Bowling alone: The collapse and revival of American community*. New York, NY: Simon & Schuster Paperbacks.

Rheingold, H. (2000). *The virtual community: Homesteading on the electronic frontier* (Revised edition). Cambridge, MA: MIT Press.

Saffo, P. (2007). *Farewell information, it's a media age*. Retrieved from http://www.saffo.com/essays/essay_farewellinfo.pdf

Soja, E. (1989). *Postmodern geographies*. London, UK: Verso.

Stark, D., & Vedres, B. (2006). Social times of network spaces: Network sequences and foreign investment in Hungary. *American Journal of Sociology*, *111*(5), 1367–1411. doi:10.1086/499507

Sveningsson, M. (2004). Ethics in Internet ethnography. In Buchanan, E. A. (Ed.), *Readings in virtual research ethics: Issues and controversies* (pp. 45–61). Hershey, PA: Information Science Pub.doi:10.4018/978-1-59140-152-0.ch003

Thompson, J. (1995). *The media and modernity: A social theory of the media*. Cambridge, UK: Polity Press.

Walther, J., Van Der Heide, B., Kim, S., Westerman, D., & Tong, S. (2008). The role of friends' appearance and behaviour on evaluations of individuals on Facebook: Are we known by the company we keep? *Human Communication Research*, *34*(1), 28–49. doi:10.1111/j.1468-2958.2007.00312.x

Warf, B., & Arias, S. (Eds.). (2008). *The spatial turn: Interdisciplinary perspectives*. London, UK: Routledge.

Wellman, B. (2002). Little boxes, glocalization, and networked individualism. In M. Tanabe, M., P. van den Besselaar, & T. Ishida (Eds.). *Digital cities II: Computational and sociological approaches, Lecture Notes in Computer Science: Vol. 2362* (pp. 10-25). Heidelberg, Germany: Springer.

Wellman, B. (2004). The three ages of internet studies: Ten, five and zero years ago. *New Media & Society*, *6*(1), 123–129. doi:10.1177/1461444804040633

Wellman, B., & Haythornthwaite, C. (Eds.). (2002). *The Internet in everyday life*. Oxford, UK: Blackwell. doi:10.1002/9780470774298

Wellman, B., Quan Haase, A., Boase, J., Chen, W., Hampton, K., & Díaz, I. (2003). The social affordances of the Internet for networked individualism. *Journal of Computer-Mediated Communication*, *8*(3).

Wesch, M. (2009). YouTube and you: Experiences of self-awareness in the context collapse of the recording webcam. *Explorations in Media Ecology*, *8*(2), 19–34.

White, H. (1992). *Identity and control: A structural theory of social action*. Princeton, NJ: Princeton Univ Press.

Wittel, A. (2001). Toward a network sociality. *Theory, Culture & Society*, *18*(6), 51–76.

ADDITIONAL READING

Bachelard, G. (1969). *The Poetics of Space* (Jolas, M., Trans.). Boston: Beacon Press.

Bakardjieva, M., & Smith, R. (2001). The internet in everyday life. *New Media & Society*, *3*(1), 67–83.

Benedikt, M. (1991). *Cyberspace: First steps*. Cambridge: MIT Press.

Boase, J., & Wellman, B. (2006). Personal relationships: On and off the Internet. In Perlman, D. (Ed.), *The Cambridge handbook of personal relationships* (pp. 709–726). Cambridge: Cambridge University Press.

Campbell, S., & Park, Y. (2008). Social implications of mobile telephony: the rise of personal communication society. *Sociology Compass*, 2(2), 371-387.

Licoppe, C. (2004). Connected presence: the emergence of a new repertoire for managing social relationships in a changing communication technoscape. *Environment and Planning. D, Society & Space*, *22*(1), 135–156. doi:10.1068/d323t

Ling, R. (2004). *The mobile connection: The cell phone's impact on society*. San Francisco: Morgan Kaufmann Publishers.

Ling, R. (2008). *New Tech, New Ties: How Mobile Communication Is Reshaping Social Cohesion*. Cambridge: MIT Press.

Lombard, M., & Ditton, T. (1997). At the heart of it all: The concept of presence. *Journal of Computer-Mediated Communication*, *3*(2).

Malpas, J. (1999). *Place and Experience: A philosophical topography*. Cambridge: Cambridge University Press. doi:10.1017/CBO9780511487606

Markham, A., & Baym, N. (Eds.). (2009). *Internet Inquiry: Conversations about method*. Los Angeles: Sage.

Papacharissi, Z. (Ed.). (2011). *A Networked Self. Identity, Community, and Culture on Social Network Sites*. New York: Routledge.

Relph, E., & Charles, E. (1976). *Place and Placelessness*. London: Pion.

Slater, D. (2002). Social relationships and identity online and offline. In Lievrouw, L., & Livingstone, S. (Eds.), *Handbook of new media: social shaping and consequences of ICTs* (pp. 533–546). London: Sage.

Spiller, N. (1998). *Digital Dreams: Architecture and the Alchemic Technologies*. London: Ellipsis Ltd.

Strate, L. (1999). The varieties of cyberspace: Problems in definition and delimitation. *Western Journal of Communication*, *63*(3), 382–412.

Thrift, N. (1995). *Spatial Formations*. London: Sage.

Tuan, Y. (1976). *Space and Place: The perspective of experience*. University of Minnesota Press.

Wellman, B. (2001). Physical place and cyberplace: The rise of personalized networking. *International Journal of Urban and Regional Research*, *25*(2), 227–252. doi:10.1111/1468-2427.00309

Wilken, Rowan. 2007. 'The Haunting Affect of Place in the Discourse of the Virtual', *Ethics, Place, & Environment: A Journal of Philosophy and Geography*, 10 (1), 49-63.

KEY TERMS AND DEFINITIONS

Context: The circumstances and relations that an interaction is situated in/by.

Convergence: The intersection point of two or more elements which are affected and have affect on each other as a result of that intersection.

Mediation: The symbolic and material system of societal structures, such as politics, economy and power in which interactions occur.

Networked Spaces: The spaces produced by the relations of intersecting social interactions. These spaces are neither online or offline specific, but are produced in the intersection of multiple relational narratives across digital and material domains.

Phenomenology: A disciplinary focus on the situated, embodied experience.

Place: A tangible, fixed and finite location understood to be singularly occupied.

Presence: A sense of proximity or of belonging – physically, emotionally and/or psychologically, often achieved in a lack of awareness of mediating systems.

Relational: Two elements which have a symbiotic connection to each other.

Social Affordances: Properties or features that are perceived as enabling social action.

Space: The abstract, limitless location of material properties which subjects learn.

Chapter 3
Registry Culture and Networked Sociability:
Building Individual Identity through Information Records

José María Zavala Pérez
Universidad Complutense de Madrid, Spain

ABSTRACT

The rise of individualism and the enhanced prominence of subjectivity that challenge inherited identities and references entail the achievement of wider margins for anonymity and personal fulfillment. On the other hand, increased registry habits generate tons of detailed information, which collides with an apparently rejected chance to better protect privacy. Identity and sociability are key concepts to understand this voluntary disclosure exerted in a context of networked individualism. New patterns of social interaction arise, and new models have to be designed to comprehend the space between individual and society. The circulation of such a great amount of information is often categorized as "surveillance," but the control of others is just one of the possible benefits that individuals can obtain from these available flows.

INTRODUCTION

"Since you wake up every morning you start leaving a trace of 'bits'; every time you use your mobile phone, your computer, or the credit card you are leaving a trace". Martin Cooper, inventor of the mobile telephone, at the 31th Conference for Data Protection and Privacy.

The arrival of the information society and the central role of ITCs have been followed by an increase in the use of expressions like "age of surveillance" or "surveillance society". This trend is not only visible in "frightening" magazine articles and TV-shows based on "orwellian" predictions, it is also present in academical circles[1], embedded in its language to the extent that some scholars describe their field directly as "surveillance studies" or they declare to research any aspect of the "surveillance societies".

The purpose of this text it is not to state if the surveillance practices have increased significantly enough as for classifying our societies under such a name. This premise might be a generalized biased approach caused by the growing application of new technologies to the art of watching each

DOI: 10.4018/978-1-61350-338-6.ch003

other. Nevertheless, at first sight it may also be concluded that we enjoy wider levels of anonymity than we suppose.

The underlying question here refers to the manner in which these analyses undermine the role of individual's active decisions, conscious positions and deliberate actions. While researching surveillance processes, structural connections are excessively remarked and they become a privileged place in the foreground. At the same time, the control of personal information is depicted as a task performed by a cast of experts (whether bureaucrats or marketing managers) who hold the *only* responsibility in the surveillance relationships and the monopoly of data management.

Of course it is essential to approach this subject having in mind the actual asymmetry of power, and it is precisely due to the subtle nature of power relationships in the network society that it would be a big mistake to ignore the minor actions of control. Therefore, current analyses of surveillance cannot exclude those acts which take place between friends, relatives, acquaintances, etc. Moreover, it is unavoidable to point out along this "soft surveillance" the overcome of unidirectionality through the voluntary contribution of information to be shared, *so that* others can watch at the same time that are being watched.

After shielding our homes, sometimes even with cutting edge security systems, we leave a lot of locks to let the others see, know and judge a wide portion of what is happening in our lives. This way, a significant amount of data is revealed: what we do, where we are, with whom we spend the time with, what we have, what we think... This trend weakens the traditional approach that describes an image in which the experts of knowledge and information dream of full dictatorial powers that would let them record each movement of the citizens/workers/consumers. In the context of a network society, the old dualizing hierarchies get blurred and are more difficult to appreciate. The scheme that divides surveillance into "watchers" (empowered) *versus* "watched" (submitted) has to be profoundly reviewed. In networked structures, information flows circulate according to such complex patterns that it is impossible to continue sustaining analyses based *exclusively* on the useful but confusing and biasing traditional dichotomies.

This wrong perspective makes surveillance research to get focused in two main fields: economics (companies) and politics (governments). Scholars insist in these two topics and media's agendas center their attention in these events. The necessary review to avoid this limitation does not come only from the acts of "outsourcing" that allow and foster "unqualified" personnel to run surveillance-related tasks (a tactic described both in distopyas like *1984* and in reality like the known infiltration of GDR's *Stasi* into the common people). Not only today but since the beginning of societies, what we understand as "surveillance" embraces a remarkable "third field" linked to phenomena of sociability, socialization and raw social control.

The circulation of information flows in the network society resembles to neuronal synapses: each cell is a relatively active agent that contributes to the transmission of information. An event can be experienced by an individual, who registers and shares this information throughout a network with other individuals, that receive it and may amplify it in an infinite sequence. Individuals do not just portray external facts, they also may share information about hundreds of personal issues: what they feel, where they find themselves at any given moment, what they think, what are their recently acquired belongings, which music they like, which people they meet… in short: *who* they are.

Western modern societies are affected by an identity crisis related to individualistic trends which might be overcome by network interconnections. This shift would mean the change from a "mass-individualism" to what Barry Wellman calls "networked individualism". In this context, the problem of generating and communicating identities becomes a perennial, continuous, infinite question. The enhanced prominence of subjectivity against inherited identities and references makes individuals to be aware of the fact that each gesture, each action, each personal object says something about them. In that act of communication, they have the hard task of being active subjects that make all that information available to others. This anxiety for sharing contrasts with the hermetic structure of hive-shaped modern urban models but also helps to understand the transition from a "mass-individualism" to a "networked individualism".

The objectives of this chapter are:

- To question the predominance of organizational perspectives in "surveillance studies" and the consequent focus on economical and political issues.
- To reclaim a purely "social" dimension of the vague concept of "surveillance", linked to the question of sociability. This includes the remark of voluntary acts of information sharing against the premise of coercion in the study of mutual control.
- To promote the use of terms ("register", "record", "trackability") that highlight this character, instead of those associated to unidirectional relationships ("surveillance", "control", "privacy violation").
- To analyze the paradox arisen when the wish of anonymity collides with the resulting "hyperpresence" that comes from social relations in a networked society.

BACKGROUND

As stated in the previous section, the main approaches of the so-called "surveillance studies" and privacy concerns in general, focus their attention on organizational factors, like those derived from the arrival of an "informational capitalism" (Castells, 2010, p. 94). As consequence of this, we obtain a reduced or even biased view that shows the image of a society in which a mass of threatened citizens have to fight constantly against huge organizations–companies and governments–which lead us to an "informational totalitarianism". It is important to point out that privacy problems are not only caused by the wrong management of *data* (e.g. variables that are able to be statistically stored and managed), they also involve a wide range of forms of *information* (e.g. complex facts and thoughts that define characters).

Lyon's (1994) concept of "Surveillance society" defines it as the resulting product of the watching acts performed by governments and companies: "Precise details of our personal lives are collected, stored, retrieved and processed every day within huge computer databases belonging to big corporations and government departments. This is the 'surveillance society'" (p.3).

According to this premise, since surveillance is carried out exclusively by *organizations*, it means to understand it as an *organized* activity, which may promote the flourish of conspiracy theories. Nonetheless, it is important to have in mind the publishing date of this definition. Common "unqualified" users are now able to take advantage of new technologies for their humble surveillance purposes: the arrival of the web 2.0 and the spread of articles and services which used to be only typical of detectives, allow today individuals to know and control their social networks in a more sophisticated way. And this kind of "microsurveillance" has nothing to do with large databases or organizations.

Yet, there is a recent questioning of the old panopticon-based perspectives. Fuchs (2009) notices the opposition of a rather critical view of surveillance (something dangerous and negative), represented by Foucault, and a rather "neutral" position, defended by authors like Giddens, Albrechtslund and Haggerty.

One of the clearest critics to the dominating frameworks in this field is provided by Albrechtslund (2008) by attacking the "hierarchical" and "vertical" concept of surveillance. He warns of the inability to analyze online social networking phenomena under the idea of surveillance as a "hierarchical system of power". Furthermore, he points out interesting consequences of the proposed "horizontal" perspective for subjectivity and identity. But the use in this context of adjectives like "participatory" and "empowering" has to be made with caution. Because as Lyon (2006) reminds, "while in principle everyone can indeed watch everyone else in mediated ways–screening the results– some forms of watching carry more weight than others" (p. 39).

Mark Andrejevic (2005) introduces an interesting approach through his concept of "lateral surveillance" or "peer to peer monitoring". Yet, this idea remains as an "offload" of monitoring practices from a saturated panopticon forced to outsource some of its duties into the common people. The persisting image of *a* gaze (which involves a watcher object and a watched subject) insists on secrecy, espionage, voyeurism and thus uncertainty or ignorance of the surveillance actions.

Mathiesen's (1997) concept of "synopticon" –the many watching the few– brings a new interesting perspective that complements the insufficient metaphor of the panopticon. Nonetheless, like most of the theorists, he still focuses his analyses in a *watching* activity, which seems to occur, this time bidirectionally, between two parties. Mathiesen's proposal is akin to the idea of "sousveillance":

One way to challenge and problematize both surveillance and acquiescence to it is to resituate these technologies of control on individuals, offering panoptic technologies to help them observe those in authority. We call this inverse panopticon "sousveillance" from the French words for "sous" (below) and "veiller" to watch. (Mann, Nolam & Wellman, 2003, p. 332)

But the top-down bias cannot be just solved with the bottom up counterpart. There is a need to remark the complex phenomenon of the many seeing and being exposed *to the many*. In this sense, now it is possible to imagine a "networked surveillance" or "surveillance networks", whose uncertainty and invisibility are not only based on the fact that it is not possible to know if the watcher is active in a certain moment; the problem now is to identify who is actually the watcher and what are the pursued goals; we cannot control the information flows because everyone is potentially an active agent (even if involuntarily) of watching processes. Moreover, as Koskela's (2004) contributions suggest, watching activities (i.e., to seek information) have to be completed with self-exhibition (to provide information).

Haggerty and Ericson (2000) do not only sense the overrepresentation of Orwell's omnipresent "Big Brother" and Foucault's interpretation of Bentham's panopticon on surveillance's imaginary; they also contribute to solve the problems of directionality and agency with their idea of "surveillant assemblage".

These authors criticize the analyses based on discrete technologies and social practices and remark the complexity of contemporary surveillance by describing it in terms of "flows" and as a product of "desires": "a range of desires now energize and serve to coalesce the surveillant assemblage, including the desires for control, governance, security, profit and entertainment" (p. 609). Borrowing the idea of "assemblage" from Deleuze and Guattari, Haggerty and Ericson provide a useful contribution to fight the purely structural and passive approaches to surveillance routines and guess the rather chaotic essence of the actual situation:

While not a complete democratic leveling of the hierarchy of surveillance, these developments cumulatively highlight a fractured rhizomatic crisscrossing of the gaze such that no major population groups stand irrefutably above or outside of the surveillant assemblage. (p. 618)

Questioning the vertical and hierarchical schemes often used to research this field does not mean to ignore or refute the coercive and threatening potential of surveillance or to justify it. Different perspectives have to be taken into account and the complexity of control and watching in modern societies has to be accepted.

INDIVIDUALIZATION, REGISTRY AND NETWORKED SOCIABILITY

A New Individualism

I start from the premise that new trends on control, watching and surveillance, whether "lateral", "participatory", "sousvillance", or understood as an "assemblage" are only possible thanks to new interaction patterns among individuals.

The culture of modernity (Picó, 1999) questions the "old" collective bonds and brings new common references through changes in economics (capitalist production and consumption), politics (democratic procedures), beliefs and cognition (scientific knowledge). This shift from traditional to modern societies can be described as a change towards an "industrial society" (Spencer, 1885), a society guided under the principle of "organic solidarity" (Durkheim, 1997), a model of "*Gesellschaft*" (Tönnies, 1979), etc. All these concepts refer to a new social context with wider levels of anonymity and individual freedom, and a minor perception of coercion from the group. Such a situation enables the progressive development of individual subjectivities in detriment of the role that collective identities and communities had played traditionally.

Simmel (1969, p. 204) places the birth of individuality at the Italian Renaissance, when it appeared as a wish of distinction. Since the eighteenth century, the figure of the individual is, at the same time, bearer of freedom, by breaking a set of illegitimate bounds and spreading the Reason, and bearer of equality, due to the necessary generalization experienced. Differentiation and leveling will be two basic consequences of individualization.

In the conjunction of a crisis of symbolic identities (Dubar, 2000) and a boom of subjectivism (Sibilia, 2008), individualism reaches in the twentieth century its maximum peak, leaving the citizens naked before huge collective references. State-based and even global cognitive frames embed the prefix "mass-" in our language. Some of the competences that once belonged to pre-state groups, are now a task for the State or for individuals. For this exposition is interesting to point out, in the first case, tasks of protection and control (Elias, 1991, p. 120) and in the second, the building of own's identity (Bauman, 2001, p. 144).

This double process of emancipation and empowerment of individuals, may also be perceived as negative, and several authors have remarked a "dramatic" side.

Durkheim (1951) sees individualization as a problem of "isolation" in a mass society and shows his fears of an "excessive individualism" (p. 209). Ulrich Beck and Elisabeth Beck-Gernsheim (2002) distinguish between the individualization as a synonym for autonomy (influenced by the neoliberal perspective) and as a synonym for "anomie" (following Durkheim's statements). While the first perception is linked with the idea of freedom and self-liberation, the latter refers to problems of "disintegration", and they even suggest the existence of signs of "hedonism" and "egoism". Other concepts that have been associated with the idea of individualization are "uncertainty" (Bauman, 2001), "narcissism" (Lipovetsky, 1983), or "nihilism" (Gomá, 2009), among much others.

Immediately arises a stereotype that describes the urban contemporary figure: an independent, autonomous citizen that lives alone and whose relationships are numerous but soft and eternally temporary. In short: a "we-less I" (Elias, 1991, p. 199).

Unavoidably, the old sociological debate started by Durkheim and Weber, that faces the analyses based on structural explanations with those that center their attention on the human action, arises once again. Since underestimating one of both extremes in this continuum would be misleading, Giddens (1979, p. 53) states that "[action and structure] presuppose one another". In this sense, Peter L. Berger affirms that "society defines us, but is in turn defined by us" (1963, p. 129). And Elias (1991, p. 202) wonders himself already in 1987 if we may have reached a "perfect we-I balance".

The way to achieve an emancipated individual is reinforced in the late modernity. Whether as "high" (Giddens, 1990) or "liquid" (Bauman, 2000), communal references damaged by the impersonality of modern social life and the flexible character of identities leave wider spaces for individual fulfillment.

After the generalized panic before an individualistic –narcissistic, hedonistic, nihilistic– future, the information society, which is not a mere broadening in the use of new technologies but implies deep changes in social relations, incites new curiosities on the development of shared identities, social bounds and community-building trends. The frameworks that once helped to contextualize industrial societies are now in crisis. Elias (1991, p. 20) suggests that the social conditions that determine the development of a person define the possibilities of individualization for each place and period, and the current context has been widely accepted as a "networked" society (Castells, 2010).

Our contemporary society is not just extremely complex, differentiated and individualistic; it is also interconnected in a huge global network. Thus, it would not be savvy to focus our attention on the loss of bounds while ignoring the development of connections. Facing the pessimism before an apparent less prominent role of communities, shared identities and social groups, Barry Wellman (2001, 2002) describes this trend as "networked individualism".

According to Wellman (2002), changes in the building of communities take place from a "little boxes" model to individualized networks through an intermediate process of "glocalization". The idea of "little boxes" "connotes people socially and cognitively encapsulated by homogeneous, broadly-embracing groups". This pattern is based on contact between households ("door-to-door") and the routines are subject to the "awareness, sanction and control of the settlement". When "glocalization" arises, household and workgroups become the primary units of activity and communities are defined socially rather than spatially. Relationships get "privatized" since they turn more deliberate and selective. Under the model of "networked individualism", a personalized and wireless world connects people through person-to-person and role-to-role interactions (2001, p. 231).

Wellman (2001) defines "community" as "networks of interpersonal ties that provide sociability, support, information, a sense of belonging, and social identity" (p. 228), and this description is as valid for densely-knit traditional groups as for the interest-based structures that conform personalized networks. In this sense, he remarks the specialized nature of relationships and communities: "Many interpersonal ties are based only on the specialized roles that people play –not the whole persons. People must maintain differentiated portfolios of ties to obtain a variety of needed and wanted resources" (p. 245). Nonetheless, it is important to take into account, that parallel to this partial interactions, individuals risk themselves to be exposed as a whole: for instance, when a name is *googled* to achieve the maximal information possible from a person or when in social network sites people share information indistinctly with acquaintances, friends, neighbors, relatives and workmates. In this circumstances, *belonging* to groups loses importance against the fact of *being* part of networks and having so much contacts as possible. Networks help us to define others (in terms of "friend", "friend of", "child of", "neighbor", "workmate", etc.) the same way that group categories helped us to categorize people when they were more effective (in terms of nationality, religious ascription, ethnicity, etc.).

Networked individualism seems to approximate to the dream of a "reconciliation" between individual and society, the "balance" claimed by Elias. To some extent, it constitutes a privatized or customized society. Instead of a "we", it provides a balanced "me with others" that prevents isolation but also limits uncomfortable constraints.

Heritage, Customization, and Single Identity

Once solved the misleading conceptualization of individualism as a necessarily isolating, selfish, anomic trend, it is required to make some thoughts about how identity is built under conditions of networked individualism. Shared identities are said to be in crisis, (Dubar, 2000), but in fact are just those inherited, imposed and obligatory identities which, to a great extent, are not accepted anymore. And if they are, this may not be just as result of socialization but a rather a consequence of conscious and voluntary choice. According to Bauman (2001), "''individualization' consists in transforming human 'identity' from a 'given' into a 'task'" (p. 144). In Elias' words (1991), the balance between the "we-identity" and the "I-identity" is inclined towards the second (p. 196). But this does not mean that the modern human being is rejecting the advantages of being part of communities.

In order to analyze the contemporary management of social and personal identities, it is advisable to apply a "Sociology of *tags*" –that means, an analysis based in the logic of networks– instead of a "Sociology of categories". "Tags" make possible to identify sets of individuals, but anyone *can create them* instantly, at any given moment, just typing and entering them into the communication highways. And the success of a concept defined by a "tag" can vary from just a handful of followers to millions of them. Communities are not anymore closed sets of individuals with common profiles. Traditional categories as nationality, religion, even ethnicity are not always the best references to understand the logic of networks. Individuals choose to a great extent their own "tags", that is, adjectives and nouns that identify them).

While Leighton and Wellman (1979) affirm that communities are best defined by interaction, Paula Sibilia (2008) holds that subjectivity is created in the interaction and communication with others. Connecting both extremes it is possible to think of a single process that feeds shared objectivation as well as individual distinction, through the *communication* of identities. Computer-mediated communication enables a customized and efficient way to express common attitudes, beliefs, tastes, values, etc. and get in touch with those who share them. But at the same time, it provides means, especially since the spread of Web 2.0 services, to be differentiated and original, that is, to be an individual.

The possibility to manage identities individually in networked societies does not imply that personalized images are created *outside* of society. These are rather configured *in* society: individualities are "socially produced" (Bauman, 2001, p. 144), "shaped and bound in the nature of their psychical self-regulation by a particular network of functions" (Elias, 1991, p. 60). The advantages of identity customization are counterbalanced by drawbacks like uncertainty and instability. The weight of customs is replaced by the responsibility of this new "task", the arrival of "precarious freedoms" (Beck & Beck-Gernsheim, 2002, p. 16) is supposed to cause a lack of guidelines. Identities have to be continuously checked and, if necessary, updated. That is why Bauman (2001) suggests using rather the term "identification", a never-ending, always incomplete, unfinished and open activity (p. 152).

Symbolic communication has been always an essential means to create and pass on identity. The resulting resources help to define both intra and intergroups. Symbols tell us who we are and who the others are. And the same way identities are being affected by individualization, so does communication. Media abandon the mass-logic and offer new personalized possibilities like web-streaming, TV on demand, *YouTube*... Communication is essential when traditional societies, characterized by regularities and routines, are replaced by modern societies that work with a faster rhythm. The psychological conditions of urban contexts imply a constant exchange of impressions, and the modern individual is thus used to differences and changes (Simmel, 1969, p. 410).

Through networked individualism, the communication of identity elements tends to "annihilate" the symbol. Symbols summarize values, ideals and beliefs that remain stable. But nowadays it is possible to communicate ways of life in real time and with a high level of detail. Several devices and infrastructures allow to reproduce accurately those experiences and moments (e.g. through geolocalization, pictures and videos, etc.) that define us. The continuous symbolic update leads to a narrowing distance between the significant and the signifier.

Now, the individual, emancipated from the binding group identities, is able to knit a personalized network in one's own way: a customized "we" which in fact is a "me-with-others" since the sense of belonging is not far developed and mutual consciousness is nonexistent. In the case of Social Network Sites (SNS[2]), it is possible to find whole pre-existing networks which are more similar to the concept of groups, and on the other hand, ego-centered networks, which start from a certain profile. In the second case, a user does not *belong* to a group, rather a number of contacts agree to *belong* to this user's network. In ego-centered networks, the individual is the founder and main manager of its own network (Garton, Haythornthwaite & Wellman, 1997).

The way networks are managed defines how identity or identities are communicated to others. The increasing options for anonymity provided by modern urban contexts allow a complete customization of personal identity. It is possible and sometimes advisable to have a "multiple personality" or at least, to hide some aspects of our life to certain persons with whom we interact: religious beliefs, sexual orientation or political attitudes are just some examples. But the technification of our social relations may hinder this adaptation, due to a high level of transparency and the loss of secrecy, a process that is incompatible with the management of different profiles or "masks". According to the website founder, only a 5% of *Facebook* users classify their contacts through *friend lists*[3]. This means, that an unworried share of information through SNS leads to present the same personal image to all the contacts. The ability to cheat people with the uncertainty of mobile phones will be invalidated as geolocalization through GSP-technology get normalized. An overwhelming flow of information to be shared with others and the omnipresent devices that reveal details of our acts make difficult to adapt the image given to friends, relatives and co-workers.

Registry: Between Surveillance and Privacy

The raw matter ultimately involved in issues related to surveillance and privacy is no other than information. Whether as numbers, written words, audio or video, information can always be converted to 'zeros and ones', that is, binary language. Undoubtedly, one of the features of the information society is that more and more data remain and *are able* to remain recorded: it is possible to register numerous activities and expressed thoughts using devices accessible to common users that may store and share the recorded information. Melucci describes the process with these words:

Information has become a central resource and complex systems depend on it for their survival and development. In the last two decades the capability of collecting, processing, and transferring information has been developed to an extent unsurpassed in all of human history. That increases the artificial or constructed characteristics of social life; large parts of our experiences occur in a socially produced environment. The media represent and reflect our actions, and individuals incorporate and reproduce these messages in a type of self-reinforcing spiral. Where are the 'nature' and 'reality' outside the cultural representations and images we receive from and produce for our social world? (Melucci, 1989, p. 83).

The theoretical difficulties explained at the beginning of the chapter reveal that the very concept of "surveillance" is problematic. Analyses of variations on what "privacy" means try to approach the problem of who-knows-what. One thing is sure: what converges between the "offensive" aspect of surveillance and the "defensive" aspect of privacy is the exchanged, stolen or protected object: personal information.

Today, not only governments and companies own technologies to manage information. Common people have in their hands numerous resources to digitalize, store, share and access to up-to-date facts regarding themselves and others: cameras and peripherals, hard disks, web-2.0 platforms, etc. A great extent of the daily experiences, summarized as pictures, videos, news *feeds* or *weblog* entries, are dumped into computers, in what Melucci (1989) calls a 'cultural surplus': "a widening of choices available to individuals and groups far beyond their possibility of actually experiencing them" (p. 83). This mediated nature of information, in conjunction with networked structures, accelerates the speed and range of flows. Moreover, much of the information that is not mediated, is recoverable through advanced technologies (e.g. DNA-traces).

Even though political and economical actors sometimes take advantage of the voluntarily shared information, this can be originally generated for other purposes related to issues like sociability. So, before asking ourselves if surveillance has increased or not –regardless of what we consider as "surveillance"–, or if privacy issues are more present in our minds or not, it is to remark that the amount of registered information grows each day. It seems that a lack of trust in our memory and our senses leads us to keep our experiences and thoughts in storage devices.

It is even possible to dispense with problematic terms as "surveillance" (that implies asymmetric power conditions) and force a conceptual renovation: The *registry* of information leaves a *record* that allows *keeping track* of individuals. What is not registered cannot be shown (shared) or watched (known).

The concept of "registry" aims to embrace the variety of moments on which a piece of personal information is made potentially accessible to others. Giddens (1987, p. 154) already proposed to distinguish between surveillance as "accumulation, coding and retrieval of information" and as "the direct supervision of the activities of some individuals or groups by others". The availability of information does not imply necessarily its supervision to control individuals. If the analysis of information flows is excessively linked to ideas like "surveillance" or "control", investigations are constricted to certain actors and purposes. The dynamization of information flows which are able to be accessed is result of millions of daily acts of registry. These acts are performed by a multiple agency and are product, to a great extent, of voluntary decisions. More and more, individuals contribute for themselves providing information and generating structures that allow its circulation.

As a result of this trend, billions of pieces of our lives remain recorded and accessible on digital media. Some numbers give us an idea of this situation[4]:

- More than 30 billion pieces of content (web links, news stories, blog posts, notes, photo albums, etc.) shared each month in *Facebook*. 10% of these are photos.
- 35 hours of video uploaded to *YouTube* every minute. 25 billion "tweets" sent in 2010.
- 152 million blogs are online.

These are just some examples. But there are much more trackable inputs: Mobile phone calls and messages, e-mails, *Foursquare* check-in's, CCTV recordings, credit card payments, etc. All these actions provide hints of the actions or properties of a person.

The use of registry devices may appear a normal habit today. Nonetheless, as biotechnology evolves, these devices are going to be more directly embedded in the human body and more capable to communicate and register different forms of information. This is the case for nanobots, that flowing through the blood torrent, should be able in the future to make early diagnosis; implantable RFID-chips are also an expression of cyborg-oriented registry devices; following this trend, Daniel Yoon recently designed the "Blackberry Empathy Phone", that would allow users "to see not only their friends activities and updates, but also how they are feeling through the use of a biometric ring that reads the wearers emotional state"[5]. The visual artist Wafaa Bilal will wear for a year a surgically-implanted camera in the back of his head, in order to capture images at one-minute intervals that will be transmitted to monitors at a museum in Qatar[6]. This embedding of devices in the human bodies remarks the prominent role of individualization in the process of registry.

J. L. Marzo (2002) refers to Western societies as "cultures of registry and archive" and reminds that writing is one of the first ways that this civilization had to classify and organize. Nevertheless, Marzo states that contemporary technologies are product of this social and cultural characteristic, that is, they are the result of "preexisting forces and needs" and not the other way around. This idea collides with Castells' (2010) premise of "dialectical interaction" between technology and society (p. 5). Current registry technologies give the possibility to leave individualized records at a significantly higher level (with more and more detailed information) than the one demanded by the "preexisting forces and needs" what ultimately transforms the social habits.

This capability of classifying and organizing individuals is not only reciprocal but also reflective. That is why, when referring to registry it does not make sense to think of a coercive background. The possibilities, means and tasks of registry have been spread –sometimes outsourced– to "unqualified" users (common citizens instead of bureaucrats and marketers). This spread must not be described as "democratization", since this term would suggest a sound change in power relations. Both "surveillance" (in the traditional sense, that is, from "above") and "sousvillance" (what implies a leveling of power relations and is exerted from "below"), as well as "peer to peer monitoring", are practices related to the management of personal information, and take place in a context of networked registry, that knits a universe of resources similar to the Haggerty and Ericsson's application of Deleuze and Guattari's concept of "assemblage". A huge network of individualized information allows infinite combinations for the use of these resources: control, knowledge, sociability, personal identity management, different kinds of surveillance, political resistances, profit, etc.

Recent trends to registry are linked to an exaggerated transparency, to the so-called "right to forget" and to the digitalization of memory.

Transparency only takes place if the registered information is potentially accessed. Otherwise, secrecy and privacy still have a chance to play a significant role in the social life. But the interconnection of the storage devices, independently of the existence of safeguards (passwords, encoded communications, privacy settings, etc.), is the base for all the possibilities of information omnipresence. "Unplugged" non-digital notebooks, pictures or videos, which undoubtedly are registry means, do not feed the transparency spiral if they are kept far enough from communication networks.

Currently there is a debate about the "right to forget" that has pushed the EU to take actions in order to review the data protection guidelines. Each month hundreds of privacy conflicts related to information accessible through Internet arise (Rosen, 2010): employers who know too much, blogs that reveal more than they should, uncontrolled pictures of lightly dressed girls, cameras that were supposed to be turned off... Even in the context of large urban societies, the past can be unavoidable, no matter how far an individual moves. When accessing to personal information is sometimes as easy as *googleing* a name, the right to forget (and thus, to be forgotten) must be well protected. The dream of a rational management of human memory has promoted research focused in the development of a drug that would help to erase what a person do not want to remember (Sibilia, 2008, p. 148). Nonetheless, since the storage of memories is shared between human and non-human resources, a major part of the problem rests in technological devices with uncertain locations (like web servers or hard disks that belong to unknown users). In the same way like Borges' character "Funes the memorious", an indeterminate network of human and non-human elements tends to register as much information (both static and dynamic) as possible.

The problem of these features related to registry (transparency, problems to be forgotten, digitalization of memory) is that individuals are not the exclusive managers of their personal information. Therefore, the structural character of registration processes effectively exists. But it is also a process activated and dynamized by *all kind* of individuals, not only by a group of professionals that work with numbers. In this activity are involved those who *give* information, those who *collect* it and those who *share and spread* it.

Political actors try to establish legal requirements for organizations, designed under the ideal premise of "minimum information necessary collected". But this aspiration is diametrically opposed to the nature of an informational economy and a culture of registry, where underlies the pretension to collect the maximum information possible (which does not have to be always obviously useful). The legal barriers to information access do not only ignore the paradox that they imply, they also presuppose that threats to privacy come mainly from organized actors. When companies whose value rests on the supply, exchange or management of information have a central place in the economical landscape (*Google*, *Facebook*, *Microsoft...*); when governments try to control each movement (through biometric technologies) and each communication (through protocol registration); when social relations have been "digitalized" and the old concept of "seeing and being seen" reach unimagined extremes; then, legislative initiatives cannot stop a complex logic that increases the volume of known, registered, accessible information. Measures against identifiable organizations that own large databases are totally useless before the mass of information dumped into digital devices each day.

The idea of "registry" may be seen as vague and even useless, since it embraces a lot of different actions and includes several grades of willfulness and consciousness in the sharing of personal information. One thing is sure: the reference to conspiracies, "orwellian" nightmares and panoptical structures has to be self-limited and done with caution. The active role of nodes and the networked shape of interconnected actors collide with the idea of *apriori* autocratic and hierarchical ways to obtain information. However, the registry of information is not always totally conscious. If users do not read the terms of use, software license agreements or privacy policies, if citizens do not react against the proliferation of public and private CCTV-cameras, if SNS-members do not bother themselves to customize the privacy settings, it does not mean that a threatening power aspires to control and watch all the individuals.

Changes in willfulness of registry also have to be considered. There are much cases of registry devices that at first where not widespread, and just certain individuals acquired them to obtain advantages. After some time, these registry devices became so common that the norm turned around: not to have them would entail a clear disadvantage. This is the case for cellular phones: first they meant to enjoy an additional comfort, but nowadays, not having such a device places people in the worst side of the digital divide and entails serious economical and social drawbacks. Webcams used to be an additional peripheral that now comes integrated in personal computers. Electronic payment systems are now very common and will probably tend to be indispensable.

The institutionalization of registry practices can of course generate "centralizable" and even passively coercive structures of information, since the rejection to participate in them entails different drawbacks. The use of telephone is a typical case: on the one hand, telecommunications can be tapped by central organizations, and on the other, avoiding this technology would cause isolation. But in the very origin of these structures we can find deliberate contributions to knit information networks, which are done to obtain a personal benefit (in terms of sociability or economical advantages). Personal information is the currency used in a free-market-based relation.

An important issue has to do with the different uses of the information recorded and the differences between the devices that feed the huge amount of data collected. Of course, there take place acts of surveillance and control, but they only mean a part of what can be done with the input generated by lots of information that is there, and it has been given willingly to a great extent. Those surveillance acts are not the base for the generation of the information flows, they just take advantage of them. The registry facilitates activities of control *a posteriori*, which are more effective and individualized; it does not involve a systematized control, this would be applied in the moment of access to the targeted data.

Therefore, the picture of an "eye that watches everything" competes with that of a decentralized (but eventually "centralizable") network of individual contributions that introduce all kind of data in it. The first one refers to a structure of control that keeps track of individuals and the second one to a network of individual actions that generate trackable information.

Among the devices that are able to register information, some of them are specifically designed for this purpose, but others are not. Thus, the idea of registry is not only linked to technologies thought expressly to collect information (cameras, microphones, RFID-chips, etc.), it refers also to devices and interfaces that, independently of their use, are able to generate a record of information potentially accessed.

It is also to be remarked the individualized nature of registry. Devices like mobile phones or personal computers and interfaces like web 2.0 applications feed the global flows of information according to the "person-to-person connectivity" (Wellman, 2002). Each actor is a potential information producer, what Sibilia (2008) defines as "I-narrator" and "I-author". Cultural communication has been thus turned around: from a unidirectional structure of passive spectators that swallowed what mass-media offered them, to a network of active extreme "prosumers" (Toffler, 1981) that are able to customize their social expressions. Personalized but interconnected at the same time. Here is the long-time claimed balance between individual and society.

Anonymity vs. Hyperpresence: An Individualized Management of Sociability

At this point, several questions arise. Among them: How to manage sociability in a context of high individualization? Which is the goal of the massive input of information generated by the multiple nodes? Each question answers the other one. The resource that dynamizes sociability is information, freely given in huge amounts to trigger networked interaction.

There is a clear paradox resulting from the contrast between the potential anonymity allowed by a context of modernity, which enables individuals to hide a broad portion of their lives to others, and the global trend to communicate a wide part of what we do and who we are. This contradiction is not the same as the one described by Barnes (2006) as "privacy paradox", that opposes a high level of information disclosure amongst teenagers and a high demand of privacy protection to face the collection of data by organizations. The paradox that I try to point out is between a context in which anonymity and privacy are more feasible than in pre-modern societies, but individuals reject them to obtain certain social advantages (identity and sociability). Based on words of Hamelink, Barnes states that higher degrees of social organization imply the expansion of social control mechanisms and therefore, the increase of information collection. Nevertheless, simple societies have also high levels of control to avoid deviation and transformation, and modernization opens wide spaces for individualism and anonymity. Control mechanisms get sophisticated but not necessarily more invasive. It needs to be remarked once again that a large part of the data collection requires the active or passive acceptance of individuals.

Figure 1. Dynamization of information flows: Registry and access

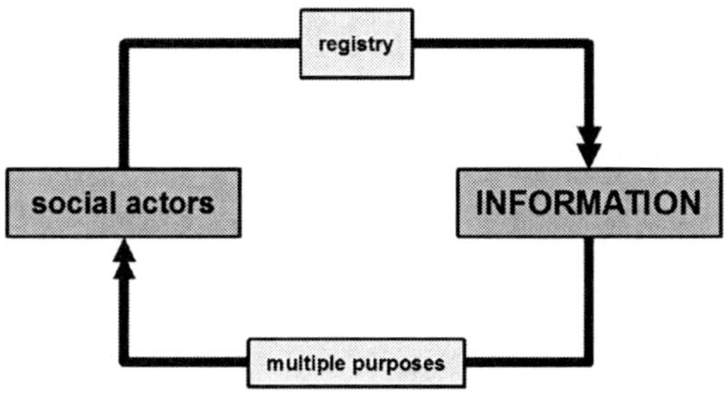

Two processes comprise the base of the link between sociability and such an extreme exchange of information: to "know" and to "tell". It is necessary to "be aware" of the current trends and news, because they define the norms. But it is also important to "tell" in order to participate in contexts of social interaction, to identify oneself and to co-create norms. In this situation, individuals give and get, that is, exchange, the "raw matter" of sociability in networked societies: information.

According to Simmel (1969), through sociability remains what he called "forms" independently of the "contents" that caused them (p. 41). Sociability is the pure social interaction, without direct references to personal interests or the obtaining of resources that institutionalized this kind of practices. That is why, in the daily tremendous exchange of information made through registry and communication, it does not make sense to appeal to concrete goals –like surveillance, political interests or economic profit–, since it is caused by different factors, and sociability is one of them.

The "know-and-show" logic that underlies these processes ("to see and to be seen"), may be understood, among other explanations, as an endogamic attitude that pursues the preservation of own norms and traditions and that prevents deviation. But since the small groups transferred to the State numerous competences, "individual people, once they are grown up, increasingly leave behind the close, local protective groups based on blood", at the same time that "groups' cohesion breaks down as they lose their protective and control functions" (Elias, 1991, p. 120). Although now the State has the valid criteria of what is wrong and what is right (the legal frame) and is the only organization legitimated to exercise control and surveillance, individuals still "play" (using Simmel's words) to judge and watch. Sociability has a sense *per se* and may be an important motivation for the the dynamization of networks against other causes like the mobilization of resources.

Sociability is related to socialization, and thus, to integration. The lack of cohesion arisen from crisis in the shared values that facilitated individualization does not have to be solved necessarily by new common goals or ideas that threat back the possibilities for individual development. A complex system of networked communication may provide apparently a way to knit the social fabric.

In the context of a SNS, when users publicly recognize that they have a certain interest they are not just giving hints about their "networked identity". Then, users are also taking advantage of the sociability resources available in these environments. If these interests are shared with others, then they will be a possible common point to *connect* with real or potential contacts and play the sociability game with them. In *Facebook*, when users answer "I like this" to a certain *feed*, they are not just saying something about themselves, they are also winking their friends and making them know that they are aware of their news, of what they say, think and feel, and that they remember them. It is a way to keep up the networked links, which have to be constantly updated like a contract that needs to be frequently renewed.

A large part of the research related to privacy and technologies focuses on phenomena that occur in SNSs[7]. Due to their origins and development, SNSs have created the "illusion of privacy", they seemed at the beginning to offer a "semi-private space" (Barnes, 2006). A significative number of conflicts started by inadequate information disclosure and announced by the media helped to increase sensitivity to privacy concerns. Since SNSs are a relatively recent phenomenon and are constantly transformed (available types of content, privacy configuration, embedding and indexing possibilities...), the observable patterns and behaviors are only valid for a short-term perspective.

Anonymity allows having broader margins for personal fulfillment, since it frees individuals from fighting the informal mechanisms against deviation. Then, why do they establish forms of social participation that entail such grades of transparency and hyperpresence? In current networked societies, interaction promotes the disclosure through words, photos, videos and coordinates. These elements are registered with the help of different "bionic prostheses" like keyboards, cameras or chips.

Foucault (1977) refers to isolation as an important element of prison, an individualizing punishment that may even make the prisoner to become insane (p. 236). The question is if the opposite of isolation, the "hyperpresence", will ever be also considered as torture. Playing with Warhol's famous sentence ("In the future, everyone will be world-famous for 15 minutes"), the British artist Bansky created a sculpture of a television with the inscription "In the future, everyone will be anonymous for 15 minutes". Following the spirit of Mies van der Rohe's "Farnsworth House" and Philip Johnson's "Glass House", the Museum of Modern Art of New York organized in 1999 an exhibition called "The Un-Private House". The project pretended to show the work of twenty six architects whose designs were full of glass walls and open spaces, aimed at reflecting the evolving cultural definition of privacy.

The increasing levels of transparency and openness to the world threat the valuable anonymity that only mass-societies can provide. A possible answer to the resulting contradiction could be a supposed laxity of moral criteria. If, always that the legal frame is respected, any kind of attitude is accepted and all ways of life fit in a society, then everything can be disclosed to anyone without major consequences. That may be the premise hold by figures like Mark Zuckerberg, *Facebook* founder, who stated that privacy is no longer a social norm (Johnson, 2010) or Eric Schmidt, *Google*'s CEO, who said that "If you have something that you do not want anyone to know, maybe you should not be doing it in the first place" (Wardrop, 2010). According to this assumption, it would not make a difference to reveal personal facts (even some types of sensitive information) to friends, relatives, neighbors or potential employers. Many users already manage their privacy in this way: their personal *weblog*, which shows a detailed CV, links to other social media resources where friendship, kinship and professional issues get mixed up. Every social media interface dreams of "centralizing" the information exchanged through other analogue services by providing "gadgets" or interconnection facilities. There have been already several attempts to unify all the digital ID's in a single one. The project for an "integrated digital. me userware" (*di.me*)[8] pretends to concentrate the management of digital identities in a single one, but showing different customized "digital faces" adjusted to the context. This system would go beyond the person-to-person logic to work based on the role-to-role connectivity (Wellman, 2002). Nonetheless, in order to control the use of different "digital masks", a single interface should have access to a great amount of personal information regarding one person.

Both anonymity and hyperpresence help to the achievement of personal fulfillment. While the first protects individuals from a collective gaze that judges and submits, the latter enables a communication process that fosters the customization of identities. Networked individualism overcomes the limits of group-based sociability: each individual takes from different networks the identity elements that compose the full image to be shared.

To prevent the isolation threat arisen from individualistic trends, the network society provides useful means: it enables to keep up existing social ties regardless of the location but also helps to create new ones through affinity communities. The structure of a networked individualism helps to solve the problem of a "lonely crowd" and to knit a social bridge to cross the abyss that may emerge between individuals and masses.

The opposite side, a situation of total transparency involves obvious privacy conflicts. Solove (2007b), based on statements of other authors agrees that "privacy" is a concept hard to define. But the difficulty to limit the meaning of privacy should not weaken the need to protect it. Solove explains the problems arisen by the "nothing to hide" argument, like "the underlying assumption that privacy is about hiding bad things" (p. 764). Privacy references may also change, and the concept of what is illegal, wrong, or just unmentionable does not remain stable. Additionally, in western societies is not possible to find individuals with no privacy concerns at all. There is always something that a person does not want to share unnecessarily with the rest.

To better understand the cultural changes regarding the patterns of information exchange, it is useful to borrow the Luft and Ingham's (1955) scheme called "Johari Window". This analytic tool helps to understand the interpersonal relationships and shows the crossing of two axes that represent knowledge access (by oneself and by others), resulting four quadrants (figure 2).

The variations in the flows of information generated by the increase of registry practices change the ways that the room "open" and, to a lesser extent, the room "blind" are configured within this scheme. Thus, the wise management of information filters, like the use of "digital faces" or the selective publication in social media, is the key to control how much of ourselves do we want that others achieve to know.

The invitation to share information publicly with others implies also to leave *updated* hints of the personal situation. The lack of strong references for social guidance is counteracted by the high volume of soft hints that reveal common values, appreciated practices and acceptable ways of conduct. Social emulation would be impossible if there were not available clear examples to imitate. This information is provided through networked infrastructures that communicate individuals. Here, the patterns of emulation do not involve an accurate imitation of established models but a customized appropriation of identity elements from different networks and nodes. At the same time, individuals have to share their experiences in order to make others know about their social engagement, to be judged and guided about their positioning in a social map.

Solutions and Recommendations

Some approaches to surveillance imply the idea of huge powerful structures that collect illegitimately as much information as possible. Undoubtedly, since the information society gives major value to this resource, some organizations aspire to act this way. But the image of a *panopticon* ignores the fact that individuals also contribute voluntarily to shape information networks.

It is recommendable to be aware of the different motivations that may cause the cession and disclosure of personal information. Networked sociability demands a constant exchange of personalized, updated and detailed information that helps to the forge of identities and to the development of a sense of belonging.

Therefore, it is important to take a look at the activities that take place in the nodes at the extremes, and not only to what happens with central servers and offices. It is essential to analyze what is done with the information that individuals share, but also how and why it came to be shared. Information can be used for different purposes, but it cannot be used at all if it is not previously *registered*, and this process reveals much about data exchange.

Figure 2. Johari window. Adapted from Luft and Ingham, 1955

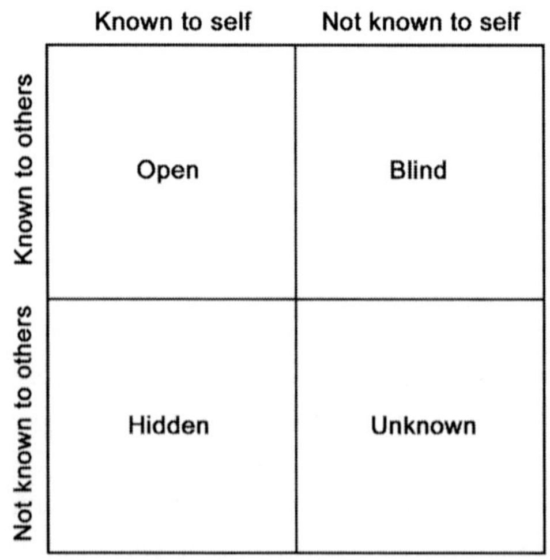

FUTURE RESEARCH DIRECTIONS

Networked societies generate complex structures of information exchange. The scheme, under which operates the system of devices and networks that makes possible this constant flow of bits, is an enigma for average users. The tendency to store a great part of the data in the so-called "Cloud" invites to think of communication structures as "centralizable" networks. If storage devices are connected to networks, then risk and fragility come into scene, but if users do not even know where these devices are located, then there will be necessary a high level of mutual trust.

Another subject interesting to deal with is the asymmetry of power that differences of information and uncertainty may generate in microsocial contexts. Individuals can use information to control the activities of peers and place themselves in an advantageous position. Also related to this question, it would be useful to analyze the differences of information exchange online and offline in networked societies, and to compare the reciprocal and reflective dimensions of registry.

Privacy is a major issue regarding networked sociability. Thus, it is necessary to analyze which image do individuals want to configure before others: Do people want to build and manage a single identity or an *ad hoc* customizable one for each situation? Do people really care about privacy or on the contrary, transparency will become finally the social norm?

CONCLUSION

The use of expressions like "surveillance societies" or "age of surveillance" may be misleading. Even the use (and abuse) of the word "surveillance" itself can foster the image of a rigid hierarchical structure of power and communication. The enhanced employment of sophisticated technologies in the field of surveillance does not involve that modern societies have increased their watching and control needs. By contrast, what has increased is the general registry of information, that implies the record, storage and potential circulation of this, but with a variety of objectives and uses. Among them, of course, there are surveillance practices, but this term does not have to be a privileged concept. The dynamization of information flows may be caused by and used for political or economical interests (from bureaucrats and managers but also from citizens and consumers). Nevertheless, non-instrumental objectives are also present in this process, like the old game of sociability.

There is a visible paradox in the opposition between the willfulness of registry and the possibility to stay anonymous. Individualized patterns are characteristic of modern societies and facilitate acceptable levels of privacy, but at the same time, hundreds of people provide hints to form a public realm full of information. Networked individualism requires the continuous flow of personal information to guarantee a networked sociability. This saturation of information generates a mechanism to participate in social contexts. Registry devices play a fundamental role: they allow individuals to summarize their customized identity in a digital format, resulting a complex mix obtained through the sharing of actions, locations, company, thoughts, feelings, etc.

Such a situation fosters several questions: Is it the end for secrecy? Do people really want to be anonymous? Is this a period of transition that creates conflicts about what is legitimate to be publicly shared? Which kind of society could accept a "total transparency" if it is not moral and culturally ready?

Even though the original motivation for the willful sharing of information through registry devices can be based in voluntary individual contributions, the resulting output may be used by different actors for rather ignoble ends. There is no *panopticon* at all. But it makes sense to ask ourselves if the existing networks and infrastructures are potentially "centralizable". The joint action of thousands of people can knit an enormous network that users exploit for individual purposes related to economy, politics or sociability. But if the circumstances change and certain actors abuse of their privileged access to each node of those networks, could these structures be transformed in permanent traps?

REFERENCES

Acquisti, A., & Gross, R. (2005). Information revelation and privacy in online social networks (The Facebook case). *Proceedings of the 2005 ACM Workshop on Privacy in the Electronic Society*, (pp. 71–80). Retrieved from http://www.heinz.cmu.edu/~acquisti/papers/privacy-facebook-gross-acquisti.pdf

Acquisti, A., & Gross, R. (2006). Imagined communities: Awareness, information sharing, and privacy on the Facebook. *Proceedings from Privacy Enhancing Technologies Workshop*, Cambridge, UK.

Albrechtsund, A. (2008). Online social networking as participatory surveillance. *First Monday*, *13*(3). Retrieved from http://firstmonday.org/htbin/cgiwrap/bin/ojs/index.php/fm/article/view/2142/1949.

Andrejevic, M. (2005). The work of watching one another: Lateral surveillance, risk, and governance. *Surveillance & Society*, *2*(4), 479–497. Retrieved from http://www.surveillance-and-society.org/articles2(4)/lateral.pdf.

Article 29 Data Protection Working Party. (2009). *Opinion 5/2009 on online social networking*. Retrieved from http://ec.europa.eu/justice/policies/privacy/docs/wpdocs/2009/wp163_en.pdf

Barnes, S. B. (2006). A privacy paradox: Social networking in the United States. *First Monday*, *11*(9). Retrieved from http://firstmonday.org/htbin/cgiwrap/bin/ojs/index.php/fm/article/view/1394/1312.

Bauman, Z. (2000). *Liquid modernity*. Cambridge, UK: Polity.

Bauman, Z. (2001). *The individualized society*. Cambridge, UK: Polity.

Beck, U., & Beck-Gernsheim, E. (2002). *Individualization: Institutionalized individualism and its social and political consequences*. London, UK: SAGE.

Berger, P. L. (1963). *Invitation to sociology: A humanistic perspective*. New York, NY: Anchor Books.

boyd, d. m., & Ellison, N. B. (2007). Social network sites: Definition, history, and scholarship. *Journal of Computer-Mediated Communication. 13*(1). Retrieved from http://jcmc.indiana.edu/vol13/issue1/boyd.ellison.html

Castells, M. (2010). The information age: Economy, society and culture.: *Vol. I. The rise of the network society* (2nd ed.). West Sussex, UK: Wiley-Blackwell.

Dubar, C. (2000). *La crise des identités. L'interprétation d'une mutation*. Paris, France: PUF.

Durkheim, E. (1951). *Suicide: A study in sociology*. New York, NY: Free Press.

Durkheim, E. (1997). *The division of labor in society*. New York, NY: Free Press.

Elias, N. (1991). *The society of individuals*. Oxford, UK: Basil Blackwell.

Foucault, M. (1977). *Discipline and punish: The birth of the prison*. London, UK: Penguin Books.

Fuchs, C. (2009). *Social networking sites and the surveillance society. A critical case study of the usage of Studivz, Facebook, and Myspace by students in Salzburg in the context of electronic surveillance*. Salzburg, Austria: Forschungsgruppe Unified Theory of Information. Retrieved from http://fuchs.icts.sbg.ac.at/SNS_Surveillance_Fuchs.pdf

Gandy, O. H. (1989). Information privacy and the crisis of control. In Raboy, P. M., & Bruck, P. A. (Eds.), *Communication for and against democracy* (pp. 59–73). Montreal, Canada: Black Rose Books.

Garton, L., Haythornthwaite, C., & Wellman, B. (1997). Studying online social networks. *Journal of Computer-Mediated Communication*, *3*(1). Retrieved from http://jcmc.indiana.edu/vol3/issue1/garton.html.

Giddens, A. (1979). *Central problems in social theory. Action, structure, and contradiction in social analysis*. Berkeley, CA: University of California Press.

Giddens, A. (1987). *Social theory and modern sociology*. Cambridge, UK: Polity Press.

Giddens, A. (1991). *The consequences of modernity*. Stanford, CA: Stanford University Press.

Gomá, J. (2009). *Ejemplaridad pública*. Madrid, Spain: Taurus.

Haggerty, K. D., & Ericson, R. V. (2000). The surveillant assemblage. *The British Journal of Sociology*, *51*(4), 605–622. doi:10.1080/00071310020015280

Hinduja, S., & Patchin, J. W. (2008). Personal information of adolescents on the Internet: A quantitative content analysis of MySpace. *Journal of Adolescence*, *31*(1), 125–146. doi:10.1016/j.adolescence.2007.05.004

Johnson, B. (2010, January 11). Privacy no longer a social norm, says Facebook founder. *The Guardian*. Retrieved from http://www.guardian.co.uk/technology/2010/jan/11/facebook-privacy

Koskela, H. (2004). Webcams, TV shows and mobile phones: Empowering exhibitionism. *Surveillance & Society*, *2*(2/3), 199–215. Retrieved from http://www.surveillance-and-society.org/articles2(2)/webcams.pdf.

Leighton, B., & Wellman, B. (1979). Networks, neighborhoods and communities. *Urban Affairs Quarterly*, *14*, 363–390. doi:10.1177/107808747901400305

Lipovetsky, G. (1983). *L'ère du vide. Essais sur l'individualisme contemporain*. Paris, France: Éditions Gallimard.

Livingstone, S. (2008). Taking risky opportunities in youthful content creation: Teenagers' use of social networking sites for intimacy, privacy and self-expression. *New Media & Society*, *10*(3), 393–411. Retrieved from http://eprints.lse.ac.uk/27072/. doi:10.1177/1461444808089415

Luft, J., & Ingham, H. (1955). The Johari window, a graphic model of interpersonal awareness. In *Proceedings of the Western Training Laboratory in Group Development*. Los Angeles, CA: UCLA.

Lyon, D. (1994). *The electronic eye. The rise of surveillance society*. Minneapolis, MN: University of Minnesota Press.

Lyon, D. (2006). 9/11, synopticon and scopophilia: Watching and being watched. In Haggerty, K. D., & Ericson, R. V. (Eds.), *The new politics of surveillance and visibility* (pp. 35–54). Toronto, Canada: University of Toronto Press.

Mann, S., Nolam, J., & Wellman, B. (2003). Sousveillance: Inventing and using wearable computing devices for data collection in surveillance environments. *Surveillance & Society*, *1*(3), 331–355. Retrieved from http://www.surveillance-and-society.org/articles1%283%29/sousveillance.pdf.

Marzo, J. L. (2002). Cultura de registro. In Fundació Tàpies, et al. (Eds.), *Culturas de archivo*. Barcelona, Spain: Editor. English version retrieved from http://www.soymenos.net/registry_culture.pdf

Mathiesen, T. (1997). The viewer society: Michel Foucault's panopticon revisited. *Theoretical Criminology*, *1*(2), 215–234. doi:10.1177/1362480697001002003

Melucci, A. (1989). *Nomads of the present. Social movements and individual needs in contemporary society*. London, UK: Hutchinson Radius.

Picó, J. (1999). *Cultura y modernidad. Seducciones y desengaños de la cultura moderna*. Madrid, Spain: Alianza Editorial.

Rosen, J. (2010, July 21). The web means the end of forgetting. *New York Times*. Retrieved from http://www.nytimes.com/2010/07/25/magazine/25privacy-t2.html

Sibilia, P. (2008). *La intimidad como espectáculo*. Buenos Aires, Argentina: Fondo de Cultura Económica.

Simmel, G. (1969). *The sociology of Georg Simmel*. New York, NY: Free Press.

Solove, D. J. (2007a). Privacy in an overexposed world. In *The future of reputation*. New Haven, CT: Yale University Press. Retrieved from http://docs.law.gwu.edu/facweb/dsolove/Future-of-Reputation/text/futureofreputation-ch7.pdf

Solove, D. J. (2007b). "I've got nothing to hide" and other misunderstandings of privacy. *The San Diego Law Review*, *44*, 745–772. http://ssrn.com/abstract=998565.

Spencer, H. (1885). *The principles of sociology*. London, UK: Williams and Norgate.

Toffler, A. (1981). *The third wave*. New York, NY: Bantam Books.

Tönnies, F. (1979). *Gemeinschaft und Gesellschaft. Grundbegriffe der reinen Soziologie*. Darmstadt, Germany: Wissenschaftliche Buchgesellschaft.

Utz, S., & Krämer, N. (2009). The privacy paradox on social network sites revisited: The role of individual characteristics and group norms. *Cyberpsychology: Journal of Psychosocial Research on Cyberspace, 3*(2). Retrieved from http://www.cyberpsychology.eu/view.php?cisloclanku=2009111001&article=1

Wardrop, M. (2010, August 18). Young will have to change names to escape cyber past, warns Google's Eric Schmidt. *The Telegraph*. Retrieved from http://www.telegraph.co.uk/technology/google/7951269/Young-will-have-to-change-names-to-escape-cyber-past-warns-Googles-Eric-Schmidt.html

Wellman, B. (2001). Physical place and cyber-Place: The rise of personalized networking. *International Journal of Urban and Regional Research*, *25*(2), 227–252. doi:10.1111/1468-2427.00309

Wellman, B. (2002). Little boxes, glocalization, and networked individualism. In M. Tanabe, P. van den Besselaar, & T. Ishida (Eds.), *Computational and sociological approaches* (pp. 11-25). Berlin, Germany: Springer-Verlag. Retrieved from http://homes.chass.utoronto.ca/~wellman/publications/littleboxes/littlebox.PDF

ADDITIONAL READING

Arendt, H. (1998). *The human condition*. London, UK; Chicago, IL: The University Chicago Press.

Ball, K., & Webster, F. (Eds.). (2003). *The intensification of surveillance. Crime, terrorism and warfare in the information age. London, UK.* Sterling, VA: Pluto Press.

Béjar, H. (1990). *El ámbito íntimo. Privacidad, individualismo y modernidad*. Madrid, Spain: Alianza.

Bentham, J. (2008). *The panopticon; or the inspection house*. London, UK: T. Payne.

Donner, F. J. (1980). *The age of surveillance*. New York, NY: Alfred A. Knopf.

Echeverría, J. (1999): *Los señores del aire: Telépolis y el tercer entorno*. Barcelona, Spain: Destino.

Flaherty, D. (1986). Government surveillance and bureaucratic accountability: Data protection agencies in western societies. *Science, Technology & Human Values*, *11*(1), 7–18.

Gálvez, A. M., & Tirado, F. (2006). *Sociabilidad en pantalla. Un estudio de la interacción en los entornos virtuales*. Barcelona, Spain: Editorial UOC.

Hampton, K. N. (2004). Sociability online, offline. In Castells, M. (Ed.), *The network society. A cross-cultural perspective. Cheltelham, UK.* Massachusetts, MA: Edward Elgar.

Hampton, K. N., Livio, O., & Goulet, L. S. (2010). The social life of wireless urban spaces: internet use, social networks, and the public realm. *The Journal of Communication*, *4*(60), 701–722. doi:10.1111/j.1460-2466.2010.01510.x

Koskela, H. (2003). 'Cam era' – the contemporary urban Panopticon. *Surveillance & Society*, *1*(3), 292–313. Retrieved from http://www.surveillance-and-society.org/articles1%283%29/camera.pdf.

Lyon, D. (1988). *The information society: issues and illusions*. Cambridge, UK: Polity Press.

Lyon, D. (2003). *Surveillance after September 11*. Cambridge, UK: Polity Press.

Marx, G. T. (1988). *Undercover: police surveillance in America*. Berkeley, CA: Univ. of California Press.

Marx, G. T. (2001). Identity and anonymity: some conceptual distinctions and issues for research. In Caplan, J., & Torpey, J. (Eds.), *Documenting individual identity*. New Jersey, NJ: Princeton University Press.

Masuda, J. (1983). *The information society as post-industrial society*. Bethesda, MD: World Future Society.

Mead, G. H. (1934). *Mind, self, and society*. Chicago, IL: University of Chicago Press.

Murakami Wood, D., & Webster, C. W. R. (2010). The normality of living in surveillance societies. In van der Hof, S., & Groothuis, M. (Eds.), *Innovating government: normative, policy and technological dimensions of modern government* (pp. 130–140). Cambridge, UK: Cambridge University Press / Asser Press.

Riesman, D. (1966). *The lonely crowd: a study of changing American character*. New Haven, CT: Yale University.

Roman, J. (1998). *La democrátie des individus. Paris, France: Calmann-Lévy, Rule, J. (1974). Private lives and public surveillance: social control in the computer age*. New York, NY: Schocken Books.

Rybczynski, W. (1987). *Home. A short history of an idea*. New York, NY: Penguin Books.

Sennet, R. (1978). *The fall of the public man*. New York, NY: Vintage Books.

Wellman, B., et al. (2003). The social affordances of the internet for networked individualism. *Journal of Computer-Mediated Communication, 8*(3). HTML-version retrieved from: http://jcmc.indiana.edu/vol8/issue3/wellman.html

Whitaker, R. (1999). *The end of privacy: how total surveillance is becoming a reality*. New York, NY: The New Press.

KEY TERMS AND DEFINITIONS

Customized Identity: The complex image of an individual resulting from a process of communication with others. It comprises multiple "pieces" of identity that may be shared with others, creating common connections that foster sociability. Individualized identities can be shared as a single image or adapted to the specific social circumstances of interaction.

Information Glows: Circulating information that acts as a "blood torrent" to activate networked sociability. They are dynamized by individuals through a communication structure that starts with the activity of registry devices and ends up with the access to information.

Networked Sociability: All those interactions that enable individuals to keep social ties, to belong and to participate in a network society. They also allow the creation and reproduction of individual and group identities. These social exchanges are understood as recreational actions without a clear instrumental or material basis, that is, they are not caused by needs but by the deliberate impulse to interact with others. In a network society, sociability is not limited to the location, and interactions that overcome time and space limitations play a significant role.

Record: The output that results from registry actions. Individuals may keep track of others if they have access to their records.

Registry: The process that permits to save a piece of personal information into an external medium. Registry devices make the knowledge of facts and experiences potentially accessible to others through communication networks. Registry actions may collect different aspects of personal information: activities, localizations, dates, interactions between two persons, preferences, feelings, etc. This process generates several types of resources: video, audio, pictures, texts and *microblogging* entries, comments, coordinates, telecommunication protocols...

SNS: Abbreviation for "Social Network Services" or "Social Network Sites". These are services based on web-technology that: provide tools that users employ to publish their own materials; give the chance to share personal information in order to generate a user profile to depict individual aspects; make possible to create a list of users of the same service with whom there is any kind of relationship. SNS are widely-used platforms to exchange personal registered information.

Surveillance: The art of monitoring others. It aims at the knowledge of facts, actions and changes regarding one or more individuals. Surveillance procedures involve different means that produce diverse indicators and resources according to the aspects that are being analyzed. The French origin of this word ("watching over") suggests an asymmetry of power and the relative ignorance of this situation from the monitored object.

ENDNOTES

1. This was already noticed by Gandy (1989, p. 59) from literature published in the 70s and 80s. Gary T. Marx and David Flaherty helped with their texts to think of a "surveillance society". Nowadays it is illustrative to take notice of the amount and the name of blogs dedicated to this topic: "Surveillance Studies", "Surveillance Project", "Surveillance and Society", etc.
2. Interesting definitions of SNSs can be found in boyd & Ellison (2007) and Art. 29 Data Protection Working Party (2009).
3. http://www.socialmeteor.com/2010/10/06/facebook-groups-get-by-with-a-little-help-from-your-friends/
4. "Internet 2010 in numbers" from *Royal Pingdom* (http://royal.pingdom.com/2011/01/12/internet-2010-in-numbers/). *Facebook* statistics page (http://www.facebook.com/press/info.php?statistics). February 2011.
5. http://es.engadget.com/2010/11/29/blackberry-empathy-phone-la-bb-del-futuro/
6. http://www.wafaabilal.com/
7. Barnes (2006), Acquisti & Gross (2005, 2006), Solove (2007a), Hinduja & Patchin (2008), Livingstone (2008), Utz & Krämer (2009), Fuchs (2009).
8. http://www.dime-project.eu

Chapter 4
The Challenge of Audience Research on Web 2.0:
The Possibilities, Problems, and Perspectives of Sentiment Analysis

Romana Andò
Sapienza University of Rome, Italy

ABSTRACT

One of the latest developments in audience research deals with the analysis of the views and opinions that individuals express in the social media web, where audiences share videos, comments, and grass-roots productions about media contents. The wealth of information available on the web, the power of world of mouth, the relevance of phenomena such as blogs, microblogs, and social network sites, combined with the urgent need to monitor, control, and predict audience behavior has led empirical research – both academic and market-driven – to exhibit a renewed interest in quantitative research, with the aim of transforming the depth of content and the interpretative frames produced by audiences in standardized search categories. The aim of this chapter is, therefore, to reflect on sentiment analysis and its applications to the social web, reflecting on the opportunity to apply the instrument to media audiences, considering the context of the research, the critical issues relating to this approach, and the perspectives which relate to quantitative study.

INTRODUCTION

Web 2.0 (O'Reilly, 2005) has significantly re-shaped different aspects of media audiences' contexts and practices.

The first change which has been brought about by Web 2.0 is related to the recent spread of convergent technologies, through which audiences can feel as if they are inhabiting a wider media space (Jenkins, 2006). This refers to a media space which they can not only cross as *space-time interpolators* – as Thompson (1995) wrote about the television and its function as a window out into the world – but one they can navigate, therefore seamlessly becoming a diffused audience (Abercrombie, & Longhurst 1998) because of the pervasiveness of online and offline media.

DOI: 10.4018/978-1-61350-338-6.ch004

As the most recent theories on networked individualism have stated (e.g. Wellman, 2001; Castells, 1996; Rheingold, 2003; Marinelli, 2004; Comunello 2006; 2010) – thereby underlining the central role of the individual in the seamless co-ordination of online and offline networks – media audiences have coherent experiences in the online world and in the physical one; they can easily manage their social activities with other subjects, in environments where they can connect with others with whom they can exchange symbolic materials. The authenticity and ease of online relationships, together with their continuity with the offline world, has led us to study 'audiences on-line' – audiences that use the Internet as a space for a larger life experience, which is highly integrated with the features and performances they already experience offline – and not so-called "online audiences", described as "online communities, online identities, online sociolinguistic patterns, cybercuture(s) relationships that emerge through CMC, and various other online social interactive human elements" (Kozinets, 2010, p. 64). The lives and cultures of online audiences are directly related to the online world, and the Internet itself becomes both a field and an object of research.

The second important change which has been introduced by Web 2.0 is that audiences have started to connect with each other once again, thanks to online sharing platforms, and they use these connections to perceive themselves as part of an audience (Livingstone, 2005). They are becoming more visible and noisy (Livingstone, 2004), and closer to the audiences that used to attend Shakespearean drama – expressing comments in real time, directly praising or criticizing texts – rather than being the passive couch potatoes described by large part of the existing scientific literature on television.

Audiences are aware that they are living in a world inhabited by other audiences, and they interpret their audiencehood knowing that other players will act as readers of their enunciative and textual products (Fiske, 1992). In the online context, the audience can be seen as a mediated product or as a performance in itself, as the barriers between the audience and the performance are being meticulously – and continuously – reconfigured.

Therefore, "this self-representation and self-performance of the audience-as-text therefore creates a second order or implied commodification insofar as the online fan audience consumes a textual construction of itself alongside the originating commodity-text, with the valued novelties of the latter crossing over into the equally novel and similarly valued speculations, rewritings and framings of the former" (Hills, 2002, p. 177).

Interactive technologies can also significantly shorten the distance between the performer and the audience; nowadays, audiences are often both producers and consumers of texts, borrowing their practices and their relationships with media companies from fans (Jenkins, 2006). Therefore, audiences are more productive in a semiotic and enunciative way (Fiske, 1992) and their textual production has definitely increased, flooding the Internet with textual material.

The aforementioned elements of Web 2.0 require a revision of the analytical models which have thus far been adopted. These models pose a huge methodological challenge for empirical research, both for academic research and for the objectives and needs of the market.

Together with the explorative methods which are typical of the ethnographic approach – and of the more recent netnographic approach (e.g. Hine,2000; Baym & Markham, 2009; Kozinets, 2010) – quantitative research tools are emerging in audience studies: rather than relying on the mere detection of consumer behavior, they are designed to measure phenomena and are increasingly focused on determining the relationships between different audiences and on assessing audience involvement, evaluation and engagement with the media content.

In this chapter, I will focus on web-based sentiment analysis, on its interpretative criticalities and its prospects for development in audience studies. I will start by (1) providing an operational definition of sentiment analysis; (2) describing the current application fields of the approach; (3) comparing it with other audience measurement methods, with particular attention to the difference between qualitative and quantitative approaches; (4) discussing the possibilities, problems and perspectives of applying sentiment analysis to the opinions and the comments expressed by the audiences.

BACKGROUND

My main idea is borrowed from the personal influence approach (Katz & Lazarsfeld, 1955), which states that individuals always tend to seek support from the experiences of others while deciding what to consume. However, in the Web 2.0 era, opinion leaders are no longer those inhabiting the local context: they are elective, and consumers find them on the Internet because they have similar tastes. This is not all: in addition to seeking advice and reviews from others, audiences love to test their own tastes, to reaffirm their choices and to use the temporary alliances they find as a trigger for the management of their own identities and social relations.

The transition from the newness – both academic and economic – of the phenomenon of the online audience to its normalization coincides methodologically with the use of quantitative research alongside the (more exploratory) ethnographic approaches, in an attempt to blend different methodologies. Once a phenomenon is found, it needs to be measured (quantitative research on samples of fans from websites and blogs; quantitative thematic analysis of forums; blogs; social network sites), meaning that quantity becomes a value (topic and posts are used as an index of fans' activity) and opinions and judgments are central (sentiment analysis and opinion mining). We should also study the level of technological and encyclopedic skills (media literacy index; e.g. Buckingham 2003; Livingstone, 2003), build a map of cross-media consumption, identify connections between different objects of fandom (*trajectories of taste*) and value the relational dimension of fandom (social network sites, community and social network analysis).

This is not just a new field of research in which we can observe audiences as lurkers: we not only have a privileged view of an online phenomenon which might be visible offline, but we are also experiencing a redefinition of a more general phenomenon, the social existence of which extends beyond online interactions and the Internet (although they may play an important role in the practices of being an audience) and continually adapts and molds itself to the existing cultures and contexts of its use.

I believe that Web 2.0 is an amazing resource with which to study audiences, and I have explained and highlighted this in the past, through research and writing on both methodologies and objectives (Andò & Marinelli, 2010). I also think that the enthusiasm for the visibility of audiences and their extraordinarily relevant enunciative activity – for the profusion of data, the supposed simplicity of real-time observations and the rapidity of information collection and retrieval, together with the transformation of the media system and the dissatisfaction felt about most traditional methodologies of audience research – should not exempt us from producing a methodological reflection on the new challenges of audience research.

Nowadays, we are facing a gradual but steady process of normalization of fandom and an expansion of the domain of the word "fandom" itself, which is gradually leading us to reconsider audiences using the traditional interpretive schemes (Andò & Marinelli, 2010). This familiarity with the phenomenon, together with the availability and accessibility of the online world, is pushing both academic research and the market to develop new research tools and new interpretive strategies.

One of the most interesting and challenging new research methods on audience media consumption and reception is sentiment analysis. Sentiment analysis (or 'opinion mining') is the computational study of opinions, sentiments and emotions expressed in text (Liu, 2010).

To get to the heart of the matter, sentiment analysis is based on the application of automated methods of analysis to online conversations and social media, with the aim of finding the different focuses that most recent researches have already pointed out (Tianxia, 2008):

1. Identifying words or phrases bearing opinions;
2. Identifying the general orientation of these opinions (in particular, looking for adjectives, adverbs and verbs);
3. Classifying sentences or documents by the polarity of their opinions.

The recent growth of Internet documents – especially online reviews (product reviews, movie reviews and so on) – within blogs, social network sites (SNS) and microblogs holds a significant interest in the application of this research method, as documented by Pang and Lee (2008). The precondition is clearly the significant development of blogging and microblogging platforms on the web, their dynamism and openness (i.e. vs message boards) for crawler searches, their multi-thematic nature and, above all, the fact that these platforms are the places in which individuals express their subjectivity and their relationships through comments, reviews, ratings, experiences and suggestions.

The application fields which have so far been explored with sentiment analysis vary from the political (where politicians use opinion assessment to obtain real-time feedback on government issues) to the commercial (where the key is the monitoring of brands and levels of loyalty) to the media field, with particular reference to film reviews, which are often used as an indicator of future box-office results. In all of these cases, a descriptive (measuring the phenomenon) and provisional (trying to read opinions as anticipatory of consumption behaviors) approach is adopted.

While using sentiment analysis as a research method, we think that when an individual is interested in a media product:

- He/she could express evaluations in its regard;
- These evaluations could be impromptu and/or rationally or emotionally based (opinion and/or sentiment);
- These evaluations will be read, assessed and appropriated by others, who will relate to an object/product and evaluate it having borrowed attitudes and motivations from the web (theories of personal influence and opinion leaders, as described in early personal influence research, Lazarsfeld, Berelson, & Gaudet, 1944).

In short, sentiment analysis is an empirical method which allows to translate human emotions and opinions, mainly those expressed in the online world, into hard data, using automated tools (i.e., crawlers) to discern, extract and process attitudinal information found in on line text (e.g. blogs; microblogs, forum) (Liu, 2010; Baloglu & Aktas, 2010; Bai, 2010; Parik & Movassate, 2009; Pang & Lee, 2008; Boiy, Hens, Deschact, Moens, 2007; Zhuang, Jing, Zhu, 2006). A SAS (Sentiment Analysis' software) crawler locates and extracts texts – comments and opinions - from different digital sources within a selected dataset. Then, it assigns the sentiment values expressed in all available text collections, identifying trends and creating graphical reports that describe the expressed feelings of consumers in real time. The output can help decision makers to evaluate trends, predict future outcomes, minimize risks and capitalize on opportunities.

From the point of view of brands (and the market), sentiment analysis means the availability of a great deal of data which would otherwise not be traceable (i.e., through other methods of market survey) and the transformation of customers' subjective opinions into statistically quantifiable and readable data over time, and often in real time. It is, therefore, possible to weigh the popularity of a product or a brand, to quantify the number of times it is mentioned and to identify the polarity – positive or negative – of consumers' opinions.

From a sociological point of view like mine, instead, sentiment analysis provides answers to three inalienable requirements for the researcher (Andò & Marinelli, 2010):

1. Certify the existence of a certain phenomenon (textual productivity is not just the result of our speculations on Web 2.0, word of mouth and on the role of social networks);
2. Objectify and measure it, in order to quantify the online buzz and to make it a manageable and controllable research object;
3. Understand the positive or negative polar opinions on consumer products, including media products, and trying to use them for forecasting and development;
4. Find connections with the broader socio-cultural background (Andò, 2010).

SENTIMENT ANALYSIS: LOOKING FOR AUDIENCES' TASTES AND OPINIONS

Why could it be useful to apply sentiment analysis to audience studies?

The lack of reciprocity between the audience and the issuer of a message in a mediated quasi-interaction has already been reported by Thompson (1995) as a significant risk factor for broadcasters, who have no control over the invisible audience and cannot design their communications in a reflexive manner. In spite of the discriminatory habit of the audiences between popular and unpopular texts (Fiske, 1989), this highly dangerous way of communicating was balanced by media scarcity in the early years of television and by the lack of significant competitors, both for content and entertainment platforms.

Nowadays, these behaviors are no longer commonplace, and audiences manifest everyday – in real time and in the multiple spaces the web offers them – the tastes and competences they gain from the products and the strategic policies of media companies. To some extent, Web 2.0 has finally made audiences aware of their bargaining power over broadcasters, and has done so by exalting their potential for connection, exchange and sharing (Jenkins, 2009).

Hence, there is a need for the market to know about audiences' tastes in greater depth, to study their opinions and engagement with media content, not so much in terms of depth (as the ethnographic approach would allow), but in terms of scope (how many people share an opinion) and visibility (where audiences share their thoughts).

Thus, sentiment analysis applied to media audiences aims to plumb grassroots-produced texts (user-generated content) in the search for a positive or negative orientation towards media content, driven by the assumption that the commented features in movie and media review are much richer than those in product review (Zhuang, Jing, & Zhu, 2006). In fact, people will not only comment on elements of media content and express their enjoyment of them (or lack thereof), but will extend their assessments to people who are relevant to media.

We need to remember that the limits of sentiment analysis which have been extensively discussed in literature (Liu, 2010) – the difficulties in interpreting the polarity of the reviews, the disambiguation of sentences and their connections to one another – are even more problematic when we try to explain the individual and social importance of media consumption in the simple terms of positive or negative positioning.

SENTIMENT ANALYSIS = RATINGS + QUALITY?

The mere application of sentiment analysis to blogs, microblogs and SNS, places where audiences express their relationship with the texts, as well as their appreciation and judgments, seems quite risky. Many of the researches which have been developed within the field of cultural studies and brought forward by audience studies are instantly and dramatically impoverished in the face of a research methodology that embraces with excessive ease the strategic approach of marketing, while laying aside deeper sociological analysis (Livingstone, 1997, Ang, 1991, Moores, 1994; Murray & Schroder & Drotner & Kline, 2003, Gillespie, 2005).

The feeling is that we are facing a challenge similar to Ang's concept of "desperately seeking the audience" (Ang, 1991), and that we have to reflect on the interpretative risk which is connected to this matter.

Quantitative research tools offer researchers the illusory certainty of being able to take the pulse of a situation, hiding behind the persuasive power of data, while the uncertainty which derives from consumption behaviours becomes less and less explicable and quantitatively justifiable.

As Mittel (2007) argues with regard to the television audience:

Television viewers are the actual people who watch television – you, your friends and family, and millions of other real people watching television. Television audiences are the way the industry thinks about viewers: categorizes them, measures them, designs programming for them, and sells them to advertisers. But there is a crucial gap between the behaviors of real viewers and the industry's understanding of audiences, a distinction that directly impacts our understanding of how the television industry functions. (Mittel, 2007)

If the need of the media industries that invest in audience research is to have knowledge in order to exert control, to observe, to acquire case histories and to manage data that can legitimize reliable forecasts regarding audience behaviours, these industries have to deal with the same limitation: although monitoring and measuring instruments can lead us to meticulous and accurate representations, their descriptive realism is not sufficient to provide a sense of control because it does not prescribe a behavior (Ang, 1991).

This leads to a vicious circle, the uncertainty of which will torment the industry until the point when a more analytical system is found. However, it could happen that, the more the look is microscopically focused on the viewer, the more we also notice how much the consumption of media is evasive (Ang, 1991).

It is obvious that when we talk about sentiment analysis, as I have said before, we are talking about something more than the head counts carried out by systems such as Nielsen or other metrics. However, I still think that sentiment analysis could be viewed too hastily as a way to correct the simple systems of statistical audience measurement, based on two central questions: *Who is watching?* and *What are they watching?* We have added the like/dislike polarity, but we are still not thinking about the *How*? or *Why*?

We are, therefore, dealing with a infinitely more complex system, one which makes the pretence of objectivity when dealing with extended panels, but which in some ways is still focused on solving the age-old problem of customer satisfaction (as it happens, e.g., with, the Italian experiences of the IQS[1], Quality and Satisfaction Index and Qualitel). What is the element that makes us move away from the idea of *quick research* towards that of *immersive research*?

MARKET RESEARCH: EMPIRICAL SOCIOLOGICAL RESEARCH. HYBRIDIZATIONS OR REWRITINGS?

Sociological research seems to be facing the risk of overlapping too quickly with the conditions of market research, being overwhelmed by the relative ease of data retrieval and the immediacy of their representation (a Twitter curve), and not realizing (until it is too late) that we are looking at a fragmented reality and are currently working without a consistent theoretical framework.

I will try to answer this question by relying on the recently re-emerged discussion about sources: what the sociologists call sources is the set of empirically accessible materials through which they find the information necessary to answer their questions. But, potentially, everything is a source of information itself: what really makes something a "source" are the questions we are trying to answer when looking at it.

What are the research questions? To what extent is academic research different from the companies who want to know the progress of their brand, which features of their products work, who the competitors are and how to orient the market by inserting surreptitiously self-produced items within the buzz?

First, I believe that anyone who is involved in media studies is perfectly aware of the difference – as expressed by John Fiske (1992) – between financial economy and cultural economy. Sentiment analysis was born in the academic research, but it is nowadays subservient to a financial logic, and not to a cultural one. As a result, maybe we should think about how to adapt sentiment analysis to our need for knowledge.

Second, tracing the life of a commercial product according to word of mouth is much easier than tracing the never-ending life of a media product. The remediation phenomenon (Bolter & Grusin, 2000) that surrounds media content – and specifically audiences' productivity and semiotic contribution to a grassroots production – makes the media an interesting research object, but one that is at the same time ephemeral, fickle and elusive.

When we talk about the media, we talk about something that is more than a brand. Nowadays, media content could quite easily become a brand and be skillfully used by consumers as a recognizable identity trait, as required by Love marketing (Roberts, 2005).

Media are even more crucial in defining our social experience, an essential dimension of everyday experience. To study the media means to deal with wherever human beings congregate both in real and virtual spaces, where they communicate, where they look for persuasion, information, entertainment, education, where they seek in a multitude of ways, and with varying degrees of success, to connect one another (Silverstone, 1999).

Therefore, the key is the relationship, the connection. This interpretation becomes even more compelling in Web 2.0: focusing on it, when I talk about social networks on the Internet – in contrast to scholars such as Barabási (2006), Watts or others linked to the "new science of networks" – I don't only refer to the technological components: main attention goes to cultures and social practices. Following this perspective, technologies enable behaviors while social practices shape technological environments.

Thirdly –and this is closely related to the second point which has already been discussed – sociology is interested in audiences, and not only in the texts they consume. Sociology is not only interested in understanding what an audience is watching and whether or not they like it, but also *how* and *why* they do so. As the why is explained by Fiske's articulation (1989) – which I still find to be decisive – I am interested in understanding how audiences make sense of media content and how they connect it to their personal experiences.

As Jenkins says about the race to study the Web 2.0,

What's so exciting is that the net discussion tends to center on those issues that are of the most interest for media researchers [...] attempts to develop aesthetic criteria for the evaluation of television and other popular texts; speculations about media authorship; critiques of ideology; and self-analysis on the netters' own involvement with the broadcast materials. (Jenkins, 1995, pp. 52-53)

As we are sociologists and interested in cultural processes, we must ask ourselves whether it is enough for us – as it seems to be for the market – to look for opinions, assess trends and follow the success/failure curve of a brand, or rather if we should rather understand the experiences themselves.

When talking about television as an engaging medium, Askwith (2007) argued that, in order to understand audience behavior, scholars need to understand the level of entertainment (*we like to watch*), the level of social connections (*did you see that?*), the level of expertise (*everyone's an expert*), the level of immersion (*being there*) and the level of identification (*we are what we watch*).

Therefore, it seems that we are not only talking about whether we like or dislike something. It has occurred to me that the key to the development of sentiment analysis should be just that. Figuring out how to fathom the infinite database of information that the Internet offers, which lexicon we should use to capture subjects' articulations and their ability to immerse themselves in media content, will make it a popular product, as Fiske would call it (1989).

It appears to me that we should use different lexicons for research, some more oriented towards understanding ratings, others focused on relating comments to individual experiences, using online and offline qualitative audience research to identify them (e.g., identifying the keywords and the transitional objects of a generation, as in the experience of the *We Search* project, a qualitative and quantitative research project using crawlers to study italian blogs [Boccia Artieri, 2010]).

The Roles of Context and Social Bonds

In my opinion, the audience model we should refer to when we carry out research on audiences should be related to our social experience. We know that we are dealing with competent audiences, who are performative and aware of their being a 'diffused audience' (Abercrombie & Longhurst, 1998). This is another key aspect on which we should focus. One of the features of the diffused audience, as theorized by Abercrombie & Longhurst (1998), is imagination: nowadays audiences – due to the pervasiveness of media, the spectacularization of everyday life and the narcissistic and performative impulses that guide their lives – are aware that they are media audiences, just like other similar audiences, and that they are imagined and imaginable as they share a common network of meanings with the media. Audiences are networks, communities that consist of shifting alliances that give further meaning to content reception and to the processing of their meanings (Fiske, 1989, Jenkins, 1992).

The first wave of fan studies was focused on fan communities – both on being connected to be fans, and on being fans to be connected. The social dimension is a distinctive feature of an audience. Comments, opinions and protests that fans produce with regard to media content gain sense and are strengthened through their involvement in a "network", both in a relational and a technological sense (Jenkins, 1992, Bacon Smith, 1992, Harrington & Bielby, 1995).

With sentiment analysis, we try to detect this rich and competent enunciative activity of audiences on the web; however, the extraction of samples of posts and comments from blogs and microblogs (but not so much from message boards) obscures both the relational value connected to these opinions and the sense of participation that exists in the convergence culture. Thus, we will use grassroots contributions from a convergence culture (*anyone can participate*), but we risk to expunge this trait from the analysis of the extracted texts.

This is primarily a theoretical problem, but it is also a methodological one: it is not accidental that sentiment analysis scholars are reflecting on the difficulties of a standardized interpretation of phrases and words that have meaning only when contextualized (i.e., the concatenation of sentences in which subjects, items for discussion and references are taken for granted; denial, which can be viewed in a positive light; and the use of judgments, the value of which can only be discriminated from their context). Considering a post (or a phrase in a post) as the minimal unit of analysis leads us to give up the richness of meaning we can only have when we connect the post to the person who is writing, as part of a broader individual profile, and when we insert it into a specific thematic context (discussion thread). In addition, nowadays, the person who is writing and discussing online has value as a media consumer, has daily trajectories of taste and affiliation to media content and those skills and abilities that we call *media literacy*, which come from his/her being more or less integrated within the media system. Without this kind of information (which many search tools are trying to obtain) about the user, we would be facing an average user, one that does not exist and cannot be properly analyzed.

On the other hand, sentiment analysis is oriented towards the identification of influential individuals, evoking the concept of personal influence and adapting it to Web 2.0 – recovering, in fact, the relational dimension of the construction and negotiation of opinions.

Another problematic area is the need to filter the presence of really active users, who produce most of the existing speeches, from the database of posts. Thus, we should create a sort of cluster related to the involvement level and to the production activities of users.

In addition, there are companies that apply research tools derived from sentiment analysis in order to take advantage of this aspect by offering to identify influential people and relate to them. In other words, after identifying where to invest and the online discussions areas that are appropriate for the product, one goal may be to specify which type of individuals to involve – consumers looking for help and support, detractors, enthusiasts of the brand who want to sponsor it (evangelists), the influential opinion leaders – and then monitor the activity outlined by word of mouth.

This example, like others that may be inferred from the observation of new trends in market research (see current web analyitics tools like ALTERIAN, BIZ360, BRANDWATCH, NIELSEN, RADIAN6, SYSOMOS)[2], shows that talking about indistinct opinions in online discussion environments is a poorly defined idea that requires more attention both in the empirical research and in terms of methodology.

It is also clear that the assessments and opinions expressed could have different levels of specific gravity, especially in terms of the impact they have on others. This has led to the importance of a necessary re-evaluation of the concept of personal influence in relation to opinion mining, and to the need to focus more on the networks of subjects and on the relationships between them (social network analysis) and less on the expression of opinions and views on a product.

ALGORITHMS VS. ETHNOGRAPHIC GAZE

How did we get to this stage in quantitative research? In the first comprehensive study on Italian fandom which was conducted in 2007 (Marinelli & Andò, 2010), we used our ethnographic experience to shift – in relation to our explorative (*Is there a phenomenon? How big is it?*) and cognitive (*What is the meaning of this?*) needs – from a qualitative to a quantitative approach. We rolled out and analyzed posts, as we were persuaded of the need to standardize our mechanisms of selection, reading and interpretation of data and, therefore, attempted to quantify the phenomenon. In retrospect, I think we have fulfilled the task of demonstrating the existence of fandom in Italy: we have interpreted it consistently and we have identified trends in practices, consumer orientation and reception, but we have not adequately understood what ties audiences to specific media content.

This interpretative problem also exists in sentiment analysis. With this kind of analysis, researchers can find quantitative data on the popularity of a product (mentions), information on the geographical origin of users who prefer a particular product, positive or negative orientation towards the same product (sentiment), but, with the lexicon which is used today, it's not possible to fully understand the reasons for attachment, loyalty and passion towards a product, nor the links between media use and everyday practices.

On the other hand, I'm fully aware that the move towards quantitative research has emerged in order to offset the limitations of the sometimes-incorrect application of the ethnographic gaze to online audiences. Netnography, in fact, entails the in-depth study of both online communities and communities online: it is based on participant observation of an online space (online fieldwork) and uses computer-mediated communication as a source of data for interpretation and an ethnographic representation of a wider phenomenon, one that is both cultural and communitarian.

Therefore, the key is not only the availability and accessibility of data, but the use of the term netnography in that case would represent the researcher's attempt to acknowledge the importance of computer-mediated-communications in the lives of cultural members, to include in their data collection between the triangulations strategies online and offline various sources of cultural understanding, and to acknowledge that, like interviews or semiotics, netnography has its own set of uniquely adapted practices and procedures that set it apart from the conduct of face-to-face ethnography (Kozinets, 2010, p. 60).

The sensation experienced so far, however, is "as if the ethnographer's own desire [is] to attain the position of a 'lurker' – invisible and supposedly all-seeing – overwhelms or displaces any interest in the technological, social and historical processes, through which this 'invisibility' has itself been constructed as a specific nodal point within mediation" (Hills, 2002, p. 175).

From Sentiment to Engagement

Regarding the very positive cultural role of Web 2.0, sociologists should expect a significant revolution in terms of audience participation and involvement, as audiences use online expression of views and comments as a trigger for broader social practices which are related to media consumption. We are dealing with a form of participation and involvement that results in commitment and engagement.

From sentiment to engagement: this seems to be a possible direction for audience research. The opinions expressed online become interesting for academic research – and probably also for the market, if *ratings* are not the only research focus.

Thus, the keyword is *engagement*: according to the dictionary, its definition is "promise or undertaking, esp. one that is formal or made in writing; agreement to marry; arrangement to go somewhere, meet somewhere or do something at a fixed time; battle" (Hornby, 1987, p. 285).

This concept is certainly closer to what an audience produces in relation to media content. Engagement is in the task of decoding (in semiotics, we talk about interpretive work) a text, and dealing with conflict over the use of its meaning (the idea of resistance used in approaches in cultural studies). Engagement is spending time consuming a media product, but it is also conceiving media use as a series of appointments at a given time, although today nothing is linked to broadcast timing any longer. Engagement is a commitment between oneself and media content. Engagement is also what characterizes audiences' critical analysis of texts, information retrieval and knowledge building, the translation of subtitles from one language to another, and creative production.

Above all, engagement is what drives the audience to perceive a seamless transition from a local experience to a mediated one, to make public their thoughts and feelings, and to be compelled to participate (an idea which is echoed in the concept of civic engagement).

On the other hand, engagement also refers to the ideas of enjoyment and emotional connection, the ability of content to entertain, involve and thrill. It is similar to the concept of love: everyone agrees that it is important, but no-one is able to define it clearly and properly, once and for all. "Engagement" translates the concepts of emotional involvement, empathy, passion, and loyalty, but – because of the potential for interpersonal connections with Web 2.0 – always tends to shift the focus from the dimension of individual perception and interpretation to a social and ultimately relational one.

If we analyze the engagement indicators developed by Brian Haven for Forrester Research (2008), we can understand the new challenges which audience research is facing:

1. **Involvement.** It is the most basic measurement of engagement (the first point of interaction with a brand) and reflects the measurable aspects of an individual's relationship with a company or a brand, such as: visits to a website or a physical store, time spent per page, and pages viewed;
2. **Interaction.** By measuring events in which individuals contribute content about a brand, request additional information, provide contact information, or purchase a product or service, it is possible to measure the depth of their involvement;
3. **Intimacy.** This relates to the affection or sentiment an individual holds for a brand, expressed through opinion, perspective, or passion for the brand;
4. **Influence.** This is to determine an individual's likelihood to encourage a fellow customer to consider or buy a brand, product, or service (brand awareness, loyalty, and the possibility of purchasing again).

CONCLUSION

In order to conclude this reflection on sentiment analysis on the Internet, it may be appropriate to think, once again, about the potentialities and the uncertainties introduced by word of mouth: it is logical to expect an explosion of online comment production (as data suggest), but researchers will also have to deal with the mutability of word of mouth and the increasing difficulty in discriminating between different opinions that people give about other points of view, in the absence of a hierarchy of roles and skills. In other words, sentiments and opinions are not stable (other than in the fact that they are difficult to detect) and they certainly do not have the same level of produced and perceived relevance (for users or for researchers).

Furthermore, interpretative and enunciative audience activity on media content is far more complex than the comments and opinions expressed by users about consumption objects (e.g. a cellular phone, a tablet), which makes sentiment application more challenging.

However, the enthusiasm of market researchers has already translated into specific tools and targeted testing. The most active actors in this field are certainly advertisers and companies which want to comprehend and take advantage of the world of mouth, with the aim of enhancing and promoting their brand. Obviously, broadcaster and content providers are also interested in sentiment analysis application.

Existing literature presents comparative analysis of current available tools. Lovett and Owyang (2010), for instance, underline that inquiring social media buzz implies a three-step activity, leading to three different kind of results. First, "listening" activity, which aims at finding internet keywords, phrases and comments about a product or a brand, or about the company's comptetitors; second, "measuring" activity, which allows to keep under control the brand/product evolution within social media in terms of reputation, influence and repetition; third, "engagement" activity, which allows to catch the consumers attention and drive them to active engagement and participation (Radian6, 2010).

Therefore, the kind of data we need to focus on creates a need for methods to be blended in audience research; to forecast future consumption choices (*How much time is spent? Where and when? How is the time spent?*) will not be enough; perhaps, even sentiment analysis itself (*What kind of opinion? What meaning does it have? Why is the user loyal?*) will not be enough; but certainly, Web 2.0 will continue to be an ideal environment where to understand the network of relationships that continually reinterpret and redirect the flow of communication.

REFERENCES

Abercrombie, N., & Longhurst, B. (1998). *Audiences: A sociological theory of performance and imagination*. London, UK: Sage.

Andò, R. (2010). (forthcoming). *Fonti informative a contenuto e tecnologie di rilevazione delle opinioni*. Tv ++ Project, Roma, Italy. *Fondazione Ugo Bordoni*.

Andò, R., & Marinelli, A. (2010). Fare ricerca sul fandom on line. Fan italiani e serie televisive. In Monaci, S., & Scifo, B. (Eds.), *Sociologia 2.0 Pratiche sociali e metodologie di ricerca sui media partecipativi* (pp. 189–221). Napoli, Italy: Scriptaweb.

Ang, I. (1991). *Desperately seeking the audience*. London, UK: Routledge. doi:10.4324/9780203321454

Askwith, I. D. (2007). *Television 2.0: Reconceptualizing TV as an engagement medium* [Thesis]. BA Individualized Study (Technology, Media & Culture) Gallatin School of Individualized Study, New York University, Master of Science in Comparative Media Studies, Massachusetts Institute of Technology.

Bacon Smith, C. (1992). *Enterprising women. Television fandom and the creation of popular myth*. Philadelphia: University of Pennsylvania Press.

Bai, X. (2010). Predicting consumer sentiments from online text. [Elsevier BV.]. *Decision Support Systems*, *50*(4), 732–742. doi:10.1016/j.dss.2010.08.024

Baloglu, A., & Aktas, M. S. (2010).BlogMiner: Web blog mining application for classification of movie reviews. *2010 Fifth International IEEE Conference on Internet and Web Application and Services*, (pp. 77-84).

Barabási, A.-L., Newman, M., & Watts, D. J. (2006). *The structure and dynamics of networks*. Princeton, NJ: Princeton University Press.

Boccia, A. G. (2010). Analisi degli user generated content e pubblici connessi: Rappresentazioni generazionali in Rete. In Monaci, S., & Scifo, B. (Eds.), *Sociologia 2.0 Pratiche sociali e metodologie di ricerca sui media partecipativi* (pp. 283–297). Napoli, Italy: Scriptaweb.

Boiy, E., Hens, P., Deschacht, K., & Moens, M.-F. (2007). Automatic sentiment analysis in on-line text, *Proceedings of the 11th International Conference on Electronic Publishing Vienna Austria (2007)ELPUB2007*

Bolter, J. D., & Grusin, R. (2000). *Remediation. Understanding new media*. Cambridge, MA: The MIT Press.

Buckingham, D. (2003). *Media education. Literacy, learning and contemporary culture*. London, UK: Polity Press-Blackwell Publishing.

Castells, M. (1996). *The rise of the network society*. Oxford, UK: Blackwell.

Comunello, F. (2006). *Reti nella rete. Teorie e definizioni tra tecnologia e società*. Milano, Italy: Guerini.

Comunello, F. (2010). *Networked sociability*. Milano, Italy: Guerini.

Fiske, J. (1989a). *Understanding popular culture*. London, UK: Routledge.

Fiske, J. (1989b). Moments of television: Neither the text nor the audience. In Thornham, S., & Marris, P. (Eds.), *Media studies: A reader* (pp. 536–546). New York, NY: NYU Press.

Fiske, J. (1992). The cultural economy of fandom. In Lewis, L. A. (Ed.), *Adoring audience. Fan culture and popular media* (pp. 30–49). London, UK: Routledge.

FreshMinds Research. (2010). *Turning conversations into insights: A comparison of social media monitoring tools*. Retrieved February 10, 2011, from www.freshminds.co.uk

Gillespie, M. (2005). *Media audiences*. London, UK: Open University Press.

Gray, J., Sandvoss, C., & Harrington, C. (Eds.). (2007). *Fandom: Identities and communities in a mediated world*. New York, NY: New York University Press.

Harrington Lee, C., & Bielby, D. (1995). *Soap fans, pursuing pleasure and making meaning in everyday life*. Philadelphia, PA: Temple University Press.

Haven, B., & Vittal, S. (with Overby, C. S., Favier, J., & Cokeh, E.). (2008). *Measuring engagement: Four steps to making engagement measurement a reality*. Cambridge, MA: Forrester Research: Hills, M. (2002). *Fan cultures*. New York, NY: Routledge.

Hornby, A. S. (1987). *Oxford advanced learners dictionary of current English*. Oxford, UK: Oxford University Press.

Jenkins, H. (1992). *Textual poachers: Television, fans and participatory culture*. London, UK: Chapman and Hall.

Jenkins, H. (2006). *Convergence culture. Where old and new media collide*. New York, NY: NYU Press.

Lazarsfeld, P. F., Berelson, B., & Gaudet, H. (1944). *The people's choice: How the voter makes up his mind in a presidential campaign*. New York, NY: Columbia University Press.

Liu, B. (2010). Sentiment analysis and subjectivity. In Indurkhia, N., & Damerau, F. J. (Eds.), *Handbook of natural language processing* (2nd ed.). Boca Raton, FL: Chapman & Hall/CRC.

Livingstone, S. (1997). The work of Elihu Katz: Conceptualizing media effects in context. In Corner, J., Schlesinger, P., & Silverstone, R. (Eds.), *International media research. A critical survey*. London, UK: Routledge.

Livingstone, S. (2003). The changing nature and uses of media literacy, *Media@lse Electronic Working Papers*, 4.

Livingstone, S. (2004). The challenge of changing audiences: Or, what is the audience researcher to do in the age of the internet? *European Journal of Communication*, *19*(1), 75–86. doi:10.1177/0267323104040695

Livingstone, S. (2005). *Audience and publics: When cultural engagement matters for the public sphere*. Bristol, UK: Intellect Books.

Lovett, J., & Owyang, J. (2010, April 21). *Social marketing analytics. A new framework for measuring results in social media.* Web Analytics Demystified and Altimeter Group.

Marinelli, A. (2004). *Connessioni. Nuovi media, nuove reti sociali.* Milano, Italy: Guerini.

Mittel, J. (2007). *Constructing an older audience*. Retrieved from http://justtv.wordpress.com

Moores, S. (1994). *Interpreting audiences: The ethnography of media consumption*. London, UK: Sage.

Murray, C., Schroder, K., Drotner, K., & Kline, S. (2003). *Researching audiences: A practical guide to methods in media audience analysis*. USA: Bloomsbury.

O'Really, T. (2005). *What is Web 2.0?* Retrieved January 10, 2010, from http://oreilly.com/web2/archive/what-is-web-20.html

Pang, B., & Lee, L. (2008). Opinion mining and sentiment analysis. *Foundations and Trends in Information Retrieval*, *2*(1-2), 1–135. doi:10.1561/1500000011

Parikh, R., & Movassate, M. (2009). *Sentiment analysis of user generated Twitter updates using various Classification techniques* (pp. 1–18). MOST.

Radian6, 2010, Social media listening, measuring and engagement primer. Retrieved January 26, 2011, from http://www.radian6.com

Rheingold, H. (2003). *Smart mobs. The next social revolution*. Cambridge, MA: Perseus Book.

Roberts, K. (2005). *Lovemarks. The future beyond brands*. New York, NY: powerHouse Book.

Sandvoss, C. (2005). *Fans: The mirror of consumption*. Cambridge, UK: Polity Press.

Silverstone, R. (1999). *Why study the media?*London, UK: Sage Publications.

Thompson, J. B. (1995). *The media and modernity. A social theory of the media*. Stanford, CA: Stanford University Press.

Tianxia, G. (2008). *Processing sentiments and opinions in text: A survey*. Department of Computer Science, School of Computing, National University of Singapore. Retrieved January 16, 2011, from http://www.comp.nus.edu.sg/~gongtian/CS6207/CS6207_Survey.pdf

Wellman, B. (2001a). Physical place and cyber place: The rise of networked individualism. *International Journal of Urban and Regional Research*, *25*(2), 227–252. doi:10.1111/1468-2427.00309

Wellman, B. (2001b). Computer networks as social networks. *Science*, *293*, 2031–2034. doi:10.1126/science.1065547

Zhuang, L., Jing, F., & Zhu, X.-Y. (2006). Movie review mining and summarization. *Proceedings of the 15th ACM International Conference on Information and Knowledge Management,* (pp. 43-50). Arlington, VA, USA, November 05 - 11, 2006.

KEY TERMS AND DEFINITIONS

Fandom: (From the noun *fan* and the affix *-dom*, as in *kingdom*) refers to the most active and innovative part of diffused audience. Fans are a kind of subculture, which is characterized by a great engagement with media contents, or actors, or characters, or singer by member of the fan group. Fans are part of participative culture and they are involved in building and spreading texts. Fans are readers that poach popular texts and interpret them in a way that is coherent with their lives.

Lexicon: In the application of sentiment analysis, lexicon is a vocabulary: a list of words that express sentiment. It is a corpus that is expanded through direct synonymy and antonymy relations, hyponymy relations, derivation, and compounding with known lexical units. A lexicon is used to analyze extracted sentences and to evaluate sentiment.

Crawler: In the application of sentiment analysis, a crawler is a software program that browses internet content, such as on line discussions, comments on blog, forum, microblog, and extracts relevant sentences, such as opinion or emotions, to be processed by sentiment analysis software.

Netnography: "Netnography is participant-observational research based in online fieldwork. It uses computer- mediated communications as a source of data to arrive at the ethnographic understanding and representation of a cultural or communal phenomenon" (Kozinets, 2010, p.60).

ENDNOTES

1 http://www.primaonline.it/wp-content/plugins/Flutter/files_flutter/1229615092file17234125748773.pdfhttp://ricerca.repubblica.it/repubblica/archivio/repubblica/2004/07/28/iqs-il-sistema-rai-dimenticato-che-ribalta.html

2 http://www.radian6.com/; http://www.alterian.com/; http://www.sysomos.com/; http://www.biz360.com; /http://Nielsen-online.com; www. http://www.brandwatch.com/

Section 2
SNS, Relational Patterns, and Identity Performances:
New Research Trends

Chapter 5
Invisible Interactions:
What Latent Social Interaction Can Tell Us about Social Relationships in Social Network Sites

Miriam J. Metzger
University of California, Santa Barbara, USA

Christo Wilson
University of California, Santa Barbara, USA

Rebekah A. Pure
University of California, Santa Barbara, USA

Ben Y. Zhao
University of California, Santa Barbara, USA

ABSTRACT

A deep understanding of user social interaction in social network sites (SNSs) can provide important insights into questions of human social and relational behavior, as well as shape the design of new social platforms and applications. Recent studies have shown that a majority of user interactions on SNSs are latent interactions—passive actions such as profile browsing that cannot be observed directly by traditional research methods. This chapter presents a new technique to capture natural latent social interaction in Renren, the most popular SNS in China. As such, it offers a better understanding of both visible (e.g., comments and wall posts) and latent (e.g., passive profile browsing) user social interactions in SNSs than has been possible to date. We show that latent interactions are much more prevalent and frequent than visible interactions, are somewhat nonreciprocal in nature, and that visits by non-friends make up a significant portion of profile views. Our results augment earlier findings on such concepts as lurking and interpersonal electronic surveillance, and in some cases, shed new light on these phenomena.

DOI: 10.4018/978-1-61350-338-6.ch005

INTRODUCTION

Popular social network sites (SNSs) like Facebook and Twitter are changing the way people communicate and interact with each other, affecting how users manage both their own identity and their relationships with others. Today's social networks already count close to one billion members worldwide. Facebook, the most popular SNS, has more than 500 million active users (Sorkin, 2010), and has surpassed Google as the most visited site on the Internet (Yarow, 2010). Increasingly, Facebook and Twitter are replacing email and search engines as users' primary interfaces to the Internet (Gannes, 2010; Kirkpatrick, 2009). This trend is likely to continue, as networks like Facebook seek to personalize the web experience by giving sites access to information about their visitors and their friends, through new platforms such as OpenGraph (http://opengraphprotocol.org).

A deep understanding of user interactions in social networks can provide important insights into questions of human social and relational behavior, as well as shape the design of social platforms and applications. For example, gauging the level of reciprocity in social interactions on SNSs can shed light on the factors that motivate social interactions. In addition, understanding how interactions are distributed between linked friends can assist in understanding information dissemination in social networks, thus identifying "popular" or "influential" users within the network (Chen, Wang, & Yang, 2009; Gruhl, Guha, Liben-Nowell, & Tomkins, 2004; Kempe, Kleinberg, & Tardos, 2003), as well as how information flows (Cha, Mislove, Adams, & Gummadi, 2008; Galuba, Aberer, Chakraborty, Despotovic, & Kellerer, 2010; Yoneki & Crowcroft, 2009). Moreover, lessons from studying how users interact through these communication tools can guide the design of new, more engaging mechanisms for social interaction and relationship management.

Initial studies of SNSs (Ahn, Han, Kwak, Moon, & Jeong, 2007; Mislove, Marcon, Gummadi, Druschel, & Bhattacharjee, 2007; Wilson, Boe, Sala, Puttaswamy, & Zhao, 2009) focused on topological characteristics of the *social graph*, which reveal patterns of explicit digital relationships (i.e., 'friend' links) between users, and have been used to approximate real-world social relationships that exist between users. However, researchers in psychology and sociology have cast doubt on the practice of inferring meaningful relationships from friend linkages alone, given how easy it is to link to others in the network whom one does not know at all or whom one barely knows (e.g., Bilge, Strufe, Balzarotti, & Kirda, 2009; boyd, 2006; Sophos, 2007). To better capture the true nature of social relationships between SNS users, recent work has shifted to measuring observable social interactions (e.g., wall posts and photo comments) between users in these networks (Chun, Kwak, Eom, Ahn, Moon, & Jeong, 2008; Leskovec & Horvitz, 2008; Viswanath, Mislove, Cha, & Gummadi, 2009; Wilson et al., 2009). By constructing and then analyzing the *visible interaction graph* to examine who actually interacts with whom across different friend links in SNSs, these studies can better distinguish close-knit, active social relationships from weak or dormant relationships, and thus derive a more accurate representation of true social relationships between social network users.

All of these studies take advantage of the fact that SNSs represent powerful environments to observe social relationships at a scale never before possible by making such interactions visible, traceable, and machine-parsable, and thus easy for researchers to capture and study. While this offers exciting promise for developing new and better models of human socio-relational behavior, some recent studies (Benevenuto, Rodrigues, Cha, & Almeida, 2009; Schneider, Feldmann, Krisnamurthy, & Willinger, 2009) are revealing that many user interactions on SNSs consist of *latent* social interactions, which involve passive actions such as profile browsing (i.e., looking at someone's profile without leaving any messages or posts).

Latent interactions within SNSs have been difficult to study because they cannot be observed by traditional network measurement techniques, including those described above, because they leave no traceable data. Moreover, most SNS privacy policies make these latent interactions invisible to researchers. The few studies that do exist (Benevenuto et al., 2009; Schneider et al., 2009) rely on clickstream data that are constrained by properties of complexity and verboseness that make it extremely difficult to gather enough data to study user latent interactions comprehensively at scale. However, a large-scale study is necessary to answer deeper questions about user behavior and social interactions in SNSs that go beyond what existing studies of social, visible, and latent interaction graphs have allowed thus far. For example, some of the questions that can be answered with comprehensive data on latent social interactions in SNSs include: To what degree are user interactions in SNS reciprocal? Do latent interactions such as profile browsing occur with the same frequency as visible actions such as user comments? What can users do to become "popular" and draw more visitors to their pages? In this chapter we begin to answer these, as well as related questions by discussing new research that looks at both visible and latent social interactions in SNSs.

Answering these sorts of questions has theoretical import as well. In fact, examining latent social interaction in SNSs can contribute new understandings to current theoretical debates surrounding social and relational behavior online. These debates include such topics as the prevalence and impacts of interpersonal electronic surveillance (including 'virtual people watching' and 'cyberstalking', for example, see boyd, 2008; Joinson, 2008, and Tokunaga, 2011 for discussions of these issues), motives for lurking behavior in online communities (e.g., Preece, Nonnecke, & Andrews, 2004; Rau, Gao, & Ding, 2008; Soroka & Rafaeli, 2006), as well as the role that SNS play in enhancing users' self-identity (e.g., Valkenburg, Peter, & Shouten, 2006) and social capital (e.g., Ellison, Steinfeild, & Lampe, 2007). For example, a great deal of concern has focused on the issue of whether SNS usage facilitates stalking (e.g., Gross & Acquisti, 2005). Recent work has suggested that this concern may be overblown because most social interaction on SNS users takes place between users who know and trust one another (Joinson, 2008; Lampe, Ellison, & Steinfield, 2006; Lenhart & Madden, 2007; Pempek, Yermolayeva, & Calvert, 2009). Data on latent social interactions by both friends and strangers within SNSs can shed new light on the prevalence and types of actual social interactions that do take place between all network users. Also, to the extent that physical stalking may be initiated by profile browsing, these data can help us better understand the extent to which SNSs play a role in stalking.

Similarly, knowing the prevalence and nature of latent social interaction in SNSs can help to better understand the ways in which people use these venues for building social capital, which is another major area of theoretical concern within SNS research (boyd & Ellison, 2007). Social capital refers to the potential benefits derived from having connections to others within a network that one can draw resources from, such as information diffusion and linking to external assets. While several studies have theorized and found evidence that visible social interactions in SNSs can increase users' social capital (e.g., Ellison, Lampe, & Steinfield, 2008; Ellison et al., 2007; Steinfield, Ellison, & Lampe, 2008), little is known whether more passive forms of social interaction in SNSs have similar effects, although latent tie theory (Haythornwaite, 2005) and theories of information propagation within networks (see Jiang, Wilson, Wang, Huang, Sha, Dai, & Zhao, 2010) suggest that they should.

Examinations of latent social interactions in SNS can also help to flesh out theories connecting SNS use and its impacts on identity and impression management. Most studies in this domain have only looked at the effects of visible social interactions or size of SNS users' social networks (i.e., number of linked friends) on impression management and identity construction (e.g., Tong, van der Heide, Langwell, & Walther, 2008; Valkenburg et al., 2006). However, according to social information processing theory (Walther, 1992), people will use any available cues in computer-mediated environments to form impressions, suggesting that latent social interactions showing one's profile popularity (i.e., knowing how many people and who has viewed your profile), may have equally important effects on users' social judgments and self-esteem.

As we shall show in this chapter, our findings on latent social interactions in SNSs in some cases support the theoretical claims made in these literatures, but also extend and challenge existing theory and research in some of these domains as well. Before reaching those conclusions, however, we describe our approach to measuring latent social interactions in SNSs in detail.

CAPTURING LATENT SOCIAL INTERACTIONS IN SNSS

Our quest for a deeper understanding of user interactions in SNSs begins by addressing the challenge of gathering data on latent interactions. To do this, we performed a large-scale crawl of the Renren social network (www.renren.com). Renren is the largest SNS in China with more than 150 million users to date (Jiang et al., 2010). Functionally, Renren is essentially a clone of Facebook, with similar structure, layout and features. Like Facebook, Renren also evolved from a university-based social network (a predecessor called Xiaonei). Unlike Facebook, however, Renren has two unique features that make it a particularly attractive platform to study user social interactions.

First, while Renren users have full privacy control over their personal profiles, their friend lists are public and unprotected by privacy mechanisms, which means that they can be crawled to produce an exhaustive snapshot of Renren's largest connected component, producing an extremely large social graph. For example, the data described in this chapter are based on a social graph with 42 million users and 1.66 billion explicit social ('friend') links. Second, and perhaps more important, Renren user profiles make a variety of information visible to both the profile owner and her visitors. Each Renren user profile includes a box that shows the total number of visitors to the profile, along with names and links to the last nine visitors ordered from most to least recent. This list is updated in real time. In addition, each photo and diary entry also has its own page that includes a count of visits by users other than the owner. These records are extremely valuable, in that they expose latent browsing events (i.e., profile visits) to crawlers. With this information, we are able to construct *latent interaction graphs* of user profile browsing behavior, granting us a unique opportunity to gather and analyze large-scale naturalistic data on latent social interaction within the Renren social network.[1]

As mentioned earlier, these data allow us to answer a number of questions about the nature of social interaction within SNSs that have been as-yet unavailable to researchers. For example, this chapter will compare the structural properties of the latent social interaction graph (i.e., profile views) against those of both visible interaction graphs (i.e., written posts and comments) and social graphs (i.e., confirmed 'friend' linkages) to answer the following questions:

1. What proportion of social interactions in SNSs is latent versus visible?
2. Do latent social interactions follow similar distribution patterns in terms of participation across users as visible interactions within the SNS user population?
3. How do social, visible, and latent interaction graphs differ in terms of (a) their social connection (average degree of separation between users), (b) how tightly or loosely connected friend relationships are within

each type of network, and (c) the likelihood of users interacting with others similar to themselves in their degree of social connectedness?

A second set of questions to be answered in this chapter revolves around a detailed examination of latent social interactions (i.e., profile visits) specifically. These include:

4. What factors (e.g., number of linked friends, account longevity, frequency of profile content updates, amount of comments) influence latent social interactions?
5. While visible social interactions are typically between linked friends, are profile visitors mostly friends or are they strangers?
6. What portion of profile visitors are repeat visitors and, of the repeat visitors, are most profile viewers friends or strangers?
7. Visible interactions tend to be highly reciprocal because social norms compel people to reply to one another when contacted via visible interactions, but to what extent are latent interactions reciprocated?

Answers to these questions will reveal new information about human behavior within SNSs environments, and will thus offer potential to advance current understandings of social interactions within online social networks that are useful to social and computer scientists alike.

CRAWLING THE RENREN SOCIAL NETWORK

As mentioned previously, Renren is best characterized as Facebook's Chinese twin, with most or all of Facebook's features, layout, and a similar user interface. Users maintain personal profiles, upload photos, write diary entries (blogs), and establish bidirectional social links with their friends. Renren users inform their friends about recent events with 140 character status updates, much like tweets on Twitter. Similar to the Facebook news feed, all user-generated updates and comments are tagged with the sender's name and a time stamp.

Renren organizes users into membership-based networks, much like Facebook used to. Networks represent schools, companies, or geographic regions. Membership in school and company networks require authentication. Students must offer an IP address, email address, or student credential from the associated university. Corporate email addresses are needed for users to join corporate networks. Renren's default privacy policy makes profiles of users in geographic networks private. This makes them difficult to crawl (Wilson, Boe, Sala, Puttaswamy, & Zhao, 2009). Fortunately, profiles of users in authenticated networks are public by default to other members of the same network, which is a feature that allowed us to access user profiles within the Peking University (PKU) network, by creating nearly unlimited authenticated accounts using our own block of IP addresses.

We crawled the entire Renren network from April 2009 to June 2009, and again from September to November of 2009.[2] For our study, we use data from our last crawl, which was an exhaustive snapshot that included 42,115,509 users and 1,657,273,875 friendship links. In addition to the complete crawl, we also performed smaller, more detailed crawls of the PKU network between September and November of 2009 (90 days) to collect information about users' profiles and interaction patterns. Since we collected the network memberships of all users during our complete crawl, we were able to isolate the 100,973 members of the PKU network to seed our detailed crawl. Of these users, 61,405 users had the default, permissive privacy policy, enabling us to collect their detailed information. This covers the majority of users (60.8%) in the PKU network, and provides overall network coverage similar to other studies that have crawled SNS regional networks (Wilson et al., 2009).

As part of our PKU crawls, we gathered all comments generated by users in message board posts, diary entries, photos, and status updates. These data form the basis of our analysis of visible social interactions. Our dataset represents the complete record of public visible interactions between users in the PKU network. In total, 19,782,140 comments were collected, with 1,218,911 of them originating in the September to November 2009 timeframe.[3]

In addition to visible interactions generated by users in the PKU network, we also recorded the recent visitor records displayed on each user's profile via successive crawls. These data form the basis of our study of latent social interactions.[4] Overall, from the 61,405 user profiles we crawled, we obtained a total of 8,034,664 total records of visits to user profiles in the PKU network, but after integrating the raw results, we were left with 1,863,168 unique profile visit events. The high reduction (77%) is because most profiles receive few page views, and thus overlaps between successively crawled results are very high. Although Renren does not show individual recent visitors of user diaries and photos, it does display the total number of visits, which we crawled as well.[5]

Our Renren dataset is larger than most previously studied SNS datasets, the exception being recent studies of the Twitter network (Cha, Haddadi, Benevenuto & Gummadi, 2010; Kwak, Lee, Park, & Moon, 2010). However, our dataset shares similar properties with social network datasets collected in prior studies (Chun, Kwak, Eom, Ahn, Moon, & Jeong, 2008; Mislove, Marcon, Gummadi, Druschel, & Bhattacharjee, 2007; Wilson et al., 2009). This suggests that the Renren network is quite similar to other popular social networks in terms of the network's structural properties, which are derived from user behavior. For greater detail on the methods used to extract the data for this study, please see Jiang et al. (2010).

PARTICIPATION IN LATENT VERSUS VISIBLE SOCIAL INTERACTIONS ACROSS USERS

We compared latent (i.e., viewing others' profiles) and visible (i.e., leaving posts and comments on others' profiles) social interactions to see how they differ in terms of prevalence. To understand the level of participation of users in both latent and visible interactions, we examined the contribution of different users to both kinds of interactions. The bulk of all visible interactions can be attributed to a very small, highly interactive portion of the user base: 28% of users account for nearly all such interactions. In contrast, latent interactions are quite prevalent across the entire population, with more than 93% of all users contributing to latent interaction events (see Figure 1). This confirms that latent interactions are more prevalent in Renren than visible interactions—users are more active in viewing profiles than they are in leaving comments—potentially because of a sense of anonymity in profile browsing.

Next, for each user, we analyzed the distribution of their latent and visible interactions across their social links. Aggregating across all users, the percentage of friends involved in these events show that roughly 80% of users only interact visibly with 5% of their friends, and no users interact with more than 40% of their friends. By contrast, about 80% of users view 20% or more of their friends' profiles, and a small portion of the population views all of their friends' profiles regularly. Thus, although not all social links are equally active, latent interactions cover a wider range of friends than do visible interactions.

To get a sense of how many visible comments are generated by latent interactions, we examined the average number of comments per page view for a variety of pages on Renren, including profiles, diary entries, and photos. Recall that along with visible comments, Renren keeps a visitor counter for each photo and diary entry. For diary

Figure 1. Distribution of visible and latent interactions

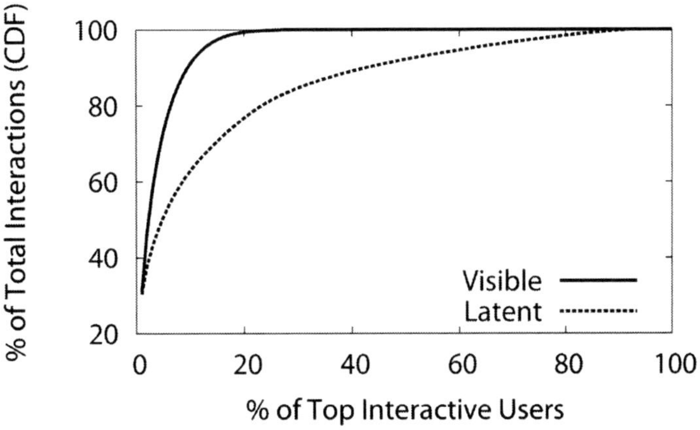

entry and photo views, the conversion rate is very low: 99% of users have less than 0.2 comments for every photo view, and 85% people have less than 0.2 comments for every diary view. This indicates that most users are passive information consumers: they view/read content and then move on without commenting themselves. By contrast, profile views have a higher conversion rate. Interestingly, 13% of users have a view/comment ratio greater than 1. This is because these users use profile comments as a form of instant messaging chat, leaving multiple responses and replies upon each visit.

Finally, we analyzed the repeat activity frequency for latent and visible interactions on Renren. In particular, we examined the likelihood that users will repeatedly interact with the same profile page after they have viewed or commented on it once. The data show that 80% of users view a given profile fewer than two times. However, 80% of users leave an average of 3.4 comments, almost twice the number of latent interactions. This result makes sense intuitively: for most types of information, users only need to view it once to consume the data. However, comments can stimulate flurries of dialog on a given page, resulting in many consecutive interactions.

Understanding Latent Social Interactions: Profile Views and Viewing Behavior

Because our work focuses on the analysis of latent interactions and the role they play in SNSs, we examined profile viewing behavior by analyzing the histories of visits to user profiles in Renren. This allowed an understanding of the popularity of latent social interaction both in terms of profile views of individual profiles and their viewing of others' profiles. It also enabled us to examine the composition of profile visitors and reciprocity in latent social interactions.

Popularity

Our analysis of the distribution of latent interactions across the Renren user base showed that the number of views a user's profile receives (i.e., profile "*popularity*") is not evenly spread across the population: only 518 people (1%) are popular enough to receive more than 10,000 views. Conversely, the majority of users (57%) exhibit very low popularity with less than 100 total profile views. Moreover, popular users receive many more views per day: 141 users (0.2%) are viewed more than 20 times a day on average, with the most popular profile being viewed more than 600

Figure 2. Percentage of strangers in profile visitors

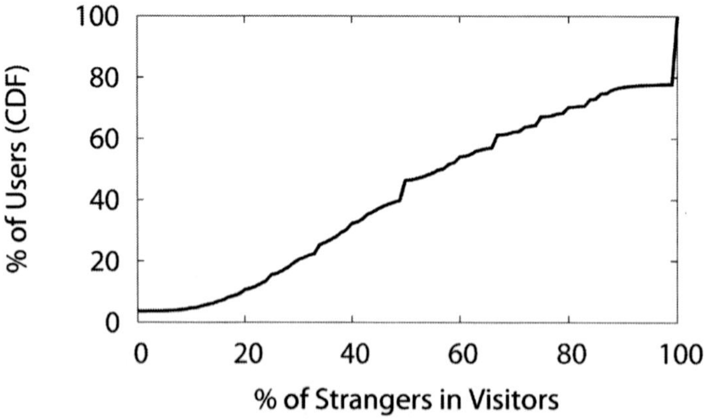

times a day. Most users (85.5%) receive less than one visit per day on average. This indicates that latent interactions are highly skewed towards a very popular subset of the population.

Consumption

Our analysis also showed that the popularity of users does not necessarily correspond to their profile viewing behavior. We define *consumption* as the number of others' profiles a user views. In Renren, the top 1% most popular users have 9% overlap with the top 1% biggest profile consumers. Those users represent a hard-core contingent of social network users who are extremely active. For the most part, however, users with high numbers of incoming latent interactions do not overlap with the people generating those interactions, (e.g., profiles of celebrities are viewed by many users, but they are inactive in viewing others' pages). This means that many (presumably average) users actively visit others, but are not visited in return. The degree of reciprocation in latent interactions is explored in greater detail below.

Composition of Profile Visitors: Friends or Strangers?

While visible social interactions are typically between linked friends, we sought to understand whether this was also true for latent social interactions. To answer this question, we analyzed the composition of visitors to user profiles to determine whether profile visitors were mostly friends or strangers. We define a stranger as any user who is not a direct linked friend of the target user. Like Facebook, Renren's default privacy settings allow users in the same campus network to browse each other's profiles. The results are fairly evenly divided: roughly 45% of users receive less than half of their profile visits from strangers. Or conversely, a slight majority of the population receives most of their profile views from strangers (see Figure 2, which shows the percentage of visitors that are strangers).

To understand what component of a profile's visitors are strangers, and how far away they are from the profile owner in the social network, we grouped the owners of profiles together by their number of friends ("social degree") and computed the average breakdown of their visitors into users who are friends (1-hop), friends-of- friends (2-hop), and other visitors (2+ hops). We see that for users with relatively few (<100) friends, the large majority of their visitors are complete strangers, with very few friends-of-friends visiting. For well-connected users with 100–1,000 friends, the majority of their visitors are direct friends, and also a significant number of friends-of-friends. Finally, for extremely popular users with more

Figure 3. Breakdown of profile visitors by owner's social degree

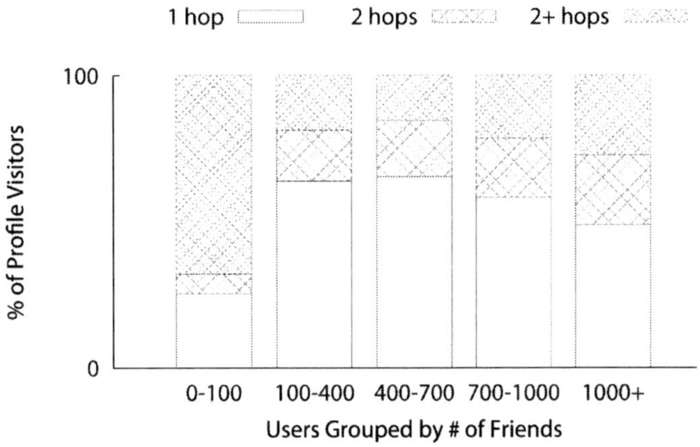

than 1,000 friends, their notoriety is such that they start to attract more strangers to visit their profiles. Figure 3 illustrates these results. These results confirm findings from previous work that discovered many Orkut users browse profiles two or more hops away on the social network (Benevenuto, Rodrigues, Cha, & Almeida, 2009).

Repeat Visitors

The portion of profile visitors that are repeat visitors was calculated from the percentage of repeated visitors for each profile. Roughly 70% of users have less than 50% repeat visitors, meaning that the majority of visitors do not browse the same profile twice (see Figure 4). This indicates that the long tail of latent interactions is generated by users randomly browsing others in the social network.

Most repeat visits occur on the same day as the initial visit, as shown by the probability density function (PDF) of the interval time between repeat visits (see Figure 5). The graph peaks on day 0, meaning that users are most likely to return to a viewed profile on the same day. We will examine the causes for this behavior more closely in a later section of this chapter. The probability for repeated views decreases with time, except for a noticeable peak at day 7. Interestingly, this shows that many users periodically check on their friends on a weekly basis. We confirmed that this feature is not an artifact introduced by our crawler or the use of RSS feeds by Renren users. Instead, we believe it may be due to the tendency for many users to browse their friends' profiles over the weekend.

Unlike friends, strangers do not tend to build long-term relationships with profile owners. Intuitively, this would seem to indicate that repeat profile viewing behavior should favor friends over strangers. To investigate this we computed the average number of visits for strangers and friends for each profile. Surprisingly, our results indicate that the repeat profile viewing behavior for friends and strangers is very similar, with friends only edging out strangers by only a small margin. This demonstrates that when considering information dissemination via latent interactions, the significance of non-friend strangers should not be overlooked.

Reciprocity in Latent Social Interaction

Social norms compel users to reply to one another when contacted via visible interactions (e.g., comments). Prior work has shown that these visible interactions are largely reciprocal between linked friends on SNSs (Wilson et al., 2009). However, is this true of latent interactions? Since Renren

Figure 4. Ratio of repeat profile visitors

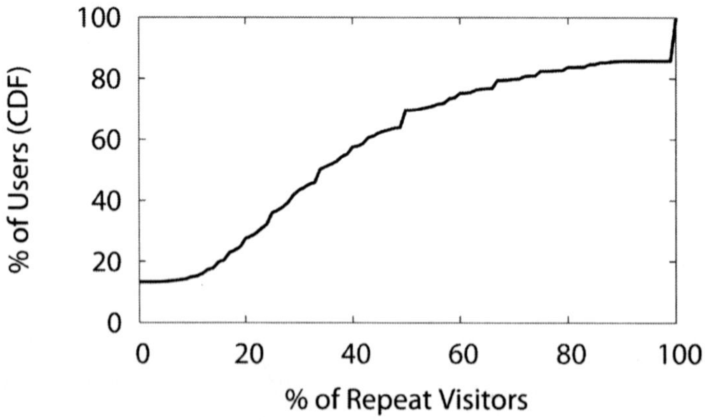

Figure 5. Interval time between repeat profile visits

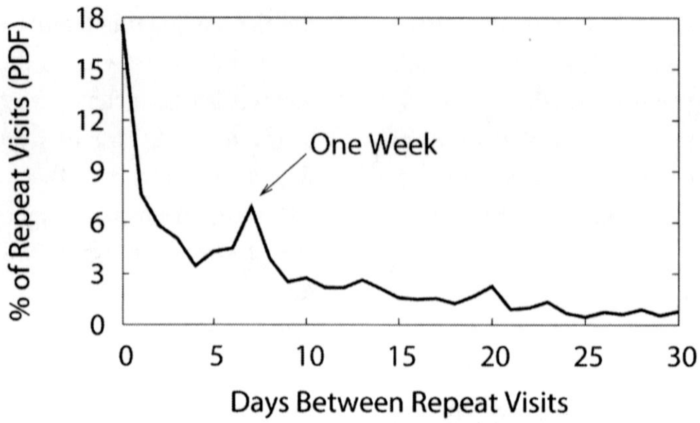

users have full access to the list of recent visitors to their profile, it is possible for people to pay return visits to browse the profiles of their visitors. The question is, does visiting other users' profiles actually trigger reciprocal visits?

As the first step towards looking more deeply at reciprocity of latent interactions in Renren, we constructed the set of visitors who view each user profile, and the set of people who are visited by each user. Then, we computed the intersection and union of these two sets for every user. Intuitively, intersections include people who view a given user profile and are also visited by that user—in other words, the latent interactions are reciprocated. Unions contain all latent relationships for a given user, including all users who viewed them, or they viewed. The ratio of intersection size to union size for each user represents the number of reciprocated latent interactions divided by the total number of latent relationships. For more than 93% of users, less than 10% of latent relationships are reciprocated. This demonstrates that incoming profile views have little influence on user's profile browsing behavior. This is surprising, especially considering the fact that users know that their visits to a profile are visible to its owner through the visitor history feature. Friends had higher probability of reciprocal visits than did strangers and, in comparison to visible interactions, latent interactions showed much less reciprocity.[6]

We next examined how reciprocal profile visits vary over time, for both strangers and friends. We compute the number of reciprocal visits that take place within 90 days after the initial visit. Not surprisingly, more profile visits are reciprocated as more time elapses. However, reciprocity remains low overall. Even across the entire 90-day period, 73% of users receive no reciprocal page views from strangers, and 45% of users obtain no reciprocal page views from friends. This demonstrates that even with Renren's visitor history feature, visiting other user profiles is not sufficient to generate reciprocal visits.

FACTORS IMPACTING LATENT SOCIAL INTERACTIONS

As discussed earlier, not all users in Renren are the target of equal numbers of latent interactions. Understanding the factors that may impact latent interactions can help us to understand the popularity of individual users (i.e., the number of views a profile receives). This is important because popularity is likely to be correlated with sources of significant information dissemination and because, as an underlying social goal, popularity can drive individuals' behavior within SNSs. There are several potential factors that could influence latent social interaction by attracting profile visitors, for example, the degree to which a user maintains an active presence in the SNS by adding or updating their profile content, including status updates, diary entries, photos, and shared links to content on the web; how often a user leaves comments on others' profiles; the number of linked friends they have in the network; and how long a user has been active in the network. To examine these, we analyzed whether (a) the number of friends a user has, (b) the longevity of a user's SNS account, (c) the frequency of uploading new user-generated content (i.e., status updates, diary entries, photos, and shared links); and (d) the frequency of leaving comments influence the number of latent social interactions (i.e., profile views) a user has.[7]

The data show that all factors increase with popularity such that users with the most profile views (latent interactions) also have the most friends, the oldest accounts, and generate the largest amounts of content/visible interactions. To reach this conclusion, we divided users into four groups based on their profile viewership "popularity," and calculated both the average value of these factors in each group, as well as the correlation between each factor and user popularity within each group (see Table 1, correlations are shown in parenthesis beside the average value for each factor).[8] Although all factors exhibit high correlation with the low viewership popularity (those whose profiles were rarely viewed by others) and "all users" categories, this is an artifact of the tied ranks among the many low activity users (0-100 profile views category). All of these users exhibit very low interactivity and number of friends, thus leading to high levels of correlation. Previous work has observed similar artifacts when analyzing all users in a large SNS dataset (Cha et al., 2010).

For the two medium popularity groups (100-1,000 and 1,000-10,000 profile views), number of friends had the highest correlation with profile views. Users in these categories can be broadly defined as normal social network users. They are not celebrities; they simply use the SNS for its intended purpose of sharing information with friends. This is reflected in the fact that users in these categories show relatively high levels of correlation across all user-generated content categories. Account lifetime is a less important factor for users in the 1,000-10,000 popularity range, given the ease with which users can quickly amass hundreds of friends on SNSs.

No factor has strong correlation with profile views for users in the high popularity group. Correlations for photos and shared links are even negative. This is an important finding, as it shows popularity is not trivially gained simply by having lots of friends, or producing copious amounts of

Table 1. Average value of factors affecting user popularity and correlations of factors with each user popularity category

User Popularity (i.e., profile views)	Friends	Lifetime	Diary	Photo	Status	Share	Comment
0-100	16 (.15)	35 (.55)	1 (.51)	3 (.47)	1 (.50)	1 (.50)	2 (.54)
100-1,000	131 (.56)	423 (.41)	11 (.33)	41 (.24)	27 (.36)	43 (.41)	96 (.45)
1,000-10,000	401 (.43)	792 (.24)	50 (.18)	125 (.10)	115 (.18)	155 (.23)	596 (.28)
>10,000	708 (.02)	869 (.02)	117 (.02)	251 (.03)	236 (.01)	273 (.05)	1581 (.01)
all users	112 (.73)	263 (.75)	12 (.70)	34 (.61)	28 (.69)	39 (.72)	134 (.76)

Note: Average values are shown in the table cells; Spearman rank correlation coefficients for each average value are shown in parentheses.

user-generated content. Therefore, there must be other factors outside the scope of our study that contribute to determine users' profile popularity. One possibility is that quality, rather than quantity, of content may be a significant draw to attract visitors. Another possibility is that real-world celebrity status is the most important determining factor of online viewership popularity.

COMPARING SOCIAL, VISIBLE, AND LATENT INTERACTION GRAPH PROPERTIES

Thus far, our results have demonstrated significant differences between latent and visible interaction patterns on Renren. To summarize these key differences briefly, latent interactions are more numerous, non-reciprocal, and often connect non-friend strangers. These results are likely to have profound implications on applications that leverage social graphs (e.g., knowing what percentage of people are passive consumers versus active producers of information in social review systems such as Yelp, Delicious, or other recommendation systems could be useful in enhancing user trust of these systems, as well as in designing new systems to encourage active participation), and thus warrant the construction of a new model to capture the properties of latent social interactions. We call this new model a latent interaction graph.

While previous studies have constructed visible interaction graphs by connecting users from the social graph who have visibly interacted one or more times (Wilson et al., 2009), a *latent interaction graph* is defined as a set of users that are connected via links representing latent interaction events between them. We constructed latent interaction graphs from our Renren data using profile views as the latent interactions. We use user comments as the visible interaction data to construct *visible interaction graphs* for Renren.[9] Finally, we constructed the *social graph* for Renren, which reflects explicit friendship linkages between users in the network. We use these data to understand how the three types of graphs differ in terms of (a) how tightly or loosely connected friend relationships are within each type of network, (b) the likelihood of users interacting with others similar to themselves in their degree of social connectedness, and (c) their social connection, defined in terms of the average degree of separation between users.

Relationship Strength

To determine relationship strength in the three graphs, a clustering coefficient was calculated which shows the level of local connectivity between nodes (i.e., users or events) in a network. The data show that the average clustering coefficients for the latent interaction graph (.03) and for the visible interaction graph (.05), are both much less than that of the social graph (.18). This is because not all friend links are accurate indicators of active social relationships between those linked users, and friend links with no interactions are removed in interaction graphs. This produces loose connections between neighbors, and thus relatively low clustering coefficients in the interaction graphs. Because a portion of the latent interactions to a profile is from strangers who randomly browse the network, it is unlikely that a user will share mutual friends with strangers, which further lowers the clustering coefficients in latent interaction graphs. These findings make sense since many people in SNSs do not actually talk to all of their linked friends, and linked friends who do talk to each other are more likely to have a closer relationship than those who merely browse others users' profiles.

Heterogeneity of Association

Assortativity is the likelihood that users establish links to other users of similar social degree (i.e., users with few friends connect to other users with few friends, and users with many friends connect to others who have many friends). Renren latent interaction graph is disassortative (-.06). This makes sense intuitively because latent social interactions are highly skewed towards a small subset of extremely popular users (e.g., celebrities, physically attractive users), as described earlier. In contrast, the other two graphs are both assortative, with the social graph (.23) being more assortative than the visible interaction graph (.05). This also makes sense because, unlike latent interactions, explicit social friend links and visible interactions tend to be based on relationships that are bidirectional (e.g., users typically befriend and write wall messages to those whom they have an established real-world relationship with). Generally speaking, relationships tend to form between similar, rather than dissimilar, people (Fehr, 2008; McPherson, Smith-Lovin, & Cook, 2001).

Social Connection

The degree of social connection within these graphs is reflected in the average path length, which is the average of all-pairs-shortest-paths in the network. In the case of Renren, the average path length of the latent interaction graph (4.02) falls between that of the visible interaction graph (5.43) and the social graph (3.64). Average path length of a graph decreases when the number of connections inside the graph increases, because more connections means it is easier to find shorter paths between users. The social graph is the most highly connected of the three types of graphs studied here, and thus has the shortest average path length. Because in the visible interaction graph, links between friends who do not talk to one another are removed, the sheer number of connections in this graph is lower than in the social graph and thus the average path length is higher. The average path length for latent interactions falls between these two other graphs because people browse profiles a lot more than they write visible comments, but still not quite enough to cover the original social graph (i.e., most people do not view the profiles of all of their friends within a given timeframe such as a week or month).

FUTURE RESEARCH DIRECTIONS

Our comprehensive study of both visible and latent user interactions in the Renren SNS shows that latent user interactions make up the large majority of user activity events. We do not claim, however, that our results are necessarily generalizable to other SNSs or to SNS users situated in other cultures. Sociopolitical circumstances (e.g., the extent of government control on expression) and cultural norms (e.g., collectivism versus individualism, conceptions of personal privacy, etc.) vary nationally and across the globe, and certainly may impact people's behavior both online and off. Moreover, different SNS systems have different interfaces, user etiquettes, and data control mechanisms, which of course likely also influence user behavior. That said, it is possible that our main findings hold true for other SNSs that allow users to passively browse profiles of non-friends and see some of their personal information. Most systems do this, including even Facebook, although the amount of viewable information there depends on each profile owner's privacy settings. It is also possible that in systems that do not reveal who has browsed a user's profile, such as Facebook, latent social interaction could be *more* prevalent than in Renren since they pose no risk of exposure to users, and yet less reciprocated since they are invisible to users. Recall, however, that even in Renren reciprocity in profile views was low. At the same time, in systems like Facebook where users know they can see only limited profile information for network members they are not linked to, latent social interactions could be *less* prevalent than in Renren. Overall, then it is difficult to say just how similar or different our results might be for users of other SNSs.

Another limitation of the current study is that we are only able to analyze data from users with public profiles in the network (as discussed earlier, luckily this is the default setting in Renren), and of course the behavior of users with public profiles may differ from those with private profiles. The foregoing points highlight the need for research across different SNS systems and across users in culturally diverse settings. This is not easy, however, as Facebook and many other SNSs do not release visitor log data even to academic researchers. One way that future research could try to circumvent this problem is to get data from a major social game company like Zynga, the creator of Farmville. Close to a fifth of the Facebook population plays Zynga games, and the games actively encourage browsing behavior (e.g., "visit my farm!"). Of course, the context for interactions is different here from profile browsing, but Zynga's user population is both very large and highly motivated. It would be interesting to examine whether their data refute or support our Renren findings.

Future research will also need to examine a wider age range of SNS users. The PKU network on Renren is dominated by college students, and yet other age groups may exhibit different types or frequencies of behaviors in SNSs. Studies of generational differences in behavior on SNS are just beginning to appear in the literature (Lenhart, Purcell, Smith, & Zickuhr, 2010; Pfeil, Arjan, & Zaphiris, 2009), and they show some important age-related differences in usage and friending patterns, which may indicate differences in latent social interactions as well. Relatedly, densification is a term describing what happens to SNSs as they themselves get older. Since most people do not do substantial amounts of un-friending in SNSs, and users are continually joining, average social degrees continually rise. Densification may lead to time-varying changes in interaction patterns, as people's friend-of-friend circles grow exponentially. Follow up studies could examine what, if any, effect densification and time dynamics have on social interaction patterns in SNSs.

Finally, future research on latent social interaction in SNSs should include user studies to examine both users' motivations for engaging in latent social interactions as well as their attitudes towards SNS browsing, by self and by others. Results of user studies would be useful in several ways. First, they could help to confirm (or disconfirm) some of our conclusions, such as the lack of reciprocity in latent social behaviors. Second, user studies would allow data to be collected from a wider array of SNS users, as well as from users who have private profiles, as long as they would be willing to self-report their behaviors accurately. At a larger level, user studies would allow for a much deeper understanding of the importance, utility, and meaning of latent social behavior to users in SNS environments.

CONCLUSION

Our study of Renren reveals a new perspective on social interaction within online social networks. This chapter uses novel methodology in computer science to capture latent social interactions in SNSs. Our data include detailed visit histories to the profiles of 61,405 Renren users over a 90-day period. We compute a single visitor history for each profile by using a new technique to merge visitor logs from multiple consecutive crawls. We then analyze profile visit histories to study important social scientific questions concerning user popularity and reciprocity for profile browsing behavior, and the link between passive profile browsing and (inter)active comments.

Indeed, the concept of latent social interaction overlaps with two widely studied phenomena in the social sciences: lurking and interpersonal electronic surveillance (IES). Lurking occurs when people use an online community to read messages posted by others without posting messages themselves. Lurkers have thus been defined as "a persistent, yet silent audience" (Soroka & Rafaeli, 2006). Interpersonal electronic surveillance is defined as "surreptitious strategies individuals use over communication technologies to gain awareness of another user's offline and/or online behaviors" (Tokunaga, 2011, p. 706). IES is a general term closely related to concepts such as horizontal or participatory surveillance (Albrechtslund, 2008), peer-to-peer monitoring (Andrejevic, 2005), social surveillance (Steinfield et al., 2008), and social searching (Lampe et al., 2006).

Although lurking is common and expected in traditional communication systems (e.g., one-way mass media), it would not seem to be a hallmark of newer interactive media. Indeed, lurking seems to fly in the face of the participatory culture of Web 2.0. Soroka and Rafaeli (2006) argue that newer forms of communication, including SNSs, are fundamentally about interactivity (see also Pempek et al., 2009). It is interesting, then, that studies of many online communities find a great deal of lurking (Katz, 1998; Pempek et al., 2009; Preece et al., 2004). Our data on the prevalence of latent versus visible interactions confirm that many SNS users engage in lurking. The amount of lurking in online environments is unknown and estimates vary widely. Some studies report lurking by about 50-60% of community or network members, whereas others put the number at about 90% (Soroka & Rafaeli, 2006). These studies tend to be based on rather small sample sizes. Moreover, estimates based on social scientific studies may systematically underestimate the amount of lurking, and particularly the amount of viewing strangers' profiles in SNSs due to stigma associated with 'cyberstalking' (or virtual people-watching) and resulting social desirability response biases in survey-based studies.

Our study provides another view of the prevalence of lurking, based on actual SNS user behavior, rather than self-reports. Similar to prior research in other contexts, we find that many more users engage in latent social interaction (lurking via profile viewing) than in visible social interaction in Renren. Furthermore, we see that most users (80%) interact visibly with only a very small subset (5%) of their friends, and yet a majority of users view a sizable portion of their friends' profiles on at least a weekly basis. Of course, there are two types of lurking possible in SNSs: viewing friends' profiles and viewing strangers' profiles. Pempek et al.'s (2009) survey of undergraduate Facebook users found that 70% report viewing friends' profiles, which is very similar to our results. However, their estimate of stranger profile browsing was only 9%, whereas we found that most Renren users received a majority of their profile views from strangers. This was especially true for Renren users with few friends and those with many friends, while the middle groups got most of their profile views from direct friends. Interestingly, we also found that the frequency of repeat profile views from friends and strangers was very similar. Our data offer nuance, and in some ways refute, Pempek et al. as well as others who claim that interactions in SNS are predominantly between people who know and trust each other, as this does not appear to be the case for latent social interactions. We will return to this point later.

Explanations for lurking in online communities include things such as needing to learn about the community before actively participating, allowing participants to gain a sense of belonging at low cost, fear of negative reaction from community, and information overload (Preece et al., 2004; Soroka & Rafaeli, 2006). The logic of information overload theory is that, as the number of interactive posters within a community increases, it is difficult for individuals to keep up with and respond to the flow of messages. Limitations in both human cognitive ability to process massive amounts of information and time constraints lead to a preference for lurking. As mentioned earlier, our data on latent social interaction in Renren certainly support the notion that a great deal of lurking takes place in SNSs, which is consistent with information overload theory. The theory further implies that users with more friends will lurk more than users with fewer friends, given that each friend connection opens exponentially more opportunities for social interaction with that person that can be monitored or responded to on the SNS. Although our data do not speak to this directly, we find that having more friends results in a higher number of incoming views to one's own profile, but that this does not necessarily trigger reciprocal latent (or visible) social interaction. It may be the case that lurking itself contributes to overload, and thus is not reciprocated. These findings suggest that further investigation of information overload theory, as well as other motives for lurking in SNSs, are warranted.

Rau et al. (2008) indeed point out that motivations for lurking on SNSs may be different than in other types of online communities. Online communities (e.g., online forums, USENET groups, etc.) differ from SNSs in that SNSs satisfy social-emotional needs, rather than informational needs, and people on SNSs are connected to individual users, rather than a large community. Rau et al. found that SNS users lurk on SNSs because they believe that their social-emotional needs may not be satisfied even if they were to post. Further, they found that SNS users are not motivated to post on the profiles of users whom they seldom talk to, or with whom they only discuss shallow topics. Rau et al. also find that affective intimacy with friends in the network negatively influences lurking behavior. These findings are consistent with our data that show differences in lurking behavior among users with greater numbers of profile views. Users who get a lot of profile views may not feel intimately connected to their viewers and are thus not compelled to interact with them visibly or otherwise. Together, these results call for future social science research to build on our findings on latent social interactions by focusing on explanations for lurking in SNS environments.

As with lurking, naturalistic behavioral data on latent social interactions can go beyond what has been revealed by social science research methods about SNS interaction in terms of interpersonal electronic surveillance. Early concerns of SNS use focused on the dangers of social surveillance and 'stalking' by strangers on these sites (see boyd, 2008 for a discussion of the "moral panic" surrounding sexual predators and SNS usage). However, more recent studies based on user surveys found that most self-reported SNS social interactions are between real-world friends or contacts rather than strangers (Joinson, 2008; Lampe et al., 2006; Lenhart & Madden, 2007; Pempek et al., 2009). Our data contradict these findings to show that a sizable portion of social interactions on SNSs do take place between strangers and that passive social browsing is an important component of SNS use. Our data also add nuance to the largely survey-based literature by showing that profile views of Renren users who possess a middle range of friends on the network (between 100-1,000) are mostly from their known friends, whereas profile views of users with very few (< 100) and very many (over 1,000) linked friends are mostly from strangers. Overall, then, our data indicate that the moral panic surrounding cyberstalking may be more justified for some types of SNS users than for others.

The negative connotation surrounding IES is not surprising because, according to latent tie theory (Haythornwaite, 2005), SNSs are a communication channel that opens possibilities for greater numbers of connections to others. The connotation may not be warranted, however, because latent social interaction is mostly between friends for a sizable portion of the user base, and because even weak connections can lead to positive outcomes, such as greater social capital (Albrechtslund, 2008; Donath & boyd, 2004; Haythornwaite, 2005; Steinfield et al., 2008). The connection between social capital and SNSs is based on Granovetter's (1982) "strength of weak ties" argument (Ellison et al., 2007), which says that personal and social benefits can accrue from even loose connections between people, as they can provide access to new information and resources that are unavailable through one's more intimate network. Steinfield et al. (2008) found this to be the case in that more avid users of Facebook (in terms of time on the SNS and number of friends) reported greater social capital.

Latent social interactions between friends or strangers in SNSs may be considered a form of 'weak ties' in that mere profile browsing might also activate previously dormant or non-existent ties between users, which the user could then benefit from. For example, via profile browsing, a user could learn about common concerns, efforts, or interests of her fellow SNS members, which could motivate her to activate a relationship. A form of social capital may even exist when latent social interaction events produce no action or reciprocation, simply by the transmission of information from one user to another in the network. That is, when a user browses a profile, information on the browsed page is naturally propagated to the viewer. In an experiment comparing information dissemination across social, visible, and latent interaction graphs, Jiang et al. (2010) found that the latent interaction graph was most efficient for transmitting information between users. This is due to the fact that latent interactions require less time and effort to perform than visible interactions, and so they happen more frequently. Thus, the potential for activation between users is high. Also, social graphs can only spread information between linked friends, and so they are less efficient for information dissemination because there are far fewer formal connections (i.e., friend links) than there are informal latent interactions between users.

Understanding latent social interactions may also shed light on processes of identity management in SNSs. Donath and boyd (2004) and boyd and Heer (2006) found that impression management motivated Friendster users to establish formal friend links to certain others on the network (e.g., to interesting or physically attractive people) because such public displays of connection serve as important identity signals to others, as well as provide self-validation. Although it is obvious why having a lot of friends on the SNS can make users feel good about themselves, it could also be that seeing that one's profile attracts a lot of visitors may similarly enhance users' self-esteem. Of course, this effect would be limited to SNSs that make or allow profile visitors visible to users, such as Renren. As mentioned at the outset of this chapter, Facebook itself does not afford this capability, and nor does its terms of service allow third party applications that make latent social interactions visible to Facebook users. This highlights the need for researchers to collect data beyond those available in Facebook to understand how processes of identity management may vary across different SNSs.

To conclude, our study reveals interesting insights into the nature of user behavior in SNSs. We observe that user behavior is different for latent compared to other types of social interactions via SNSs: more users participate in latent social interaction, users do not feel the need to reciprocate profile visits, and visits by non-friends make up a significant portion of views to most user profiles. We also see that visits to user profiles generate more active interactions (comments) than visits to photos or diary pages. Using profile browsing events, we construct latent interaction graphs as a more accurate representation of peer social interactions. Analysis of these graphs derived from our Renren dataset reveal characteristics that fall between visible interaction graphs and social graphs. This confirms the intuition that latent interactions are less limited by constraints such as time and energy, but more meaningful than the formal 'friend' linkages that are provided by the social graph alone.

Finally, our study includes an exhaustive crawl of the largest connected component in the Renren social graph. The resulting graph is one of the biggest of its kind, with more than 42 million nodes and 1.6 billion edges. Other than a proprietary Cyworld dataset, this is the only social graph we know of that covers 100% of a large social graph component. Given its size and comprehensiveness, we are currently investigating different options for sharing this dataset with the research community.

REFERENCES

Ahn, Y.-Y., Han, S., Kwak, H., Moon, S. B., & Jeong, H. (2007). Analysis of topological characteristics of huge online social networking services. *Proceedings of the 16th International Conference on World Wide Web (WWW'07)*, Banff, Alberta, Canada.

Albrechtslund, A. (2008). Online social networking as participatory surveillance. *First Monday, 13*(3).

Andrejevic, M. (2005). The work of watching one another: Lateral surveillance, risk, and governance. *Surveillance & Society, 2*(4), 479–497.

Benevenuto, F., Rodrigues, T., Cha, M., & Almeida, V. (2009). Characterizing user behavior in online social networks. *Proceedings of the ACM Internet Measurement Conference (IMC'09)*, Chicago, IL.

Bilge, L., Strufe, T., Balzarotti, D., & Kirda, E. (2009). All your contacts belong to us: Automated identity theft attacks on social networks. *Proceedings of the 18th International Conference on World Wide Web (WWW'09)*, Madrid, Spain. boyd, d. (2006). Friends, Friendsters, and MySpace Top 8: Writing community into being on social network sites. *First Monday, 11*(12). boyd, d. (2008). *Taken out of context: American teen sociality in networked publics* (Doctoral dissertation). University of California, Berkeley, CA.

boyd, d., & Heer, J. (2006). Profiles as conversation: Networked identity performance on Friendster. *Proceedings of the 39th Hawaiian International Conference on System Sciences*, Kauai, HI.

Cha, M., Haddadi, H., Benevenuto, F., & Gummadi, K. (2010). Measuring user influence in Twitter: The million follower fallacy. *Proceedings of the 4th International AAAI Conference on Weblogs and Social Media (ICWSM),* Washington, DC.

Cha, M., Mislove, A., Adams, B., & Gummadi, K. (2008). Characterizing social cascades in Flickr. *Proceedings of the ACM Workshop on Online Social Networks (WOSN'08)*, Seattle, WA.

Chen, W., Wand, Y., & Yang, S. (2009). Efficient influence maximization in social networks. *Proceedings of the ACM Conference on Knowledge Discovery and Data Mining,* Paris, France.

Chun, H., Kwak, H., Eom, Y. H., Ahn, Y.-Y., Moon, S. B., & Jeong, H. (2008). Comparison of online social relations in volume vs. interaction: A case study of Cyworld. *Proceedings of the ACM Internet Measurement Conference (IMC'08)*, Vouliagmeni, Greece.

Donath, J., & boyd, d. (2004). Public displays of connection. *BT Technology Journal*, *22*(4), 71–82. doi:10.1023/B:BTTJ.0000047585.06264.cc

Ellison, N., Lampe, C., & Steinfield, C. (2008, May). *Net worth: Facebook use and changes in social capital over time*. Paper presented at the annual meeting of the International Communication Association, TBA, Montreal, Quebec, Canada.

Ellison, N., Steinfield, C., & Lampe, C. (2007). The benefits of Facebook "friends": Exploring the relationship between college students' use of online social networks and social capital. *Journal of Computer-Mediated Communication*, *12*(3).

Fehr, B. (2008). Friendship formation. In Sprecher, S., Wenzel, A., & Harvey, J. (Eds.), *Handbook of relationship initiation* (pp. 29–54). New York, NY: Taylor & Francis.

Galuba, W., Aberer, K., Chakraborty, D., Despotovic, Z., & Kellerer, W. (2010). Outtweeting the Twitterers? Predicting information cascades in microblogs. *Proceedings of the ACM Workshop on Online Social Networks* (*WOSN'10*), Boston, MA.

Gannes, L. (2010). *When social replaces search, what can you do to monetize?* Retrieved October 29, 2010, from http://gigaom.com/2010/03/24/when-social-replaces-search-what-can-you-do-to-monetize/

Granovetter, M. (1983). The strength of weak ties: A network theory revisited. *Sociological Theory*, *1*(1), 201–233. doi:10.2307/202051

Gruhl, D., Guah, R., Liben-Nowell, D., & Tomkins, A. (2004). Information diffusion through blogspace. *Proceedings of the 13th International Conference on World Wide Web (WWW'04)*, New York, NY.

Haythornthwaite, C. (2005). Social networks and Internet connectivity effects. *Information Communication and Society*, *8*(2), 125–147. doi:10.1080/13691180500146185

Jiang, J., Wilson, C., Wang, X., Huang, P., Sha, W., Dai, Y., & Zhao, B. Y. (2010). Understanding latent social interactions in online social networks. *Proceedings of the ACM Internet Measurement Conference (IMC'10)*, Melbourne, Australia.

Joinson, A. N. (2008). Looking at, looking up, or keeping up with people? Motives and uses of Facebook. In *Proceedings of the 26th Annual SIGCHI Conference on Human Factors in Computing Systems* (Florence, Italy, April 05-10 2008), CHI '08, ACM, New York, (pp. 1027-1036).

Katz, J. (1998). *Luring the lurkers*. Retrieved October 30, 2010, from http://slashdot.org/features/98/12/28/1745252.shtml

Kempe, D., Kleinberg, J. M., & Tardos, Ï. (2003). Maximizing the spread of influence through a social network. *Proceedings of the ACM Conference on Knowledge Discovery and Data Mining*, Washington, DC.

Kirkpatrick, M. (2009). *Social networking now more popular than email, report finds*. Retrieved August 12, 2010, from http://www.readwriteweb.com/archives/social_networking_now_more_popular_than_email.php

Kwak, H., Lee, C., Park, H., & Moon, S. (2010). What is Twitter, a social network or a news media? Proceedings of the *19th International Conference on World Wide Web (WWW'10),* Raleigh, North Carolina.

Lampe, C., Ellison, N., & Steinfield, C. (2006). A Face(book) in the crowd: Social searching vs. social browsing. *Proceedings of the Conference on Computer-Supported Cooperative Work* (CSCW'06), (pp. 167-170). Banff, Alberta.

Lenhart, A., Madden, M., Macgill, A., & Smith, A. (2007, December 19). *Teens and social media*. Pew Internet & American Life Project. Retrieved October 28, 2010, from http://www.pewinternet.org/Reports/2007/Teens-Privacy-and-Online-Social-Networks.aspx

Leskovec, J., & Horvitz, E. (2008). Planetary-scale views on a large instant-messaging network. *Proceedings of the 17th International Conference on World Wide Web (WWW'08),* Beijing, China.

McPherson, M., Smith-Lovin, L., & Cook, J. (2001). Birds of a feather: Homophility in social networks. *Annual Review of Sociology, 27*, 415–444. doi:10.1146/annurev.soc.27.1.415

Mislove, A., Marcon, M., Gummadi, P. K., Druschel, P., & Bhattacharjee, B. (2007). Measurement and analysis of online social networks. *Proceedings of the ACM Internet Measurement Conference (IMC'07)*, San Diego, CA.

Pempek, T. A., Yermolayeya, Y. A., & Calvert, S. L. (2009). College students' social networking experiences on Facebook. *Journal of Applied Developmental Psychology, 30*(3), 227–238. doi:10.1016/j.appdev.2008.12.010

Preece, J., Nonnecke, B., & Andrews, D. (2004). The top five reasons for lurking: Improving community experiences for everyone. *Computers in Human Behavior, 20*(2), 201–223. doi:10.1016/j.chb.2003.10.015

Rau, P.-L. P., Gao, Q., & Ding, Y. (2008). Relationship between the level of intimacy and lurking in online social network services. *Computers in Human Behavior, 24*(6), 2757–2770. doi:10.1016/j.chb.2008.04.001

Schneider, F., Feldmann, A., Krishnamurthy, B., & Willinger, W. (2009). Understanding online social network usage from a network perspective. *Proceedings of the ACM Internet Measurement Conference (IMC'09)*, Chicago, IL.

Sophos. (2007). *Facebook ID probe shows 41% of users happy to reveal all to potential identity thieves*. Retrieved October 15, 2010, from http://www.sophos.com/pressoffice/news/articles/2007/08/facebook.html/

Sorkin, A. R. (2010, July 22). Facebook tops 500 million users. *New York Times Blog*. Retrieved August 11, 2010, from http://dealbook.blogs.nytimes.com/2010/07/22/facebook-tops-500-million-users/

Soroka, V., & Rafaeli, S. (2006). Invisible participants: How cultural capital relates to lurking behavior. *Proceedings of the 15th International Conference on World Wide Web (WWW'06)*, Edinburgh, Scotland.

Steinfield, C., Ellison, N., & Lampe, C. (2008). Social capital, self-esteem, and use of online social network sites: A longitudinal analysis. *Journal of Applied Developmental Psychology, 29*(6), 434–445. doi:10.1016/j.appdev.2008.07.002

Tokunaga, R. S. (2011). Social networking site or social surveillance site? Understanding the use of interpersonal electronic surveillance in romantic relationships. *Computers in Human Behavior, 27*(2), 705–713. doi:10.1016/j.chb.2010.08.014

Tong, S. T., van der Heide, B., Langwell, L., & Walther, J. B. (2008). Too much of a good thing? The relationship between number of friends and interpersonal impressions on Facebook. *Journal of Computer-Mediated Communication, 13*(3), 531–549. doi:10.1111/j.1083-6101.2008.00409.x

Valkenburg, P. M., Peter, J., & Schouten, A. P. (2006). Friend networking sites and their relationship to adolescents' well-being and social self-esteem. *Cyberpsychology & Behavior, 9*(5), 584–590. doi:10.1089/cpb.2006.9.584

Viswanath, B., Mislove, A., Cha, M., & Gummadi, K. P. (2009). On the evolution of user interaction in facebook. *Proceedings of the ACM Workshop on Online Social Networks (WOSN'09)*, Barcelona, Spain.

Walther, J. B. (1992). Interpersonal effects in computer-mediated interaction: A relational perspective. *Communication Research, 19*, 52–90. doi:10.1177/009365092019001003

Wilson, C., Boe, B., Sala, A., Puttaswamy, K. P. N., & Zhao, B. Y. (2009). User interactions in social networks and their implications. *Proceedings of the ACM SIGOPS Eurosys '09*, Nuremberg, Bavaria.

Yarow, J. (2010). *Facebook was more popular in the U.S. than Google last week.* Retrieved October 30, 2010, from http://www.businessinsider.com/facebook-was-more-popular-in-the-us-than-google-last-week-2010-3

Yoneki, E., & Crowcroft, J. (2009). GIS: Geographical information cascade in online social networks. *Proceedings of the International Conference on Network Science (NetSci),* Venice, Italy.

ADDITIONAL READING

Amaral, L. A. N., Scala, A., Barthelemy, M., & Stanley, H. E. (2000). Classes of small-world networks. In *Proceedings of the National Academy of Sciences*, pp. 11149-11152.

Barabasi, A. L., & Albert, R. (1999). Emergence of scaling in random networks. *Science*, 286.

Boyd, D. M., & Ellison, N. B. (2008). Social network sites: Definition, history, and scholarship. *Journal of Computer-Mediated Communication, 13*(1), 210–230. doi:10.1111/j.1083-6101.2007.00393.x

Brin, S., & Page, L. (1998). The anatomy of a large-scale hypertextual web search engine. *Computer Networks and ISDN Systems, 30*(1-7), 107-117.

Cha, M., Kwak, H., Rodriguez, P., Ahn, Y.-Y., & Moon, S. (2007). I tube, you tube, everybody tubes: analyzing the world's largest user generated content video system. In *Proceedings of the 7th ACM SIGCOMM conference on Internet measurement* (IMC '07).

Cho, J., & Garcia-Molina, H. (2002). Parallel crawlers. In *Proceedings of the World Wide Web conference*, pp. 124-135.

Cho, J., Garcia-Molina, H., & Page, L. (1998). Efficient crawling through URL ordering. *Computer Networks and ISDN Systems, 30*(1-7), 161-172.

Erdos, P., & Renyi, A. (1960). *On the evolution of random graphs*. Mathematical Institute of the Hungarian Academy of Science.

Gjoka, M., Kurant, M., Butts, C. T., & Markopoulou, A. (2010). A walk in Facebook: Uniform sampling of users in online social networks. In *Proceedings of the IEEE Infocom.*

Gross, R., & Acquisti, A. (2005). Information revelation and privacy in online social networks (the Facebook case). *Proceedings of Privacy in the Electronic Society (WPES'05)* (pp. 71-80). Alexandria, VA: Association of Computing Machinery.

Hargittai, E., & Hsieh, Y.-P. (2010). Predictors and consequences of differentiated practices on social network sites. *Information Communication and Society, 13*(4), 515–536. doi:10.1080/13691181003639866

Leskovec, J., & Faloutsos, C. (2006). Sampling from large graphs. In *Proceedings of the Knowledge Discovery and Data Mining* conference, pp. 631-636.

Leskovec, J., Kleinberg, J., & Faloutsos, C. (2005). Graphs over time: Densification laws, shrinking diameters and possible explanations. In *Proceedings of ACM Knowledge Discovery and Data Mining*.

Lovász, L. (1993). Random walks on graphs: A survey. *Combinatorics*, *2*, 1–46.

Milgram, S. (1967). The small world problem. *Psychology Today*, *6*, 62–67.

Milgram, S. (1977). *The familiar stranger: an aspect of urban anonymity*. Addison-Wesley.

Pinkerton, B. (1994). Finding what people want: Experiences with the webcrawler. In *Proceedings of the World Wide Web conference*.

Ryberg, T., & Larsen, M. C. (2008). Networked identities: Understanding relationships between strong and weak ties in networked environments. *Journal of Computer Assisted Learning*, *24*(2), 103–115. doi:10.1111/j.1365-2729.2007.00272.x

Slonje, R., & Smith, P. K. (2008). Cyberbullying: Another main type of bullying? *Scandinavian Journal of Psychology*, *49*(2), 147–154. doi:10.1111/j.1467-9450.2007.00611.x

Spitzberg, B. H., & Hoobler, G. (2002). Cyberstalking and the technologies of interpersonal terrorism. *New Media & Society*, *4*(1), 71. doi:10.1177/14614440222226271

Thelwall, M. (2009). Social network sites: Users and uses. In Marvin, V. Z. (Ed.), *Advances in computers* (*Vol. 76*, pp. 19–73). Elsevier.

Watts, D. J., & Strogatz, S. (1998). Collective dynamics of 'small-world' networks. *Nature*, *393*, 440–442. doi:10.1038/30918

Wight, N., Varey, A., & Chesney, T. (2005). An investigation of sociability measurements in online communities. *International Journal of Web Based Communities*, *1*(4), 400–411. doi:10.1504/IJWBC.2005.008106

KEY TERMS AND DEFINITIONS

Assortativity: is a mathematical calculation that shows the likelihood that users establish links to other users of similar social degree

Average Path Length: is the average of all-pairs-shortest-paths in a network

Clustering Coefficient: is a mathematical calculation that shows the degree of local connectivity between nodes (i.e., users or events) in a network

Consumption: is the number of other network members' profiles a user views

Cyberstalking: includes threatening behavior or unwanted advances directed at another using the Internet and other forms of online and computer communications

Information Overload Theory: says that as the number of interactive posters within a network increases, it is difficult for individuals to keep up with and respond to the flow of messages

Interpersonal Electronic Surveillance: refers to surreptitious strategies that individuals use over communication technologies to gain awareness of another user's offline and/or online behaviors

Latent Interaction Graph: shows a set of users in a network who are connected via links representing latent interaction events between them (i.e., profile views)

Latent Social Interactions: consist of passive views of a network member's profile by other network members

Latent Tie Theory: says that the introduction of any new medium for communication between network members creates latent ties which are technically possible but not yet activated socially

Lurking: is when people use an online community to read messages posted by others without posting messages themselves

Network Crawl: is a method of capturing specific types of data from a network that begins by collecting data from a set of "seed" members, and from this generating a new list of members to visit until all or some desired number of network members are visited

Popularity: is the number of views a network member's profile receives

Probability Density Function: is a mathematical function describing the likelihood of a random variable (e.g., profile browsing behavior) having a specific value, such that in our study it shows the probability of a network member returning to a previously-viewed profile

Reciprocity: is the degree to which users in a network will visit the profile of other users who have viewed their own profile

Social Capital: refers to potential benefits derived from having connections with others within a network that one can draw resources from, such as information diffusion and linking to external assets

Social Degree: is the number of explicit friendship linkages a user has in a network

Social Graph: shows a set of users in a network who are connected via explicit friendship linkages between them

Tie Strength: is the degree of closeness of relations between users in a network, which is influenced by such things as the types of exchanges, frequency of contact, intimacy, duration of the relationship, etc. between individual network members

Visible Interaction Graph: shows a set of users in a network who are connected via visible interaction events between them (i.e., comments and wall posts)

Visible Social Interactions: consist of active communication events (e.g., comments generated by users in message board posts, diary entries, photos, and status updates) between users in a network

ENDNOTES

1 Like Facebook, a Renren user's homepage includes a number of friend recommendations that encourage formation of new friend relationships. Renren lists three users with the most number of mutual friends on each page. In addition, Renren shows a list of eight "popular users" at the very bottom of the page. These popular users are randomly selected from the 100 users with the most friends in the university network. Friend lists in Renren are always public, which contrasts with most other SNSs, where full social graph crawls are prevented by user privacy policies that hide friendship links from the public. Moreover, comments in Renren are threaded, which enabled us to precisely distinguish the intended target of each comment. One other difference between Renren and Facebook is that each standard user is limited to a maximum of 1,000 friends. Users may pay a subscription fee to increase this limit to 2,000. From our data, we saw that very few users (0.3%) took advantage of this feature.

2 We seeded crawlers with the 30 most popular users' profiles, and performed a breadth-first traversal of the social graph. During the crawl, we collected unique userIDs, network affiliations, and friendship links to other users.

3 This study focused on the structure of social graphs and interactions between users. Since we did not need any actual content of comments, photos, or user profiles, we waited for crawls to complete, then went through our data to anonymize userIDs and strip any private data from our dataset to protect user privacy. In addition, all user IDs were hashed to random IDs, and all timestamps were replaced with relative sequence numbers. Our group has visited and held research meetings with technical teams at Renren, and they are aware of our ongoing research.

4 Crawling Renren for recent visitor records is complicated by two things. First, each user's profile only lists the last nine visitors. This

means that our crawler must be constantly revisiting users in order to glean representative data, as new visitors will cause older visitors to fall off the list. Clearly we could not crawl every user continuously. Frequent crawls leave the ID of our crawler on the visitor log of profiles, which has generated unhappy feedback from profile owners. In addition, Renren imposes multiple per-account rate limits that slow our crawler significantly despite our large number of crawler accounts. Thus, we designed our crawler to be self-adapting. This means that we track the popularity and level of dynamics in different user profiles, and allocate most of our requests to heavily trafficked user profiles, while guaranteeing a minimum crawl rate (1/day) for low traffic users. The individual lists from each crawl contain overlapping results, which we integrate into a single history. The second challenge to crawling recent visitor records is that each visitor is only shown in the list once, even if they visit multiple times. Repeat visits simply cause that user to return to the top of the list, erasing their old position. This makes identifying overlapping sets of visitors from the iterative crawls difficult. To solve these two challenges, we use a log-integration algorithm to concatenate the individual recent visitor lists observed during each successive crawl. More specifically, some overlapping sets of visitors exist in successive crawl data, and our main task is to find new visitors and remove overlaps. There are two kinds of incoming visitors: new users, who do not appear in the previous list, and repeat users, who appear in the prior list at a different relative position. The first kind of incoming visitor is easily identified, since his record is completely new to the recent visitor list. New visitors provide a useful checkpoint for purposes of log-integration, since other users behind them in the list are also necessarily new incoming visitors. The second type of incoming visitor, repeat users, can be detected by looking for changes in sequence of the recent visitor list. If a user repeatedly visits the same profile in-between two visits of other users, nothing changes in the recent visitor list. Therefore, consecutive repeat visits are ignored by our crawler.

We were concerned that our crawls might not be frequent enough to capture all visit events to a given profile. To address this concern, we took a closer look at the impact of crawler frequency on missing visits. First, we take all of the profiles we crawled for visit histories, and computed their average daily visit count between September and November 2009. Most users (99.3%) receive 8 or fewer visits per day on average. Since Renren shows 9 latest visitors, crawling a profile once every day should be sufficient to capture all visits. While our crawler adapts to allocate more crawl requests to popular, frequently visited profiles, we guarantee that every profile is crawled at least once every 24 hours. Next, we select 1,000 random PKU users and crawl their recent visitors every 15 minutes for 2 days. We use the data collected to simulate five frequencies for crawling process, namely 15 minutes, 30 minutes, 1 hour, 12 hours and 1 day. Then we use the log-integration algorithm to concatenate the individual recent visitor lists at different crawling frequencies. For every person, we computed the number of visits missed by the crawler when we reduce the frequency, beginning with visits every 15 minutes. This shows that for 88% of users, there are no additional visits missed when we reduce the crawler rate from once every 15 minutes to once per day. Only for a very small group of users (0.7%) is the number of missing visits greater than 10 when crawling at once per day. Moreover, less than 0.7% of all users receive more than nine visits per day. Only these users would require more than one crawl per day to collect a full history of their visits. Since we allocate the bulk of our crawler requests to these high popularity users (and crawl once per day for the rest), we are relatively confident that very few visits are missed by our crawls.

6 To calculate this, we quantified the lack of reciprocity for latent interactions by calculating a reciprocity coefficient (see Jiang et al., 2010). The reciprocity coefficient is measured between -1 and 1, where positive values indicate reciprocity, and negative values anti-reciprocity. The reciprocity coefficient of profile visits on Renren is only 0.23. In contrast, reciprocity of visible comments on Renren is 0.49, and the reciprocity of visible interactions on Cyworld is 0.78.

7 For account longevity we measure the number of days in between a user joining and leaving Renren. Neither of these pieces of information is provided by Renren, and thus must be estimated. Join date can be approximated by the timestamp of the first comment received by a user, since the comment is likely to be a "welcome message" from a friend greeting the new user (Wilson et al., 2009). Because abandoned and inactive accounts can still receive comments, the best estimate of departure time is the timestamp of the last comment left by a user.

8 Given the drastic differences in size of each popularity group, we used Spearman's rank correlations (Spearman's ρ), which is a nonparametric measure of the correlation between two variables and is thus more appropriate for this analysis.

9 We restrict our social, latent, and visible interaction graphs to only contain users from the PKU network, since these are the only users for which we have complete interaction records. Note that we only consider interactions that occur between users in the PKU network, as it is possible for interactions to originate from or target users outside the network for whom we have limited information. Also note that because non-friend strangers can view user's profiles, the latent interaction graph will contain links between users who are not friends in the social graph. Our formulation of interaction graphs uses an unweighted graph. We do not attempt to derive a weight scheme for interaction graphs analyzed in this paper, but leave exploration of this facet of latent interaction graphs to future work.

Chapter 6
Social Network Site Use among Dutch Students:
Effects of Time and Platform

Sonja Utz
VU University Amsterdam, The Netherlands

ABSTRACT

This chapter compares the SNS use of Dutch students across time and platforms. Between 2009 (n = 194) and 2010 (n = 212), many users migrated from Hyves, the hitherto largest Dutch SNS, to Facebook. Comparisons between the two years showed that SNS use remained relatively stable over time; only self-disclosure increased remarkably. However, there were several differences between the platforms. Facebook users were more active, they disclosed more about themselves, but they reacted also more to their friends. There were no effects of time and platform on positive or negative consequences of social interaction on SNS, indicating that the preference for a SNS is more a question of the current trend. In contrast to the assumption that SNS are especially useful to stay in touch with acquaintances, the respondents used them mainly for conversation with close friends. The implications of these findings are discussed.

INTRODUCTION

Within only a few years, social network sites (SNS) have become part of everyday life for most adolescents and young adults (Ellison, Steinfield, & Lampe, 2007). On these sites, users present themselves on profiles and display and maintain their relationships with others. The profiles on SNS are public or at least semi-public. Many users have hundreds of SNS friends, therefore, even comments posted on private profiles are visible to a large audience. Thereby, communication on SNS blurs the distinction between interpersonal and mass communication.

DOI: 10.4018/978-1-61350-338-6.ch006

The enormous popularity of SNS and the public display of private information has instigated many researchers to study the phenomenon. These studies focus often on a specific aspect, such as dealing with privacy issues (Dwyer, Hiltz, & Passerini, 2007; Lenhart & Madden, 2007; Utz & Krämer, 2009), self-presentation (Donath, 2007; Krämer & Winter, 2008; Mehdizadeh, 2010; Zhao, Grasmuck, & Martin, 2008), impression formation (Tong, Van Der Heide, Langwell, & Walther, 2008; Utz, 2010; Walther, Van Der Heide, Hamel, & Shulman, 2009; Walther, Van Der Heide, Kim, Westerman, & Tong, 2008) or the consequences of SNS use for different types of relationships (Ellison et al., 2007; Utz & Beukeboom, 2011; Valenzuela, Park, & Kee, 2009). However, descriptive studies with a broader focus that describe in depth how people actually use these sites are still rare. Descriptive studies using a random selection of SNS profiles or a representative sample of the population or specific subgroups are important because online-surveys posted on SNS are often filled in by the most active users and might therefore show a biased picture. Parks (2008) for example randomly selected MySpace profiles and found that despite of the hype around MySpace many profiles were abandoned or not used very intensively. Another deficit of the present studies is that the vast majority focuses on American college students and on Facebook, the largest SNS. To fully understand SNS use, studies that examine different countries and different platforms are needed.

Comparisons across time are also important because the popularity of SNS as well as the features of SNS change over time. Till now, there is no paper that compares SNS use across time *and* platform. To fill this gap, the present chapter presents the data of two surveys conducted in subsequent years among Dutch students. Within this year, many people switched from Hyves, the largest Dutch SNS, to Facebook. This migration to Facebook allows a comparison of SNS use across time as well as across platforms. The chapter will report adoption patterns and self- and other-centered forms of SNS use.

BACKGROUND

SNS are "web-based services that allow individuals to (1) construct a public or semi-public profile within a bounded system, (2) articulate a list of other users with whom they share a connection, and (3) view and traverse their list of connections and those made by others within the system" (Boyd & Ellison, 2007). The explicit display of the personal network and the (semi-)public maintenance of social relationships make SNS an interesting venue for researchers.

Due to this combination of features – online profiles and networking opportunities -, SNS can be used in a more self-centered and/or a more other-centered way. Using SNS mainly as a platform for self-presentation is a rather self-centered way of using SNS, whereas using SNS to communicate with friends and acquaintances or to engage in group discussions is considered as other-focused way of SNS use. A somewhat similar distinction in identity as display and identity as connection has been made by Livingstone (2008). The present research examined both types of behaviors.

In the following paragraphs, an overview over the most frequently studied aspects and consequences of SNS use will be given, before the results of prior studies that compared SNS use across platforms and time will be summarized.

Privacy Settings

The fact that SNS users put a lot of personal information on their (semi-)public profiles while stating that they are concerned about their privacy has received much attention by the media as well as scholars. Barnes (2006) coined the term privacy paradox to describe this phenomenon. Various dangers of putting sensitive information online have been stressed: reputation damages, leading even to dismissal or rejection at job interviews, (identity) theft, harassment or stalking (Debatin, Lovejoy, Horn, & Hughes, 2009). Users have basically two options: restrict the access to their profile or think carefully about what to put on the SNS. Allowing only friends to access the profile information still bears some dangers, especially because most users have hundreds of friends and add also vague acquaintances or even strangers (Parks, 2010). Gross and Acquisti (2005) analyzed 4000 Facebook profiles and found that only a small number of users had restricted the access to their profiles. In a similar vein, Thelwall (2008) reported that only 27% of MySpace profiles were set to private. Some studies tried to solve the paradox by arguing that SNS users have a different definition of privacy. For teenagers and adolescents it is more important that they are in control about what information about them is available than whether it is available (Livingstone, 2006, 2008). However, there are also studies showing that dealing with privacy issues has changed over time and that many users nowadays restrict the access to their profile. For example, Utz and Krämer (2009) found in three studies on Dutch and German SNS that the vast majority of users has changed the default privacy settings into more restrictive settings. These findings support the claim by Lewis, Kaufman, and Christakis (2008) that the widespread adoption of SNS as well as the attention that media paid to the privacy issues have led to a privacy movement. Lewis et al. (2008) argue that people are more aware of the dangers and choose therefore more restrictive privacy settings. In line with these assumptions, Young and Quan-Hase (2009) report that people also use other privacy protection strategies such as sending private messages instead of writing wall postings, excluding personal information on the profile, untagging themselves from images, or deleting messages posted to their Facebook walls.

Self-Centered SNS Use

Self-presentation is a central part of SNS. Users are invited to upload a profile picture and fill in information about their age, relationship status, educational background, hometown, interests, favorite music, favorite movies, favorite sports, and so on. Related to the question how people present themselves on SNS is the question how people form impressions of others based on the information provided in a profile. Several studies have focused on the relationship between personality characteristics and self presentation. The effects were usually weak to moderate, and not always consistent across studies. The best predictors were extraversion and openness to experience. Extraverted individuals fill in more fields of their profile and use more often non-standard profile pictures than introverted individuals do (Krämer & Winter, 2008). Extraverted individuals have also more friends on the SNS than introverted individuals (Ross, et al., 2009; Wehrli, 2008). Openness to experience is for example related to the number of features used (Amichai-Hamburger & Vinitzky, 2010).

Related to these findings is the question how realistic self presentation on SNS are. Do people present themselves like they are in real life, or do they present an optimized and idealized picture? Gosling, Gaddis, and Vazire (2007) reported that people were able to reliable predict the personality of individuals based on their Facebook profiles. These results indicate that the self-presentations are realistic at least to a certain degree. Donath (2007) argues that self-presentations on SNS are more realistic than in other online venues because the public display of the social network functions as a social control mechanisms. If a person lies, the friends would write astonished comments on the profile. Back et al. (2010) found that Facebook profiles reflect actual personality rather than self-idealized personality. Nevertheless, it can be assumed that people are somewhat selective and tend to use pictures on which they look great (Siibak, 2009) or talk mainly about positive and self-enhancing experiences.

Some people even argue that SNS are an optimal venue for people high in narcissism or might even increase narcissim (Rosen, 2007). Indeed, Buffardi and Campbell (2008) found that narcissistic individuals presented themselves in a more self-promoting way. Similar results were reported by Mehdizadeh (2010). However, narcissistic people really believe in their superiority, so their selfpromoting self-presentation again reflects their personality.

Closely related to self presentation is the issue of self-disclosure. Self-disclosure addresses the amount of personal information disclosed to others. Self-disclosure plays a central role in relationship formation. According to social penetration theory, depth and breadth of self-disclosure increase with increasing intimacy of relationships (Altman & Taylor, 1973). On SNS, self-disclosure is no longer a dyadic or small-group phenomenon. Instead, self-disclosure it visible at leat for all friends. Surprisingly, self-disclosure is independent from privacy concerns (Tufekci, 2008a). Thus, it is not the case that mainly people who do not care about privacy engage in detailed online self-disclosure. The privacy calculus approach views self-disclosure as a trade-off between privacy concerns and the perceived benefits of self-disclosure (Krasnova, Spiekermann, Koroleva, & Hildebrand, 2010). As long as the benefits prevail, people will show high levels of self-disclosure regardless of their privacy concerns. Self-disclosure serves a social goal and helps to establish and maintain social relationships (Young & Quan-Haase, 2009). Moroever, Christofides, Muise, and Desmarais (2009) reported that self-disclosure is related to the need for popularity, indicating that individuals who strive to become popular on the SNS reveal more about themselves. However, social factors like perceived norms also play a role (Mesch & Beker, 2010).

Other-Centered SNS Use

Many studies found that the main reason for using SNS is keeping in touch with friends and acquaintances (e.g. Ellison et al., 2007; Lenhart & Madden, 2007; Livingstone, 2008). Tufekci (2008b) coined the term social grooming to describe this other-centered form of SNS use. As a consequence, SNS use increases social capital (Ellison et al., 2007; Steinfield, Ellison, & Lampe, 2008; Valenzuela et al., 2009). Social capital can be distinguished in strong and weak ties (Putnam, 2000). Strong ties are ties with close friends and family members. These ties usually provide emotional support and are also called bonding social capital. Weak ties are ties with acquaintances who provide mainly informational support; these ties are also called bridging social capital. SNS are well suited to stay in contact with weak ties. Especially people with low self-esteem benefit from SNS use by increasing their bridging social capital (Ellison et al., 2007).

However, SNS use can also have negative impacts on interpersonal relationships. Muise, Christofides, and Desmarais (2009) found that the information provided about one's partner on a SNS can lead to jealousy. Especially individuals with low self-esteem are prone to experience SNS jealousy, and they do more so the higher their need for popularity (Utz & Beukeboom, 2011). However, SNS use could also have negative impacts on relationships with "friends", for example, if somebody refuses to accept a friendship request or if people do not get full access to profiles of friends.

Prior research on the effects of SNS use on social relationships or social capital has used rather general indicators of SNS use. In depth studies that systematically examine how superficial or intimate the (semi-) public communication on SNS is, are missing. Raacke and Bonds-Raacke (2008) assessed how happy and excited people were when they received messages on their profile and found only moderate levels of happiness and excitement. Bellur, Oeldorf-Hirsch and High (2008) reported in a conference paper that social support is perceived as more appropriate if there is not too much emotion displayed, indicating that the norm might be to engage rather in superficial chitchat than in emotional and very intimate discussions. The present chapter will fill this gap by examining which situations elicit more reactions and how far people are affected by reactions they receive on their profile.

Prior Comparisons across Platforms and Time

Hargittai (2008) found in a study on American college students that demographic data predicted preferences for a SNS. For example, Hispanic students preferred MySpace, whereas Asian and Asian American students preferred Xanga and Friendster. Whereas Hargittai (2008) focused on the choice of a SNS, other authors compared the use of SNS. Dwyer, Hiltz, and Passerini (2007) for example compared trust and privacy concerns of Facebook and MySpace users. They found similar levels of privacy concerns, but higher trust in the SNS among the Facebook users. Fogel and Nehmad (2009) also found higher trust in Facebook than in MySpace. Tufekci (2008a) on the other hand found that more Facebook users used their real name, while more MySpace users restricted the access to their profile.

Some studies only reported different adoption patterns, but did not analyze in detail differences in usage (e.g. Shim, 2008, for Cyworld vs. Facebook in Korea vs. the USA). If differences in usage were studied, they were usually attributed to cultural differences. For example, Cho (2010) focused on the dimension individualism-collectivism and found that individuals from collectivistic cultures had more tight friendships on the SNS and lower levels of self-disclosure. Unfortunately, many of these studies suffer from small sample sizes or other problems, for an overview see Vitkauskaite (2010). Thus, there are only a few studies that explicitly compare different SNS because even when respondents used different sites, the data were often collapsed across SNS (Raacke & Bonds-Raacke, 2008; Utz & Beukeboom, 2011).

There are also not many comparison across time. Some authors describe the rise and fall of different SNS (Boyd & Ellison, 2007; Torkjazi, Rejaie, & Willinger, 2009) on a general level. For example, Friendster used to be very popular, then came MySpace and currently Facebook is the most dominant SNS worldwide. Real longitudinal studies are scarce. Steinfield et al. (2008) used a mixed design. They surveyed two random samples of students in subsequent years and sent the survey also to the ones who had completed the first wave. However, the focus of this study was to examine effects of SNS use and not so much comparison of SNS use across time. In another paper, Lampe, Ellison, and Steinfiled (2008) compared Facebook use over three years (2006 – 2008), using again data of American students. Within this time, several feature changes occurred: Facebook opened its network also to people outside of high schools and universities, news feed and mini-feeds were introduced, new privacy settings were made available, and the application platform was launched. Lampe et al. (2008) found that Facebook use remained consistent over time. For some items, there was an increase from 2006 to 2007, but values went down to the 2006 level in 2008. Number of Facebook friends and minutes per day on Facebook as well as agreement to statements like "Facebook is part of my everyday activity" increased between 2006 and 2007, but remained stable at this high level in 2008. Some differences, such as the expected visits from total strangers from the same university, can be explained with a change of the features, in this case, the removal of the "browse network" option. With regard to privacy settings, the number of users who used the default privacy settings dropped from 64% in 2006 to 45% and 48% in 2007 and 2008. Interestingly, privacy concerns did not change over the years.

A similar cross-sectional approach is taken in the present chapter. Dutch students were surveyed in 2009 and 2010. However, because Facebook gained popularity from 2009 to 2010, the present chapter does not only examine SNS use across years, but also across platforms.

Facebook is probably well-known because it is currently the largest SNS worldwide. It started in 2004 as a network only available for Harvard students that was later opened for all students of American universities. In September 2005, a high school version was launched, and since September 2006 it is open for everyone with a valid email-address aged 13 or older. Thus, Dutch students could only join Facebook from 2006 on. Facebook has currently (August 2011) more than 750 million active users. In 2009 when the first survey was taken, there were 300 million active users. Hyves was also founded in 2004. In August 2011, it had more than 11 million members. The majority are Dutch, and most communication is also in Dutch. The Netherlands have 16 million inhabitants, so Hyves is clearly the market leader in this country. Hyves is like Facebook a leisure-oriented SNS, and the features are quite similar. People create a profile, upload a picture and can fill in demographic data such as age, relationships status or education as well as interests, favorite movies, music, books, or brands. Moreover, they can connect to friends and acquaintances, and this network is displayed on the profile. Hyves users can also join groups or upload pictures and movies. The two SNS got even more similar when Hyves gave *buzz* a central place in 2008 and changed the profile page in 2009. *Buzz* is information about events in the social circle, a feature similar to the News Feed in Facebook. Before the change, this information had to be pulled from the profiles of friends. There are also some differences between the two platforms. On Facebook, social games such as FarmVille and MafiaWars and applications are more prominent, whereas Hyves offers its users the possibility to host their own blog on their profile, thereby instigating also longer communication. The mean age of the Hyves users was 23 in 2007 and is now 30, indicating that Hyves is no longer predominantly used by students. There are more female (56%) than male users (44%), and the average number of friends is 101 (130 on Facebook).

First, descriptive data on SNS adoption will be reported, and it will be examined whether users of different platforms and from different cohorts differ in important personality measures. Next, the paper will examine privacy concerns and settings before it focuses in more detail on self-centered and other-centered forms of usage.

With regard to time effects, different predictions can be made. SNS became more and more part of a daily routine, and this could be reflected in the frequency of use, the number of SNS friends or the level of self-disclosure. Dealing with privacy is also constantly in the flux. Utz and Krämer (2009) found that many Dutch SNS users restricted the access to their profiles to "only friends" but speculated that this might take some of the fun of SNS. Therefore, it could be that people change to "friends of friends" after a while. On the other hand, it could be that SNS are already so integrated into daily life that little differences occur. Lampe et al. (2008) did find much more changes between 2006 and 2007 than between 2007 and 2008. Hyves already started in 2004, so it could be that SNS use in the Netherlands already reached this stable level.

The chapter focuses on Dutch users, but there could still be differences between the platforms. The Netherlands are a small country (roughly 300km from North to South, 200 km from West to East), so it is easy to keep in touch if friends move to a different city. Facebook was in the beginning restricted to American high school students but became more and more international. Thus, it could be that Facebook attracts more open-minded and cosmopolitan people, whereas the more conservative and locally orientated people stay at Hyves. Communication on Hyves could be more cozy and intimate; this should be reflected in differences in self-disclosure.

METHOD

Samples

In 2009 (n = 194) and 2010 (n = 212), an online survey was held among all students who followed a course on interpersonal communication. Participation was part of course credit, therefore the sample is representative for communication science students. Although students of social sciences might not be representative for the whole population of the Netherlands, students still form a majority of SNS users.

Measures

- *Demographics.* Age and gender were assessed.
- *Personality characteristics.* The Big Five (extraversion, agreeableness, openness to experience, emotional stability, conscientiousness) were assessed with the ten-item short personality inventory by Gosling, Rentfrouw, and Swann (2003). Need to belong was measured with the scale by Leary, Kelly, Cottrell, and Schreindorfer (2001). To assess need for popularity, seven items of the scale by Santor, Messervey, and Kusumakar (2000) were used. Self-esteem was assessed with the scale by Rosenberg (1965). Answers were given on 7-point scales. *SNS adoption.* Respondents were presented with a list of SNS and asked to indicate on which of these they had a profile, which SNS they used regularly, and which of these SNS was their main SNS. They were then instructed to answer all following questions with regard to their main SNS.
- *SNS use.* Frequency of login (1 = less than once a month – 5 = several times a day) and duration of membership were assessed. The answer categories for the latter were 1= "since a few weeks", 2= "2-6 months", 3= "6-12 months", 4= "1-2 years", 5= "2-3years", and 6= "more than 3 years". Respondents also indicated the number of SNS friends. The Likert-items of the SNS intensity scale by Ellison et al. (2007) were used to measure the psychological meaning of SNS use. Example items are "My favorite SNS is part of my everyday activity."
- *Privacy concerns and settings.* To measure privacy concerns, respondents indicated their agreement with five statements like "Compared with other subjects on my mind, personal privacy is very important" on seven-point scales (partly based on Malhotra, Kim, & Agarwal, 2004). To assess privacy settings, they indicated for various categories such as pictures or email address who could view this part of their profile. The answer categories were "only friends", "friends of friends", "all members of the SNS", or "everybody".
- *Profile maintenance.* Respondents indicated how often they engaged in various behaviors such as "uploading pictures" or "updating their status". The scale ranged from 1= "almost never" to 7= "daily" (Utz & Beukeboom, 2011).
- *Strategic self-presentation.* Five items assessed how far people used the internet for strategic self presentation. An example is: "I use the internet to influence my image". Agreement was given on a 7-point scale. This scale was also used by Utz and Krämer (2009).
- *Manipulation of the profile.* Respondents were asked whether they exaggerate or make up information and whether they have ever purposely done something to

cool or popular on a SNS. These items were adapted from Zywica and Danowski (2008). Answer categories ranged from 1= "never" to 4= "often".

- *Self-disclosure*. Seventeen items tapped various aspects of self-disclosure. Respondents were asked how likely they were to talk about various topics. Answers were given on 7-point scales. Actual wall postings and status updates served as input for the development of the items. Exploratory factor analyses showed that they could be grouped into three scales. The first assessed self-disclosure about mainly positive events (e.g. holiday, accomplishments), the second captured self-disclosure about products or opinions (happiness or disappointment about products, political opinions), and the third assessed self-disclosure about feelings (e.g. falling in love, anger, shame).
- *Social grooming*. In a similar vein like the measurement of profile maintenance, respondents indicated how often they used SNS to maintain relationships. The scale contained six items; an example item is "leaving comments on the profiles of friends" (Utz & Beukeboom, 2011).
- *Reacting on other users*. Eight items assessed in more detail what triggered reactions on a SNS. Respondents were asked how likely they were to react to four different types of events: birthday, upload of nice pictures, when the target was happy or when the target was sad (according to the status update). Respondents answered these questions for two targets: a close friend and an acquaintance. Answers were given on 7-point scales ranging from 1= "very unlikely" to 7= "very likely".
- *Positive and negative consequences of SNS use*. In a similar vein it was assessed how people reacted on the comments of others. Respondents were asked how likely they were to become happy when close friends respectively acquaintances wrote on their wall or tried to cheer them up. Another four items captured negative aspects, e.g. "be disappointed because somebody does not accept your friendship invitation". Answers were again given on 7-point scales.

RESULTS

Comparison of the Samples

In both samples, about 71% of the respondents were female (2009: 71.1%, 2010: 71.7%), and the mean age was also virtually identical (*M*s = 21.41 and 21.45). As can be seen in Table 1, the two samples were also quite similar with regard to personality traits. Only for extraversion and emotional stability marginally significant differences occurred, $t(404) = 1.68, p < .10$ for extraversion and $t(404) = -1.69, p < .10$ for emotional stability. The participants in 2010 scored lower on extraversion, but higher on emotional stability. Because these differences are only marginally significant and point to opposite directions, it is assumed that the two samples are quite comparable with regard to gender distribution, age and basic personality characteristics.

SNS Adoption

In 2009, 91.8% of the respondents had a profile on at least one SNS. In 2010, this percentage was risen to 93.4%. Table 2 displays on which SNS the respondents had a profile, which of these profiles they used regularly and which SNS they used mainly.

Table 2 shows that people have accounts on several SNS. Only the four most often mentioned SNS are displayed in the table, but respondents also had accounts on a variety of smaller and/or less well-known SNS. Not all SNS were used

Table 1. Means and standard deviations for the personality characteristics of the two samples

	2009		2010	
	M	*SD*	*M*	*SD*
Big Five: extraversion	5.03	1.78	4.83	1.20
Big Five: agreeableness	4.35	0.75	4.38	0.75
Big Five: conscientiousness	4.92	1.28	5.01	1.14
Big Five: openness to experience	5.26	1.00	5.25	1.04
Big Five: emotional stability	4.68	1.28	4.88	1.10
Self-esteem	5.36	0.87	5.33	0.87
Need to belong	4.54	0.75	4.59	0.84
Need for popularity	2.82	1.03	2.71	1.10
Satisfaction with life	4.97	1.11	5.10	1.08

regularly, but the majority of the respondents used at least one SNS regularly. Moreover, there was a clear move from Hyves to Facebook. Although many respondents still had a Hyves account in 2010, more and more used Facebook regularly and half of them identified Facebook as their main SNS in 2010.

To check whether the regular users use several SNS regularly, or whether they visit only one SNS regularly, the crossed distribution of platform and regular use was calculated. An interesting change over time occurred. In 2009, only 20% of the respondents who used Hyves regularly also used Facebook regularly, whereas almost 60% focused on one SNS (48% Hyves, 11% Facebook). In 2010, 36% used both SNS regularly. The percentage of users focusing on one SNS has decreased to 47% and the preference has shifted to Facebook (19% Hyves, 28% Facebook).

SNS Use and Personality

First, it was examined whether people who have a profile on at least one SNS differ from people who do not have a profile on at least one SNS. Less than 10% of the respondents had no profile, therefore, the samples were collapsed across both years.

Comparisons with the Big Five, need to belong, need for popularity, and self-esteem as dependent variable showed that SNS users differed from non-users only in their need to belong, $F(1,403) = 4.67, p < .05$, and self-esteem, $F(1,403) = 11.18, p < .05$. SNS users had a higher need to belong ($M = 4.59$) than non-users ($M = 4.26$). At the same time, they had a lower self-esteem ($M = 5.30$) than non-users ($M = 5.85$).

Next, it was examined whether Hyves and Facebook attract different people. Differences between Hyves and Facebook users would indicate selection effects. There were no gender effects, but Facebook attracted older individuals ($M = 22.25$) than Hyves ($M = 20.78$), $F(1,354) = 14.36, p < .001$.

With regard to the personality measures, there were only two marginal effects. Hyves users tended to be more extravert ($M = 5.03$) than Facebook users ($M = 4.80$), $F(1,355) = 3.05, p < .10$, whereas Facebook users tended to score higher on openness to experience ($M = 5.35$) than Hyves users ($M = 5.17$), $F(1,355) = 2.77, p < .10$.

Table 2. SNS adoption across the two samples

	2009			2010		
	Have a profile	**Use regularly**	**Main SNS**	**Have a profile**	**Use regularly**	**Main SNS**
Hyves	86.1%	67.5%	79.2%	81.6%	55.2%	**45.5%**
Facebook	49.0%	30.9%	15.7%	74.1%	64.2%	**50.0%**
MySpace	9.3%	1.0%	0%	6.6%	0.5%	**0.5%**
LinkedIn	13.4%	5.7%	2.2%	20.3%	5.7%	**1.5%**

The latter makes sense when one considers that Hyves was the dominant Dutch SNS and Facebook is the newcomer. People with a high openness to experience are more willing to try out new online environments.

SNS Usage Statistics

After having established that the two samples are not fundamentally different on important personality characteristics, I now turn to the question how SNS use differs across time and platform.

First, the effects of time and platform on the very general usage indicators duration of membership and login frequency were examined. With regard to duration of membership, an effect of time occurred, $F(1,354) = 9.73$, $p < .01$. Not surprisingly, respondents of 2010 have been a member for a longer time ($M = 4.65$, corresponds to 2-3 years) than respondents from 2009 ($M = 4.19$, 1-2 years). There was also an effect of platform, $F(1,354) = 69.57$, $p < .001$. Respondents have been longer a member of Hyves ($M = 5.05$) than of Facebook ($M = 3.81$). These data are in line with the adoption rates and indicate again that Facebook gained popularity in the Netherlands during the last year.

For the login frequency, only an effect of platform was found. Facebook users logged in more often ($M = 4.12$) than Hyves users ($M = 3.73$), $F(1,354) = 7.43$, $p < .01$. This result also implies that Hyves is losing users whereas Facebook is gaining in attractiveness. However, Hyves users still reported more friends ($M = 256$) than Facebook users ($M = 200$), $F(1,354) = 9.35$, $p < .01$. When SNS intensity, the variable that captures more the psychological meaning of SNS use, was used as dependent variable, a crossover interaction between time and platform was found, $F(1,353) = 5.50$, $p < .001$. Whereas the intensity of Hyves use dropped from 2009 to 2010 (*M*s = 2.70 and 2.49, respectively), the intensity of Facebook use increased (*M*s = 2.45 and 2.69, respectively).

Privacy Settings and Privacy Concerns

There were no effects of time or platform on privacy settings, all *F*s < 1. In line with earlier findings by Utz and Krämer (2009), people protected their profiles. Email address and cell phone number were the most protected elements of a profile; about 85% of the respondents made those only available for friends. Roughly 55% of the respondents made also pictures, wall postings and status updates only available for friends, another 20% granted also friends of friends access to these data. Only about 10% of the respondents had a completely public profile.

Interestingly, there were differences in privacy concerns. A main effect of time, $F(1,354) = 6.80$, $p < .05$, indicated that privacy concerns were higher in 2009 ($M = 4.27$) than in 2010 ($M = 3.90$). A main effect of platform, $F(1,354) = 7.02$, $p < .05$ showed that Facebook users ($M = 4.27$) were more concerned than Hyves users ($M = 3.90$). However, these two main effects were qualified by a marginally significant interaction, $F(1,354) = 3.60$, $p < .10$ showing that Facebook users in 2009 ($M = 4.59$) differed from the other three groups (all *M*s between 3.85 an 3.95). In 2009, only 28 people used mainly Facebook, so this interaction should be treated with some caution.

Self-Centered SNS Use

The dataset contained several indicators of self-centered use: the scale profile maintenance that captured self-centered behaviors such as uploading pictures or updating the status updates, strategic self-presentation, a scale measuring the *motivation* to deliberately use the internet to present oneself in a favorable way, two items on the tendency to exaggerate information/make up information as more *behavioral* indicators and self-disclosure as more content-related measures.

Login frequency was included as a covariate in the following analyses because Facebook users were more active on their SNS. For profile maintenance, marginal effects of platform and time occurred that were qualified by the marginal two-way interaction between these two variables, $Fs(1,353) = 3.51$, 2.93, and 3.26, respectively, all $p < .10$. Facebook users engaged in 2009 ($M = 2.63$) more often in profile maintenance than Hyves users ($M = 2.25$) did. In 2010, this difference was no longer significant and Facebook users decreased their engagement in profile building to the same level as Hyves users ($Ms = 2.27$ and 2.26, respectively). In 2009, only a small group of early adopters used Facebook. They were obviously very active in creating their new profile.

There were no significant effects of time and/or platform on strategic self-presentation, all $Fs < 1.23$, or manipulation of the profile, all $Fs < 1$. In general, respondents did neither agree nor disagree with the items assessing the deliberate use of the internet for self-presentation ($M = 3.91$ on a 7-point scale), and they also did not exaggerate information ($M = 1.12$) or put purposely things on the SNS to look cool ($M = 1.49$ on 4-point scales from 1= "never" to 4= "often").

In Table 3, the means for all four groups and the three self-disclosure scales are displayed. As can be seen, most SNS users talk about positive experiences. Products/opinions and feelings are less often discussed.

The analyses showed time effects for self-disclosure of positive experiences, $F(1,354) = 4.57$, $p < .05$, and self-disclosure of products, $F(1,354) = 4.31$, $p < .05$. People in 2010 disclosed more about positive experiences ($M = 4.05$) and products/opinions ($M = 2.78$) than they did in 2009 ($Ms = 3.60$ and 2.42, respectively). There was no difference in the disclosure of feelings ($Ms = 2.30$ and 2.24). There were also main effects of platform. Facebook users disclosed more about products/opinions ($M = 3.02$) and their feelings ($M = 2.47$) than Hyves users did ($Ms = 2.18$ for products/opinions and 2.08 for feelings), $F(1,353) = 22.90$, $p < .001$ and $F(1,353) = 6.38$, $p < .001$.

Table 3. Self-disclosure across time and platform

	Hyves		Facebook	
	2009	2010	2009	2010
Positive experiences	3.53	3.95	3.66	4.16
Products and opinions	1.88	2.48	2.95	3.09
Feelings	1.97	2.19	2.51	2.42

Other-Centered Usage

For the scale social grooming, no significant effects occurred, all $Fs < 1$. Interestingly, users of both SNS engaged more in social grooming ($M = 3.81$) than in profile maintenance ($M = 2.28$).

To analyze social interactions in more detail, the eight items on reaction to other users were analyzed with a repeated measurements analyses of variance, treating event (birthday, uploaded pictures, happiness, sadness) and target (friend vs. acquaintance) as repeated measurements factor. Login frequency was included as a covariate to control for the higher activity of Facebook users.

As can be seen in Table 4, respondents were overall most likely to react on the birthday of a person, followed by comments on pictures. Reactions on emotions, either happiness or sadness, were least common, but did not differ from each other, $F(3,1059) = 56.18$, $p < .001$. There was also a clear main effect of target, $F(1,353) = 113.70$, $p < .001$, indicating that people are much more likely to react to a friend than to an acquaintance. A main effect of platform showed that Facebook users were more likely to react than Hyves users, $F(1,353) = 11.10$, $p < .001$. However, this effect was qualified by an interaction between platform and time, $F(1,353) = 7.05$, $p < .001$. The difference between platforms was mainly driven by the very active early Facebook adopters in 2009; in 2010, the differences between the two platforms decreased. Or, put in other words, Facebook users decreased social reactions, whereas Hyves users increased social reactions. An interaction effect between platform and event, $F(3,1059) = 5.05$, $p < .05$, further revealed that Hyves and Facebook users did not differ in reactions to birthdays, but that Facebook users were more likely to react to the other three types of events.

Next, the positive and negative consequences of social interactions on SNS were examined, again controlling for login frequency. For the positive consequences, a repeated analyses of variance showed mainly that people were more happy when they got reactions from a good friend ($M = 4.89$) than from an acquaintance ($M = 4.46$), $F(1,353) = 26.03$, $p < .001$. However, there were no effects of time and platform besides a difficult to interpret four-way interaction. There were also no significant effects of time or platform on negative consequences, all Fs < 1, and the mean of the scale was with $M = 3.38$ below the scale-midpoint.

DISCUSSION

This study compared SNS use of Dutch students across time and platforms. The results showed that Facebook gained popularity in the Netherlands. More respondents had an account, used it regularly or declared it as their favorite SNS in 2010 than in 2009. Facebook users were also more active on their SNS site: they logged in more frequently, worked more on their profile, disclosed more, and reacted more often to their friends. There were also some interesting time-effects, but they were often qualified by an interaction with platform and indicated that the small group of respondents who primarily used Facebook already in 2009, was a peculiar group of early adopters. They had higher privacy concerns and spent more time on creating and updating their profile. For both SNS, increases in self-disclosure about positive experiences and products or opinions over time were found.

Table 4. Reaction to other users as a function of time and platform

	Hyves		Facebook	
	2009	2010	2009	2010
Friend has birthday	5.61	5.74	5.74	5.63
uploads nice pictures	4.60	5.10	5.04	5.12
is happy	3.96	4.40	4.87	4.61
is sad	4.01	4.29	4.90	4.48
Acquaintance has birthday	4.23	4.27	4.73	4.30
uploads nice pictures	2.96	3.45	4.25	3.63
is happy	2.32	2.79	3.85	2.96
is sad	2.30	2.71	3.61	2.84

Personality and SNS Adoption

Interestingly, there was a significant difference between individuals who had a profile on at least one SNS and people who did not. SNS users had a higher need to belong and lower levels of self-esteem. This is an interesting finding that might indicate that there is a strong norm or peer pressure to be a member of a SNS. This is already expressed in the high adoption rate of more than 90%. Obviously, only people with a lower need to belong and at the same time a high self-esteem can resist the pressure to use SNS.

An alternative explanation is that SNS use lowers self-esteem and increases the need to belong. The latter would be somewhat counter-intuitive because SNS are mainly used to stay in touch with friends and acquaintances. However, it could be that these SNS contacts remain relatively superficial and that these superficial contacts increase the need for meaningful interpersonal relationships. If SNS use causes higher need to belong and lower self-esteem, the effects should be stronger for people who are more intensive users. Additional analyses showed that self-esteem and need to belong are unrelated to membership duration and login frequency. Thus, it seems rather a selection effect than a socialization effect.

Facebook and Hyves users differed only marginally in extraversion and openness to experience. Hyves users tended to be more extraverted, whereas Facebook users tended to be more open to experience. However, the 2009 sample was also marginally more extraverted, and then Hyves was the dominant SNS, so this might also be due to the sample. The latter finding confirms the expectation that the somewhat more traditional or conservative users stick to Hyves whereas the ones that like to try new things started to use Facebook. Facebook attracted also somewhat older users, probably because they have more international experiences and more friends that moved to a different city or country.

Many studies reported that SNS are part of the life of American students (Ellison et al., 2007; Lenhart & Madden, 2007; Ross et al., 2009); the current results show that the same holds true for Dutch students of social sciences. More than 90% had an account, and two-thirds were active on at least one SNS. The percentage of individuals who actively used both SNS also increased from 2009 to 2010. There are two possible explanations for this change. First, it could be due to the migration from Hyves to Facebook. Some friends are probably still on only one of the two SNS, so people need to use both SNS regularly if they want to stay in touch with all of their friends. Second, SNS use might have become such a routine that people easily manage to maintain several active accounts. SNS use can be time-consuming - two thirds log in daily or even several times a day - so it seems more plausible that people are active on both SNS because not all of their friends migrated to Facebook yet. However, future research is needed to answer this question.

Privacy Settings and Privacy Concerns

Interestingly, time and platform had no effect on privacy settings. However, the actual settings were even more restrictive than the ones reported by Utz and Krämer (2009). Utz and Krämer (2009) collected data among Hyves users in June 2008 and in September 2008. The present results are in line with the earlier finding that there is a shift towards more restrictive profiles. They are not in line with the conjecture that too much restriction might lessen the fun of social networking and result eventually in somewhat less restrictive privacy settings.

Surprisingly, there were differences in privacy concerns. Facebook users had higher privacy concerns than Hyves users, but this effect was mainly driven by differences in 2009. Facebook has more often been criticized for its treatment of privacy issues, and it was relatively new for the Dutch in 2009. Early adopters might also have had higher concerns because Facebook is larger, more international and more commercially orientated than Hyves, therefore the potential dangers of data misuse are also larger. However, in 2010, users of both platforms did no longer differ in their privacy concerns. Moreover, they scored slightly below the midpoint of the scale, indicating that Dutch students are not really concerned about privacy issues on the Internet.

Self-Centered SNS Use

The study also revealed interesting time and platform effects on self-disclosure. Facebook users showed higher levels of self-disclosure about positive experiences and feelings. In general, feelings were least disclosed, indicating that (semi-)public communication on SNS remains rather superficial. Still, it is interesting that the levels are higher on Facebook. It could have been expected that the smaller Dutch SNS provides a safer haven for self-disclosure. The data show that is the other way around. Probably people feel more safe on the more anonymous platform. Although not assessed, it seems plausible that Facebook users have a more heterogeneous network. Facebook users were also two years older, and are thus likely to have more international experiences and friends that moved away. Therefore, it might be more important for Facebook users to keep friends updated about what is going on in their life. This would also explain why there are no differences in self-disclosure on products or opinions. Talking about products and opinions is more closely related to profiling oneself as smart customer or influential person. Across time, the more self-promoting types of self-disclosure increased. Respondents disclosed more about positive experiences and products/opinions in 2010 than in 2009. This could indicate that people feel more comfortable on SNS, but it could also indicate that SNS create an optimal venue for narcissistic people that promote themselves.

Other-Centered SNS Use

As in other studies, it was also found for Dutch students that they use SNS mainly for the maintenance of relationships and less so for self-presentation. The scores on the scale social grooming were much higher than the ones on profile maintenance. However, a closer look at social interactions showed that the respondents mainly interacted with close friends. That people communicate more with close friends than with less close friends and weak acquaintances has been shown before, also for long-distance friendships (Utz, 2007). However, it is often argued that SNS are especially useful for maintaining weak ties (Ellison et al., 2007). Facebook and Hyves did not distinguish between close friends and acquaintances; the status updates of all people in the network are displayed equally in the News Feed. Therefore, SNS would offer an easy tool to also react on the events in the life of acquaintances. Interestingly, people still differentiate between their SNS friends and interact mainly within the circle of close friends.

There was an interesting discrepancy between Facebook and Hyves users in the type of reactions. Both groups were most likely to react to the birthday of another person, but Facebook users reacted significantly more often to other events such as nice pictures, happiness or sadness of the target than Hyves users did. Facebook seems to be more social than Hyves. However, there is also an interesting development over time: Facebook users reacted less to their SNS friends, whereas Hyves users interacted more. This pattern could be explained by the fact that Facebook was used in 2009 only by a small group of very active early adopters, and a feature change in Hyves. In 2009, Facebook already had News feeds which pushed information about SNS friends in the profile, whereas Hyves users had to visit the profiles of their friends to get the latest information. However, a few weeks after the data collection in 2009, Hyves introduced a new homepage. Since then, buzz, a feature similar to the News Feed on Facebook, is directly displayed when a user logs in. If information is directly presented when people log in, they are obviously more likely to react on it than when they first have to pull it from the friend's profile.

In general, respondents were least likely to react when a SNS friend indicated to be sad. There are two alternative explanations for this finding. First, it could be that SNS communication is rather superficial, and the goal is more to keep others in the loop and stay in touch, but not to provide social support. Therefore, people do not engage in comforting others. The second explanation is that people do care, but use different media or even face-to-face contacts to comfort their friends. This would be in line with earlier findings on long-distance friendships. Although people communicated with close friends more across different media, the more intimate topics were discussed via the phone and not via email (Utz, 2007).

Respondents did not only react more to friends than to acquaintances, they also become more happy when they received messages from a close friend than when they received messages from an acquaintance. Anecdotal evidence oven suggests that SNS allow people to re-connect with lost contacts, but the present results suggest that people are in general more happy when they interact with their close friends. Again, this suggests that SNS are mainly used for staying in the loop. People like the gossip character, getting information and some ambient awareness of what their acquaintances are doing, but they do not want to engage in conversations or intensify the relationship. This can be a useful strategy because having intimate conversation with hundreds of SNS friends might go beyond the cognitive capacity of individuals. Thus, the main function of SNS with regard to weak ties seems to be to stay in touch and to be able to re-activate the ties easily when – but only when – necessary.

Variables not Affected by Time or Platform

Despite the reported differences, there were also many variables on which no effects of time and platform occurred: privacy settings, strategic self-presentation, manipulation of information, social grooming, and positive as well as negative consequences of interactions on SNS. Thus, people use both platforms in a similar way, and although they are somewhat more active on Facebook, they receive similar benefits. It seems that the preference for a certain SNS is rather driven by the current trend and the critical amount of friends on the platform, but not so much by the features of the SNS. Friendster was replaced by MySpace, which was then overtaken by Facebook. In this regard, SNS seem to be rather common-bond than common-identity groups (Prentice, Miller, & Lightdale, 1994; Ren, Kraut, & Kiesler, 2007). In common-bond groups, attachment to the group is based on interpersonal relationships, whereas it is based on the group prototype in common-identity groups. As a consequence, people migrate easily to a different group when the most popular member of a common-bond group moves on to another group. Members of common-identity groups stay because they identify with the goals and norms of the group.

LIMITATIONS AND FUTURE RESEARCH DIRECTIONS

Although this study revealed interesting results, there are also some limitations. In 2009, the group of Facebook users was relatively small, so some of the platform effects should be viewed with caution. Moreover, only students of the social sciences were in the sample. All students following a specific course participated, so the results do not suffer from self-selection and can be generalized to this population. However, the results might not hold for all SNS users. Students from other faculties might show slightly different behavior, and students' SNS use might differ from the SNS use of working individuals (Watkins & Lee, 2010). Almost no respondent used the business network LinkedIn as main SNS; this might be different for the working population. Also, more and more elder people start to use SNS, and they might also use them in a different way. Another limitation is that about 70% of the sample were female. Males and females might differ in their SNS use. The focus of this chapter was comparison across time and platform within a specific user group, but future research should conduct similar comparisons with broader samples and look also at gender differences. Another limitation is the cross-sectional design. A similar group of students was surveyed in each year, but real longitudinal studies would be even better suited to capture changes in SNS use. The sample consisted of Dutch students or at least of students living in the Netherlands. The Netherlands are a small country; thus it is easier to stay in touch with friends who moved to a different city. The role of SNS in maintaining weak ties might therefore be more important for people from larger countries or with a more international network. The Netherlands have an individualistic culture which is at the same time characterized by low power distance and low masculinity. Future research could examine whether the same patterns are found in more collectivistic cultures or cultures with a higher power distance.

The study found some interesting results that can instigate further research. First, it is not clear yet whether Facebook really induces more activity of whether the higher activity on Facebook is caused by its current popularity. More studies in the following years are needed.

Although SNS are an optimal venue to stay in touch with weak ties, respondents used them primarily to communicate with close friends. Future research could examine the communicative functions of SNS in more detail. It seems as if people want to keep updated about the lives of their acquaintances, but do not want to engage in too much conversation or intensify the relationship. Respondents, especially Hyves users, did also react more on birthdays than on the emotions of their friends or acquaintances. One post-hoc explanation was that people might use other media to comfort their friends. Media-choice studies that examine which media are selected for specific purpose are needed to confirm this explanation. Media choice studies have a long tradition, but have not included SNS so far.

Another interesting finding that deserves more research is the increase in self-disclosure over time. Especially self-disclosure about positive experiences increased. This could be an indicator that SNS indeed increase narcissism (Rosen, 2007). The present study relied on self report; future research could take a more qualitative approach and analyze self-disclosure in status updates in more detail. It would also be interesting to examine the relationships between self-disclosure and narcissism or need for popularity. Privacy concerns and settings could also be an influence factor.

During the research period, Hyves introduced more and more features that are similar to the ones in Facebook; both platforms are leisure-oriented SNS and they dominated their local market. Future research should examine also the use of smaller niche-SNS that differentiate themselves more clearly from Facebook.

SNS are constantly changing. For example, while I was writing this book chapter, Facebook announced new profile pages for 2011; the first users could already test these profiles. School and current work shall be displayed more centrally in the basic information section and accompanied by pictures the person was recently tagged with. Moreover, it should be possible to highlight important friends. As the discussion section of the announcement on http://blog.facebook.com/blog.php?post=462201327130 shows, not all people were happy with these changes. Regardless of the question whether Facebook will take the comments of the users serious, this is just one example of the permanent change of SNS and their central features. Introducing new features or displaying other information more centrally can alter the social processes on a specific SNS, but can also influence migration pattern from one SNS to the other. Future studies should thus examine the interplay between technological features and social and psychological processes.

CONCLUSION

This study compared SNS use across time and platform and documented the migration of Dutch students from Hyves to Facebook. The paper contributed to the field of SNS research in several ways. It reports detailed descriptive data about the SNS use by Dutch students. According to Parks (2008), descriptive analyses of the SNS use of specific populations are missing; instead, the literature often focuses on the very active users. Till now, there are also only a few studies that examine SNS use over time. By focusing on Dutch students, the paper also allows to test the generalizability of findings that are based on American college students. The comparison across the two platforms also allows to test the universality of earlier findings on SNS use.

There were several interesting findings. A first important finding was that SNS users had lower levels of self-esteem and a higher need to belong than non-users, indicating that there is some social pressure to become a member of a SNS. For the majority of the respondents, SNS use is part of the daily routine. SNS use remained also relatively stable over time, indicating again that SNS are no longer a new medium for Dutch students. The privacy settings have also become even stricter. This implies that students are well aware of the dangers of making personal information or compromising pictures public.

The only change over time was an increase in self-disclosure. People did not talk so much about feelings, but about self-promoting topics such as positive experiences or products and opinions. Thus, the function of self-disclosure on SNS seems to be positive self-presentation rather than creating intimacy. Nevertheless, respondents engaged more in social grooming than in profile maintenance. However, they communicated mostly with close friends. Again, respondents were more likely to react when the friend had birthday or has uploaded nice pictures, but not when the friend expressed feelings. The semi-public communication on SNS is thus rather superficial. People like to passively read what their acquaintances are doing, but they do not use the potential of SNS to intensify the relationships with acquaintances by actively reacting on comments and status updates. It might be interesting to examine in a few years whether active SNS users are better able to reactivate social capital from their weak ties than less active SNS users or non-users.

There were also clear differences between platforms. Facebook users logged in more often. Even when controlling for login frequency, they showed higher levels of self-disclosure, but gave also more social support to their SNS friends. These two processes might also intensify each other – if there is more self-disclosure, there is also more to react on. These differences cannot be explained by cultural differences because all participants were Dutch or lived at least in the Netherlands. Thus, the differences in usage might reflect different norms; in Facebook, social interaction seems to play a more important role.

Taken together, the results suggest that SNS have become an indispensable tool for many Dutch students. They are used for interaction with close friends and keeping informed about acquaintances. However, which SNS is used is influenced by the current fashion. Future research will show whether Facebook will stay the most popular SNS.

REFERENCES

Altman, I., & Taylor, D. (1973). *Social penetration: The development of interpersonal relationships*. New York, NY: Holt, Rinehart, & Winston.

Amichai-Hamburger, Y., & Vinitzky, G. (2010). Social network use and personality. *Computers in Human Behavior*, *26*, 1289–1295. doi:10.1016/j.chb.2010.03.018

Back, M., Stopfer, J., Vazire, S., Gaddis, S., Schmukle, S., & Egloff, B. (2010). Facebook profiles reflect actual personality, not self-idealization. *Psychological Science*, *21*(3), 372–374. doi:10.1177/0956797609360756

Barnes, S. (2006). A privacy paradox: Social networking in the United States. *First Monday*, *11*(9), 11–15.

Bellur, S., Oeldorf-Hirsch, A., & High, A. (2008). *Misery doesn't love company: An exploration of emotional bandwidth on online social networks*. Paper presented at the annual meeting of the International Communication Association, Montreal, Canada.

boyd, D., & Ellison, N. (2007). Social network sites: Definition, history, and scholarship. *Journal of Computer-Mediated Communication*, *13*(1), 210–230.

Buffardi, L. E., & Campbell, W. K. (2008). Narcissism and social networking web sites. *Personality and Social Psychology Bulletin*, *34*(10), 1303–1314. doi:10.1177/0146167208320061

Cho, S. (2010). *A cross-cultural comparison of Korean and American social network sites: Exploring cultural differences in social relationships and self-presentation*. New Brunswick, NJ: Rutgers State University.

Christofides, E., Muise, A., & Desmarais, S. (2009). Information disclosure and control on Facebook: Are they two sides of the same coin or two different processes? *Cyberpsychology & Behavior*, *12*(3), 341–345. doi:10.1089/cpb.2008.0226

Debatin, B., Lovejoy, J., Horn, A., & Hughes, B. (2009). Facebook and online privacy: Attitudes, behaviors, and unintended consequences. *Journal of Computer-Mediated Communication*, *15*(1), 83–108. doi:10.1111/j.1083-6101.2009.01494.x

Donath, J. (2007). Signals in social supernets. *Journal of Computer-Mediated Communication*, *13*(1), 231–251. doi:10.1111/j.1083-6101.2007.00394.x

Dwyer, C., Hiltz, S., & Passerini, K. (2007). *Trust and privacy concern within social networking sites: A comparison of Facebook and MySpace.* Paper presented at the AMCIS 2007, Keystone, CO.

Ellison, N., Steinfield, C., & Lampe, C. (2007). The benefits of Facebook "friends:" Social capital and college students' use of online social network sites. *Journal of Computer-Mediated Communication*, *12*(4), 1143–1168. doi:10.1111/j.1083-6101.2007.00367.x

Fogel, J., & Nehmad, E. (2009). Internet social network communities: Risk taking, trust, and privacy concerns. *Computers in Human Behavior*, *25*(1), 153–160. doi:10.1016/j.chb.2008.08.006

Gosling, S. D., Gaddis, D., & Vazire, S. (2007). *Personality impressions based on Facebook profiles.* Paper presented at the ICWSM, Boulder, Colorado, USA.

Gosling, S. D., Rentfrow, P. J., & Swann, W. B. (2003). A very brief measure of the Big-Five personality domains. *Journal of Research in Personality*, *37*(6), 504–528. doi:10.1016/S0092-6566(03)00046-1

Gross, R., & Acquisti, A. (2005). *Information revelation and privacy in online social networks.* Paper presented at the ACM, Alexandria, VA.

Krämer, N. C., & Winter, S. (2008). Impression management 2.0: The relationship of self-esteem, extraversion, self-efficacy, and self-presentation within social networking sites. *Journal of Media Psychology: Theories, Methods, and Applications*, *20*(3), 106–116. doi:10.1027/1864-1105.20.3.106

Krasnova, H., Spiekermann, S., Koroleva, K., & Hildebrand, T. (2010). Online social networks: Why we disclose. *Journal of Information Technology*, *25*(2), 109–125. doi:10.1057/jit.2010.6

Lampe, C., Ellison, N., & Steinfield, C. (2008). *Changes in use and perception of Facebook.* Paper presented at the CSCW, San Diego, CA.

Leary, M., Kelly, K., Cottrell, C., & Schreindorfer, L. (2001). *Individual differences in the need to belong: Mapping the nomological network*. Unpublished Paper. Wake Forest University.

Lenhart, A., & Madden, M. (2007). *Teens, privacy & online social networks: How teens manage their online identities and personal information in the age of MySpace*. Retrieved December 8, 2010, from http://www.pewinternet.org/Reports/2007/Teens-Privacy-and-Online-Social-Networks.aspx?r=1

Lewis, K., Kaufman, J., & Christakis, N. (2008). The taste for privacy: An analysis of college student privacy settings in an online social network. *Journal of Computer-Mediated Communication*, *14*, 79–100. doi:10.1111/j.1083-6101.2008.01432.x

Livingstone, S. (2006). Children's privacy online: experimenting with boundaries within and beyond the family. In Kraut, R., Brynin, M., & Kiesler, S. (Eds.), *Computers, phones, and the Internet: Domesticating Information Technology* (pp. 128–144). Oxford, UK: Oxford University Press.

Livingstone, S. (2008). Taking risky opportunities in youthful content creation: Teenagers' use of social networking sites for intimacy, privacy, and self-expression. *New Media & Society, 10*(3), 393–411. doi:10.1177/1461444808089415

Malhotra, N. K., Kim, S. S., & Agarwal, J. (2004). Internet users' information privacy concerns (IUIPC): The construct, the scale, and a causal model. *Information Systems Research, 15*(4), 336–355. doi:10.1287/isre.1040.0032

Mehdizadeh, S. (2010). Self-presentation 2.0: Narcissism and self-esteem on Facebook. *Cyberpsychology, Behavior, and Social Networking, 13*(4), 357–364. doi:10.1089/cyber.2009.0257

Mesch, G. S., & Beker, G. (2010). Are norms of disclosure of online and offline personal information associated with the disclosure of personal information online? *Human Communication Research, 36*(4), 570–592. doi:10.1111/j.1468-2958.2010.01389.x

Muise, A., Christofides, E., & Desmarais, S. (2009). More information than you ever wanted: Does Facebook bring out the green-eyed monster of jealousy? *Cyberpsychology & Behavior, 12*(4), 441–444. doi:10.1089/cpb.2008.0263

Parks, M. R. (2008). *Characterizing the communicative affordances of MySpace: A place for friends or a friendless place?* Paper presented at the annual meeting of the International Communication Association, Montreal, Canada.

Parks, M. R. (2010). *Who are Facebook friends? Exploring the composition of Facebook friend networks.* Paper presented at the Annual Meeting of the International Communication Association, Singapore, Singapore.

Prentice, D., Miller, D., & Lightdale, J. (1994). Asymmetries in attachments to groups and to their members: Distinguishing between common-identity and common-bond groups. *Personality and Social Psychology Bulletin, 20*(5), 484–493. doi:10.1177/0146167294205005

Putnam, R. (2000). *Bowling alone: The collapse and revival of American community.* Simon and Schuster.

Raacke, J., & Bonds-Raacke, J. (2008). MySpace and Facebook: Applying the uses and gratifications theory to exploring friend-networking sites. *Cyberpsychology & Behavior, 11*(2), 169–174. doi:10.1089/cpb.2007.0056

Ren, Y., Kraut, R., & Kiesler, S. (2007). Applying common bond and identity theory to design of online communities. *Organization Studies, 28*, 377–408. doi:10.1177/0170840607076007

Rosen, C. (2007). Virtual friendship and the new narcissism. *New Atlantis (Washington, D.C.), 17*(Summer), 15–31.

Rosenberg, M. (1965). *Society and the adolescent self-image.* Princeton, NJ: Princeton University Press.

Ross, C., Orr, E. S., Sisic, M., Arseneault, J. M., Simmering, M. G., & Orr, R. R. (2009). Personality and motivations associated with Facebook use. *Computers in Human Behavior, 25*(2), 578–586. doi:10.1016/j.chb.2008.12.024

Santor, D. A., Messervey, D., & Kusumakar, V. (2000). Measuring peer pressure, popularity, and conformity in adolescent boys and girls: Predicting school performance, sexual attitudes, and substance abuse. *Journal of Youth and Adolescence*, *29*(2), 163–182. doi:10.1023/A:1005152515264

Shim, J. (2008). Social networking sites: A brief comparison of usage in the US and Korea. *Decision Line*, *39*(5), 16–18.

Siibak, A. (2009). Constructing the self through the photo selection-visual impression management on Social Networking Websites. *Cyberpsychology: Journal of Psychosocial Research on Cyberspace*, *3*(1). Retrieved December 9, 2010, from http://cyberpsychology.eu/view.php?cisloclanku=2009061501&article=1

Steinfield, C., Ellison, N. B., & Lampe, C. (2008). Social capital, self-esteem, and use of online social network sites: A longitudinal analysis. *Journal of Applied Developmental Psychology*, *29*(6), 434–445. doi:10.1016/j.appdev.2008.07.002

Thelwall, M. (2008). Social networks, gender, and friending: An analysis of MySpace member profiles. *Journal of the American Society for Information Science and Technology*, *59*(8), 1321–1330. doi:10.1002/asi.20835

Tong, S. T., Van Der Heide, B., Langwell, L., & Walther, J. B. (2008). Too much of a good thing? The relationship between number of friends and interpersonal impressions on Facebook. *Journal of Computer-Mediated Communication*, *13*(3), 531–549. doi:10.1111/j.1083-6101.2008.00409.x

Torkjazi, M., Rejaie, R., & Willinger, W. (2009). *Hot today, gone tomorrow: On the migration of MySpace users*. Paper presented at the 2nd ACM Workshop on Online Social Networks, Barcelona, Spain.

Tufekci, Z. (2008a). Can you see me now? Audience and disclosure regulation in online social network sites. *Bulletin of Science, Technology & Society*, *28*(1), 20–36. doi:10.1177/0270467607311484

Tufekci, Z. (2008b). Grooming, gossip, Facebook and Myspace. *Information Communication and Society*, *11*(4), 544–564. doi:10.1080/13691180801999050

Utz, S. (2007). Media use in long-distance friendships. *Information Communication and Society*, *10*(5), 694–713. doi:10.1080/13691180701658046

Utz, S. (2010). Show me your friends and I will tell you what type of person you are: How one's profile, number of friends, and type of friends influence impression formation on social network sites. *Journal of Computer-Mediated Communication*, *15*(2), 314–335. doi:10.1111/j.1083-6101.2010.01522.x

Utz, S., & Beukeboom, C. (2011). The role of social network sites in romantic relationships: Effects on jealousy and relationship happiness. *Journal of Computer-Mediated Communication*, *16*(4), 511–527. doi:10.1111/j.1083-6101.2011.01552.x

Utz, S., & Krämer, N. (2009). The privacy paradox on social network sites revisited: The role of individual characteristics and group norms. *Cyberpsychology: Journal of Psychosocial Research on Cyberspace*, *3*(2). Retrieved December 9, 2010, from http://cyberpsychology.eu/view.php?cisloclanku=2009111001&article=2

Valenzuela, S., Park, N., & Kee, P. F. (2009). Is there social capital in a social network site? Facebook use and college students' life satisfaction, trust, and participation. *Journal of Computer-Mediated Communication*, *14*, 875–901. doi:10.1111/j.1083-6101.2009.01474.x

Vitkauskaite, E. (2010). Overview of research on cross-cultural impact on social networking sites. *Ekonomika ir vadyba, 15*, 844-848.

Walther, J. B., Van Der Heide, B., & Hamel, L., M., & Shulman, H. C. (2009). Self-generated versus other-generated statements and impressions in computer-mediated communication: A test of warranting theory using Facebook. *Communication Research*, *36*(2), 229–253. doi:10.1177/0093650208330251

Walther, J. B., Van Der Heide, B., Kim, S.-Y., Westerman, D., & Tong, S. T. (2008). The role of friends' appearance and behavior on evaluations of individuals on Facebook: Are we known by the company we keep? *Human Communication Research*, *34*(1), 28–49. doi:10.1111/j.1468-2958.2007.00312.x

Watkins, C. S., & Lee, E. H. (2010). *Got Facebook? Investigating what's social about social media.* Retrieved December 9, 2010, from http://www.theyoungandthedigital.com/wp-content/uploads/2010/11/watkins_lee_facebookstudy-nov-18.pdf

Wehrli, S. (2008). *Personality on social network sites: An application of the five factor model.*

Young, A. L., & Quan-Haase, A. (2009). *Information revelation and internet privacy concerns on social network sites: A case study of Facebook.* Paper presented at the Fourth International Conference on Communities and Technologies, University Park, PA.

Zhao, S., Grasmuck, S., & Martin, J. (2008). Identity construction on Facebook: Digital empowerment in anchored relationships. *Computers in Human Behavior*, *24*(5), 1816–1836. doi:10.1016/j.chb.2008.02.012

Zywica, J., & Danowski, J. (2008). The faces of Facebookers: Investigating social enhancement and social compensation hypotheses; predicting Facebook and offline popularity from sociability and self-esteem, and mapping the meanings of popularity with semantic networks. *Journal of Computer-Mediated Communication*, *14*, 1–34. doi:10.1111/j.1083-6101.2008.01429.x

ADDITIONAL READING

Antheunis, M. L., Valkenburg, P. M., & Peter, J. (2010). Getting acquainted through social network sites: Testing a model of online uncertainty reduction and social attraction. *Computers in Human Behavior*, *26*(1), 100–109. doi:10.1016/j.chb.2009.07.005

Back, M., Stopfer, J., Vazire, S., Gaddis, S., Schmukle, S., & Egloff, B. (2010). Facebook profiles reflect actual personality, not self-idealization. *Psychological Science*, *21*(3), 372–374. doi:10.1177/0956797609360756

Baker, L. R., & Oswald, D. L. (2010). Shyness and online social networking services. *Journal of Social and Personal Relationships*, *27*(7), 873–889. doi:10.1177/0265407510375261

boyd, d. (2006). Friends, friendsters, and top 8: writing community into being on social network sites. *First Monday*, *11*(2). Retrieved January 23, 2011 from http://firstmonday.org/htbin/cgiwrap/bin/ojs/index.php/fm/article/view/1418/1336

Burke, M., Marlow, C., & Lento, T. (2009). *Feed me: motivating newcomer contribution in social network sites.* Paper presented at the Proceedings of the 27th international conference on Human factors in computing systems, Boston, MA, USA.

Derlega, V., & Chaikin, A. (1977). Privacy and self-disclosure in social relationships. *The Journal of Social Issues*, *33*(3), 102–115. doi:10.1111/j.1540-4560.1977.tb01885.x

Donath, J., & boyd, D. (2004). Public displays of connection. *BT Technology Journal*, *22*(4), 71–82. doi:10.1023/B:BTTJ.0000047585.06264.cc

Gangadharbatla, H. (2008). Facebook Me: Collective Self-Esteem, Need to Belong, and Internet Self-Efficacy as Predictors of the iGeneration's Attitudes toward Social Networking Sites. *Journal of Interactive Advertising*, *8*(2), 1–28.

Hargittai, E. (2008). Whose space? Differences among users and non-users of social network sites. *Journal of Computer-Mediated Communication, 13*(1), 276–297. doi:10.1111/j.1083-6101.2007.00396.x

Jiang, L. C., Bazarova, N. N., & Hancock, J. T. (2011). The disclosure–intimacy link in computer-mediated communication: An attributional extension of the hyperpersonal model. *Human Communication Research, 37*(1), 58–77. doi:10.1111/j.1468-2958.2010.01393.x

Kim, J., & Lee, J.-E. R. The Facebook paths to happiness: Effects of the number of Facebook friends and self-presentation on subjective well-being. *Cyberpsychology, Behavior, and Social Networking, 0*(0), null.

Krasnova, H., Günther, O., Spiekermann, S., & Koroleva, K. (2009). Privacy concerns and identity in online social networks. *Identity in the Information Society, 2*(1), 39–63. doi:10.1007/s12394-009-0019-1

Krasnova, H., Kolesnikova, E., & Guenther, O. (2009). " It won't happen to me!": Self-disclosure in online social networks. *AMCIS 2009 Proceedings*, paper 343.

Ledbetter, A., Mazer, J., DeGroot, J., Meyer, K., Mao, Y., & Swafford, B. (2011). Attitudes toward online social connection and self-disclosure as predictors of Facebook communication and relational closeness. *Communication Research, 38*, 27–53. doi:10.1177/0093650210365537

Lee, D.-H., Im, S., & Taylor, C. R. (2008). Voluntary self-disclosure of information on the Internet: A multimethod study of the motivations and consequences of disclosing information on blogs. *Psychology and Marketing, 25*(7), 692–710. doi:10.1002/mar.20232

Mendelson, A., & Papacharissi, Z. (2010). Look at us: collective narcissism in college student Facebook photo galleries. In Papacharissi, Z. (Ed.), *A Networked Self: Identity, Connectivity and Culture on Social Network Sites*. New York: Routledge.

Mod, G. (2010). Reading romance: The impact Facebook rituals can have on a romantic relationship. *Journal of Comparative Research in Anthropology and Sociology, 1*(2), 61–77.

Neumann-Braun, K., & Autenrieth, U. P. (Eds.). (2011). *Freundschaft und Gemeinschaft im Social Web [Friendship and community in the social web]*. Baden-Baden: Nomos Edition Reinhard Fischer.

Orr, E. S., Sisic, M., Ross, C., Simmering, M. G., Arseneault, J. M., & Orr, R. R. (2009). The influence of shyness on the use of Facebook in an undergraduate sample. *Cyberpsychology & Behavior, 12*(3), 337–340. doi:10.1089/cpb.2008.0214

Papacharissi, Z. (2010). *A Networked Self: Identity, Community, and Culture on Social Network Sites*. Routledge.

Pempek, T. A., Yermolayeva, Y. A., & Calvert, S. L. (2009). College students' social networking experiences on Facebook. *Journal of Applied Developmental Psychology, 30*(3), 227–238. doi:10.1016/j.appdev.2008.12.010

Peter, J., Valkenburg, P. M., & Schouten, A. P. (2005). Developing a model of adolescent friendship formation on the Internet. *Cyberpsychology & Behavior, 8*(5), 423–430. doi:10.1089/cpb.2005.8.423

Pike, J., Bateman, P., & Butler, B. (2009). I didn't know you could see that: The effect of social networking environment characteristics on publicness and self-disclosure. *AMCIS 2009 Proceedings*, 421.

Urista, M., Dong, Q., & Day, K. (2009). Explaining why young adults use MySpace and Facebook through uses and gratifications theory. *Human Communication A Journal of the Pacific and Asian Communication Association, 12*(2), 215-230.

Utz, S. (2004). Enter your e-mail address: How German Internet users manage their e-mail addresses. *Cyberpsychology & Behavior, 7*(2), 241–246. doi:10.1089/109493104323024492

Utz, S. (2009). The (potential) benefits of campaigning via Social Network Sites. *Journal of Computer-Mediated Communication, 14*, 221–243. doi:10.1111/j.1083-6101.2009.01438.x

Viseu, A., Clement, A., & Aspinall, J. (2004). Situating Privacy Online. *Information Communication and Society, 7*(1), 92–114. doi:10.1080/1369118042000208924

Young, A. L., & Quan-Haase, A. (2009). *Information revelation and internet privacy concerns on social network sites: a case study of facebook.* Paper presented at the fourth international conference on Communities and technologies, University Park, PA, USA.

KEY TERMS AND DEFINITIONS

Hyves: The most popular SNS in the Netherlands. Hyves has more than 10 million registered users and is a leisure-oriented SNS.

Other-Centered SNS Use: Communicating with SNS friends and other SNS users (e.g. reading status updates, reacting on postings of SNS friends, initiating new relationships, joining groups).

Privacy Concerns: Being aware of the privacy risks that can arise from internet and social media use.

Privacy Settings: The profile settings people chose to determine who can view various parts of their profile (e.g. email address, birthday, address). Options are usually friends only, friends of friends, every user of the SNS, everyone.

Self-Centered SNS Use: Working on the own profile in order to present oneself in a desired way (choosing/changing a profile picture, uploading pictures, status updates, filling in fields in the profile).

Self-Disclosure: Revealing information about oneself, e.g., emotions, experiences, or attitudes.

Strategic Self-Presentation: Using the internet deliberately to create a favorable impression.

Chapter 7
Sociability in Social Network Sites:
Facebook as Trial Platform for Social Behavioral Patterns

Bernadette Kneidinger
University of Vienna, Austria

ABSTRACT

This chapter discusses the potential of social network sites (SNS) as sources for both social feedback and trial platforms for social behavioral patterns. With the findings of an online survey and 40 qualitative interviews of Facebook users, this chapter analyzes how social network sites are used for "communicative self-presentation" and how users provoke and handle positive as well as negative social reactions from other users that become part of their own identity presentations in the online network. Finally, the combination of studies shows that social feedback is not only one of the main motives for using SNS, but can also cause self-reflection processes in users. Additionally, it appears that men and women handle social feedback on SNS quite differently.

INTRODUCTION

Until recently, social networks were characterized by a diffuse and unseizable nature, a fact that has changed completely since the rapid increase of SNS on the internet. On these virtual platforms, users′ social relationship structures are manifested and become an integral part of users' self-presentations in the network. Therefore, it is not surprising that SNS have become a "social space" for more than 600 million Facebook users from all over the world. In what way do the online visualized relationship networks correspond with relationship structures in reality, and in what way

DOI: 10.4018/978-1-61350-338-6.ch007

do different identity facets and behavioral patterns in social relationship maintenance appear in the virtual environment compared to those in real life? These questions will be answered within this chapter by using the results of qualitative and quantitative surveys of Facebook users.

As an introduction, we start with an analysis of the main motives for using SNS like Facebook. It will be shown that SNS are used primarily for social reasons, especially the reactivation of former relationships and the fostering of existing relationships. In contrast, socializing with unknown people does not happen frequently on SNS but occurs rather often in real life.

Based on these initial findings of the survey that identify the maintenance of social contacts as the main motive for Facebook use, the question arises of how relationship-fostering really transpires on SNS. In what way can these online contacts be seen as sources of social feedback that form an important aspect of online and offline identity construction? Can gender-specific differences be observed in using Facebook as a channel for social feedback?

To answer these questions, usage habits of SNS are analyzed. It appears that interaction via the online social network is characterized by a merging of communication, information, and self-presentation, a characteristic that will be summarized in the chapter as "communicative self-presentation." Using the status message tool in Facebook as an example, it will be illustrated how certain features of Facebook can be used for communicative self-presentation. Furthermore, the analysis shows the dominance of personality-oriented messages that express either current activities or intimate feelings of the user. A variety of qualitative interviews with Facebook users reveals that the majority of status messages are published not just for the sake of publication itself but with a strong intention to provoke reactions and social feedback from other people. Thus, the online social network becomes a more or less protected trial platform for certain behavioral patterns, attitudes, and opinions (Döring, 2003; McKenna et al., 2002; Schachtner, 2008; Steinfield et al., 2008). As will be shown later in this chapter, the expectation of social feedback in response to publications forms one of the most important motivators for actively using the network (Ibrahim, 2009; Kollock, 1999; Kramer & Winter, 2008; Young, 2010).

Finally, based on these findings of the high significance of social feedback processes on SNS, we look at the question of how negative social reactions to publications and activities in the network are experienced and in the different ways men and women handle such negative feedback.

BACKGROUND

SNS: Both a Blessing and a Curse for Social Relationships?

The importance for social change that SNS have can be seen quite evidently in the statistics of the largest social network, Facebook. As of January 2011, Facebook has more than 600 million users who, on average, spend more than 700 billion minutes per month on the online social network (Facebook statistics, January 2011). Hence, Facebook is used intensively by an incredibly large group of people for networking and most of them see the internet as a "social space" where their social interactions take place to a bigger and bigger extent (Donath & boyd, 2004, p. 71). It is not surprising that the question arises how these forms of online-based networking can affect real-life social relationships and the individual identity construction process.

Opinions about that question are quite different. They range from technical critical views that fear the isolation and the loss of sense of reality of the users (Kraut et al., 1998) and describe computer-mediated communication as poor environments because of the lack of nonverbal cues (Daft & Lengel, 1984; Kiesler, Siegal, McGuire, 1984; Mesch & Talmud, 2006; van Dijk, 1999) and in consequence as impersonal, superficial, and hostile (Benninger, 1987; Berry, 1993) to very positive opinions that view SNS as a further step toward the democratization of society and the establishment of contacts and open-minded communication (Haste & Hogan, 2006; Rice & Love, 1987; Sproull & Kiesler 1986). Especially for people who have problems with social interactions, or who are confronted quite regularly with prejudices because they have some kind of disability, or who are timid or lack of self-confidence, SNS can form an ideal (trial-) platform for social interactions (Amichai-Hamburger & Ben Artzi, 2003; Donath & boyd, 2004; Mesch & Talmud, 2006, p. 30).

As a further aspect of the increasing significance of SNS, the transition from a traditional "community" to a "networked individualism" has to be mentioned (Von Kardorff, 2006, p. 80; Wellman, 2001a, 2001b). Wellman describes this as a transformation from "door-to-door" interactions ("little boxes"), which represent traditional face-to-face contacts, to "place-to-place" interactions that connect households via cheaper and faster transportation technologies as well as via the telephone ("glocalisation"). Finally, there are the "person-to-person" interactions ("networked individuals") that become possible due to mobile phones and mobile internet devices that can connect people with other people independently from the geographic location. (Chua et al., 2009, p. 4; Wellman, 2002; Wellman & Tindall, 1993). This expresses the trend moving away from traditional community construction toward egocentric networks. The individual stands at the core and the individual network is constructed around the person (Kayahara, 2006). For this reason, Wellman and Boase speak about "personal communities" (Wellman & Boase, 2004). The new networks are no longer space or time dependent; they are very flexible and often constructed at an individual's work station without any face-to-face interactions with other people. Because of such trends, the question arises in what way traditional concepts like "community", as defined by Toennis in his distinction between "Gemeinschaft" (community) and "Gesellschaft" (society) as groupings that are based on a shared feeling of togetherness (Toennies 1887), are still adequate and valid. Bauman also discusses the changing forms and significance of "community" as a place of security "in an insecure world" (Bauman 2001). Thiedke prefers the term "virtual collectivization" (Thiedke, 2008, p. 68) that results from changing communication opportunities and new life situations. It seems that "community" in the traditional sense only partially exists in an era of global social computer networks because it is no longer based on geographic closeness or regular face-to-face interactions, but nevertheless it allows similar feelings of belonging together. Although that cannot be equated with a real disappearance of social togetherness, it does mean a transformation of it. According to Wellman and Haythornthwaite, "The internet is not destroying community but it is responding to, resonating with, and extending the types of community that have already become prevalent in the developed Western world: for local and distant ties, strong and weak ties, kin and friends" (2001, p. 4). Thus, new forms of social togetherness seem to be developing, as Chua et al. (2009, p.5) highlight based on a range of empirical findings: "the internet is in fact seamlessly integrated with personal communities and is rarely a separate second life in itself" (cf. Boase et al., 2006; Quan-Haase & Wellman, 2008; Veenhof et al., 2008; Wang & Wellman, 2009; Wellman & Hogan, 2004).

Identity Construction in the Virtual World

Identity is an essential part of each human being and is constantly transformed and rebuilt during a lifetime and through interactions with other people (Arnett, 2000; Erikson, 1959; Giddens 1991). According to Bauman, identity becomes even more important in an era where "community" in the traditional sense is in danger because of globalization and changing political, technological and social environments (Bauman 2001). Additionally, identity is a multifaceted and fluid construct– depending on the interaction partners or situations, different aspects of one's identity are activated and shown (boyd, 2002; Jenkins, 2004). This indicates quite clearly that identity is a highly social construct because other people influence the identity with their more or less direct reactions or social feedback processes (Buckingham, 2008, p. 3; Goffman, 1981; Mead, 1988). Each human being has to be aware of what aspects of identity are necessary or acceptable in various social interaction situations. Children and teenagers especially test different forms of social behavioral patterns so that they can internalize what behavior is accepted or beneficial and what behavior causes problems, criticisms, or negative feedback (Swindler, 1986). In real life this process of identity construction appears in a quite subliminal way, but it becomes obvious on SNS where each user presents himself proverbially with his virtual profile (Salimkhan, Manago, & Greenfield, 2010). Almost all users try to describe themselves as positively as possible and create a self-image that provokes lots of positive social reactions. With the booming of social network sites, the virtual self-presentation becomes an integral part of one's identity management (Livingstone, 2008). SNS become quite similar to a "stage," as Goffman (1959, 1996) called it in his famous book "The Presentation of Self in Everyday Life." Willems & Pranz also see a "stage and dramaturgy of self-thematization" (2008, p. 189) in the internet.

As already mentioned, identity is a multifaceted construct and SNS offer many tools to represent oneself (Manago, Graham, Greenfield, & Salimkhan, 2008). It starts with the opportunity to represent oneself with a profile picture that forms the equivalent to the first impression we get from someone we meet for the first time in real life. Additionally, users can post other photos or videos which show themselves, but also other people, their pets, or holiday pictures - all things that are important to the users and say something about them (Mikkola et al., 2008). The selection of photos happens quite consciously; users always intend to show themselves as attractively and interestingly as possible (Siibak, 2009; Strano, 2008). In this way, users can create a visualization of their identity.

Identity construction happens in a visual and a communicative way. In SNS, written communication gains much importance, which allows a precise reflection of transmitted messages. Users present themselves and their lives by describing their own activities, emotions, interests, and so on. One form of this written self-presentation is the "wall" in SNS, where nearly all activities of a user are filed along with other users′ comments to them. The (virtual) identity appears as a combination of self-presentation and the corresponding social reactions of others. This form of identity construction in an interactive way is reminiscent of Mead′s (1988) distinction between "me" and "I," which expresses the fact that the individual identity of a person is generated in the combination of the individual's self-perception ("I") and the perception of the person by the "generalized others" ("me").

The "wall" gives clear insight into what a user is doing, thinking, and feeling, as well as how others rate and handle those messages.

Besides the active forms of identity construction, posting messages, and publishing photos of oneself, there is also a more passive form of identity construction, for example, the comments or "like it" statements of other users (Back et al., 2010; Walther et al. 2008, p. 29). The number and listing of friends also express a form of identity construction. By displaying a connection to another user, the profile owner also expresses something about himself (Salimkhan, Manago, & Greenfield, 2010), and the number of friends can be seen as an expression of one's social capital

(Workman, 2008; Walther et al., 2008). Additionally, the public display of connections can be seen as an implicit verification of identity (Donath & boyd, 2004; Walther & Parks, 2002; p. 33).

The variety of communication and self-presentation tools of SNS (Krämer & Winter, 2008; Raacke & Bond-Raacke, 2008) indicates that these virtual networks can be used as trial platforms to test different social behavioral patterns as well as activate different aspects of users' identity (Ellison, Heino, & Gibbs, 2006).

In contrast to other online communities, such as online game communities or communities in anonymous chat forums, where the users can really create virtual identities that are independent of the real-life identity (Turkle, 1995), personal identity on SNS matches the real-life image of users because these networks are used primarily for interactions with already known associates (Ambady & Skowronski, 2008; Ebersbach et al., 2008; Funder, 1999; Gosling et al., 2007;Hall & Bernieri, 2001; Kenny, 1994; Kneidinger, 2010; Lampe et al., 2006; Machilek et al., 2004; Vazire & Gosling, 2004). The creation of a totally new self-image would cause incredibility because most of the online "friends" already have real-life knowledge of the individual and his or her social behavior ("extended real-life hypothesis" Back et al., 2010). One issue with identity construction and activation on SNS is the heterogeneity of relationship networks. Whereas in real life humans activate different identity facets depending on their interaction partners, e.g., they behave differently in interactions with close friends than with working colleagues, on SNS they have to present the same self-image to all of their different relationship groups (Donath & boyd, 2004). This can cause problems when some relationship groups get to know new personality traits of a Facebook user that do not fit the previous image of the person. Maybe this problem will be solved in the future by offering the opportunity to create different profiles for different relationship groups, but at the moment this is only possible for single messages or photo publications. The main profile information is the same for all "friend" types, except when a user specifies in detail which information which type of "friend" can see.

This problem of open identity construction independent of various social relationship groups also offers new opportunities for "self-monitoring" (Kumru & Thompson 2003) and social feedback because the online social network allows users to obtain social reactions to their own personality from a large number of people (Manago et al, 2008; Siibak, 2009, Valkenburg et al., 2006; Zhao et al., 2008). In face-to-face interactions only a small group of mostly close friends or family members represents the main sources of social feedback. In the online environment, these feedback processes can be opened to a much bigger reference group. The question arises whether users really appreciate social feedback on the SNS and how they handle positive as well as negative reactions. This question is interesting for analyzing different forms of identity construction online and offline. SNS, in particular, stimulate the users to create an online image of themselves and allow to test different aspects of one's own identity. Additionally, as it will be shown in the results of the studies, the expectation of social feedback forms one of the main motivators for publishing actively in the network.

The Studies: Methodology

To answer questions about social behavioral patterns and the effects of SNS on users, subjective user experiences were collected and the potential of Facebook as a trial platform for social behavioral patterns was analyzed. The following results are based on an online survey of 700 Facebook users from German speaking countries (Austria, Germany, and Switzerland). Forty individuals from this online survey were selected to participate in qualitative interviews that provide a deeper insight into the subjective usage motivations and the individual strategies to handle different forms of social feedback on Facebook. Twenty-four women and 16 men between the ages of 18 and 45 participated in the interviews. All of them have an above average educational level and two-thirds are students. The qualitative interviews were recorded, transcribed, and analyzed with a quantitative content analysis according to Mayring (2003). For the online survey, users were selected according to two main criteria: gender and age. In total, 364 men and 336 women answered the online survey, most of them have an above average educational level, 60% are students. The participants are between 15 and 66 years of age, with the average age being 26.8 years. Due to the quite good distribution of gender and age aspects, the online survey can reveal differences between men and women as well as differences between the age groups. More problematic is the concentration of very high-educated users. This is a problem of many studies about social network site usage because a lot of them focus primarily on college students (cf. Aquisti & Gross, 2006; Ellison et al., 2007; Lampe et al., 2006; Walther et al., 2008) which represent a user group with a higher educational level and younger age than the majority of society. Additionally, the online survey faces the problem of representativeness as the majority of online studies because of the following facts: Firstly, the whole population of all Facebook users cannot be exactly measured because of the constantly changing user numbers. So, it is nearly impossible to define a clear sampling frame (Couper, 2000). Secondly, participation in such online surveys requires the user's willingness and a specific interest in the topic of study. So it has to be assumed that highly involved people are more likely to participate in the study. But as Matsuo et al. (2004: 3998) point out, this problem of self-selection is no more problematic in online surveys than in mail or telephone surveys where the contacted individuals are free to decide if they would like to participate or not. And Gosling et al. (2004) even mention the high motivation of those people who participate in internet surveys as one advantage of the method compared to traditional offline surveys. Thus, we can assume that the presented studies do not claim representativeness, but nevertheless they can provide insight into the possible potentials of SNS and their effects on real relationships and the social behavior of their active users. The findings of such explorative studies can be used as groundwork for more representative surveys.

The Motives for Facebook Use

To answer the question of what motivates people to join Facebook, users were asked in the online survey and in the qualitative interviews about their motives for Facebook use.

The interviewees indicate that maintenance and reactivation of social relationships are the main motivators, especially for women (cf. Park et al., 2009; Raacke & Bonds-Raacke, 2008; Ridings & Gefen, 2004). Facebook is used because it offers the opportunity to get up-to-date information about friends, family members, or acquaintances easily.

My friends are very important for me and I'd like to know what they are doing and how they are feeling... and so I use Facebook almost all day and have the best insight into my friends' lives. (26-year-old female user)

Facebook is especially significant when it comes to maintaining contact with people who live abroad. Besides the various communication opportunities, Facebook enables the users to exchange photos or videos, so that they can really get a visual impression of what a friend is doing.

Another motivation mentioned spontaneously is the various communication opportunities via chat, message box, the wall or comments on photos, activities, and so on.

I use Facebook mainly for communicating with my friends... I don't have to write an SMS, but I write something on the wall when there is a party or something special has happened. And when you know that your friends are on Facebook and they read it, they write something back and so you get feedback[1]. (18-year-old female user)

Well, I think Facebook makes single life easier because you are not alone when you come home. You see some of your friends online and can talk with them without having to call them or leave the house[1] (31-year-old male user)

However, Facebook is also used for entertainment or amusement purposes; it offers various games and quizzes. In addition, amusement is also experienced by reading the publications of other users, for example, funny wall messages or links to entertaining web contents.

Facebook is very very important in my life. (...) It´s funny with all these status messages and internet links and certainly the small silly games and the looking after my farm. It's simple, when you are bored you can use it every time[1]. (22-year-old female user)

The fourth motive of Facebook use is the possibility to exchange information. This information can focus on events or private interests but also on professional purposes:

I use Facebook mainly for professional needs. I try to get people in our group and to inform people about and invite them to events[1]. (38-year-old male user)

Facebook seems to combine a big variety of communicative, informative, and entertaining needs and so one user described it as a "multi-functional platform":

I use Facebook to maintain social contacts, to stay up to date about events, to view photos or videos. Basically you do not need any other homepage than Facebook because there you get everything; it´s like television, music and radio and the whole nine yards. In some way I really use it 'multimedially'[1]. (23- year-old male Facebook user)

These findings correspond for the most part with the findings of the quantitative online survey. The findings of the qualitative interviews are used to modify the questionnaire of Ellison et al. (2006, 2007; Steinfield et al., 2008) in order to adapt it to the German speaking users and a more heterogeneous sample that does not only consist of college students as in the US study.

The items are analyzed with a factor analysis (principal component, varimax rotation, KMO=0.752) and four dimensions of usage motivators are extracted:

- **Motive 1 "information function":** items *"to get information," "to publish information," "to use groups or fan sites of Facebook," "to use Facebook as an alternative to other email/chat programs."* This dimension presents information exchange as the main motivator. Facebook groups and fan sites are used to communicate and exchange information with people with similar interests and the online social network is seen as an alternative to other computer-mediated communication forms.
- **Motive 2 "networking function":** items *"to establish new contacts," "to flirt," "to be a part of the Facebook community," "for professional relationship management."* This dimension focuses around the main motivation of networking with others, even less known or new people, which seems to be the case especially with professional contacts. Also, the feeling of being a part of the Facebook community is an important aspect.

- **Motive 3 "amusement function":** items *"to pass spare time," "to play games."* Facebook is an entertainment tool, and, by using it, boredom is avoided and spare time is filled.
- **Motive 4 "private contact maintenance":** items *"to maintain private contacts," "to refresh former relationships."* Similar to the first survey, this dimension represents private relationship management focused primarily on the maintenance and fostering of pre-existing relationships.

Table 1. Motives for Facebook use: Men vs. women

		N	mean	significance
motive 1: information	men	360	2.42	**
	women	334	2.22	
motive 2: networking	men	360	2.10	***
	women	332	1.93	
motive 3: amusement	men	361	2.05	***
	women	335	2.30	
motive 4: private contact maintenance	men	361	3.30	**
	women	336	3.44	

***<0.001, **<0.01, *<0.05

The users are asked how strongly they agree or disagree with the user motives and it appears that the most important usage motive is the private contact maintenance (mean=3.36[2], explained variance=12.7%), followed by the information function (mean=2.32[2], explained variance=17.2%), and the amusement function (mean=2.16[2], explained variance=13.7%). Least important is the motive of networking (mean=2.01[2], explained variance=15.7%). This ranking of different motive-dimensions for Facebook use reflects the findings of the U.S. study, which also indicates that social reasons form the main motivators for Facebook use (Barker, 2009; Ellison et al., 2006), and reflects the results of Park et al. (2009) and Raacke/Bond-Raacke (2008) about the main motives for using SNS.

Similar to the findings of previous studies (Barker, 2009; Gross et al., 2002; Jonier et al., 2005; Rainie, 2003), interesting differences can be observed in the usage motives when the sexes are compared. Traditional gender differences seem to be reproduced in the usage habits of SNS. Men more often articulate information and networking as the strongest motivators for their Facebook use, while women mention more often the reasons of amusement and social relationship maintenance.

The age of users also has an effect on usage motives. It appears that the younger a user, the more important the aspect of amusement is. With increasing age, the aspects of information exchange and of networking gain in significance. No age differences were observed for the motive of social relationship maintenance; it seems to be the most important usage aspect of Facebook for all age groups.

The data indicate that motivation for Facebook use can be explained by a merging of different factors. Users' needs for information, communication, and entertainment are gratified at the same time, and most needs are determined by users' individual interests and personality characteristics. This form of merging usage motives and habits may be called "communicative self-presentation." This label is chosen to describe the quite egocentric form of information transfer and communication in the network, which is reminiscent of the term of "networked individualism" (Wellman, 2002). Nearly all users' messages have a strong connection to the individual's interests, attitudes, and activities and, in this way of communication, they are the direct or indirect form of self-presentation in the network. Facebook's "status message" tool illustrates how communicative self-presentation is realized in SNS. This tool is especially well suited for the analysis of communicative self-presentation because it is used for a lot of different publications and usage forms, as it will be illustrated in the following paragraph.

The Status Message as a Tool for "Communicative Self-Presentation"

To identify the potential of the status message as a tool for "communicative self-presentation", i.e., the merging of communicative, informative, and self-presentation usage aspects with a strong concentration on the individual author, the users have been asked what they post in their status messages and why they write certain things. It appears that three main types of status messages can be distinguished:

1. Information oriented messages (links to news, events, etc.)
2. Entertainment oriented messages (jokes, dictums, funny links, etc.)
3. Information about one's own life (activities, emotions, etc.)

The most used type seems to be the information about one's own life; nearly half of the interviewees mentioned this spontaneously. The users post such messages to inform their network of friends about their activities, but also about emotions and feelings. This seems to conform to Wellman's thesis of the "networked individualism" (Wellman, 2002), where the individual user forms the core of the social network, and therefore information about individual life becomes most important. Interestingly, it seems to be a frequent practice that the status messages are formulated in a quite indirect and ambiguous way, so that only those people who have a closer connection to the poster understand the real background of a message. Another reason for ambiguous messages can be that the communicator wants to attract greater attention from the whole network.

Personally, I never write very explicitly. I prefer to write a little bit hidden. I don't like to open myself too much to all the others[1]*. (22-year-old female user)*

Yeah, the thing is that people who really know me know what I'd like to say and they can laugh about it. (...)[1]*. (20- year-old female user)*

The second most mentioned type of status messages are the information-oriented statements with which users post links to interesting (media) information or events but also express their opinions on certain topics.

I use the status message really manifold. I push things that I like. (...) I give things away on Facebook. I help friends who are looking for a new apartment. I use it to publish news. I find out a lot about the status message of others. Last week, for example, I got news of the death of two former work colleagues, information that I wouldn't have got without Facebook. So, Facebook really has news worth, but on a very personal level[1]*. (23-year-old male user)*

The least used type of status messages are the entertainment-oriented statements. Most of them are just funny statements or links to entertaining contents or videos. Some users explicitly say that they publish messages with the intention to entertain other people, for example, by posting jokes or funny dictums.

Gosh, no idea... Most of the time I post slogans or something funny. Very very seldom do I write really serious things. But actually I don't know why I post. I think it's always funny when other people comment on your messages[1]*. (23-year-old female Facebook user)*

In total, status message is used in a quite ambivalent way, with aspects of pure information transmission as well as forms of communicative self-presentation by expressing personal activities and emotions.

Considering the findings in the qualitative interviews, seven expressions of status messages are formulated and the users are asked how frequently they use each of them. Thereby, with a factor analysis (principal component analysis, varimax rotation, KMO=0.812), four types of status messages are identified:

- **Type 1 "general information":** items *"political statements," "neutral information, e.g., links to media news, events, etc."* In this case, the status message is used as a tool for information exchange, whereby these publications are also published with the expectation of reactions and comments of other users on the informational messages.
- **Type 2 "individual oriented information":** items *"emotional expressions, e.g., feelings, sentiments," "personal activities."* All information from this type is focused on the publisher himself. The user tells his friends about his personal experiences, feelings, and opinions. Thus, the individual is the center of the message.
- **Type 3 "search for social support":** item *"request for help/support."* This type is represented by only one item that implies a very special aim of the user. The status message is published with the sole aim to get social support from friends or acquaintances. This support can even happen in a material way and in real life, but quite often it happens in the form of supporting words or expressions of compassion and consolation. Here the individual user is also the center of communication.
- **Type 4 "amusement":** items *"questions," "jokes."* Here the status message is used as an entertainment tool with which the user can share funny links, jokes, or provocative questions with other users. This type is less focused on the individual user than the other three types.

The most used form of status message seems to be type 2, the individual oriented messages (mean=2.34[3]), followed by "general information" (mean=1.96[3]), and amusing messages (mean=1.91[3]). Explicit requests for social support are published comparatively rarely (mean=1.66[3]).

The aspect of the search for social support was identified as an important gratification of Facebook use by Ridings & Gefen (2004). But, compared to the findings of the qualitative interviews, it can be supposed that although social support is not requested explicitly in the status message, it forms an integral part of the individually oriented message, with which personal emotions are expressed that should also provoke reactions from other users.

As a next step, we analyze the motives leading to a publication in the status message. It appears that the status message is primarily appreciated because it allows the fast and easy transmission of information to a huge number of people in the network. Additionally, status messages are seen as good ways to initiate communication with friends because they form a kind of public communication that can be commented on quite easily by other members.

Well, if I read a funny status message, I certainly click on the "Like it"-button or write an addlebrained comment to the statement[1]. (22-year-old female user)

I really like to comment on status messages of friends... Status messages are a cool thing because they help strike up a conversation. One friend posts something and the others start commenting on it, and so a conversation starts[1]. (23-year-old male user)

There are a lot of reasons why a user posts a status message in his or her profile. The most important factor seems to be the expectation of friends' reactions. This corresponds with the findings of Ibrahim (2009), Kollock (1999); Kramer and Winter (2008) and Young (2010). More than half of the interviewees report spontaneously that they really wait for these feedback comments from their friends. In some cases, real frustration is experienced when nobody comments on a posting. The user motive "search for attention" and self-presentation is closely connected with the expectation of social feedback:

Yeah, I really like to get a reaction to my postings. I intentionally write provocative or funny things in my status[1]*. (22-year-old male user)*

I really think that status message is used to fulfill the need for attention. Why else would somebody write something like 'I'm ill'? People just write such things because they like to read 'Ah, you poor thing'. That's the way it is. I think when you read such things, you really know that this person expects and hopes that you write some comments[1]*. (23-year-old female user)*

When I'm in a bad mood or I'm ill, I post it as message because I'd like that someone writes 'Get well soon!' or something like that[1]*. (22-year-old female user)*

These quotations clearly indicate that the status message is not used just for the one-sided exchange of information, but first and foremost for the interactive communication inspired by social feedback about one's own publications. The latter aspect can be seen as an indicator that status messages are appropriate for testing behavioral patterns, opinions, and activities from the societal viewpoint. One's own position is tested and evaluated by others, and so the user gets important information about how this is perceived and rated by other people. At the same time, all comments of the friends become an integral part of one's own virtual and multi-faceted self image (Döring, 2003), by expressing that a person gets social support from his friends and by this his sociability is expressed in the network.

According to these findings of the qualitative interviews, in the online survey Facebook users are confronted with six possible reasons why they write a status message. With a factor analysis (principal component analysis, varimax rotation, KMO=0.783) the items are once again classified into motive types.

There appear to be three reasons why someone publishes a status message in his profile:

- **Motive 1 "general information exchange":** items *"to publish information," "to get attention for specific topics," "to initiate discussions/communication."* Here the motivation to exchange information and discuss different topics forms the main motivation.
- **Motive 2 "self-expression":** items *"to provoke emotions/compassion in others," "to get attention for myself."* In this motive-dimension, the aspect of self-presentation appears quite evidently. This self-presentation is in nearly all cases combined with an implicit expectation of social reaction and even social support.
- **Motive 3 "amusement":** item *"to avoid boredom."* This motive is represented by only one item that describes the factor of writing a status message just for fun or filling spare time. The content of the publication does not seem to have high importance for the user.

The "general information motivation" dominates the ranking list of the three motivation-dimensions for the status message (mean=2.69[4]), followed by "amusement" (mean=2.17[4]), and the "self expression" (mean=2.07[4]).

In this context, the status message seems to be used primarily for general information transfer, but "self expression" seems to be less important. These findings are surprising when compared to the results from the qualitative interviews, where the users express the high importance of personal messages. It appears that a tendency toward socially desirable responses has distorted the results of the quantitative survey.

To prove this assumption, the question about the usage motives for the status message is also asked in a reflexive form, i.e., the users are asked what they think are the most important usage motivators of other users for the status message. The same motive items are used and classified into the three motive-dimensions. The comparison of the self-estimation and the estimation about the usage motives of others shows interesting differences. In total, all three motives are estimated as more important for other users than for the self-descriptions. As the most important motive for other users the dimension of "amusement" (mean=3.31[4]) is mentioned, followed by "self expression" (mean=3.25[4]). Clearly far behind is "general information exchange" (mean=2.99[4]) as a motive of other users. The highest differences between the self-estimation and the estimation of the motivations of others can be observed for the "self expression" that is evaluated for the estimation of others' motives 1.19 points higher than for the self-estimation. For factor "amusement" the estimation for other users is 1.14 points higher than the self-image, and the smallest difference is found for the motive of the "general information exchange" (estimations of other 0.3 points higher than self-estimation).

These clear differences between the evaluation of self-motivations and those of other users, especially in the dimension that is focused primarily on self-presentation, can be seen as an indicator of socially desirable answers in the self-estimation. Whereas the motive of the "general information exchange" can be seen as desirable, the motivation of self expression or amusement seems to be less accepted in society and so it is reported as a motive of others rather than as a motive for one's own use of the status message.

In summary, the status message is a tool for "communicative self-presentation" because it combines traditional information exchange about general topics and entertaining aspects with an expression of one's own activities and emotions up to the possibility to request social support. Nearly all status messages have a strong connection to the user who publishes it, so that the status message is really used as a kind of "stage" (Goffman 1959, 1996), to present one's own life, and nearly all messages are written with the expectation of social reactions.

Interesting differences can be observed between men and women. Whereas men rate status messages exchanging general information of highest significance, women write status messages mainly because they want to express individually oriented information. No gender differences can be detected for the amusement motive. Women seem to have a higher affinity for publishing personal status messages, while men prefer the exchange of general information. These findings correspond with the results of Ross (2008), who found that women are more likely to publish emotional messages and show more self-disclosure in their interaction on SNS than men.

Especially interesting from a sociological viewpoint is the usage of Facebook as a channel for social feedback. At the moment, Facebook offers two tools for expressing social reactions: the comment function, available alongside the status messages, pictures, and other publications and activities of online friends; and the "like" button, with which a user can express with just one click that he or she likes the message or activity of another user. (Interestingly enough, a "dislike" button does not yet exist.)

How to Handle Negative Social Feedback on SNS

Based on the finding that the majority of activities and publications on SNS happen with the expectation to realize an interactive dialogue with other users who give social feedback to messages, the question of how users handle these social reactions should be answered. The importance of comments from other users can be seen quite clearly in the descriptions of the interviewed users who express disappointment if they get no reactions to their publications.

It is interesting that the users do not only get positive reactions but also critical and negative comments. More than one-third of the 700 asked users (36.5%) report that they have already experienced negative reactions to their own publications or activities on Facebook. But how do the users handle negative social feedback? To answer these questions, the users are confronted with seven possible reactions to these negative comments and evaluate the way in which they would react.

Most of the users (78.5%) would mitigate the negative reaction by adding their own comment to it. Another good reaction is ignoring the negative comment (45.3%). Deleting the negative statement is considered a possible reaction by one third of the users (33.0%). Acts of revenge do not represent a good answer to critics; just 10.9% of the users would write negative statements on the wall of the personal critic. Just as small is the acceptance of deleting the critic from the friends list on Facebook (9.1%).

Just how much influence such negative comments can have on the personal identity and the self-confidence of the users can be seen in the facts that at least one quarter of the users (23.4%) would feel insecure and 10.9% would start to reflect their own attitudes and activities.

In this context, the gender differences are very interesting. Whereas only one quarter of the men (25.4%) would delete a negative comment from their wall, 40% of women would do so ($Chi^2=27.726$, $p<0.001$). Additionally, women would delete the critic significantly more often from their friends list (women 11.1%, men 6.5%; $Chi^2=8.806$, $p<0.05$). Slight gender differences can also be found in acts of revenge, which are realized significantly more often by men than women (women 10.3%, men 11.5%, $Chi^2=8.212$, $p<0.05$).

No gender differences seem to exist in ignoring the negative feedback (women 46.7%, men 44.4%) or in mitigating the comment by adding a comment to the critic (women 77.8%, men 79.7%).

Furthermore, there are some differences in the personal consequences of negative social feedback between men and women. Whereas both men and women would reflect on their own attitudes and activities because of such negative reactions (women 55%, men 50.5%), women are made to feel more insecure than men. One third of the women (33.2%) report that their self-esteem would suffer from negative social feedback, but only 14.8% of men would also react in this way ($Chi^2=37.92$, $p<0.001$). Thus, negative social feedback on SNS seems to be of much higher risk for the self-esteem of women than for men.

In summary, it can be demonstrated quite clearly what influences social feedback on SNS can have on the real life personalities of the users. Negative feedback in the virtual environment can be as problematic as negative reactions in real life contacts. Nevertheless, one of the main motivators to publish messages on Facebook is the expectation to receive social feedback about one's own attitudes, opinions, and activities. That indicates quite clearly that Facebook is really used as a platform for social evaluation and for getting information about the social acceptance of one's own position. Positive as well as negative reactions from other users can activate a process of self-reflection which can help provide a better impression and knowledge of oneself.

LIMITATIONS OF THE STUDY

The findings of the presented studies can give some insights into the usage motives and habits of the social network site Facebook and especially into the significance of social feedback processes in the interaction between the network members. But all findings have to be interpreted by considering the fact that the results merely represent the using habits of a certain part of Facebook users and cannot be seen as representative for all of the 600 million Facebook users. Additionally, the study was focused on the Facebook usage in German speaking countries, where the network is relatively new. So it could be supposed that the using habits as well as the handling of social feedback in such virtual networks could change when the Facebook penetration in these countries increases and the social network sites become more routine. Additionally, the problem of undefined population has to be mentioned. As in other online surveys (cf. Baym & Ledbetter, 2009; Acquisti & Gross, 2006, Walther et al., 2008), it is quite impossible to determine the whole population of Facebook users because these numbers change daily. Therefore, the findings of this chapter should be seen as a kind of status quo analysis of a part of Facebook users in German speaking countries and should not be interpreted as representative for all Facebook or even SNS users in general. It can be supposed that other SNS can also satisfy other user needs. Nevertheless, the combination of qualitative and quantitative survey should give an initial insight into possible usage motivators and usage habits of SNS and how people handle different forms of social feedback in the (virtual) network.

CONCLUSION AND FUTURE RESEARCH DIRECTIONS

Facebook as a trial platform for social behavioral patterns - this thesis can be verified by analyzing the usage habits and motives of different user types and how important the factor of social reactions is as a motive for publishing actively in the network. The expectation of an interactive dialogue with a high degree of mutual social evaluation makes SNS an ideal platform for testing different identity facets of the self, including individual interests, opinions, and attitudes. Therefore, it is important that SNS play a decisive role in the everyday communication mix of the users, but it does not replace traditional interaction forms in real life such as face-to-face conversations and telephone calls. The two spheres of communication – traditional offline communication and computer-mediated communication on the online social network – supplement and influence each other. The users appreciate Facebook mainly because of the opportunity to maintain and foster offline social relationships in the online network. But also a form of self-presentation and strongly subjective focused information transfer that can be described as a form of "communicative self-presentation" - play decisive roles in the usage motivation of SNS. Because of the high willingness of Facebook users to express their own opinions about friends' messages, the online social network creates frequent and open social feedback processes. Additionally, the large number of "friends" in the network and the absence of communication barriers that often make face-to-face conversation less open than online conversation (Tidwell & Walther, 2002) increase the number of potential feedback givers in the user's social network. Whereas in real life only close friends express their personal thoughts about the attitudes or activities of a person, on Facebook less intimate acquaintances also become potential feedback givers. Thus, the evaluation in the network is based on a much broader view of society than the real life contact. This can be seen as a great advantage of socializing on SNS, but also as a new danger because negative reactions are possible, and that can make users feel insecure and uncomfortable. This can be a problem especially for women who are more likely to publish personal and emotional message and at the same time are more likely to be made insecure by negative comments on the social network site. So members of networking sites have to learn to handle this new mass of social feedback reactions, especially those comments that express critical or negative evaluation. For future research it would be interesting if different levels of social bonding and relationship strength cause different user reactions and consequences for individual identity construction as well as social relationship maintenance. For example, it should be asked whether feedback from less intimate acquaintances causes as much individual consequences for the self-image and the reflection of personal attitudes or behavioral patterns as feedback from close friends or family members. Additionally, the technical development of Facebook must be kept in mind, because in some countries a "dislike" button is being tested. It will be interesting to observe whether such a button for articulating negative feedback would increase the number of negative mutual reactions of users and what consequences these new forms of negative evaluation would have for online socializing in general.

REFERENCES

Ambady, N., & Skowronski, J. (Eds.). (2008). *First impressions*. New York, NY: Guilford.

Amichai-Hamburger, Y., & Ben Artzi, E. (2003). Loneliness and Internet use. *Computers in Human Behavior*, *19*, 71–80. doi:10.1016/S0747-5632(02)00014-6

Aquisti, A., & Gross, R. (2006). Imagined communities: Awareness, information sharing, and privacy on the Facebook. In G. Danezis & P. Golle (Eds.), *Privacy enhancing technologies, 4258*, 36-58.

Arnett, J. J. (2000). Emerging adulthood: A theory of development from the late teens through the twenties. *The American Psychologist*, *55*, 469–480. doi:10.1037/0003-066X.55.5.469

Back, M. D., Stopfer, J. M., Vazire, S., Gaddis, S., Schmukle, S. C., Egloff, B., & Gosling, S. D. (2010). Facebook profiles reflect actual personality, not self-idealization. *Psychological Science*, *21*(3), 372–374. doi:10.1177/0956797609360756

Barker, V. (2009). Older adolescents' motivations for social network site use: The influence of gender, group identity, and collective self-esteem. *Cyberpsychology & Behavior*, *12*(2), 209–213. doi:10.1089/cpb.2008.0228

Bauman, Z. (2001). *Community. Seeking safety in an insecure world.* Cambridge, UK: Polity.

Baym, N. K., & Ledbetter, A. (2009). Tunes that bind? *Information Communication and Society*, *12*(3), 408–427. doi:10.1080/13691180802635430

Berry, W. (1993). *Sex, economy, freedom, and community*. New York, NY: Pantheon.

Boase, J., Horrigan, J., Wellman, B., & Rainie, L. (2006). *The strength of Internet ties*. Washington, D.C.: The Pew Internet and American Life Project.

boyd, d. (2002). *Faceted Id/entity: Managing representation in a digital world.* MIT Master's Thesis, Cambridge, MA.

Buckingham, D. (2008). Introducing identity. In Buckingham, D. (Ed.), *Youth, identity, and digital media* (pp. 1–24). Cambridge, MA: The MIT Press.

Butt, S., & Phillips, J. G. (2008). Personality and self report mobile phone use. *Computers in Human Behavior*, *24*(2), 346–360. doi:10.1016/j.chb.2007.01.019

Chua, V., Madej, J., & Wellman, B. (2009). Personal communities: The world according to me. Extended version of book chapter. In Carrington, P., & Scott, J. (Eds.), *Handbook of social network analysis*. Cambridge: Cambridge University Press.

Couper, M. P. (2000). Web surveys: A review of issues and approaches. *Public Opinion Quarterly*, *64*, 464–494. doi:10.1086/318641

Donath, J., & boyd, D. (2004). Public displays of connection. *BT Technology Journal*, *22*(4), 71–82. doi:10.1023/B:BTTJ.0000047585.06264.cc

Döring, N. (2003). *Sozialpsychologie des Internet: Die Bedeutung des Internet für Kommunikationsprozesse, Identitäten, soziale Beziehungen und Gruppen*. Göttingen, Germany: Hogrefe.

Ebersbach, A., Glaser, M., & Heigl, R. (2008). *Social Web*. Konstanz, Germany: UKV.

Ellison, N., Steinfield, C., & Lampe, C. (2006, June). *Spatially bounded online social networks and social capital. The role of Facebook*. Paper presented at the Annual Conference of International Communication Association ICA, in Dresden, Germany.

Ellison, N. B., Steinfield, C., & Lampe, C. (2007). The benefits of Facebook "friends:" Social capital and college students' use of online social network sites. *Journal of Computer-Mediated Communication, 12*(4). doi:10.1111/j.1083-6101.2007.00367.x

Erikson, E. H. (1959). *Identity in the life cycle*. New York, NY: Norton.

Feld, S. L. (1981). The focused organisation of social ties. *American Journal of Sociology, 86*(5), 1015–1035. doi:10.1086/227352

Funder, D. C. (1999). *Personality judgment: A realistic approach to person perception*. San Diego, CA: Academic Press.

Giddens, A. (1991). *Modernity and self-identity*. Cambridge, UK: Polity.

Goffman, E. (1959). *Presentation of self in everyday life*. Garden City, NY: Doubleday Anchor Book.

Goffman, E. (1996). *Wir alle spielen Theater. Die Selbstdarstellung im Alltag*. München, Germany: Piper.

Gosling, S. D., Gaddis, S., & Vazire, S. (2007, March). *Personality impressions based on Facebook profiles*. Paper presented at the International Conference on Weblogs and Social Media 2007, Boulder, CO.

Gosling, S. D., Vazire, S., Srivastava, S., & John, O. P. (2004). Should we trust web-based studies? A comparative analysis of six preconceptions. *The American Psychologist, 59*(2), 93–104. doi:10.1037/0003-066X.59.2.93

Gross, E. F., Juvonen, J., & Gable, S. L. (2002). Internet use and well-being in adolescence. *The Journal of Social Issues, 58*, 75–90. doi:10.1111/1540-4560.00249

Hall, J. A., & Bernieri, F. J. (Eds.). (2001). *Interpersonal sensitivity: Theory and measurement*. New York, NY: Erlbaum.

Haste, H., & Hogan, A. (2006). Beyond conventional civic participation, beyond the moral-political divide: Young people and contemporary debates about citizenship. *Journal of Moral Education, 35*(4), 473–493. doi:10.1080/03057240601012238

Ibrahim, Y. (2009). Social Networking Sites (SNS) and the 'narcissistic turn': The politics of self-exposure. In Rummler, S., & Ng, K. B. (Eds.), *Collaborative technologies and applications for interactive information design: Emerging trends in user experiences* (pp. 82–95). Hershey, PA: Idea Group Inc. doi:10.4018/978-1-60566-727-0.ch006

Jenkins, R. (2004). *Social identity*. London, UK: Routledge. doi:10.4324/9780203463352

Jonier, R., Gavin, J., & Duffield, J. (2005). Gender, Internet identification, and Internet anxiety: Correlates of Internet use. *Cyberpsychology & Behavior, 8*, 371–376. doi:10.1089/cpb.2005.8.371

Kenny, D. A. (1994). *Interpersonal perception: A social relations analysis*. New York, NY: Guilford.

Kneidinger, B. (2010). *Facebook und Co. Eine soziologische Analyse von Interaktionsformen in Online Social Networks.* Wiesbaden, Germany: VS.

Kollock, P. (1999). The economies of online cooperation: Gifts and public goods in cyberspace. In Smith, M., & Kollock, P. (Eds.), *Communities in cyberspace* (pp. 29–59). London, UK: Routledge.

Kramer, N. C., & Winter, S. (2008). Impression management 2.0. The relationship of self-esteem, extraversion, self-efficacy, and self-presentation within social networking sites. *Journal of Media Psychology, 20*, 106–116. doi:10.1027/1864-1105.20.3.106

Kraut, R., Patterson, M., Lumark, V., Kiesler, S., Mukhopadhyay, T., & Scherlis, W. (1998). The Internet paradox: A social technology that reduces social involvement and psychological well-being. *The American Psychologist, 53*, 1017–1032. doi:10.1037/0003-066X.53.9.1017

Kumru, A., & Thompson, R. A. (2003). Ego identity status and self-monitoring behavior in adolescents. *Journal of Adolescent Research, 1*, 1–16.

Lampe, C., Ellison, N., & Steinfield, C. (2006). A Face(book) in the crowd: Social searching vs. social browsing. *Proceedings of the 2006 20th Anniversary Conference on Computer-Supported Cooperative Work* (CSCW 2006), (pp. 167-170). New York, NY: ACM Press.

Livingstone, S. (2008). Taking risky opportunities in youthful context creation: Teenagers' use of social networking sites for intimacy, privacy and self-expression. *New Media & Society, 10*(3), 393–411. doi:10.1177/1461444808089415

Machilek, F., Schütz, A., & Marcus, B. (2004). Selbstdarsteller oder Menschen wie du und ich? Intentionen und Persönlichkeitsmerkmale von Homepagebesitzer/inne/n [Self-promoters or ordinary people? Intention and personality of homepage owners]. *Zeitschrift für Medienpsychologie, 16*, 88–98. doi:10.1026/1617-6383.16.3.88

Manago, A., Graham, M., Greenfield, P., & Salimkhan, G. (2008). Self-presentation and gender on MySpace. *Journal of Applied Developmental Psychology, 29*, 446–458. doi:10.1016/j.appdev.2008.07.001

Matsuo, H., McIntyre, K. P., Tomazic, T., & Katz, B. (2004). The online survey: Its contributions and potential problems. *Proceeding of the Survey Research Methods Section*, ASA 2004, (pp. 3998-4000).

Mayring, P. (2003). *Qualitative Inhaltsanalyse. Grundlagen und Techniken* (8th ed.). Weinheim, Germany: Beltz.

McKenna, K. Y. A., Green, A. S., & Gleason, M. E. G. (2002). Relationship formation on the Internet: What is the big attraction? *The Journal of Social Issues, 58*(1), 9–31. doi:10.1111/1540-4560.00246

Mead, G. H. (1988). *Geist, Identität und Gesellschaft aus der Sicht des Sozialbehaviorismus.* Frankfurt am Main, Germany: Suhrkamp.

Mesch, G. S., & Talmud, I. (2006). Online friendship formation, communication channels, and social closeness. *International Journal of Internet Science, 1*(1), 29–44.

Mikkola, H., Oinas, M.-M., & Kumpulainen, K. (2008). Net-based identity and body image among young IRC-gallery users. In K. McFerrin, R. Weber, R. Carlsen, & D. A. Willis (Eds.). *Proceedings of Society for Information Technology and Teacher Education International Conference 2008*, (pp. 3080-3085), Chesapeake, VA: AACE.

Park, N., Kee, K. F., & Valenzuela, S. (2009). Being immersed in social networking environment: Facebook groups, uses and gratifications, and social outcomes. *Cyberpsychology & Behavior, 12*(10), 1–5.

Quan-Haase, A., & Wellman, B. with Witte, J. & Hampton, K. (2002). Capitalizing on the net. In B. Wellman, C. Haythornwaite (Eds.), *The Internet in everyday life* (pp. 291-324). Oxford, UK: Blackwell.

Raacke, J., & Bonds-Raacke, J. (2008). MySpace and Facebook. Applying the uses and gratifications theory to exploring friend-networking sites. *Cyberpsychology & Behavior, 11*(2), 169–175. doi:10.1089/cpb.2007.0056

Rainie, L. (2003). *Teenage life online: The rise of the networked generation*. Paper presented at the Youth.Net Conference. Singapore.

Rice, R. E., & Love, G. (1987). Electronic emotion: Socio-emotional content in a computer mediated communication network. *Communication Research, 14*, 85–108. doi:10.1177/009365087014001005

Ridings, C. M., & Gefen, D. (2004). Virtual community attraction: Why people hang out online. *Journal for Computer-Mediated Communication, 4*. Retrieved October 10, 2010, from http://jcmc.indiana.edu/vol10/issue1/ridings_gefen.html

Ross, C. (2008). *"What's up? LOL!" Optimism and gender differences in social support on Facebook.com*. Thesis, Ohio State University, Ohio.

Ross, C., Orr, E. S., Arseneault, J. M., Simmering, M. G., & Orr, R. R. (2009). Personality and motivations associated with Facebook use. *Computers in Human Behavior, 25*, 578–586. doi:10.1016/j.chb.2008.12.024

Salimkhan, G., Manago, A. M., & Greenfield, P. M. (2010). The construction of the virtual self on MySpace. *Cyberpsychology: Journal of Psychosocial Research on Cyberspace, 4*(1), article 1.

Siibak, A. (2009). Constructing the self through the photo selection – Visual impression management on social networking websites. *Cyberpsychology: Journal of Psychosocial Research on Cyberspace, 3*, article 1.

Siibak, A. (2010). Constructing masculinity on a social networking site. *Young: Nordic Journal of Youth Research, 18*(4), 403–425.

Sproul, L., & Kiesler, S. (1986). Reducing social context cues: Electronic mail in organizational communication. *Management Science, 32*(11), 1492–1512. doi:10.1287/mnsc.32.11.1492

Steinfield, C., Ellison, N. B., & Lampe, C. (2008). Social capital, self-esteem, and use of online social network sites: A longitudinal analysis. *Journal of Applied Developmental Psychology, 29*, 434–445. doi:10.1016/j.appdev.2008.07.002

Strano, M. M. (2008). User descriptions and interpretations of self-presentation through Facebook profile images. *Cyberpsychology: Journal of Psychological Research on Cyberspace, 2*(2), article 5.

Swindler, A. (1986). Culture in action: Symbols and strategies. *American Sociological Review, 51*(2), 273–286. doi:10.2307/2095521

Thiedke, U. (2008). Die Gemeinschaften der Eigensinnigen. Interaktionsmediale Kommunikationsbedingungen und virtuelle Gemeinschaften. In Von Gross, F., Marotzki, W., & Sander, U. (Eds.), *Internet - Bildung - Gemeinschaft* (pp. 45–73). Wiesbaden, Germany: VS Verlag. doi:10.1007/978-3-531-90793-2_4

Tidwell, L. C., & Walther, J. B. (2002). Computer-mediated communication effects on disclosure, impressions, and interpersonal evaluations: Getting to know one another a bit at a time. *Human Communication Research, 28*(3), 317–348. doi:10.1111/j.1468-2958.2002.tb00811.x

Toennis, F. (1887). *Gemeinschaft und Gesellschaft. Abhandlung des Communismus und des Socialismus als empirische Culturformen*. Leipzig, Germany: Fues.

Turkle, S. (1995). *Life on the screen: Identity in the age of the Internet*. New York, NY: Simon & Schuster.

Valkenburg, P. M., Jochen, P., & Schouten, A. P. (2006). Friend networking sites and their relationship to adolescents' well-being and self-esteem. *Cyberpsychology & Behavior*, *9*, 584–590. doi:10.1089/cpb.2006.9.584

Van Dijk, J. (1999). *The network society. Social aspects of new media*. London, UK: Sage.

Vazire, S., & Gosling, S. D. (2004). E-perceptions: Personality impressions based on personal websites. *Journal of Personality and Social Psychology*, *87*, 123–132. doi:10.1037/0022-3514.87.1.123

Veenhof, B., Wellman, B., Quell, C., & Hogan, B. (2008). *How Canadians' use of the Internet affects social life and civic participation*. (Connectedness report series: F0004M-16, December 4.29).

Von Kardorff, E. (2006). Virtuelle Netzwerke - eine neue Form der Vergesellschaftung? In Holstein, B., & Straus, F. (Eds.), *Qualitative Netzwerkanalyse. Konzepte, Methoden, Anwendungen* (pp. 61–97). Wiesbaden: VS Verlag.

Walther, J. B., & Parks, M. R. (2002). Cues filtered out, cues filtered in: Computer-mediated communication and relationships. In Knapp, M. L., & Daly, J. A. (Eds.), *Handbook of interpersonal communication* (3rd ed., pp. 529–563). Thousand Oaks, CA: Sage.

Walther, J. B., Van der Heide, B., Kim, S.-Y., Westerman, D., & Tom Tong, S. (2008). The role of friends' appearance and behavior on evaluations of individuals on Facebook: Are we known by the company we keep? *Human Communication Research*, *34*, 28–49. doi:10.1111/j.1468-2958.2007.00312.x

Wang, H., & Wellman, B. (2009). (forthcoming). Social connectivity in America. *The American Behavioral Scientist*, *52*.

Wellman, B. (2001a). Physical place and cyber place: The rise of personalized networking. *International Journal of Urban and Regional Research*, *25*(2), 227–252. doi:10.1111/1468-2427.00309

Wellman, B. (2001b). *The persistence and transformation of community: From neighbourhood groups to social networks*. Ottawa: Report to the Law Commission of Canada.

Wellman, B. (2002). Little boxes, glocalization, and networked individualism. In Tanabe, M., Van den Besselaar, P., & Ishida, T. (Eds.), *Digital cities* (pp. 10–25). Berlin, Germany: Springer Verlag.

Wellman, B., Boase, J., Horrigan, J. B., & Rainie, L. (2006). *The strength of Internet ties*. Washington: Pew Internet & American Life Project.

Wellman, B., & Haythornthwaite, C. (Eds.). (2001). *The Internet in everyday life*. Oxford, UK: Blackwell Publishers.

Wellman, B., & Hogan, B. (2004). The immanent Internet. In McKay, J. (Ed.), *Netting citizens* (pp. 54–80). Edinburgh, UK: Saint Andrew Press.

Wellman, B., & Tindall, D. (1993). Reach out and touch some bodies. *Progress in Communication Science*, *12*, 63–94.

Willems, H., & Pranz, S. (2008). Formationen und Transformationen der Selbstthematisierung. Von der unmittelbaren Interaktion zum Internet. In Willems, H. (Ed.), *Weltweite Welten. Internet-Figurationen aus wissenssoziologischer Perspektive* (pp. 189–222). Wiesbaden, Germany: VS Verlag.

Wolfradt, U., & Doll, J. (2001). Motives of adolescents to use the Internet as a function of personality traits, personal and social factors. *Journal of Educational Computing Research*, *24*(1), 13–27. doi:10.2190/ANPM-LN97-AUT2-D2EJ

Workman, T. A. (2008, February). *Responding to the YouTube and MySpace generation: Thinking digitally about today's college student.* Paper presented at the 29th Annual National Conference on Law and Higher Education, Stetson University College of Law.

Zhao, S., Grasmack, S., & Martin, J. (2008). Identity construction on Facebook: Digital empowerment in anchored relationships. *Computers in Human Behavior, 24*, 1816–1836. doi:10.1016/j.chb.2008.02.012

ADDITIONAL READING

Bargh, J. A., & McKenna, K. Y.. The Internet and social life. *Annual Review of Psychology, 55*, 573–590. doi:10.1146/annurev.psych.55.090902.141922

Batinic, B., Reips, U.-D., & Bosnjak, M. (2002) (Eds.). *Online Social Sciences*, Seattle: Hofgrefe.

Boase, J., & Wellman, B. (2004). Personal Relationships: On and Off the Internet. In Perlman, D., & Vangelisti, A. L. (Eds.), *Handbook of Personal Relations* (pp. 1–19). Oxford: Blackwell.

Castells, M. (1996). *The Rise of Network Society*. Oxford: Blackwell Publishers.

Franzen, A. (2000). Does the Internet make us lonely? *European Sociological Review, 16*(4), 427–438. doi:10.1093/esr/16.4.427

Franzen, A. (2003). Social Capital and the Internet: Evidence from Swiss Panel Data. *Kyklos, 56*, 341–360. doi:10.1046/j.0023-5962.2003.00224.x

Haythornthwaite, C. (2002). Strong, weak and latent ties and the impact of the new media. *The Information Society, 18*, 385–401. doi:10.1080/01972240290108195

Haythornthwaite, C. (2002). Strong, weak and latent ties and the impact of the new media. *The Information Society, 18*, 385–401. doi:10.1080/01972240290108195

Joinson, A. N. (2001). Self disclosure in CMC: The role of self awareness and visual anonymity. *European Journal of Social Psychology, 31*, 177–192. doi:10.1002/ejsp.36

Kiesler, S., Siegel, J., & McGuire, T. W. (1984). Social Psychological Aspects of Computer-Mediated Communication. *The American Psychologist, 39*, 1123–1134. doi:10.1037/0003-066X.39.10.1123

Kraut, R., Kiesler, S., Boneva, B., Cummings, J., Helgeson, V., & Crawford, A. (2002). Internet Paradox Revisited. *The Journal of Social Issues, 58*, 49–74. doi:10.1111/1540-4560.00248

McKenna, K., & Bargh, J. (2000). Plan 9 from cyberspace: The implications of the Internet for personality and social psychology. *Personality and Social Psychology Review, 4*, 57–75. doi:10.1207/S15327957PSPR0401_6

Ploderer, B., Howard, S., & Thomas, P. (2008, November). *Being Online, Living Offline: The Influence of Social Ties over the Appropriation of Social Network Sites.* Paper presented at CSCW 08, in San Diego, California.

Walther, J. B. (1992). Interpersonal Effects in Computer-Mediated Interaction: A Relational Perspective. *Communication Research, 19*, 52–90. doi:10.1177/009365092019001003

Wellman, B. (1996). An Electronic Group is Virtually a Social Network. In Kiesler, S. (Ed.), *Cultures of the Internet* (pp. 179–205). Hillsdale: Lawrence Erlbaum.

Wellman, B., & Berkowitz, S. D. (2008) (Eds.). *Social Structures. A Network Approach.* United Kingdom et al.

Wilson, C., Boe, B., Puttaswamy, K. P. N., & Zhao, B. Y. (2009, April). *User Interactions in Social Networks and their Implications.* Paper presented at the EuroSys 09, in Nürnberg, Germany.

Wolak, J., Mitchell, K. J., & Finkelhor, D. (2003). Escaping or connecting? Characteristics of youth who form close online relationships. *Journal of Adolescence*, *26*, 105–119. doi:10.1016/S0140-1971(02)00114-8

KEY TERMS AND DEFINITIONS

Communicative Self-Presentation: A new form of self-presentation which can be realized especially on SNS. The main characteristic is the merging of communicative, informative, and self-presentation usage aspects. Nearly all communication acts and information transfers are focused on the individual author of the message and so become an integral and more subliminal part of the self-presentation.

Online Identity: This term should be distinguished from "virtual identity," which stands more for a kind of false and artificial identity form that has nothing in common with a user's real life identity. Online identity describes the identity that a user represents in the social web where he interacts with a lot of people with whom he already maintains contact in real life. Online identity is never totally fictional or false but always fits the real life identity of a user. It is just the representation of his or her identity in the online environment.

Online Social Feedback: A special form of social feedback that happens in an online environment, especially on SNS, and is characterized by the expression of one's own evaluation of other's publications, activities and personal attitudes in view of the whole social network of a user.

Online Social Relationships: The opposite of traditional relationships that are based on real life interactions. Online social relationships describe all forms of friendship or acquaintanceship that are actually established and formed in the online environment without any prior real life contact.

Social Space: Does not necessarily mean a physical place; can be positioned in the virtual environment without any physical or geographical connection. Social space describes a real or virtual "area" where people can interact with each other.

Social Support: A collective term for all forms of help an individual gets from others. This can include material support (e.g., money) and physical support (e.g., help with building a house) but also emotional support (e.g., consolation) and cognitive support (e.g., advice).

Using Gratifications: Represent the benefits users get from their active utilization of something, especially used for benefits from different forms of media use. Using gratifications are influenced by two different aspects: (a) the expectation about the using benefits; and (b) the already experienced benefits that a user gets by using a medium, e.g., an online social network.

ENDNOTES

1. All citations are translated from German to English
2. 4-point scale: 1= I strongly disagree, 2= I disagree, 3= I agree, 4= I strongly agree
3. 4-point scale: 1= never, 4=very often
4. 4-point scale: 1 = not important, 4 = very important

Chapter 8
Branding Identity:*
Facebook, Brands, and Self Construction

Geraldina Roberti
University of L'Aquila, Italy

Alberto Marinelli
Sapienza University of Rome, Italy

ABSTRACT

The driving force of consumption has shifted from the need for something to the desire for it. This change implies that we, as researchers, should pay attention to the relationship dynamics which link consumers with certain products and brands - autonomously chosen according to the individuals' personalities, sub-cultures, and increasingly, to their offline and online relationships.

Such processes seem to be emphasized by Social Network Sites; in this chapter we analyze a sample of posts published on Facebook by fans of successful brands, in order to try and understand if consumption is more related to individuals' identities and expressions or if it is still connected to the product itself and its qualities. We will try to observe the dynamics of brand appropriation and the mechanisms through which individuals include lovemarks (Roberts, 2006) among the identity resources they use to express themselves and to experiment - with no substantial differences between mediated and face to face relationships - their experience in the world.

INTRODUCTION[1]

The experimental research we carried out has two different aims: on one hand, to identify the main dimensions that connect individuals and brands in the process of identity construction; on the other, to analyze how Social Network Sites enable an expression of these projective connections in real-time and within a shared relational context. Our hypothesis is that brands participate in the construction of one's self identity: they offer suggestions, moods and symbolic materials from which consumers can freely draw on to represent their self- images and share them with others.

DOI: 10.4018/978-1-61350-338-6.ch008

The analysis was conducted by monitoring the buzz generated on Facebook - the most widespread non-professional social network - by four popular international brands, belonging to different product categories: Ferrero's Nutella for what concerns mass consumption goods, Prada for fashion, Piaggio's Vespa and Mercedes' Smart respectively for scooters and cars. The decision to monitor Facebook is related both to the widespread diffusion of this social network in Italy (in September 2010 the platform had about 16.5 million Italian users) and to the substantial coherence between the identified brand profiles and the age of the platform users (about 37 years old according to the latest data provided by Facebook Ad Platform).

To aggregate user generated contents referring to single brands of different kinds (even cultural and political), Facebook introduced "social pages" in June 2010 (in Italy), to which users that are "fans" of a brand find themselves enrolled. These social pages have not been considered in our research due to their recent release and because of the marketing intent they are mainly characterized by, since they are promoted (or managed) by people appointed by brands. Considering the objectives of our research, we preferred to focus on free, nearly unconscious expressions, often produced by the users as the consequence of an association of ideas. We, therefore, excluded from our analysis any activity coordinated by the brands using viral marketing strategies to promote or create attention and opinions about specific products (Libai, Bolton, Bügel, de Ruyter, Götz, Risselada, & Stephen, 2010).

In this paper, after assessing the topic of identity construction in the light of the transformations that characterize the postmodern age, we will identify the dimensions of consumption – and of brand appropriation – connected to the definition of the self. We will, then, analyze how people can find a space to represent, share and store for future memory this process of self-definition on Facebook personal news feeds, where heterogeneous symbolic and expressive materials are consistently inserted in a profile.

The cognitive, creative and emotional investment of each consumer in their preferred brand indicates that the driving force of consumption has shifted from the need for something to the desire for it. It is seen as the transfer of the symbolic value of consumption from the object-product to the subject-producer of sense, a consumer who is increasingly more capable of transforming his/her identity in a project and who uses brands to give form to and express his/her own identity processes (Fabris, 2010).

The mechanisms of appropriation and incorporation of specific products and brands in the communication dynamics of Social Network Sites could offer researchers an innovative perspective when reading the definition of postmodern identity processes.

IDENTITY AS A PROJECT[2]

The feeling of insecurity and precariousness which runs through the postmodern age - and which makes it so difficult to schematize - has deep repercussions on the most important social processes, and first of all, on the construction of identities. In fact, the apparently irreversible crisis of the traditional systems of meaning allows individuals to develop new experiences and gives them a lot of freedom in the design of their own life-path; at the same time, though, it deprives subjects of any solid social anchorage and exposes them to instability and uncertainty.

As Erikson (1950) states, we start conceptualizing identity when it historically becomes a problem: when it appears to be more autonomous, no longer inevitably subjected to "social fate", but also more fragile and subject to changes because of the deterioration of both community connections and social status caused by modernization

(Sciolla, 2007). According to Bauman's interpretation (1997), the concept of identity derives from the crisis of the sense of belonging, when it stops being determined once and for all and it becomes a project individuals can individually follow. The growing de-institutionalization which characterizes the postmodern world weakens the level of normativity of the social context (Touraine, 1997) and serves for a less tight control of the individual's actions and for new possibilities of personal self-determination. Questioning an ultra-socialized model of the self produces, as a consequence, the individual's rediscovery of autonomy, since he's asked to personally perform tasks which in the past were prerogative of different social entities. This sort of *tyranny of possibilities*, as defined by Hannah Arendt (1958), attributes to individuals the responsibility to bring order to fragmented and contradictory experiences, in the attempt to trace one's own original life-path. Thus, the arising of the procedural and voluntary aspect of identity formation allows the individual to choose freely from which ambits and symbolic materials to draw on. As Bauman (2001) says, the determination of the social collocation in the postmodern world is replaced by a sort of self-determination, which gives the individual the possibility to change aspects of his/her own self on the basis of a personal project. With the pluralization of the worlds in which the social experience is built (Berger & Luckmann, 1966), identities themselves are a source of sense, since the reflective attitude of the self is used to coherently put together the different options each individual has at his/her disposal (Giddens, 1991).

We have to remember that, in the past, the concept of identity was used to combine experiences that happened diachronically during the whole course of an individual's life. In the postmodern age, rather, those experiences seem to happen at the same time, simultaneously, forcing the individual to look for some kind of synchronic coherence. Such a need – that has to be interpreted through the persistency / change dialectic that characterizes identity – should not be confused with a request for continuity, since the postmodern individual generally perceives continuity as a barrier, a possible obstacle to the spreading of his/her freedom of choice.

Since the individual's path of life seems a sort of oscillation between different social worlds (Berger, Berger,& Kellner, 1973), it is up to the single individual to determine, from time to time, how to create relationships and which aspects of his/her identity to privilege and in which context to set his/her social relationships. In this way, we obtain temporary and revocable affiliations, based on the sharing of feelings and lifestyles; emotional communities (Weber, 1922) to which the social actor can temporarily – and reversibly – adhere.

In the complex dynamics of identity construction – with the weakening of the theoretical foundation of identity, considered more as a flow than as a structure – both the social and interactive nature of the formation of the self and the centrality of the mechanisms of social recognition seem quite obvious. Symbolic interactionism had already recognized the importance of social relationships in the process of definition of the self (see Mead, 1934), since social actors acquire the ability to see themselves as individuals with identities that are also defined through daily interactions with Significant Others. As Schutz (1967) suggests, the reciprocal recognition of each other through the attribution of an identity is nothing else than the effect of those acts of typification that individuals use daily to rationalize and simplify the world they live in.

In the fragmented context of postmodern society, consumption gains an increasingly important role in the process of self definition: it affects both the presentation of one's self in interpersonal relationships and the appropriation of symbolic values that are incorporated in specific consumer goods.

The New Dimensions of Consumption[3]

Regardless of what was once believed, it seems that contemporary culture is shaped by consumption, not production[4]. In an attempt to fully understand postmodern society we need to consider the meanings carried by consumer goods, since they seem to be loaded with information that individuals use to organize reality, including symbolically. Successful products and brands have gradually become vectors of culturally attributed meanings, which have little or nothing in common with economic-utilitaristic logics. On one hand, consumer goods are tools for identity negotiation and experimentation, therefore assuming a strong expressive valence; on the other, they have an important communicational value, since goods – the visible side of culture – allow individuals to establish social relationships (see Douglas & Isherwood, 1979). Consumption is transformed into a sort of identity investment, becoming an expression of the social actors' way of being – and of representing themselves – at the same time, though, it allows for the definition of the dimensions of belonging and inclusion, even if it does so only as a consequence of fragile and occasional relationships[5]. In this sense, the possibility the individual has to enter and leave different spheres of belonging – to which he/she can gain access thanks to consumption – stresses, on one hand, a dangerous precariousness in the mechanisms of social affiliation (Beck, 1997) and emphasizes, on the other, the multiple ambits of experimentation in which individuals can define themselves. The fruition of a certain good – or of a specific brand – allows individuals to take possession of the symbolic values the objects carry and to perform (Goffman, 1959), through the act of consumption, different aspects of their personality.

We can say that, when the freedom of having is replaced by the freedom of being (Melucci, 1991), we confer an expressive dimension to the universe of consumption, implicitly attributing the status of cultural objects to goods. Within such a process, it seems obvious that products and brands gain a new evocative ability and end up becoming the entrance key to those possible worlds the individual must choose from. Therefore, we are involved in a continuous *re-sematization* of consumer goods which naturally acquire distinctive valences and meanings for identity when they are inserted in the fruition models of social actors. This new craft consumer (Campbell, 2005) uses the products he/she buys with great discretion, completing and re-elaborating them in creative and original ways - sometimes far removed from the original intentions of the commodity's producer. This ability to re-interpret objects and brands in a subjective way resembles the mechanisms of textual cooperation that Eco analyzed (1979): products and brands – considered semiotically open – offer their interlocutors values and patterns of life that consumers are asked to actively integrate drawing on their experience. In this way, social actors use goods as material to exchange information about the world, their aspirations and the values they recognize in themselves. Therefore, in the following pages we will try to understand how individuals practically use the universes of meanings represented by products to set their relationships and to define – even if only temporally and in a flexible way – their own identity.

The Research[6]

The monitoring we carried on was performed on 3 non-consecutive working and weekend days, dividing the day into three time ranges (11:00 a.m. - 1:00 p.m.; 5:00 p-m. - 7:00 p.m.; 10:00 p.m. - 12:00 p.m.) and starting Wednesday, the 30th of June 2010[7]. In addition, considering the necessity to verify the reliability of the results, we repeated the analysis on Friday, the 30th of July, exactly four weeks after the beginning of the research, in order to crosscheck the formulated research hypothesis.

We must add that, since this was an explorative survey, our methodological approach was mainly qualitative and it aimed at aggregating the published posts in macro-categories that could stress the different identity and expressive intents connected to the brands. As Hine (2005) suggests, "there is a considerable evidence that within a research setting, people also disclose more about themselves online compared to in offline equivalents, and that much of that disclosure is more candid" (p. 25).

As a consequence of the privacy protection policies adopted by Facebook, it was possible to gain access only to the posts published by users with an open profile, therefore visible to all the platform members. The over 7.000 posts analyzed[8] (see tab. 1) represent a minor – though significant – part of what has been said by the users about the 4 brands.

Our methodological approach didn't allow us to analyze - and segment - users based on traditional socio-demographic variables, since the only discriminating factor in our selection of the posts was the mentioning of one of the four brands. On the other hand, the goal of a non-standardized research generally is to analyze a specific process or to understand the meanings attributed to it; not to analyze the relationships between variables or to get to statistically relevant results. We can say that "[…] one real strength of qualitative research is that it can use naturally occurring data to find the sequences ("how") in which participants' meanings ("what") are deployed and thereby establish the character of some phenomenon" (Silverman, 2006, p. 44).

Table 1. Number of brand posts per day

	Nutella	Prada	Vespa	Smart
30.06.2010	2088	119	228	102
02.07.2010	1332	164	177	143
04.07.2010	909	140	91	40
30.07.2010	1287	145	278	103
Total	**5616**	**568**	**774**	**388**

Source: our elaboration.

In our research, we wanted to stress out the richness and the depth of the texts we analyzed, using non-standardized criteria that we thought were more coherent to understand the complexity of the social phenomena we studied.

TALKING ABOUT OURSELVES THROUGH BRANDS[9]

- *"Questa sono io. Rido sempre, ho sempre fame, sono sempre in ritardo, mi incazzo facilmente, vivo di musica, darei la vita per le persone che amo (pochissime), preferisco un paio di jeans a una gonna, preferisco mangiare un Big Mac piuttosto che fare una cazzo di dieta xD, adoro la nutella, adoro il mare odio il caldo e sono un po' pazza" [nutella_30.07.2010_11-13]*[10]

This is how a girl we intercepted on Facebook, following the trail of the connection with the brand Nutella, describes herself. It seems a perfect expression of the way we can use some brands to talk about ourselves on social network sites, describing our identity according to the brands and consumer goods we are surrounded by.

Individuals use symbolic and expressive values that brands carry to make their own social presentation, as a consequence of the fact that nowadays it is easy to find brands with a strong identity, capable of offering life models in which consumers can identify themselves. From this point of view, brands end up acting as a relational platform "[…] where individuals that share both consumption choices and a similar vision of the world can meet each other" (Fabris, 2008; p. 382).

Among the identity resources used by individuals to represent themselves and to mediate their own relationships with the world, the dynamics of appropriation carried out by social actors and the mechanisms of inclusion of certain *lovemarks* (Roberts, 2006) give brands a very strong social and cultural value (Minestroni, 2010).

The observation of the appropriation and re-semantization of brands inside social network sites (boyd, Ellison, 2007) leads us to understand some fundamental differences which strengthen the process itself. First of all, through those forms of relationships typical of networked sociability (Castells et al., 2006; Marinelli, 2004; Comunello, 2010) consumers conquer a space of their own, a place where they can freely express their opinions; one which does not naturally overthrow the power of producers (and marketing strategies), but balances it with irreverent and "unorthodox", "grassroots requests" (Bartoletti, 2009). In this new expressive space, the sharing of images and values that come from brands has a structural valence for individuals - both in their ostentation of the self and in their activation of relationships. For this reason, as Henry Jenkins notices, "in the spreadable media landscape, companies must find ways not simply to motivate consumers to talk about their brands but also enable them to talk through their brands" (Jenkins et al., 2010). For those who manage brands, declarations of loyalty represent a resource they need to use and strengthen, even through "infiltrations" (for promotional purposes) in the relational networks.

Quite a few of the links we found in our research refer to "engagement proposals" launched on institutional pages (financed by the brands) and which are in harmony with the perceptions and the relational intents of the audience.

Secondly, it is the technological nature of Social Network Sites that gives shape to the self-reflective paths of subjects: the possibility to observe and describe oneself, becoming a transparent and open subject, is a default resource guaranteed by the system. Whether it has the syncopated, punctiform, fragmented form of Social Network Sites – like the "status update" (What's on your mind?) on Facebook and, even more, on Twitter – or the longer and more conversational form of a blog, certain dimensions do not change: the collocation inside a flow, observable in terms of time and space; the expectation of a response (usually asynchronous, but potentially in real time); the activation of other possible conversations and links to repositories, pictures and consumer goods. Brands enter naturally in this new form of talking about oneself in public: they draw distinctive features of identity, they evoke generational practices, they accompany daily life and penetrate deeply in both personal and shared memories.

Posting Identities[11]

In contemporary society, consumption practices play an important role in the process of construction of the self. Such a role is amplified by the possibilities to experiment and to share enabled by new media: through web-based interactions, individuals can represent themselves, creatively designing the profile and image they propose to others. Nowadays, we have to overcome those interpretations which view the life on the screen (Turkle, 1996) as a sort of virtual dimension, capable of transporting social actors in a parallel dimension[12]. Instead, we need to include – without any substantial difference – online experiences among the representations of the self and the social interactions individuals experiment everyday (Castells, 2001). Social actors can implement their relational potential through Social Network Sites: using, in the relationships they establish on line, the representations of their selves related with the symbolic meanings incorporated in brands and consumer goods. This process is particularly performed by younger generations, heavy users of Social Networking platforms and of Web 2.0. These environments allow users to define their identities and to describe their sense of belonging through the construction and mutual sharing of an online profile. SNS are becoming a communicational environment in which the multiple and contingent postmodern self can observe itself through interactions on the News Feed, allowing everybody to choose how to talk about themselves and which aspects of their personality to privilege during the narration.

Thus, as Figure1 shows us, identity seems to be a dialectic pole to which are referred both the consumptions of social actors and their representations on Social Network Sites; users seem to be perfectly capable of using personal pages on SNS to draw the profile of their identity and to recompose their consumption choices in a description of their selves that is often original.

Therefore, reading Facebook messages in this perspective could become both a useful indicator to reconstruct users' identities and maps of belonging and a way to interpret meanings and values attributed to brands by social actors.

The analysis of such conversations could, in fact, allow us to identify more clearly the role nowadays played by "the world of goods" (Douglas and Isherwood, 1979) in the representations people use to manage their social relationships, highlighting the symbolic dimensions of consumption that have become so significant for the postmodern social actor. Inside these dynamics, material goods assume a social dimension, allowing individuals to use them – as fences or bridges – to communicate with others and to express themselves both in their offline and online relationships. The constant increase of Facebook users – 600 million by the end of 2010 – is an indicator of the ability of individuals to unify their

Figure 1. The triangle identity-consumptions-social network sites

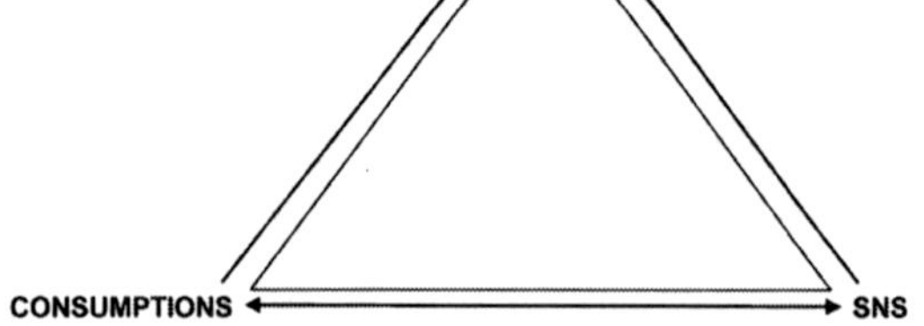

various relational spheres (lived in presence or through technological mediation) and it provides researchers with important material to reflect on the dynamics of identity building. If, as the latest data indicates, everyday over 35 million people update their profile on Facebook – inserting observations, comments, links and personal material (such as photos and videos)[13] – the analysis of posts published on users' walls can effectively be a useful indicator of the ways in which users present themselves and the modalities through which they interact with the reality surrounding them, using consumer goods and the relationships they vehiculate as an input. However, it is important to add that if social relationships mediated by technology – and first of all by social networks – increase the ways through which it is possible to communicate, think and act, at the same time, they seem to favor the *disembedding* modalities of experience described some years ago by Giddens (1990). In other words, they seem to encourage relationships that are not mediated by physical presence: this process frees social activities from located contexts. Perhaps the answer to the demand of re-embedding of the postmodern self could come exactly from the integration of the two dimensions of social interaction: in presence and mediated. Cooley (1967) has stressed how the identity of an individual was, at least partially, a social construction, verified and consolidated through the interaction with others. Nowadays, though, it seems obvious that the ambit of relationships capable of producing sense has grown and has reached the Web, letting us understand the continuity of the social experience lived inside and outside technological networks.

Interacting with the Brands[14]

We have acknowledged the ability of individuals to build their own identity in an original way, using meanings they appropriate from their lifestyles and the products they consume, but we still need to stress how, in postmodern society, the concept of brand has been reformulated.

In the past consumers mainly demanded a quality product, while today, in addition to good quality, they expect brands to establish a dialectic relationship with them. As the authors of the Cluetrain Manifesto[15] affirmed more than ten years ago, markets are not only a place for transactions but they are increasingly becoming spaces for conversations; environments where companies and customers communicate horizontally, as equals, building together the values and the images brands are carriers of. Brands are increasingly focusing on immaterial and affective values, on the construction of atmospheres and worlds that consumers are asked to share emotionally. From this point of view, the identity of a brand crosses symbolic and highly imaginative territories – which have little to do with the objective characteristics of a product and, instead, aim to a sort of identification of the audience with the message proposed by the brand.

Analyzing our sample more deeply, the first observations concern the structural characteristics of the posts selected and are transversal towards the four brands analyzed. First of all, we can observe – consistently with what a 2010 research by the social media company Vitrue on production and consumption behaviors towards Facebook posts[16] – that Wednesday is the day in which the greatest number of messages is published, while the number of messages considerably decreases on Sundays or during the weekend (Table 2)[17]. For what concerns time ranges, Table 3 shows that the sharing of messages increases in the afternoon, in comparison with the other times of the day (data confirmed by the trend of the hours of use provided by Vitrue)[18].

The messages reveal how consumers have an empathetic affinity with the brand and how their consumption behaviors often are a mechanism of projection or identification. One of the elements that emerges more clearly from our analysis is the relationship between the symbolic universes described by the brands and the aspirations of social actors, and it seems to be relatively independent from the product category the brand refers to. Facebook users who choose to insert a reference of any kind to a brand on their walls are perfectly able to identify its connotative meaning, to coherently adapt it to their profile and to use the semantic aura that surrounds each brand in function of their own social presentation:

"Costiera:Vespa=Mare:Me" [vespa_30.06.2010_11-13][19]

"Soddisfatta dello shopping appena fatto. Chanel, Prada, Gucci, Fendi.. Pane per i miei denti!" [prada_30.07.2010_11-13][20]

"Lampi..tuoni...fulmini e saette...in una serata come qst il massimo del piacere e restare a casa a guardare un film, mangiando un cornetto con la nutella e magari dividere tutto qst con la persona del tuo cuore!!!!!" [nutella_30.07.2010_22-24][21]

Table 2. Messages divided per day of the week

Day	Number of posts
Wednesday 30.06.2010	2537
Friday 02.07.2010	1816
Sunday 04.07.2010	1180
Friday 30.07.2010	1813
Total	**7346**

Source: our elaboration.

Table 3. Messages divided per time-range

Time-range	Number of posts
11:00 a.m. - 1:00 p.m.	2538
5:00 p-m. - 7:00 p.m.	2750
10:00 p.m. - 12:00 p.m.	2058
Total	**7346**

Source: our elaboration.

"Il 98% delle donne che guidano la smart sono gnocche. È statisticamente provato che le gnocche viaggiano solo su un certo tipo di autovetture... solitamente del valore, potenza e design direttamente proporzionali alla quantità di gnoccaggine della stessa..." [smart_30.06.2010_11-13][22]

Hence, social actors select in which brand to invest emotionally, and they determine their consumption pathways on the basis of their definition of themselves. A more aware use of the new technologies has transformed the relationship with brands into a fully bidirectional exchange and the consumer is, increasingly, the one that determines interaction' modalities and conditions, claiming the possibility to underline even the negative elements of a consumption experience:

"Il prossimo che mi dice che la cioccolata e la nutella rendono felici lo ammazzo" [nutella_30.07.2010_22-24][23]

"As long as I live I will never speak to a women wearing prada DnG and or Gucci" [prada_ 30.06.2010_ 22-24]

The wealth of the data we have gathered allows us to make a further step in the analysis, since consumption has gradually become a creator of sense. An overall broader reflection leads us to consider the meaning users give to the act of publishing something on a profile (a consideration, a link, the sharing of a comment, a photo, etc): the content of our sample of messages seems to indicate the ability of the social actors to use *narration* as a tool to steady their self, to present themselves socially through a story and to put their identity on stage[24].

"Prendi una sera d'estate....prendi l'aria calda che ti passa tra i capelli...vestiti comodi e infradito....mettici anche una buona compagna....il tutto su una vespa che ha la tua età...condito con un pizzico di pazzia...." [vespa_02.07.2010_11-13][25]

Therefore, even if consumption choices have gradually lost their ostentatious nature[26] to become more and more an expressive moment – as Fabris (2010) stresses – it is still possible to classify *Facebook* messages according to whether the element that started them is connected to identity projections and personal memories or if it originates from lifestyles connected to a brand.

We could divide our sample in two macro-categories: in the first, communication is centered on the *subjective* dimension, while in the second the *object of consumption* (the brand) itself is the point of reference in the narration. The principle of congruence that shapes the individual's temporal and symbolic continuity is usually found in the egocentrism of the individual him/herself and in his/her ability to build an original and conscious life story to use when communicating with others. In some cases, though, the product/brand could be a driving force of the identification process.

Among the examples of messages where the social actor is placed in the foreground, we can find:

"Ha voglia di pane e nutella senza essere in stato interessante" [nutella_30.06.2010_22-24][27]

"Fake has never been in style, stop rockin' it like an in season Prada bag. Always be a first-rate version of yourself, instead of a second-rate version of somebody else. Have another beautiful day FB" [prada_02.07.2010_17-19]

"Eating strawberries and nutella, watching Edward Scissorhands... trying to forget the things attacking me from all different directions..." [nutella_30.06.2010_17-19]

"Andare in giro come un bellimbusto sulla mia Vespa" [vespa_30.07.2010_17-19][28]

The messages that find their main communicative trigger in the expressive dimensions of the brand bear different forms of communication, where the focus is on the "personality" of the product:

"I have chosen prada n i think my eyes have adjusted to my glasses!" [prada_30.06.2010_11-13]

"Se ho te...ho tutto....grazie 1000 vespa [vespa_30.07.2010_11-13][29]

"Nutella sandwiches and peanut butter bumpers cereal make me a happy man" [nutella_30.06.2010_22-24]

"Finalmente la macchina =)) SMART I LOVE YOU =))" [smart_30.07.2010_22-24][30]

Carrying on our analysis, we can observe that users interact with the brands through different modalities, as if the relationship between consumers and products summoned different aspects of the social actors' personalities. After an analysis of our sample, we can classify the messages according to three different brand approaches:

- Emotional approach
- Competent approach
- Critical approach

In the emotional approach, the consumer reveals an intense emotional investment connecting him/her to the product, which we see as a commodity with a strong symbolic value for the social actor's identity. As we know, it has become quite usual for brands to invest in a communication strategy based on the language of emotions, on the involvement of the consumer and on the passion the brand is able to arouse. According to Kevin Roberts (2006), CEO worldwide of Saatchi & Saatchi, this is the only way a brand is able to transform itself into a *lovemark*: a brand capable of establishing a relationship of almost love with its audience.

"There's a difference between like and love. Because, I like my Skechers, but I love my Prada backpack" [prada_ 30.06.2010_22-24]

"Wendy torna da me... ci vuole un miracolo.. un estate senza Vespa è la fine" [vespa_04.07.2010_22-24][31]

"Oh my prada !!!!.....u gave me love and helped me find d sun..and everytime dat i am down...u always come around...and get my feet back on d ground.....:) [prada_30.07.2010_17-19]

"Io nn sn come la nutella... io vivo in simbiosi con la nutella!!! siamo una cosa sola..." [nutella_04.07.2010_11-13][32]

In the competent approach, instead, what emerges is the deep knowledge of the brand, of its characteristics and of the experiences that it allows to experiment:

"Mai provare la tenuta di strada di una smart sul bagnato se non si ha la giusta quantità di adrenalina nel sangue!!!!" [smart_30.07.2010_22-24][33]

"Do you know what Nutella is? We had a conversation one day at a dinner table about Nutella. What is your favorite way to eat Nutella ? mine is eating directly from the jar with a nice fat spoon! Can you believe that they are now telling us that it is not that good for you! Have you ever seen "Death by Nutella " on the news?! NO!! so please, let us all live in peace!" [nutella_30.07.2010_22-24]

"Albicocche alla nutella, Anelli alla nutella, Baci di dama, Banana split alla nutella, Barchette di nutella...: la Nutella è come il bianco...sta bene su tutto!!" [nutella_02.07.2010_11-13][34]

"Oggi ho fatto un altro passo importante per riavere in perfetto stato d'uso la vespa dei miei 14 anni.....fra un po'...torno ad andare in vespetta !!!!!!! yuppieee !!!!!!!!!!" [vespa_30.07.2010_22-24][35]

Finally, in the critical approach, the relationship connecting the consumer to the brand implies a sort of deliberate distance from the product and from the cultural model it represents, with a clear argumentation about the most controversial aspects:

"Flashy cars, beautiful houses, millions of dollars,designers,D&G, Abrecombie n fitch,GUCCI, Prada, d most beautiful girls on earth,d sexiest physique n what hav u...........whc one of dis wil u take along wen u die......? VANITY....dats wat dis world is....so no mata wat u do, always think of dis..." [prada_30.07.2010_11-13]

"ODIO LE RAGAZZE CON LA SMART, STRONZEEE" [smart_30.07.2010_17-19][36]

"Dear FB, men do NOT wear flip flops, especially to work. Maybe on the beach, beyond that if your a man wearing flip flops F@CK YOU! You probably ride a vespa.... Grrrrrr" [vespa_02.07.2010_22-24]

"Io vengo dalla vecchia scuola faccio parte di quelli che da piccoli giocavano con le fionde ed erano contenti a guardar gli alberi con le loro fronde è tutto uno strano giro piu o meno come se guardi giu da un burrone e ti viene il capogiro è da qui che veniamo dalla strada nn siamo abituati a portare robba prada.." [prada_30.07.2010_11-13][37]

"Provo un odio irrefrenabile per qualsiasi smart in circolazione è ufficiale:D" [smart_02.07.2010_11-13][38]

"No matter how hoochie koochie you get with Gucci, no matter how breathless u become in a prada dressing room, no matter how cute a pair of chanel eyelet hot pants are, if a particular style is unflattering on u, u can look, well, tacky!!! Unless u don't mind getting rid of certain items every season, stay away from overly trendy pieces when shopping for your basic wardrobe. Clothes say more about you than you can" [prada_04.07.2010_17-19]

Thus, it is clear that the relationship between consumer and brand is deeply rooted in the emotional and cognitive system of the individual, and that it is able to transform the world of things into a sort of language, used to express oneself and communicate with others (Douglas, Isherwood, 1979), even through network technologies. If consumption is one of the places in which the battle to define and shape culture is fought, perhaps we can identify one of the traits of today's society in the social actors' relationship with brands.

A Classification of the Brands' Functions[39]

We have seen that brands have become a sort of medium for our interactions with the world. Nowadays, brands cleverly build universes of symbols and values around themselves, and it is in these universes that consumers mirrors their self and combine them according to their personality and lifestyle. The prevailing dimension which connects consumers and brands is the engagement: the emotional and empathetic involvement of the audience in the worlds of meanings represented by the brands. We could define it as the passage from the transaction to the relationship, underlining the closeness between producers and consumers in the creation of the cultural value of a brand (Gummesson, 2002).

Therefore, we need to try and understand how the relationship between individual and brand can be concretely articulated, identifying the different functions attributed to the brands by the social actors. In the light of what has been said so far, we have identified four main functions, which seem to be related to four different areas of the self:

1. expressive function
2. evocative function
3. aspirational function
4. aggregative function

In the expressive function - referring to the expressive value of a brand - consumers use the brand to express their feelings, their most personal sensations or an intimate aspect of their self, thus revealing the ability of the brand to break through the symbolic and emotional dimension of the social actors:

"Comiendo Nutella..corazón vacío...barriga llena! " [nutella_30.06.2010_22-24]

"Per questa settimana lavoro chiuso! Fatto shopping per coccolarmi un po'...(un bel paio di Prada e di Hogan)...e adesso...viviamoci il week end!" [prada_02.07.2010_17-19][40]

"Milly, stop eating Nutella out of the jar, get a life and go and meet your friends..." [nutella_02.07.2010_22-24]

"Non sono un intenditore.. ma per me ha un valore molto affettivo...io sono un meridionale pur vivendo a roma..e ci sono nato su vespa e ape 50 ;)....per questo le adoro" [vespa_02.07.2010_17-19][41]

"Quando e bello ke le persone ke ti vedono nella makina nuova e dikono mo te le presa e a me nn mi piace kosi, preferisco l'audi a3 ... bello io o 18 anni e cio la smart tu tieni 20 anni e stai a piedi, la gelosia e una brutta kosaaa ___ aaa quanda e bella la mia smarttt" [smart_30.06.2010_22-24][42]

"Terminarte un bote de nutella en dos dias que significa? a) cochi b) hambre c) tristesa d) ninguna de las tres" [nutella_30.07.2010_17-19]

We can, instead, identify an evocative function when people use a brand to gain access to dimensions such as memory and nostalgia; when consumers use a brand to think about moments of their past with a certain sense of loss and want to share them with others:

"Ti ricordi il barattolo da 5 chili di nutella alla cambusa??? Curava le nostre cosiddette "mancanze d'affetto". Però devo dire che la nutella funziona veramente...xD" [nutella_04.07.2010_17-19][43]

"Mamma miaaaaaa...e chi la vende!!!troppi ricordi la mia smart!!!!un pezzo di vita" [smart_30.06.2010_17-19][44]

"Qui se souvient de ces bons moments à passer devant la Tv en regardant cette serie mythique qui sent bon le Nutella et autres gouters. J'aimerai tant redevenir un enfant pour revivre ces moments intenses avec encore le petillement dans les yeux d'un enfant qui decouvre la premiere fois Goldorak" [nutella_04.07.2010_11-13]

"COSTIERA AMALFITANA LA SPIAGGIA DEI MIEI 15 ANNI.... IO, TU E LA VESPA 50...." [vespa_04.07.2010_11-13][45]

"ATTENZIONE!!!!!!!!RAGAAAAAAA!!!!!! X tutti quelli ke insieme a me Hanno vissuto belle e lunghe passeggiate KON LA MIA SUPER E SEXY CAR!!!!!! ti amo tanto pikkola smart mi manki tanto!!! Rimarrai nel my Cuoricino!!!!!!!" [smart_30.06.2010_22-24][46]

"NEI CASETTI DEI RICORDI HO TROVATO QUESTA CANZONE...........MIO DIO QUANTE VOLTE D'ADOLESCENTI L'ABBIAMO CANTATA A SQUARCIAGOLA SULLA TUA VESPA GIALLA!!!!" [vespa_30.07.2010_22-24][47]

Brands seem to have a more instrumental role in the aspirational function, as if the social actors used them to outline a sort of ideal image of themselves, or to express their closeness to a clearly recognizable style of life:

"In love with my new PRADA bag... so sexy!!!" [prada_02.07.2010_22-24]

"Ed oggi è contentissima perché ha comprato le sue prime scarpe di prada !!!!!!! =)" [prada_04.07.2010_11-13][48]

"I love my new scooter! Viva la Belle e Italiano Piaggio Vespa ! Uhh... I don't speak Italian..." [vespa_30.06.2010_17-19]

"Ho preso la macchina... LA SMART!!! Che figa!!!" [smart_30.06.2010_22-24][49]

"La vespa è uno stile di vita!!!" [vespa_02.07.2010_17-19][50]

"Took my first step toward my Italian conversion... bought my first pair of Prada shoes" [prada_30.06.2010_17-19]

"La VESPA è sempre la VESPA ha uno stile intramontabile" [vespa_30.06.2010_11-13][51]

"La smart è trendy" [smart_02.07.2010_11-13][52]

"Ella parece importada de italia ella solo viste marc jacobs, guy laroche,versace gafas prada ella usa vestidos de guess, carteras nine west o louis vuitton, los zapatos deben ser gucci o coach usa perfume marca chanel ella solo viste de Armani exchange ella esta a otro nivel....." [prada_04.07.2010_22-24]

We can split the last function, the aggregative one, according to two different typologies: on one hand, there are the messages where products seem an occasion to socialize and meet other people, anticipating possible interactions in presence; on the other hand, we can find messages which use the possibilities of *social engagement* offered by the social network sites and are based on diffusive behaviors such as the "like" function or the sharing of links[53]. This way we can obtain a *social interaction with little engagement*, typical of social networking, which allows users to experiment a sort of community dimension thanks to the Web. Thus, we participate in a sort of worldwide sharing of racking passions, puns and ironic wisecracks that users choose to publish on their profiles.

We can insert in the first typology messages of the following kind:

"Get ready to go for a Vespa ride around the bay with some other Vespa rider, what a day, sun is all out, full power!" [vespa_04.07.2010_17-19]

"Fresas, nutella y movie night con mi familia [nutella_30.06.2010_22-24]

"POSSESSORI E FAN VESPA CASTROVILLARI. GRUPPO DEDICATO AI POSSESSORI ED AGLI ESTIMATORI DELLA MITICA VESPA - CITTA' DI CASTROVILLARI" [vespa_30.06.2010_22-24][54]

"=) cm al pigiama party a mezzanotte e mezza a mangiare nutella, troppo bello =) ihihihi" [nutella_30.07.2010_22-24][55]

"2° Raduno Smart Varese: Luogo: Varese, Ora: domenica 4 luglio 2010 9.00.00" [smart_02.07.2010_17-19][56]

"à la recherche des anciens du vespa club de charleroi des années 1950.... avis aux amateurs et connaisseurs toutes les infos sont les bienvenues !" [vespa_04.07.2010_11-13]

In the second typology we could identify slightly different aggregative and engagement modalities:

"Se anche a te piacciono le crepes alla nutella, metti mi piace e condividi" [nutella_example of a shared message][57]

"Una Smart Costa 10.000 Euro Chiavi In Mano... Una station wagon costa 18.000 ma almeno chiavi sdraiato!" [smart_example of a shared message][58]

"Noi... che con la Vespa almeno una volta, abbiamo fatto una riparazione in strada" [vespa_example of a shared message][59]

"Salve, sono Claudio Silvestri, ex cuoco della Nazionale. Forse ai ragazzi ho dato troppa Nutella!" [nutella_example of a shared message][60]

"I get money, I get paper, I get girls of different flavors. I buy gucci I buy prada, I spend dolla afta dolla" [prada_example of a shared message]

In addition, with reference to the first kind of messages, we want to stress how Social Network Sites foster the creation of brand tribes: communities of consumers united by their passion for a product or a brand capable of becoming a sort of cult object. Through Facebook posts, the most motivated fans can exchange their impressions, share information and knowledge, or simply experiment a feeling of integration and group belonging, though using rather slack participation modalities. Therefore, brands become a sort of social aggregator, a postmodern totem capable of gathering individuals around themselves – subjects that are often different in their socio-demographic characteristics, but united by an emotional, flexible and voluntary bond[61]. A sort of community aspiration that, according to Bauman (1997), is destined to fail because it tries to find a form of stability in a changeable and evanescent environment. Instead, positive reflections are provided by the ability of the self to create itself through social relationships, more and more grounded by common consumption practices and the sharing of social meanings related to the brands.

The data we analyzed allows us to make another closing observation: though understanding the risks connected to an excessive dependence by consumption – and sharing part of the concern expressed i.e. by Bauman (2007) on the possible commercialization of interpersonal relationships – we must stress that consumers have acquired the ability to organize dissonant fruition practices, even if they are inserted in consumption models characterized by a certain coherence. As a consequence of their personal projection of the self, social actors are able to buy strongly interconnected clusters of products or to establish new connections between semantically distant brands and goods. We are talking about savvy and experienced consumers, who choose their belongings and prove to be able to manage the relationship with the brands with reasonable awareness, as the following messages indicate:

"J. Lindeberg suit, Hugo boss shirt, prada sunglasses, Ted baker tie...yes I'm an explosion of brandnames! Ugh!" [prada_30.06.2010_22-24]

"Imagine every one put in on fashion designed cloths (Gucci Prada saun john...) dat wat i wil do when i rule" [prada_02.07.2010_22-24]

"Fred Perry, Adidas, bermuda, testa rasata e giornata in Vespa....." [vespa_04.07.2010_22-24][62]

"I say prada on my feet and polo on my body.." [prada_30.07.2010_17-19]

"LA VOGLIOOOOOO HELLO KITTY SMART: SIIIIII NON È CHIC DI PIÙ" [smart_04.07.2010_22-24][63]

"Tu ragazza tutta gucci e Prada k pensi di essere stilosa ... blea ti sbagli di grosso..." [prada_30.06.2010_22-24][64]

FUTURE TRENDS[65]

In this research, we have found and analyzed the wealth of expressive forms employed by networked publics (Ito, 2008) and their habit to consider social network walls as a surface on which to project sensations, feelings and expectations, capable of assuming a relevant meaning in identity construction processes. If we compare the relationship and expressive contexts in Social Network Sites with the off line ones, it's clear that the online context gives researchers the huge advantage of making visible such dynamics and making them the subject of systematic observation.

For SNS users themselves, the possibility to trace their activities leads to a stronger awareness of the communication and relational dynamics. Therefore, the communication practices experimented in Social Network Sites enable a form of self-reflection which could be difficult to manage through face to face relationships: when a subject is "connected" he/she can, in fact, benefit from a privileged point of view to observe him/herself and the memory of his/her communication intentions expressed through creative forms (the different posts on Facebook feeds).

The analysis we have proposed aims at reconstructing the processes of self construction and the value that brands assume in the objectification (on a Facebook wall) and sharing of these processes.

The same forms of expression can also be read according to marketing objectives, since they represent an extraordinary repertoire to reconstruct the values of brands and the many different ways individuals appropriate them. The analysis so far carried out in literature has been centered on sentiment and opinion research (Boiy, Hens, Deschacht, & Moens, 2007; Pang & Lee, 2008) and the huge databases built have been mostly examined with the objective of estimating the more or less positive perception of brands within the communication flows exchanged by the social actors through the Internet (not only in Social Network Sites, but also blogs, web pages, etc.). On one hand, these analyses satisfy brands' constant need to estimate their position in the consumers' perception; on the other they make it difficult for us to use the data produced by market researchers for scientific objectives and compare them with our research.

Still, we believe that some of the methodologies used for the automatic recovery and indexing of databases could be used, instead, to evaluate how brand values and expressions can foster identity processes of each single individual. We are also certain that these kinds of analyses could be valorized by those who are responsible of brand positioning, since the younger generations seem to multiply and contaminate their lifestyles as a consequence of a weaker and temporary sense of belonging. Young consumers have, indeed, learned to attribute unusual meanings to their own original practices of fruition. These meanings can end up surprising companies and producers, but could also offer new semantic universes for the brands to explore. In this dialectic between continuity and innovation, the brands could therefore learn how to exploit these expressions of unpredictable and elusive consumers, who escape the traditional marketing categories and demand equality when dealing with brands (Christodoulides, 2009).

At the same time, the economic crisis we are facing has forced individuals to partly rethink their lifestyle, focusing not so much – and not only – on a drastic reduction of their spending power, but also on the re-allocation of the available resources characterized by sobriety and respect of the environment. These new consumers demand a bigger effort from the brands: more responsible behavior and a renewed attention towards the real needs of individuals and society. Thus, in the light of these dynamics it seems necessary for researchers who focus on the market to develop a different sensitivity, elaborating multidisciplinary methodologies capable of understanding the complexity of consumption behaviors. New opportunities of knowledge can emerge from the contamination of approaches and from dialogue, though respecting – and maintaining distinct – the specific research aims.

CONCLUSION[66]

Our research has considered one of the most recent and particular expressive forms of postmodern identity, an identity that is open and structured through a multiplicity of heterogeneous social practices, such as the conversations that take place in Social Network Sites. In this continuous process of observation and definition of the individual's identity, the symbolic materials offered by consumption are used by social actors for the creation of their self, but also as a tool for classification and social recognition. The postmodern condition has accustomed social actors to read in the practices of fruition a non verbal expression of the senses of belonging and distinction (Roberti, 2006). These practices are increasingly expressed in a symbolic way, both in the physical spaces and in the communicational exchange made possible by the technological development of the Internet.

The uncertainty of the paths which lead to the construction of an identity, together with the fragility of the community of reference, led individuals to continuously experiment new systems of interpretation in the attempt of finding a stable way to re-embed[67] their existence. The strong emotional investment in the symbolic values connected to the sphere of consumption – and to the projection of the individual's identity towards the brands – could indicate the need to identify anchorages, though fragile and changeable (Bauman 1997), which can partially surrogate the stronger senses of belonging that post-modernity seems to have swept away. In our opinion, the appropriation and rewriting of brands' values allow the construction of an identity that can be used in different relational contexts. The expressions - apparently ephemeral and more or less correlated to real consumption practices - used as describers of feelings, desires and expectations, are not immediately functional to the acquisition of a social status. They are, instead, useful to create new relationships and to build elective social bonds, since it is through others that we become ourselves (Mead, 1934). The sample of messages we have analyzed clearly reveal the users' ability to use brands in an active way: to "tell their story" and to use the distinctive features of consumption goods to trace the boundaries of their new forms of recognition and belonging.

The new experiences of "digital intimacy" offered by Social Network Sites acquire an objective importance – especially among younger generations – because they let users experiment on their identity projections without having to pay too much in terms of control and social acceptance. The communication flow can, therefore, be strengthened through a real-time sharing of emotions and a simple way to link to the symbolic, expressive and value dimensions of the brand; through this process, it acquires those characteristics that are related to a specific generational sense of belonging.

We still need to understand – in the next years, refining our analysis tools – if the competences that networked publics have acquired through their manipulation and sharing of objects and symbols will be able to safeguard their need for authenticity and free personal expression, even while facing growing investments in brand promotion.

REFERENCES

Arendt, H. (1958). *The human condition*. Chicago, IL: University of Chicago Press.

Bartoletti, R. (2009). Il lato B della Barbie: la rivincita dei consumatori nel social web. In Mazzoli, L. (Ed.), *Network effect. Quando la rete diventa pop* (pp. 57–74). Torino, Italy: Codice Edizioni.

Bauman, Z. (1997). *Postmodernity and its discontents*. Oxford, UK: Blackwell.

Bauman, Z. (2001). *The individualized society*. Cambridge, UK: Polity Press.

Bauman, Z. (2007). *Consuming life*. Cambridge, UK: Polity Press.

Beck, U. (1997). *Eigenes Leben. Ausfluge in die unbekannte Gesellschaft, in der wir leben.* Munchen, Germany: Beck.

Berger, P., Berger, B., & Kellner, H. (1973). *The homeless mind.* Harmondsworth, UK: Penguin Books.

Berger, P., & Luckmann, T. (1966). *The social construction of reality.* New York, NY: Doubleday.

Boiy, E., Hens, P., Deschacht, K., & Moens, M. (2007). Automatic sentiment analysis in on-line text. *Proceedings ELPUB2007 Conference on Electronic Publishing – Vienna, Austria – June 2007,* (pp. 349-360).

boyd, d., & Ellison, N. B. (2007). Social network sites: Definition, history, and scholarship. *Journal of Computer Mediated Communication, 13.*

Campbell, C. (2005). The craft consumer. *Journal of Consumer Culture, 5,* 23–42. doi:10.1177/1469540505049843

Castells, M. (2001). *Internet galaxy.* London, UK: Oxford University Press.

Castells, M., & Fernandez-Ardèvol, M. Linchuan, Qiu J., & Sey, A. (2006). *Mobile communication and society. A global perspective.* Cambridge, MA: The MIT Press.

Christodoulides, G. (2009). Branding in the post-internet era. *Marketing Theory, 9*(1), 141–144. doi:10.1177/1470593108100071

Comunello, F. (2010). *Networked sociability.* Milano, Italy: Guerini.

Cooley, C. H. (1967). *Human nature and the social order.* New York, NY: Schocken.

Cova, B. (1997). Community and consumption. *European Journal of Marketing, 31*(3-4), 297–316. doi:10.1108/03090569710162380

Douglas, M., & Isherwood, B. (1979). *The world of goods.* New York, NY: Basic Books.

Eco, U. (1979). *Lector in fabula.* Milano, Italy: Bompiani.

Erikson, E. (1950). *Childhood and society.* New York, NY: Norton.

Fabris, G. (2008). *Societing. Il marketing nella società postmoderna.* Milano, Italy: Egea.

Fabris, G. (2010). *La società post-crescita. Consumi e stili di vita.* Milano, Italy: Egea.

Featherstone, M. (1990). *Consumer culture and postmodernism.* London, UK: Sage.

Giddens, A. (1990). *The consequences of modernity.* Cambridge, UK: Polity Press.

Giddens, A. (1991). *Modernity and self-identity.* Cambridge, UK: Polity Press.

Goffman, E. (1959). *The presentation of self in everyday life.* New York, NY: Doubleday.

Gummesson, E. (2002). *Total relationship marketing.* Woburn, MA: Butterworth-Heinemann.

Hine, C. (Ed.). (2005). *Virtual methods: Issues in social research on the Internet.* Oxford, UK: Berg.

Ito, M. (2008). Introduction. In Varnelis, K. (Ed.), *Networked publics.* Cambridge, MA: MIT Press.

Jenkins, H., Green, J., Xiaochang, L., & Domb Krauskopf, A. (2010). *If it doesn't spread is dead. Creating value in a spreadable marketplace. Convergence Culture Consortium.* MIT.

Levine, R., Locke, C., Searls, D., & Weinberger, D. (2000). *The cluetrain manifesto.* Cambridge, MA: Perseus Book.

Libai, B., Bolton, R., Bügel, M. S., de Ruyter, K., Götz, O., Risselada, H., & Stephen, A. T. (2010). Customer-to-customer interactions: Broadening the scope of word of mouth research. *Journal of Service Research, 13,* 267–282. doi:10.1177/1094670510375600

Marinelli, A. (2004). *Connessioni. Nuovi media, nuove relazioni sociali.* Milano, Italy: Guerini.

Mead, G. H. (1934). *Mind, self and society*. Chicago, IL: University of Chicago Press.

Melucci, A. (1991). *Il gioco dell'io. Il cambiamento di sé in una società globale*. Milano, Italy: Feltrinelli.

Minestroni, L. (2010). *Il manuale della marca. Consumatore, cultura, società*. Bologna, Italy: Fausto Lupetti editore.

Pang, B., & Lee, L. (2008). Opinion mining and sentiment analysis. *Foundations and Trends in Information Retrieval*, *2*(1-2), 1–135. doi:10.1561/1500000011

Roberti, G. (2006). Percorsi identitari giovanili. In Bovone, L., & Volontè, P. (Eds.), *Comunicare le identità. Percorsi della soggettività nell'età contemporanea*. Milano, Italy: FrancoAngeli.

Roberts, K. (2006). The *lovemarks effects. Winning in the consumer revolution*. New York, NY: powerHouse books.

Schutz, A. (1967). *The phenomenology of the social world*. Evanston, IL: Northwestern University Press.

Sciolla, L. (2007). Dimenticare l'identità o le concezioni riduzioniste dell'identità? Note sulle oscillazioni di un concetto. *La società degli individui, 29*, 33-45.

Silverman, D. (2006). *Interpreting qualitative data*. London, UK: Sage.

Touraine, A. (1997). *Pourrons-nous vivre ensemble? Egaux et différents*. Paris, France: Fayard.

Turkle, S. (1996). *Life on the screen: Identity in the Age of the Internet*. New York, NY: Simon & Schuster.

Veblen, T. (1899). *The theory of the leisure class*. London, UK: Macmillan.

Weber, M. (1922). *Wirtschaft und Gesellschaft*. Tubingen, Germany: Mohr.

ADDITIONAL READING

Abimbola, T. (2009). Story Telling to Move Markets, Audiences, People and Brands. *Journal of Consumer Marketing*, *26*(4), 304–305.

Arvidsson, A. (2006). *Brands: Meaning and Value in Media Culture*. London, UK: Routledge.

Bauman, Z. (1999). *La società dell'incertezza*, Bologna: il Mulino.

Beer, D. & Burrows, R., (2010). Consumption, Prosumption and Participatory Web Cultures: An introduction. *Journal of Consumer Culture*, March, 10, 3-12.

Crane, D. (2000). *Fashion and its social agendas. Class, gender, and identity in clothing*. Chicago, IL: University of Chicago Press.

De Certeau, M. (1990). *L'invention du quotidien*. Paris: Gallimard.

Douglas, M. (1996). *Thought Styles*. London, UK: Sage Publications.

Frechette, B. (2010). Brand Digital: Simple Ways Top Brands Succeed in the Digital World. *Journal of Consumer Marketing*, *27*(3), 273–293.

Fuchs, C., & Diamantopoulos, A. (2010). Evaluating the effectiveness of brand-positioning strategies from a consumer perspective. *European Journal of Marketing*, *44*(11/12), 1763–1786. doi:10.1108/03090561011079873

Griswold, W. (1994). *Cultures and Societes in a Changing World*, Thounsand Oaks/CA: Pine Forge Press.

Holt, D. (2006). Toward a sociology of branding. *Journal of Consumer Culture*, (November): 6, 299–302.

Lantieri, T., & Chiagouris, L. (2009). Brand trust in an age without trust: expert opinions. *Journal of Consumer Marketing*, *26*(2), 78–86. doi:10.1108/07363760910940447

Lyotard, J. F. (1979). *La condition postmoderne*. Paris: Minuit.

Maffesoli, M. (1988). *Le temps des tribus. Le declin de l'individualisme dans les societes de masse*. Paris: Meridiens Klincksieck.

Miller, D. (2008). *The Comfort of the Things*. Cambridge, UK: Polity Press.

Parker, B. (2009). A comparison of brand personality and brand user-imagery congruence. *Journal of Consumer Marketing, 26*(3), 175–184. doi:10.1108/07363760910954118

Paterson, M. (2006). *Consumption and Everyday Life*. London, UK: Routledge.

Phau, I., & Teah, M. (2009). Devil wears (counterfeit) Prada: a study of antecedents and outcomes of attitudes towards counterfeits of luxury brands. *Journal of Consumer Marketing, 26*(1), 15–27. doi:10.1108/07363760910927019

Ritzer, G., & Jurgenson, N. (2010). Production, Consumption, Prosumption: The nature of capitalism in the age of the digital 'prosumer'. *Journal of Consumer Culture*, (March): 10, 13–36.

Wellman, B. (1997). An electronic group is virtually a social network. In Kiesler, S. (Ed.), *Culture of the Internet* (pp. 179–205). Hillsdale, NJ: Lawrence Erlbaum.

Wellman, B. (2001). Physical Place and Cyberplace: The Rise of Personalized Networking. *International Journal of Urban and Regional Research, 25*, 227–252. doi:10.1111/1468-2427.00309

Wellman, B., & Haythornthwhite, C. (2002). *The Internet in Everyday Life*. Oxford, UK: Blackwell Publishing. doi:10.1002/9780470774298

KEY TERMS AND DEFINITIONS

Brand: Sum of the distinctive aspects, both material and immaterial, which identify a product, a service or a company. Today we tend to affirm that a brand consists of the totality of what is said about it by its producers and consumers.

Consumption Society: Indicates the passage from an industrial society based on production to a social model based on consumption, intended more and more as a tool of communication, social relationship and identity definition.

Facebook: Indicates the most widespread and well-known Social Network Site, with over 500 million active users, founded in 2004 by Mark Zuckerberg. Its mission is to "help people communicate more efficiently with their friends, family and coworkers".

Networked Publics: Indicates a linked set of social, cultural and technological developments that have accompanied people's engagement with digitally networked media. It is used as an alternative to terms such as 'audience' or 'consumer'.

Post-Modernity: Indicates the overcoming (or for some the embedding) of certain principles of modernity such as the faith in progress and in great collective ideas (among which enlightenment, idealism, marxism), in favor of a stronger relativism, of widespread uncertainty and of an increase of social complexity.

Social Network Sites: Indicates those "web-based services that allow individuals to (1) construct a public or semi-public profile within a bounded system, (2) articulate a list of other users with whom they share a connection, and (3) view and traverse their list of connections and those made by others within the system. The nature and nomenclature of these connections may vary from site to site" (boyd, Ellison, 2007).

ENDNOTES

* This paper is the result of a common reflection of the authors. However, for standard academic practice, we indicate the writer of each paragraph.

1 By Alberto Marinelli.

2 By Geraldina Roberti.

3 By Geraldina Roberti.

4 On the relationship between consumption and postmodernity see Featherstone, 1990.

5 It is Bauman (2007) who affirms that a society of consumers tends to fragment social groups, allowing only the creation of temporary and inconsistent relationships.

6 By Geraldina Roberti.

7 The other two selected days were Friday, July 2 and Sunday July 4, 2010.

8 For what concerns the language, while in the counting we considered all the messages about the four brands, the analysis of the texts concerned only those published in Italian, English, French and Spanish.

9 By Alberto Marinelli.

10 In reporting examples chosen from the messages gathered, we decided to respect, compatibly with the comprehensibility of the text, the original graphical forms, lexicon and syntax:
"This is me. I'm always laughing, I'm always hungry, I'm always late, I get angry easily, I live of music, I would give my life for the people I love (very few), I prefer a pair of jeans to a skirt, I prefer to eat a Big Mac, rather than go on a (f@cking) diet, I adore nutella, I adore the sea, I hate heat and I'm a bit crazy".

11 By Geraldina Roberti.

12 On these topics see Marinelli, 2004.

13 For all the data see http://mashable.com/2010/02/10/*Facebook*-growth-infographic/

14 By Geraldina Roberti.

15 See Levine et alii, 2000.

16 Anatomy of a *Facebook* Post: Vitrue's Data Behind Effective Social Media Marketing, from http://vitrue.com/blog/2010/09/21/anatomy-of-a-*Facebook*-post-vitrue/

17 This element, however, like also the following one, ought to be integrated intersecting the data concerning the messages created with structural variables connected to the users' country of origin.

18 Ibidem

19 "Sea cost:Vespa=Sea:Me".

20 "Satisfied with the shopping just done. Chanel, Prada, Gucci, Fendi.. I met my match!".

21 "Lightning..thunder...Flashes and bolts... in an evening like this the maximum of pleasure is to stay at home and to watch a film, eating a bread and nutella and maybe sharing it with the person you love!!!!!".

22 "98% of the women who drive smarts are cool. It is statistically proved that only cool women drive such a kind of vehicle... usually the value, the power and the design are directly proportional to their coolness...".

23 "I will kill the next person who tells me that chocolate and nutella make us happy".

24 Although, in some case, a bad management of such dynamics could cause the development of such an hypertrophic and awkward self that it could prevent from seeing reality as it is.

25 "Consider a summer evening....consider the hot hair that goes through your hair...comfortable clothes and flip-flops....add some good company....All of which on a vespa of the same age as you...flavored with a touch of madness....".

26 In this case, we obviously refer to Veblen, 1899.

27 "I want bread and nutella without being pregnant".

28 "To go around like a cool guy on my Vespa".

29 "If I have you...I have everything....Thank you so much vespa".

30 "At last the car =)) SMART I LOVE YOU =))".

31 "Wendy back to me...I need a miracle.. A summer without a Vespa is the end".

32 "I am not like nutella... I live in symbiosis with nutella!!! We are one thing".

33 "Never try the road-holding of a smart when its wet unless you have the right amount of adrenalin in your blood!!!!".

34 "Apricots with nutella, Pasta rings with nutella, Banana split with nutella, Barchette with nutella...: Nutella is like the color white...It goes with everything!!".

35 "Today I made another important step to have my vespa of when I was 14 in perfect condition....In a while I will...go back using my vespetta !!!!!!! yuppieee !!!!!!!!!!".

36 "I HATE GIRLS WITH A SMART, SHIT".

37 "I come from the old school I am one of those who when they were children played with slings and were happy to look at the trees with their leaves It is all a strange round like as if you are looking down a cliff and you feel dizzy. From here we move to the road. We are not used to wearing prada..".

38 "I feel uncontrollable hatred for any smart in circulation. It is official:D".

39 By Geraldina Roberti.

40 "For this week work is over! I did some shopping to take care of myself a little...(a nice pair of Prada and of Hogan)...and now... let's live the weekend!".

41 I'm not an expert..but for me it has an emotional value...I am a southern man, although I live in Rome..and I was born on the vespa and ape 50 ;)....for this reason I adore them".

42 "How nice it is when people see you in your new car and they say to you that they prefer the Audi A3 … Cool. I am 18 and I have a Smart. You are 20 and you are on foot. Jealousy is a bad thing ___ aaa how beautiful my Smart is".

43 "Do you remember the 5 kilo jar of nutella??? It cured our so called "lack of affection". But I have to say that nutella really works xD".

44 "Mamma miaaaaaa...and who will ever sell it!!!Too many memories with my smart!!!! A piece of life".

45 "AMALFI COAST THE BEACH OF WHEN I WAS 15.... YOU, ME AND THE VESPA 50....".

46 "BE CAREFUL!!!!!!!GIRL!!!!! To all those who had long and love l rides with me in MY SUPER SEXY CAR!!!!!!ti I love you little Smart. I miss you a lot!!! You will remain in my little heart!!!!!!!".

47 "IN MY MEMORY I HAVE FOUND THIS SONG...........MY GOD HOW MANY TIMES WE SANG IT OUT LOUD ON MY YELLOW VESPA WHEN WE WERE TEENAGERS!!!!".

48 "And today she is very happy because she has bought her first pair of prada shoes!!!!!!! =)".

49 "I have bought a car... A SMART!!! How cool it is!!!".

50 "The vespa is a style of life!!!".

51 "The VESPA is always a VESPA. It has an ageless style".

52 The Smart is trendy".

53 On these topics see. Comunello, 2010.

54 "CASTROVILLARI VESPA OWNERS AND FANS. GROUP DESTINED TO THE OWNERS AND THE FANS OF THE MYTHICAL VESPA - CITTA' DI CASTROVILLARI".

55 "=) Such as the pyjama party at half past twelve to eat nutella, too nice =) ihihihi".

56 "2° Smart gathering Varese: Place: Varese, Time: Sunday, July 4, 2010 9.00.00".

57 "If you life nutella crepes too, put I like and share".

58 "A Smart costs 10.000 Euro ready for the road... A station wagon costs 18.000, but at least you make love lying down!".

[59] "Those... who at least once with a Vespa, made repairs on the side of the road".

[60] "Hello, I am Claudio Silvestri, ex-chef of the National Football Team. Perhaps I gave the footballers too much Nutella!".

[61] There is a vast scientific literature on the relationship between consumption and new forms of community. See, however, Cova, 1997.

[62] "Fred Perry, Adidas, bermuda, shaved head and a day out on my Vespa.....".

[63] "I WANT IT: A HELLO KITTY SMART: YES. IT'S NOT CHIC. IT'S MORE".

[64] "You girl all Gucci and Prada who thinks to be stylish ... Well you are wrong in a big way...".

[65] By Alberto Marinelli and Geraldina Roberti.

[66] By Alberto Marinelli and Geraldina Roberti.

[67] On these topics see Giddens, 1990.

Chapter 9
Checking in at the Urban Playground:
Digital Geographies and Electronic Flâneurs

Martin Berg
Halmstad University, Sweden

ABSTRACT

Taking its point of departure in a critical discussion of the imagined dividing line between physical and digital spaces, this chapter demonstrates a socio-spatial turn in Internet studies and sets out to explore the meaning of locative technologies as an illuminating example of how such spatial boundaries increasingly collapse. Being empirically grounded in an analysis of twelve qualitative interviews with users of the applications Foursquare and Gowalla, this chapter focuses on the interplay between what is termed electronic flâneurs and digital geographies, and demonstrates in what ways the use of locative technologies provokes changes at two levels in the social realm: first, by adding a communicative digital layer to the spatial organisation of physical space, and second, by adding a spatially bound layer to interactions in digital space.[1]

INTRODUCTION

Ever since the early days of Internet studies, a problematic detachment between physical and digital spaces has been a recurring theme, often conceptualised in ontological rather than practical terms. Even though the conceptual division between "online" and "offline" could plausibly refer to the practical conditions of social interaction (which is how it is used in this chapter), it has often been understood as designating a difference between "virtual" and "real". Having operated as the dominant assumption for several years,

DOI: 10.4018/978-1-61350-338-6.ch009

predominantly through the trope of "cyberspace", this imagined dividing line is nowadays rarely regarded as a feasible construct. On the contrary, it has become a widespread assumption that physical and digital spaces increasingly merge thus blurring the boundaries between online and offline modes of interaction, which in turn renders the overused dichotomy between "real" and "virtual" terminally obsolete. The last few years have witnessed significant changes in the nature of online communication, not the least because of the proliferation of (mobile) social network sites (SNS) which points at the de-domestication of Internet use as well as a fundamental intertwining of physical and digital spaces. Taking these changes seriously and further elaborating an understanding of their social implications, this chapter considers the emergence of what could be termed the "socio-spatial turn" in Internet studies. Particularly focusing on the possible relationship between digitally mediated social interactions and physical (urban) space, the initial parts of this chapter deal with earlier perceptions of the Internet as a facilitating factor in the articulation of identities and social relations without necessary interdependence on either temporal or spatial boundaries. As will be demonstrated, the previously prevailing era of online anonymity and thereby associated corporeal absence was altogether forgotten and substituted by a regime of personally centred networks by the early 2000s. Significantly, in 2006, Time Magazine tapped into these processes of change when awarding "You" the honour of being the person of the year (Han, 2010). This example from popular discourse does not only suggest that the era of anonymity had ended but also, in consequence, that the Internet had gone through a fundamental make over. Much has happened since the birth of "the social web" and nowadays, traversing the informational highway is no longer confined to take place from the security of domestic spaces but is increasingly performed through mobile devices. In conjunction with the increment of mobile Internet access, the development of "locative technologies" and the use of "locative mobile social networks" (de Souza e Silva & Frith, 2010; de Souza e Silva & Sutko, 2009) have experienced a nearly immeasurable upsurge which has troubled predominant perceptions of interactions in digital space profoundly.

As of today, there are a handful of locative technologies and among these, Foursquare and Gowalla are the most widely used.[2] Substantially, these are mobile applications that allow users to engage in location-based interaction by means of mobile devices through which place-specific information can be created, consumed and shared. Although these applications are different regarding graphical user interface and basic functionality, they are both promoted as a facilitator of interaction through a communicative layer intimately bound up with physical spaces and places. Foursquare as well as Gowalla are said to make it possible for users to share their location with friends by "checking in" at digital spots (i.e. a digital representation of places), provide commentaries on others' locations and urban activities while at the same time receiving rewards of different sorts. Their basic functionality is thus a question of adding different forms of metadata to geographically identifiable places for distributing social interaction in digital spaces to various sites in physical space and vice versa. Locative technologies such as Foursquare and Gowalla are often depicted as providing a platform for exploring the city, establishing interpersonal relations and keeping up with current events in the urban landscape.

Gowalla (2010) is presented as a service through which it is possible to "[k]eep up with your friends, share the places you go, and discover the extraordinary in the world around you". The core graphical user interface consists of the "Passport" in which it is possible to collect stamps from visited places. Gowalla informs that "[i]t's pretty much like stamping your passport in real life. Only without the jetlag and customs forms". One of the crucial features is the possibility to interact with the places and the information posted from your friends' check-ins. Taking and sharing photos, commenting on places and sharing highlights, make such an interaction possible. Occasionally, upon check-in, users can find virtual items that function as digital souvenirs. These items are added to the Passport in which information is provided about what items are carried and which ones that are missing. In a similar vein, Foursquare (2010) invites its users to "unlock your world and find happiness just around the corner" and, furthermore, become "more aware of all the incredible things around you". The application is explained through a six step process that consists of "finding friends", "checking in", "learning tips", "getting out", "gaining power" and "using it everywhere". It is a way of gaining knowledge about where your "friends are hanging out" and it is possible to see if they are geographically nearby looking at their recent check-in. One special feature is the ability to become "mayor" at places visited frequently which functions as temporary label for demarcating that the user in question is the most regular client. The ways in which both Gowalla and Foursquare are depicted clearly point at the assumption that these applications are designed for use in conjunction with physical space. However, even though these descriptions of Foursquare and Gowalla are commercially viable and remarkably enchanting, it is nevertheless vital to further explore to what extent the users of these applications perceive a difference between forms of interaction in physical as well as digital spaces.

The purpose of this chapter is to explore the ways in which the locative technologies Gowalla and Foursquare are deployed in everyday life and how users understand their utilisation of these technologies as a (social) practice. It will highlight different challenges to the distinction between physical and digital spaces by addressing the act of "checking in" as a social process through which socio-spatial information is gathered and interpersonally shared. The increasing use of locative technologies points at a fundamental change of the urban landscape and the possibilities to navigate it by means of mobile devices. As a result of the consolidation of physical and digital spaces, the urban landscape shows signs of turning into a digitally fostered playground on which social interaction through check-ins, exchange of messages, images and video lay the foundation of a new way of experiencing urban life (de Souza e Silva & Hjorth, 2009). It appears that the city dweller, using locative technologies, literally turns into an electronic flâneur with a possibility to transgress and reinterpret physical as well as geographical boundaries through the creation, use and sharing of digital spots.[3] Putting a digital geography into play, digitally mediated interactions provide a challenge to current understandings of the social as well as built environment (Zook, Dodge, Aoyama & Townsend, 2004). Are we thus facing an extension of physical space and perhaps even the emergence of a regulating layer that operates socially on the level of playful interaction? This chapter suggests that users of locative technologies, to a large extent, strive a striking a balance between digital and physical spaces as integral parts of their everyday lives. Rather than understanding digital space as a detached social realm with a proper set of discursive regulatory mechanisms and procedures, the emergence of a highly playful but inescapably commercial geography is located. It is thus not a question of a playground without social and discursive constraints but rather one by which social interaction and the presentation of self is both regulated and disciplined.

Methodological Remarks

The arguments pursued in this chapter are empirically grounded in an analysis of twelve qualitative and thematically organised conversational interviews with users of Gowalla and Foursquare in the urban area of Malmö, Sweden.[4] Departing from the fact that a vast array of research demonstrates the increased importance of new media and social technologies for social interaction (Crang, Crosbie & Graham, 2007), this study has aimed at an empirical grounding of theoretical arguments. Taking their point of departure in a general discussion of SNS and the perceived differences between online/offline as well as their embedding in everyday life, the interviews focused perceptions of locative technologies, strategies for self-presentation and interpersonal communication, mainly by focusing of the practice of checking in at different places as well as partaking in the creation and consumption of information that forms the basis of digital geographies.[5] The empirical material aims at providing a nuanced understanding of the ways in which these technologies are used as communicative devices and as a means for interacting with people and places. This is a vital example of emerging forms of social interaction and establishment of interpersonal relationships that provides a significant contribution to an understanding of networked sociability as well as the blurring of the boundaries between digital and physical spaces. The importance of doing empirical studies within this field of research has been underscored by Hine whom maintains that "[a] key challenge for the future is to develop forms of ethnography that take seriously the social reality of online settings, whilst also exploring their embedding within everyday life" (2008, p. 258). Whilst Hine's suggestion should be taken seriously, much has clearly happened during the few years that have passed since its publication. During the last year or so, a number of locative technologies have emerged that constitute a challenge to the formerly popular distinction between online and offline space and this development has functioned as a rationale for this study.

BACKGROUND

Ever since the early years of Internet studies, sci-fi narratives and metaphorical figures such as "cyberspace" (Gibson, 1984) have been important sources for envisaging possible implications of the rising network society and the socio-structural changes that it is assumed to provoke. Exploring the history of Internet studies, Wellman (2004) maintains that it is distinguished by three different "ages". Initially, the Internet was regarded "a technological marvel" (p. 124) assumed to not only transform the world but also provide a foundation for global connectivity beyond the constraints of time and space. Subsequently, researchers moved away from the "eloquent euphoria" (p. 127) of the first age, by studying Internet communication as a phenomenon embedded in everyday life activities. Wellman contends that is was a time in which the population of the Internet had changed "from a world of Internet wizards to a world of ordinary people routinely using the Internet" (p. 125). The second age was thus characterised by social scientific studies and documentation of the constant proliferation of users as well as uses of the Internet. These studies demonstrated that Internet use seemed to foster offline social relationships and strengthen social ties in offline settings. Finally, the third age of Internet studies is characterised by rather different conditions which allow for a theoretically driven analysis that can seriously take into account that "[t]he Internet is helping each person to become a communication and information switchboard, between persons, networks, and institutions" (p. 127). Although the field of Internet studies has undergone quite dramatic changes, it is vital to acknowledge that the early "cyber-theorists" of the first euphoric age frequently regarded digital space as a distinct social realm, not only assumed to be spatially unbound but also characterised by the absence of corporeal matter. Putting terms like "cyberspace" and "virtual reality" into practice, leading theorists such as Rheingold (1995), Turkle (1995) and Benedikt (2000/1991) gave voice to a utopian futurism that routinely desired social interaction to take place without any necessary reliance on either space, place or time as impeding factors. In this sense, cyberspace was often positioned as not only the antithesis of urban space but also, and perhaps more intriguingly, as its very antidote. Instead of getting stuck in traffic, delayed by public transport and consumed by the hubbub of urban space, urban dwellers were assumed to resort to cyberspace where they, leaving their bodies and troubles of everyday life behind, could traverse the digital highways as electronic flâneurs. These ideas have led several commentators to propose that digital communication would threaten the cultural and social life of the city (Light, 1999; Mitchell, 2000/1995, 2003). However, arguing that this conception has no significant bearing, Graham (2004) makes clear that urbanisation and the intensified use of digital communication are mutually supporting factors in processes of cultural and social change. Even though this appears to be a plausible interpretation, historical accounts of communication and interaction in digital space were often underpinned by a rather different presumption.

Understanding cyberspace as an immaterial environment, it was frequently considered to be "an apparently anti-spatial world where digital streams of information, data, images and video [...] seemed to operate like some giant nervous system for the planet" (Graham, 2004, p. 7). It could be argued, as Batty (1993) among others has done, that digital space (or "cyberspace" as he prefers to term it), due to its invisibility to our direct senses, is a different form of space that might become interwoven with and layered on top of the foundations of geographic space. On the whole, early attempts to theorise cyberspace reverberated McLuhan's (2001/1964) vision of the emergence of new social forms through the rise of the "global village" which was unavoidably expected to put the city in a rather problematic situation. In this account, spatial proximity was rendered both undesirable and purposeless in the era of digital communication and replaced by the newborn pleasures of spatially unbound interaction. Understanding the above mentioned interpretations of the Internet from a present-day perspective, they clearly expressed more of a visionary image than a realistic portrayal. It is worthwhile to observe, however, that several interpretations of this kind are typically marked by a futurism that is routinely bringing "nerdwords" into play (Gauntlett, 2004). This state of affairs stem from the fact that Internet studies, whether scientific or commercial, as Holmes (2005) asserts, often strive at capturing a sort of "cybergeist" and thus, as Cavanagh (2007) suggests, conform to a "cult of the new". Even though it is tempting to immerse oneself in futuristic sci-fi narratives, it is decisive to remember that the Internet and interaction in digital space necessarily need to be grasped considering the social and political reality of everyday life in the offline sphere (Robins & Webster, 1999).

From Cyberspace to Everyday Life: A Social Turn

The past few years have witnessed an increased criticism towards the distinction between physical and digital spaces of interaction and several researchers have attuned to the changing conditions by understanding digital space as an integral part of everyday life (see for instance Bakardjieva, 2005; Wellman & Haythornthwaite, 2002). In contrast to the notion of digital space as a separate social realm, current conceptualisations increasingly situate digital space as deeply embedded in everyday life and as a challenge to the contemporary modes of societal organisation in physical space.[6] At this point, the Internet is thus frequently recognised as an infrastructure that to a large extent is used for bringing into play the social web through which people immerse themselves in activities such as sharing, sorting and categorising data that is reviewed and commented upon. The social web can be regarded as a "cluster of technologies, devices, and applications that support the proliferation of social spaces in the Internet" (Castells, 2009, p. 65). These changes suggest that the popular view of online communication as mediated through portals (Lash, 2002, 2006) needs to be read in light of Wellman's idea that "[t]he person has become the portal" (2004, p. 127).

One of the core features of the social web is found in the phenomenon of SNS which, according to boyd and Ellison (2007), demarcate a shift in the ways that online communities are organised. In their account, SNS are portrayed as applications on the social web that allows for the construction of a public or semi-public profile through which it is possible to put on display a list of shared social connections which, in turn, makes it viable to browse the social connections of other users. Research has demonstrated that SNS are mainly used to maintain and sustain offline relationships (Ellison, Steinfield & Lampe, 2007). This thought is further validated by Lampe, Ellison, and Steinfield (2006) whom make clear that the searching for people to which the users of SNS already have an offline relation is vastly more frequent than the act of flickering through the profiles of strangers as a means for establishing a social relationship. Following this line of thought, Vergeer and Pelzer (2009) maintain that online and offline networks supplement rather than replace each other and these findings are further supported by Valenzuela, Park and Kee (2009) whom argue that engagement in SNS enhances social relationships in the offline realm (see also McKenna, Green & Gleason, 2002). Similar ideas have been elaborated by Boyd (2008b) whom suggests that SNS can be regarded as a "networked public" that support social interaction in the same sense as offline spaces would do. In overall terms, the primary function of SNS is the facilitation of communication with people that are already part of one's extended social network. Understood in such way, the emergence of SNS implied a fundamental shift from social interaction in thematically organised online communities to SNS that are centred on people's personal, or as Boyd and Ellison (2007) put it, "egocentric" networks. In this sense, they maintain that SNS do not primarily serve to initiate relationships with strangers but rather to articulate and make one's social network visible. By demonstrating the social connections to others, an establishment of latent social ties is facilitated and thus, as Haythorntwaite (2005) has demonstrated in depth, a form of connectivity emerges that makes otherwise unconnected others connect.

As indicated above, the basic advantage of SNS is the ability to establish social relationships and perform a self-presentation, observe each other and exhibit social relations through the graphical user interface. Following this line of thought, Beer and Burrows maintain that SNS can be regarded as "dynamic matrices of information through which people observe others, expand the network, make new "friends", edit and update content, blog, remix, post, respond, share files, exhibit, tag and so on" (2007, p. 2.1). Importantly, however, this kind of social applications provide, as Kozinets has put it, a "new level of voyeurism and exhibitionism" (2010, p. 71) that is substantially different from the interactional scene in physical space. Being assumed to facilitate social interaction and collaboration, the social web has triggered several theorists to argue that the culture of today is a participatory one (Jenkins, 2006) largely inhabited by the prosumer (Beer & Burrows, 2010; Ritzer & Jurgenson, 2010) which, in turn, not only constitutes a new social category but also, and more surprisingly, is nearly perceived of as a form of life with a radically different kind of individuality and a lust for shouldering the conditions of late-modern communicative capitalism (Dean, 2005, 2010a, 2010b). Beer and Burrows (2007) underscore the importance of understanding SNS in the context of what Thrift (2005) has termed "knowing capitalism". Thrift argues that "software has come to intervene in nearly all aspects of everyday life and has begun to sink into its taken-for-granted background" (Thrift, 2005, p. 153). Following this line of thought, Beer and Burrows point at the importance of recognising

SNS as commercial spaces since they routinely are used to harvest information about the users, thus pointing at a problematic aspect of their being free to use.

The rapid emergence of SNS has prompted researchers to discuss the possible implications of the modes of social organisation it allows for. Even though a vast array of issues are being considered in this research context, the relationship between processes of impression management, friending strategies and privacy concerns stand out as the most important themes. As mentioned earlier, one core characteristic of SNS is the public display of connections and this is a feature that allows for a negotiation of self while at the same time serving as a means for connecting with others (Boyd, 2004) and provides a possibility to validate the identity information that is found in other users' profiles (Donath & Boyd, 2004). Understood in such a way, different parts of the public profile can be regarded as mechanisms of self-presentation (Boyd & Heer, 2006), not the least since it has been demonstrated that "wall postings" on Facebook is an important part of how profile owners are perceived (Walther, Van Der Heide, Kim, Westerman & Tong, 2008) and that their listing of interests functions as an arena for taste performances (Liu, 2008). Clearly, people carefully construct their online self-presentation and it is often performed considering anticipated offline interaction (Ellison, Heino & Gibbs, 2006). Importantly, however, it has been pointed out that there is a certain discrepancy between social popularity online and offline and this is a factor that provides a problematic aspect of SNS as a means for self- presentation (Utz, 2010).

Evidently, there is a large amount of factors outside the immediacy of personal action that affects the processes of self-presentation. An important aspect of this state of affairs is that SNS, in contrast to common practice offline, allow for the creation of a very large extended network. Making a distinction between "Friends" on SNS and the "friends" of everyday life, Boyd (2006) argues that the first kind provides a means for users to imagine an audience that, in turn, serves as a guide for their action. Criticising such a distinction, Beer (2008) calls for an understanding of SNS as changing the understandings of friendship in general which, since SNS are becoming part of the cultural mainstream, could be remediated and indeed shaped by the version of friendship provided by SNS. Due to the recent upsurge of SNS as well as mobile and locative technologies, Beer argues that social life as such has become mediated to such an extent that the notion of life "offline" is no longer a feasible construct. Furthermore, he maintains that "these technologies are so mundane and integrated in how we live, why try to understand them by separating them out of our routines, how we live, how we connect with people and form relationships and so on" (2008, p. 521).

During the last few years, privacy concerns on SNS have been widely discussed, not the least because of the inherent risk that personal information could be harvested and used for commercial purposes. Early accounts of these issues illuminated a disconnection between users' desire for privacy protection and their actual behaviour (Acquisti & Gross, 2006). Even though Stutzman (2006) have pointed out that the public nature of SNS remains unknown for a large number of users, the level of desired privacy appears to relate to perceived trust and usage goals (Dwyer, Hiltz & Passerini, 2007). Technological changes, by which the users of Facebook, for instance, have been haunted regularly during the last few years, affect the notions of privacy, not the least by disrupting the users' sense of control over impression management (Boyd, 2008a). However arguing that SNS can threaten personal privacy, Debatin et al. (2009) assert that the perceived benefits of online social networking most often compensate for the risks associated with the disclosure of personal information. In addition, they argue that the use of Facebook is deeply integrated in everyday life to such an extent that it has its own routines and rites.

This thought is further elaborated by Sadeh et al. (2009) in arguing that privacy concerns in mobile social networks depend on the time spent using a specific application since users tend to be more comfortable with disclosing personal data over time. Measures for enhancing the conditions of personal integrity has been taken in different forms and, as Boyd and Ellison (2007) make clear, the majority of SNS demand a bi-directional confirmation process for the establishment of friendships. Importantly, the development of location aware mobile technologies that are equipped with camera devices could possibly provoke a shift in the ways that privacy concerns are understood since they, in contrast to regular SNS, facilitate a detailed place-specific tracking of other individuals (de Souza e Silva & Sutko, 2009).

Making Place Matter: A Spatial Turn

The enormous increase in mobile communication that has become reality during the last few years has changed the use of the Internet and particularly the use of SNS since people increasingly use mobile devices to connect to each other and their extended networks. If the development of the social web and SNS marked a social turn in the history of the Internet, a tentative suggestion would be that the emergence of locative technologies, correspondingly, marks a spatial turn. Understanding contemporary society and culture as characterised by an ephemerality while arguing that communication and space are deeply bound up with each other, Jansson and Falkheimer (2006) point at the necessity for a general spatial turn in media studies (whereas Soja [1999, 2009] calls for a general transdisciplinary spatial turn). This necessity is further illuminated when the intersection between mobile technology and SNS is considered. Several researchers have suggested that the boundaries between public and private are blurred because of mobile communication technologies (for instance Höflich, 2006; Puro, 2002; Sheller, 2004; Sheller & Urry, 2003) and Wilken (2008) has called for an examination of the ways in which these technologies shape (the experience of) places while mobile communication increasingly becomes integrated in everyday life activities.

When online communication is no longer confined to the security of domestic spaces but rather ubiquitous and intensely used in conjunction with urban life, the imagined boundary between physical and digital spaces increasingly appears to be implausible. Importantly, earlier studies have demonstrated that mobile technology accelerates the informational exchange which in turn has deep effects on the "urban metabolism" (Townsend, 2000). Along with other researchers, Humphreys (2010) understand the proliferation of mobile social networks as an important factor in the transformation of social interaction and maintains that it can provide the foundation for a rearrangement of socio-spatial practices and a negotiation of public space since it facilitates novel informational flows. Arguing that mobile social networks make it easier to interact in public with others, Humphreys suggest that this kind of technology needs to be positioned in the relational borderland between communication technology and urban life. Although the use of mobile social networks primarily consist of online communication, their ability to facilitate the exchange of social or locational information catalyses offline interaction.

What is here termed a spatial turn in Internet studies cannot be reduced to the increasing use of mobile technology but rather needs to be understood considering more overarching questions of media, mediation and late-modern social processes. Numerous researchers have endeavoured to theorise the conditions of late-modern society with certain respect to its increasing mediatisation. In this context, Giddens (1991) positioned the dissociation of time and space as a significant attribute of late modernity along with Beck and Beck-Gernsheim (2002) whom positioned processes of individualisation at the heart of late-modernity (see also Han, 2010; Harvey, 1990). More specifically, Meyrowitz (1985) provided an early account of how electronic media affected people's perception of space and provoked changes at the level of community and social roles. These are but singular examples, but it seems that contemporary society is not so much bound up with institutional arrangements as it is concerned with network connections which, by default, emphasise individuality.

Elaborating these thoughts profoundly, Castells (2001/1996) argues that a new spatial logic which he terms "space of flows" follows the rise of the network society. Positioning space and time as deeply intertwined, Castells notes that space normally brings together practices that are temporally simultaneous. Partly due to the increasing number of circuits of electronic exchange, space as well as time have taken on new characteristics which provide the foundation for a transformation of the urban landscape. Although people continue to live in "the space of places", social practices are nowadays supported and structured by "the space of flows" which implies that the meaning and social dynamic of places is heavily altered. In a similar vein yet focusing specifically on the interrelationship between media and modernity, Thompson (1995) underscores that any understanding of communication networks needs to reconsider the idea that its singular function is to transmit information. Instead, he suggests that it intervenes in the social world by allowing for new forms of action and interaction which fundamentally reorganise the social realm. Arguing that "the use of communication media transforms the spatial and temporal organization of social life" (p. 4), Thompson maintains that social bonds that include physically absent others are established. Consequently, these developments have "resulted in the uncoupling of space and time, in the sense that spatial distanciation no longer required temporal distanciation" (p. 32). An important aspect of Thompson's argument is that these changes has paved way for a "despatialized simultaneity" which has profoundly expanded the spatial horizons in contemporary society thus altering the conditions for experienced belonging and perceptions of time and space. Following this line of thought, communications media transform social action to by transcending the boundaries of the immediate social context thus making it potentially directed towards an indefinite range of recipients.

Understanding locative technologies while taking into account the theoretical framework above, their practical meaning clearly needs to be situated in a broader social context as well as regarded as an important mediator of symbolic content. An early account of this kind of technology demonstrated that it facilitated the experience of closeness in the urban setting while at the same time providing a means for congregation as well as avoidance (Humphreys, 2010). Asserting that the use of locative technologies simultaneously involve a combination of communication, collaboration and social interaction on both a physical and digital level, de Souza e Silva and Sutko (2009) propose that it provides an opportunity to engage in novel forms of exploring (and navigating) urban as well as digital spaces. Although they largely understand the use of such technologies in the context of socio-spatial gaming, de Souza e Silva and Sutko provide a functional nomenclature for understanding the meaning of applications like Gowalla and Foursquare. Suggesting that locative-mobile social networks facilitate the establishment of a dynamic relationship between physical as well as digital spaces and the people that populate them, they claim that this state of affairs results in the emergence of a "playful layer that is formed on top of physical spaces" which consequently leads to a "reconfiguring [of] urban spaces into ludic experiences" (2009, p. 6). In order to develop this thought further, they bring the metaphorical figure of the flâneur into play since it, as they maintain, draws attention to the possibility of playful activity to reshape urban space thus calling for an understanding of the city as consisting of "spaces to be explored, rather than circulatory spaces, in which the main purpose of movement is to travel from point to point" (2009, p. 6).

Understanding the flâneur as an actor whom aimlessly and without any explicit destination traverses the urban playground, de Souza e Silva and Sutko maintain that his (or her) "wandering and detracted gaze" leads to a reterritorialisation of the city by means of merging "the "serious" space of the city (designed to promote the circulation of people) with the ludic activity of casual walk, thus eliminating the boundaries that separate a distinct and separate playful space from ordinary life spaces" (2009, p. 7). The idea that locative technologies provide an additional communicative layer to the geography and social topography of urban space is worthwhile only when considering urban space as a multilayered phenomenon. In his Production of Space, Lefebvre (1999/1974) sets out to grasp the complexity of spatial arrangements. Understanding the city as divided into different yet interrelated levels, he provides a foundation for conceptualising the meaning of locative technologies in a contemporary urban setting. Drawing on his understanding of space as a product of social action, de Souza e Silva and Sutko argue that the playful spaces that emerge from the use of locative technologies correspond to his notion of lived space. This thought can be further elaborated by turning to Anderson (2004) whom, by using the term "cosmopolitan canopy", maintains that spatial location implies an inclination to act in a manner that corresponds to a shared assumption about the place in question.

Even though locative technologies facilitate the emergence of a playful, or at least communicative, layer through which physical and digital spaces are allowed to intermingle, this chapter pursues an understanding of these technologies that is underpinned by Huizinga's (1998/1944) suggestion that play always implies a certain amount of seriousness. As will be demonstrated later on in this chapter, locative technologies such as Foursquare and Gowalla are used in a manner that is not only playful but also firmly interlaced with preoccupations of (prospective) social transactions in physical space. It is often maintained that the act of checking in at different places is accompanied by a certain degree of anxiety and desire for pleasing a digitally present yet spatially distant other. These technologies appear to provide more than adding a digital layer to urban space, as de Souza e Silva and Sutko (2009) suggest, since they also, and what is more important, are adding a spatial (and thus physical) layer to digital space. It appears to be the case that "[t]he information order is inescapable. It gives us no longer an outside place to stand" (Lash, 2002, p. xii).

CHECKING IN AT THE URBAN PLAYGROUND

Although several research reports (for instance Medierådet, 2010) demonstrate that interactions in digital space are perceived as an integral part of everyday life, it is important to remember that some fundamental differences between physical and digital spaces persist. The absence of corporeal matter in digital space limits the interactive mechanisms to the sensory faculties of sight and hearing, but this state of affairs does not imply that bodies (or places, for that sake) are rendered unimportant. On the contrary, the very prerequisite for the intelligibility of locative technologies hinges on the fact that people, with their bodies and senses, are (not) located at certain places. This entails that an exploration of the ways in which locative technologies are used in different social contexts is significant. In so doing, it is crucial to question whether interaction in digital space renders spatial proximity purposeless and/or undesirable and, furthermore, to examine if such an interaction takes place at a radical distance from the social realm in physical space. In the following sections it will be demonstrated that the use of locative technologies involves a dual social process since they are used for sharing place-specific information, on the one hand, and gathering such information from members of the personal social network, on the other hand. These aspects of the utilisation are linked through a multitude of network connections, interconnected social networks and flows of social interaction in different forms and intensities. The remainder of this section endeavours to explore these notions in depth to establish an understanding of how locative technologies are used in everyday life and to what extent such applications contribute to the amalgamation of experiences in physical and digital space.

Dissolved Boundaries, Embedded Social Action

In almost every case, the interviews were opened up by discussing the personal experiences of online interaction and most of the interviewees touched upon the division between digital and physical spaces when conversing about questions of anonymity and privacy concerns. Clearly, the complexities of such a division were something they had carefully reflected upon and, in overall terms, the prevailing thought was that digital and physical spaces are largely inseparable. At several occasions, the interviewees returned to the idea that these spaces have become fused into a communicative social realm and expressed an inclination for striking a balance between experiences gained in digital and physical spaces. Jessica, a 30 years old communications officer, recalls the earlier situation and suggests: "nowadays, the digital wild and crazy of the 90's has started to collide with reality". In a similar vein, and relating to notions of anonymity, Amanda, a 26 years old communications manager, maintains that there is no significant difference between these spaces since they are equally a playground for initiating and sustaining relationships, "but through other channels and slightly different ways of expressing oneself". Following this thread, David, a 28 years old graphic designer, recalls his early days of browsing and chatting on the Internet and asserts that in his case, anonymity has never been an issue. Instead, he explains, using the Internet was a means for establishing social ties based on interest rather than geographical proximity. Even though he clearly understands the Internet as all but anonymous, David contends that some properties of digital interaction makes it different from its physical parallel. Suggesting that interaction in digital spaces puts the actor in a social "safe-mode" in which, at least to some extent, a "pre-talk" is facilitated, David appears to understand SNS as providing a functional filter through which the other is scrutinised. In his account, it appears to be a question of evaluating the other from a safe distance or, as David explains, pointing at the current situation, "the idea that people friend each other on Facebook and chat a bit on Facebook and then sort of become a couple [...] I think that has made quite a lot for people's close relationships". David's view of digital communication is vastly similar to the accounts provided by the other interviewees and it points at the idea that digital interaction is to some extent characterised by rationalisation and calculability. As several researchers have argued, for instance Ritzer (2004), these are significant facets of late modern society and provide an important context when David explains that interaction in digital space allows for an evaluation of other people, thus making it easier to meet them in person (or decide not to do so).

Understood in such a way, what happens in digital space does certainly not stay digital but on the contrary materialise, penetrate and act on processes and events in physical space. It is thus often assumed that actions in digital space demand a perceived authenticity by the subject acting "back stage" (Goffman, 1990/1956). This idea is backed up by Amanda whom says: "you have to live up to what you give the impression of; if you check in at the arts gallery, you kind of have to live up to that [...] maybe it sounds a bit harsh, but you should at least have an interest". Similarly, Michael, a guy in his thirties, makes clear that providing information about offline actions and places necessarily implies that he stands as a guarantee for its validity. In line with this understanding, several interviewees maintained that on SNS it is appropriate to be "personal, but not private" and it appears to be the case that this is said as a precaution and a strategy for keeping a distance between what occurs in digital and physical space. Subjected to the gaze of the other, the "private" thus never comes into the limelight but is rather reduced to the fictionalised and highly narrated notion of the "personal". This, however, is not an easy task but rather, as Jessica explains, "a balancing act" and it is thus not very surprising that check-ins with a potential to evoke a desired social response are preferred in favour of others, as will be demonstrated later on in this chapter. It is in this context that locative technologies such as Gowalla and Foursquare need to be understood. Even though these applications are but examples of mechanisms that challenge the imagined division between digital and physical spaces, their entrenchment in physical space draws this thought to its extreme.

Checking In: The Electronic Flâneur, a Botanist of the Digital Sidewalk

Taken together, the interviews provide a rich account of the practice of "checking in" and give voice to a conceptualisation of locative technologies as a mechanism through which a complex interplay between self-presentation, social interaction, space and place is put into play. In contrast to the anonymous and disembodied subject of "cyberspace", the trope of the electronic flâneur is here deployed to comprehend actors that are deeply involved in complex social relationships, wandering on the frail boundary between digital and physical spaces. In so doing, the electronic flâneur challenges the very feasibility of such a boundary since both of these spaces appear to be interwoven and subjects of mutual penetration. Elaborating these ideas further, this section is devoted to three interrelated themes, namely the check-in as a device for social filtering, distant interaction and strategic self-presentation.

On the surface, the act of "checking in" is often presented in a very instrumental manner. Even though the interviewees often explained that the use of locative technologies had some primary purpose (such as gaming, keeping up with friends, trying to figure out new business ventures or simply using it as a pastime), they all expressed a view of these technologies as fundamentally social and deeply embedded in everyday life activities. One of the basic tenets of the practice of checking in appears to involve the establishment of social relationships to a variety of places which are used as a means for sharing information about oneself as well as visited places to the members of one's extended network. Although sharing place-specific information, providing suggestions or simply being amusing could well be regarded as ways of providing others with a "social surplus value", as Amanda puts it, checking in often comprises an early stage of a social process which occasionally results in an offline encounter.

In the interviews, several ways of conceptualising this aspect of the check-in surface and most notably, both David and Jennifer, an advertising creative in her thirties, explain that it can be understood as an invitation for meeting up, whereas Amanda makes clear that it is an invitation to dialogue. Several interviewees provide examples of how the check-in have resulted in different forms of serendipitous gatherings of which some have blossomed out to friendships while others have simply remained a temporary acquaintance. Understanding the check-in as related to the establishment of social relationships is crucial since it lays the foundation for comprehending questions of self-presentation and social presence in digital space. Checking in at different places involves the marking of a simultaneous presence at a vast array of places thus increasing the number of potential social contact surfaces independent of time and space. This implies that the imaginable recipients of check-in data fluctuate in character and number since there is always an indefinite range of potential recipients involved, as Thompson (1995) suggested, although in a context very different from this. Being used as a means for establishing relationships of different kinds, the check-in thus metaphorically becomes a way of scattering breadcrumbs in the trails of one's journey through the urban landscape while simultaneously laying the foundation for a spatial dispersion of the self. Taken together, these ideas point at a relationship between self and other that appears to be sustained by and bound up with places of different kinds.

A majority of the interviewees make clear that these technologies are used as a means for navigating not only the urban landscape but also, and what is more important, there and others' social network. In overall terms, check-in data facilitates the sorting out of people with similar interests and tastes, since it provides information about movement patterns in physical space that are considered to be important for experiencing a similarity. Understood in such a way, these technologies allow for a filtering of the flows of information in people's extended networks thus making it possible to differentiate between individuals with whom one could possibly experience either strong or weak ties (Granovetter, 1973). Importantly, places serve as a nexus in the social and informational flows thus being an important factor in the filtering of social interactions. At several occasions, the interviewees suggested that the check-in, to some extent, contributes to a sense of order in an otherwise disordered social context characterised by a multitude of actors, messages and potential social relationships. In this sense, shared places help discerning similarities between actors thus allowing for a "pre-talk", as David expresses it, and other forms of interpersonal evaluation prior to the establishment of a social interaction offline. Michael maintains that checking in at the same places as other individuals is part of such an evaluative procedure since a shared place can function as an important piece in a social jigsaw puzzle. Explaining that it is often a question of discerning patterns of movement to find out a commonality of interests, David says: "you check out who've been around at a place [...] for example, it's possible to see who've been here a couple of hours ago". At several occasions, the interviewees explained that checking in facilitates the establishment of social relations, not the least by flickering through other people's check-ins for discovering mutual friends and place-specific relationships. One illuminating example of these processes is the spontaneous emergence of social ties through ousting the "mayor" of a place in Foursquare. Amanda concludes that such an experience provides an impression of commonality and says: "if a person has checked in there many times, then we have to have something in common". This sort of events often trigger an urge to embellish such an embryonic social relationship through, as Amanda maintains, "checking out the person in question just to see what other places this person's got". If the check-in should be regarded as an utterly social practice, then it follows that the electronic flâneur, to achieve a meaningful existence, unceasingly depends on the others' activity. Taking part of other people's check-ins, an increased knowledge of both people and places emerges and clearly, checking in at the same place as others indicates a commonality since, as Amanda puts it, "it has to lie something in the fact that they check-in at a certain place". This assumption is often operationalised in a strategic fashion since being at the same places as other (influential) people and checking in there provides a foundation for establishing a relationship in physical space.

Following this line of thought, it does not come as a surprise that a number of the interviewees pointed out that the possibility to comment upon other people's check-ins is an important feature.[7] Arguing that this is one of the most significant aspects of locative technologies, David maintains that it allows for "exploring the city and spreading information about lovely places". Similarly, Jessica as well as Robert, a tech savvy 35-year old, explain that commenting on check-ins is an important part of these technologies since it establishes social interaction, to some extent. Facilitating distant interaction this way, these technologies enable a communicative flow that is deeply bound up with places without the necessity of bodily presence. Although checking in at places which correspond to an actual locale in physical space is common, there is a possibility that people check in at imaginary places (such as for instance "the rabbit-hole to China" or "the world's ugliest fountain") which implies that, as will be further elaborated in the next section, place-specific interaction is not always bound up with the actual geography of physical space. Rather, space appears to be constructed by flows to a higher extent than it is linked to the space of places which entails that the digital geography as such appears to be an important point of reference.

Even though the possibility to mediate communication and interaction through places in digital space is an important feature of locative technologies, their ability to make physical and digital space interpenetrate is significant. This state of affairs provides a foundation for one of the most important aspects of the use of locative technologies that surfaced in the interviews, namely their significance for strategic self-presentation. To a large extent, the interviewees suggest that checking in at places is, however performed routinely, associated with a great deal of reflection and sometimes even meticulous preparation. For instance, Jessica maintains that she puts down "quite an effort in formulating myself on the Internet because it increases the chances to receive funny comments [...] just so that someone will see it and think it's amusing". It is thus important, she adds, not to simply deliver information or images but rather, "to create some sort of narrative of the things you publish". A similar account is provided by Amanda whom explains that she often chooses not to check in at all places to which she pays a visit, "but rather choose the ones that will strengthen my personal brand the most, so to speak". Understanding places as an important part of her self-presentation, Amanda makes clear that places as such are integral parts of her personal "brand". This entails that the check-in serves at, as Humphreys (2010) has demonstrated (even though not sufficiently accounting for the socio-structural circumstances involved), facilitating the meeting up with friends as well as the possibility of avoiding certain social encounters. Being aware of which places that are selected for check-in does thus not primarily appear to be a question of privacy concerns as earlier research on SNS has demonstrated but rather implicates a connection to possible outcomes in the offline social realm. When sharing check-in data, it is not primarily the intrinsic qualities of the place that are at stake but rather the possible reaction from one's social network.

Checking in at a place is an act that is directed towards other individuals and, similar to what one could expect from a setting in physical space, certain positive aspects of the user's urban life are revealed. At times, this is achieved by checking in at some places but avoid doing it at others and is a question of, as Jessica maintains, "glorifying life a bit, no one need to see the failures". Facilitating a favourable self-presentation of this sort, the use of locative technologies could be understood as a means for legitimising one's social network. Amanda, for instance, points at a complexity in the relationship between check-ins and the social network in arguing that checking in a certain places has a possibility to "confirm that you're doing right in having each other as friends" and that fighting over mayorships on Foursquare might provide a feeling of being "right in your context". In a similar vein, Jessica asserts that it is more favourable to check in at socially accepted and/or desired places and informs that "one becomes a bit cocky being at the gym and noticing that one is top of the leader board [...] It doesn't mean anything but [...] it's just in your face!". This theme was discussed by several interviewees and Michael, for instance, makes clear that these technologies are used to construct a "myth" about oneself; about the places you visit, your journeys". Similarly, Rebecca maintains that they are used as a means for shaping one's identity, which is a perception comparable to Jennifer's whom argue that they are used for "telling other people who you are". Self-presentation and places are thus intimately connected and Daniel, a tech geek in his late thirties, explains that he avoids checking in a certain places since some information is simply not meant for others and it is important to remain in control. Yet another way of handling these issues is expressed by Jennifer whom reveals that she occasionally checks in at nearby places that are slightly more "cool" instead of checking in at the place where she is actually situated. Clearly, locative technologies are not simply used as a means for connecting with existing friends but are rather associated with a possibility to establish spontaneous connections and interactions. Checking in must therefore be situated in a complex web of interrelated factors that, taken together, provide a means for self-presentation. It does thus not come as a surprise that the interviewees often suggest that actions and interactions in digital space are performed strategically to evoke desired effects in physical space. Andrew, a 37 year old Internet entrepreneur, provides an illuminating example of this inclination and maintains that checking in is associated with calculation and tactics since it, one way or the other, serves at generating some sort of social surplus value. A similar thought is expressed by Jessica whom explains that it is a question of putting on display "all that raises your status [...] you have a desire to share positive experiences".

Linking up the statements above, it becomes clear that locative technologies and the act of checking in is of a complex nature. It could certainly be regarded as a mechanism that allows individuals to not only extend their personal social network but also provides an opportunity to facilitate distant presence at digital representations of places in physical space. Hence, these technologies make it possible to be digitally present yet spatially dispersed. Such a dispersed presence provides an opportunity to engage in a strategic self-presentation that transgresses temporal as well as spatial boundaries although they are deeply bound up with the geography of physical space. The possibility to engage in self presentation in different yet parallel contexts is an important feature of locative technologies and provides a foundation for understanding the electronic flâneur as an inherently playful, yet notoriously conscious actor. Clearly, locative technologies are largely used in a fashion that implies a rationalisation of social relations while at the same time being subjected to a commercialisation of both the social realm and the self. Checking in is often surrounded by a high level of calculability and is thought of as deeply related to potential offline encounters. In contrast to self-presentation on SNS, locative technologies seem to foster a self-presentation that is performed by establishing relationships to places which are put on display. It is thus a question of strategically sharing place-specific occurrences online to evoke (and avoid) certain effects in the offline social realm. In Baudelaire's original account of the flâneur, it was often assumed to be a "botanist of the sidewalk" and, in a sense, an observer that was always detached from the immediate social surroundings while strolling the urban neighbourhoods. Traversing urban space as a digital billboard, the electronic flâneur differs from this figure quite dramatically since it is highly regulated and always on guard to protect its fragile yet valuable personal brand. At hand, is thus an actor which could simultaneously be regarded as a stroller of the city streets thus participating in and portraying the city as well as an actor that not only experiences the city reflexively and with a high level of calculability but also participates in a social context through which the city and the urban landscape is provided with meaning. This does not only prove the distinction between physical and digital space to be fundamentally blurred but demonstrates as well that actions and interactions in physical space are often governed by the social and informational flow in digital space (and vice versa).

Checking Out: Digital Geographies and Spatially (Un)Bound Pleasures

Traversing the urban playground, checking in by means of locative technologies and thus being distantly present on a vast array of places, the electronic flâneur establishes social relationships in a variety of ways. An integral part of the processes associated with the act of "checking in" is, curiously enough, the act of "checking out" other people and places. As a whole, the interviews suggest that digital interaction is seldom performed without spatial references but is rather intimately connected with the digital representation of physical space. Several examples of how these spaces converge and interpenetrate are found in the interviews and by illuminating some of them, an understanding is established of the complexity attached to locative technologies and the emergence of digital geographies.

The use of locative technologies and the creation of spots allow for the emergence of a digital geography and this is a theme that was touched upon in a number of the interviews. Commenting her use of these technologies, Jennifer states that "there's sort of a virtual map over Malmö, like a layer or a web" and in a similar fashion Robert explains that "it's like a digital layer on top of the city; there's a darn lot of information that we get mobile access to". Sometimes the spots are intimately bound up with the physical geography of the city whereas the other times take the form of imaginary places. Even though some of the interviewees find the humorous creation of imaginary spots desirable, others, such as Matthew, an entrepreneur in his late 20s, and Daniel make clear that the correspondence to the physical geography is essential. Arguing that social organisation in digital space is characterised by a certain degree of undesired "messiness" and exemplifying with the possibility to create geographical spots through locative technologies, Matthew declares that "there is something missing in these applications; they aren't rooted in reality and I don't fancy the anarchy in people's adding of places". In contrast to his view, Jennifer underscores that part of the fun with locative technologies disappears when there is too much of a similarity between the physical and digital geography. Although Daniel explains his view of locative technologies as providing "a map on top of the map" he finds it decisive to strive at a precise digital cartography. Arguably, this view needs to be understood while considering the fact that several interviewees declared that they use locative technologies to gain an extended knowledge about the city. Rebecca, for instance, reveals that she finds it hard to remember street addresses and thus uses the digital "map" to find a café or a restaurant whenever necessary. Importantly, however, she explains that gaining knowledge about a certain place is not only a question of browsing nearby spots but is something that includes her social network for validating purposes. Understood in this way, the place in itself is not sufficient for attracting her interest since the members of her network also need to have some sort of relationship to the place in question. Traversing the urban playground thus becomes a question of, as Rebecca puts it, "following in the footsteps of one's friends".

Although it is often argued that these technologies are used to gain knowledge about the city, it appears to be done in a rather passive and socially subjected fashion. Several informants state that they seldom search for information about places actively, but are rather inclined to be affected by actions performed by the members of their personal social network. An informative example of this state of affairs is provided by Jessica whom maintains that it is more a question of taking notice of other people's check-ins than actively browsing the place archives. Although she receives this information passively, she clearly states that it has an impact on what places she chooses to visit. A similar conception is expressed by Christopher, a 20-year old computer science student, whom points out that check-ins are quite useful when it comes to learning about the city since they can be regarded as "recommendations from like-minded people". In this sense, gaining an understanding of the city or, more correctly, apprehend the behavioural patterns of the individuals that form your extended network is quite easily done. Jessica exemplifies this thought, saying: "you can see where people check in even if you're not friends on Twitter or Facebook". Taking this idea one step further, Robert explains that these technologies make him move around in the city and that they serve as a map for finding out where to buy pizza, for instance.

Several interviewees shed light over the fact that locative technologies prompt a curiosity and spark an interest for acquiring further information about the city due to the ability to take part of other, known as well as unknown, people's check-ins. A reason behind this state of affairs is not the least that checking in at the same place as others lays the foundation for the occurrence of unexpected social relations. Jessica, for instance, tells the story of how she once took notice of another person regularly checking in at places similar to hers which made her wonder, as she puts it, "who the fuck is that person? We've almost got exactly the same movement patterns!". Similar experiences are described by several interviewees and could well be contextualised by Rebecca whom explains that checking in is "a way of making yourself public; it is like a public business card with a photo". Even though the users rarely search for places actively by means of locative technologies, the majority of the informants agree that they have contributed to an increased knowledge of the city. It appears to be the case, however, that they inform themselves indirectly by looking, gazing and taking notice of where the other is located. Despite the fact that this indicates a certain degree of passivity, Jessica explains that the use of locative technologies easily develops into a social mechanism through which it is not only possible to keep a check on what is going on but also to experience, to some extent, a distant presence: "even though not acting [...] you experience a participation despite the fact that you're not actually interacting with those people for real". A similar thought is expressed by Jennifer whom explains that she frequently partakes in other people's activities at a distance but often ends up thinking "oh my god, it would be fun being at [a night club], but where to find an instant babysitter?"

Relating interpersonal communication to places and thus dissolving the boundaries between physical and digital spaces, locative technologies and their mediation of distant interaction facilitate the experience of community without being dependent on proximity in time and space. As was discussed in the former section, the interviewees shared stories about the possibility to being distantly present, such as for instance hanging out with friends without leaving the comfort of one's home. Several informants explain that they make use of locative technologies to find out where their friends are located thus making it possible for them to coincide. It could well be argued that a presence at multiple sites becomes facilitated this way with a possibility to transgress geographical obstacles in order to experience a spatial proximity. Importantly, it is not a question of being geographically situated in physical space but rather of establishing a digital connection to a place and the social interactions occurring at it. In this way, the physical geography is by no means rendered futile but rather, a transmutation of physical space is provoked by the enmeshment in the digital communicative layer provided by locative technologies. Hence, it is again possible to return to the idea that locative technologies facilitate a distant presence and this thought is further illustrated by Amanda whom informs that "sometimes you don't know what to do on a Friday evening and sometimes you're too tired to do anything but then it feels like you can partake in the night out even if you're staying in". Understanding the use of locative technologies as a means for taking part in social situations at a distance, Amanda maintains that "you feel a lot less lonely these days". However accentuating a rather different aspect of this state of affairs, Rebecca explains that checking in is a way of telling her friends where she is and says that she uses these technologies in order to figure out what other people that are present in the same locale as she is. In a sense, she thus endeavours to explore the immediate offline setting by means of online technology.

Providing a possibility to partake in different and, at times, parallel social settings at a distance, locative technologies can be used as a means for experiencing a sense of community. A number of interviewees touched upon this theme while suggesting that these technologies allow for keeping a check on people in the extended network thus shortening the temporal as well as spatial distance to others. Importantly, this occurs, as Jennifer makes clear, on two different levels since it is a question of relating to both known and unknown people. Furthermore, Jennifer explains that locative technologies can provide a sense of community, even though there are clear limitations. Sharing a story about being situated in a large crowd at one of the city squares while noticing how a large amount of her friends checked in at the same place, she tells about the frustration in not being able to find her friends among all the other people. However, it is clear that the very experience of being at the same place as others is strengthened when mediated by locative technologies. A similar idea is put forward by Amanda whom continues her reasoning about the possibility to be digitally together with her friends that are having a night out in town: "if my friends have spent a night out and I feel like; no, I'm just too tired, then I still have the possibility to see where they've checked in and [...] the dialogue is so much closer than just asking, yeah, so what were you up to?". Considering these statements, it seems fruitful to understand locative technologies as a mechanism that facilitates a certain form of intimacy and feeling of community. It is not only a question of being able to see what other people are doing, but rather that their actions, so to speak, are delivered automatically.

In line with what was touched upon earlier, several informants frequently return to the idea that the personal "feed" is of crucial importance to their social practice and use of locative technologies. It is not unusual that this is understood as an automatised condensation of a generalised other that constantly supplies response and information (Lash, 2006). Taken together, the statements above suggest that the digital geographies that emerge from the use of locative technologies are utterly social. The electronic flâneur, traversing digital and physical spaces while "prosuming" these geographies is largely a passive observer, expecting to be guided by the social feed and the activity of others. This intricate manifestation of a tension between a digital voyeurism and exhibitionism makes it plausible to question from where the activity comes if the majority of users are only passively engaged or, as Amanda indicated, acting to entertain people. When it comes to locative technologies, the feed often takes a peculiar form since it is not simply a question of automatic delivery of social updates but also the deliverance of socially anchored representations of space. The electronic flâneur is thus situated in a rather strange situation since no effort is demanded to partake in the urban events but instead, they can be conveniently received from a safe distance. Hence, an example of passive activity or, to use a more suiting concept, interpassivity (cf. Dean, 2010b; van Oenen, 2008; Žižek, 1999) surfaces. In place of the individual flâneur, the digital representation of the city appears to act on its own thus providing, as Žižek puts it, a "sense of being active through another subject who does the job for me" (1999, p. 104). It seems fair to ask if the electronic flâneurs are checking out the activity of other users or if it could possibly be that they are the ones who are being checked out by the social feed and by the gaze of a system that increasingly gives the impression of sustaining an interpassivity rather than invigorating social interaction, critical dialogue and mutual recognition.

In the above, two major themes have surfaced that are equally important for understanding locative technologies and the emergence of digital geographies. First, it has been demonstrated that locative technologies allow for a distant presence thus transgressing spatial boundaries. Taken as a whole the arguments above indicate that the use of locative technologies supports an alternate understanding of the urban playground that challenges earlier assumptions of interaction in digital space. In contrast to the assumption that interaction in digital space would render spatial proximity unnecessary, locative technologies clearly involve social processes through which geographical spaces are interpenetrated by digital communication and, vice versa, that online interactions are bound up with representations of physical space. This, in turn, makes up a serious challenge to the imagined distinction between digital and physical spaces. Second, these technologies are largely dependent upon informational feeds and thus promote an interpassivity rather than interactivity. In overall terms, these technologies facilitate the rise of an array of geographies which, when converging into a "cosmopolitan canopy" (Anderson, 2004), provide an altered perception of the city while at the same time rendering possible diverse modes of social interaction in, through and by means of the city in as a point of reference.

FUTURE RESEARCH DIRECTIONS

There are several important research themes that go beyond the scope of this particular study but nevertheless prove to be closely related to its core arguments. Researching the Internet and its social appropriations is a tricky endeavour since there are different temporal logics at play. This is why it is important not to forget basic social processes and sociologically viable categories such as actor, structure and agency, for instance. In the case of locative technologies, further research of the importance of the feed and the notion of interpassivity is needed. It is important to elucidate whether the technological development is making it easier to interact, collaborate and participate in social settings or if it is rather an example of systems of knowing with an automatised feed that are acting in place of the individual actor. In conjunction with this important question, it is pivotal to further investigate the significance of communicative capitalism that increasingly appears to make up the very foundation of SNS and similar applications.

CONCLUSION

At the outset of this chapter, previous discussions about the problematic division between online and offline social spaces were introduced. It has been demonstrated that checking in at the urban playground is a fundamentally social act that brings together different aspects of physical as well as digital spaces. It is not, however, a question of a playful use of locative technologies but rather one that is deeply associated with a constant awareness of the other and of the social mechanisms of late modern society. The use of locative technologies brings forth an electronic flâneur that is partly strolling and partly sneaking around while observing the actions of the other. Even though these technologies are intentionally used as a means for interaction and overcoming spatio-temporal obstacles, they also position the actor in a state of interpassivity through which the social network acts on its own behalf. Locative technologies thus not only entail a mechanism that makes it effortless to traverse urban space but also the establishment of a regulatory device that puts individual patterns of movement on display while simultaneously monitoring individual self-presentation and the virtual co-presence of other individuals. In other words, it is a question of processes similar to what de Souza e Silva and Sutko (2009) have termed "co-surveillance".

Despite the difficulties associated with the use of locative technologies, they are often used in a range of imaginative ways. Most importantly, they allow for a social filtering and a distant presence at places that transgress temporal and spatial boundaries while facilitating a presentation of self that is dispersed and scattered around the urban landscape. Most importantly, the interviews suggest that drawing a boundary between digital and physical spaces is a difficult task since they are often understood as parallel and intertwined. At the same time, however, digital space appears to be founded on its own logic with an apparent relationship to communicative capitalism. The electronic flâneur appears to be quite lonely yet highly interconnected and, in a sense, very anxious; as if its very existence hinges upon social recognition, in digital as well as physical space. In a similar vein, locative technologies facilitate the emergence of digital geographies through which physical spaces are understood and traversed with the social network and the check-ins of other users as points of reference. In overall terms, the deployment of locative technologies such as Foursquare and Gowalla provokes changes at two levels in the social realm. First, it adds a communicative digital layer to the spatial organisation of physical space. Second, it adds a spatially bound layer to interactions in digital space thus connecting the flows of bits and bytes to places in physical space.

REFERENCES

Acquisti, A., & Gross, R. (2006). Imagined communities: Awareness, information sharing, and privacy on the Facebook. In G. Danezis & P. Golle (Eds.), Privacy Enhancing Technologies, 6th International Workshop, PET 2006 (pp. 36-58). New York, NY: Springer.

Anderson, E. (2004). The cosmopolitan canopy. *The Annals of the American Academy of Political and Social Science*, *595*(1), 14–31. doi:10.1177/0002716204266833

Atkinson, R., & Willis, P. (2007). Charting the Ludodrome: The mediation of urban and simulated space and rise of the flâneur electronique. *Information Communication and Society*, *10*(6), 818–845. doi:10.1080/13691180701751007

Bakardjieva, M. (2005). *Internet society: The Internet in everyday life*. London, UK: Sage.

Batty, M. (1993). The geography of cyberspace. *Environment and Planning. B, Planning & Design*, *20*(6), 615–617.

Beck, U., & Beck-Gernsheim, E. (2002). *Individualization: Institutionalized individualism and its social and political consequences*. London, UK: Sage.

Beer, D. (2008). Social network(ing) sites...revisiting the story so far: A response to danah boyd & Nicole Ellison. *Journal of Computer-Mediated Communication*, *13*(5), 516–529. doi:10.1111/j.1083-6101.2008.00408.x

Beer, D., & Burrows, R. (2007). Sociology and, of and in Web 2.0: Some initial considerations. *Sociological Research Online*, *12*(5), 17. doi:10.5153/sro.1560

Beer, D., & Burrows, R. (2010). Consumption, prosumption and participatory Web cultures: An introduction. *Journal of Consumer Culture*, *10*(1), 3–12. doi:10.1177/1469540509354009

Bell, M. (2011, February 20). Personal communication with McClain Bell, Gowalla/Allison & Partners].

Benedikt, M. (2000). Cyberspace: First steps. In Bell, D., & Kennedy, B. M. (Eds.), *The cybercultures reader* (pp. 29–44). London, UK: Routledge. (Original work published 1991)

Benjamin, W. (Ed.). (1990). *The arcades project*. Cambridge, UK: Belknap Press.

Boyd, D. (2004). Friendster and publicly articulated social networks. Conference on Human Factors and Computing Systems (CHI 2004), April 24-29. Vienna, Austria: ACM.

Boyd, D. (2006). Friends, Friendsters, and MySpace Top 8: Writing community into being on social network sites. *First Monday*, *11*(12).

Boyd, D. (2008a). Facebook's privacy trainwreck: Exposure, invasion, and social convergence. *Convergence*, *14*(1), 13–20.

Boyd, D. (2008b). Why youth (heart) social network sites: The role of networked publics in teenage social life. In Buckingham, D. (Ed.), *Youth, identity, and digital media* (pp. 119–142). Cambridge, UK: The MIT Press.

Boyd, D., & Heer, J. (2006). Profiles as conversation: Networked identity performance on Friendster. Proceedings of the Hawai'i International Conference on System Sciences (HICSS-39), Persistent Conversation Track, January 4-7. Kauai, HI: IEEE Computer Society.

Boyd, D. M., & Ellison, N. B. (2007). Social network sites: Definition, history, and scholarship. *Journal of Computer-Mediated Communication*, *13*(1), 210–230. doi:10.1111/j.1083-6101.2007.00393.x

Castells, M. (2001). *The rise of the network society* (2nd ed.). Oxford, UK: Blackwell. (Original work published 1996)

Castells, M. (2009). *Communication power*. Oxford, NY: Oxford University Press.

Cavanagh, A. (2007). *Sociology in the age of the Internet*. Berkshire, UK: Open University Press.

Crang, M., Crosbie, T., & Graham, S. (2007). Technology, time - space, and the remediation of neighbourhood life. *Environment & Planning A*, *39*(10), 2405–2423. doi:10.1068/a38353

Cross, M. (2011, February 18). [Personal communication with Meghan Cross, Foursquare/Kaplow PR].

de Souza e Silva, A. & Hjorth, L. (2009). Playful urban spaces: A historical approach to mobile games. *Simulation & Gaming*, *40*(5), 602–602. doi:10.1177/1046878109333723

de Souza e Silva. A., & Sutko, D. M. (2009). Merging digital and urban playspaces: An introduction to the field. In A. de Souza e Silva & D. M. Sutko (Eds.), Digital cityscapes: Merging digital and urban playspaces (pp. 1-20). New York, NY: Peter Lang.

de Souza e Silva, A., & Frith, J. (2010). Locative mobile social networks: Mapping communication and location in urban spaces. *Mobilities*, *5*(4), 485–505. doi:10.1080/17450101.2010.510332

Dean, J. (2005). Communicative capitalism: Circulation and the foreclosure of politics. *Cultural Politics*, *1*(1), 51–74. doi:10.2752/174321905778054845

Dean, J. (2010a). *Blog theory: Feedback and capture in the circuits of drive*. Cambridge, UK: Polity Press.

Dean, J. (2010b). The real Internet. *International Journal of Žižek Studies*, *4*(1). http://zizekstudies.org/index.php/ijzs/article/view/242/322.

Debatin, B., Lovejoy, J. P., Horn, A.-K., & Hughes, B. N. (2009). Facebook and online privacy: Attitudes, behaviors, and unintended consequences. *Journal of Computer-Mediated Communication, 15*(1), 83–108. doi:10.1111/j.1083-6101.2009.01494.x

Donath, J., & boyd, d. (2004). Public displays of connection. *BT Technology Journal, 22*(4), 71–82. doi:10.1023/B:BTTJ.0000047585.06264.cc

Dwyer, C., Hiltz, S. R., & Passerini, K. (2007). Trust and privacy concern within social networking sites: A comparison of Facebook and MySpace. Proceedings of the Thirteenth Americas Conference on Information Systems, Keystone, Colorado, August 9-12.

Ellison, N., Heino, R., & Gibbs, J. (2006). Managing impressions online: Self-presentation processes in the online dating environment. *Journal of Computer-Mediated Communication, 11*(2), 415–441. doi:10.1111/j.1083-6101.2006.00020.x

Ellison, N. B., Steinfield, C., & Lampe, C. (2007). The benefits of Facebook "friends": Social capital and college students' use of online social network sites. *Journal of Computer-Mediated Communication, 12*, 1143–1168. doi:10.1111/j.1083-6101.2007.00367.x

Featherstone, M. (1998). The flâneur, the city and virtual public life. *Urban Studies (Edinburgh, Scotland), 35*(5-6), 909–926. doi:10.1080/0042098984619

Foursquare. (2010). How to unlock your world with Foursquare. Retrieved November 22, 2010, from http://www.howcast.com/videos/386406-How-To-Unlock-Your-World-With-Foursquare

Gauntlett, D. (2004). Web studies: What's new. In Gauntlett, D., & Horsley, R. (Eds.), *Web studies*. London, UK: Arnold.

Gibson, W. (1984). *Neuromancer*. New York, NY: Ace Books.

Giddens, A. (1991). *Modernity and self-identity: Self and society in the late modern age*. Stanford, CA: Stanford University Press.

Goffman, E. (1990). *The presentation of self in everyday life*. London, UK: Penguin. (Original work published 1956)

Gowalla. (2010). Home. Retrieved November 22, 2010, from http://gowalla.com/

Graham, S. (2004). *The cybercities reader*. London, UK: Routledge.

Granovetter, M. S. (1973). The strength of weak ties. *American Journal of Sociology, 78*(6), 1360–1380. doi:10.1086/225469

Han, S. (2010). Theorizing new media: Reflexivity, knowledge, and the Web 2.0. *Sociological Inquiry, 80*(2), 200–214. doi:10.1111/j.1475-682X.2010.00327.x

Hartmann, M. (2004). *Technologies and utopias: The cyberflaneur and the experience of "being online"*. Munich, Germany: Verlag Reinhard Fischer.

Harvey, D. (1990). *The condition of postmodernity: An enquiry into the origins of cultural change*. Oxford, UK: Blackwell.

Haythornthwaite, C. (2005). Social networks and internet connectivity effects. *Information Communication and Society, 8*(2), 125–148. doi:10.1080/13691180500146185

Hine, C. (2008). Virtual ethnography: Modes, varieties, affordances. In Fielding, N., Lee, R. M., & Blank, G. (Eds.), *The SAGE handbook of online research methods* (pp. 257–270). London, UK: Sage.

Höflich, J. R. (2006). The mobile phone and the dynamic between private and public communication: Results of an international exploratory study. Knowledge. *Technology and Policy, 19*(2), 58–68. doi:10.1007/s12130-006-1024-4

Holmes, D. (2005). *Communication theory: Media, technology and society*. London, UK: Sage.

Huizinga, J. (1998). *Homo Ludens: A study of the play-element in culture*. London, UK: Routledge. (Original work published 1944)

Humphreys, L. (2010). Mobile social networks and urban public space. *New Media & Society, 12*(5), 763–778. doi:10.1177/1461444809349578

Jansson, A., & Falkheimer, J. (2006). Towards a geography of communication. In Jansson, A., & Falkheimer, J. (Eds.), *Geographies of communication: The spatial turn in media studies* (pp. 9–25). Gothenburg, Sweden: Nordicom.

Jenkins, H. (2006). *Convergence culture: Where old and new media collide*. New York, NY: New York University Press.

Kozinets, R. V. (2010). *Netnography: Doing ethnographic research online*. London, UK: Sage.

Lampe, C., Ellison, N., & Steinfield, C. (2006). A Face(book) in the crowd: Social searching vs. social browsing. CSCW '06: Proceedings of the 2006 20th Anniversary Conference on Computer Supported Cooperative Work.

Lash, S. (2002). *Critique of information*. London, UK: Sage.

Lash, S. (2006). Dialectic of information? A response to Taylor. *Information Communication and Society, 9*(5), 572–582. doi:10.1080/13691180600965542

Lefebvre, H. (1999). *The production of space*. Oxford, UK: Blackwell. (Original work published 1974)

Li, C., & Bernoff, J. (2008). *Groundswell: Winning in a world transformed by social technologies*. Boston, UK: Harvard Business Press.

Light, J. S. (1999). From city space to cyberspace. In Crang, M., Crang, P., & May, J. (Eds.), *Virtual geographies: Bodies, spaces and relations* (pp. 109–130). London, UK: Routledge.

Liu, H. (2008). Social network profiles as taste performances. *Journal of Computer-Mediated Communication, 13*, 252–275. doi:10.1111/j.1083-6101.2007.00395.x

McKenna, K., Y. A., Green, A. S., & Gleason, M. E. J. (2002). Relationship formation on the Internet: What's the big attraction? *The Journal of Social Issues, 58*(1), 9–31. doi:10.1111/1540-4560.00246

McLuhan, M. (2001). *Understanding media: The extensions of man*. London, NY: Routledge. (Original work published 1964)

Medierådet. (2010). *Ungar & Medier 2010: Fakta om Barns och Ungas Anvandning och Upplevelser av Medier*. Stockholm, Sweden: Kulturdepartementet.

Meyrowitz, J. (1985). *No sense of place: The impact of electronic media on social behavior*. Oxford, UK: Oxford University Press.

Mitchell, W. J. (2000). *City of bits: Space, place, and the Infobahn*. Cambridge, MA: MIT Press. (Original work published 1995)

Mitchell, W. J. (2003). *Me++: The cyborg self and the networked city*. Cambridge, MA: MIT Press.

Puro, J.-P. (2002). Finland: A mobile culture. In Katz, J. E., & Aakhus, M. (Eds.), *Perpetual contact: Mobile communication, private talk, public performance* (pp. 19–29). Cambridge, MA: Cambridge University Press.

Qualman, E. (2009). *Socialnomics: How social media transforms the way we live and do business*. Hoboken, NJ: Wiley.

Rheingold, H. (1995). *The virtual community: Finding connection in a computerized world.* London, UK: Minerva.

Ritzer, G. (2004). *The McDonaldization of society*. London, UK: Pine Forge Press.

Ritzer, G., & Jurgenson, N. (2010). Production, consumption, prosumption: The Nature of capitalism in the age of the digital "prosumer". *Journal of Consumer Culture, 10*(1), 13–36. doi:10.1177/1469540509354673

Robins, K., & Webster, F. (1999). *Times of the technoculture: From the information society to the virtual life*. London, UK: Routledge.

Sadeh, N., Hong, J., Cranor, L., Fette, I., Kelley, P., Prabaker, M., & Rao, J. (2009). Understanding and capturing people's privacy policies in a mobile social networking application. *Personal and Ubiquitous Computing, 13*, 401–412. doi:10.1007/s00779-008-0214-3

Sheller, M. (2004). Mobile publics: Beyond the network perspective. *Environment and Planning. D, Society & Space, 22*(1), 39–52. doi:10.1068/d324t

Sheller, M., & Urry, J. (2003). Mobile transformations of "public" and "private" life. *Theory, Culture & Society, 20*(3), 107–125. doi:10.1177/02632764030203007

Shields, R. (2006). Flanerie for cyborgs. *Theory, Culture & Society, 23*(7-8), 209–220. doi:10.1177/0263276406069233

Shirky, C. (2009). *Here comes everybody: How change happens when people come together*. London: Penguin.

Shirky, C. (2010). *Cognitive surplus: Creativity and generosity in a connected age*. New York, NY: The Penguin Press.

Simmel, G. (1950). The metropolis and mental life. In Wolff, K. H. (Ed.), *The sociology of Georg Simmel* (pp. 409–424). New York, NY: Free Press.

Soja, E. W. (1999). Thirdspace: Expanding the scope of the geopolitical imagination. In Massey, D., Allen, J., & Sarre, P. (Eds.), *Human geography today* (pp. 260–278). Cambridge, UK: Polity Press.

Soja, E. W. (2009). Thirdspace: Toward a new consciousness of space and spatiality. In Ikas, K., & Wagner, G. (Eds.), *Communicating in the third space* (pp. 49–61). New York, NY: Routledge.

Stutzman, F. (2006). An evaluation of identity-sharing behavior in social network communities. International Digital and Media Arts Journal, 3(1).

Tapscott, D., & Williams, A. D. (2008). *Wikinomics: How mass collaboration changes everything*. London, UK: Atlantic Books.

Thompson, J. B. (1995). *The media and modernity: A social theory of the media*. Stanford, CA: Stanford University Press.

Thrift, N. (2005). *Knowing capitalism*. London, UK: Sage.

Townsend, A. M. (2000). Life in the real-time city: Mobile telephones and urban metabolism. *Journal of Urban Technology, 7*(2), 85–104. doi:10.1080/713684114

Turkle, S. (1995). Life on the screen: Identity in the Age of the Internet. London, UK: Phoenix.

Utz, S. (2010). Show me your friends and i will tell you what type of person you are: How one's profile, number of friends, and type of friends influence impression formation on social network sites. *Journal of Computer-Mediated Communication, 15*(2), 314–335. doi:10.1111/j.1083-6101.2010.01522.x

Valenzuela, S., Park, N., & Kee, K. F. (2009). Is there social capital in a social network site? Facebook use and college students' life satisfaction, trust, and participation. *Journal of Computer-Mediated Communication, 14*(4), 875–901. doi:10.1111/j.1083-6101.2009.01474.x

Van Dijck, J., & Nieborg, D. (2009). Wikinomics and its discontents: A critical analysis of Web 2.0 business manifestos. *New Media & Society*, *11*(5), 855–874. doi:10.1177/1461444809105356

van Oenen, G. (2008). Interpassivity revisited: A critical and historical reappraisal of interpassive phenomena. *International Journal of Žižek Studies*, *2*(2). http://zizekstudies.org/index.php/ijzs/article/view/96/230.

Vergeer, M., & Pelzer, B. (2009). Consequences of media and Internet use for offline and online network capital and well-being. A causal model approach. *Journal of Computer-Mediated Communication*, *15*(1), 189–210. doi:10.1111/j.1083-6101.2009.01499.x

Walther, J. B., Van Der Heide, B., Kim, S.-Y., Westerman, D., & Tong, S. T. (2008). the role of friends' appearance and behavior on evaluations of individuals on Facebook: Are we known by the company we keep? *Human Communication Research*, *34*(1), 28–49. doi:10.1111/j.1468-2958.2007.00312.x

Weinstein, D., & Weinstein, M. A. (1991). Georg Simmel: Sociological Flâneur Bricoleur. *Theory, Culture & Society*, *8*(3), 151–168. doi:10.1177/026327691008003011

Wellman, B. (2004). The three ages of Internet Studies: Ten, five and zero years ago. *New Media & Society*, *6*(1), 123–129. doi:10.1177/1461444804040633

Wellman, B., & Haythornthwaite, C. A. (Eds.). (2002). *The Internet in everyday life*. Oxford, UK: Blackwell. doi:10.1002/9780470774298

Wilken, R. (2008). Mobilizing place: Mobile media, peripatetics, and the renegotiation of urban places. *Journal of Urban Technology*, *15*(3), 39–55. doi:10.1080/10630730802677939

Žižek, S. (1999). Is it possible to traverse the fantasy in cyberspace? In Wright, E., & Wright, E. (Eds.), *The Žižek reader*. Oxford, UK: Blackwell.

Zook, M., Dodge, M., Aoyama, Y., & Townsend, A. (2004). New digital geographies: Information, communication, and place. In Brunn, S. D., Cutter, S. L., & Harrington, J. W. (Eds.), *Geography and technology* (pp. 155–176). Dordrecht, The Netherlands: Kluwer Academic Publishers.

KEY TERMS AND DEFINITIONS

Electronic Flâneur: A metaphorical figure used in order to encircle the actor that traverses urban space by means of locative technologies.

Digital Geography: Geographical metadata that is added to the physical geography which bears a possibility to both correspond and diverge from the actual appearance of physical space.

Digital Space/Physical Space: A conceptual dichotomy that refers to different yet interrelated social realms and that could be regarded as closely related to online/offline.

Locative Technologies: Mobile applications allowing users to create, share and consume place-specific information and engage in location-based interaction.

Online/Offline: A conceptual dichotomy that refers to the practical conditions of social interaction as being either mediated by the Internet or not.

Social Network Sites (SNS): Online communities centred around the individual which often include a public or semi-public profile and the public display of social connections which facilitate the browsing of others' personal network.

Social Web: A series of applications that in different ways allow users to share, sort, review, comment and categorise user generated data which in turn supports the emergence of social spaces.

ENDNOTES

1 The research for this chapter was made possible by financial support from the Bank of Sweden Tercentenary Foundation.

2 Internationally, Foursquare is closing in on 6.5 million users and attracts more than 25,000 new users every day. Every day, over 2 million check-ins are performed around the globe. Foursquare does not provide usage statistics by country but reveals that 40% of the users are situated outside of USA (Cross, 2011). However not providing any specific numbers of active users, Gowalla informs that Sweden has the second highest user base worldwide for Gowalla, after USA and that Malmö is a city with very high check-in activity (Bell, 2011). Worth mentioning is that Facebook launched "Places', a service similar to those of Gowalla and Foursquare, during the writing this chapter (however subsequent to the fieldwork).

3 The concept of "electronic flâneur" was originally formulated by Mitchell (2000/1995) and has been deployed by several researchers in a range of studies (for instance Atkinson & Willis, 2007; Featherstone, 1998; Hartmann, 2004; Shields, 2006). Originally, the trope of the flâneur was formulated by Baudelaire but has been theoretically elaborated by theorists such as Benjamin (1990) and Simmel (1950). See also Weinstein and Weinstein (1991) for an important review of Simmel's significance.

4 Malmö is the third largest city in Sweden and is situated in the Øresund Region, a transnational region in which Copenhagen, capital of Denmark is the largest urban area. In total, the region has a population of approximately 3.7 million habitants. However not being the largest city in the area, Malmö has in recent years undergone a fundamental transformation from industrial to postindustrial city and is nowadays regarded as an important venue for the media industry.

5 The interviews included 8 men and 4 women in the ages between 20 and late thirties (not all interviewees agreed to disclose their actual age) that all could be considered to be early adopters of locative technologies. The majority of the interviewees worked within the media, communications and/or the creative industry. The length of the interviews ranged from 50 to 100 minutes (mean 70 minutes). All quotations have been translated from Swedish to English and are moderately rephrased for linguistic reasons.

6 It is not unusual that the implications of the social web are interpreted in commercially popularised accounts (such as Li & Bernoff, 2008; Qualman, 2009; Shirky, 2009, 2010; Tapscott & Williams, 2008) which could be termed, following van Dijck and Nieborg (2009), "Web 2.0 business manifestos".

7 At the time of undertaking the fieldwork this was a possibility for social interaction that was exclusively provided by Gowalla. Recently, however, it was recently implemented in Foursquare as well.

Section 3

Social Media and Institutions:

New Research Trends

Chapter 10
Revived and Refreshed:
Selective Exposure to Blogs and Political Web Sites for Political Information

Thomas J. Johnson
University of Texas at Austin, USA

Shannon L. Bichard
Texas Tech University, USA

Weiwu Zhang
Texas Tech University, USA

ABSTRACT

This study uses an online panel of Internet users to examine the degree to which those who visit U.S. political websites and blogs practice selective exposure as they construct their individual political networks. Specifically, the analysis addresses the extent to which individuals say they visit websites and blogs with which they agree and disagree. The findings indicate strong support for the detection of selective exposure in this context. Reliance on political websites and blogs as well as partisanship emerged as predictors of selective exposure for political information after controlling for demographic and political factors.

INTRODUCTION

As the number of people who seek out U.S. election news from the four major networks has declined, the number of people seeking more partisan sources such as cable television, political Web sites and blogs has been on the rise (Pew Research, 2008a; 2008b, 2010; Project for Excellence, 2008). Partisans increasingly are seeking out media that support their viewpoints and consequently voters could have received a completely different view of the 2008 U.S. presidential campaign depending on which sources they sought out (Project for Excellence, 2008). For instance, the majority of MSNBC viewers were Democrats and the news they saw was more supportive of Barack Obama and more critical of John McCain than the news media generally (Project for Excellence, 2008).

DOI: 10.4018/978-1-61350-338-6.ch010

MSNBC viewers were also more likely to hear about Sarah Palin's $150,000 wardrobe spending spree and Colin Powell's decision to endorse Obama than Fox News viewers, who were more likely than MSNBC viewers to hear about Obama's connection to the ACORN community organization that was linked to voter fraud (Pew Research, 2008).

Selective exposure to more partisan sources such as political Web sites and blogs is an important topic to explore because of the democratic implications of people only searching out views congenial to their opinions and beliefs. While some researchers suggest that selective exposure may actually motivate people to participate in politics and help them to organize political information meaningfully (Schudson, 1995), others fear selective exposure will contribute to existing problems in democracy. For instance, some researchers claim that engaging in partisan selective exposure will lead people to develop more polarized attitudes and more fragmented political networks (Iyengar & Hahn, 2009; Meffert et al. 2006; Sunstein, 2001; Prior, 2002). Polarized views could lead to a more biased processing of information and to less tolerance of opposing viewpoints (Mutz, 2002). Selective exposure may also produce a less informed electorate as democratic theory suggests that citizens should gather and critically evaluate a range of opinions before reaching decisions (Delli Carpini & Keeter, 1996).

While several studies have examined selective exposure to the Internet as a whole (Bimber & Davis, 2003; Garrett, 2009), few studies could be found that have explored selective exposure to different components of the Internet such as political Web sites and blogs (Johnson et al., 2009; in press; Stroud, 2006, 2008, 2010). Studies suggest that selective exposure effects are stronger for more partisan content (Best et al., 2005; Stroud, 2010), and therefore, selective exposure may be stronger for political blogs and political Web sites that often employ and engage a more partisan network (Johnson et al., 2008; Papacharissi, 2004; Thompson, 2003; Trammell Tarkowski, Hofmokl, & Sapp 2006). While selective exposure tends to look at whether individuals actively seek out stories that conform to their partisan biases, fewer studies explore whether people avoid conflicting information. Finally, while studies have linked motivations for seeking out sources to political attitudes, cognitions and behaviors (Shah, Kwak, & Holbert, 2001; Shah et al., 2005) as well as to credibility (Johnson et al., 2007; Johnson et al., in press), few researchers have analyzed the connection between gratifications and selective exposure. Those studies that have explored the gratifications and selective exposure association have typically examined how gratifications predict exposure to specific media genres (Hawkins et al., 2001; Kim and Rubin, 1997), not the degree to which different gratifications predict selective exposure and the management of individual networks.

This study employs an online panel of Internet users in the United States to investigate the degree to which those who rely on political Web sites and blogs practice selective exposure. More specifically, this study will examine whether those who rely on political Web sites and blogs for political information will be more likely to say that they visit sites and blogs that they agree with versus those they disagree with. This study will also focus on whether people are significantly more likely to practice selective exposure with blogs than political Web sites and whether people are more likely to seek out information that conforms to their beliefs than avoid information that confronts their beliefs. Finally, this study will explore the degree to which reliance, motivations for seeking out blogs and political Web sites and degree of partisanship predict amount of selective exposure to political Web sites and blogs after controlling for demographic and political factors. This study, then, will show how people manage their own social networks on political blogs and websites by examining one way people try to control information overload: through selective exposure to information that accords with their beliefs and avoiding sites that challenge their worldview.

The literature review will explain selective exposure and partisan selective exposure and show how it is linked to network society and individualism. The literature review will specifically examine selective exposure to political websites and blogs and then explore factors that explain selective exposure including political and demographic measures as well as reliance. Finally, because network individualism literature suggests that people seek out information that satisfies their needs, this study will examine the link between selective exposure and uses and gratifications.

BACKGROUND

Selective Exposure

Selective exposure arose out of cognitive dissonance theory, which proposes that when individuals are exposed to information or events that are inconsistent with their own beliefs, it causes a state of discomfort or dissonance (Festinger, 1957). Festinger argues that selective exposure is one of the mechanisms used to reduce feelings of dissonance. To reduce dissonance, individuals will seek out information that supports their beliefs or actively avoid information that challenges those views (Festinger, 1957). However, studies that have examined the degree to which selective exposure reduces dissonance have produced mixed results at best (Kinder, 2003; Sears & Freedman, 1967; Zaller, 1992).

Studies have found more robust results when they decouple selective exposure from its cognitive dissonance moorings and instead study it as an information-processing technique. Selective exposure is an efficient way to process information because, as information-processing theories such as the elaboration likelihood model (Petty & Cacioppo, 1986) suggest, people are cognitive misers. That is, they look at ways to simplify their information-processing tasks (Taylor, 1981). Information-processing researchers indicate that people need to exert more cognitive energy to process information that challenges their predispositions (Edwards & Smith, 1996) than information that supports their views, which is also likely to bring greater rewards (Edwards & Smith, 1996). Therefore, it is not a desire to reduce dissonance that leads to selective exposure, but a desire to process information more efficiently. Similarly, people perceive that media outlets and messages differ in quality and people select those that are perceived to be of higher quality. Those sources determined to be of higher quality, however, are those expressing consonant views, which is judged to be more convincing and legitimate than contradictory information (Fischer Jonas, Frey, & Schulz-Hardt, 2005; Miller, McHoskey, Bane, & Dowd, 1993; Nimmo, 1990). Studies that have examined selective exposure as an information-processing technique have consistently found support for the theory, particularly when the study focuses on partisan information (Stroud, 2006; 2008; 2010).

Scholars have increasingly explored selective exposure during the last decade because of its perceived effects on the U.S. political system. The chasm between blue and red states demonstrates that the country has become increasingly polarized (Iyengar & Hahn, 2009; Stroud, 2010; Sunstein, 2001). Scholars have attributed the increase in polarization, at least in part, to the rise of more partisan sources and people's increased tendency to seek out media, messages, and social networks that support their political predispositions (Iyengar & Hahn, 2009). Increased polarization may make it more difficult for politicians to find a shared political agenda and therefore blunt the government's abilities to create policies responsive to public needs. Increased polarization through selective exposure may also lead to people questioning the political legitimacy of politicians that do not share their political viewpoints (Stroud, 2006; 2008).

Selective exposure decreases political tolerance of other political viewpoints, making it difficult to achieve consensus on issues needed to solve political and social problems (Stroud, 2006). Finally, selective exposure may not produce informed citizens who can make reasoned judgments. Democratic theorists argue that to make informed decisions, individuals must seek out information from all sides and weigh the arguments before reaching a decision (Delli Karpini & Keeter, 1996). On the other hand, selective exposure may be linked to several positive democratic indicators. Those who are politically knowledgeable are likely to seek out information and maintain networks that support their political views because they know where they stand on issues. Similarly because partisanship leads to selective exposure and partisans report high levels of political interest and activity, those who are politically interested and active report higher levels of selective exposure (Mutz, 2002; 2006; Stroud, 2006).

Network Society and Selective Exposure

The rise of mobile communication and Web 2.0, which is characterized by a more user-centered design, and information sharing and collaboration represented by wikis, blogs and social network sites, have accelerated society's century long transformation from neighborhood groups to a network society, a social structure based on information and communication technologies that is global in nature (Castells & Cardoso, 2005; Wellman, Boas, & Chen, 2002). This transformation affects not only the organization of communication, but also society is well. Networks are the basic units of society and therefore affect all domains of social life as the key social structures and activities are centered around digital information networks (Castells, 2007, 2008; Castells & Cardoso, 2005; Wellman, 2001).

While the 20th century was dominated by one-way forms of communication such as newspapers and televisions owned by large multinational corporations, the new network society has created a huge growth in horizontal networks of interactive communication in addition to, but independent from, media organizations and governments. This growing horizontal communication has created a new form of socialized communication: mass self-communication (Castells, 2007). The new communication system of the 21st century is mass communication that it is diffused through the Internet and can reach a global audience. But it is also self-communication in that communication messages are often created by individuals or groups through blogs, text messages, wikis, social media sites and other networked forms of communication allowing people to communicate with each other without going through channels created by media corporations (Castells, 2007; Castells & Cardoso, 2005).

Relationships in contemporary society are not with one particular group of tightly knit individuals, but rather many relationships with multiple small groups of individuals (Wellman et al., 2002). In this sense, social networks today are marked by networked individualism. In networked individualism, society has moved from a mass media system to a networked society in which relationships are not limited to a particular geographic group of densely-knit individuals, but multiple relationships with multiple groups or individuals that includes close friends and family, acquaintances, as well as people who do not know each other or who only know each other to a small extent. These relationships are not bound by place, but can easily be maintained over great distances (Boase & Wellman, 2005; Wellman, 2001; Wellman, Quan-Haase, Boase, & Chen, 2003). Because it is rare for two people to have exactly the same set of relationships, every individual has his own personal community that they can communicate with through text messaging, blogs, social media and other networked sources as well as through more traditional sources such as telephone and face-to-face communication (Boase & Wellman, 2005; Castells, 2007). Computer-mediated communication allow personalization with people having control over what sources they get messages from and what information they seek (Wellman et al., 2003). Behavior in these individual networks is driven by their individual needs and preferences (Foth & Hearn, 200; Wellman et al., 2003). These personal communities supply the social elements people need: support, sociability, information, social identities, and a sense of belonging (Wellman et al., 2002, 2003)

The concept of networked individualism may sound like a system in which people are isolated from the rest of society; it is actually a transformation of sociability. The more people use the Internet, the more social contact they have with their friends, the more friends they have and the more overall contact they have with friends because online communication is cheaper, quicker and more efficient than visiting, telephoning or writing letters (Boase & Wellman, 2005; Hampton, Sessions, Her, & Rainie, 2009; Wang & Wellman, 2010). Online network communication does not replace offline communication, but supplements face-to-face and other forms of offline communication (Castells & Cordoso, 2005; Wellman et al., 2002, 2003). Also, social relationships that begin online are continued in the offline world and vice versa (boyd & Ellison, 2007; Castells, 2001; Foth & Hearn, 2007). The Internet allows individuals to decide which networks they want to invest their time and effort with, allowing them to create "portfolios of sociability" (Castells, 2001).

While authors such as Wellman and Castells don't directly mention selective exposure, clearly their ideas about the network society, network individualism and mass self-communication are in line with selective exposure. These researchers don't see people communicating in a vast public sphere, but rather with multiple networks of people who share their own interests (Wellman et al, 2003). They see the individual as the driving force in social networks, seeking out information that satisfies their individual needs. Castells (2007) describes mass self-communication as being "self-generated in content, self-directed in emission, and self-selected in reception by many that communicate with many" (pg. 248). Wellman and Castells also see the potential danger in networked communities, noting that it will create a fragmented citizenship, a fear raised about selective exposure (Castells & Cardoso, 2005; Wellman, et al., 2003). Perhaps the major distinction between the works of Wellman and Castells and selective exposure scholars is that the latter focus on the selection of information supporting one's viewpoints, while Wellman and Castells center more on the selection of individuals for connection at a more social level.

Partisan Selective Exposure

Research suggests that personally relevant beliefs, ones that are central to a person's interests or self-identity, are more likely to influence information selection than non-relevant ones because relevant beliefs are more accessible in memory and are therefore more likely to guide exposure decisions (Donsbach, 1991; Price & Tewksbury, 1997). Political partisanship has been demonstrated to be a construct that is easily accessible to memory and therefore one that helps dictate exposure decisions (Green, Palmquist, & Schickler, 2002; Lau, 1989). Researchers have suggested that selective exposure consistently influences choice of political content (Lowin, 1967; Stroud, 2006, 2008, 2010).

Both survey (Ziemke, 1980) and experimental studies (Bartlett, Drew, Fahle, & Watts, 1974; Chaffee & McLeod, 1973; Redlawski, 2002; Meffert et al., 2006) have found a relationship between people's partisan leanings and exposure to media content. That is, they are more likely to select information sources and political content that supports their political beliefs and avoid information that contradicts those beliefs.

People are more likely to expose themselves to both media (Donsbach, 1991; Chaffee et al., 2001; Meffert et al., 2006) and to candidate materials such as speeches or pamphlets (Chaffee & McLeod, 2001; Ziemke, 1980) about their preferred candidate. They are also more likely to search out information on issues of importance to them such as affirmative action or gun control (Taber & Lodge,, 2006). Finally, people may rely on certain media that they believe conform more to their political views. For instance, Republicans are more likely to watch Fox News Network or follow #tcot on Twitter and Democrats are more likely to view CNN or be fans of Nancy Pelosi's Facebook page (Pew Research, 2010).

Internet and Selective Exposure

The range of opinions available online far exceed those available in the traditional media (Albrecht, 2003). Further, because the Internet is interactive, people have greater power to seek out information from political Web sites that supports their predispositions and they have more control over what sites they visit (Garrett, 2009). Not surprisingly, then, studies find strong support for the claim that people actively seek out information online that supports their political beliefs (Bimber & Davis, 2003; Mutz & Martin, 2001). On the other hand, studies find less support for the claim that people avoid information that does not support their political views (Baruh, 2004; DiMaggio & Sato, 2003; Iyengar & Hahn, 2009), although Chaffee and associates (2001) found that people paid attention to both information that supported their views and information that countered it.

Critiques of selective exposure have noted that a failing of selective exposure research was the tendency to focus on whether people seek out supportive information, without much emphasis on whether people avoid conflicting information in the media (Cotton, 1985). This study will explore the degree to which those who rely on political Web sites and blogs for political information not only self-select supportive information, but also avoid information that doesn't accord with their political views.

Blogs and Selective Exposure

Few studies have examined whether people practice selective exposure when they visit blogs. But because studies suggest blogs advocate a particular point of view and attract likeminded individuals (Johnson et al., 2007; Perlmutter, 2008; Thompson, 2003; Trammell et al., 2006), selective exposure to blogs is likely stronger than to political Web sites (Johnson et al., 2009).

Blogs can foster a sense of community among users. Users can locate blogs that share their viewpoints as well as discuss their views with the site creator and other users on the site. Bloggers can link their blogs to other sites that share their views (Thompson, 2003) and political blogs that express a partisan viewpoint overwhelmingly link to sites with a similar ideology (Sunstein, 2007). While traditional journalists claim to adhere to objectivity, bloggers contend that one strength of blogs is that they can discuss issues from specific ideological perspectives (Bruns, 2006; Johnson et al., 2007; Perlmutter, 2008) and they provide opinionated, thoughtful analysis of the news that is missing from the mainstream media (Bruns, 2006).

Political Measures and Selective Exposure

There is a strong link between selective exposure and political measures such as degree of partisanship, ideology and political interest. Factors such as partisanship or personal relevance of an issue are key to understanding whether someone will seek out information that supports his or her position (Chaffee et al., 2001; Donsbach, 1991; Ziemke, 1980).

Degree of partisanship drives selective exposure to political Web sites as several studies indicate that partisans are more likely to rely on sites agreeable to their political opinions (Bimber & Davis, 2003; Garrett, 2009;; Mutz & Martin, 2001), and selective exposure is higher for more personally relevant attitudes and beliefs (Brannon, Tagler & Eagly, 2007). But studies suggest that other factors such as political interest and reliance may influence selective exposure. Stroud (2006, 2008, 2010) notes that those who are motivated to consume political information in partisan ways would be more likely to practice selective exposure. Results indicate that political interest predicted selective exposure to talk radio, cable news, and the Internet, and that the relationship flowed from interest to selective exposure not vice versa. Stroud (2008, 2010) posits that political interest is linked to reliance that, in turn, helps explain political selective exposure. Partisans, because they are more politically interested, are more likely to rely on the media for political information and seek out sources that support their point of view. Most studies exploring ideology have examined the degree to which liberals or conservatives visit ideologically similar Web sites (Chaffee et al., 2001; Best et al., 2005; Stroud, 2008). However, studies found that liberals were more likely than conservatives to practice selective exposure to both Web sites (Johnson et al., in press) and blogs (Johnson et al., 2009). These findings run counter to studies that suggest that liberals are more accepting of minority opinions and of groups who are not part of the mainstream when compared with conservatives (Bobo & Licari, 1989; Keum et al., 2005).

Media Reliance and Selective Exposure

Because traditional news media and their online counterparts adhere to balance and objectivity, reliance on these media may be unrelated to selective exposure (Best et al., 2005; Mutz & Martin, 2001). Selective exposure may be more strongly linked to more partisan sources such as political Web sites or blogs because audience members may seek out sites that hold the same views they do. The more individuals rely on blogs or political Web sites, the more likely they will practice selective exposure (Johnson et al., 2009, in press).

Media Motives and Selective Exposure

Motives for seeking out information may also impact selective exposure (Hoffner, Fujioka, Ye & Ibrahim, 2009). Relying on the Internet for information seeking or surveillance of the environment has been linked to increased political and civic engagement and political knowledge (Shah et al., 2005; Shah et al., 2001). On the other hand, relying on the Internet for entertainment or habitual needs tends to be unrelated or negatively related to political measures (Norris & Jones, 1998). Results for communication variables depend on how they are measured. Norris and Jones (1998) found that being an expressive (those who engaged in political discussion online or posted their opinions on bulletin boards and newsgroups) was unrelated to political knowledge and participation. Similarly, Shah and associates (Shah et al., 2001) failed to find a relationship between using the Internet for social recreation (playing a game or participating in a chat room or on-line forum) and civic engagement. On the other hand, when Shah and associates (2005) later examined interactive civic messaging and measured it in terms of using e-mail to discuss politics, contact political players or to recruit or organize, they did find that it predicted civic participation. The communication measure used in this study will be closer to one employed by Norris and Jones (1998), which found little influence on political attitudes.

Studies that have explored the influence of gratifications on Internet credibility suggest that informational needs predict credibility better than entertainment ones (Flanagin & Metzger, 2000) and that social surveillance measures (using the Internet to seek out a variety of viewpoints and to learn about others' opinions) predicted credibility, but not as strongly as information ones (Johnson et al., 2007).

Because information needs predict the same political variables connected to selective exposure and because people judge information they agree with as more credible than information they disagree with, using the Internet for information needs should lead to selective exposure to political Web sites and blogs. Entertainment needs should be unrelated to selective exposure. Communication may be positively related to selective exposure, but the relationship should be weaker than for information.

Hypotheses and Research Questions

The current analysis seeks to address the following hypotheses and research questions in order to better understand the process and motivations for selective exposure to information on Web sites and blogs.

H1: Respondents who use political Web sites and blogs for political information will be more likely to say that they visit sites and blogs that they agree with than those they disagree with.

H2: Those who use political blogs will be more likely to practice selective exposure than those who rely on political Web sites.

H3: The more partisan respondents are, the more they will selectively expose themselves to information on (a) political Web sites and (b) blogs. after controlling for political and demographic variables

H4: The more politically interested respondents are, the more they will selectively expose themselves to information on (a) political Web sites and (b) blogs. after controlling for political and demographic variables

H5: The more people rely on (a) political Web sites and (b) blogs, the more they will practice selective exposure after controlling for political and demographic variables.

H6: The more people rely on (a) political Web sites and (b) blogs for information needs, the more they will practice selective exposure after controlling for political and demographic variables

H7: Reliance on (a) political Web sites and (b) blogs for entertainment needs will be negatively related to selective exposure after controlling for political and demographic variables

H8: Reliance on (a) political Web sites and (b) blogs for information needs will more strongly predict selective exposure than entertainment or communication needs after controlling for political and demographic variables

R1: Will liberals or conservatives be more likely to selectively expose themselves to information on political Web sites and blogs?

R2: Will people who rely on political Web sites and blogs for communication needs be more likely to practice selective exposure?

METHODS

Data Collection

An online panel of Internet users was used to analyze the practice of selective exposure. The panel was operated by a media research lab at a major U.S. university and contains consumers who have chosen to participate in Web-based research. An online survey was posted from September 13 through September 23, 2007 and e-mail invitations were sent to 5,000 panel members who said they used the Internet to search for political information and were eligible to vote in the United States. Respondents were also offered the opportunity to participate in a cash drawing as an incentive for their involvement. This sample yielded 772 completed surveys, a 15.4% response rate. Past research indicates that Internet surveys typically garner lower response rates often due to fear of spam or issues of confidentiality (Cook et al., 2000; Sills & Song, 2002).

Measures

Demographic Variables. Close to 60 percent (59.8%) of the sample respondents were female. The median age was 44 years old (SD = 12.7). On average, respondents reported obtaining a four-year college degree (SD = 1.1). These variables closely resembled the panel demographics as provided by the research lab used in this study. Participants also reported a median household income between $65,001 and $80,000. With respect to ideology, 41.2% considered themselves moderate, 21.8% conservative, and 22.5% liberal. Also, 31.6% identified themselves as Republicans, 36.4% Democrats, 27.6% Independents, with the remainder responding "Libertarian" or "Green Party." The strength of party affiliation was measured with an 11-point scale where "1" meant "very weak party affiliation" and "11" meant "very strong party affiliation." The respondents exhibited fairly strong party affiliation with an average of 6.8 (SD = 2.7). On the same 11-point scale ranging from "1" "absolutely not interested in politics" to "11" "absolutely interested in politics," participants reported a strong interest in politics in general (M = 7.6, SD = 2.5).

Definitions for blog and Web site. The survey instrument offered an introduction for respondents defining blogs and Web sites. Political blogs were defined as news or discussion-oriented Web sites that were hosted by a blogger. Political Web sites were defined as Web sites posted by an individual or organization about a political issue, organization, or individual.

Motivations for using Internet for political information. There were three dimensions of people's motivations for using political Web sites or blogs for political information: (1) information needs; (2) entertainment needs; and (3) communication needs.

Political Web site information needs was an additive measure of four items: to find specific political information that one is looking for; to keep up with the main issues of the day; for information one can't get from traditional media; and to find out about issues affecting people like oneself. Responses were given on a 5-point scale where "1" meant "strongly disagree" and "5" meant "strongly agree" (Cronbach's alpha =.75). The same questions were asked and summed to build an index of *blog information needs* (Cronbach's alpha =.83).

Entertainment needs for political Web sites or blogs was an additive measure of two items. On the same 5-point scale, respondents were asked the extent to which they agreed or disagreed with the following two statements: because it is entertaining; because it helps one to relax. Responses were summed to form an index of *political website entertainment needs* (Inter-item correlation =.53) and *blog entertainment needs* (Inter-item correlation =.47).

Communication needs for political Web sites or blogs was an additive measure of five items. On the same 5-point scale, respondents were asked to indicate the extent to which they agreed or disagreed with the following statements: to give one something to talk about with others; to use as ammunition in arguments with others; to let one's opinions be known; to be in contact with like-minded people; and to learn about other people's opinions. Responses were summed to build an index of *political Web site communication needs* (Cronbach's alpha =.76) and *blog communication needs* (Cronbach's alpha =.79).

Reliance on online sources for political information. Respondents were asked a series of questions regarding the extent to which they relied on seven online sources for political information: blogs (M = 1.71, SD =.99), broadcast television news sites (M = 2.72, SD = 1.2), cable television news sites (M = 2.85, SD = 1.2), newspaper sites (M = 2.84, SD = 1.3), electronic mailing lists/bulletin boards (M = 1.87, SD = 1.1), chat rooms/instant messaging (M = 1.35, SD =.7) and politically oriented Web sites (M = 2.15, SD = 1.2). The variables were measured on a 5-point scale varying from "1" for "don't rely on at all" to "5" for "heavily rely on."

Selective Exposure. Respondents used a 5-point scale to indicate the frequency of visits to political Web sites and blogs that provide information about specific issues or policies that they agreed with and those Web sites and blogs that provide information about specific issues or policies that they disagreed with ranging from "1" "never visited" to "5" "very often visited." Responses for visiting sites that respondents "disagree" with were reverse coded so that higher scores indicated more selective exposure and lower scores meant less selective exposure. The two questions were summed to form an index of *selective exposure to political Web sites* as well as an index of *selective exposure to political blogs.*

Data Analysis

T-tests were conducted to test H1: People who rely on political Web sites and blogs for political information will be more likely to say that they visit sites and blogs that they agree with than those they disagree with and H2: Those who rely on blogs will be more likely to practice selective exposure than those who rely on political Web sites. Hierarchical regression analysis was then used to test Hypotheses 3-8 and answer Research Questions 1-2 and examine whether motivations for using political Web sites and blogs, and reliance on online sources for political information significantly predict selective exposure to blogs and political Web sites after controlling for demographic and political variables. Specifically, selective exposure to blogs and political Web sites are the dependent variables, with the following four blocks of independent variables entered in this order: Block 1: demographics (gender, age, education, income, and income); Block 2: political variables (political interest, strength of party affiliation, and ideology); Block 3: motivations for political Web sites and blogs variables (website information needs, entertainment needs, and communication needs; blog information needs, entertainment needs, and communication needs); Block 4 reliance on online sources for political information (reliance on blogs, online broadcast TV news sites, online cable TV news sites, online newspapers sites, online political Web sites, electronic mailing lists/bulletin boards, and chatrooms/instant messaging).

RESULTS

The first hypothesis proposed that individuals who rely on political Web sites and political blogs would be more likely to say that they visit sites or blogs that they agree with than those they disagree with. To test this hypothesis, paired-samples T-tests were conducted. As demonstrated in Tables 1 and 2, the results indicate strong support for H1. With respect to political Web sites, individuals are more likely to visit sites that they agree with (M = 2.43, SD =1.15) than those that they disagree with (M = 2.10, SD =.98), (t (771) = 11.92, p <.001). Similarly, when visiting political blogs, respondents indicated that they are more likely to visit blogs that they agree with (M = 1.73, SD = 1.10) than those that they disagree with (M = 1.55, SD =.88), (t (771) = 8.22, p<.001).

Hypothesis 2 posited that those who rely on blogs will be more likely to practice selective exposure than those who rely on political Web sites. A T-test was conducted for the analysis (Table 3) and indicated little difference between selective exposure to political Web sites (M = 3.16, SD =.37) and selective exposure to political blogs (M = 3.09, SD =.31), (t (771) = -5.29, p<.001), Therefore, hypothesis 2 was not supported.

Table 1. T-Test Comparing Selective Exposure to Political Web Sites Respondents Agreed With and Those Respondents Disagreed With

Selective Exposure	N	Mean	SD	T Test
Political web sites R agreed with	772	2.43	1.15	T (771) = 11.92 P<.001
Political web sites R disagreed with	772	2.10	.98	

Note: #=.10, * = p <.05, ** = p <.01, *** = p<.001

Table 2. T-Test Comparing Selective Exposure to Political Blogs Respondents Agreed With and Those Respondents Disagreed With

Selective Exposure	N	Mean	SD	T Test
Political blogs R agreed with	772	1.73	1.10	T (771) = 8.22 p<.001
Political blogs R disagreed with	772	1.55	.88	

Note: #=.10, * = p <.05, ** = p <.01, *** = p<.001

Table 3. T-Test Comparing Selective Exposure to Political Web Sites and Political Blogs

Selective Exposure	N	Mean	SD	T Test
Political Web sites	772	3.16	.37	T (771) = -5.29 p<.001
Political Blogs	772	3.09	.31	

Note: #=.10, * = p <.05, ** = p <.01, *** = p<.001

The remaining hypotheses (3-8) were tested utilizing hierarchical regression. Research questions 1 and 2 were also answered via hierarchical regression analyses.

The third hypothesis speculated a positive relationship between the strength of party affiliation and selective exposure to political Web sites and blogs. As seen from Table 4, the more people feel strongly affiliated with a political party, the more likely they went to political Web sites and blogs (β =.13, p<.10, β =.15, p<.05, respectively) that they agree with. Therefore, H3 was supported.

Hypothesis 4 predicted a positive relationship between general political interest and selective exposure to political Web sites and blogs. According to Table 4, general interest was not a significant predictor of either selective exposure to political Web sites or selective exposure to blogs. So H4 was not supported.

Research question 1 inquired as to whether liberals or conservatives would be more likely to practice selective exposure to political websites and blogs. Table 4 indicates that ideology was not a significant predictor of selective exposure to political websites or blogs. Therefore, there is no significant difference between liberals and conservatives regarding their selective exposure behavior.

The fifth hypothesis under scrutiny asserts that the more people rely on Web sites and blogs, the more likely they will practice selective exposure to these sources. Table 4 demonstrates that the more respondents relied on blogs, the more likely they went to political blogs that they agreed with (β =.29, p<.001). As expected, the more respondents relied on politically oriented Web sites, the more likely they went to political Web sites and blogs that they agreed with (β=.21, p<.05; β=.17, p<.05). Reliance on political Web sites predicted selective exposure to those Internet components, but reliance on blogs was not a significant predictor of selective exposure to political Web sites. Therefore, hypothesis H5 was supported.

Hypothesis 6 predicted the positive relationship between reliance on political Web sites and blogs for information needs and the practice of selective

Table 4. Predicting Selecting Exposure

	Selective exposure to political Web sites	Selective exposure to political blogs
Demographics		
Age	.003	-.04
Gender (female coded higher)	.04	.04
Education	.25**	.22**
Income	-.12	-.06
R^2 (%)	**11.0****	**12.6*****
Political Variables		
Ideology (liberal coded higher)	.002	.09
Strength of party affiliation	.13#	.15*
General political interest	.09	.06
Incremental R^2 (%) Motivations for Political Website and Blog Uses	**4.1***	**4.6***
Web info needs	.01	-.05
Web entertainment needs	.01	-.10
Web comm. needs	-.03	.09
Blog info needs	-.01	.09
Blog entertainment needs	-.04	.09
Blog comm. needs	.07	-.17
Incremental R^2 (%)	**1.4**	**5.8***
Reliance on Online Sources for Political Information		
Blogs	.08	.29***
Online broadcast TV news sites	-.17#	-.07
Online cable TV news sites	-.06	-.04
Online newspaper sites	-.10	-.11
Electronic mailing lists/bulletin boards	.02	-.04
Chat rooms/Instant messaging	-.20*	-.10
Politically oriented Web sites	.21*	.17*
Incremental R^2 (%)	**11.1****	**11.0*****
Total R^2 (%)	**27.6****	**33.9*****

β represents final standardized regression coefficients.
Note: #=.10, * = p <.05, ** = p <.01, *** = p<.001

exposure. As seen from Table 4, neither reliance on political Web sites nor blogs for information needs were positively related to selective exposure. Therefore, H6 was not supported.

Hypothesis 7 posited that there would be a negative relationship between reliance on political Web sites and blogs for entertainment needs and selective exposure. Table 4 indicated no relationship was found. Therefore, H7 was not supported.

The eighth hypothesis proposed that reliance on political Web sites and blogs for information needs would be stronger predictors of selective exposure than for entertainment or communication needs. As seen from Table 4, none of the political Web site and blog gratifications measures were statistically significant. Therefore, H8 was not supported.

The second research question assessed whether reliance on political Web sites and blogs for communication needs would predict selective exposure. Again, Table 4 showed that neither reliance on political Web sites or reliance on blogs for communication needs was a statistically significant predictor of selective exposure behavior.

DISCUSSION

Cotton (1985) acknowledged that a shortcoming of selective exposure research was the tendency to focus on whether people seek out supportive information, without an emphasis on whether people avoid conflicting information in the media. The current research addressed this criticism directly and found that those who rely on political Web sites and blogs are more likely to seek out information they agree with than to avoid information they disagree with. This finding parallels past research indicating less support for the claim that people avoid information that does not support their political views (Baruh, 2004; DiMaggio & Sato, 2003). Past studies also suggest that people need to expend more cognitive energy to process information that challenges their predispositions (Edwards & Smith, 1996). In turn, it requires less effort to process supportive information, which is also likely to bring greater rewards (Edwards & Smith, 1996; Ziemke, 1980). This need for cognitive efficiency and the rampant increase in the availability of media sources make it easier and more likely that users will seek out information that supports their predispositions (Mutz & Martin, 2001; Sunstein, 2001) or to avoid political information altogether (Atre & Katz, 2005; Prior, 2002).

This analysis posited that those who rely on blogs would practice selective exposure to a higher degree than those who rely on political Web sites. The results indicated no statistical difference between the two. This is somewhat surprising due to the strong partisan content revealed on blogs. Studies have indicated that selective exposure effects are stronger for more partisan content (Bennett, 2002; Best et al., 2005). However, while political Web sites are more likely than blogs to feature nonpartisan information, there are a plethora of issue-oriented, party and candidate Web sites that do present a strong partisan perspective (Bichard, 2006). Therefore, those seeking out partisan content can rely on political Web sites as easily as blogs, and reliance scores suggest they do rely on political Web sites more for partisan information.

Partisanship did appear to increase the practice of selective exposure after controlling for political and demographic variables. The more strongly affiliated with a political party, the more likely individuals went to political Web sites and blogs that shared their views. This is congruent with past studies consistently finding a relationship between partisan leanings and exposure to media and media content (Bartlett et al., 1974; Chaffee & McLeod, 1973; Meffert et al., 2006; Ziemke, 1980). Stroud (2006, 2008) noted that those who are motivated to consume political information in partisan ways are more likely to practice selective exposure. Additional studies suggest that the sheer amount of media information available has increased selective exposure efforts, specifically those with partisan content (Bennett, 2002; Best et al., 2005).

As hypothesized, reliance on both politically oriented Web sites and blogs predicted selective exposure to the respective online platforms after controlling for political and demographic variables. This is understandable considering that individuals often attribute more credibility to sources with which they are familiar. Past analyses have indicated that reliance is a consistently strong predictor of credibility perceptions (Banning & Trammell, 2006; Johnson & Kaye, 2004).

Past studies have paid little attention to the influence of motivations for using sources on selective exposure. However, studies have found that searching out sources to gratify informational needs predicts both political attitudes and behaviors as well as media credibility (Flanagin & Metzger, 2000; Shah et al., 2005; Shah et al., 2001). Furthermore, relying on the Internet to satisfy information needs has proven a much stronger predictor of credibility and political attitudes and behaviors than relying on the Internet to gratify entertainment needs. Results for communication needs are mixed, depending on how such needs are measured. While this study found reliance strongly predicted selective exposure to political blogs and Web sites, motivations for using these sources had no influence.

Research has suggested that reliance is an important measure of such factors as selective exposure and credibility (Johnson et al., 2007) because those who heavily rely on blogs and Web sites are savvy users who know which blogs have the partisan information they are seeking. Knowing what sites contain information that supports your already held beliefs, then, has a much stronger influence on why you practice selective exposure than what motivates you to seek out information in the first place.

CONCLUSION

The current research attempted to revive the analysis of selective exposure, but in the context of new media networks. The analysis utilized an online panel of Internet users to investigate the degree to which those who rely on political Web sites and blogs practice selective exposure. This study also examined whether people who used blogs practiced selective exposure more than those who relied on political Web sites. Finally, the study examined how well reliance, motivations for using blogs and political Web sites, and partisanship predicted political exposure after controlling for demographic and political variables.

The question of whether people practice selective exposure to information has important implications for the democratic system. These implications are especially significant in an era of new media and consumer empowerment. The ability to self-direct and select information while managing individual networks can lead to polarization. Castells (2007) description of mass self-communication recognizes the potential danger in homogeneous networked communities. Democratic deliberation and debate depends on an informed citizenry who are familiar with different perspectives on social and political issues. Our findings indicate that Internet users do practice selective exposure when accessing political Web sites and blogs, although substantial numbers who rely on political Web sites say they seek out neutral or balanced information. This practice of selective exposure limits the amount of conflicting information individuals are exposed to and therefore limits the ability of citizens to engage in a deliberative debate on issues. While many hoped that the Internet would bring about more deliberation and less polarization, our research suggests that online media reliance and partisanship propel selective exposure to Web sites and blogs. This perpetuation of individual biases limits the development of a collective identity in our networked society. Selective exposure to information online threatens this goal of creating collective identity with shared values and may instead create polarization in our society (Best et al., 2005; Stroud, 2006). Our research indicates that those who rely on political Web sites and blogs are more likely to seek out information they agree with than to avoid information they disagree with. This polarizing behavior could lead to a more biased processing of information (Meffert et al., 2006) and to less tolerance of opposing viewpoints (Mutz, 2002).

FUTURE RESEARCH DIRECTIONS

Survey analysis does not provide a causal direction, but offers only one snapshot of respondent views. Future study may wish to examine the self-reported data of subjects over a period of time to capture a more complete analysis of selective exposure to Internet components. Specific social networks could also be identified for investigation and analysis. Future research with a larger more diverse sample may be helpful to discover the degree to which people seek out supportive information online and avoid information that challenges their views. These could also include a more in depth look into the motivations for exposure as it may vary with a more diverse sample. Research collected during a political campaign would also provide a useful context for understanding such measures. Finally, future studies may want to look at selective exposure to more specific content including social networking sites, media sites and blogs as well as candidate and issue-oriented Web sites and blogs to provide a more detailed understanding of the relationship between political content and selective exposure.

REFERENCES

Albrecht, S. (2003). Whose voice is heard in online deliberation? A study of participation and representation in political debates on the Internet. *Information Communication and Society*, *9*, 62–82. doi:10.1080/13691180500519548

Atre, J., & Katz, E. (2005, May). *What's killing television news? Experimentally assessing the effects of multiple channels on media choice.* Paper presented at the International Communication Association Conference, New York, NY.

Banning, S., & Trammell, K. D. (2006, August). *Revisiting the issue of blog credibility: A national survey.* Paper presented at the Annual Conference of the Association for Education in Journalism & Mass Communication, San Francisco, CA.

Bartlett, D. L., Drew, P. B., Fahle, E. G., & Watts, W. A. (1974). Selective exposure to a presidential campaign appeal. *Public Opinion Quarterly*, *38*, 264–270. doi:10.1086/268158

Baruh, L. (2004). Audience surveillance and the right to read: Anonymous reading in interactive media. *Knowledge Technology and Policy*, *1*, 59–73. doi:10.1007/BF02687076

Bennett, S. E. (2002). Predicting Americans' exposure to political talk radio in 1996, 1998, and 2000. *The Harvard International Journal of Press/Politics*, *7*, 9–22.

Best, S. J., Chmielewski, B., & Krueger, B. S. (2005). Selective exposure to online foreign news during the conflict with Iraq. *Harvard Journal of Press/Politics*, *10*(4), 52-70.

Bichard, S. L. (2006). Building blogs: A multi-dimensional analysis of the distribution of frames on the 2004 presidential candidate websites. *Journalism & Mass Communication Quarterly*, *82*, 329–345.

Bimber, B., & Davis, R. (2003). *Campaigning online: The internet in U.S. elections*. Oxford, UK: Oxford University Press.

Boase, J., & Wellman, B. (2006). Personal relationships: On and off the Internet. In Vangelisti, A. L., & Perlman, D. (Eds.), *The Cambridge handbook of personal relationships* (pp. 709–725). Cambridge, UK: Cambridge University Press.

Bobo, L., & Licari, F. C. (1989). Educational and political tolerance: Testing the effects of cognitive sophistication and target group affect. *Public Opinion Quarterly*, *53*, 285–308. doi:10.1086/269154

Brannon, L. A., Tagler, M. J., & Eagly, A. H. (2007). The moderating role of attitude strength in selective exposure to information. *Journal of Experimental Social Psychology*, *43*, 611. doi:10.1016/j.jesp.2006.05.001

Bruns, A. (2006). The practice of news blogging. In Bruns, A., & Jacobs, J. (Eds.), *Uses of blogs* (pp. 11–22). New York, NY: Peter Lang.

Castells, M. (2001). *The Internet galaxy. Reflections on the Internet, business and society*. Oxford, UK: Oxford University Press.

Castells, M. (2007). Communication, power and counter-power in the network society. *International Journal of Communication, 1*, 238–266.

Castells, M. (2008). *The new public sphere:* Global civil society, communication networks, and global governace *The American Academy of Political and Social Science, 616*, 78-93,

Castells, M., & Cardoso, G. (Eds.). (2005). *The network society: From knowledge to policy*. Washington, DC: The John Hopkins University.

Chaffee, S. H., & McLeod, J. M. (1973). Individuals vs. social predictors of information seeking. *The Journalism Quarterly, 50*, 237–245.

Chaffee, S. H., Saphir, M. N., Grap, J., Sandvig, C., & Hahn, K. S. (2001). Attention to counter-attitudinal messages in a state election campaign. *Political Communication, 18*, 247–272. doi:10.1080/10584600152400338

Cook, C., Heath, F. M., & Thompson, R. L. (2000). A meta-analysis of response rates in Web-or Internet- based surveys. *Educational and Psychological Measurement, 60*, 821–826. doi:10.1177/00131640021970934

Cotton, J. L. (1985). Cognitive dissonance in selective exposure. In Zillmann, D., & Bryant, J. (Eds.), *Selective exposure to communication* (pp. 11–33). Hillsdale, NJ: Erlbaum.

Delli Carpini, M. X., & Keeter, S. (1996). *What Americans know about politics and why it matters*. New Haven, CT: Yale University Press.

DiMaggio, & Sato, K. (2003, August). *Does the Internet Balkanize political attention? A test of the Sunstein thesis.* Paper presented at the Annual Meeting of the American Sociological Association, Atlanta, GA.

Donsbach, W. (1991). Exposure to political content in newspapers: The impact of cognitive dissonance on reader's selectivity. *European Journal of Communication, 6*, 155–186. doi:10.1177/0267323191006002003

Edwards, K., & Smith, E. E. (1996). A disconfirmation bias in the evaluation of arguments. *Journal of Personality and Social Psychology, 71*(1), 5–24. doi:10.1037/0022-3514.71.1.5

Festinger, L. (1957). *A theory of cognitive dissonance*. Stanford, CA: Stanford University Press.

Fischer, P., Jonas, E., Frey, D., & Schulz-Hardt, S. (2005). Selective exposure to information: The impact of information limits. *European Journal of Social Psychology, 35*, 469–492. doi:10.1002/ejsp.264

Flanagin, A. J., & Metzger, M. J. (2000). Perceptions of Internet information credibility. *Journalism & Mass Communication Quarterly, 77*, 515–540.

Forh, M., & Hearn, G. (2007). Networked individualism of urban residents: Discovering the communicative ecology in inner-city apartment buildings. *Information Communication and Society, 10*, 748–772.

Garrett, R. K. (2009). Echo chambers online? Politically motivated selective exposure among Internet news users. *Journal of Computer-Mediated Communication, 14*, 265–285. doi:10.1111/j.1083-6101.2009.01440.x

Green, D., Palmquist, B., & Schickler, E. (2002). *Partisan hearts & minds: Political parties and the social identities of voters*. New Haven, CT: Yale University Press.

Hampton, K., Sessions, L., Her, E. J., & Rainie, L. (2009). *Social Isolation and new technology: How the Internet and mobile phones impact Americans'social networks.* Retrieved from http://www.pewinternet.org/ ~/media// Files/Reports /2009/ PIP_Tech_and_Social_Isolation.pdf

Hawkins, R. P., Pingree, S., Hitchon, J., Gorham, B. W., Kannaovakun, P., Gilligan, E., & Schmidt, T. (2001). Predicting selection and activity in television genre viewing. *Media Psychology, 3,* 237–263. doi:10.1207/S1532785XMEP0303_02

Hoffner, C. A., Fujioka, Y., Ye, J., & Ibrahim, A. G. S. (2009). Why we match: Factors affecting exposure to tragic television news. *Mass Communication & Society, 12*(2), 193–216. doi:10.1080/15205430802095042

Iyengar, S., & Hahn, L. (2009). Red media, blue media: Evidence of ideological selectivity in media use. *The Journal of Communication, 59,* 19–39. doi:10.1111/j.1460-2466.2008.01402.x

Johnson, T. J., Bichard, S. L., & Zhang, W. (2009). Communication communities or cyberghettos? A path analysis model examining factors that explain selective exposure to blogs. *Journal of Computer-Mediated Communication, 15*(1), 60–82. doi:10.1111/j.1083-6101.2009.01492.x

Johnson, T. J., & Kaye, B. K. (2004). Wag the blog: How reliance on traditional media and the Internet influence perceptions of credibility of Weblogs among blog users. *Journalism & Mass Communication Quarterly, 81*(3), 622–642.

Johnson, T. J., Kaye, B. K., Bichard, S. L., & Wong, W. J. (2007). Every blog has its day: Politically interested Internet users' perceptions of blog credibility. *Journal of Computer-Mediated Communication, 13,* article 6.

Johnson, T. J., Zhang, W., & Bichard, S. L. (in press). Voices of convergence or conflict? A path analysis investigation of selective exposure to political Web sites. *Social Science Computer Review.* doi:.doi:10.1177/0894439310379962

Keum, H., Hillback, E. D., Rojas, H., de Zuniga, H. G., Shah, D. V., & McLeod, D. M. (2005). Personifying the radical: How news framing polarizes security concerns and tolerance judgments. *Human Communication Research, 21,* 337–364. doi:10.1093/hcr/31.3.337

Kim, J., & Rubin, A. M. (1997). The variable influence of audience activity on media effects. *Communication Research, 24,* 107–135. doi:10.1177/009365097024002001

Kinder, D. R. (2003). Communication and politics in the age of information. In Sears, D. O., Huddy, L., & Jervis, R. (Eds.), *Oxford handbook of political psychology* (pp. 357–393). Oxford, UK: Oxford University Press.

Lau, R. R. (1989). Construct accessibility and electoral choice. *Political Behavior, 11*(1), 5–32. doi:10.1007/BF00993365

Lowin, A. (1967). Approach and avoidance: Alternate modes of selective exposure to information. *Journal of Personality and Social Psychology, 6*(1), 1–9. doi:10.1037/h0024531

Meffert, M. F., Chung, S., Joiner, A. J., Waks, L., & Garst, J. (2006). The effects of negativity and motivated information processing during a political campaign. *The Journal of Communication, 56*(1), 27–51. doi:10.1111/j.1460-2466.2006.00003.x

Miller, A. G., McHoskey, J. W., Bane, C. M., & Dowd, T. G. (1993). The attitude polarization phenomenon: Role of response measure, attitude extremity, and behavioral consequences of reported attitude change. *Journal of Personality and Social Psychology, 64*(4), 561–574. doi:10.1037/0022-3514.64.4.561

Mutz, D. C. (2002). Cross-cutting social networks: Testing democratic theory in practice. *The American Political Science Review*, *96*(1), 111–126. doi:10.1017/S0003055402004264

Mutz, D. C., & Martin, P. S. (2001). Facilitating communication across lines of political difference: The role of mass media. *The American Political Science Review*, *95*(1), 97–114.

Nimmo, D. (1990). Principles of information seeking in information processing: A preliminary political analysis. In Kraus, S. (Ed.), *Mass communication and political information processing* (pp. 3–17). Hillsdale, NJ: Lawrence Erlbaum Associates.

Norris, P. A., & Jones, D. (1998). Virtual democracy. *The Harvard International Journal of Press/Politics*, *3*, 474–480. doi:10.1177/1081180X98003002001

Papacharissi, Z. (2007). The blogger revolution? Audiences as media producers. M. Tremayne (Ed), *Blogging, citizenship, and the future of media* (pp. 21-39). New York: Routledge.

Perlmutter, D. D. (2008). *Blog wars*. New York, NY: Oxford University Press.

Petty, R., & Cacioppo, J. (1986). *Communication and persuasion: Central and peripheral routes to attitude change*. New York, NY: Springer-Verlag Pew Research Center. (2008a, December 15). *Internet now major source of campaign news: Continuing partisan divide in cable TV news audience.* Retrieved from http://people-press.org/report

Pew Research Center. (2008b, December 15). *Key news audiences now blend online and traditional sources: Audience segments in a changing news environment*. Retrieved from http://people-press/org/reports

Pew Research Center. (2010). *Americans spending more time following the news: Ideological news source: Who watches and why?* Retrieved from http://pewresearch.org/pubs/1725/where-people-get-news-print-online-readership-cable-news-viewers

Prior, M. (2002). Liberated viewers, polarized voters - The implications of increased media choice for democratic politics. *The Good Society*, *11*(3), 10–16. doi:10.1353/gso.2003.0016

Schudson, M. (1995). *The power of news*. Cambridge, MA: Harvard University Press.

Sears, D. O., & Freedman, J. L. (1967). Selective exposure to information: A critical review. *Public Opinion Quarterly*, *31*, 194–213. doi:10.1086/267513

Shah, D. V., Cho, J., Eveland, W. P. Jr, & Kwak, N. (2005). Information and expression in a digital age: Modeling Internet effects on civic participation. *Communication Research*, *32*, 531–565. doi:10.1177/0093650205279209

Shah, D. V., Kwak, N., & Holbert, R. L. (2001). Connecting and disconnecting with civic life: Patterns of Internet use and the production of social capital. *Political Communication*, *18*, 141–162. doi:10.1080/105846001750322952

Sills, S. J., & Song, C. (2002). Innovations in survey research: An application of Web surveys. *Social Science Computer Review*, *20*, 22–30. doi:10.1177/089443930202000103

Stroud, N. J. (2006). *Selective exposure to partisan information.* Unpublished dissertation, University of Pennsylvania, Philadelphia, PA.

Stroud, N. J. (2008). Media use and political predispositions: Revisiting the concept of selective exposure. *Political Behavior*, *30*, 341–366. doi:10.1007/s11109-007-9050-9

Stroud, N. J. (2010). Polarization and partisan selective exposure. *The Journal of Communication, 60*, 556–576. doi:10.1111/j.1460-2466.2010.01497.x

Sunstein, C. R. (2001). *Republic.com*. Princeton, NJ: Princeton University Press.

Sunstein, C. R. (2007). *Republic.com 2.0*. Princeton, NJ: Princeton University Press.

Taber, C. S., & Lodge, M. (2006). Motivated skepticism in the evaluation of political Beliefs. *American Journal of Political Science, 50*(3), 755–769. doi:10.1111/j.1540-5907.2006.00214.x

Taylor, S. E. (1981). The interface of cognitive and social psychology. In Harvey, J. H. (Ed.), *Cognition, social behavior, and the environment* (pp. 189–211). Hillsdale, NJ: Lawrence Erlbaum Associates.

Thompson, G. (2003). Weblogs, warblogs, the public sphere, and bubbles. *Transformations, 7*, 1–12.

Trammell, K. D., Tarkowski, A., Hofmokl, J., & Sapp, A. M. (2006). Rzeczpospolita blogow [Republic of Blog]: Examining Polish bloggers through content analysis. *Journal of Computer-Mediated Communication, 11*, article 2. Retrieved from http://jcmc.indiana.edu/vol11/ issue3.trammell.html

Wall, M. (2006). Blogging Gulf War II. *Journalism Studies, 7*(1), 111–126. doi:10.1080/14616700500450392

Wang, H., & Wellman, B. (2010). Social connectivity in America: Changes in adult friendship network size from 2002 to 2007. *The American Behavioral Scientist, 53*, 1148–1169. doi:10.1177/0002764209356247

Wellman, B. (2001). Physical place and cyberspace: The rise of personalized networking. *International Journal of Urban and Regional Research, 25*, 227–252. doi:10.1111/1468-2427.00309

Wellman, B., Boase, J., & Chen, W. (2002). The networked nature of community: Online and offline. *IT & Society, 1*, 151–165.

Wellman, B., Quan-Haase, A., Boase, J., Chen, W., Hampton, K., Isla de Diaz, I., & Miyata, K. (2003). The social affordances of the Internet for networked individualism. *Journal of Computer Mediated Communication, 8*. Retrieved from http://jcmc.indiana.edu/vol8/issue3/wellman.html

Zaller, J. R. (1992). *The nature and origins of mass opinion*. Cambridge, UK: Cambridge University Press.

Ziemke, D. A. (1980). Selective exposure in a presidential campaign contingent on certainty and salience. In Nimmo, D. (Ed.), *Communication yearbook* (*Vol. 4*, pp. 497–511). New Brunswick, NJ: Transaction Books.

ADDITIONAL READING

Baldassarri, D., & Bearman, P. (2007). Dynamics of political polarization. *American Sociological Review, 72*, 784–811. doi:10.1177/000312240707200507

Boulianne, S. (2009). Does Internet use affect engagement? A meta-analysis of research. *Political Communication, 26*, 193–211. doi:10.1080/10584600902854363

Brundidge, J. (2008, May). *The contemporary media environment and breadth of communication: The contribution of the Internet to the heterogeneity of political discussion networks.* Paper presented at the International Communication Association Conference, Montreal, Canada.

Brundidge, J. (2010). Encountering "difference" in the contemporary public sphere: The contribution of the Internet to the heterogeneity of political discussion. *The Journal of Communication, 60*, 680–700. doi:10.1111/j.1460-2466.2010.01509.x

Choi, J. H., Watt, J. H., & Lynch, M. (2006). Perceptions of news credibility about the war in Iraq: Why war opponents perceived the Internet as the most credible medium. *Journal of Computer-Mediated Communication, 12*, 11. Retrieved from http://jcmc.indiana.edu/vol12/issue1.choi.html. doi:10.1111/j.1083-6101.2006.00322.x

Davis, S., Elin, L., & Reeher, G. (2004). *Click on democracy: The internet's power to change political apathy into civic action*. Boulder, CO: Westview Press.

Delli Carpini, M. (2004). Mediating democratic engagement: The impact of communications on citizens' involvement in political and civic life. In Kaid, L. L. (Ed.), *Handbook of Political Communication Research* (pp. 395–434). Mahwah, NJ: Lawrence Erlbaum Associates.

Delli Carpini, M. X. (2000). Gen.com: Youth, civic engagement, and the new information environment. *Political Communication, 17*(4), 341–349. doi:10.1080/10584600050178942

Graf, J., & Aday, S. (2008). Selective attention to online political information. *Journal of Broadcasting & Electronic Media, 52*, 86–100. doi:10.1080/08838150701820874

Hardy, B. W., & Scheufele, D. A. (2005). Examining differential gains of Internet use: Comparing the moderating role of talk and online interactions. *The Journal of Communication, 55*(1), 71–84. doi:10.1111/j.1460-2466.2005.tb02659.x

Hill, K. A., & Hughes, J. E. (1998). *Cyberpolitics: Citizen activism in the age of the Internet*. Lanham, MD: Roman & Littlefield Publishers.

Horrigan, J. Garrett, K., & Resnick, P. (2004). The Internet and democratic debate: Wired Americans hear more points of view about candidates and key issues than other citizens. *Pew Research Center,* Retrieved October 27, 2004 from http://www.pewinternet.org/reports

Horrigan, J. (2007). A typology of information and communication technology users. Retrieved from http://www.pewinternet.org/pdfs/ PIP_ICT_Typology.pdf

Iyengar, S., Hahn, K. S., Krosnick, J. A., & Walker, J. (2008). Selective exposure to campaign communication: The role of anticipated agreement and issue public membership. *The Journal of Politics, 70*, 186–200. doi:10.1017/S0022381607080139

Jennings, M. K., & Zeitner, B. (2003). Internet use and civic engagement: A longitudinal analysis. *Public Opinion Quarterly, 67*, 311–334. doi:10.1086/376947

Johnson, T. J. Zhang, W., Bichard, S. L., & Kaye, B.K. (2008, November). *Shut up and listen: The influence of selective exposure to blogs and political Websites on political tolerance.* Paper presented at the annual meeting of the Midwest Association for Public Opinion Research.

Johnson, T. J., & Kaye, B. K. (2003). A boost or a bust for democracy? How the Web influenced political attitudes and behaviors in the 1996 and 2000 presidential elections. *The Harvard International Journal of Press/Politics, 8*(3), 9–34. doi:10.1177/1081180X03008003002

Johnson, T. J., & Kaye, B. K. (2006). Blog day afternoon: Are blogs stealing audiences away from traditional media sources? in Ralph Berenger (ed.), *Cybermedia go to war* (316-333). Spokane, WA: Marquette Books.

Johnson, T. J., & Kaye, B. K. (2009, November). *The dark side of the boon?: Credibility, selective exposure and the proliferation of online sources of political information*. Paper presented at the Midwest Association for Public Opinion Research, Chicago, Illinois.

Jones, S. G. (Ed.). (1995). *CyberSociety: Computer-mediated communication and community*. Thousand Oaks, CA: Sage Publications.

Kaye, B. K. (2007). Blog use motivations: An exploratory study. In Tremayne, M. (Ed.), *Blogging, citizenship, and the future of media* (pp. 127–148). New York: Routledge.

Kaye, B. K., & Johnson, T. J. (2004). Weblogs as a source of information about the 2003 Iraq War. In Berenger, R. D. (Ed.), *Global media goes to war: Role of news and entertainment media during the 2003 Iraq War* (pp. 291–301). Spokane, WA: Marquette Books.

Kaye, B. K., & Johnson, T. J. (2004). A web for all reasons: Uses and gratifications of Internet components for political information. *Telematics and Informatics, 21*, 197–223. doi:10.1016/S0736-5853(03)00037-6

Kaye, B. K., & Johnson, T. J. (2006). The age of reasons: Motives for using different components of the Internet for political information. In Williams, A. P., & Tedesco, J. C. (Eds.), *The Internet election: perspectives on the Web in campaign 2004*. Lanham, MD: Rowman & Littlefield.

Kenski, K., & Stroud, N. J. (2006). Connections between Internet use and political efficacy, knowledge, and participation. *Journal of Broadcasting & Electronic Media, 50*(2), 173–192. doi:10.1207/s15506878jobem5002_1

Knobloch-Westerwick, S., & Meng, J. (2009). Looking the other way: Selective exposure to attitude-consistent and counter-attitudinal political information. *Communication Research, 36*, 426–448. doi:10.1177/0093650209333030

Kraut, R., Patterson, M., Lundmark, V., Kiesler, S., Mukopadhyay, T., & Scherlis, W. (1998). Internet paradox: A social technology that reduces social involvement and psychological well-being? *The American Psychologist, 53*, 1017–1031. doi:10.1037/0003-066X.53.9.1017

Lawson-Borders, G., & Kirk, R. (2005). Blogs in campaign communication. *The American Political Science Review, 80*(2), 505–520.

Melican, D. B., & Dixon, T. L. (2008). News on the Net: Credibility, selective exposure, and racial prejudice. *Communication Research, 35*, 151–168. doi:10.1177/0093650207313157

Moy, P., Manosevitch, E., Stamm, K., & Dunsmore, K. (2005). Linking dimensions of Internet use and civic engagement. *Journalism & Mass Communication Quarterly, 82*, 571–586.

Scheufele, D. A., Nisbit, M. C., Brossard, D., & Nisbet, E. C. (2004). Social structure and citizenship: Examining the impact of social setting, network homogeneity, and information variables on political participation. *Political Communication, 21*, 315–338. doi:10.1080/10584600490481389

Shah, D. V., Schmierbach, M., Hawkins, J., Espino, R., & Donavan, J. (2002). Nonrecursive models of Internet use and community engagement: Questioning whether time spent online erodes social capital. *Journalism & Mass Communication Quarterly, 79*(4), 964–987.

Stromer-Galley, J. (2003). Diversity of political conversations on the Internet: Users' perspectives. *Journal of Computer-Mediated Communication*. Retrieved from http://jcmc.indiana.edu/ vol8/issue3/stromergalley.html.

Stroud, N. J. (2007). Media effects, selective exposure, and *Fahrenheit 9/11*. *Political Communication, 24*, 415–432. doi:10.1080/10584600701641565

Sweetser, K. D., & Weaver-Lariscy, R. (2007). *Candidates make good friends: An analysis of candidates' use of Facebook*. Chicago, IL: National Communication Association.

Tedesco, J. C., & Kaid, L. L. (2000, November). *Candidate web sites and voter effects: Investigating uses and gratifications*. Paper presented at the annual meeting of the National Communication Association, Seattle.

Tian, Y. (2006). Political use and perceived effects of the Internet: A case study of the 2004 election. *Communication Research Reports*, *23*, 129–137. doi:10.1080/08824090600669103

Wellman, B., Haase, A. Q., Witte, J., & Hampton, K. (2001). Does the internet increase, decrease, or supplement social capital? Social networks, participation, and community commitment. *The American Behavioral Scientist*, *45*, 436–456. doi:10.1177/00027640121957286

Wojciewszak, M. E., & Mutz, D. C. (2009). Online groups and political discourse: Do online discussion spaces facilitate exposure to political disagreement? *The Journal of Communication*, *59*, 40–56. doi:10.1111/j.1460-2466.2008.01403.x

Zhang, W., Johnson, T., Seltzer, T., & Bichard, S. (2010). The revolution will be networked: The influence of social network sites on political attitudes and behaviors. *Social Science Computer Review*, *28*, 75–92. doi:10.1177/0894439309335162

KEY TERMS AND DEFINITIONS

Cognitive Dissonance Theory: When individuals are exposed to information or events that are inconsistent with their own beliefs, it causes a state of discomfort or dissonance.

Cognitive Misers: Individuals look for ways to simplify their information-gathering and processing tasks.

Partisan Selective Exposure: The degree that individuals seek out partisan information that supports their political position or avoid partisan information that challenges their beliefs.

Personally Relevant Beliefs: Beliefs that are central to a person's interests or self-identity.

Polarization: The degree to which individuals take increasingly extreme positions.

Political Blogs: News or discussion-oriented Web sites that are hosted by a blogger.

Political Web Sites: Websites posted by an individual or an organization about a political issue, organization or individual.

Selective Exposure: The degree individuals seek out information that supports their political position or avoid information that challenges their beliefs.

Chapter 11

Net Gain?

Selective Exposure and Selective Avoidance of Social Network Sites

Barbara K. Kaye
University of Tennessee-Knoxville, USA

Thomas J. Johnson
University of Texas-Austin, USA

ABSTRACT

This study examined the influence of motivations for, and reliance, on social network sites on selective exposure (purposely seeking agreeable political information) and selective avoidance (purposely dodging disagreeable political information). The results are based on an online survey that was posted during the four-week period surrounding the 2008 presidential election. The responses from 1,530 politically interested social network users revealed five primary motivations were found for accessing social network sites: (1) political information seeking, (2) anti-traditional media sentiment, (3) expression/affiliation, (4) political guidance/judgments, and (5) personal fulfillment. Of these five motivations, the latter three predict selective exposure but none predict selective avoidance. Reliance is not a predictor of selectivity, but gender and several political characteristics are predictors of both selective exposure and selective avoidance.

INTRODUCTION

Social networking is often used to widen social circles and boost online social standing, but more so it has evolved into a powerful tool that links individuals ideologically, politically, culturally, and professionally. Beyond simply connecting individuals to each other, social network sites (SNS) have profoundly changed the way people interact and with whom they interact. Social network users are exposed to people, ideas, and opinions to which they would otherwise not have access. This exposure, in turn, has altered and intensified networkers' worldviews.

DOI: 10.4018/978-1-61350-338-6.ch011

Social networks today are marked by network individualism where every individual has his or her own personal community that ranges from close friends and family to people unknown outside of the electronic network. People communicate to their own personal networked community through social media such as blogs, text messaging and SNS as well as through more traditional sources such as telephone and person-to-person communication (Boase & Wellman, 2005; Castells, 2007). While personal networks can supply important elements of community to individuals such as support, sociability, information, social identity and a sense of belonging (Wellman, Boase & Chen, 2002, Wellman et al., 2003), there is also a fear is that SNS are another way for online users to block out opposing views and expose themselves to only agreeable information (Castells, 2005; Wellman, et al., 2003). Ultimately, the consequences of such selectivity are an even more polarized and fragmented electorate (Stroud, 2008, 2010; Sunstein, 2001) and less tolerance for opposing viewpoints (Mutz, 2002).

Ordinary citizens are using SNS as a way to sway their network of friends to a particular political point of view or candidate. For instance, 40% of all social network users and 50% of those under the age of 30 used SNS to obtain or share information about politics and the 2008 presidential election campaign. Specifically, 29% of SNS users sought their friends' political interests or affiliations and 22% looked for information about a candidate or campaign (Smith & Rainie, 2008). Further, about 28 percent of all Internet users get news or political information from friends they follow on Facebook and about 13% of online users have become a fan or friend of a journalist or news organization (Purcell, Rainie, Mitchell, Rosenstiel, & Olmstead, 2010).

Barack Obama and his staff recognized the powerful influence of social network sites and thus relied heavily on them to drum up support for his 2008 bid for the presidency. Pundits claim that this use of social networks contributed to Obama's victory in what is dubbed the "Facebook Effect" (Fraser & Dutta, 2008; Kenski, Hardy, & Jamieson, 2010).

Considering the effect SNS use had on the election, and its influence on a politically polarized world and on the way individuals manage their social and political relationships, it is important to understand the reasons for turning to SNS and what information is being sought. Therefore, this chapter focuses on whether reliance on social network sites and motivations for accessing these venues strengthen the propensity for social network users to avoid political information they disagree with or to look for only what they are favorably inclined toward. This chapter relies on the responses of individuals who completed a survey that was posted online during the four weeks surrounding the 2008 presidential election.

LITERATURE REVIEW

Selective Exposure/ Selective Avoidance

The proliferation of online outlets of political information, many that advocate a particular point of view, has moved information selectivity into the forefront of media research. Media consumers cannot possibly access more than a miniscule portion of online information so they have become adept at choosing what to view and what to ignore. The psychological process of such information selection is complex and often leads to behaviors known as selective exposure and selective avoidance (known together as selectivity) (Smith, Farbrigar & Norris, 2008; Stroud, 2006, 2008).

Selective exposure is when people search for information that supports their political dispositions. Selective avoidance is when people ignore information that challenges their beliefs and opinions. Individuals seem to search for information that supports their views more often than they avoid information that challenges their beliefs (Chaffee, Saphir, Grap, Sandvig, & Hahn, 2001; Donsbach, 2001; Graf & Aday, 2008), but this finding should be interpreted carefully because survey respondents may think it is more socially acceptable to state they seek information rather than avoid it. Also, individuals who view issues as important to them personally, who have greater interest in politics and a stronger party affiliation purposely seek counter information to learn what the other side thinks so they can deploy arguments against their opponents' claims (Knobloch-Westerwick & Meng, 2009).

Selectivity and Social Networking Sites

With the countless number of political sources online it is easy to locate supportive reports and avoid disagreeable ones (Bennett & Iyengar, 2008; Galston, 2003; Sunstein, 2001), thus increasing the opportunity for selectivity (Best, Chmielewski, & Krueger, 2005; Garrett, 2009; Smith, 2009). Online interactivity facilitates selectivity to partisan information by allowing users to control what information appears on their computer screen (Bimber & Davis, 2003; Garrett, 2009; Johnson, Bichard, & Zhang, 2009; Johnson, Zhang & Bichard, in press; Mutz & Martin, 2001; Stroud, 2006, 2008, 2010). Social media also enhance selectivity by allowing communication that bypasses corporate media and other gatekeeping sources (Castells, 2005, 2007). By choosing what networks they what to invest their time and effort with social network users create their own "portfolios of sociability" (Castells, 2001).

The nature of social network sites seems both to encourage and hinder selectivity. On sites like Facebook users have considerable control over who can be a friend and who cannot, and they usually select friends from among those who they are acquainted with offline (boyd & Ellison, 2007). And because users often manage their network profile to project a certain image of themselves (Tufekci, 2008), when they get friend requests from strangers they are likely to be from those who share similar outlooks on life. When individuals limit the size of their SNS pool of friends to those they know personally, they limit their exposure to only those who are likely to share similar values and interests and they avoid coming into contact with those who challenge their opinions. In addition to individual associations, SNS users often create or join groups or fan pages that are comprised of others with similar beliefs, interests, ideas and values (Kushin & Kitchener, 2009; Woolley, Limperos & Oliver, 2010). The consequence of belonging to such homogeneous groups is that it may lead to selectivity (Walsh, 2003).

On the other hand, SNS also facilitate casting a wide net within which to capture a diverse set of friends from which to learn opposing viewpoints and opinions (Mutz, 2002). In particular, SNS friends often post links and videos on status updates or on wall posts that challenge the status quo. Users might also join groups and fan pages that run counter to their views, thus reducing selective exposure and selective avoidance.

Motivations and Social Network Sites

The rise of the Internet has led to resurgence in uses and gratifications research, which is based on the premise that audience members are active and goal directed. Consumers are aware of, and are able to explain, their motivations for using the media and that they actively choose specific content and media that satisfy their needs (Blumler, 1979; Katz, Blumler & Gurevitch, 1974; Katz, Gurevitch & Haas, 1973; McLeod & Becker, 1981; Palmgreen, 1984). The tenets of uses and gratifications can be applied to the study of the Internet and its specific components because users actively seek content and choose what sites and sources to access (Bucy, 2004; Ruggiero, 2000; Stovall, 2004).

Each component of the Internet gratifies particular needs. What needs are satisfied depends on how the source functions, and levels and types of interactivity it allows (Levy & Windahl, 1985; Ruggiero, 2000). There are two major types of interactivity: content and interpersonal (Bucy, 2004). Content interactivity is when users control how information is selected, delivered and presented, through such means as clicking on a story link or downloading photos or videos. Internet components like web sites, on which users largely interact with content, primarily serve information-seeking needs. Interpersonal interactivity is person-to-person communication, delivered both synchronously (such as instant messaging and chatting) and asynchronously (such as social networking or e-mailing).

Content interactivity satisfies the need for accessing information not available in traditional media, to check on the accuracy of traditional media and to keep up with the main issues of the day (Kaye & Johnson, 2004, 2006). In general, both synchronous and asynchronous interpersonal interactivity, largely serve social needs such as putting users in contact with likeminded people and providing a forum of expression (Stafford, Stafford & Schkade, 2004).

Researchers are just beginning to explore what needs social network sites gratify, with most studies looking at network sites in general, though some examine aspects of SNS such as groups and fan pages (Park, Kee & Valenzuela, 2009). SNS satisfy social needs such as relationship maintenance, communicating with friends and making new friends (Bumgarner, 2007; Park, et al., 2009; Quan-Haase & Young, 2010; Raake & Bonds-Raake, 2008; Sheldon, 2008). Social network use also gratifies social information seeking needs such as learning about events and social functions (Raake & Bonds-Raake, 2008), as well as social convenience needs such as being able to communicate easily or to get hold of someone quickly (Nyland, 2007). Users are also motivated to rely on SNS for entertainment, to pass time, and for personal expression (Bumgarner, 2007; Nyland, 2007; Sheldon, 2008).

More recently researchers have realized that many online users connect to SNS to keep up with political happenings. More than just looking for political information, these users are specifically turning to SNS for something to talk about with others, to contact like-minded people, for ongoing political debates and arguments, to keep up with political issues, to learn something new and because they are a convenient way to find political news (Kaye, 2010a). Additionally, SNS satisfy the need "to meet other supporters" and "to find out what other people have to say about the candidate" (Ancu & Cozma, 2009). Kaye (2010a) notes that because political blogs and social network sites share several characteristics such as offering news and opinion, promoting discussion and community, and providing an online space for communicating with others that users may be seek out blogs and social media sites for similar reasons. For instance, one of the major motivations for using blogs is because users do not trust the traditional media and they turn to blogs for information they cannot get from traditional media and to check on the facts presented in mainstream sources (Ekdale, Namkoong, Fung & Perlmutter, 2010; Johnson & Kaye, 2009; Kaye, 2005, 2007, 2010b; Kaye & Johnson, 2006). Similarly, shared links are often from sources not connected to the media and there seems little connection between the focus of social media posts and issues stressed in the media (Project for Excellence in Journalism, 2010).

Selectivity, Reliance, Motivations, and Social Network Sites

The media that people rely on influence the degree to which they practice selectivity. For example, reliance on traditional broadcast and print media and their online counterparts is not conducive to selectivity because these sources are perceived as presenting all sides of an issue (Best et al, 2005). However, partisan and alternative sources such as talk radio, cable TV news, political Web sites and blogs are magnets for selectivity (Johnson, Zhang & Bichard, in press, Johnson, Bichard & Zhang, 2011 2009; Stroud, 2006, 2008, 2010).

Reliance and selectivity are linked because the more individuals rely on partisan/alternative sources for political news and information, the more familiar they become with the ones that support or contradict their views. The more users agree with content, they more heavily they rely on the source, and conversely, if they dislike the content, they'll shun the source. Therefore, the more experienced and familiar users becomes with social networks, the more they will rely on them, and the more knowledge they will have about which ones contain information that support their points of view (Johnson & Kaye, 2004, 2009; Johnson, Kaye, Bichard & Wong, 2007)

Just as reliance may influence the degree of selectivity so might motivations for using a particular source, whether traditional or online (Atkin, 1985, Kim, 2007). Users are typically selective in their media choices, including SNS, to ensure they visit sources that will satisfy their needs and preferences (Castells, 2005; Hoffner et al., 2009; Kim, 2007; Wellman et al., 2003).

But motivations and selectivity may be only tenuously linked. For example, Johnson, et al., (2011) examined both reliance as well as informational, entertainment and communication motives for seeking political blogs and web sites that support the users' political positions. While reliance proved to be among the strongest predictors of selective exposure to both political web sites and blogs, motivations proved unrelated to selectivity.

Research Questions

This chapter investigates the motivations for using social network sites, and whether motivations and reliance influence the propensity for selective exposure and selective avoidance. Specifically, this study asks the following research questions.

RQ1. *Does reliance on social network sites predict selective exposure (purposely seeking agreeable information)?*

RQ2. *Does reliance on social network sites predict selective avoidance (avoiding contrary information)?*

RQ3. *Do motivations for using social network sites predict selective exposure (purposely seeking agreeable information)?*

RQ4. *Do motivations for using social network sites predict selective avoidance (avoiding contrary information)?*

METHOD

This study's findings are based on the responses to a survey that was available online during the four weeks surrounding the 2008 presidential election. As in other published studies (Johnson & Kaye, 2004, 2009, 2010) the survey's URL and a request to participate was placed on hundreds of politically oriented websites, blogs and social network sites of diverse political ideologies as well as on the discussion boards of traditional media.[1] The survey was comprised of questions that asked about reliance on social network sites, motivations for using SNS, political attitudes, and demographic characteristics.

Respondents were encouraged to "snowball" the survey by clicking on a link that automatically forwarded it to politically interested friends. The survey was completed by 4,241 respondents. The survey software recorded the number of individuals who accessed the survey and the number who completed it – resulting in a cooperation rate of 26.2%

Study Variables

Selective Exposure and Selective Avoidance. Respondents were asked on a 1-10 scale how likely they are to access online sources that *share* their point of view about political issues, and how likely they are to connect to online sources that *challenge* their point of view about political issues.

Reliance. Reliance on social network sites for political information was measured on a five-point scale: (1) never rely, (2) rarely rely, (3) sometimes rely, (4) rely, (5) heavily rely.

Motivations for Using Social Network Sites. Respondents marked their level of agreement with 32 reasons for accessing social network sites on a scale that ranged from (1) strongly disagree to (5) strongly agree.

Political Attributes. Respondents marked their levels of political knowledge, political interest, knowledge of, and interest in, the 2008 presidential campaign, and the strength of their political party ties on a 1-10 scale. Political ideology was measured on a five-point scale: (1) very liberal, (2) liberal, (3) moderate, (4) conservative, (5) very conservative. Self-efficacy and trust were assessed using a five-point scale that ranged from (1) strongly disagree to (5) strongly agree. The measures were taken from the National Election Studies. Self-efficacy is comprised of the following four statements: "I consider myself well qualified to participate in politics," "I feel I could do as good of a job in public office as most other people," "I think that I am better informed about politics and government than most people," and I feel that I have a pretty good understanding of the important political issues facing our country." Trust in the government was measured by "Most of our leaders are devoted to the service of our country," "Politicians never tell us what they really think," and "I don't think public officials care much about what people like me think." The trust and efficacy measures were combined into separate self-efficacy and trust indices. Reliability for the self-efficacy index is.70, for trust it is.73.

Demographics. Respondents were asked their gender, age as of their last birthday, and estimated income for 2008. They also selected their highest level of education from a list that ranged from "less than high school" to "terminal degree," such as Ph.D., M.D., J.D.

DATA ANALYSIS

Frequencies were run on the reliance variable. Respondents who "never" rely on social network sites were excluded from further analysis. Of the total sample, 1,230 respondents rely on social network sites.

Mean scores were derived to determine the likelihood of practicing selective exposure and selective avoidance by accessing online sources that share or challenge existing views, levels of reliance on social network sites, political attributes (political knowledge, political interest, election knowledge, election interest, ideology, strength of party association, trust in the government, self-efficacy) and demographics (gender, age, education, income).

Factor analysis categorized the 32 motivational items into five factors. Reliability scores range from.717 to.929.

The first set of hierarchical regressions were run to ascertain whether reliance on social network sites predicts if users avoid information that challenges their views or seek information that shares their view. Demographics were entered in the first block followed by the political variables in the second block. Reliance on social network sites was entered as the third block.

The second set of regressions tested whether motivations for using social network sites predict if users avoid contrary information or look for content that fits their worldview. Demographics were entered in the first block with political variables in the second block and each of the motivations was entered separately into the third block. A total of five regressions (one for each motivation as independent variable) were run for both selective exposure and selective avoidance.

RESULTS

Respondent Profile

Respondents have a greater tendency to access online sources that *share* their views (m=7.94, range=1-10) than ones that *challenge* their beliefs (m=5.71, range=1-10). Specifically, slightly more than 8 in ten (84.0%) are very likely to visit sources they agree with and 4 in ten (40.3%) very often link to sources that challenge their views. Moreover, 18.0% said they rarely seek contrary information. When seeking political news and information on social network sites, only 16.2% rely on/heavily rely on them with the remaining sometimes/rarely rely on them.

Slightly more 8 of ten (82.5%) of respondents are highly self-efficacious but they are not very trusting of the government. Only 13.1% is highly trusting, 65.4% is moderately trusting and 21.5% express little trust.

Slightly less than three-quarters of respondents consider themselves very knowledgeable (73.7%) about politics, and 8 in ten (80.6%) are very interested in politics. About nine in ten reported that they were very knowledgeable about (88.1%) and very interested in (90.5%) the 2008 presidential election. Slightly more than one-quarter (26.2%) are politically conservative/very conservative, 20.7% moderate, and 53.1% liberal/very liberal. Respondents are also moderately tied to their political party of choice (m=6.8, range 1-10).

Males comprise 6 of 10 (59.1%) of the 1,230 social network users. The typical respondent has a college degree or higher (74.2%), earns $68,600 per year, is white (90.0%), and 41.9 years of age.

Respondents are motivated to use social network sites for five primary reasons: (1) political information seeking, (2) anti-traditional media sentiment, (3) expression/affiliation, (4) political guidance/judgments, and 5) personal fulfillment. The five factors explain 66.85% of the variance:

1. **Political Information Seeking.** Social network sites are used to seek up-to-date and in-depth information about politics and current issues. Respondents turn to SNS for a wide variety of viewpoints and opinions. They also enjoy debating politics and learning from others networkers.
2. **Anti-Traditional Media Sentiment.** Respondents access SNS because they are independent of traditional media, which they view with suspicion. Users would rather rely on the word of their SNS friends than on big media gatekeepers. SNS users feel they get information that the mainstream media omit or gloss over.
3. **Expression/Affiliation.** SNS are used to express personal viewpoints, to feel politically involved and to connect with like-minded individuals. They are also interested in learning different perspectives and gathering information to talk about with others.
4. **Political Guidance/Judgments.** Respondents use SNS for support and validation of their own opinions and to help them make up their minds on how to vote. They feel that social network sites inform them of candidate stances on issues and about their personal characteristics.
5. **Personal Fulfillment.** Using social network sites are relaxing and entertaining, and bring close the excitement of election races (Table 1).

Research Questions

The study first asks if reliance on social network sites predicts selective *exposure*. The data show that relying on social network sites does not lead to purposely seeking agreeable information. Instead, high levels of political interest, election knowledge, election interest, but low political knowledge, strength of party ties, low trust in the government, liberalism and being female

Table 1. Motivations for using social network sites for political information

F1 POLITICAL INFO SEEKING	
Eigenvalue 13.59 - Variance Explained 42.4%, Reliability.923	
for a wide variety of political information	.751
because I want to learn something new	.729
to get a wide variety of viewpoints	.686
to keep up with political issues	.676
for the ongoing political debates and arguments	.657
because it's interesting	.629
for political news analysis	.599
for depth of political information	.598
for links to more political information sources	.590
F2 ANTI-TRADITIONAL MEDIA SENTIMENT	
Eigenvalue 3.50-Variance Explained 10.9%, Reliability.929	
because I don't trust traditional media	.889
to avoid traditional media bias	.886
to check on the accuracy of traditional media	.718
for information I can't get from traditional media	.684
because they are independent from traditional media	.683
for credible political information	.531
F3 EXPRESSION/AFFILIATION	
Eigenvalue 1.79 - Variance Explained 5.6%, Reliability.841	
to be in contact with like-minded people	.841
to feel politically involved	.679
to express my opinions	.668
to give me something to talk about with others	.650
for specific political perspectives (i.e. conservative, libertarian, liberal)	.527
to find out about issues affecting people like myself	.504
F4 POLITICAL GUIDANCE/JUDGMENTS	
Eigenvalue 1.35 - Variance Explained 4.2%, Reliability.873	
to see how the candidates stand on various issues	.789
to judge the personal qualities of candidates	.768
to help make up my mind how to vote in an election	.689
to find specific political information that I'm looking for	.561
for unbiased viewpoints	.553
to remind me of my candidates strong points	.531
to judge who is likely to win an election	.468
F5 PERSONAL FULFILLMENT	
Eigenvalue 1.15 - Variance Explained 3.6%, Reliability.717	
because it helps me to relax	.792
because it is entertaining	.547
to enjoy the excitement of an election race	.546

(to use as ammunition in arguments with others did not load on any of the factors) determine a likelihood of accessing supportive political information (Table 2). The second research question examined the influence of reliance on SNS on selective *avoidance*. Reliance is also not a significant predictor of selective exposure. Instead, males who are strongly partisan but not very interested in politics and who were not very interested in the election are likely to selectively avoid information with which they disagree (Table 2).

The study now turns attention from reliance to motivations as predictors of selectivity. Three of the five motivations for using social network sites predict selective *exposure*. Individuals who are motivated to use SNS because they enjoy expressing themselves and affiliating with others, seek political guidance and desire personal fulfillment are most likely to choose information they find agreeable. They also lean liberal, do not trust the government and are very interested in politics. Using SNS for seeking political information and anti-traditional media sentiment does not predict selective exposure (Table 3).

In contrast, none of the motivations are predictors of selective *avoidance*. Instead, several political characteristics mitigate the influence of motivations on selective avoidance. Generally, users with low election knowledge but who are political liberals with strong party ties were most likely to avoid disagreeable information.

Table 2. Hierarchical regression analysis of reliance as a predictor of selective exposure and selective avoidance

	Selective Exposure	*Selective Avoidance*[1]
Predictor Variables		
Gender[2]	-.09*	.08*
Age	.01	.01
Education	-.02	.03
Income	-.01	.00
R2	**.021**	**.018**
Politics Knowledge	-.11**	-.00
Political Interest	.26***	-.15**
Election Knowledge	.16**	-.09
Election Interest	.08*	-.10**
Strength of Party Ties	.09*	.15***
Political Ideology	-.09*	-.03
Trust	-.10**	-.02
Efficacy	.06	-.03
R2	**.222**	**.110**
R2 Change	**.201**	**.092**
Sig. of Change	**.000**	**.000**
Rely on Social Network Sites	.00	-.02
R2	**.222**	**.110**
R2 Change	**.000**	**.000**
Adjusted R	**.212**	**.099**
Sig. of Change	**.897**	**.595**

*p<.05, **p<.01, ***p<.001

1. Reverse coded. Positive betas indicate respondents do practice selective avoidance, negative betas indicated they do not.

2. Positive = male, negative=female

DISCUSSION

Overview of Findings

This study set out to discover the relationships among motivations for using social network sites and reliance on them and selective exposure and selective avoidance. The motivational findings show that users connect to SNS for five primary reasons: (1) political information seeking, (2) anti-traditional media sentiment, (3) expression/affiliation, (4) political guidance/judgments, and (5) personal fulfillment. These motivations can be further classified as either content or interpersonal needs as identified by Bucy (2004). For instance, political information seeking, political guidance

Table 3. Hierarchical regression analysis of motivations for using sns as predictors of selective exposure

	Select Exp.	*Select Exp.*	*Select Exp.*	*Select Exp.*	*Select Exp.*
Predictor Variables					
Gender[1]	-.04	-.02	-.03	-.02	-.02
Age	-.03	.06	-.00	.03	
Education	-.03	-.00	.01	.01	-.02
Income	-.00	.01	.04	.02	-.00
R2	**.024**	**.027**	**.028**	**.025**	**.025**
Political Knowledge	-.13	-.13	-.07	-.07	-.10
Political Interest	.42***	.40***	.38***	.35***	.41***
Election Knowledge	.18	.18	.14	.19	13
Election Interest	.02	.02	-.02	.02	.02
Strength of Party Ties	.10	.09	.06	.05	.07
Political Ideology	-.13*	-.13*	-.12*	-.11	-.12
Trust	-.16**	-.12	-.16**	-.13*	-.18**
Efficacy	.02	.03	.02	.04	.05
R2	**.318**	**.305**	**.306**	**.282**	**.303**
R2 Change	**.294**	**.278**	**.278**	**.257**	**.279**
Sig. of Change	**.000**	**.000**	**.000**	**.000**	**.000**
F1 Political Info. Seeking	.08				
F2 Anti-Traditional Media		.13			
F3 Expression/Affiliation			.30***		
F4 Political Guide/Judge				.14*	
F5 Personal Fulfillment					.18**
R2	**.323**	**.315**	**.375**	**.299**	**.333**
R2 Change	**.005**	**.011**	**.070**	**.017**	**.030**
Adjusted R	**.279**	**.271**	**.334**	**.254**	**.163**
Sig. of Change	**.214**	**.079**	**.000**	**.026**	**.003**

*p<.05, **p<.01, ***p<.001

1. Positive = male, negative=female

and personal fulfillment satisfy content needs as users engage in person-to-content activities by clicking on links, watching video, scanning through photo libraries and reading.

This study focuses on whether there is a connection between motivations for using SNS and selectivity, and if the link is robust enough such that motivations predict selective exposure and selective avoidance. The findings indicate that the interpersonal motivations of expression/affiliation, personal fulfillment, and political guidance predict selective exposure. Being true to their name, social network sites are strongly used for interpersonal contact, which is similar to conclusions drawn by other researchers (Bumgarner, 2007; Raake & Bonds-Raake, 2008; Sheldon, 2008).

The content motivations, political seeking and anti-traditional media, do not predict either selective exposure or selective avoidance. It seems that individuals are driven to SNS to satisfy interpersonal needs but not content needs. Online users are

Table 4. Hierarchical regression analysis of motivations for using sns as predictors of selective avoidance[1]

	Select	*Select*	*Select*	*Select*	*Select*
	Avoid	*Avoid*	*Avoid*	*Avoid*	*Avoid*
Predictor Variables	.09	.09	.08	.11	.09
Gender[2]	.00	-.01	.00	.02	.02
Age	-.01	.00	-.03	-.02	-.02
Education	.05	.05	.06	.06	.05
Income					
R2	**.043**	**.042**	**.035**	**.042**	**.044**
Political Knowledge	.07	.08	.13	.08	.06
Political Interest	-.07	-.07	-.08	-.08	-.07
Election Knowledge	-.21	-.24**	-.24**	-.21	-.19
Election Interest	-.05	-.05	-.05	-.07	-.07
Strength of Party Ties	.24**	.22**	.23**	.25***	.24***
Political Ideology	-.15*	-.17**	-.17**	-.15**	-.15*
Trust	-.07	-.06	-.06	-.08	-.07
Efficacy	-.10	-.11	-.15	-.12	-.11
R2	**.185**	**.186**	**.189**	**.191**	**.187**
R2 Change	**.142**	**.143**	**.154**	**.149**	**.144**
Sig. of Change	**.000**	**.000**	**.000**	**.000**	**.000**
F1 Political Info. Seeking	-.07				
F2 Anti-Traditional Media		.05			
F3 Expression/Affiliation			-.01		
F4 Political Guide/Judge				-.01	
F5 Personal Fulfillment					.04
R2	**.189**	**.187**	**.189**	**.191**	**.189**
R2 Change	**.004**	**.001**	**.000**	**.000**	**.002**
Adjusted R	**.137**	**.135**	**.136**	**.140**	**.037**
Sig. of Change	**.292**	**.549**	**.883**	**.859**	**.555**

*p<.05, **p<.01, ***p<.001

*Reverse coded. Positive betas indicate respondents do practice selective avoidance, negative betas indicated they do not.

2. Positive = male, negative=female

drawn to other sources, such as blogs, to gratify content needs (Kaye, 2010b). Presumably, online users rely on friends and those within their social circles to satisfy interpersonal needs, but look to reporters and experts, such as those write for media sites and blogs, for fulfilling content needs.

In addition to investigating the relationship between motivations and selectivity, this study investigated whether *reliance* on social network sites predicts selective exposure (deliberately seeking agreeable information) or selective avoidance (purposely ignoring contrary information) while using SNS for political information. Reliance however, does not influence whether SNS users seek agreeable or disagreeable information.

Lastly, this study found a few associations among demographic characteristics, and political attributes and motivations, reliance, selective exposure and selective avoidance. In general, liberal females who are interested in politics but not very politically savvy, and who do not trust the government are more likely to insulate themselves within a cocoon of agreeable information. In contrast, liberal males who are politically disinterested but claim strong party ties tend to shun disagreeable information

Implications of Findings

Motivations

The reasons for linking to SNS found in this study are similar to the reason that users are drawn to blogs (Kaye, 2007, 2010b). The similar motivations for using SNS and blogs suggest that interactive Internet communications fulfill needs in a way that traditional media cannot. The personal and interactive nature of the SNS and its ability to link people globally through common interests is unprecedented.

But caution must also be taken. Just because there are so many electronic information distribution points and such a wide variety of opinions, viewpoints and beliefs, does not necessarily mean that online use leads to enlightenment and acceptance of what is different from one's worldview.

It is precisely the availability of almost unlimited information that gives online users the ability to choose what to attend to and what to ignore. Before the 1980s, when there are only a few outlets, such as one local newspaper or several local broadcast stations, media consumers were limited to information that was accessible within time and space limitations, and gatekeeping restrictions. But now that the Internet offers innumerable outlets of information and control over what content is viewed, it facilitates both selective exposure and selective avoidance.

SNS users are selective with whom they interact and tend to prefer like-minded individuals with whom they feel comfortable expressing their opinions. There is no argument or negativity when setting forth a viewpoint that others in the network agree with. For example, this study found that social network sites are accessed for political guidance, such as help with making voting decisions. It is logical then, that users would deliberately seek out networks that are inhabited by those with similar political positions. Commonalities boost affinity whereas as differences are polarizing. Further, agreement requires less cognitive energy to process than disagreement (Edwards & Smith, 1996).

As with non-mediated interpersonal friendships where close friends usually share similar political beliefs (Mutz, 2002), cyber social circles are characterized by network individualism where every participant is part of a personal community of likeminded persons (Boase & Wellman, 2005; Castells, 2007). Within these cyber-networks individuals feel free to express themselves and they gain much personal fulfillment in doing so. The downside, however, is that despite connections to millions of individual others, users tend to associate with those who share similar ideas and beliefs, which limits their range of opinion and information.

Reliance

This study found that reliance on SNS is not a predictor of either selective exposure or selective avoidance. Yet reliance on other online sources does influence selectivity because the more familiar individuals become with a source through using it, the more they adept the become at selecting or avoid information (Johnson & Kaye, 2004, 2009; Johnson et al., 2007; Johnson et al., 2011).

But as this study shows, respondents are motivated to use SNS to gratify interpersonal needs rather than content needs. And perhaps, whether users agree or disagree with their friends is not as important as the connection itself. Informational/ content needs are more readily satisfied when users find agreeable information. But because the respondents in this study are not motivated to use SNS for content needs, it follows that reliance would not influence selectivity.-

Moreover, only 16.2% of this study's SNS users rely on/heavily rely on these sites for political information. This study in general indicates that users may be drawn to SNS to for political reasons, but they do not heavily rely on them. It could be that they merely use political information found on SNS as a back-up to what they learn from other resources, to find information to use in counter-arguments with others (Knobloch-Westerwick & Meng, 2010), to become politically involved, or for superficial reasons, like to see what issues their friends support, to read about a candidate's blunder, but they do not rely on what they read or hear as the last word in politics. But as SNS become a part of everyday communication, and the Internet continues to clog up with superfluous and contradictory information, online users could seek the haven of known and homogenous social networks and come to rely more heavily on them to learn about political happenings. Thus, heavy reliance on SNS could lead to selective exposure and selective avoidance.

Who practices selective exposure and selective avoidance on SNS also depends on various personal characteristics and political attitudes. This study found that those who practice selective exposure are different from those who selectively avoid what they see as negative information.

A strong affiliation to a political party is the one commonality between these two groups. Thus, those who identify strongly with a political party look for information that conforms to the party line and avoid information that presents their party in a negative light. Presumably, because those who practice selective exposure lean liberal, the combination of ideology and party ties lead these users to look for information that supports Democratic party views. Whether conservatives have a tendency to practice selective exposure or selective avoidance may not have emerged in this study because only one-quarter of this study's respondent's reported being conservative.

Solutions and Recommendations

Scholars and political observers have lamented the rise of more partisan news sources such as blogs, worrying that people will increasingly congregate on sites that support their political views and shun those that challenge their beliefs. Indeed, stronger reliance on blogs and cable news has increased the likelihood of selective exposure (Johnson et al., in press; Johnson et al, 2009; Stroud, 2006, 2008, 2010).

It is everyone's responsibility to uphold the Internet as a free and democratic venue for political expression and decision-making (Kaye, Johnson, & Muhlberger, in press). Online components can easily become forums for the disaffected and discontented and rather than reaching rational consensus inhabitants create a bully pulpit from which to intimate others to their way of thinking. The perils of such an Internet are many, but perhaps the biggest threat is to the strongest reason to using components such as SNS – to communicate with diverse others who espouse a variety of opinions and viewpoints that are used to bring about change for the greater good (Kaye, Johnson & Muhlberger, in press).

Based on this chapter's findings and on other research, it is easy for SNS users to find themselves in a network of similar others and thus unwittingly promote an insular worldview. But perhaps SNS users can help minimize selective exposure and selective avoidance. Individuals who use SNS should take care that they do not block the democratic process, either purposely or inadvertently, by setting up or belonging to networks that espouse one particular point of view and do not tolerate dissension. Rather, SNS users could make it a point to connect with people from all walks of life and who hold different political opinions. Social network sites are a powerful tool that should used to promote diversity, democracy, political involvement, and political inclusion. But to do so requires participants to embrace the positive and open their minds and work together toward a greater good.

FUTURE RESEARCH DIRECTIONS

Uses and gratifications is a strong framework from which to investigate how people use the media, especially a new medium like the Internet. Many uses and gratifications studies adapted motivational items from studies of other media. For example, Kaye's (2005) study of reasons for using blogs, adapted items from Web use and television use research. The current study modified its motivational items from those used in an earlier study of blog use (Johnson & Kaye, 2009; Kaye & Johnson, 2006). But because SNS are so very different from other online components, perhaps motivations should be derived from open-ended responses from SNS users. Motivations unique to SNS might be revealed.

A past study indicates that motivations for using political blogs and websites are not predictors of selectivity (Johnson, et al, 2011), whereas in the current study three of the five motivations are strong predictors of selective exposure. Additional research is needed to understand the influence of motivations and reliance for using online sources, such as Facebook, Twitter and others, before speculating why they predict selectivity of information presented on some sources but not on others.

It should also be noted that this study measures self-reported selective exposure and avoidance rather than actual behavior. Respondents may be more likely to admit to selective exposure than selective avoidance because they may think it is more socially acceptable to state they seeking out information rather than trying to avoid it (Chaffee et al., 2001). Perhaps an experiment in which politically interested SNS users are observed using various networks would reveal different selectivity tendencies.

CONCLUSION

Selective exposure and avoidance has been blamed for creating a more polarized and fragmented society (Stroud 2008, 2010; Sunstein, 2001) and for reducing tolerance for opposing positions. By their very nature, social network sites have the capability of expanding democratic deliberation and reducing polarization and selectivity.

Because this study found that reliance is not related to selective exposure or avoidance, it seems that heavier SNS users are no more likely to be selective than lighter users. Hopefully in the future as people are more experienced with social network sites and the political content available to them, they will click on links to information that challenge their values and beliefs because such information often comes from people they know and trust. Hopefully the SNS of the future will truly be venues for the open-minded and places where selective exposure and selective avoidance are minimal.

REFERENCES

Ancu, M., & Cozma, R. (2009). MySpace politics: Use and gratifications of befriending candidates. *Journal of Broadcasting & Electronic Media*, *53*, 567–583. doi:10.1080/08838150903333064

Atkin, C. K. (1985). Informational utility and selective exposure to entertainment media. In Zillmann, D., & Bryant, J. (Eds.), *Selective exposure to communication* (pp. 63–92). Hillsdale, NJ: Lawrence Erlbaum.

Bennett, W. L., & Iyengar, S. (2008). A new era of minimal effects? The changing foundation of political communication. *The Journal of Communication, 58*, 707–737. doi:10.1111/j.1460-2466.2008.00410.x

Best, S. J., Chmielewski, B., & Krueger, B. S. (2005). Selective exposure to online foreign news during the conflict with Iraq. *Harvard Journal of Press/Politics, 10*(4), 52-7.

Bimber, B., & Davis, R. (2003). *Campaigning online: The Internet in U.S. elections*. Oxford, UK: Oxford University Press.

Blumler, J. G. (1979). The role of theory in uses and gratifications studies. *Communication Research, 6*, 9–36. doi:10.1177/009365027900600102

Boase, J., & Wellman, B. (2006). Personal relationships: On and off the Internet. In Vangelisti, A. L., & Perlman, D. (Eds.), *The Cambridge handbook of personal relationships* (pp. 709–725). Cambridge, UK: Cambridge University Press.

boyd, d. m., & Ellison, N. B. (2007). Social network sites: Definition, history, and scholarship. *Journal of Computer-Mediated Communication, 13*(1), article 11. Retrieved from http://jcmc.indiana.edu/vol13/issue1/bod.ellison.html

Bucy, E. P. (2004). Second generation net news: Interactivity and information accessibility in the online environment. *The International Journal on Media Management, 6*, 102–113. doi:10.1080/14241277.2004.9669386

Bumgarner, B. A. (2007). You have been poked: Exploring the uses and gratifications of Facebook among emerging adults. *First Monday, 12*(11). Retrieved from http://firstmonday.org/ htbin/ cgiwrap/bin/ojs/index.php/fm/article/ viewArticle/2026/1897.

Castells, M. (2001). *The Internet galaxy. Reflections on the Internet, business and society*. Oxford, UK: Oxford University Press.

Castells, M. (2005). The network society: From knowledge to policy. In Castells, M., & Cardoso, G. (Eds.), *The network society: From knowledge to policy* (pp. 3–21). Washington, DC: The John Hopkins University.

Castells, M. (2007). Communication, power and counter-power in the network society. *International Journal of Communication, 1*, 238–266.

Chaffee, S. H., Saphir, M. N., Grap, J., Sandvig, C., & Hahn, K. S. (2001). Attention to counter-attitudinal messages in a state election campaign. *Political Communication, 18*, 247–272. doi:10.1080/10584600152400338

Donsbach, W. (1991). Exposure to political content in newspapers: The impact of cognitive dissonance on reader's selectivity. *European Journal of Communication, 6*, 155–186. doi:10.1177/0267323191006002003

Edwards, K., & Smith, E. E. (1996). A disconfirmation bias in the evaluation of arguments. *Journal of Personality and Social Psychology, 71*(1), 5–24. doi:10.1037/0022-3514.71.1.5

Ekdale, B., Namkoong, K., Fung, T. K. F., & Perlmutter, D. D. (2010). Why blog? (then and now): Exploring the motivations for blogging by popular American political bloggers. *New Media & Society, 12*, 217–234. doi:10.1177/1461444809341440

Fraser, M., & Dutta, S. (2008, November, 19). Barack Obama and the Facebook election. *U. S. News & World Report*. Retrieved from http://www.unew.com/articles/opinion/2008/11/19/barck-obama-and-the-facebook-election

Galston, W. A. (2003). If political fragmentation is the problem, is the Internet the solution? In Anderson, D. M., & Cornfield, M. (Eds.), *The civic web: Online politics and democratic values* (pp. 35–44). Oxford, UK: Rowman & Littlefield.

Garrett, R. K. (2009). Echo chambers online? Politically motivated selective exposure among Internet news users. *Journal of Computer-Mediated Communication, 14*, 265–285. doi:10.1111/j.1083-6101.2009.01440.x

Graf, J., & Aday, S. (2008). Selective attention to online political information. *Journal of Broadcasting & Electronic Media, 52*, 86–100. doi:10.1080/08838150701820874

Hoffner, C. A., Fujikota, Y., Ye, J., & Ibrahim, A. G. S. (2009). Why we watch: Factors affecting exposure to tragic television news. *Mass Communication & Society, 12*, 193–216. doi:10.1080/15205430802095042

Johnson, T. J., Bichard, S. L., & Zhang, W. (2009). Communication communities or cyberghettos? A path analysis model examining factors that explain selective exposure to blogs. *Journal of Computer-Mediated Communication, 15*(1), 60–82. doi:10.1111/j.1083-6101.2009.01492.x

Johnson, T. J., Bichard, S. L., & Zhang, W. (2011). Revived and refreshed: Selective exposure to blogs and political Websites. In Comunello, F. (Ed.), *Networked sociability and individualism" Technology fo personal and professional relationships Hershey*. PA: IGI Global.

Johnson, T. J., & Kaye, B. K. (2004). Wag the blog: How reliance on traditional media and the Internet influence perceptions of credibility of weblogs among blog users. *Journalism & Mass Communication Quarterly, 81*(3), 622–642.

Johnson, T. J., & Kaye, B. K. (2009). In blog we trust: Deciphering credibility of components of the Internet among politically interested Internet users. *Computers in Human Communication, 25*, 175–182.

Johnson, T. J., & Kaye, B. K. (2010). Choosing is believing? How web gratifications and reliance affect Internet credibility among politically interested users. *Atlantic Journal of Communication, 18*(1), 1–21. doi:10.1080/15456870903340431

Johnson, T. J., Kaye, B. K., Bichard, S. L., & Wong, W. J. (2007). Every blog has its day: Politically interested Internet users' perceptions of blog credibility. *Journal of Computer-Mediated Communication, 13*, article 6. Retrieved from http://jcmc.indiana.edu/vol13/issue1/ johnson.html

Johnson, T. J., Zhang, W., & Bichard, S. L. (in press). Voices of convergence or conflict? A path analysis investigation of selective exposure to political Web sites. *Social Science Computer Review*.

Katz, E., Blumler, J., & Gurevitch, M. (1974). Utilization of mass communication by the individual. In Blumler, J., & Katz, E. (Eds.), *The uses of mass communication: Current perspectives on gratifications research* (pp. 19–34). Beverly Hills, CA: Sage.

Katz, E., Gurevitch, M., & Haas, H. (1973). On the use of the mass media for important things. *American Sociological Review, 38*, 164–181. doi:10.2307/2094393

Kaye, B. K. (2005). It's a blog, blog, blog, blog world: Users and uses of weblogs. *Atlantic Journal of Communication, 13*(2), 73–95. doi:10.1207/s15456889ajc1302_2

Kaye, B. K. (2007). Blog use motivations: An exploratory study. In Tremayne, M. (Ed.), *Blogging, citizenship, and the future of media* (pp. 127–148). New York, NY: Routledge.

Kaye, B. K. (2010a). Between Barack and a net place: Users and uses of social network sites and blogs for political information. In Papacharissi, Z. (Ed.), *The networked self: Identity, community and culture on social network sites* (pp. 208–231). New York, NY: Routledge.

Kaye, B. K. (2010b). Going to the blogs: Exploring the uses and gratifications of blogs. *Atlantic Journal of Communication*, *18*(4), 194–206. doi :10.1080/15456870.2010.505904

Kaye, B. K., & Johnson, T. J. (2004). A Web for all reasons: Uses and gratifications of Internet resources for political information. *Telematics and Informatics*, *21*(3), 197–223. doi:10.1016/ S0736-5853(03)00037-6

Kaye, B. K., & Johnson, T. J. (2006). The age of reasons: Motives for using different components of the Internet for political information. In Williams, A. P., & Tedesco, J. C. (Eds.), *The Internet election: Perspectives on the role of the Web in campaign 2004*.

Kaye, B. K., Johnson, T. J., & Muhlberger, P. (in press). I can speak freely now: Blogs as a source of democratic deliberation. In Dumova, T., & Fiordo, R. (Eds.), *Blogging the global society: Cultural, political and geographical aspects*. Hershey, PA: IGI Global.

Kenski, K., Hardy, B. W., & Jamieson, K. H. (2010). *The Obama victory: How media, money, and message shaped the 2008 election*. Oxford: Oxford University Press.

Kim, Y. M. (2007). How intrinsic and extrinsic motivations interact in selectivity: Investigating the moderating effects of situational information processing goals in issue public's web behavior. *Communication Research*, *34*, 185–211. doi:10.1177/0093650206298069

Knobloch-Westerwick, S., & Meng, J. (2009). Looking the other way: Selective exposure to attitude-consistent and counterattitudinal political information. *Communication Research*, *36*, 426–448. doi:10.1177/0093650209333030

Kushin, M. T., & Kitchener, K. (2009). Getting political on social network sites: Exploring online political discourse on Facebook. *First Monday*, *14*(11). Retrieved from http://firstmonday.org/ htbin/cgiwrap/bin/ojs/index.php/ fm/article/ viewArticle/2645/2350.

Levy, M. R., & Windahl, S. (1985). The concept of audience activity. In K. E. Rosengren, L. A. Wenner, & P. Palmgreen (Eds.), *Media gratifications research: Current perspectives (pp.* 109-122). Beverly Hills, CA: Sage.

McLeod, J. M., & Becker, L. B. (1981). The uses and gratifications approach. In Nimmo, D. D., & Sanders, K. R. (Eds.), *Handbook of political Communication* (pp. 67–100). Beverly Hills, CA: Sage.

Mutz, D. C. (2002). Cross-cutting social networks: Testing democratic theory in practice. *The American Political Science Review*, *96*(1), 111–126. doi:10.1017/S0003055402004264

Mutz, D. C., & Martin, P. S. (2001). Facilitating communication across lines of political difference: The role of mass media. *The American Political Science Review*, *95*(1), 97–114.

Nyland, R. (2007). *The gratification niches of Internet social networking, e-mail, and face-to-face communication.* (Unpublished master's thesis), Brigham Young University.

Palmgreen, P. (1984). Uses and gratifications: A theoretical perspective. In Bostrom, R. N. (Ed.), *Communication yearbook 8* (pp. 61–72). Beverly Hills, CA: Sage Publications, Inc.

Park, N., Kee, K. F., & Valenzuela, S. (2009). Being immersed in social networking environment: Facebook groups, uses and gratifications, and social outcomes. *Cyberpsychology & Behavior*, *12*, 729–733. doi:10.1089/cpb.2009.0003

Project for Excellence in Journalism. (2010). *How blogs and social media agendas relate and differ from the traditional press.* Retrieved from http://www.journalism.org/analysis_report/new_media_old_media

Purcell, K., Rainie, L., Mitchell, A., Rosenstiel, T., & Olmstead, K. (2010). *Understanding the participatory news consumer.* Retrieved from http://www.pewinternet.org/Reports/2010/Online-News.aspx?r=1

Quan-Haase, A., & Young, A. L. (2010). Uses and gratifications of social media: A comparison of Facebook and instant messaging. *Bulletin of Science, Technology & Society, 30*, 350–361. doi:10.1177/0270467610380009

Raake, J., & Bonds-Raake, J. (2008). MySpace and Facebook: Applying the uses and gratifications theory to exploring friend-networking sites. *Cyberpsychology & Behavior, 22*, 169–174. doi:10.1089/cpb.2007.0056

Ruggiero, T. (2000). Uses and gratifications theory in the 21st century. *Mass Communication & Society, 3*, 3–37. doi:10.1207/S15327825MCS0301_02

Sheldon, P. (2008). Student favorite: Facebook and motives for its use. *Southwestern Mass Communication Journal, 23*, 39–55.

Smith, A. (2009). The Internet's role in campaign 2008. Retrieved from http://www.pewinternet.org/ Reports/2009/6--The-Internets-Role-in-Campaign-2008.aspx

Smith, A., & Rainie, L. (2008, June 15). *The Internet and the 2008 election.* Pew Internet & American Life Project. Retrieved from http://www.pewinternet.org/Reports/2008/The-Internet-and-the-2008-Election.aspx

Smith, S. M., Fabrigar, L. R., & Norris, M. E. (2008). Reflecting on six decades of selective exposure research: Progress, challenges and opportunities. *Social and Personality Psychology Compass, 2*, 464–493. doi:10.1111/j.1751-9004.2007.00060.x

Stafford, T. F., Stafford, M. R., & Schkade, L. L. (2004). Determining uses and gratifications for the Internet. *Decision Sciences, 35*, 259–288. doi:10.1111/j.00117315.2004.02524.x

Stovall, J. G. (2004). *Web journalism: Practices and promise of a new medium.* New York, NY: Pearson.

Stroud, N. J. (2006). *Selective exposure to partisan information.* Unpublished dissertation, University of Pennsylvania, Philadelphia, PA.

Stroud, N. J. (2008). Media use and political predispositions: Revisiting the concept of selective exposure. *Political Behavior, 30*, 341–366. doi:10.1007/s11109-007-9050-9

Stroud, N. J. (2010). Polarization and partisan selective exposure. *The Journal of Communication, 60*, 556–576. doi:10.1111/j.1460-2466.2010.01497.x

Sunstein, C. R. (2001). *Republic.com.* Princeton, NJ: Princeton University Press.

Tufekci, Z. (2008). Can you see me now? Audience and disclosure regulation in online social network sites. *Bulletin of Science, Technology & Society, 28*, 21–37.

Walsh, K. C. (2003). *Talking about politics: Informal groups and social identity in American life.* Chicago, IL: University of Chicago Press.

Wellman, B., Boase, J., & Chen, W. (2002). The networked nature of community: Online and offline. *IT & Society, 1*, 151–165.

Wellman, B., Quan-Haase, A., Boase, J., Chen, W., Hampton, K., Isla de Diaz, I., & Miyata, K. (2003). The social affordances of the Internet for networked individualism. *Journal of Computer-Mediated Communication, 8*. Retrieved from http://jcmc.indiana.edu/vol8/issue3/wellman.html.

Woolley, J. A., Limperos, A. M., & Oliver, M. B. (2010). The 2008 presidential election, 2.0: A content analysis of user-generated political Facebook groups. *Mass Communication & Society, 13*(5), 584–607. doi:10.1080/15205436.2010.516864

Ziemke, D. A. (1980). Selective exposure in a presidential campaign contingent on certainty and salience. In Nimmo, D. (Ed.), *Communication Yearbook* (*Vol. 4*, pp. 497–511). New Brunswick, NJ: Transaction Books.

ADDITIONAL READING

Bowman, S., & Willis, C. (2003). *We media: How audiences are shaping the future of news and information*. Reston, VA: The Media Center at the American Press Institute.

Fernandes, J., Giurcanu, M., Bowers, K. W., & Neely, J. C. (2010). The writing on the wall: A content analysis of college students' Facebook groups for the 2008 presidential election. *Mass Communication & Society, 13*, 653–675. doi:10.1080/15205436.2010.516865

Garrett, R. K. (2006, June). *Seeking similarity, not avoiding difference: Reframing the ideological selective exposure debate* Paper presented at the annual meeting of the International Communication Association, Dresden, Germany.

Meffert, M. F., Chung, S., Joiner, A. J., Waks, L., & Garst, J. (2006). The effects of negativity and motivated information processing during a political campaign. *The Journal of Communication, 56*(1), 27–51. doi:10.1111/j.1460-2466.2006.00003.x

Melican, D. B., & Dixon, T. L. (2008). News on the Net: Credibility, selective exposure, and racial prejudice. *Communication Research, 35*, 151–168. doi:10.1177/0093650207313157

KEY TERMS AND DEFINITIONS

Motivations: The psychological reasons that compel people to use a particular medium. Individuals are motivated to use particular sources to gratify their needs.

Reliance: An attitude toward media and information sources that goes beyond merely using a source. Reliance assumes trust and belief in media content and that media is important in one's life.

Selective Avoidance: The act of purposely dodging information that is contrary to one's worldview.

Selective Exposure: The act of purposely choosing only information that is agreeable and in accordance with existing beliefs and opinions.

Selectivity: A behavior wherein media users purposely select and evade particular information. Selectivity comprises both selective exposure and selective avoidance.

Social Network Sites: Online sites that contain user generated content for social purposes. Users create a social circle of friends that includes those they know in real life and those they know only online. Users post a profile or biography and express their views, opinions, beliefs and observations and "converse" with others through their social network. They also link their friends to information on other websites.

Uses and Gratifications: A theoretical framework from the perspective of how people use the media. It asserts that people are aware of their needs and are drawn to the media that best satisfy those needs.

ENDNOTE

1 To promote the survey, the authors created a Facebook Group, The Internet and the 2008 Election. Those who joined were asked to complete the survey. Notices of the survey were also posted on 37 MySpace and 86 Facebook groups representing various political ideologies, candidates, and issues. Notices were also posted on 11 media and 55 political websites and 70 blogs as well as 12 political and educational listservs/mailing lists and political newsgroups.

Chapter 12
Public Administrations and Citizens 2.0:
Exploring Digital Public Communication Strategies and Civic Interaction within Italian Municipality Pages on Facebook

Alessandro Lovari
Università degli Studi di Siena, Italy

Lorenza Parisi
Sapienza Università di Roma, Italy

ABSTRACT[1]

The aim of this chapter is to describe how the use of social media, especially the use of social network sites, is influencing public communication strategies and online users' interactions. We conducted an exploratory analysis of the prevalent use of Facebook pages by Italian municipalities examining the characteristics of the online interactions emerging in the communication strategies of four Italian provincial capitals: Rimini, Reggio Emilia, Modena, and Venezia. We compared the four municipality pages on Facebook looking at the number of users, age composition, and gender. Then we carried out a content analysis to describe the prevalent kinds of posts published in the municipality Walls on Facebook. We concluded that Italian municipalities are now adopting different communication strategies on Facebook: each municipality proposes a particular content mix that creates a specific communication flow addressed toward citizens.

DOI: 10.4018/978-1-61350-338-6.ch012

INTRODUCTION

Digital media and technologies are strongly modifying public administrations. Their impact is evident on administrative procedures, data management, functioning and delivering of public services and, moreover, on the communication between public organisations and citizens (Contini and Lanzara, 2009; Faccioli, 2000; Pieterson and Ebbers, 2008; West, 2005).

The growth and development of Web 2.0 technologies (O'Reilly, 2005) has deeply changed the functioning and management of public administrations and government agencies. Above all there is a general request for a new phase of transparency, openness and participation (Sirianni, 2009; Noveck, 2009) where citizens can have an active role in stimulating innovative practices of communication and dialogue (van Dijck, 2009; Shirky, 2008; Tapscott, 2009). Moreover, using participatory and social media (Kaplan and Haelein, 2010; Rheingold, 2008; Shirky, 2008) citizens can contribute to creating new services or reshaping existing ones, remixing data and activities (Hilgers and Ihl, 2010), a typical process of our convergence culture (Jenkins, 2006). In this scenario social media, and in particular social network sites (boyd and Ellison, 2007), play an important role in re-defining relationships, power dynamics and communication strategies between institutions and citizens (Bennet, 2008; Castells, 2009; Dahlgren, 2009). Analysing best practices diffused worldwide it seems probable that nowadays social network sites, and Facebook in particular, could be strategic applications for enhancing transparency interaction between administrations and citizens. This is clearly evident in Italy where the great success and penetration of this platform is creating a lot of interest and expectations among users, public administrators and social media consultants. In Italy in January 2011 Facebook counts 18 million users, around 75% of Italian Internet users. Nevertheless in Europe and in Italy in particular there is a lack of in depth research analysing the real use of these online interactive spaces by public institutions and municipalities. The aim of this chapter is to provide an exploratory description of the prevalent uses of Facebook pages by Italian municipalities. Therefore we examined the characteristics of online interaction and communication strategies emerging in the Facebook Pages of four Italian capital cities of province: Rimini, Modena, Reggio Emilia and Venezia[2].

In conclusion the chapter will provide answers to the following research questions:

1. What are the contents generally published by municipalities in their institutional Facebook pages?
2. What are the general traits of the users of a municipality Facebook Page?
3. What are the prevalent kinds of questions, comments and proposals posted by users on the municipality Facebook Walls?
4. What are the contents that better stimulate an high level of participation of users in terms of number of comments and appreciation ('like') of the messages?

BACKGROUND[3]

Web 2.0 and online communities such as blogs and, above all, social network sites are widely adopted and used in the network society (Nielsen, 2009; The Economist, 2010). Whereas a few years ago these platforms were supposed to connect only peers and friends (Boyd & Ellison, 2007; Boyd, 2008) in recent years social network sites (SNS) have been increasingly used by politicians, companies, brands and institutions to interact with users (Coleman, 2005; Tapscott, 2009; Qualman, 2010; Rheingold, 2008). It is evident that these digital participative media are influencing the way public administrations communicate with citizens and the public (Masini, Lovari & Benenati, 2009).

In the public sector the use of social media is becoming a hot issue: on one side institutions and government agencies are creating interactive online platforms to better communicate with citizens and stake-holders; on the other side media consumption patterns reveal an increasing importance of social media in citizens' communication mix. In this scenario public administrations are evaluating social media, and social network sites in particular, as an opportunity and a challenge (Quocirca, 2007; Human Capital Institute, 2010). Some institutions in North America, Europe and Asia are adopting social network sites with an internal focused purpose such as to stimulate employee learning and development or, most often, with an external function to foster communication and civic participation (Human Capital Institute, 2010; Serrat, 2010). The positive echo of these innovations in communication is influencing many public agencies all over the world, stimulating institutions and public managers to create or colonize interactive and participatory platforms to connect with citizens. At the same time there is still the dilemma of the tangible impact these media can have on governments, in terms of privacy issues, data management and culture of trust (Fyfe & Crookal, 2010) and many applications of Web 2.0 to the public sector seem to follow a rhetorical strategy of business manifestos rather than developing concrete solutions for enhancing co-creation and citizen participation (Van Dijck & Nieborg, 2009).

How Public Sector is Using Social Media

Several research papers limit their analysis in describing the advantages institutions can gain by adopting social media as additional channels to inform citizens within a multichannel communication strategy. Broadly speaking, there is a lack of mature analysis into the emerging use of social media among citizens and institutions, in particular by municipal governments, especially in Europe. According to Nabatchi and Mergel (2010) social media can increase citizen involvement toward public sector policies and decision making processes. To describe this phenomenon they adopt a spectrum (ranging from information, collaboration and then empowerment), claiming that social and digital platforms could be a strategic means to increase transparency and participation in the public sector. Only a small number of contributions describe how several agencies are pragmatically using these media to enhance e-participation, to collect solicitations and comments about public policies, to conduct online public meetings and to raise attention on specific issues or problems (Osimo, 2008; Lovari & Parisi, 2010; Bryer, 2010; Waller, 2010). To summarise the results of various research papers, public administrations are developing web 2.0 services or social media applications to satisfy several different aims:

a. To inform citizens about public services and opportunities. For example many different institutions such as municipalities, counties, states or universities opened YouTube channels, MySpace profiles, Facebook Fan Pages or Twitter accounts (Bryer, 2010; Waller, 2010).
b. To promote specific campaigns or sectors. For example the American Centers for Disease Control and Prevention's use of social media strategy for preventing the peanut salmonella outbreak and the H1N1 flu (Mergel, 2010); or the specific Facebook Pages created by Hong Kong, Israel and Macau Ministries of Tourism to promote their countries (Kuzma, 2010).
c. To collect citizens' views about civic problems, service problems and potential solutions to inefficacy of public services (Nabatchi & Mergel, 2010; Noveck, 2010; Sirianni, 2009). For example "FixMyStreet.com" is a UK website designed to identify and report problems related to the poor con-

ditions of streets and public areas and infrastructures; the "Virginia Idea Forum" allows citizens to submit ideas about improvements for state government; "MyIdea4CA.com" is a Twitter forum created by California Governor Schwarzenegger for discussing ideas over a vast range of issues, from transportation to pollution.

Following the Obama 'Open Government' strategies, harnessing the power of public engagement to influence the conversation across various spheres of cross-influence (Monte, 2009), several international public administrations are investing resources in defining novel social media strategies. At the same time several scholars began to observe the presence of administrations in the social web, trying to define the characteristics these institutional social platforms should have in order to be useful for citizens. Mergel (2010) identified three different strategies of social media colonization by public administrations, starting from an analysis of the existing platforms in the USA: (a) 'push strategy', in which a social medium is used as an additional tool and as an extension of an existing Internet presence; (b) 'pull strategy' using social media applications to bring publics back to the institutions' websites; (c) 'networking strategy', where institutions adopt social media to stimulate interaction with users and reach specific publics in order to share and create knowledge.

Instead, Lee and Elser (2010) proposed nine commandments public administrations should follow to reach an effective social media strategy, such as to identify a tangible mission-related reason for their use, to commit to their maintenance and updating, or to integrate with the existing institutional communication activities.

Focusing on social network sites, scholars and policy makers differently evaluate the opportunity for public agencies, and in particular municipalities, to join social networking sites such as Facebook. Some experts consider SNS a platform that encourages civic participation and engagement (Bryer, 2010; Cole, 2009; Jenkins, 2009); others say SNS are tools to monitor issues and to resolve problems, involving citizens in sharing knowledge and in cooperating (Danis et al., 2009; Hilgers & Ihl, 2010; Noveck 2010); others look at SNS as a medium that could be used to inform the public in case of emergencies and natural disasters (American Red Cross, 2010; Roberts, 2010). On the other side some scholars consider these spaces private platforms believing they are not appropriate for public institutions and only serve to stimulate social voyeurism and gossip among users (Keen, 2007). On the whole, few research studies have been carried out to investigate the emerging use of social network sites in the public and non-profit sector: for example, Kuzma (2010) analysed how Asian countries are colonizing Facebook, Twitter and YouTube and which different communication strategies are adopted in order to interact with local residents and international tourists; Waters et al. (2009) investigated the role social network sites can play to increase the awareness or to trigger donor participation for non-profit organizations. Furthermore social networks sites, and Facebook in particular, started to be studied in terms of the interaction between students and universities; several empirical studies were carried out on different aspects: i.e. the function of Facebook as relationship enabler between students and faculty members (Hewitt & Forte, 2006; Mazer, Murphy & Simonds); the privacy issues (Lewis, Kaufman & Christakis, 2008); the Facebook effect for building social capital (Ellison, Steinfield & Lampe 2007; Valenzuela, Park, and Kee, 2009) and the role of this SNS for communicating with students and alumni (Aquilani & Lovari 2009; Lewis, 2010)

Moreover we should consider that even if public administrations decide not to be present in SNS, their activities and services are in any case the subject of discussion among Internet and social network sites users (Solis & Breakenridge, 2009). In Facebook we observed that public services become the subject of public conversations in the Facebook Walls even if institutions (municipalities, hospitals, universities, etc) are not present on the network with a specific Page or profile. For example we noticed online that the Facebook Pages of several counterfeit agency or municipalities show the logo of the institution in the profile picture even if they are managed by private citizens.

Social Media for Enhancing Participation: The Role of Citizens

Adopting a citizen perspective, some studies have been carried out to investigate how social media are modifying online user behaviour toward public administrations. Lindmark (2009) reports that citizens through web 2.0 tools can play an active role at different levels in the delivery of public services: for example they can become content providers; they can be quality managers commenting and evaluating issues and topics proposed by administrations; they can test applications in a perpetual beta process; or they can contribute to developing innovative services through the creation of collective intelligence. On the whole the unique nature of citizen participation in the Web is still a manifold and ambiguous topic, which remains difficult to investigate. Ferro and Molinari (2010) argue that e-participation should be evaluated according to three different dimensions:

"a. counting how many postings were added by the different contributors to the electronic debates; b. using the sheer number of registered users, possibly normalised for the target population size; c. considering the number of independent visitors (views) to the pilot web-site coming from the pilot area." (Ferro & Molinari, 2010, p. 58).

Focusing on social media, research conducted by Pew Research Center (Smith, 2010) defines 'government social media users' as those citizens using digital tools other than web-sites to search and get information from government agencies and institutions. In particular 5% of American Internet users follow or are 'friends' of a government or public body on social network sites; these users are more engaged in information seeking than in actively participating in posting comments and messages (Smith, 2010). The same study reports the existence of citizens who actively participate in online debates about government policies or public issues: these people, called 'online government participators', represent 23% of Internet users and their conversations take place not only in the official blogs or fan pages, but also in a broader online environment (Smith, 2010).

A Specific Case Study: Italians and Facebook

As we already stated, social network sites, and Facebook in particular, seem to be the killer applications for enhanced transparency and interaction between public administrations and citizens. This is clearly evident in Italy where the big success and penetration of Facebook is raising interest and expectations among users, policy makers and social media experts (Comunello, 2010). In fact in fall 2008 Facebook started to be widely adopted in Italy and today (February 2011) Facebook has more than 18 million users. During 2009 the impressive growth of users encouraged many Italian public administrations, especially municipalities, to experiment with a presence in this online interactive platform. In Italy some municipalities started to look at SNS as useful shortcuts to recover or create a dialogue with citizens, especially with the younger generation who are the most common users of these media, in order to counter widespread and permanent disillusionment with politics and public affairs. Nowadays this adoption has been accelerated due to an intense broadcasting media coverage about Facebook and its potential role to connect citizens to public institutions. To summarize, Italian institutions are beginning to understand the 'power' of social media (since social networks permeate citizens' personal networks) and consider these platforms crucial in re-assign a value to public institutions.

EXPLORING PUBLIC COMMUNICATION STRATEGIES WITHIN ITALIAN MUNICIPALITY PAGES ON FACEBOOK

Methodology[4]

We decided to analyse four Facebook municipalities Pages selecting four capital cities of province that satisfied the following conditions:

- municipality of medium-large size (number of residents between 100,000 and 300,000);
- the presence in the first 30 positions of Italian rating regarding the so called "Digital Cities" (9° Rapporto Città Digitali, 2006);
- institutional Facebook pages that has been created during the year 2009. This decision was taken in order to analyse 6 months of online interaction with citizens.[5]

We choose a case study four cities located in the Northern Italy: Rimini, Reggio Emilia, Modena and Venezia. Three of them belong to Emilia Romagna Region, while Venezia is located in the Veneto Region. All these four cities are known for proposing some best practices in public communication, in particular related to the implementation of digital networks and web 2.0 strategies. For example Venezia is renowned for many projects related to technological innovation (like the creation of an open municipality wireless network and for the "IRIS" application, software designed to allow citizens to report needs in a given area) while Modena is well known for its innovative use of multi-channel strategies to communicate with citizens. Three of the four municipality Facebook pages we analysed are *Like Pages* (former *Fan Pages*). Only the Reggio Emilia municipality uses a Facebook Profile.

We decided to observe the characteristics of the four municipalities' Facebook Pages[6] manually 'rewinding' the posts published on the Walls during six months of online activities, from 1st December 2009 to 25th May 2010. This was inevitable given that, thus far, software collecting and archiving social interactions in social network sites cannot work on Facebook Pages as the technical characteristics of these Pages make it laborious to automatically save data (e.g. status update, comments, likes, sharing) appearing in real time on Facebook.

Afterwards to describe the general characteristics of the online users (age, sex, etc.) a quantitative analysis was conducted using Facebook statistical data (Facebook Insight) provided by each municipality. We then manually counted the number of posts published by the municipalities and users, annotating the latter only when municipalities allowed citizens to post messages on their Walls. Later we conducted a qualitative analysis categorising the content of each post. We slightly modified a typology already tested in a previous pilot case-study about the Facebook profile of Spello, an Italian municipality

Finally we provided a questionnaire to the employers responsible of each municipality Facebook Page in order to better understand how they manage the communication flow on Facebook (i.e. creation of the agenda, organisation of the back-office, routines and practices adopted).

Main Characteristics of the Municipalities' Facebook Pages[7]

Exploring the Mission of the Pages

Table 1 summarises the general characteristics of the case studies in terms of: date of creation; name of the office managing the Page; number of employers in charge of the service.

A comparison across the offices managing the Facebook Pages showed an heterogeneity of the structures involved: a signal that the management of social networking site presence is not yet strongly institutionalised in public administrations. There were also differences in terms of the number of items available in the Facebook Page menu: for instance, besides to the popular Wall, info, photo and boxes tabs, Modena and Venezia enhanced their pages with other tools like "Rss/blog", while Rimini created sections for "notes" and "discussion".

We carried out four interviews with the municipal Facebook managers to delineate the different missions of the four Facebook Pages.

The communications manager of the Rimini Fan Page stated they decided to use Facebook as an additional channel to interact with the Municipal Office for Public Relations (URP). They started using Facebook in November 2009 based on a low profile strategy, to test the potential to harmonise the platform with the Citizen Relationship Management system and the back-office structures. It is the only case within our study where citizens are not only enabled to comment on posts written by the administrator, but can also publicly post requests of information and opinions. We observed that the municipality has a specific policy to reply to inquiries and uses the Facebook platform to enhance the dialogue with its public. The communications manager clearly described the procedure: each user request published on Facebook is classified with an official identification number which is communicated to users via Facebook; after that it is submitted to a central back office structure called "Punto di Ascolto" (Listening Point). Then the request is transmitted to the appropriate municipal office to be answered, and later on it is posted on Facebook (unless it contains sensitive data). The "listening" activity is described by the mission of the Page publicly reported in the Facebook information box that claims:

"All citizens (residents or not) can ask for information, express opinions, suggestions and critics related to the municipality services and public offices. They can raise specific questions about administrative proceeding. They can also join discussion about general interest themes that could help the municipality to better understand public opinion on collective civic issues related to the improvement of public services".

Table 1. General characteristics of the Facebook pages

Name of the Facebook Page	Date of creation	Name of the office managing the Page	Number of employers in charge of the service
Comune di Rimini	November 2009	URP (Office for public relations)	3 part-time
Comune di Reggio nell'Emilia	February 2009	Servizio comunicazione, relazioni esterne e marketing del Comune (Communication, External Relations and Marketing Office)	1 full time
Città di Modena	March 2009	Servizio Comunicazione del Comune (Communication Service)	4 part-time
Comune di Venezia	2009	Ufficio stampa (Press Office)	Not available

Reggio Emilia manages the oldest Page within our case studies (created in February 2009) and is the only municipality using a Facebook Profile. On May 2010 the Reggio Emilia Profile reached the maximum number of users allowed on Facebook Profile (n=5000) and later started to publish posts only on the municipality *Like Page* named "Città di Reggio nell'Emilia". This latter Page was created in April 2010 and in November 2010 counted around 4700 members. The Facebook profile and the Like Page are managed by the same municipal structure. On the Like Page the municipality opened five groups of discussions to exchange experiences among residents and to enhance citizen participation. The mission of the Page is the following:

"This space is open to everyone willing to participate, express points of view about specific issues, solutions and personal experiences. Join our groups and give your support!"

Continuing our analysis, the Modena Facebook Like Page uses a multi-channel strategy. The declared aim of the Page is:

"This space, like the web-site, interactive services, and 'physical' services (URP, Youth Information Office, etc.) is open to everyone who wants to communicate, to access to services, and who wants to participate and share points of view about city and civic issues".

The municipality publishes a significant amount of video and images to enrich the Facebook posts published in the Wall.

To conclude our overview, the Venezia Like Page is managed by the municipal Press Office. We observed a strong effort to build an innovative digital flow of public communication through a co-ordinated and integrated use of social media such as Facebook Pages, Twitter account, YouTube channel and RSS feed. The mission of the Venezia Like Page is not clearly published in the Facebook information box.

Growing Patterns, Age, and Gender of Users

Table 2 shows the demographics of the four Municipalities' Facebook Pages (in terms of users' age and gender) and it compares the number of residents with the number of each municipality Facebook Page users.

The number of Facebook users on municipality Pages does not seem correlated with the number of city residents. The number of users seems based on the date of creation of the Page: i.e. Modena has more users probably due to the fact that it's Like Page was one of the first to be created (March 2009), while Rimini has the smallest number of users given that it started in November 2009. This finding is similar to a preferential attachment process (Barabasi and Albert, 1999). The age of users extensively varies according to the different municipalities. 13-17 years old users are the first visitors of the Reggio Emilia profile (26%), followed by the 18-24 (24%) and 25-34 (24%) age ranges, while in Rimini this category of users is the least numerous. On the contrary Rimini has 34% of visitors aged 35-44. Also Venezia Like Page has an older public: 28% of users are between 25-34 and 27% are between 35-44 years old. Furthermore Venezia and Rimini are the two Pages with the highest presence of fans over 55 years old. According to the evolution of Italian Facebook users we noted that early adopters of the municipality Pages were young adults, while the other age ranges have grown rapidly in the last months of our analysis.

Moreover table n. 2 underlines a difference in terms of users' gender. Modena is the only Page that female use slightly more than men (52% versus 48%). Gender is equally represented in Reggio

Table 2. Characteristics of the 4 municipalities Facebook pages in terms of: number of city residents, number of Facebook users, age composition and gender of the followers

Municipality	City residents	Number of users, 25th May 2010	Age ranges	Gender
Comune di Rimini	140,000	683	13-17 (2%) 18-24 (10%) 25-34 (28%) 35-44 (34%) 45-54 (16%) over 55 (9%)	54% Male 46% Female
Comune di Venezia	270,000	2524	13-17 (3%) 18-24 (14%) 25-34 (28%) 35-44 (27%) 45-54 (17%) over 55 (10%)	55% Male 45% Female
Comune di Reggio nell'Emilia	160,000	3527	13-17 (26%) 18-24 (24%) 25-34 (24%) 35-44 (15%) 45-54 (7%) over 55 (3%)	50% Male 50% Female
Comune di Modena	180,000	5659 (26th April)	13-17 (9%) 18-24 (29%) 25-34 (30%) 35-44 (20%) 45-54 (9%) over 55 (4%)	48% Male 52% Female

Emilia. On the whole in Venezia there are more male than female users (55% versus 45%) as is the case in Rimini (56% versus 44%). We did not use Facebook geographical data describing users' cities of residence (hometown) since we evaluated the data provided by "Facebook Insight" as incomplete and questionable. This means we cannot know exactly how many Facebook users live in the city of which they are fan (or "they like"). However according to the content analysis of the posts, to the interviews conducted with the Facebook municipality managers and to our previous research experience (Lovari and Parisi, 2009) we can assume that resident citizens account for about half of users. This area warrants further investigation and future research efforts.

As Figure 1 and Figure 2 show, during the six months time range the number of users in Rimini and Reggio Emilia municipality Like Pages grew linearly according to a monotone function. As Figure 3 displays, the number of Modena Facebook Page users intensively grew at the beginning of February, around the 10th March and at beginning of April, producing a non-linear growth pattern. We verified that these steps were correlated to the presence of a higher number of users commenting the historical and cultural quizzes the municipality posted. As figure n. 4 shows on the Venezia Page we observed an increase in the number of network members during the day (30th March) of the mayoral elections. During that day the Venezia municipality Facebook administrators continuously posted real time electoral data. These posts (n=45) triggered impressive interaction among users commenting the polls. In 24 hours we counted 485 comments and 285 likes.[8] In one day the number of users grew from 1975 to 2294.

To conclude, Modena and Venezia network growing trends show that elevated user interaction within the municipal network, in terms of com-

Figure 1. Rimini municipality Facebook Like Page number of users growth

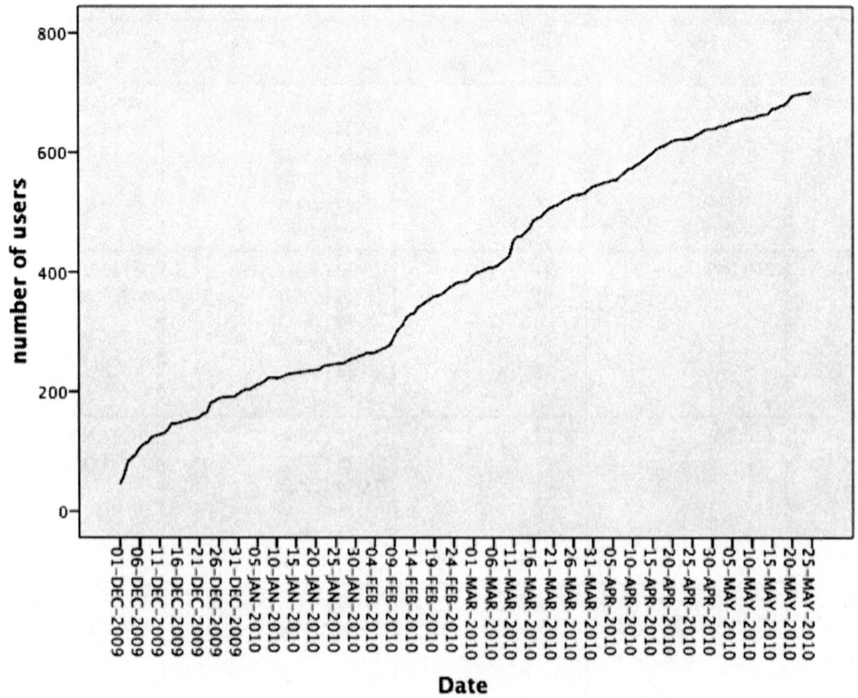

Figure 2. Reggio Emilia municipality Facebook Like Page number of users growth

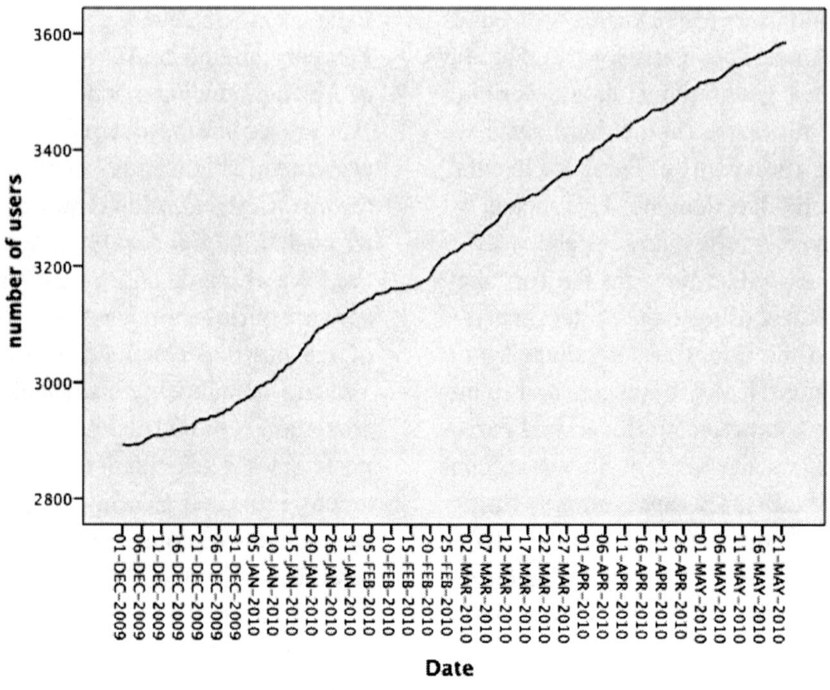

Figure 3. Modena municipality Facebook Like Page number of users growth

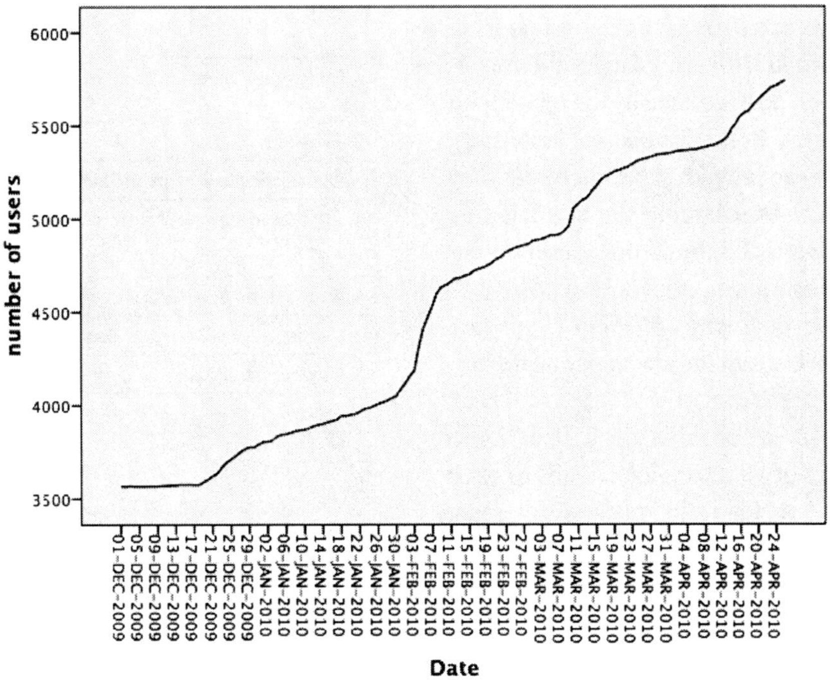

Figure 4. Venezia municipality Facebook Like Page number of users growth

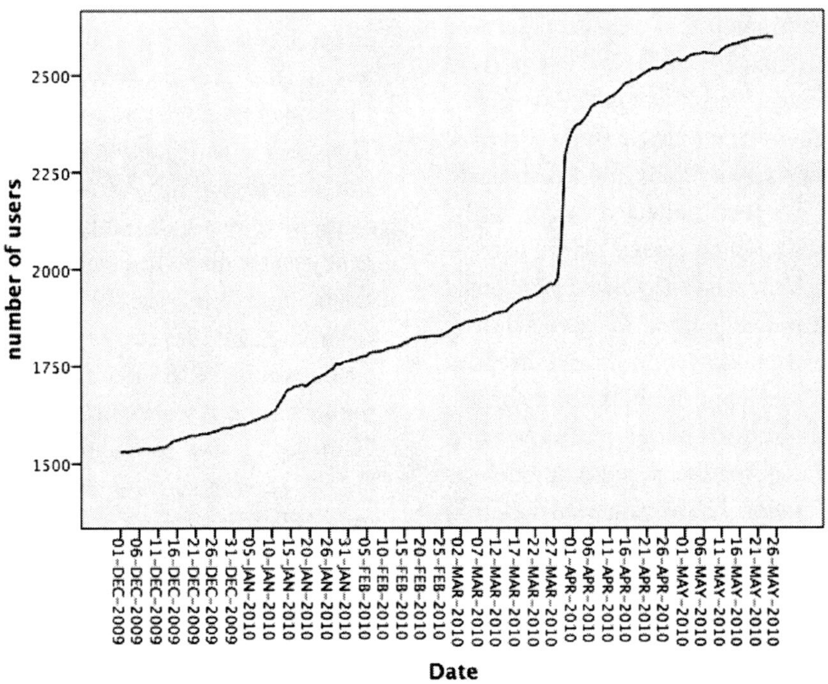

ments and likes, provokes an immediate increase in the overall number of users. We observed that users' comments and likes are decisive factors to produce substantial network growth in terms of new users. In fact, posts created by the municipality are visible only in the Facebook Home Page of the users who are already fans, therefore they do not contribute to enlarging the municipality relationship network. On the contrary, users' comments and likes on municipality posts gain visibility on all the personal Walls of every single fan. In that way, since social networks permeate citizens' personal networks, the content of each commented or liked post also gains visibility in the Home Pages of all Facebook friends of each municipality's Fan Page. In other words, user interaction constitutes a powerful potential multiplier for municipality communication flows and it effectively creates a real opportunity for the municipality to come into contact with new users.

Toward a Classification of Facebook Municipality Contents[9]

Following a comparison in terms of users, we conducted a content analysis of the posts published on the four municipality Walls. We categorised the messages using a classification that we previously tested for another empirical study (Parisi & Lovari, 2010) and that we slightly modified during the analysis of the posts collected in our study. Table 3 describes the nine categories we used.

Starting with Venezia we classified 146[10] posts published by the municipality. As Figure 5 shows, the most recurrent category is "information about public services and opportunities for citizens" (28.8%) that publicises various traditional and innovative services for the population such as "People mover" (a local light train transportation from Mestre to Venice), the possibility of a garden to cultivate for older people ("Orto a Ca' Noghera"), public competition for jobs, water taxi for disabled people, a social service guide in English, Romanian and Bangladeshi, a gas and

Table 3. List of the categories we used to describe the kind of contents published on municipalities Facebook Pages

1. Information about public services and opportunities for citizens
2. Events promotion
3. Online communication self-promotion
4. Alert about emergencies and services problems
5. Call for civic participation
6. News related to municipality life
7. Culture and civic heritage discovery
8. City images display
9. Other

energy bonus for residents, a refund for elderly victims of robbery ("Ocio al tacuin"), etc. The category "events promotion" (21.9%) contains posts such as the famous Venetian Carnival ("Carnevale di Venezia"), local pedestrian competitions ("Su e zo per i ponti"), art exhibitions ("Gli ebrei a Venezia") and music festivals such as the "Heineken Jammin' Festival". Posts under the label "alert about emergencies and services problems" (17.8%) report breaking news that could affect the city, such as sudden high and low flood levels (the service was updated even during Christmas Eve), the pollution rate related to the Thermoelectric plant in Marghera, the airport situation regarding ash from the Icelandic volcano, the closing of public parking or the emergency snow plan. The category "news related to municipality life" (15.8%) publicises information regarding city life, such as the number of people participating in Venice Carnival or the official request to be selected to host the 2020 Olympic Games. "Online municipality communication" (12.3%) collects messages where the municipality publicises different digital media used for communicating with citizens: Twitter channel, video news, RSS feed, newsletter and web 2.0 platforms such as "Comunicare Venezia" (Communicate Venice) or "Venice Connected". The category "call for civic participation" (1.4%) includes the request for citizens' participation in online forums and the "5 x 1000" communication campaign, a call for residents to give a percentage of taxes to the municipality.

Ad we already noted Rimini is the only municipality in our study allowing users to post messages on its Wall. Out of a total of 125 posts, 67 messages were posted by the municipality and 59 by users. Rimini Like Page is used as an additional means to contact the URP (Office for public relations), like a physical front office transferred online. Citizens use this page to communicate directly with the municipality but they are not particularly talkative among each other according to the small number of comments we counted over a period of six months (n=14). As Figure 6 shows citizens mainly use the Facebook Page to request information (n=26) such as a bonus for public housing, welfare for the unemployed, etc; to signal service probliems (n=13) related above all to the poor conditions of schools, traffic congestion and parking and to express their opinion (n=12) on decisions to improve public services and city life. Greetings and compliments are marginal (n=6) in the communication flow[11].

The municipality of Modena uses the Like page differently compared to the two case studies mentioned above. In six months the municipality posted a total of 154 posts. It is evident from the Wall that the editorial board managing the content implemented a well defined strategy to attract users. Every day the municipality uploads different content according to a weekly schedule: for example on Monday is for the scheduled day for a column on "I misteri di Modena" (Modena's mysteries), while on Wednesday the Facebook Page hosts the posts "Il Comune informa" (The municipality informs) and on Friday "Che fare in città" (Things to do in the city). This planning informs users in advance about what is happening on the municipality Page and builds user loyalty. Moreover, we noted that two categories of contents are published on the Modena Wall that do not appear on the Venezia and Rimini Walls. We defined these additional categories as "culture

Figure 5. Frequencies of different categories of posts published in Venezia Like Page (%)

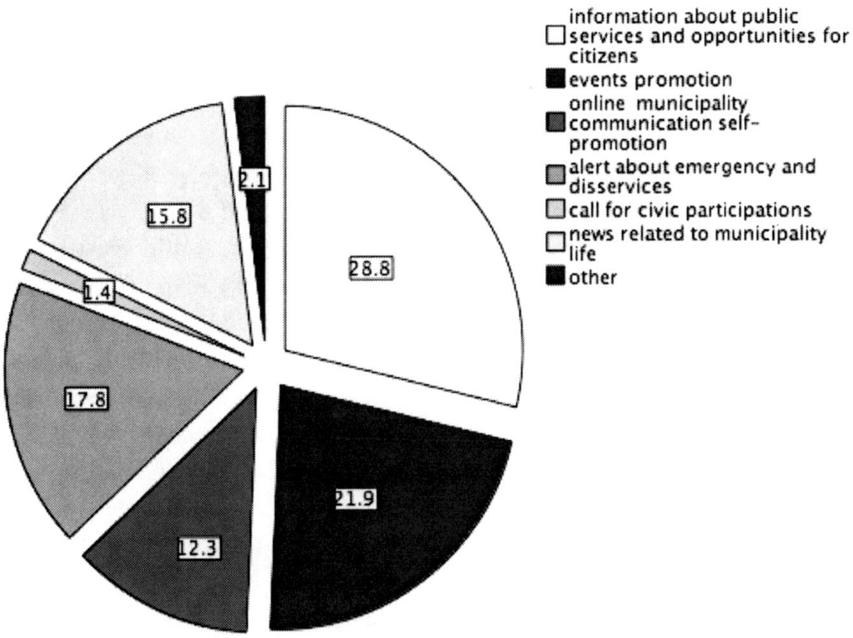

Figure 6. Frequency of the typology of posts published by users in the Rimini Like Page

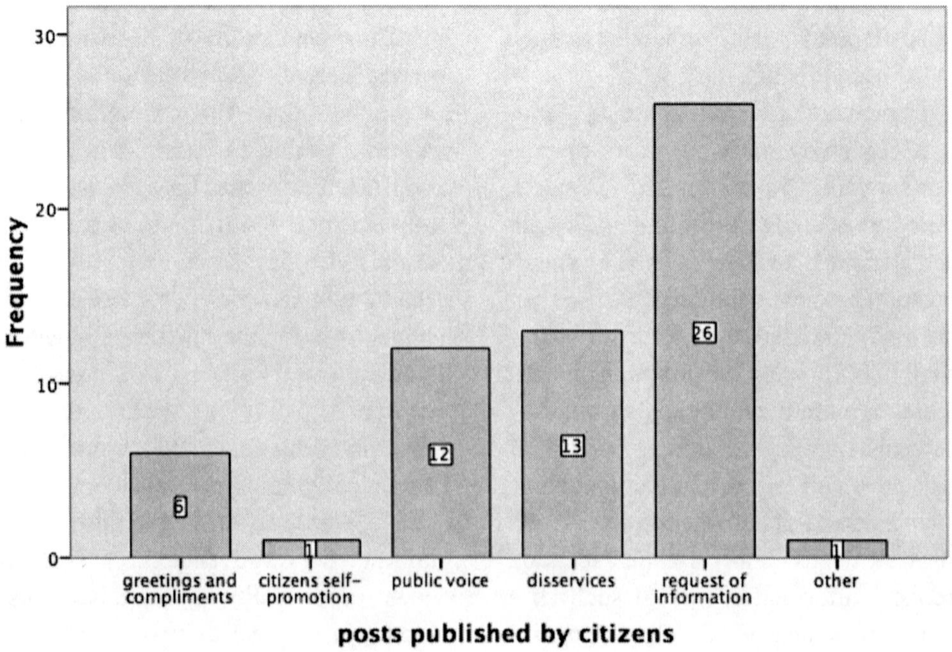

and civic heritage discovery" and "city images display". The first one collects historical and cultural quizzes created to encourage citizen participation. These involve solving mysteries related to city places (squares, churches, historical buildings, etc.) or important persons, such as politicians, poets or musicians, born or raised in Modena. For example, the quizzes "Indovina chi è?" (Guess who?) and "Indovina indov'e'?" (Guess where?). The solutions to the quizzes are published weekly and users are very active in using personal knowledge and memory to solve puzzles. The second category contains images of the city, like those taken during the winter snow or public events. Figure7 shows how these categories of content comprise the Modena Facebook communication strategy. Posts containing content referred to "culture and civic heritage discovery" are the most frequent category (44.2%); subsequently "events promotion" gained an important role in the communication mix (20.1%). "City images" have high visibility (7.1%). Compared to the other municipalities' communication strategies posts containing "information about public services and opportunities for citizens" are marginal (5.8%).

Our last case study is the Reggio Emilia Fan Page. To analyse the posts we applied our standard typology even though the municipality has a specific publishing policy. As Figure 8 highlights, out of the total 884 posts, 787 (617 + 170) are published by the administration while 47 are notes, videos or images in which the Reggio Emilia Municipality has been tagged by citizens and other users (non-profit organisations, other public bodies, tourists, etc). The vast majority of posts (n=617) are messages labelled "Riceviamo e Condividiamo" (Received and Forwarded). These are news items produced by different individuals or groups in the territory of Reggio Emilia that the municipality receives and publishes on its Wall. Thus the Reggio Emilia Facebook Page

Figure 7. Frequencies of the different categories of posts published in Modena Like Page (%)

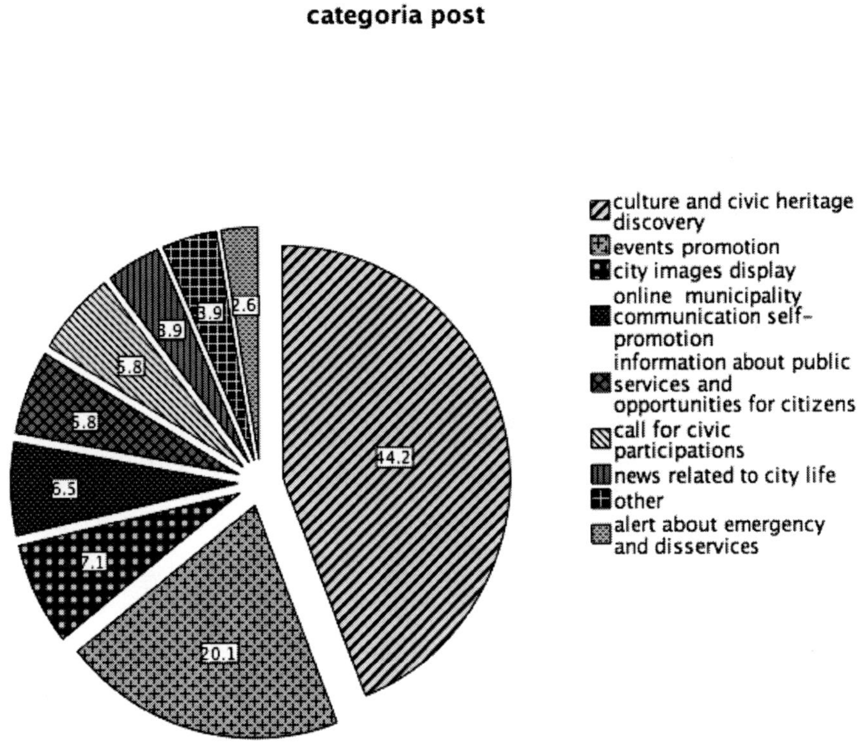

becomes a big public Wall in which grassroots events and activities regarding social and civic life find visibility. Over six months 617 events were promoted by fans and friends, with an average of 3.39 posts per day. This is certainly a sign of institutional cohesion, demonstrating a close relationship between the municipality and actors in the Reggio Emilia area.

To compare the contents published by the four sample municipalities we excluded from the Reggio Emilia content analysis both the 'Received and Forwarded' events and the contents where the municipality is tagged by other users. Figure 9 shows how the Reggio Emilia communication mix is essentially focused on events promotion (72.4%), even if the Facebook Profile is occasionally used to post alerts directed at to citizens about emergencies and service problems (10%), as happened during the snow storms that paralysed the city and forced the closure of public schools.

To conclude this section of our study we compared the contents published by the four municipalities to highlights the different production within the six month period (Figure 10).

Figure 10 shows that Reggio Emilia dedicates more attention to promoting events organized by the municipality or by different local actors. Rimini and Venezia give more relevance to information about public services and opportunities for citizens. Finally Venezia posts the highest number of messages related to 'emergencies and alerts' while the call for participation strategy is more prevalent o then Modena and Rimini Walls. As we already observed Modena publishes several posts inviting users to discover local culture and heritage.

Figure 8. Reggio Emilia Facebook Profile posts' distribution (frequency)

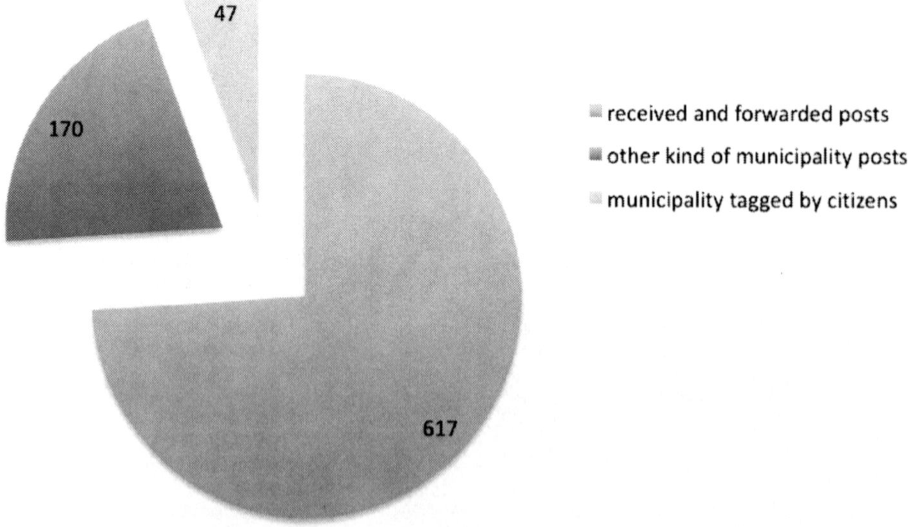

Forms and Characteristics of Users' Activation and Participation[12]

Table 4 shows how user interaction with the municipality (in terms of number of comments and likes) differs according to the type of published content and to the different communication strategies implemented by the three municipalities in question.[13] Modena municipality Facebook Page is the more dynamic: it obtained on average 10 total interactions (comments + likes) for each post published. Reggio Emilia got on average 1 interaction per post, while the Venezia Like Page[14] had on average 5 total interactions.

In general in all the Pages the number of likes is more than the number of comments. These data suggest that commenting is considered in general less impulsive than expressing "like" and it demands interest in the topic involved. The Modena Page attracts the highest level of interaction with users: it records 1244 likes and 1213 comments. The category producing the highest number of likes and comments is "Culture and civic heritage discovery" (364 likes and 757 comments) followed by 'City image display' (324 likes; 96 comments): this demonstrates the large-scale participation of citizens (from different age ranges) activated by the municipal communication strategies. The various quizzes related to the history, locations and famous residents of the city create a positive impetus to solve puzzles, generating a large number of interactions. Thus citizens publicly express their pleasure in finding out more about the city through the Facebook content. Excluding these civic posts, Modena users pressed the "like" button particularly in relation to events (n=197) and city news (n=112); while they mostly commented on messages related to "call for civic participation" (n=87) and "alerts for emergencies" (n=84). In the Venezia Facebook Page the highest number of likes is recorded under the category "event" (n=134), followed by "information about public services" (n=106); while the topics most frequently commented by users are "news related to city life" and "alert about emergencies and service problems". Among Reggio Emilia users likes are concentrated on the category "events" (n=145), and the action of commenting is more addressed to "alerts of emergencies and service problems" (n=19).

Figure 9. Frequencies of the different categories of posts published in Reggio Emilia Profile Page (%)

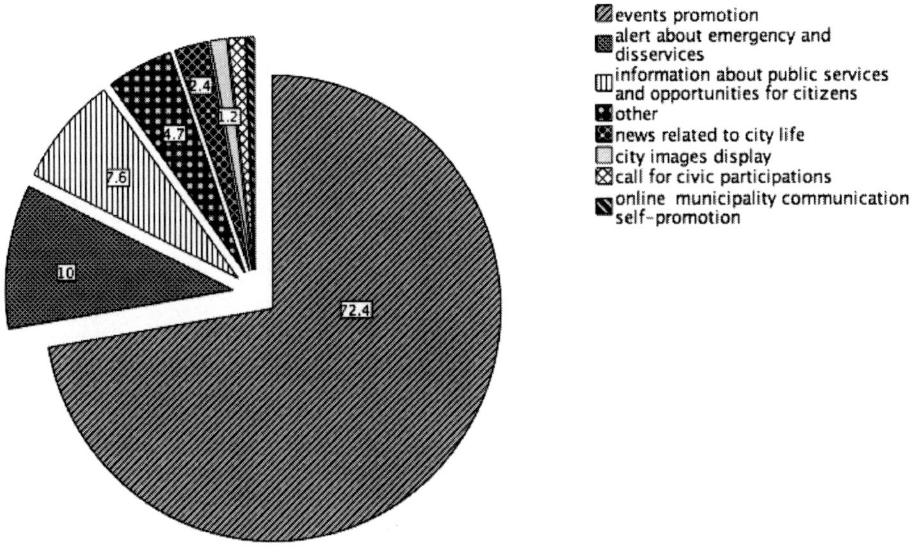

Figure 10. Comparison among the four municipalities contents of the posts published in the Facebook

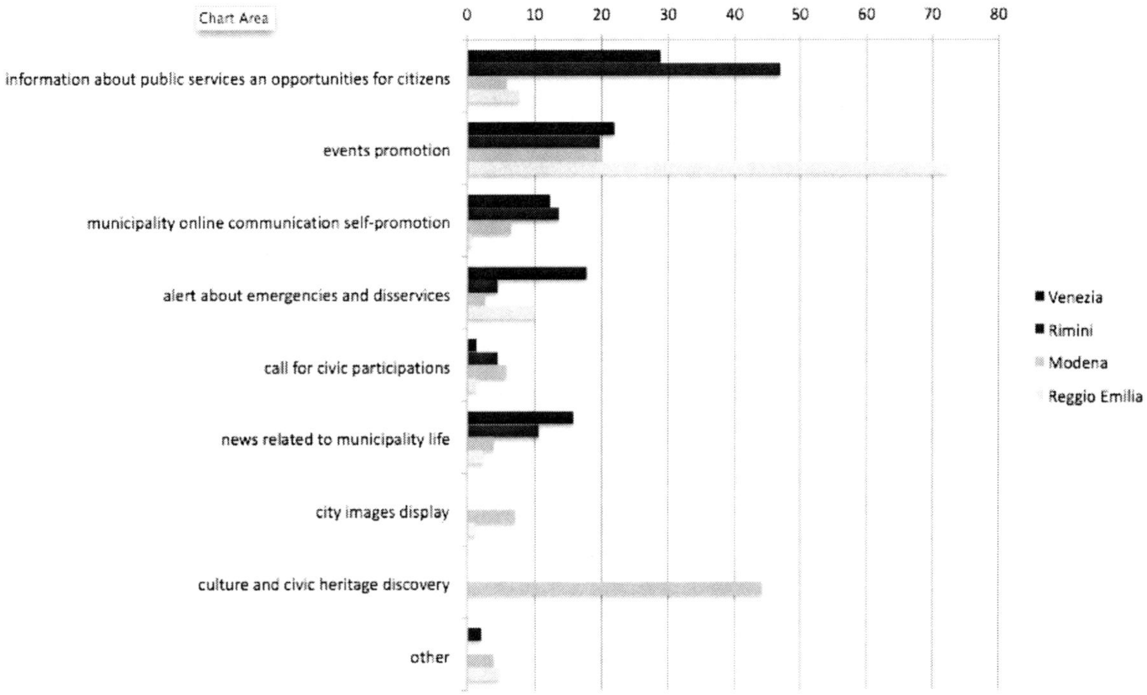

Table 4. Six month user interaction in terms of likes and comments in the Venezia, Reggio Emilia and Modena Facebook Pages

Typology of contents posted	Venezia		Reggio Emilia		Modena	
	like	comments	like	comments	like	Comment
Information about public services and opportunities for citizens	106	19	18	5	39	13
Events promotion	**134**	42	**145**	11	197	60
Online communication self-promotion	75	10	1	0	60	21
Alert about emergencies and service problems	24	47	13	**19**	17	84
Call for civic participation	3	16	2	0	53	87
News related to municipality life	93	**52**	7	0	112	21
Culture and civic heritage discovery	0	0	0	0	**364**	**757**
City images display	0	0	12	1	324	96
Other	35	17	5	0	78	74
Total	**470**	**203**	**203**	**36**	**1244**	**1213**

Findings and Discussion[15]

Looking at the online activities of four different municipalities our analysis provided an exploratory description of the prevalent uses of Facebook Pages by Italian municipalities. The municipalities in our sample are using Facebook adopting a multichannel communication strategy addressed to different kinds of publics according to their different communication strategies (Bryer, 2010; Mergel, 2010). Moreover, Facebook municipality Pages seem to attract the interest of various kind of users: not only residents but also tourists, former residents or just curious people interested in what is going on in the cities (Kuzma, 2010). All the Pages seem to respect many of the nine commandments to reach an effective social media strategy (Lee and Elser 2010): they are constantly updated, integrated with the existing public communication flow and managed by specific offices; only in the Venezia Facebook Page is the mission not clearly stated but it can be deduced from analysis of the posts.

Our study shows that content promoted by municipalities can reach a wider public using the 'power' of social networks sites: citizens' personal networks act as effective multipliers and let public communication better circulate through the net. Moreover, the contents that each municipality publishes (e.g. news, images, videos) seems to affect the overall image of the city. At the same time social networks appear to be used by institutions not only as a tow-down channel to download information but also as a place to signal in real time service problems, collect proposals and express citizens' public voice (Nabatchi and Mergel, 2010). In particular, municipalities on Facebook are examples of place-based institutions experimenting an online presence that modifies the communication flow between a digital space and the local territory. The Facebook Like Page appears like a 'public forum' where citizens can find news related to city life, share ideas and access information that in the past was only accessible through face to face interactions. Our research confirmed an increasing dialogue between online and offline spaces (Varnelis, 2008). At the same time it reveals that social interactions in online space produce concrete and tangible effects on daily life, in terms of enhancing the sense of belonging toward a territory and trust toward institutions.

Furthermore the content analysis of the Facebook institutional pages and the outcomes of the interviews with the four municipality communication managers outlined four different communication strategies that vary according to the different offices managing the service. On the whole, municipality Facebook Pages appear to be used: (1) as an expansion of the Office for Public Relations; (2) as a tool for enhancing civic memory and belonging; (3) as a civic online Wall to publish news and events; (4) as an online local newspaper to inform users about municipality services and civic interest news.

In particular:

1. The first example of a use of municipality Facebook Page is the one carried out by the municipality of Rimini. This municipality uses the Facebook Like Page as an expansion of the Office for Public Relations. This online space is used to publish news regarding city opportunities and public services and to host and reply to questions and inquiries raised by residents. It is a innovative use of the Facebook platform that encourages the use of this space not only to disseminate information but it also represents an additional channel to listen to citizens' needs and resolve problems.
2. The municipality of Modena activates interaction with its residents mainly publishing on the Facebook Like Page contents that are related to cultural and civic life. The decision to organise weekly scheduled quizzes seems an excellent idea to stimulate the interest of fans and to revitalise a common sense of belonging to city life and history. The mechanism of quizzes, enriched by pictures and videos, raises the attention of users from different age ranges: while young people are challenged to find places and recognise famous residents of the city, adults and elderly citizens use Facebook to publicly convey their memories of the past. Using Facebook as a tool for civic memory and belonging could be considered another specific example of the various uses experimented by Italian municipalities on Facebook.
3. Reggio Emilia adopts a third different use. The municipality massively disseminates and makes visible on its Facebook Profile news and events that are created by different actors in Reggio Emilia territory. This makes the online Page a civic online Wall where users can find opportunities provided by the municipality and by others institutional and social actors.
4. In the Venezia Facebook Pages we observed a coherent multi-channel communication strategy (i.e. the link between the institutional Twitter account and the posts on Facebook). Moreover since the employers in charge of the Page work in the Press Office, the publication of news related to municipal civic life is heavily emphasised on the Wall (i.e. the real-time publication of information on the mayoral election). In conclusion this Like Page appears similar to an online newspaper where users are informed about municipality services and news of civic interest.

All four platforms follow specific communication strategies that can be linked to the typology proposed by Mergel (2010): for example Venezia seems to use a 'push strategy', while Modena adopts a 'networking strategy', stimulating interaction with users in order to share and create knowledge. At the same time these four Pages are strategically used to inform and support citizens in case of emergencies and alerts related to city life, such as floods, smog emergencies, traffic bans or snow. This is a common use of these social network sites, as mentioned in the literature review (American Red Cross, 2010; Roberts, 2010) and it is extremely useful for citizens and local residents.

In conclusion, we believe that, in order to strategically manage social network sites, public administrations need to recruit and to train skilled human resources to manage these services. Before creating and managing an institutional presence in the social web, public communication officers need to know the technical characteristics of these interactive platforms and the social impacts these media can have on the relations between administrations and citizens,. Indeed "history shows that when new media are introduced communicators tend to use them in the same way they used the old media; [...] practictioners first used online media as an information dump, in the same way they used traditional media, newsletters, and publications" (Grunig, 2009, p.6). On the contrary, communicators should develop a social media plan, strategically choosing the platforms (Facebook, Twitter, YouTube, Flickr, etc) in order to reach specific objectives and to interact with different publics; it is also important to allocate people and resources to the management of social media and to adopt clear policies to post contents and reply to citizens' inquiries. In particular, municipalities willing to experiment with a presence on Facebook to foster civic participation and encourage users to express their opinion should periodically publish valuable contents in their Walls and frequently reply to users' messages and comments. Citizens will populate these institutional social spaces only if they are able to find useful contents and services and if they see that their public voice is listened to by administrations (Rheingold, 2008)

FUTURE RESEARCH DIRECTIONS[16]

In our opinion, in literature there is a lack of analytic research exploring the interaction between public administration and citizens through social media. In particular there is a need for empirical studies to verify whether social network sites, and Facebook in particular, are activating innovative and participative communication practices, or whether administrations are simply replicating traditional communication practices, enriched by participatory media. Moreover, cross-national comparisons are also lacking. The creation of dedicated software to automatically collect and save data appearing on Facebook (e.g. status update, comments, numbers of likes and sharing) would certainly facilitate the research of scholars studying internet-based social interactions.

Moreover, it may be important to investigate the uses and results people seek when they become friends or "likers" of a public administration on Facebook. Is the act to be connected with a institution an impulse action? Is it a marker of identity and belonging, or does it satisfiy specific needs and expectations? These shifts could be very interesting for improving more effective public interfaces in social web applications and in particular for social scientists doing research in this field.

Finally, as regards the specific topic of our research, further studies should be done to investigate how many users of each municipality Facebook Like Pages are citizens living in the cities. As we noted, the "Facebook Insight" tool only offers questionable data. This research issue deserves future investigation. It is crucial, in order to implement new strategies and to better communicate with the public, to be aware of the general characteristics of the actual users of the Facebook Page (citizens, tourists, journalists, etc.).

CONCLUSION

Social media and web 2.0 applications offer valuable tools to create a dialogue between public administrations and citizens, enhancing their participation in civic life. Our research explored some of the uses emerging in the online communication of four Italian Municipalities' Facebook Pages. Facebook Pages are used by Municipalities for different purposes: (1) as an expansion of the Office for Public Relations; (2) as a tool for enhancing civic memory and belonging; (3) as a civic online Wall to publish news and events; (4) as an online local newspaper to inform users about municipal services and civic interest news.

In conclusion, the case studies we presented reveal that Facebook Pages can represent a useful online platform to enhance dialogue between public administrations and their citizens. In fact, through social network sites public administrations can obtain valuable access to citizens' personal networks and share their messages within the same online spaces where citizens comment on their everyday lives. On the whole, social media seem to offer significant opportunities for institutions willing to enrich their communication mix within a multi-channel strategy and avoid a traditional top-down and broadcast flow of communication.

REFERENCES

American Red Cross. (2010). *The case for integrating crisis response with social media*. Retrieved February 25, 2011, from http://www.scribd.com/doc/35737608/White-Paper-The-Case-for-Integrating-Crisis-Response-With-Social-Media

Aquilani, B., & Lovari, A. (2009, August). *Social networks and university communication: Is Facebook a new opportunity? An Italian exploratory study*. Paper presented at the 12th International QMOD and Toulon-Verona Conference on Quality and Service Sciences (ICQSS), Verona, Italy.

Barabasi, A. L., & Albert, R. (1999). Emergence of scaling in random networks. *Science*, *286*(5439), 509–512. doi:10.1126/science.286.5439.509

Bennet, W. L. (Ed.). (2008). *Civic life online: Learning how digital media can engage youth*. Cambridge, MA: MIT Press.

boyd, d. m., & Ellison, N. B. (2007). Social network sites: Definition, history and scholarship. *Journal of Computer-Mediated Communication*, *13*(1), 210-230.

boyd, d. m. (2008). Why youth (heart) social network sites: The role of networked publics in teenage social life. In D. Buckingham (Ed.), *Youth, identity, and digital media* (pp.1-26). Cambridge, MA: MIT Press.

Bryer, T. (2010). Across the great divide: Social media and networking for citizens engagement. In J. H. Svara, & J. Denhardt (Eds.), *Connected communities, local government as partners in citizens engagement and community building* (pp. 73-79). Retrieved March 10, 2011, from http://www.tlgconference.org/communityconnectionswhitepaper.pdf.

Castells, M. (1996). *The rise of the network society*. Malden, MA: Blackwell.

Castells, M. (2009). *Communication power*. Oxford, UK: Oxford University Press.

Coleman, S. (2005). *Remixing citizenship. Democracy and young people's use of internet*. Retrieved December 13, 2010, from http://cypi.carnegieuktrust.org.uk/files/Carnegie_v3LRES_0.pdf

Comunello, F. (2010). *Networked sociability*. Roma, Italy: Guerini Scientifica.

Contini, F., & Lanzara, G. F. (2009). *ICT and innovation in the public sector. European studies in the making of e-government*. New York, NY: Palgrave Macmillan.

Dahlgren, P. (2009). *Media and political engagement: Citizens, communication and democracy*. Cambridge, UK: Cambridge University Press.

Ellison, N., Steinfield, C., & Lampe, C. (2007). The benefits of Facebook "friends:" Social capital and college students use of online social network sites. *Journal of Computer-Mediated Communication*, *12*(4), 1143–1168. doi:10.1111/j.1083-6101.2007.00367.x

Faccioli, F. (2000). *Comunicazione pubblica e cultura del servizio*. Roma, Italy: Carocci.

Ferro, E., & Molinari, F. (2010). Making sense of Gov 2.0 strategies: No citizens, no party. *Journal of eDemocracy and Open Government, 2*(1), 56-68.

Fyfe, T., & Crookal, P. (2010). *Social media and public sector policy dilemmas*. Toronto, Canada: Institute of Public Administration of Canada.

Grunig, J. E. (2009). Paradigms of global public relations in an age of digitalization. *PRism, 6*(2), 1-19, Retrieved March 18, 2011, from http://www.prismjournal.org

Hewitt, A., & Forte, A. (2009). *Crossing boundaries: Identity management and student/faculty relationships on the Facebook.* Poster presented at CSCW Bauff, Alberta, Retrieved February 25, 2011, from http://www.cc.gatech.edu/~aforte/HewittForteCSCWPoster2006.pdf

Hilgers, D., & Ihl, C. (2010). Citizensourcing: Applying the concept of open innovation to the public sector. *International Journal of Public Participation, 4*(1), 67–88.

Human Capital Institute (Ed.). (2010). Social networking in government: Opportunities & challenges. Retrieved December 13, 2010, from http://www.hci.org/lib/social-networking-government-opportunities-challenges-part-1

Jenkins, H. (2006). *Convergence culture*. New York, NY: NYU Press.

Jenkins, H. (2009). *Confronting the challenges of participatory culture. Media education for the 21st century*. Cambridge, MA: MIT Press.

Keen, A. (2007). *The cult of the amateur. How today's internet is killing our culture*. New York, NY: Doubleday.

Kuzma, J. (2010). Asian government usage of Web 2.0 Social Media. *European Journal of ePractice, 9,* 71-83, Retrieved March 11, 2011, from http://www.eupractice.eu

Lee, M., & Lee Elser, E. (2010). *The nine commandments of social media in public administration: A dual-generation perspective. PA Times, 33(3).* Washington, DC: American Society for Public Administration.

Lewis, B. K. (2010). Social media and strategic communication: Attitudes and perceptions among college students. [from http://www.prsa.org/Intelligence/PRJournal]. *The Public Relations Journal, 4*(3), 1–23. Retrieved January 27, 2011.

Lewis, K., Kaufman, J., & Christakis, N. (2008). The taste for privacy: An analysis of college student privacy settings in an online social network. *Journal of Computer-Mediated Communication, 14*, 79–100. doi:10.1111/j.1083-6101.2008.01432.x

Lindmark, S. (2009). *Web 2.0: Where does Europe stand?* JRC European Commission. Retrieved December 13, 2010, from http://ftp.jrc.es/EURdoc/JRC53035.pdf

Lovari, A., & Parisi, L. (2009, November). *Amministrazioni pubbliche in ascolto. Prove di customer satisfaction attraverso la lente dei social network site*. Paper presented at the conference *Reti socievoli, convegno Pic AIS,* Urbino, Italy.

Lovari, A., & Parisi, L. (2010). *Pubbliche amministrazioni e cittadini 2.0, Esplorando forme di partecipazione civica e relazionalità.* Paper presented at AIS Conference, Milano, Italy.

Masini, M., Lovari, A., & Benenati, S. (Eds.). (2009). *Comunicazione pubblica digitale*. Acireale-Roma, Italy: Bonanno Editore.

Mazer, J. P., Murphy, R. E., & Simonds, C. J. (2007). I'll see you on "Facebook": The effects of computer-mediated teacher self-disclosure on student motivation, affective learning, and classroom climate. *Communication Education, 56*(1), 1–17. doi:10.1080/03634520601009710

Mergel, I. (2010). *Gov 2.0 revisited: Social media strategies in the public sector. PA Times, 33(3)*. Washington, DC: American Society for Public Administration.

Monte, L. (2009). *The social pulpit. Barack Obama, social media toolkit*. Retrieved March 15, 2011, from http://www.edelman.com

Nabatchi, T., & Mergel, I. (2010). Participation 2.0: Using Internet and social media: technologies to promote distributed democracy and create digital neighborhoods. In J. H. Svara, & J. Denhardt (Eds.), *Connected communities, local government as partners in citizens engagement and community building* (pp. 80-87). Retrieved March 10, 2011, from http://www.tlgconference.org/communityconnectionswhitepaper.pdf

Nielsen, (Ed.). (2009). *Global faces and network place. A Nielsen report on social networking's new global footprint*. Retrieved December 13, 2010, from http://blog.nielsen.com/nielsenwire/wp-content/uploads/2009/03/nielsen_globalfaces_mar09.pdf

Noveck, B. S. (2009). *Wiki government: How technology can make government better, democracy stronger, and citizens more powerful*. Washington, DC: Brookings Institution Press.

O'Reilly, T. (2005). What is Web 2.0? Design patterns and business models for the next generation of software. Retrieved December 13, 2010, from www.oreillynet.com

Osimo, D. (2008). *Web 2.0 in government: Why and how?* European Commission, Joint Research Centre. Retrieved December 13, 2010, from http//ftp.jrc.es/EURdoc/JRC45269.pdf

Pieterson, W., & Ebbers, W. (2008). The use of service channel by citizens in the Netherlands: Implications for multi-channel management. *International Review of Administrative Sciences, 74*(1), 95–110. doi:10.1177/0020852307085736

Qualman, E. (2010). *Socialnomics. How social media transforms the way we live and do business*. Hoboken, NJ: John Wiley & Sons.

Quocirca, (Ed.). (2007). Social networking and opportunities in the public sector. Retrieved December 13, 2010, from www.quocirca.com

Rheingold, H. (2008). Using participatory media and public voice to encourage civic engagement. In Bennet, L. (Ed.), *Civic life online* (pp. 97–118). Cambridge, MA: McArthur Foundation.

Roberts, N. C. (2010). Open-source, Web-based platforms for public engagement during disasters. In J. H. Svara, & J. Denhardt (Eds.), *Connected communities, local government as partners in citizens engagement and community building* (pp. 88-94), Retrieved March 10, 2011, from http://www.tlgconference.org/communityconnectionswhitepaper.pdf

Serrat, O. (2010). *Social media and the public sector*. Asian Development Bank Report. Retrieved December 13, 2010, from http://www.adb.org/documents/information/knowledge-solutions/social-media-and-the-public-sector.pdf

Shirky, C. (2008). *Here comes everybody. Revolution doesn't happen when society adopts new technology, it happens when society adopts new behaviours*. New York, NY: Penguin Books.

Sirianni, C. (2009). *Investing in democracy: Engaging citizens in collaborative governance*. Washington, DC: Brookings Press.

Smith, A. (2010). *Governmento: The internet gives citizens new paths to government services and information*. Pew Internet & American Life Project. Retrieved December 13, 2010, from http://pewinternet.org/Reports/2010/Government-Online.aspx

Solis, B., & Breakenridge, D. (2009). *Putting the public back in public relations*. Upper Saddle River, NJ: Pearson Education.

Tapscott, D. (2009). *Grown up digital. How the Net generation is changing your world.* New York, NY: McGraw Hill.

The Economist (Ed.). (2010). *A world of connections. A special report on social networking.* Retrieved December 13, 2010, from http://www.economist.com/node/15351002

Valenzuela, S., Park, N., & Kee, K. (2009). Is there social capital in a social network site? Facebook use and college students' life satisfaction, trust, and participation. *Journal of Computer-Mediated Communication, 14*(4), 875–901. doi:10.1111/j.1083-6101.2009.01474.x

Van Dijck, J. (2009). Users like you? Theorizing agency in user generated content. *Media Culture & Society, 31*(1), 41–58. doi:10.1177/0163443708098245

Van Dijck, J., & Nieborg, D. (2009). Wikinomics and its discontents: A critical analysis of Web 2.0 business manifestos. *New Media & Society, 11*(5), 855–874. doi:10.1177/1461444809105356

Varnelis, K. (Ed.). (2008). *Networked publics.* Cambridge, MA: MIT Press.

Waller, S. N. (2010). *Social media for public parks and recreation organizations: Bridging the communication gap. PA Times, 33(3).* Washington, DC: American Society for Public Administration.

Waters, R. D., Burnett, E., Lamm, A., & Lucas, J. (2009). Engaging stakeholders through social networking: How nonprofit organizations are using Facebook. *Public Relations Review, 35*(2), 102–106. doi:10.1016/j.pubrev.2009.01.006

West, D. M. (2005). *Digital government. Technology and public sector performance.* Princeton, NJ: Princeton University Press.

ADDITIONAL READING

Bakardjieva, M. (2011). The Internet in Everyday Life: Exploring the Tenets and Contributions of Diverse Approaches. In Consalvo, M., & Ess, C. (Eds.), *The handbook of internet studies* (pp. 59–82). Chichester: Wiley-Blackwell. doi:10.1002/9781444314861.ch4

Barabási, A. L. (2002). *Linked. The new Science of networks.* Cambridge, MA: Perseus Publishing.

Baym, N. K., & Ledbetter, A. (2009). Tunes that Bind?: Predicting Friendship Strength in a Music-Based Social Network. *Information Communication and Society, 12*(3), 408–427. doi:10.1080/13691180802635430

Beer, D. (2008). Social network(ing) sites. Revisiting the story so far: A response to danah boyd & Nicole Ellison. *Journal of Computer-Mediated Communication, 13*(2), 516–529. doi:10.1111/j.1083-6101.2008.00408.x

Benkler, Y. (2006). *The Wealth of Networks: How Social Production Trasforms Markets and Freedom.* New Haven, CT: Yale University Press.

Bertot, J. C., Jaeger, P. T., & Grimes, J. M. (2010). Using ICTs to create a culture of trasparency: E-government and social media as openness and anti-corruption tools for societies. *Government Information Quarterly, 27*(3), 264–271. doi:10.1016/j.giq.2010.03.001

Bolter, J. D., & Grusin, R. (1999). *Remediation. Understanding New Media.* Cambridge, MA: MIT Press.

Brabham, D. C. (2008). Crowdsourcing as a Model for Problem Solving: An introduction and Cases. *Convergence: The International Journal of Research into Media Technologies, 14*(1), 75–90. doi:10.1177/1354856507084420

Consalvo, M., & Ess, C. (Eds.). (2011). *The handbook of internet studies.* Chichester: Wiley-Blackwell. doi:10.1002/9781444314861

Gross, R., & Acquisti, A. (2005). Information revelation and privacy in online social networks (the Facebook case), *ACM Workshop on Privacy and the Electronic Society* (WPES)

Himanen, P. (2001). *The hacker ethic and the spirit of information age*. London: Random House.

Hodge, M. (2006). The Fourth Amendment and privacy issues on the "new" Internet: Facebook.com and MySpace.com. *Southern Illinois University Law Journal. Southern Illinois University at Carbondale. School of Law, 31*, 95–123.

Howe, J. (2008). *Crowdsourcing: why the power of the crowd is driving the future of business*. New York, NY: Crown Pyblishing Group.

Ito, M. (Ed.). (2009). *Hanging Out, Messing Around and Geeking Out: Kids living and learning with New Medi*. Cambridge, MA: MIT Press.

Macnamara, J. (2010). Public communication practices in the Web 2.0-3.0 mediascape: The case for PRevolution, *Prism* 7(3), 1-13. Retrieved March 15, 2011, from http://www.prismjournal.org

Marinelli, A. (2004). *Connessioni. Nuovi media, nuove relazioni sociali*. Milano: Guerini.

Morcellini, M., & Mazza, B. (Eds.). (2008). *Oltre l'individualismo. Comunicazione, nuovi diritti e capitale sociale*. Milano: Franco Angeli.

Stutzman, F. (2006). An Evaluation of Identity-Sharing Behavior in Social Network Communities. *International Digital and Media Arts Journal, 3*(1), 1–7.

KEY TERMS AND DEFINITIONS

Civic Participation: The act of participating in the social and civic life of a specific territory, such as the active presence in the public debates and events. It also includes the need of citizens to be informed about civic issues.

Facebook: The most famous social network site to support internet mediated social interactions.

Multi-Channel Strategies: Strategies adopted by public administration to deliver services and to communicate using different media and targeting to various kind of users.

Public Administration: Public institutions at various level (local, regional, national) providing services to citizens and stakeholders.

Public Communication: The communication flow created and managed by public administrations in order to inform citizens, media and other social and economic actors about the policies and services they deliver.

Social Media: Digital media based on web 2.0 applications that enable users to create, share and discuss contents online.

Social Network Sites (SNS): web 2.0 applications used to publish semi-public profiles. Through SNS users are connected whit their friends and can relate to other users for different aims (such as social, professional, ludic ones).

ENDNOTES

1 The concept of the chapter is the result of a process of dialogue and sharing ideas between the authors. The attribution of each paragraph is indicated each time. The introduction and the conclusion of the chapter are written together.

2 We would like to thank the four managers of the municipality Facebook Pages who kindly collaborated with us providing access to statistical data and other useful information about the institutional use of the Facebook Pages.

3 By Alessandro Lovari.

4 By Lorenza Parisi.

5 For these reasons we excluded some Facebook Fan pages like Torino, Genova and Udine because of the city size (over 300,000) and other like Lucca and Arezzo, since the pages have been created only in 2010.

6 In May 2010 Reggio Emilia profile reached the maximum number of users (5000) and nowadays the municipality is asking users to join the new municipality *Like Page.* We think *Like Pages* will become the standard for municipalities that want to communicate on Facebook, having no limit in number of users and providing full access to Facebook statistical data.

7 By Alessandro Lovari.

8 During 6 months of activities in Venezia Facebook Like Page we counted 1457 total interaction (comments + like).

9 By Lorenza Parisi.

10 We excluded 45 posts containing specific posts about the mayor poll published on 30th March 2010.

11 These results differs to the ones we obtained analysing the Facebook Profile of the municipality of Spello (Lovari and Parisi, 2009). In the case study related to the Municipality of Spello we classified the citizens' posts noticing that the majority of the messages were greetings (40%) and citizens' self promotion (20%). This denote that Rimini Like Page users are using the Facebook platform to interact with the municipality and to express opinions and critics about public services, according to the proposed mission.

12 By Lorenza Parisi.

13 Rimini Page has been excluded for hosting a marginal number of comments and likes.

14 1 In this analysis we do not considered the users' interaction on the Venezia Like Page on 30th of March. That day the Municipality only posted messages about the polls (n=45) creating an huge interaction among the users and the municipality (485 comments and 285 likes).

15 By Lorenza Parisi.

16 By Lorenza Parisi.

Chapter 13
Networked Individualism, Constructions of Community, and Religious Identity:
The Case of Emerging Church Bloggers in Australia

Paul Emerson Teusner
RMIT University, Melbourne

ABSTRACT

This chapter offers a contribution to the ongoing research into networked individualism in late modern society from the perspective of religion online. Using a sample of weblogs created by Australians involved in the "emerging church movement," this chapter will explore how the Internet has enabled individuals to seek relationships with others and discern a religious identity beyond the confines of local faith communities and denominational institutions. Here we will see how those who use blogs to form religious networks must negotiate constructions of communal identities, not just offline, but within the blogosphere. These negotiations represent a postmodern quest for authentic religious expression and practice, which is found in the flow of information among a myriad of traditional and new sources.

INTRODUCTION

This chapter explores the use of blogging technology to fuel networked individualism's impact on religious identity. It draws from a study of Christian bloggers in Australia to highlight how people use the technology to negotiate membership to Christian communities, both online and offline, and form their own relationships that foster faith identity. It suggests implications for the future role of religious institutions in public discourses on religion, the place of local faith communities in fostering religious identity of individuals, and the impact of being online on expressing religious identity offline.

For many Christians, participation in the local congregation or faith community is considered the basic cell from which one's religious identity is formed. The congregation's participation in a wider institution connects its members to a wider, even global, community to the effect that one's identity could be defined by membership

DOI: 10.4018/978-1-61350-338-6.ch013

in a denomination: "I am Roman Catholic", "I am Southern Baptist" or "I am Methodist", for example. We know, however, that mobility and use of telecommunication technologies have meant people have a range of sources of religious information, and settings for social interaction (Giddens, 1991). Ecumenism has encouraged Christians to explore other expressions of Christian faith, while liberal pluralism has meant that Christian churches sit alongside, communicate with, and even compete with, other religions (Finke & Stark, 2005). As such churches in late modernity can no longer assume they are their members' sole source of information, support and religious development (Bauman, 1998).

Recent research has shown that the Internet provides an alternative space for the construction of religious identity, free from the constraints of institutional authority, and with the potential to create and explore new symbolic practices (Lövheim & Linderman, 2005). Blogging also promises a democratisation of voices and the freedom to express personal views on public religious issues, and the capacity to create global networks to share information and resources, find support and care, and build trusting relationships (Beer & Burrows, 2007; Campbell, 2005; Cheong, Halavais, & Kwon, 2008). For those who feel excluded from, or silenced in their local faith communities, and those who find cultural and symbolic practices of local churches foreign, find in the blogosphere a place to say something and be heard.

A study of thirty such bloggers, from a variety of Protestant and Evangelical faith traditions in Australia, will be used a case study. These thirty use phrases like "in exile from their denomination", "looking for something different", or even "churchless" to describe their sense of affiliation with the tradition of their upbringing, and use blogging to confess their needs and seek like minds. Blogging promises the exploration and development of religious identity in an open parliament on the cultural, symbolic, institutional, economic and theological practices of the modern Church. Online they are introduced to a global movement of bloggers, sometimes called the "emerging church" or "missional" movement. They find here that discursive practices have developed that determine bloggers' place within the movement, and that even patterns of authority have emerged. Ironically, those who use blogging to negotiate their place in the Christian Church offline discover that they must also negotiate their belonging to an online community.

This chapter asks, to what extent do these bloggers seek belonging in an online community, or simply a position within a network of connections, from which to construct individual religious identities? A study of posts and conversations in these blog sites, together with information collected from interviews with the sites' authors, will show that bloggers in the study find in the blogosphere a place to explore their religious identities away from the constraints of institutional churches offline. Moreover, the study will show that while they identify with values of the online emerging church movement to varying degrees, generally they prefer to see themselves "on the outskirts" of the movement, rather than actively involved in it.

BACKGROUND

Researching Religion Online

These questions find themselves within a tradition of researching religious identity and practice on the Internet, which began in the middle of the 1990s (see Brasher, 1996). Along this tradition, it may be argued, that researchers into religion online have moved from a focus on what particular religious ideas, practices and values appear online toward an interest in how Internet technologies and religious values interact in all spheres of everyday life.

First projects of research into religion online, what Højsgaard and Warburg (2005) considered "the first wave" of research in the field, considered web sites as destinations that users "arrive at" when they type in URLs or click hyperlinks. Such research seemed primarily concerned with questions of such journeys and destinations. These pieces of fact-finding endeavoured to answer "What does online religion look like?", "What can people do online and why would they do it?", or "What kind of people go online for religion and why?"

For example, in 2004, Hoover, Clark and Rainie published a report for the Pew Internet and American Life series based on a widespread and in depth study of American Internet users. They asked simple questions of their sample, including "Do you go to the Internet for religious purposes?". They found that most users of religious Internet sites were active participants in religious activities offline, and that Internet use was to enhance religious activity in other parts of their lives.

This "first wave" of research into online religion sought to uncover the phenomenon of religious practice on the Internet, as an evolutionary step of a differently technologised society. As Wellman noticed in other contexts of Internet research in this period, early investigations "insisted on looking at online phenomena in isolation. They assumed that only things that happened on the internet were relevant to understanding the internet" (2004: 124). Some research did focus on how religious life online compares to offline religion, and even evaluated its merits and pitfalls against what we knew about religious life in the "real world" (see Helland, 2002; Karaflogka, 2002). In doing so, however, it tended, mostly, to start with preconceived understandings of "what religious practice" was, evident in its methodologies. What was considered a religious web site, or what could be seen as a purely religious practice, was based on their similarities with what we saw in mosques and coven gatherings and dangling from car rear-view mirrors.

Højsgaard and Warburg believe, as do I, that while talk of "waves" of research into online religion implies some chronological development, it is perhaps better to see them as shifts in focus which have generally occurred over time, but not universally. Some research products fit into different "waves" at different times, based on different circumstances, and different universities, research traditions and countries.

Indeed, a few years would pass since the aforementioned works before the first extensive study of religion in the blogosphere was published. From a sample of two hundred Christian blogs and interviews with 49 authors, Cheong, Halavais and Kwon (2008) used both quantitative and qualitative measures to analyse religious content online, motivations for blogging, and links between religious blogs and other online information. The following claims were made:

1. That some users find the act of blogging a part of their regular religious practice, as a response to religious experiences recognised in daily living.
2. That bloggers linked to such a number of external sites that have little or no religious content, that the researchers could say bloggers did not limit their exposure to only religious content.
3. That blogs are a vehicle for mission to readers, through the promotion of Christian responses to world events and issues, and the engagement of readers in conversation about participation in society as religious people.
4. That blogging has a function for entertainment and escapism.

The authors conclude that the blogosphere provides for the faithful an environment where the religious and the secular are explored, expressed and debated equally and freely, where other social environments may be perceived to favour one over the other. In the blogosphere, claim the authors, the profane and sacred spheres merge.

Adopting a uses and gratifications approach to the sample, the research did not extend beyond an analysis of the relationship between the technology and the primary user, appearing to take an atomistic approach to analysis of blog content and bloggers' interaction with the technology. Indeed it lacks study of interaction between bloggers and their readership. The authors make note of this exclusion, prompting future research to "expand the investigation by delving into more posts that constitute blog texts within a religious tradition and investigate the links of individual blog posts. As blogs offer an alternative in religious self-expression, future research could investigate the implications of critical communicative shifts on traditional religious norms, including governing sanctions and concepts of religious authority and leadership" (p. 127).

Like Cheong, Halavais and Kwon's work, studies of religion online in the first "wave" tended to approach their data as content to be considered as composed and consumed by individual users. The next "wave" would approach the Internet as sites for, through interaction between users, the creation, modification and reinforcement of religious norms, practices and structures.

For Højsgaard and Warburg the "second wave" of research into religion online focussed more on the nature of religious practice online. It included rites of passage, ritual and the placement of authority in online Wiccan groups (see Helland, 2005), identity formation among adolescents (see Lövheim, 2004), the establishment of trust in email groups (see Campbell, 2005). It also included discursive constructions of the technology itself, within religious communities and structures of power (see Dawson, 2005; O'Leary, 2005).

The "third wave", whose advent was heralded by Højsgaard and Warburg but not yet complete, was to be what can be researched about the impact of Cyborg religion on religion in the offline world. It would include comparisons of structures of authority and knowledge between online and offline groups, such as the study of Barker (2005) on cult groupings, and of Campbell (2007) on how religious authority is asserted in online conversations about religion.

These new "waves" took a detour from quantitative approaches to online religion - counting sites, users, demographics, to consider ethnographic pursuits and sociological ponderings about the humans who were doing the religion in this world. Yet as the first wave showed a presumption about what is religious, these sets of work tend to make presumptions about the Internet, specifically, as a realm of being religious that is discrete and separate from the world outside.

However, increasing access to high-speed Internet connections in the developed world, prolific use of mobile media devices, and the popularity of Web 2.0 applications have changed the nature of being online. Firstly, we are aware that being online is no longer a discrete step. For many who have enjoyed Internet access for years, and for those who have made it to adulthood without knowing life before the Web, Cyberspace need not be a place we need to make time or room for, but is something constantly within reach. As Pang suggested:

Why is cyberspace coming to an end? Our experience of interacting with digital information is changing. We're moving to a world in which we (or objects acting on our behalf) are online all the time, everywhere. Designers and computer scientists are also trying hard to create a new generation of devices and interfaces that don't monopolize out attention, but ride on the edges of our awareness. We'll no longer have to choose between cyberspace and the world; we'll constantly access the first while being fully part of the second. Because of this, the idea of cyberspace as separate from the real world will collapse. (quoted in Thomas, 2006)

With this in mind, research into religion online moves away from questions "Where is the religious Internet and what will it do for me?" and "What can we do online that we can't do offline and vice versa?" and "What will happen to me when I go online, who will I meet and what will

I become?". Rather, questions will be more like "What is religious about the Internet that I create, gather, rear, mould and cultivate?"

Presumptions about what makes an online practice a religious one, and what makes a religious practice an online one, may be overcome in this fourth wave, as the research tradition experiences a new shift of focus. Lövheim recognises it well, calling researchers like this one to reconsider the "purpose and the social contexts of interaction with religion online". Firstly, we must ask less about users' "relation to religious communities on the Internet", as if online religious communities can tell us all we need to know about online religion. Instead we must consider how religion is a component of the wider "social contexts organized through and in connection to new media". Secondly, we must ask less about Internet as a place where religion is done in peculiar, unique or traditional ways, and more about how the Internet is one "context for negotiations of the place and value of religion in the wider society and culture". (Lövheim, 2008)

Blogging and the Challenge to "Community"

In the first few years of the twenty-first century, weblogs, known more conveniently as blogs, were by far the most popular platform for user-generated content on the Internet. According to a 2006 press release by Technorati, in that year the blogosphere contained approximately 57 million sites, and the number was growing by 100,000 daily (Sifry, 2006). In 2008, Technorati's "About" page claims those numbers are 112.8 million and 175,000, respectively (Technorati, 2008). Last year, while total figures were not provided, Technorati reported that personal blogs comprised a smaller proportion of the total number of blogs than in previous years, and professional blogs are on the rise. Technorati (2010) suggests that users of blogs for personal purposes are switching to social networking sites like Facebook, or microblogging tools like Twitter.

Blogs have emerged in the last decade to become an important vehicle for self-publishing and expression online. Blogging was introduced in 1999 as a platform by which personal web pages could easily be updated, without having to edit the entire page. Users would enter text that would appear as "posts," arranged in reverse chronological order, so that the web page would resemble an online journal, made publicly available on the Net. Over time, new features were added to the blogging platform, which facilitated the conversational element of this medium. "Comments" features enabled readers of blog pages to respond to posts with their own opinions, starting a conversation between blog authors ("bloggers") and their audiences via entire threads of interactions recorded online. "Permalinks" allowed posts and their ensuing comments to have their own URL, thereby enabling bloggers to refer back to a previous article via these links. "Tagging" allowed bloggers to assign one or more keywords to a blog post that could later be sorted by topic for readers. These features also allowed search engines to identify and collect the permalinks and tags of multiple bloggers' posts so they could be easily sorted and accessed by readers. Technorati, a search engine that collects information from blog pages and arranges them according to tags, made blog posts further accessible to a wider audience. The search engine also allows posts to be ranked by popularity, or "authority," as determined by the number of permalinks published on other blogs within a given time period (Blood, 2004; Bortree, 2005; Kumar, Novak, Raghavan, & Tomkins, 2004). These features became important tools to help facilitate online conversation as well as to analyse the influence of blogging conversation in society.

These new additions to the technology have enabled blogs to evolve from a simple web publishing tool to a global social networking platform, where each blog page becomes a site for interaction between multiple users and where issues of public interest can be explored and discussed across a multitude of sites, offering a wide range of opinions and perspectives. Thus, in the last decade the blogosphere – a term referring to the entire collective of blogs on the Internet – has rapidly emerged as an important alternative source of information, challenging the power of institutional media and the authority of voices that are prominent therein (Beer & Burrows, 2007; Efimova & de Moor, 2005). It is important to note that, while blogs are used for social networking, they are not classified as "social network sites", or SNS. SNS are, according to boyd and Ellison (2007, p. 211) bounded sites, where members connect through pages or profiles. For example, Facebook users connect with one another all within the domain of facebook.com. Blogs, on the other hand, are hosted by a multitude ofdomains and powered by a variety of different software platforms.

Blogs don't exist in isolation from each other. As authors read books, so bloggers also read others' blogs. Bloggers respond to comments made about their posts. They publish lists of their favourite bloggers on their blog's front page or sidebar. They make references to posts on other blogs, with hyperlinks so readers can follow conversations occurring over multiple sites. Bloggers recognise they are part of a blogging community, recognise common blogging etiquette and rules of behaviour, work to build friendships and relationships of collegiality and trust with other writers.

At the beginning of 2006, the time this research project began, blogging appeared to be the most popular online platform for expressions of personal beliefs and opinions about religious topics outside chat rooms and email groups. It was also relatively new context for research into online religion. In Australia, blogging was a far more popular alternative to the social network sites we know well today, e.g. Facebook. Myspace, Friendster. Over seven hundred blogs were counted by Technorati as religious blogs in Australia alone (discovered by typing in "religion" and "Australia" into Technorati's search engine on 1 March 2006), while Myspaceand Facebook were in use only by teenagers and undergraduate students (respectively).

The blogosphere presents a need to rethink the conceptualisation of community for both religion and research purposes. It is hardly a bounded community. While those involved in conversation through posts and comments on one blog may see the limits of the communicative space in the one web page, however bloggers are connected with other bloggers who are connected again with others in a way that the limits of communication cannot be drawn. Network is a better word to describe the constellation of connections that bloggers and readers navigate through the blogosphere.

This phenomenon is not new to interactions in blogs. Wellman and Leighton (1979) notice that urban sociologists began to think community as a separate concept from spatially bounded groupings, such as neighbourhoods. For the writers, community has traditionally been measured according to three principles:

Networks of interpersonal ties (outside of the household) which provide sociability and support to members, residence in a common locality; and solidarity sentiments and activities. (Wellman & Leighton 1979, p. 365)

The rise of the modern city has had urban sociologists suggest that many modes of social interaction have moved out of the neighbourhood, and consider whether the concept of community is lost to larger mechanisms of city and state institutions. Wellman and Leighton, however, suggest that:

Neighborhood relationships persist but only as specialized components of the overall primary networks. The variety of ties in which an urbanite can be involved – with distant parents, intimate friends, less intimate friends, coworkers, and so on – and the variety of networks in which these are organized can provide flexible structural bases for dealing with routine and emergency matters. ((Wellman & Leighton, 1979, p. 385)

Castells (2001) suggests that the idea of community in the offline world, as a point of comparison with online community, may be idealised beyond the reality. Modern Western life, for the author, has seen the rise of personal relationships outside families and embedded communities (schools, churches, sporting groups, workplaces) as a dominant pattern of sociability, to the embodiment of "me-centred networks".

It represents the privatization of sociability. This individualized relationship to society is a specific pattern of sociability, not a psychological attribute. It is rooted, first of all, in the individualization of the relationship between capital and labor, between workers and the work process, in the network enterprise. It is induced by the crisis of patriarchalism, and the subsequent disintegration of the traditional nuclear family, as constituted in the late nineteenth century. It is sustained (but not produced) by the new patterns of urbanization, as suburban and exurban sprawl, and the de-linking between function and meaning in the micro-places of megacities, individualize and fragment the spatial context of livelihood. And it is rationalized by the crisis of political legitimacy, as the growing distance between citizens and the states stressed the mechanisms of representation, and fosters individual withdrawal from the public sphere. The new pattern of sociability in our societies is characterized by networked individualism. (Castells, 2001, pp. 128-129)

Castells blames not the Internet on the rise of networked individualism, but sees that this pattern of sociability works best online, as it "provides an appropriate material support for the diffusion of networked individualism as the dominant form of sociability" (p. 131). Indeed, recent research into the maintenance of social capital online has found that high Internet usage, while not associated with participation in online communities *per se*, has facilitated participation in social, cultural and political networks both online and offline (see Junghee & Hyunjoo, 2010; Wellman, Haase, Witte, & Hampton, 2001).

These ideas suggest the idealisation of community in a formal religious context. Especially for post-Vatican II Catholicism and mainstream Protestantism, the congregation is highly prized as a sacrament, the face of Christ's presence on earth, the starting point and destination of the church's mission. But in a late modern society the congregation cannot singularly represent the religious identity and practice of its members, but can only be a node in the network of everyday living that informs those things.

So in these times perhaps "community" is not a description of what is, but of the ideals that either attract or repel people from engagement in religious activity. Community is a construct. The blogosphere is a place where religious people not only construct community online through their interactions, but engage in the practice of discursively reconstructing religious community as a whole.

Rheingold opened conversation and debate on theorising online community with *The Virtual Community*, in which he attempts to define community in Cyberspace as "social aggregations that emerge from the Net when enough people carry on those public discussions long enough, with sufficient human feeling, to form webs of personal relationships" (1995, p. 5). Since then, sociologists have endeavoured to define what constitutes community, and by what conditions online communities evolve, by studying online behaviour in relation to limitations and opportunities presented by the technologies used, the structure of interdependency (e.g. common interests and purposes of the group) and the effects of group characteristics on members' cognitive processes (see Matzat, 2004). These research efforts have been bound, however, by the investigation of single sites of online interaction, studying a chat room or email group, say, as if the medium constituted the primary gathering point of the community's members (Matzat, 2004, p. 69). Yet in the blogosphere, as in social networking sites and other platforms for user-generated content, there is no one site of interaction that can point to a community of users.

In his appraisal of mass media in the late twentieth century, Castells asserts that the rise of new media into dominance in society has heralded a process of diversification and decentralisation of media production and distribution. With the introduction of cable television, for example, audiences turn to different channels for different information, to find the channel tailored to the "rites and language of this audience, not only in the context but in the whole organization of the station and in the technology and design of image/broadcasting" (1996, p. 340). Music, news and weather, sport, comedy and education programming find themselves in their own channels designed for their specific content, shaping the entire medium.

Audiences, too, become as specialised, segmented and diverse as the media around them, to the point that "we are not living in a global village, but in the customized cottages globally produced and locally distributed" (1996, p. 341). Rather than connecting people from around the planet to a common agora for the sharing of stories, symbols, language and information, media have created innumerable nodes of connection that users simply pass through, in their navigation of an information culture and economy. Theorising the structuring of social relations through media is an idea about a space of flows, which, according to Hine, "in contrast to the space of place, is organized around connection rather than location. Flows of people, information, money, circulate between nodes which form a network of associations" (2000, p. 61).

Emerging Church in Australia in the Context of Secularisation and Postmodernism

Though historically as Christian as its European colonists, Australia is a multicultural and multi-religious nation, characterised by a nominally secular government and public sphere. Christianity remains the country's most popular religion, though currently in decline while other religions such as Buddhism, Hinduism, Islam and Sikhism are increasing in number. Many Christian denominations exist in Australia. The most popular are Roman Catholic, the family of mainstream Protestant traditions (such as Anglican and Baptist), and the family of Evangelical Protestant denominations (like the Assemblies of God and Apostolic churches).

Recent reports from the National Church Life Survey (Bellamy & Castle, 2004, pp. 8-10) show that in the last decade of the twentieth century church attendance in Australia was in steady decline. In 2001, 8.8% of the Australian population attended church services weekly, compared to 9.9% in 1996. Monthly attendance also fell from 20% in 1998 to 18.6% in 2002. Between 1991 and 2001, Anglican, Lutheran, Presbyterian and Salvation Army denominations closed between 2 and 9 per cent of their total congregations. The Uniting Church closed 22% of theirs, though in this decade there was an official reform of the term "congregation" as a statistical definition. In contrast, congregations belonging to the Apostolic churches, the Assemblies of God and the Church of the Nazarene grew by between 27 and 67 per cent. While these figures may suggest some Christians are moving from Catholic and mainstream Protestant to Evangelical churches, research shows these churches (such as the Assemblies of God, the Christian City Churches and the Christian Revival Crusade) have the highest incidence of "drifting out", i.e. of people leaving these churches and forsaking church attendance altogether (Sterland, Powell, & Castle, 2006, pp. 12-13).

Weber, a founding contributor to the sociology of religion, perceives secularisation in Western societies as the phenomenon where religious values and recommended behaviours are set against those of the secular world (i.e. institutions and settings outside of religious institutions like the churches), to the extent where a dichotomy is seen between sacred and profane spheres of social life. Weber does not view secularization as a logical historical process or a step in the West's social evolution. Rather, he prefers to see it as an empirical social fact, as the effect of other forces of change in modern society. (Hughey, 1979, pp. 86-89)

In fact, Weber tends to write less about secularisation as a concept than he does of "intellectualisation" and "disenchantment". He claims that when values between the religious and secular worlds are set against each other, compromises need to be made. One such compromise is the communication and exchange of religious values in secular terms within the public sphere. This, Weber suggests, has been the fate of the Protestant work ethic, which has been subsumed into the ethics of capitalism. Another is the rejection of values and behaviours in the public sphere, but an allowance for them to be communicated and exchanged in certain social spaces that are deemed not public. An example would be the removal of communal prayer in schools, but recognition of the freedom to pray, or even the encouragement to do so, in homes and places of worship. Thus in Western society the process of secularisation has involved the "privatisation" of religion.

Weber claims the main cause of such privatisation in the rationalisation of public discourse, which places value on empiricism and rational science over irrational claims of supernatural and divine interventions in history. The decline in church attendance in Western nations, according to Weber's thesis, is a product of the rationalisation of discourse in secular institutions, including education, politics and business. Modern life in the West is disenchanted with the irrational and mystical behaviours and speeches of religious institutions, and people seek alternative settings and discourses for discerning meaning and purpose. (see Bauman, 1998; Hughey, 1979)

While this thesis may account for European nations in the twentieth century and later, writers such as Casanova contend that it cannot explain for the steady high incidence of church participation in the United States of America, or countries in Asia and South America where modernisation is met with growth in attendance at Protestant Christian churches. For Casanova, the "privatisation" of religion is not the result of a disenchanted modern people, or the removal of religious speech in favour of rational, empirical or scientific discourse. Rather it is the product of an ideological campaign of modernity, both for freedom of conscience from ecclesial control, and for the progression of institutional differentiation for the capitalist economy (1994, pp. 40-42). Casanova sees the persistence of the churches to maintain a presence in the public sphere as not a resistance to secularisation but a "deprivatisation" of religion in moral response to capitalism, consumerist worldviews or their threats to traditional worldviews (1994, p. 228).

Turner's secularisation theory aligns with that of Casanova in that he sees the privatisation of religion as the result of the modernist campaign to relegate institutions founded on "ineffable" truths to the private sphere for the benefit of modern democracy and liberty.

In a democratic environment, the very idea that some truths are ineffable contradicts the ethos of modern society in which everybody assumes a right to understand or at least to have the relevant information. Democracy tends to promote plain speech and political campaigns are based on personalities and slogans and not only policies. The control of ineffable knowledge is compromised and the whole idea of hierarchically organized wisdom evaporates. We are moving from the age of revelation to the age of information where everything is, at least in principle, effable. The resulting crisis of authority is perhaps the real meaning of secularization [...]. (Casanova 2008, p. 221)

He departs from Casanova's theory in his understanding of the re-entrance of Christianity in the public sphere. For Turner, modern public religion is "low-intensity", favouring the practical, attractive and therapeutic at the expense of "authentic and viable forms of personal piety" (2008, p. 232). Even religion that appears to challenge consumer culture, like Fundamentalism, enters the public sphere as a marketplace, "selling a lifestyle based on special diets, alternative education, health regimes and mentalities" (2008, p. 233). Even if (post)modern, individualist, and consumerist society has allowed religion to speak its values, it has determined the conditions on which it can communicate.

The emerging church movement is seen in the context of religious "deprivatisation" and the conditions with which Christianity is allowed a public face. While the movement tends to defy definition, many (see Hunt, 2008) find in the emerging church movement a body of experiments in postmodern theology. Driscoll (2006) identifies the emerging church movement as the third and last in a series of models, based on their level of engagement in the public sphere. Traditional expressions of Christianity, such as Catholicism and mainstream Protestantism, are labelled "Church 1.0", that claim to retain their privileged place in modern culture, though have failed to retain an authoritative voice in postmodern culture. "Church 2.0", appealing to public audiences and engaging in a "culture war" to regain the lost position of cultural privilege, and managed as businesses that market spiritual goods and services (pp. 87-88).

For Driscoll, postmodern theology is embodied and lived out in model "3.0", which accepts that in a secularised and pluralistic society the "culture war" is won only at the expense of authentic spirituality, and therefore not worth fighting (pp. 88). For Brian McLaren, a popular American voice of the movement, the emerging church seeks an alternative to the secular dilemma, where Christians choose either "a private, personal spirituality unconnected to public life" or "a public civil religion that compromises with partisan politics" (Streett, 2006, p. 11).

Those involved in the emerging church conversation in blogs identify as "postmodern" Christians. The term "postmodern" is an for "postmodernism", which is difficult to define, but is often used in reference to recent movements in art, literature, popular culture, politics and philosophy, that aligns with some or all of the following characteristics:

1. A rejection of the "grand narrative", i.e. the notion that society is on a path of constant progress in wealth and well-being (see Lucente, 1991)
2. A rejection of the pursuit of truth that is found in an encyclopaedic knowledge of the universe (see Lucente, 1991)
3. A rhizomatised consideration of different perspectives, especially in narrative writing, that highlights both the fallacy of omniscient narration, and the voices of marginal characters (see Lucente, 1991)
4. Bricolage, that is, the placement of a text (such as writing, sound or visual art) alongside texts of other genres, movements or time periods, in order to change the meaning or value of the text (see Crimp, 1998, p. 51)
5. An embrace of the post-structuralist notion that all claims to knowledge are bound by structures of power, including those of social institutions. As such, institutions such as family, religion, science, government and even gender, are not static, but undergo fluid change (see Bauman, 1998)

For Moritz (2008, pp. 30-32), emerging churches are seen to be rooted in postmodernism, as is noticed by the following properties:

1. A recognition and rejection of modernist dichotomies such as matter/spirit, truth/value, science/religion and sacred/secular
2. A recognition that individualism and consumerism are forces of alienation in urban society and contemporary Christianity
3. A desire to retrieve and re-present ancient liturgical and devotional practices that reflect authentic community living
4. Valuing multi-media, multi-sensory communal worship
5. A disdain for systematic or academic theology

Emerging Church Bloggers and the Construction of Religious Identities

The blogosphere presents itself to the emerging church movement as a viable alternative for the sharing of religious information and communication of religious experience, away from the constraints of authority structures and social mores in traditional religious institutions and local place-based communities. It also presents itself as a vehicle for the creation of connections and formation of a communal identity for those who seek relationships beyond traditional church boundaries.

The author understands the construction of identity is, as Giddens (1991) has put it, a self-reflexive process where points of difference and similarity are mitigated within contexts of social interaction. Traditionally, local communities are provided these contexts, but increased mobility, urbanisation and use of telecommunications have given rise to what Giddens calls a "disembedding" of identity from local place (see also Lövheim, 2005; Wellman & Leighton, 1979).

So those who use blogging to make connections and discuss what it means to be religious in the emerging church context, find that constructing a religious identity involves a negotiation of two levels of tension. At the first level is the tension between their involvement in (and identification with) their local faith community offline and their personal network of connections made in the blogosphere. At the second level is the tension between their own motivations for involvement in the blogosphere and the construction of an emerging church communal identity, as is informed by prominent bloggers and other writers on the movement. How emerging bloggers in Australia deal with these tensions is the focus of this study.

EMERGING CHURCH BLOGGERS

Method

The overall goal of the following research is to determine, in the rhetoric of bloggers' posts and conversations with their audience, whether belonging to a defined and bounded online community, or participating in a fluid online network, is more important for the construction of individual religious identities.

This researcher chose to collect and analyse information from Australian blogs only, for two reasons. The first was in order to limit the sample and ensure access to bloggers for interviews. The second was that, as readers will discover, it interested the researcher to note how bloggers understood their place and voice as members of local and national institutions of religion within a global conversation.

The sites of twenty Australian bloggers were identified for the purposes of the study, found among the top results of a search on Technorati's weblog search engine after the following key phrases: 'emerging church', 'emergent church' and 'postmodern Christianity'. A further number of sites were identified through a six-month scan of comments made on the original twenty sites where links to other Australian blogs were made, and of links presented on the original twenty sites to other Australian blogs. Each of these sites mentions some connection with, or interest in talking about, the emerging church movement. Of these sites, two were authored by non-Australians who were living in Australia at the time of writing, and one was authored by an Australian living overseas. The list of blogs in the sample is in the table below.

Of the blogs identified, all may be found on any Internet search, unless they are no longer active. At the time the sample was identified and data was being collected, there were no restrictions from the general public to open and read either articles or comments posted on the sites. So for the purposes of this research, all information found on these sites is considered public documentation. The quotations used below are attributed to the author, according to their chosen and displayed username, which may not necessarily be the author's real name.[1]

Posts published to these blog sites between 1 July and 31 October 2006, and between 1 February and 31 May 2007, were collected for study. Comments made by readers of these posts and sent to the sites were also collected. Texts that expose bloggers' attitudes towards the Internet as a medium for expression and connection, and toward the emerging church movement online, are discussed here. Any spelling or grammar errors found in the original text are kept and not corrected when quoted here.

The act of conversation, in this media context, is an important sire for the exploration of identity construction. In a place where people cannot bring their physical bodies, written text is the primary mode of self-expression, above the provision of other media texts, such as sound and photography. For participants in the blogosphere, the freedom to create and share these texts is paramount for the construction of authentic identities. This section will show some posts and comments made about bloggers' attitudes to the Internet, to blogging, and about their opinions of the emerging church movement/conversation as they find it online. This section will show what values these bloggers present about the medium in which they present them, and their understanding of their place and contribution to the evolving identity of the emerging church in the blogosphere.

Posts and comments that made comment on the following topics were collected for study: attitudes toward the Internet and blogs as a vehicle for self-expression and connection with others; attitudes towards the emerging church as an appropriate label for bloggers' beliefs; attitudes towards the emerging church as a global movement. Given the number of posts and comments published during the sample period, the number of posts and conversations on these topics were surprisingly small. Therefore, a content analysis did not require any quantitative analysis. Bloggers, also surprisingly, tended not to disagree on any given issue, though they provided different perspectives, as is outlined below.

In addition, all bloggers in the sample were invited to be interviewed. 26 of all bloggers in the sample were interviewed by this researcher, either in person, where distance permitted, or over Skype or telephone. The interviews were conducted between September 2006 and May 2007. The results of the interviews are organized below according to information about their motivations for blogging, and their identification as "emerging church bloggers".

Attitudes Toward the Internet and Blogosphere

No posts or comments were found during the sample period where bloggers made a claim for the essential goodness of the Internet. Two bloggers, however, affirm the creation of an opportunity for people to share stories and make relationships outside the confines of institutional church. Making connections and developing relationships online are viewed positively by bloggers such as Cheryl and Craig, as a source of support for people who may be otherwise isolated.

i also wonder how much blogging/journalling online has become a space for people to share

Table 1. List of blogs in the study sample

Blog title	URL	Username of author(s)
[hold:: this space]	alternative.victas.uca.org.au	Cheryl
Neurotribe.net	www.neurotribe.net/blog	Stephen
A churchless faith	achurchlessfaith.blogspot.com	Chris
A foot in both places	afootinbothplaces.wordpress.com	Tim
Aropax(R) Nation	aropaxnation.blogspot.com	Dave
Backyard missionary	backyardmissionary.com	Hamo
Breathing space	breathing-space.blogspot.com	Eddie
Circle of pneuma	circleofpneuma.blogspot.com	Philjohnson
Eclectic itchings	mattstone.blogs.com	Matt
emergingBlurb	emergingblurb.blogspot.com	Garth
Exploring emerging embracing	gregtheexplorer.wordpress.com	Greg the explorer
Fernando's desk	fernandogros.com	Fernando
Jen's musings	jen-reed-candid.blogspot.com	Jen
Lionfish	underneathejetty.blogspot.com	Lionfish
Living Room >> A space for life	www.livingroom.org.au/blog	Darren Rowse
Missional diatribe	missionaldiatribe.blogspot.com	Andrew
Mountain masala	craigmitchell.typepad.com/mountain_ma-sala	Craig
No diggity	diggerrandle.com	Digger
No guarantees	noguarantees.blogspot.com	Vawz
Notyetfinished	notyetfinished.blogspot.com	Andy
Pacific highlander	pacifichighlander.postkiwi.com	Duncan
Planet telex	planettelex.bur.st	Darren
Random murmurings	random-murmurings.typepad.com/ran-dom_murmurings/	Linzc
Random thoughts by Chris	randomthoughtsbychris.blogspot.com	Chris Logan
Saintgaz strikes back	saintgazstrikesback.blogspot.com	Gaz
Signposts	signposts.org.au	Phil and Dan
SmuloSpace	johnsmulo.com	John Smulo
The forgotten ways	forgottenways.org/blog	Alan
The merry rose	themerryrose.blogspot.com	Themerryrose
The rev	reverendjohn.blogspot.com	The Rev
The X facta	xfacta.blogspot.com	Kel
TheGeoffre(y)port	geoffreport.com/wp/	Geoff
Urban stone	urbanstone.blogspot.com	Andrew Johnson
World Changers	steveaddison.net	Steve

their spiritual stories without the church, but with a number of strangers and peers and onlookers participating. (Darren. Comment to "wondering aloud". Posted 24 October 2006 in Cheryl, [hold:: this space])

While the internet is often talked about for it's 'evils' I'm constantly discovering it to be a 'sacred space' where people explore what it means to find life. (Darren Rowse. "Thinking about 'Ministry'." Living room. Posted 17 July 2006.)

One of the things that crossed my mind in a conversation about it this morning is that it might work if we go the monastic community line - a commitment to a rhythm of life, where the virtual community sustains us to live differently in our own contexts. (Cheryl. "virtual church." [hold:: this space]. Posted 24 October 2006.)

Yeah this really interests me. both personally and as I watch [my] twins online life and wonder about how much the church relies on face to face. I've always wanted to do some regular live online chat stuff as part of that too. and i like to think of people in diverse locations with some common symbols as well. (Craig. Comment to "virtual church". Posted 30 October 2006 in Cheryl, [hold:: this space].)

Others acknowledge that the blogosphere has negative potentials. Philjohnson, for example, laments the narcissistic attitude to which people approach online social media technologies. Matt and Fernando criticise those bloggers for whom counting visitors is a primary goal, to say that his objective is to connect with people.

There is much worthless material loaded onto websites and blogspots that undermines the intellectual and cultural value that ought to be manifested through this technology. So what we end up with is web-content produced by people with pretensions of "stardom" who want to be noticed, yearn for widespread recognition, and hope to experience the "glamour" of being well-regarded. (Philjonson. "Blog Hype and Digital Narcissism." Circle of pneuma. Posted 9 April 2007.)

[...] people are asking questions about the nature of "influence." I have a great comment on my blog about that. Part of what is wrong with the EC ghetto of the blogosphere is the way it is entrall to its A-list celebrities. [...] FWIW, the biggest slice of my blog's traffic comes from people who neither have blogs, nor have a predeliction to comment on them. They are people I have actually met in the real world who are engaged in ministry and teaching. That "influence" matters far more to me than a technorati ranking. (Fernando. Comment to "50 Most Influential Blogs". Posted 21 July 2006 in Matt, Eclectic itchings.)

It truely is the deep engagements that count. I prefer one good face to face conversation to a dozen blog hits. [...] And I get far more gratification out of interacting with people in comments and private emails than watching my tracker. (Matt. Comment to "50 Most Influential Blogs". Posted 21 July 2006 in Matt, Eclectic itchings.)

For Digger, blogging fulfils both personal and professional needs, regardless of any connections that may be made with readers.

Often for me I think [blogging is] about trying to help me sift through stuff that's going on in my head, but sometimes it is purely because something interests/excites/angers me and so I want to let others know.

Was also interesting thinking about the stage I went through with my blogging where I really cared how many people read my blog, and would fully just make up posts so that my readership wouldn't go down. Nowadays I couldn't really be bothered. (Digger. "Writing for readers." No diggity. Posted 17 April 2007.)

Attitudes Toward the Emerging Church

Most bloggers in the sample acknowledge a global conversation is occurring about the role of the church in postmodern society, and label this conversation either "emerging church" or "missional church". Yet bloggers show their reticence to allow these people and organisations to speak for them. Bloggers are reluctant to identify themselves as belonging to the "emerging church movement" that the above identities point to or represent.

Bloggers such as Hamo agree with some public criticisms made against the emerging church movement, calling attention to the notion that not everyone in the conversation holds exactly the same theological position, and that a few published authors do not represent everyone involved.

[...] for those who feel the need to continue writing their critiques let me offer some guidelines: [...] ***Please don't tell me what I believe!.*** *You don't know me. You probably don't know 99% of people in EC's so please don't assume you know what we believe. I am constantly amazed at some of the stuff I am apparently signed on to! I am unashamedly conservative theologically, but I am willing to ask questions and I am open to other people's questions. I think this is called 'learning'. [...] (Hamo. "Guidelines for Critiquing the Emerging Church." Backyard missionary. Posted 20 July 2006.)*

Matt writes that organisations (like "Emergent" and "Forge") that exist in Australia have no right to speak for the emerging church movement, but only participate in the conversation along with everyone else.

Actually, I should add that Fuzz Kitto is the sole official representative of Emergent in Australia. Thus 99.9% of the Emerging Church down under has no direct association with Emergent. This gives you an idea of just how off base Carson's critique is for us when he casually equates the two. (Matt. Comment to "The Amusement Index". Posted 23 July 2006 in Matt, Eclectic itchings.)

Given the label "conversation" that is applied, and given that is seen as a postmodern critique of institutional religion, painting everyone by the same brush seems absurd to bloggers such as Garth and Gaz. Moreover, bloggers such as Philjohnson and Hamo find it uneasy to accept the label "emerging church" applied to them or their blog sites, given their own personal critiques of some of its incarnations.

It's not often I talk about the emerging church but here's a definition that I find interesting. [...] "The emergent church is a "flock of singularities," meaning that it's like a bunch of different birds that all fly together in some kind of loose formation." (Gaz. "Emerging Definitions." Saintgaz strikes back. Posted 28 August 2006.)

I think 'branding' is such a pre-supposed notion.... you must have a name, you must be in a box, you must be definable. Surely a definable postmodern church movement is an oxymoron....comparison are fine, but labels tend to become inaccurate for what has burgeoned as a diverse church that has broken itself "out of the box". I'm sure my emergent notions are fleshed out in very different ways to other EC churches...and that should be a good thing as we continue to "be all things to all men" rather than just a liberal or conservative branch of the same faith. (Garth. Comment to "Guidelines for Critiquing the Emerging Church". Posted 24 July 2006 in Hamo, backyard missionary.)

I am sooo very tired of reading many inaccurate critiques of this beast that is labelled 'the emerging church'. And while it's a tag that I don't much care for (because of the associated vagaries) it is also a label that I find myself sitting under for better or worse. (Hamo. "Guidelines for Critiquing the Emerging Church." Backyard missionary. Posted 20 July 2006.)

As for myself, I really do not identify with the "emerging" tags. Quite apart from the raging arguments over what the term means and signifies, I am not pioneering a congregational experiment. [...]

Circle of Pneuma [...] is not speaking from within any specific network, tribe, or experiment that is self-consciously part of EC. (Philjohnson. "Emerging/Missional Bloggers." Circle of pneuma. Posted 28 March 2007.)

It is read in these posts and comments that bloggers approach the Internet as a space for the sharing of stories, experiences and opinions about religion beyond the confines of church. The Internet is either another "sacred place" or an opportunity to address the sacred/secular dichotomy made in modern Christian culture. Bloggers are not too naïve to appreciate that the blogosphere is not an egalitarian space. Some are wary of users' campaigns for popularity and influence within the blogosphere. These bloggers carry the "emerging" or "missional" label with some trepidation, or refuse to carry them at all. They are aware that perceptions of the movement or conversation is less diverse than the reality, and strive to let this be known.

It may be said, then, that these bloggers are more comfortable being at the edge of the emerging church conversation than at the centre of it. As they grow to understand the blogosphere as a network of nodes, they identify their sites as places where the emerging church identity is challenged and negotiated rather than reinforced in any way. They tend to see themselves as "partly in and partly out" of the circle, or reject that there is such a circle at all. There is no desire to reach all people in the emerging church online debate, but create spaces for particular conversations within a network of discussions and relationships.

Motivations for Blogging

Reasons for blogging are varied. Motivations range from developing a personal writing/journaling practice, through maintaining connections with others they've met offline, extending their social and professional networks, and contributing to online conversations in the wider blogosphere, right to creating online communities.

For six of them, blogging is either an opportunity to practise writing, or create a journal of thoughts. However for these interviewees the idea of writing for other people, to transform diary entries into discussions with others, is a key attraction to blogging over other media.

The original purpose was just to write. And I think the biggest purpose is I think to theologically reflect on, not just theology, but as theology applies to everyday life. I had a recent post on violence and how are we supposed to handle violence as Christians and deal other people's violence. It started as a discussion between me and a friend who said that he doesn't think that violence is ever acceptable and I said "I don't know about that" so I posted my thoughts and started this discussion between various people, which was interesting. (anonymous interviewee)

Conversations with others are the main purpose of blogging for the majority of interviewees. In particular, maintaining connections with people that interviewees have met in other settings motivates them to keep blogging.

I fell into blogging. [A friend] had been blogging for a while and kept encouraging me to read his stuff. [..] So I went on and had a look at his and then I realised that another friend of mine who was writing who had a link from [a friend's] site so I had a look at his and when I went to make a comment on his I had to log on, and so then I had to become a member to log on so I kind of created my own blog. And it was good procrastination from my exams at the time. [...] And then I was encouraged by people once I was blogging to keep dong it so I lasted for two months. And then after having a public kick up the pants from some [friends...] I've restarted blogging. (anonymous interviewee)

Eight interviewees identify that blogging forms part of their professional practice, and see blogging as an extension of their community and workplace. Yet these bloggers recognise that blogging offers the freedom and risk to portray a personal identity that may conflict with the expectations of others as professionals in religious settings.

The website would be seen as a very important part of my work. [...] I wanted to have an Internet presence. Resources and stuff for people to download, and to tell the story of the project. And I knew I want to have some form of archiving [...] and blogging seemed the logical way to do that, both in terms of [...] ease, the ability to post things each day, [...]. But also in a more accurate way of telling the story, instead of a month-by-month report. This way is more raw, I think, and I liked that. (anonymous interviewee)

Now that I've taken up a position [...] as "emerging generations" pastor [...] That then has prompted me to move my blog into a more public forum. Before then it was just friends and people I knew, but now I've given it more publicity. It's on my business card [...] It's been quite interesting now I'm working with people locally like other pastors. They turn up and they've read my blog. It's interesting that they've read all this stuff before they even meet me. I don't know if that's a positive or a negative yet. (anonymous interviewee)

I want to blog my experience of what's happening in the church to try and keep it distant from the views of the church, because they're my views and I don't want it to turn a pastor's blog which just reinforces the message of the week. I still want to keep it pushing boundaries of thinking church and faith and things like that. (anonymous interviewee)

I think for my personality something of that risk appeals to me. Pushing the envelope a little bit and having people respond in ways that are not always in agreeance with what I'm saying. I like that. Not always, at the same time I tend to avoid conflict so I... But I do like that edgy, pushing-the-envelope and stretching people and being stretched myself. When people disagree with me I think that's good for me, as long as they keep it nice. (anonymous interviewee)

For nine interviewees, the desire to contribute to conversations they have encountered online has motivated them to start a blog.

Creating dialogue with those who primarily see themselves as being within the broad umbrella of emerging church experiments and particularly to provide commentary on issues related to the rhetoric and slogans of missions that circulate in emerging church circles. [...] but especially with the recognition of the religious plurality especially new religions and alternate forms of spirituality which I have been engaged with since the late 1970s. [...] The concern that I have is that most of it is being ignored by those who consider themselves to be missional, and in my opinion, if they are genuinely being missional, it's going to be very difficult to avoid encountering these forms of spirituality among non-Christians. (anonymous interviewee)

Five bloggers believe their blogs to be online communities and/or discussion groups. For three of them, their blogs function as alternative religious communities, connected with the offline communities in which they work as pastors. For one, it is a forum for non-Christians to be engaged in the emerging church/missional conversation. For another, it is a community of people who have gathered to respond to the (offline) published works of the blogger.

I've actually been intentional in trying to actually engage people from other religious movements on my blog. [...] Possibly a third of the people are non-Christian. [...] There's quite a few agnostics as well. But I also get the occasional pagan, I've had a lesbian Buddhist. I have all sorts of interesting characters at different times. I quite deliberately target people from other religions. (anonymous interviewee)

The blogging thing was for [...] the reader to engage me in things I've written about, because I always think if someone's taken the time to read such a complex book I owe them some sort of responsibility. [...] Having read it, you can engage with others, having a discussion or a dialogue. And I generally let the discussions go along. I make comments along the way, but mostly I just let them roll. I'm interested in watching [discussions] evolve and unfold. [...] Honouring the audience, giving them access to the author, and to give back. (anonymous interviewee)

Nine interviewees state that being able to connect with people through their blog is vitally important for their own spiritual growth, as shown in the first example below. Yet for three of these, meeting someone online does not equate to "knowing" a person as much as an offline encounter. Two examples are given below.

Blogs helped me detox from church. I've connected with many other bloggers, many of whom are not Christians. [...] What I read on their blogs have had some impact on what thought processes are going on for me, and I'll bring that to my blog. (anonymous interviewee)

I wouldn't survive in a local church without connections like this. Talking with [other bloggers named] every other night sort of helps you survive [...] it's one thing being marginalised, it's another thing to be able to talk about it over the net. (anonymous interviewee)

It's a bit like an idiot-savant relationship. Through the blogs you know a lot about the person in a really narrow field. And it's not until you meet the person the relationship deepens, so I think people who have actually met having blogs, it's a different sort of community then. [...] It provides new opportunities but at the end of the day it's still not the same level of community. But it helps us keep in touch. (anonymous interviewee)

When asked by the interviewer about the blogs that they enjoy reading, all but one mentioned blogs outside the sample. Three did not mention any blogs within the sample. Of the twenty-six, twelve explained that they read blogs that focus on conversations that would be considered only a small sub-section of the varied conversations that appear in the emerging church blogosphere. Two claimed their interest in Christian approaches to dialogue with other faiths. Six said their interest lies in alternative worship practices and alternative "theologies of worship". One mentioned that his interest lies in church planting initiatives. The rest were interested in urban mission strategies and alternative theological methods. Of these 12, nine told the researcher they closely followed overseas blogs, from the UK and USA, and often conversed with them on each other's sites. Five of these twelve reported having met them face-to-face and used the blogs to maintain friendships and the flow of resources and information. Of the entire group of interviewees, five reported keeping in close contact through the blogs with member of the organisation, Forge, and that the blogosphere helped them stay in touch in between conferences and meetings.

Also, of the twenty-six, eight also mentioned the importance of small friendship groups that interact through the blogs. These friendships are with members of the same state, if not the same city. For these eight interviewees, local connections have given them a sense of belonging in the blogosphere.

Identification as "Emerging Church Blogger"

Given the number of references to, opinions on, and discussions about the emerging church, among all blogs in the sample, it surprised the researcher to find that only one out of all interviewees referred to himself as an emerging church blogger. While most exhibited some level of tolerance at the idea that others viewed them as emerging church bloggers, one refused the label outright.

I am not an emerging church blogger. I blog about the emerging church. (anonymous interviewee)

Indeed, fourteen interviewees shared their critique of the emerging church movement, as they saw it, both in and out of the blogosphere. These critiques ranged from bloggers' failure to engage in offline relationships to its focus on critiques of traditional theology, as is seen in these three examples.

It's a conversation that I think is only useful if it's grounded at some point. I think there's way too much abstract theology in a whole lot of these blogs. That's nice, but it needs to be grounded at some point. My site is focussed on my particular reality. (anonymous interviewee)

Emerging church could encompass a lot of doctrine that could question the unquestionable. [...] I remember reading a critique made by the established church about the American emerging church questioning the virgin birth. I thought "Hey I agree with the established church on this one". [...] but when things take on a meaning that they were never intended to have. That's what I see the emerging church questioning. (anonymous interviewee)

Given the high level of Internet access available to them, connections made or maintained online are significant in their religious life, and conversations held in blogs help make sense of offline religious experiences and relationships. Yet more important is involvement in offline settings. Many criticise emerging church conversations that are not grounded in local community and mission. Many believe that online connections do not equate to "knowing" a person until there is an offline encounter. The identity project of the emerging church blogger is not cultivated solely online, but found in the flow between online and offline environments, and in the negotiation of their meaning and significance in relation to each other.

Though content enough to be considered as one "emerging church blogger" among others, it appears the most significant online networks for some are topic-based, or based on encounters made offline. These connections may be considered a small sub-section of the entire emerging church blogosphere, and not necessarily Australian. So while accepting that they are participating in the emerging church blogosphere, their perception is that the blogosphere is a network on which they reside in a small pocket on the edge. By no means, for these interviewees, is the blogosphere a group of people where everyone knows everyone else. If there is indeed an inner circle of emerging church bloggers, they are not interested in being there.

FINDINGS

How bloggers conduct themselves online, how they construct their online religious identities, is significantly informed by the values they attribute to the Internet. These bloggers are not interested in making more Christians, or even persuade current

Christians to join the emerging church movement. As self-professed outsiders in the traditional churches they have lived and worked in, they are looking for like-minded people who will help them grow in faith. Rather than "looking for the lost", cyberspace is a place where they themselves can be "saved", or at least find something meaningful on the margins of traditional church culture.

The information shows that bloggers enter Cyberspace with both a sense of awe and a sense of purpose. With reverence to the vastness that is the world they have yet to discover and thanks for every new encounter with it, emerging church bloggers accept that what they know about God, the world and their place in it is "byte"-sized compared to the terabytes of knowledge awaiting their discovery. They embrace that their grasp of the world is only a small construction, fragile to erosion and transformation by the flow of information. For these bloggers, truth is a concept that is still seeking grounding, and cannot be pinned down by doctrine or institutional authority. If truth is a mountain, then the Internet will show you an infinite number of paths to its peak, and will present them all as equally valid, depending on where you're coming from.

These emerging church bloggers enter the blogosphere with a view to meet the "other" with a willingness to let that encounter change their worldview, even if only a little. Denominational ties only highlight how "static" modern religious identity is. Emerging church bloggers choose fluidity over stasis, and being on the margins of religion rather than building a new centre for it.

This even makes the term "emerging church blogger" a problem they must negotiate in forming their online presence. Emerging church bloggers refuse any definition of what the emerging church is. It is at once a movement and a reaction to the movement, a conversation and a practice, a community and a collection of unconnected global diasporas, a new form of organised religion, a rejection thereof, a reclamation of ancient religion, and a redefinition of the word "religion". One message comes through: as the emerging church seeks to define itself it ceases to be emerging; it joins the fray of traditions vying for relevance in a world where Christianity is regarded as generally irrelevant. So bloggers maintain a marginal identity, open to challenge and doubt, and actively valuing the beauty of being fledgling and uncertain.

Bloggers are intent on creating bonds with readers and other bloggers involved in the emerging church conversation. At the same time they are reluctant to carry the label "emerging church", choosing instead to be seen as somewhere on the margins of the network.

FUTURE THINKING ABOUT RELIGION ONLINE

The Australian emerging church blogosphere represents an ongoing change across the religious landscape of late modern society. As "me-centred networks" rise, and denominationalism gives way to the polarisation of conservative and progressive voices in the public sphere, the power of denominations to frame one's religious identity is waning. Instead, involvement in religious movements, or conversations, that connect people to networks of ideas and people, will have a greater role in the way people talk about their connection to religion. The Internet cannot claim to have started this phenomenon, but can be said to contribute to it. This case study of Australian emerging church bloggers supports the following claims, which the researcher proposes as new contributions to the field of research into online religion.

The project of identity construction for those who seek religion online is not just found in their residence in Cyberspace, but in the journeys to and from all spaces both offline and online. Thus communications and relationships in Cyberspace should not be studied in isolation.

The diminishing power of religious institutions to speak for religious people, and therefore to be points of reference for religious identity, gives way to the rise in such power of networks, both online and offline. Public religion in late modernity is marked by the fall of denominational Christianity. These institutions are becoming, among others, mere nodes in the networks of interactions that individuals use to construct their own religious identity.

The Internet does not shape how people construct religious identities as much anymore as the other way around. People express their identities by the way they shape the Internet. Those interested in researching religion online should look to the Internet not just as a haven of peculiar religious practices, or as a meeting point for discrete online communities, but as a changing and evolving social setting for the ongoing debate and dialogue on the place religion in all aspects of life, both online and offline.

CONCLUSION

This chapter has endeavoured to contribute to the ongoing research into Internet use, networked individualism, and changing patterns of sociability in late modern society, by offering a discussion from the perspective of religion online. Emerging church bloggers in Australia represent a postmodern turn in the place of religion in the public sphere, in their endeavour to create spaces for the discernment of a religious identity that challenges modern dichotomies of sacred and secular, conservative and progressive. In doing so they negotiate the construction of an online communal identity known as the "emerging church movement" with their participation and involvement in local and offline religious groups.

Thus these bloggers also show how the interplay between Internet use and networked individualism influences one's quest for belonging and purpose in a spiritual sense. In the late modern world of "me-centred networks", religious identity is formed by being "on the margins" of local communities. The case study shows that the creation of fluid, decentred and global networks plays an important role in the development of religious identity, that helps identify the inadequacies of local faith communities to foster and sustain faith identities alone, and highlights that communities constructed online face the same issues. Religious identity, therefore, is formed, supported and sustained in the flow between these groups, rather than in the groups alone.

REFERENCES

Barker, E. (2005). Crossing the boundary: New challenges to religious authority and control as a consequence of access to the Internet. In Højsgaard, M. T., & Warburg, M. (Eds.), *Religion and cyberspace* (pp. 67–85). London, UK: Routledge.

Bauman, Z. (1998). Postmodern religion. In Heelas, P., & Martin, D. (Eds.), *Religion, modernity and postmodernity* (pp. 55–78). Oxford, UK: Blackwell.

Beer, D., & Burrows, R. (2007). Sociology and, of and in Web 2.0: Some initial considerations. *Sociological Research Online*, *12*(5). Retrieved from http://www.socresonline.org.uk/12/5/17.html.

Bellamy, J., & Castle, K. (2004). *NCLS occasional paper 3: 2001 Church attendance estimates*. Sydney, Australia: NCLS.

Blood, R. (2004). How blogging software reshapes the online community. *Communications of the ACM*, *47*(12), 53–55.

Bortree, D. S. (2005). Presentation of self on the web: An ethnographic study of teenage girls' weblogs. *Education Communication and Information*, *5*(1), 25–39.

boyd, d. m., & Ellison, N. B. (2007). Social networking sites: Definition, history, and scholarship. *Journal of Computer-Mediated Communication*. 13, 210-230.

Brasher, B. (1996). Thoughts on the status of the cyborg: On technological socialization and its link to the religious function of popular culture. *Journal of the American Academy of Religion. American Academy of Religion*, *64*(4), 809–830.

Campbell, H. (2005). *Exploring religious community online: We are one in the network*. New York, NY: Peter Lang.

Campbell, H. (2007). Who's got the power? Religious authority and the Internet. *Journal of Computer-Mediated Communication*, *12*(3).

Casanova, J. (1994). *Public religions in the modern world*. Chicago, IL: University of Chicago Press.

Castells, M. (1996). The rise of the network society: *Vol. 1. The Information Age: Economy, society and culture*. Malden, MA: Blackwell.

Castells, M. (2001). *The Internet galaxy: Reflections on the Internet, business and society*. New York, NY: Oxford University Press.

Cheong, P. H., Halavais, A., & Kwon, K. (2008). The chronicles of me: Understanding blogging as a religious practice. *Journal of Media and Religion*, *7*(3), 107–131.

Crimp, D. (1998). On the museum's ruins. In Foster, H. (Ed.), *The anti-aesthetic: Essays on postmodern culture* (pp. 49–64). New York, NY: The New Press.

Dawson, L. L. (2005). The mediation of religious experience in cyberspace. In Højsgaard, M. T., & Warburg, M. (Eds.), *Religion and cyberspace* (pp. 15–37). London, UK: Routledge.

Driscoll, M. (2006). A pastoral perspective on the emergent church. *Criswell Theological Review*, *3*(2), 87–93.

Efimova, L., & de Moor, A. (2005). *Beyond personal web publishing: An exploratory study of conversational blogging practices*. Paper presented at The 38th Annual Hawaii International Conference System Sciences.

Finke, R., & Stark, R. (2005). *The churching of America, 1776-2005: Winners and losers in our religious economy*. New Jersey: Rutgers University Press.

Giddens, A. (1991). *Modernity and self-identity: Self and society in the late modern age*. San Francisco, CA: Stanford University Press.

Helland, C. (2002). Surfing for salvation. *Religion*, *32*(4), 293–302.

Helland, C. (2005). Online religion as lived religion. In O Krüger (Ed.), *Online - Heidelberg Journal of Religions on the Internet. 01.1 Special Issue on Theory and Methodology.* Retrieved 6 December, 2006, from http://online.uni-hd.de/

Hine, C. (2000). *Virtual ethnography*. London, UK: Sage.

Højsgaard, M. T., & Warburg, M. (2005). *Religion and cyberspace*. London, UK: Routledge.

Hoover, S. M., & Clark, L. S. (2004). *Faith online*. Pew Internet & American Life Project.

Hughey, M. W. (1979). The idea of secularization in the works of Max Weber: A theoretical outline. *Qualitative Sociology*, *2*(1), 85–111.

Hunt, S. (2008). The emerging church and its discontents. *Journal of Beliefs & Values*, *29*(3), 287–296.

Junghee, L., & Hyunjoo, L. (2010). The computer-mediated communication network: Exploring the linkage between the online community and social capital. *New Media & Society*, *12*, 711–727.

Karaflogka, A. (2002). Religious discourse and cyberspace. *Religion*, *32*(4), 279–291.

Kumar, R., Novak, J., Raghavan, P., & Tomkins, A. (2004). Structure and evolution of blogspace. *Communications of the ACM*, *47*(12), 39.

Lövheim, M. (2004). Young people, religious identity, and the internet. In Dawson, L. L., & Cowan, D. E. (Eds.), *Religion online: Finding faith on the Internet* (pp. 59–73). New York, NY: Routledge.

Lövheim, M. (2008). *Finding and sharing religion online? Some new questions and challenges*. Presented at Association of Internet Researchers 9.0, Copenhagen.

Lövheim, M., & Linderman, A. (2005). Constructing religious identity on the Internet. In Højsgaard, M. T., & Warburg, M. (Eds.), *Religion and cyberspace* (pp. 121–137). London, UK: Routledge.

Lucente, G. (1991). Modernism and postmodernism in Italian literature and philosophy. *Annali di Italianistica*, 9.

Matzat, U. (2004). Cooperation and community on the Internet: Past issues and present perspectives for theoretical-empirical Internet research. *Analyse & Kritik*, *26*(1), 63–90.

Moritz, J. M. (2008). Beyond strategy, towards the kingdom of God: The post-critical reconstructionist mission of the emerging church. *Dialog: A Journal of Theology*, *47*(1), 27-36.

O'Leary, S. (2005). Utopian and dystopian possibilities of networked religion in the new millennium. In Højsgaard, M. T., & Warburg, M. (Eds.), *Religion and cyberspace* (pp. 38–49). London, UK: Routledge.

Rheingold, H. (1995). *The virtual community: Finding connection in a computerized world*. London, UK: Minerva.

Sifry, D. (2006). State of the blogosphere, October, 2006. *Technorati weblog*. Retrieved 19 November 2006, from http://technorati.com/weblog/2006/11/161.html

Sterland, S., Powell, R., & Castle, K. (2006). *NCLS occasional paper 8: Inflow and outflow between denominations: 1991 to 2001*. Sydney, Australia: NCLS.

Streett, R. A. (2006). An interview with Brian McLaren. *Criswell Theological Review*, *3*(2), 5–14.

Technorati. (2008). *Technorati: About us*. Retrieved 6 May 2008, from http://technorati.com/about/

Technorati. (2010). *The state of the blogosphere 2010*. Retrieved 16 March 2011, from http://technorati.com/blogging/article/state-of-the-blogosphere-2010-introduction/

Thomas, S. (2006). The end of cyberspace and other surprises. *Convergence: The International Journal of Research into New Media Technologies*, *12*(4), 383–391.

Turner, B. S. (2008). Religious speech: The ineffable nature of religious communication in the information age. *Theory, Culture & Society*, *25*(7-8), 219–235.

Wellman, B. (2004). Three stages of internet studies: Ten, five and zero years ago. *New Media & Society*, *6*(1), 123–129.

Wellman, B., Haase, A. Q., Witte, J., & Hampton, K. (2001). Does the Internet increase, decrease, or supplement social capital? Social networks, participation, and community commitment. *The American Behavioral Scientist*, *45*, 436–455.

Wellman, B., & Leighton, B. (1979). Networks, neighborhoods, and communities: Approaches to the study of the community question. *Urban Affairs Review*, *14*, 363–390.

ADDITIONAL READING

Brasher, B. (2001). *Give Me That Online Religion*. San Francisco: Jossey-Bass.

Breward, I. (1988). *Australia: The Most Godless Place Under Heaven?*Melbourne: Lutheran Publishing House.

Bruce, S. (1996). *Religion in the Modern World: From Cathedrals to Cults*. Cambridge: Oxford University Press.

Campbell, H. (2005). *Exploring Religious Community Online: We are One in the Network*. New York: Peter Lang.

Clark, L. S. (2002). Religion on the Internet: Research Prospects and Promises. *Sociology of Religion*, *63*(4), 540.

Cohen, K. (2006). A Welcome for Blogs. *Continuum: Journal of Media & Cultural Studies*, *20*(2), 161–173.

Davis, E. (1998). *TechGnosis: Myth, Magic, and Mysticism in the Age of Information*. New York: Harmony.

Hadden, J. K., & Cowan, D. E. (Eds.). (2000). *Religion on the Internet: Research Prospects and Promises*. New York: Elsevier Science.

Højsgaard, M. T., & Warburg, M. (2005). *Religion and Cyberspace*. London: Routledge.

Hoover, S., & Clark, L. (2002). *Practicing Religion in the Age of the Media*. Columbia University Press.

Meyer, B., & Moors, A. (Eds.). (2006). *Religion, Media, And the Public Sphere*. Indianapolis: Indiana University Press.

Mitchell, J., & Marriage, S. (Eds.). (2003). *Mediating Religion: Conversations in Media, Religion and Culture*. London: T&T Clark.

Silverstone, R. (2007). *Media and morality: On the rise of the mediapolis*. Cambridge: Polity.

Smith, M., Kollock, P., Smith, M., & Kollock, P. (1998). *Communities in Cyberspace*. Routledge.

Tanner, K. (1997). *Theories of Culture: A New Agendafor Theology*. Minneapolis: Fortress Press.

KEY TERMS AND DEFINITIONS

Blog: A diminution of the term web log, referring to a web page composed of small entries, arranged in reverse chronological order, that may contain reader comments.

Blogger: A blog's author or creator.

Blogosphere: A collective term for all blog sites in the Internet.

Doctrine: One, or a set of, established beliefs or principles endorsed by a religious group or institution.

Emerging Church (or Emergent Church): A term applied to a conversation or movement for reformation within Christianity, supporting postmodernist deconstructions of contemporary theology, small local communities, and the use of modern technologies in communication. Emerging church manifests mainly in Protestant denominations in English-speaking countries.

Postmodernism: A movement found in literature, the arts, and popular culture, that challenges or rejects the principles of modernism.

Religious Identity: The communication of an individual's or group's religious, beliefs, values and attitudes, usually by way of connection or belonging to a religious group, institution or movement.

Secularisation: The process disempowerment of religious institutions in the public sphere, or the removal of religion from national identity, or the relegation of religious discourses away from the public sphere.

ENDNOTE

1 This policy was informed by the Association of Internet Researchers' report, *Ethical decision-making and Internet research*, 2002 (Retrieved 2006 from http://www.aoir.org/reports/ethics.pdf). The report acknowledges that blog material may be considered public as long as its authors consider it to be so (i.e. do not limit access tomaterial by way of usernames and passwords) and recommends samples be adults and be made aware of research being undertaken (p.5). All authors in the sample were made aware of the research and were invited to participate therein by way of interview.

Compilation of References

Abercrombie, N., & Longhurst, B. (1998). *Audiences: A sociological theory of performance and imagination*. London, UK: Sage.

Acquisti, A., & Gross, R. (2006). Imagined communities: Awareness, information sharing, and privacy on the Facebook. In P. Golle & G. Danezis (Eds.), *Proceedings of6th Workshop on Privacy Enhancing Technologies*. (pp. 36-58).Cambridge, UK: Robinson College.

Acquisti, A., & Gross, R. (2005). Information revelation and privacy in online social networks (The Facebook case). *Proceedings of the 2005 ACM Workshop on Privacy in the Electronic Society*, (pp. 71–80). Retrieved from http://www.heinz.cmu.edu/~acquisti/papers/privacy-facebook-gross-acquisti.pdf

Adler, B. T., & de Alfaro, L. (2007). A content-driven reputation system for the Wikipedia. In *Proceedings of the 16th International Conference on World Wide Web - WWW '07* (p. 261). doi:10.1145/1242572.1242608

Ahn, Y.-Y., Han, S., Kwak, H., Moon, S. B., & Jeong, H. (2007). Analysis of topological characteristics of huge online social networking services. *Proceedings of the 16th International Conference on World Wide Web (WWW* '07), Banff, Alberta, Canada.

Albrecht, S. (2003). Whose voice is heard in online deliberation? A study of participation and representation in political debates on the Internet. *Information Communication and Society*, *9*, 62–82. doi:10.1080/13691180500519548

Albrechtslund, A. (2008). Online social networking as participatory surveillance. *First Monday*, *13*(3).

Albrechtsund, A. (2008). Online social networking as participatory surveillance. *First Monday*, *13*(3). Retrieved from http://firstmonday.org/htbin/cgiwrap/bin/ojs/index.php/fm/article/view/2142/1949.

Altman, I., & Taylor, D. (1973). *Social penetration: The development of interpersonal relationships*. New York, NY: Holt, Rinehart, & Winston.

Ambady, N., & Skowronski, J. (Eds.). (2008). *First impressions*. New York, NY: Guilford.

American Red Cross. (2010). *The case for integrating crisis response with social media*. Retrieved February 25, 2011, from http://www.scribd.com/doc/35737608/White-Paper-The-Case-for-Integrating-Crisis-Response-With-Social-Media

Amichai-Hamburger, Y., & Vinitzky, G. (2010). Social network use and personality. *Computers in Human Behavior*, *26*, 1289–1295. doi:10.1016/j.chb.2010.03.018

Amichai-Hamburger, Y., & Ben Artzi, E. (2003). Loneliness and Internet use. *Computers in Human Behavior*, *19*, 71–80. doi:10.1016/S0747-5632(02)00014-6

Amit, V. (2007). Globalization through weak ties: A study of transnational networks among mobile professionals. In Amit, V. (Ed.), *Going first class* (pp. 53–71). Oxford, UK: Berghahn.

Ancu, M., & Cozma, R. (2009). MySpace politics: Use and gratifications of befriending candidates. *Journal of Broadcasting & Electronic Media*, *53*, 567–583. doi:10.1080/08838150903333064

Anderson, E. (2004). The cosmopolitan canopy. *The Annals of the American Academy of Political and Social Science, 595*(1), 14–31. doi:10.1177/0002716204266833

Andò, R. (2010). (forthcoming). *Fonti informative a contenuto e tecnologie di rilevazione delle opinioni*. Tv ++ Project, Roma, Italy. *Fondazione Ugo Bordoni*.

Andò, R., & Marinelli, A. (2010). Fare ricerca sul fandom on line. Fan italiani e serie televisive. In Monaci, S., & Scifo, B. (Eds.), *Sociologia 2.0 Pratiche sociali e metodologie di ricerca sui media partecipativi* (pp. 189–221). Napoli, Italy: Scriptaweb.

Andrejevic, M. (2005). The work of watching one another: Lateral surveillance, risk, and governance. *Surveillance & Society, 2*(4), 479–497. Retrieved from http://www.surveillance-and-society.org/articles2(4)/lateral.pdf.

Ang, I. (1991). *Desperately seeking the audience*. London, UK: Routledge. doi:10.4324/9780203321454

Aquilani, B., & Lovari, A. (2009, August). *Social networks and university communication: Is Facebook a new opportunity? An Italian exploratory study*. Paper presented at the 12th International QMOD and Toulon-Verona Conference on Quality and Service Sciences (ICQSS), Verona, Italy.

Aquisti, A., & Gross, R. (2006). Imagined communities: Awareness, information sharing, and privacy on the Facebook. In G. Danezis & P. Golle (Eds.), *Privacy enhancing technologies, 4258*, 36-58.

Arazy, O., & Nov, O. (2010). Determinants of Wikipedia quality: The roles of global and local contribution inequality. In *Proceedings of the 2010 ACM Conference on Computer Supported Cooperative Work*, (pp. 233–236).

Arendt, H. (1958). *The human condition*. Chicago, IL: University of Chicago Press.

Arnett, J. J. (2000). Emerging adulthood: A theory of development from the late teens through the twenties. *The American Psychologist, 55*, 469–480. doi:10.1037/0003-066X.55.5.469

Article 29 Data Protection Working Party. (2009). *Opinion 5/2009 on online social networking*. Retrieved from http://ec.europa.eu/justice/policies/privacy/docs/wpdocs/2009/wp163_en.pdf

Askwith, I. D. (2007). *Television 2.0: Reconceptualizing TV as an engagement medium* [Thesis]. BA Individualized Study (Technology, Media & Culture) Gallatin School of Individualized Study, New York University, Master of Science in Comparative Media Studies, Massachusetts Institute of Technology.

Atkin, C. K. (1985). Informational utility and selective exposure to entertainment media. In Zillmann, D., & Bryant, J. (Eds.), *Selective exposure to communication* (pp. 63–92). Hillsdale, NJ: Lawrence Erlbaum.

Atkinson, R., & Willis, P. (2007). Charting the Ludodrome: The mediation of urban and simulated space and rise of the flâneur electronique. *Information Communication and Society, 10*(6), 818–845. doi:10.1080/13691180701751007

Atre, J., & Katz, E. (2005, May). *What's killing television news? Experimentally assessing the effects of multiple channels on media choice*. Paper presented at the International Communication Association Conference, New York, NY.

Back, M., Stopfer, J., Vazire, S., Gaddis, S., Schmukle, S., & Egloff, B. (2010). Facebook profiles reflect actual personality, not self-idealization. *Psychological Science, 21*(3), 372–374. doi:10.1177/0956797609360756

Bacon Smith, C. (1992). *Enterprising women. Television fandom and the creation of popular myth*. Philadelphia: University of Pennsylvania Press.

Bai, X. (2010). Predicting consumer sentiments from online text. [Elsevier BV.]. *Decision Support Systems, 50*(4), 732–742. doi:10.1016/j.dss.2010.08.024

Bakardjieva, M. (2005). *Internet society: The Internet in everyday life*. London, UK: Sage.

Baker, J., & Moore, S. (2008). Distress, coping, and blogging: Comparing new MySpace users by their intention to blog. *Cyberpsychology & Behavior, 11*(1), 81–85. doi:10.1089/cpb.2007.9930

Bales, R. F. (1950). A set of categories for the analysis of small group interaction. *American Sociological Review, 15*(2), 257–263. doi:10.2307/2086790

Bales, R. F. (1965). Small group theory and research. In Merton, R., Broom, L., & Cottrell, L. (Eds.), *Sociology today*. New York, NY: Harper Torchbooks.

Bales, R. F. (1955). The equilibrium problem in small groups. In T. Parsons, R. Bales, & E. Shils, *Working papers in the theory of action*. Glencoe, IL: The Free Press.

Baloglu, A., & Aktas, M. S. (2010).BlogMiner: Web blog mining application for classification of movie reviews. *2010 Fifth International IEEE Conference on Internet and Web Application and Services,* (pp. 77-84).

Banning, S., & Trammell, K. D. (2006, August). *Revisiting the issue of blog credibility: A national survey*. Paper presented at the Annual Conference of the Association for Education in Journalism & Mass Communication, San Francisco, CA.

Barabasi, A. L., & Albert, R. (1999). Emergence of scaling in random networks. *Science, 286*(5439), 509–512. doi:10.1126/science.286.5439.509

Barabási, A.-L., Newman, M., & Watts, D. J. (2006). *The structure and dynamics of networks*. Princeton, NJ: Princeton University Press.

Barker, V. (2009). Older adolescents' motivations for social network site use: The influence of gender, group identity, and collective self-esteem. *Cyberpsychology & Behavior, 12*(2), 209–213. doi:10.1089/cpb.2008.0228

Barker, E. (2005). Crossing the boundary: New challenges to religious authority and control as a consequence of access to the Internet. In Højsgaard, M. T., & Warburg, M. (Eds.), *Religion and cyberspace* (pp. 67–85). London, UK: Routledge.

Barnes, S. (2006). A privacy paradox: Social networking in the United States. *First Monday, 11*(9), 11–15.

Bartlett, D. L., Drew, P. B., Fahle, E. G., & Watts, W. A. (1974). Selective exposure to a presidential campaign appeal. *Public Opinion Quarterly, 38*, 264–270. doi:10.1086/268158

Bartoletti, R. (2009). Il lato B della Barbie: la rivincita dei consumatori nel social web. In Mazzoli, L. (Ed.), *Network effect. Quando la rete diventa pop* (pp. 57–74). Torino, Italy: Codice Edizioni.

Baruh, L. (2004). Audience surveillance and the right to read: Anonymous reading in interactive media. *Knowledge Technology and Policy, 1*, 59–73. doi:10.1007/BF02687076

Batty, M. (1993). The geography of cyberspace. *Environment and Planning. B, Planning & Design, 20*(6), 615–617.

Bauman, Z. (2000). *Liquid modernity*. Cambridge, UK: Polity.

Bauman, Z. (2001). *The individualized society*. Cambridge, UK: Polity.

Bauman, Z. (2001). *Community. Seeking safety in an insecure world*. Cambridge, UK: Polity.

Bauman, Z. (1997). *Postmodernity and its discontents*. Oxford, UK: Blackwell.

Bauman, Z. (2007). *Consuming life*. Cambridge, UK: Polity Press.

Bauman, Z. (1998). Postmodern religion. In Heelas, P., & Martin, D. (Eds.), *Religion, modernity and postmodernity* (pp. 55–78). Oxford, UK: Blackwell.

Baym, N. (2007). The new shape of online community: The example of Swedish independent music fandom. *First Monday, 12*(8).

Baym, N. K., & Ledbetter, A. (2009). Tunes that bind? Predicting friendship strength in a music-based social network. *Information Communication and Society, 12*(3). doi:10.1080/13691180802635430

Baym, N. K., & Ledbetter, A. (2009). Tunes that bind? *Information Communication and Society, 12*(3), 408–427. doi:10.1080/13691180802635430

Beck, U., & Beck-Gernsheim, E. (2002). *Individualization: Institutionalized individualism and its social and political consequences*. London, UK: SAGE.

Beck, U. (1997). *Eigenes Leben. Ausfluge in die unbekannte Gesellschaft, in der wir leben*. Munchen, Germany: Beck.

Beer, D. (2008). Social network(ing) sites...revisiting the story so far: A response to danah boyd & Nicole Ellison. *Journal of Computer-Mediated Communication, 13*(5), 516–529. doi:10.1111/j.1083-6101.2008.00408.x

Beer, D., & Burrows, R. (2010). Consumption, prosumption and participatory Web cultures: An introduction. *Journal of Consumer Culture, 10*(1), 3–12. doi:10.1177/1469540509354009

Beer, D., & Burrows, R. (2007). Sociology and, of and in Web 2.0: Some initial considerations. *Sociological Research Online*, *12*(5). Retrieved from http://www.socresonline.org.uk/12/5/17.html.

Bell, D. (1976). *The cultural contradictions of capitalism*. New York, NY: Basic Books.

Bell, M. (2011, February 20). [Personal communication with McClain Bell, Gowalla/Allison & Partners].

Bellah, R. N., Madsen, R., Sullivan, W. M., Swidler, A., & Tipton, S. M. (1996). *Habits of the heart: Individualism and commitment in American life (Updated.)*. Berkeley, CA: University of California Press.

Bellamy, J., & Castle, K. (2004). *NCLS occasional paper 3: 2001 Church attendance estimates*. Sydney, Australia: NCLS.

Bellur, S., Oeldorf-Hirsch, A., & High, A. (2008). *Misery doesn't love company: An exploration of emotional bandwidth on online social networks*. Paper presented at the annual meeting of the International Communication Association, Montreal, Canada. boyd, D., & Ellison, N. (2007). Social network sites: Definition, history, and scholarship. *Journal of Computer-Mediated Communication*, *13*(1), 210–230.

Belson, D. (1994). *The network nation revisited* (Bachelor). New Jersey Institute of Technology. Retrieved from http://sunsite.utk.edu/FINS/Periodicals_and_Newspapers/Fins-PaN-33.txt

Benedikt, M. (2000). Cyberspace: First steps. In Bell, D., & Kennedy, B. M. (Eds.), *The cybercultures reader* (pp. 29–44). London, UK: Routledge. (Original work published 1991)

Benevenuto, F., Rodrigues, T., Cha, M., & Almeida, V. (2009). Characterizing user behavior in online social networks. *Proceedings of the ACM Internet Measurement Conference (IMC'09)*, Chicago, IL.

Benjamin, W. (Ed.). (1990). *The arcades project*. Cambridge, UK: Belknap Press.

Benkler, Y. (2002). Coase's Penguin, or, Linux and the nature of the firm. *The Yale Law Journal*, *112*(3), 369–446. Retrieved from http://www.yale.edu/yalelj/112/Benkler-WEB.pdf. doi:10.2307/1562247

Benkler, Y. (2007). *The wealth of networks: How social production transforms markets and freedom*. Yale University Press.

Bennet, W. L. (Ed.). (2008). *Civic life online: Learning how digital media can engage youth*. Cambridge, MA: MIT Press.

Bennett, S. E. (2002). Predicting Americans' exposure to political talk radio in 1996, 1998, and 2000. *The Harvard International Journal of Press/Politics*, *7*, 9–22.

Bennett, W. L., & Iyengar, S. (2008). A new era of minimal effects? The changing foundation of political communication. *The Journal of Communication*, *58*, 707–737. doi:10.1111/j.1460-2466.2008.00410.x

Berger, P. L. (1963). *Invitation to sociology: A humanistic perspective*. New York, NY: Anchor Books.

Berger, P., Berger, B., & Kellner, H. (1973). *The homeless mind*. Harmondsworth, UK: Penguin Books.

Berger, P., & Luckmann, T. (1966). *The social construction of reality*. New York, NY: Doubleday.

Berry, W. (1993). *Sex, economy, freedom, and community*. New York, NY: Pantheon.

Beschastnikh, I., Kriplean, T., & McDonald, D. W. (2008). Wikipedian self-governance in action: Motivating the policy lens. *Proc. ICWSM 2008*.

Best, S. J., Chmielewski, B., & Krueger, B. S. (2005). Selective exposure to online foreign news during the conflict with Iraq. *Harvard Journal of Press/Politics*, *10*(4), 52-70.

Bichard, S. L. (2006). Building blogs: A multi-dimensional analysis of the distribution of frames on the 2004 presidential candidate websites. *Journalism & Mass Communication Quarterly*, *82*, 329–345.

Bimber, B., & Davis, R. (2003). *Campaigning online: The internet in U.S. elections*. Oxford, UK: Oxford University Press.

Blood, R. (2004). How blogging software reshapes the online community. *Communications of the ACM*, *47*(12), 53–55.

Blumler, J. G. (1979). The role of theory in uses and gratifications studies. *Communication Research, 6*, 9–36. doi:10.1177/009365027900600102

Boase, J., Horrigan, J., Wellman, B., & Rainie, L. (2006). *The strength of Internet ties*. Washington, D.C.: The Pew Internet and American Life Project.

Boase, J., & Wellman, B. (2006). Personal relationships: On and off the Internet. In Vangelisti, A. L., & Perlman, D. (Eds.), *The Cambridge handbook of personal relationships* (pp. 709–725). Cambridge, UK: Cambridge University Press.

Bobo, L., & Licari, F. C. (1989). Educational and political tolerance: Testing the effects of cognitive sophistication and target group affect. *Public Opinion Quarterly, 53*, 285–308. doi:10.1086/269154

Boccia, A. G. (2010). Analisi degli user generated content e pubblici connessi: Rappresentazioni generazionali in Rete. In Monaci, S., & Scifo, B. (Eds.), *Sociologia 2.0 Pratiche sociali e metodologie di ricerca sui media partecipativi* (pp. 283–297). Napoli, Italy: Scriptaweb.

Bodenhamer, D. J., Corrigan, J., & Harris, T. M. (Eds.). (2010). *The spatial humanities: GIS and the future of humanities scholarship*. Indianapolis, IN: Indiana University Press.

Boiy, E., Hens, P., Deschacht, K., & Moens, M.-F. (2007). Automatic sentiment analysis in on-line text, *Proceedings of the 11th International Conference on Electronic Publishing Vienna Austria (2007)ELPUB2007*

Boiy, E., Hens, P., Deschacht, K., & Moens, M. (2007). Automatic sentiment analysis in on-line text. *Proceedings ELPUB2007 Conference on Electronic Publishing – Vienna, Austria – June 2007,* (pp. 349-360).

Bolter, J. D., & Grusin, R. (2000). *Remediation. Understanding new media*. Cambridge, MA: The MIT Press.

Bortree, D. S. (2005). Presentation of self on the web: An ethnographic study of teenage girls' weblogs. *Education Communication and Information, 5*(1), 25–39.

Bourdieu, P. (1984). *Distinctions. A social critique of the judgement of taste*. Cambridge, MA: Harvard University Press.

boyd, d. (2008). *Taken out of context: American teen sociality in networked publics*. (Doctoral dissertation), University of California-Berkeley, California.

boyd, d. (2008b). Why youth hearth social network sites. In D. Buckingham (Ed.), *Youth, identity, and digital media*. Cambridge, MA: MIT Press.

boyd, d., & Ellison, N. (2007). Social network sites: Definition, history, and scholarship. *Journal of Computer Mediated Communication, 13*(1), 210-230.

Boyd, D., & Heer, J. (2006). Profiles as conversation: Networked identity performance on Friendster. Proceedings of the Hawai'i International Conference on System Sciences (HICSS-39), Persistent Conversation Track, January 4-7. Kauai, HI: IEEE Computer Society.

Brannon, L. A., Tagler, M. J., & Eagly, A. H. (2007). The moderating role of attitude strength in selective exposure to information. *Journal of Experimental Social Psychology, 43*, 611. doi:10.1016/j.jesp.2006.05.001

Brasher, B. (1996). Thoughts on the status of the cyborg: On technological socialization and its link to the religious function of popular culture. *Journal of the American Academy of Religion. American Academy of Religion, 64*(4), 809–830.

Bruno, R. (2010). *A democracy of unequals* (Ph. D. Dissertation). West Lafayette, IN: Purdue University.

Bruns, A. (2008). *Blogs, Wikipedia, Second Life, and beyond: From production to produsage*. New York, NY: Peter Lang.

Bruns, A., & Jacobs, J. (Eds.). (2006). *Uses of blogs*. New York, NY: Peter Lang.

Bruns, A. (2006). The practice of news blogging. In Bruns, A., & Jacobs, J. (Eds.), *Uses of blogs* (pp. 11–22). New York, NY: Peter Lang.

Bryant, S. L., Forte, A., & Bruckman, A. (2005). *Becoming Wikipedian: Transformation of participation in a collaborative online encyclopedia*. Sanibel Island, FL: ACM.

Bryer, T. (2010). Across the great divide: Social media and networking for citizens engagement. In J. H. Svara, & J. Denhardt (Eds.), *Connected communities, local government as partners in citizens engagement and community building* (pp. 73-79). Retrieved March 10, 2011, from http://www.tlgconference.org/communityconnectionswhitepaper.pdf.

Buckingham, D. (2003). *Media education. Literacy, learning and contemporary culture*. London, UK: Polity Press-Blackwell Publishing.

Buckingham, D. (2008). Introducing identity. In Buckingham, D. (Ed.), *Youth, identity, and digital media* (pp. 1–24). Cambridge, MA: The MIT Press.

Bucy, E. P. (2004). Second generation net news: Interactivity and information accessibility in the online environment. *The International Journal on Media Management*, *6*, 102–113. doi:10.1080/14241277.2004.9669386

Buffardi, L. E., & Campbell, W. K. (2008). Narcissism and social networking web sites. *Personality and Social Psychology Bulletin*, *34*(10), 1303–1314. doi:10.1177/0146167208320061

Bumgarner, B. A. (2007). You have been poked: Exploring the uses and gratifications of Facebook among emerging adults. *First Monday*, *12*(11). Retrieved from http://firstmonday.org/ htbin/cgiwrap/bin/ojs/index.php/fm/article/viewArticle/2026/1897.

Burrows, R., & Ellison, N. (2004). Sorting places out? Towards a social politics of neighbourhood informatization. *Information Communication and Society*, *7*(3), 321–336. doi:10.1080/1369118042000284588

Butt, S., & Phillips, J. G. (2008). Personality and self report mobile phone use. *Computers in Human Behavior*, *24*(2), 346–360. doi:10.1016/j.chb.2007.01.019

Cameron, D. (2001). The rocket in your pocket: How mobile phones became the media by stealth. *Asia Pacific Media Educator*, *11*, 141–149.

Campbell, C. (2005). The craft consumer. [Sage Publications.]. *Journal of Consumer Culture*, *5*, 23–42. doi:10.1177/1469540505049843

Campbell, H. (2005). *Exploring religious community online: We are one in the network*. New York, NY: Peter Lang.

Campbell, H. (2007). Who's got the power? Religious authority and the Internet. *Journal of Computer-Mediated Communication*, *12*(3).

Casanova, J. (1994). *Public religions in the modern world*. Chicago, IL: University of Chicago Press.

Castells, M. (2010). The information age: Economy, society and culture.: *Vol. 1. The rise of the network society* (2nd ed.). West Sussex, UK: Wiley-Blackwell.

Castells, M. (1996). *The rise of the network society*. Oxford, UK: Blackwell.

Castells, M. (2009). *Communication power*. Oxford, NY: Oxford University Press.

Castells, M. (2001). *The Internet galaxy. Reflections on the Internet, business and society*. Oxford, UK: Oxford University Press.

Castells, M. (2007). Communication, power and counter-power in the network society. *International Journal of Communication*, *1*, 238–266.

Castells, M., & Cardoso, G. (Eds.). (2005). *The network society: From knowledge to policy*. Washington, DC: The John Hopkins University.

Castells, M. (2001). *The Internet galaxy. Reflections on the Internet, business and society*. Oxford, UK: Oxford University Press.

Castells, M. (2007). Communication, power and counter-power in the network society. *International Journal of Communication*, *1*, 238–266.

Castells, M. (2009). *Communication power*. Oxford, UK: Oxford University Press.

Castells, M. (1996). The rise of the network society: *Vol. 1. The Information Age: Economy, society and culture*. Malden, MA: Blackwell.

Castells, M. (1996). *The Information Age: Economy, society and culture, Vol. 1: The rise of the network society*. Blackwell, UK: Oxford.

Castells, M. (2008). *The new public sphere:* Global civil society, communication networks, and global governace *The American Academy of Political and Social Science*, *616*, 78-93,

Castells, M., & Fernandez-Ardèvol, M. Linchuan, Qiu J., & Sey, A. (2006). *Mobile communication and society. A global perspective*. Cambridge, MA: The MIT Press.

Cavanagh, A. (2007). *Sociology in the age of the Internet*. Berkshire, UK: Open University Press.

Cha, M., Haddadi, H., Benevenuto, F., & Gummadi, K. (2010). Measuring user influence in Twitter: The million follower fallacy. *Proceedings of the 4th International AAAI Conference on Weblogs and Social Media (ICWSM)*, Washington, DC.

Cha, M., Mislove, A., Adams, B., & Gummadi, K. (2008). Characterizing social cascades in Flickr. *Proceedings of the ACM Workshop on Online Social Networks (WOSN'08)*, Seattle, WA.

Chaffee, S. H., & McLeod, J. M. (1973). Individuals vs. social predictors of information seeking. *The Journalism Quarterly*, *50*, 237–245.

Chaffee, S. H., Saphir, M. N., Grap, J., Sandvig, C., & Hahn, K. S. (2001). Attention to counter-attitudinal messages in a state election campaign. *Political Communication*, *18*, 247–272. doi:10.1080/10584600152400338

Chen, W., Wand, Y., & Yang, S. (2009). Efficient influence maximization in social networks. *Proceedings of the ACM Conference on Knowledge Discovery and Data Mining*, Paris, France.

Cheong, P. H., Halavais, A., & Kwon, K. (2008). The chronicles of me: Understanding blogging as a religious practice. *Journal of Media and Religion*, *7*(3), 107–131.

Cho, S. (2010). *A cross-cultural comparison of Korean and American social network sites: Exploring cultural differences in social relationships and self-presentation*. New Brunswick, NJ: Rutgers State University.

Christodoulides, G. (2009). Branding in the post-internet era. *Marketing Theory*, *9*(1), 141–144. doi:10.1177/1470593108100071

Christofides, E., Muise, A., & Desmarais, S. (2009). Information disclosure and control on Facebook: Are they two sides of the same coin or two different processes? *Cyberpsychology & Behavior*, *12*(3), 341–345. doi:10.1089/cpb.2008.0226

Chua, V., Madej, J., & Wellman, B. (2009). Personal communities: The world according to me. Extended version of book chapter. In Carrington, P., & Scott, J. (Eds.), *Handbook of social network analysis*. Cambridge: Cambridge University Press.

Chun, H., Kwak, H., Eom, Y. H., Ahn, Y.-Y., Moon, S. B., & Jeong, H. (2008). Comparison of online social relations in volume vs. interaction: A case study of Cyworld. *Proceedings of the ACM Internet Measurement Conference (IMC'08)*, Vouliagmeni, Greece.

Cohen, N. (2007, March 5). A contributor to Wikipedia has his fictional side. *New York Times*. Retrieved from http://www.nytimes.com/2007/03/05/technology/05wikipedia.html?pagewanted=2&_r=1

Coleman, S. (2005). *Remixing citizenship. Democracy and young people's use of internet*. Retrieved December 13, 2010, from http://cypi.carnegieuktrust.org.uk/files/Carnegie_v3LRES_0.pdf

Computer-Mediated Communication. *13*(1), article 11. Retrieved from http://jcmc.indiana.edu/vol13/issue1/boyd.ellison.html

Comunello, F. (2006). *Reti nella rete. Teorie e definizioni tra tecnologia e società*. Milano, Italy: Guerini.

Comunello, F. (2010). *Networked sociability*. Milano, Italy: Guerini.

Contini, F., & Lanzara, G. F. (2009). *ICT and innovation in the public sector. European studies in the making of e-government*. New York, NY: Palgrave Macmillan.

Cook, C., Heath, F. M., & Thompson, R. L. (2000). A meta-analysis of response rates in Web-or Internet- based surveys. *Educational and Psychological Measurement*, *60*, 821–826. doi:10.1177/00131640021970934

Cooley, C. H. (1967). *Human nature and the social order*. New York, NY: Schocken.

Cotton, J. L. (1985). Cognitive dissonance in selective exposure. In Zillmann, D., & Bryant, J. (Eds.), *Selective exposure to communication* (pp. 11–33). Hillsdale, NJ: Erlbaum.

Couper, M. P. (2000). Web surveys: A review of issues and approaches. *Public Opinion Quarterly*, *64*, 464–494. doi:10.1086/318641

Cova, B. (1997). Community and consumption. *European Journal of Marketing*, *31*(3-4), 297–316. doi:10.1108/03090569710162380

Crang, M., Crosbie, T., & Graham, S. (2007). Technology, time - space, and the remediation of neighbourhood life. *Environment & Planning A*, *39*(10), 2405–2423. doi:10.1068/a38353

Crawford, K. (2009). Following you: Disciplines of listening in social media. *Journal of Media & Culture Studies*, *23*(4), 525–535. doi:10.1080/10304310903003270

Crimp, D. (1998). On the museum's ruins. In Foster, H. (Ed.), *The anti-aesthetic: Essays on postmodern culture* (pp. 49–64). New York, NY: The New Press.

Cross, M. (2011, February 18). [Personal communication with Meghan Cross, Foursquare/Kaplow PR].

Dahlgren, P. (2009). *Media and political engagement: Citizens, communication and democracy*. Cambridge, UK: Cambridge University Press.

Davies, J. (2004). *Wiki brainstorming and problems with wiki based collaboration.* (Master's thesis). University of York.

Dawson, L. L. (2005). The mediation of religious experience in cyberspace. In Højsgaard, M. T., & Warburg, M. (Eds.), *Religion and cyberspace* (pp. 15–37). London, UK: Routledge.

de Certeau, M. (1984). *The practice of everyday life*. Berkeley, CA: University of California Press.

de Souza e Silva, A. & Hjorth, L. (2009). Playful urban spaces: A historical approach to mobile games. *Simulation & Gaming*, *40*(5), 602–602. doi:10.1177/1046878109333723

de Souza e Silva, A., & Frith, J. (2010). Locative mobile social networks: Mapping communication and location in urban spaces. *Mobilities*, *5*(4), 485–505. doi:10.1080/17450101.2010.510332

de Souza e Silva. A., & Sutko, D. M. (2009). Merging digital and urban playspaces: An introduction to the field. In A. de Souza e Silva & D. M. Sutko (Eds.), Digital cityscapes: Merging digital and urban playspaces (pp. 1-20). New York, NY: Peter Lang.

Dean, J. (2005). Communicative capitalism: Circulation and the foreclosure of politics. *Cultural Politics*, *1*(1), 51–74. doi:10.2752/174321905778054845

Dean, J. (2010a). *Blog theory: Feedback and capture in the circuits of drive*. Cambridge, UK: Polity Press.

Dean, J. (2010b). The real Internet. *International Journal of Žižek Studies*, *4*(1). http://zizekstudies.org/index.php/ijzs/article/view/242/322.

Debatin, B., Lovejoy, J. P., Horn, A.-K., & Hughes, B. N. (2009). Facebook and online privacy: Attitudes, behaviors, and unintended consequences. *Journal of Computer-Mediated Communication*, *15*(1), 83–108. doi:10.1111/j.1083-6101.2009.01494.x

Delli Carpini, M. X., & Keeter, S. (1996). *What Americans know about politics and why it matters*. New Haven, CT: Yale University Press.

DiMaggio, & Sato, K. (2003, August). *Does the Internet Balkanize political attention? A test of the Sunstein thesis.* Paper presented at the Annual Meeting of the American Sociological Association, Atlanta, GA.

Doak, J., & Parker, G. (2005). Networked space? The challenge of meaningful participation and the new spatial planning in England. *Planning Practice and Research*, *20*(1), 23–40. doi:10.1080/02697450500261699

Donath, J., & boyd, d. (2004). Public displays of connection. *BT Technology Journal*, *22*(4), 71–82. doi:10.1023/B:BTTJ.0000047585.06264.cc

Donath, J. (2007). Signals in social supernets. *Journal of Computer-Mediated Communication*, *13*(1), 231–251. doi:10.1111/j.1083-6101.2007.00394.x

Donsbach, W. (1991). Exposure to political content in newspapers: The impact of cognitive dissonance on reader's selectivity. *European Journal of Communication*, *6*, 155–186. doi:10.1177/0267323191006002003

Döring, N. (2003). *Sozialpsychologie des Internet: Die Bedeutung des Internet für Kommunikationsprozesse, Identitäten, soziale Beziehungen und Gruppen*. Göttingen, Germany: Hogrefe.

Douglas, M., & Isherwood, B. (1979). *The world of goods*. New York, NY: Basic Books.

Dourish, P. (2004). What we talk about when we talk about context. *Personal and Ubiquitous Computing*, *8*(1), 19–30. doi:10.1007/s00779-003-0253-8

Driscoll, M. (2006). A pastoral perspective on the emergent church. *Criswell Theological Review*, *3*(2), 87–93.

Dubar, C. (2000). *La crise des identités. L'interprétation d'une mutation*. Paris, France: PUF.

Durkheim, E. (1951). *Suicide: A study in sociology*. New York, NY: Free Press.

Durkheim, E. (1997). *The division of labor in society*. New York, NY: Free Press.

Dwyer, C., Hiltz, S. R., & Passerini, K. (2007). Trust and privacy concern within social networking sites: A comparison of Facebook and MySpace. Proceedings of the Thirteenth Americas Conference on Information Systems, Keystone, Colorado, August 9-12.

Ebersbach, A., Glaser, M., & Heigl, R. (2008). *Social Web*. Konstanz, Germany: UKV.

Eco, U. (1979). *Lector in fabula*. Milano, Italy: Bompiani.

Edwards, K., & Smith, E. E. (1996). A disconfirmation bias in the evaluation of arguments. *Journal of Personality and Social Psychology*, *71*(1), 5–24. doi:10.1037/0022-3514.71.1.5

Efimova, L., & de Moor, A. (2005). *Beyond personal web publishing: An exploratory study of conversational blogging practices*. Paper presented at The 38th Annual Hawaii International Conference System Sciences.

Ekdale, B., Namkoong, K., Fung, T. K. F., & Perlmutter, D. D. (2010). Why blog? (then and now): Exploring the motivations for blogging by popular American political bloggers. *New Media & Society*, *12*, 217–234. doi:10.1177/1461444809341440

Elias, N. (1991). *The society of individuals*. Oxford, UK: Basil Blackwell.

Elliott, M. S., & Scacchi, W. (2003). *Free software developers as an occupational community: Resolving conflicts and fostering collaboration*. Sanibel Island, FL: ACM.

Ellison, N., Heino, R., & Gibbs, J. (2006). Managing impressions online: Self-presentation processes in the online dating environment. *Journal of Computer-Mediated Communication*, *11*(2). doi:10.1111/j.1083-6101.2006.00020.x

Ellison, N., Steinfield, C., & Lampe, C. (2007). The benefits of Facebook friends: Social capital and college students' use of online social network sites. *Journal of Computer-Mediated Communication*, *12*(4), 1143–1168. doi:10.1111/j.1083-6101.2007.00367.x

Ellison, N., Lampe, C., & Steinfield, C. (2008, May). *Net worth: Facebook use and changes in social capital over time*. Paper presented at the annual meeting of the International Communication Association, TBA, Montreal, Quebec, Canada.

Ellison, N., Steinfield, C., & Lampe, C. (2006, June). *Spatially bounded online social networks and social capital. The role of Facebook*. Paper presented at the Annual Conference of International Communication Association ICA, in Dresden, Germany.

Erikson, E. H. (1959). *Identity in the life cycle*. New York, NY: Norton.

Erikson, E. (1950). *Childhood and society*. New York, NY: Norton.

Fabris, G. (2008). *Societing. Il marketing nella società postmoderna*. Milano, Italy: Egea.

Fabris, G. (2010). *La società post-crescita. Consumi e stili di vita*. Milano, Italy: Egea.

Faccioli, F. (2000). *Comunicazione pubblica e cultura del servizio*. Roma, Italy: Carocci.

Featherstone, M. (1990). *Consumer culture and postmodernism*. London, UK: Sage.

Featherstone, M. (1998). The flâneur, the city and virtual public life. *Urban Studies (Edinburgh, Scotland)*, *35*(5-6), 909–926. doi:10.1080/0042098984619

Fehr, B. (2008). Friendship formation. In Sprecher, S., Wenzel, A., & Harvey, J. (Eds.), *Handbook of relationship initiation* (pp. 29–54). New York, NY: Taylor & Francis.

Feld, S. L. (1981). The focused organisation of social ties. *American Journal of Sociology*, *86*(5), 1015–1035. doi:10.1086/227352

Feller, J. (2005). *Perspectives on free and open source software*. Cambridge, MA: MIT Press.

Fernback, J. (1997). The individual within the collective: Virtual ideology and the realization of collective principles. In Jones, S. (Ed.), *Virtual culture* (pp. 36–54). Thousand Oaks, CA: Sage.

Ferro, E., & Molinari, F. (2010). Making sense of Gov 2.0 strategies: No citizens, no party. *Journal of eDemocracy and Open Government, 2*(1), 56-68.

Festinger, L. (1957). *A theory of cognitive dissonance*. Stanford, CA: Stanford University Press.

Finke, R., & Stark, R. (2005). *The churching of America, 1776-2005: Winners and losers in our religious economy*. New Jersey: Rutgers University Press.

Fischer, P., Jonas, E., Frey, D., & Schulz-Hardt, S. (2005). Selective exposure to information: The impact of information limits. *European Journal of Social Psychology, 35*, 469–492. doi:10.1002/ejsp.264

Fiske, J. (1989a). *Understanding popular culture*. London, UK: Routledge.

Fiske, J. (1992). The cultural economy of fandom. In Lewis, L. A. (Ed.), *Adoring audience. Fan culture and popular media* (pp. 30–49). London, UK: Routledge.

Fiske, J. (1989b). Moments of television: Neither the text nor the audience. In Thornham, S., & Marris, P. (Eds.), *Media studies: A reader* (pp. 536–546). New York, NY: NYU Press.

Flanagin, A. J., & Metzger, M. J. (2000). Perceptions of Internet information credibility. *Journalism & Mass Communication Quarterly, 77*, 515–540.

Fogel, J., & Nehmad, E. (2009). Internet social network communities: Risk taking, trust, and privacy concerns. *Computers in Human Behavior, 25*(1), 153–160. doi:10.1016/j.chb.2008.08.006

Forh, M., & Hearn, G. (2007). Networked individualism of urban residents: Discovering the communicative ecology in inner-city apartment buildings. *Information Communication and Society, 10*, 748–772.

Foucault, M. (1977). *Discipline and punish: The birth of the prison*. London, UK: Penguin Books.

Foursquare. (2010). How to unlock your world with Foursquare. Retrieved November 22, 2010, from http://www.howcast.com/videos/386406-How-To-Unlock-Your-World-With-Foursquare

Fox, J. (2007). Getting rich off those who work for free. *Time*. Retrieved from http://vnweb.hwwilsonweb.com/hww/jumpstart.jhtml?recid=0bc05f7a67b1790e43f188a0944caaa997c3f03c1167820e090dc389e2346f69d2c219bb19f24143&fmt=C

Fraser, M., & Dutta, S. (2008, November, 19). Barack Obama and the Facebook election. *U. S. News & World Report*. Retrieved from http://www.unew.com/articles/opinion/2008/11/19/barck-obama-and-the-facebook-election

FreshMinds Research. (2010). *Turning conversations into insights: A comparison of social media monitoring tools*. Retrieved February 10, 2011, from www.freshminds.co.uk

Fuchs, C. (2009). *Social networking sites and the surveillance society. A critical case study of the usage of Studivz, Facebook, and Myspace by students in Salzburg in the context of electronic surveillance*. Salzburg, Austria: Forschungsgruppe Unified Theory of Information. Retrieved from http://fuchs.icts.sbg.ac.at/SNS_Surveillance_Fuchs.pdf

Funder, D. C. (1999). *Personality judgment: A realistic approach to person perception*. San Diego, CA: Academic Press.

Fyfe, T., & Crookal, P. (2010). *Social media and public sector policy dilemmas*. Toronto, Canada: Institute of Public Administration of Canada.

Galston, W. A. (2003). If political fragmentation is the problem, is the Internet the solution? In Anderson, D. M., & Cornfield, M. (Eds.), *The civic web: Online politics and democratic values* (pp. 35–44). Oxford, UK: Rowman & Littlefield.

Galuba, W., Aberer, K., Chakraborty, D., Despotovic, Z., & Kellerer, W. (2010). Outtweeting the Twitterers? Predicting information cascades in microblogs. *Proceedings of the ACM Workshop on Online Social Networks (WOSN'10)*, Boston, MA.

Gandy, O. H. (1989). Information privacy and the crisis of control. In Raboy, P. M., & Bruck, P. A. (Eds.), *Communication for and against democracy* (pp. 59–73). Montreal, Canada: Black Rose Books.

Gannes, L. (2010). *When social replaces search, what can you do to monetize?* Retrieved October 29, 2010, from http://gigaom.com/2010/03/24/when-social-replaces-search-what-can-you-do-to-monetize/

Garrett, R. K. (2009). Echo chambers online? Politically motivated selective exposure among Internet news users. *Journal of Computer-Mediated Communication, 14*, 265–285. doi:10.1111/j.1083-6101.2009.01440.x

Garton, L., Haythornthwaite, C., & Wellman, B. (1997). Studying online social networks. *Journal of Computer-Mediated Communication, 3*(1). Retrieved from http://jcmc.indiana.edu/vol3/issue1/garton.html.

Gauntlett, D. (2004). Web studies: What's new. In Gauntlett, D., & Horsley, R. (Eds.), *Web studies*. London, UK: Arnold.

Gibson, J. (1986). *The ecological approach to visual perception*. Hillsdale, NJ: Laurence Erlbaum.

Gibson, W. (1984). *Neuromancer*. New York, NY: Ace Books.

Gibson, J. (1977). The theory of affordances. In Shaw, R., & Bransford, J. (Eds.), *Perceiving, acting, and knowing: Towards an ecological psychology* (pp. 67–82). Hillsdale, NJ: Laurence Erlbaum.

Giddens, A. (1979). *Central problems in social theory. Action, structure, and contradiction in social analysis*. Berkeley, CA: University of California Press.

Giddens, A. (1987). *Social theory and modern sociology*. Cambridge, UK: Polity Press.

Giddens, A. (1991). *The consequences of modernity*. Stanford, CA: Stanford University Press.

Giddens, A. (1991). *Modernity and self-identity*. Cambridge, UK: Polity.

Giddens, A. (1990). *The consequences of modernity*. Cambridge, UK: Polity Press.

Gillespie, M. (2005). *Media audiences*. London, UK: Open University Press.

Gillmor, D. (2006). *We the media: Grassroots journalism by the people, for the people*. Sebastopol, CA: O'Reilly.

Goffman, E. (1959). *Presentation of self in everyday life*. Garden City, NY: Doubleday Anchor Book.

Goffman, E. (1996). *Wir alle spielen Theater. Die Selbstdarstellung im Alltag*. München, Germany: Piper.

Goffman, E. (1959). *The presentation of self in everyday life*. New York, NY: Doubleday.

Gomá, J. (2009). *Ejemplaridad pública*. Madrid, Spain: Taurus.

Gosling, S. D., Rentfrow, P. J., & Swann, W. B. (2003). A very brief measure of the Big-Five personality domains. *Journal of Research in Personality, 37*(6), 504–528. doi:10.1016/S0092-6566(03)00046-1

Gosling, S. D., Vazire, S., Srivastava, S., & John, O. P. (2004). Should we trust web-based studies? A comparative analysis of six preconceptions. *The American Psychologist, 59*(2), 93–104. doi:10.1037/0003-066X.59.2.93

Gosling, S. D., Gaddis, D., & Vazire, S. (2007). *Personality impressions based on Facebook profiles*. Paper presented at the ICWSM, Boulder, Colorado, USA.

Gowalla. (2010). Home. Retrieved November 22, 2010, from http://gowalla.com/

Graf, J., & Aday, S. (2008). Selective attention to online political information. *Journal of Broadcasting & Electronic Media, 52*, 86–100. doi:10.1080/08838150701820874

Graham, S., & Marvin, S. (2001). *Splintering urbanism: Networked infrastructures, technological mobilities and the urban condition*. London, UK: Routledge. doi:10.4324/9780203452202

Graham, S. (2004). *The cybercities reader*. London, UK: Routledge.

Granovetter, M. (1973). The strength of weak ties. *American Journal of Sociology, 78*(6), 1360–1380. doi:10.1086/225469

Granovetter, M. (1983). The strength of weak ties: A network theory revisited. *Sociological Theory, 1*(1), 201–233. doi:10.2307/202051

Gray, J., Sandvoss, C., & Harrington, C. (Eds.). (2007). *Fandom: Identities and communities in a mediated world*. New York, NY: New York University Press.

Green, D., Palmquist, B., & Schickler, E. (2002). *Partisan hearts & minds: Political parties and the social identities of voters*. New Haven, CT: Yale University Press.

Gross, E. F., Juvonen, J., & Gable, S. L. (2002). Internet use and well-being in adolescence. *The Journal of Social Issues*, *58*, 75–90. doi:10.1111/1540-4560.00249

Gross, R., & Acquisti, A. (2005). *Information revelation and privacy in online social networks*. Paper presented at the ACM, Alexandria, VA.

Gruhl, D., Guah, R., Liben-Nowell, D., & Tomkins, A. (2004). Information diffusion through blogspace. *Proceedings of the 13th International Conference on World Wide Web (WWW'04)*, New York, NY.

Grunig, J. E. (2009). Paradigms of global public relations in an age of digitalization. *PRism*, *6*(2), 1-19, Retrieved March 18, 2011, from http://www.prismjournal.org

Gummesson, E. (2002). *Total relationship marketing*. Woburn, MA: Butterworth-Heinemann.

Hafner, K. (2006). *Growing Wikipedia refines its "anyone can edit" policy*.

Haggerty, K. D., & Ericson, R. V. (2000). The surveillant assemblage. *The British Journal of Sociology*, *51*(4), 605–622. doi:10.1080/00071310020015280

Hall, J. A., & Bernieri, F. J. (Eds.). (2001). *Interpersonal sensitivity: Theory and measurement*. New York, NY: Erlbaum.

Hampton, K., Sessions, L., Her, E. J., & Rainie, L. (2009). *Social Isolation and new technology: How the Internet and mobile phones impact Americans' social networks*. Retrieved from http://www.pewinternet.org/ ~/media// Files/Reports/2009/PIP_Tech_and_Social_Isolation.pdf

Han, S. (2010). Theorizing new media: Reflexivity, knowledge, and the Web 2.0. *Sociological Inquiry*, *80*(2), 200–214. doi:10.1111/j.1475-682X.2010.00327.x

Harrington Lee, C., & Bielby, D. (1995). *Soap fans, pursuing pleasure and making meaning in everyday life*. Philadelphia, PA: Temple University Press.

Hartmann, M. (2004). *Technologies and utopias: The cyberflaneur and the experience of "being online"*. Munich, Germany: Verlag Reinhard Fischer.

Harvey, D. (1990). *The condition of postmodernity: An enquiry into the origins of cultural change*. Oxford, UK: Blackwell.

Haste, H., & Hogan, A. (2006). Beyond conventional civic participation, beyond the moral-political divide: Young people and contemporary debates about citizenship. *Journal of Moral Education*, *35*(4), 473–493. doi:10.1080/03057240601012238

Haven, B., & Vittal, S. (with Overby, C. S., Favier, J., & Cokeh, E.). (2008). *Measuring engagement: Four steps to making engagement measurement a reality.* Cambridge, MA: Forrester Research: Hills, M. (2002). *Fan cultures*. New York, NY: Routledge.

Hawkins, R. P., Pingree, S., Hitchon, J., Gorham, B. W., Kannaovakun, P., Gilligan, E., & Schmidt, T. (2001). Predicting selection and activity in television genre viewing. *Media Psychology*, *3*, 237–263. doi:10.1207/S1532785XMEP0303_02

Haythornthwaite, C. (2005). Social networks and Internet connectivity effects. *Information Communication and Society*, *8*(2), 125–147. doi:10.1080/13691180500146185

Helland, C. (2002). Surfing for salvation. *Religion*, *32*(4), 293–302.

Helland, C. (2005). Online religion as lived religion. In O Krüger (Ed.), *Online - Heidelberg Journal of Religions on the Internet. 01.1 Special Issue on Theory and Methodology.* Retrieved 6 December, 2006, from http://online.uni-hd.de/

Hewitt, A., & Forte, A. (2009). *Crossing boundaries: Identity management and student/faculty relationships on the Facebook.* Poster presented at CSCW Bauff, Alberta, Retrieved February 25, 2011, from http://www.cc.gatech.edu/~aforte/HewittForteCSCWPoster2006.pdf

Hilgers, D., & Ihl, C. (2010). Citizensourcing: Applying the concept of open innovation to the public sector. *International Journal of Public Participation*, *4*(1), 67–88.

Hiltz, S. R., & Turoff, M. (1978). *The network nation: Human communication via computer*. Reading, MA: Addison-Wesley.

Hinduja, S., & Patchin, J. W. (2008). Personal information of adolescents on the Internet: A quantitative content analysis of MySpace. *Journal of Adolescence*, *31*(1), 125–146. doi:10.1016/j.adolescence.2007.05.004

Hine, C. (Ed.). (2005). *Virtual methods: Issues in social research on the Internet*. Oxford, UK: Berg.

Hine, C. (2008). Virtual ethnography: Modes, varieties, affordances. In Fielding, N., Lee, R. M., & Blank, G. (Eds.), *The SAGE handbook of online research methods* (pp. 257–270). London, UK: Sage.

Hoffner, C. A., Fujioka, Y., Ye, J., & Ibrahim, A. G. S. (2009). Why we match: Factors affecting exposure to tragic television news. *Mass Communication & Society*, *12*(2), 193–216. doi:10.1080/15205430802095042

Höflich, J. R. (2006). The mobile phone and the dynamic between private and public communication: Results of an international exploratory study. Knowledge. *Technology and Policy*, *19*(2), 58–68. doi:10.1007/s12130-006-1024-4

Hogan, B. (2009). *Networking in everyday life* (Doctoral dissertation). University of Toronto, Toronto.

Højsgaard, M. T., & Warburg, M. (2005). *Religion and cyberspace*. London, UK: Routledge.

Holmes, D. (2005). *Communication theory: Media, technology and society*. London, UK: Sage.

Hoover, S. M., & Clark, L. S. (2004). *Faith online*. Pew Internet & American Life Project.

Hornby, A. S. (1987). *Oxford advanced learners dictionary of current English*. Oxford, UK: Oxford University Press.

Howe, J. (2009). *Crowdsourcing: Why the power of the crowd is driving the future of business (unedited edition.)*. Crown Business.

Hughey, M. W. (1979). The idea of secularization in the works of Max Weber: A theoretical outline. *Qualitative Sociology*, *2*(1), 85–111.

Huizinga, J. (1998). *Homo Ludens: A study of the play-element in culture*. London, UK: Routledge. (Original work published 1944)

Human Capital Institute (Ed.). (2010). Social networking in government: Opportunities & challenges. Retrieved December 13, 2010, from http://www.hci.org/lib/social-networking-government-opportunities-challenges-part-1

Humphreys, L. (2010). Mobile social networks and urban public space. *New Media & Society*, *12*(5), 763–778. doi:10.1177/1461444809349578

Hunt, S. (2008). The emerging church and its discontents. *Journal of Beliefs & Values*, *29*(3), 287–296.

Ibrahim, Y. (2009). Social Networking Sites (SNS) and the 'narcissistic turn': The politics of self-exposure. In Rummler, S., & Ng, K. B. (Eds.), *Collaborative technologies and applications for interactive information design: Emerging trends in user experiences* (pp. 82–95). Hershey, PA: Idea Group Inc.doi:10.4018/978-1-60566-727-0.ch006

Inglehart, R. (1997). *Modernization and postmodernization: Cultural, economic, and political change in 43 societies*. Princeton, NJ: Princeton University Press.

Ito, M., Okabe, D., & Matsuda, M. (Eds.). (2005). *Personal, portable, pedestrian: Mobile phones in Japanese life*. Cambridge, MA: MIT Press.

Ito, M. (2008). Introduction. In Varnelis, K. (Ed.), *Networked publics*. Cambridge, MA: MIT Press.

Iyengar, S., & Hahn, L. (2009). Red media, blue media: Evidence of ideological selectivity in media use. *The Journal of Communication*, *59*, 19–39. doi:10.1111/j.1460-2466.2008.01402.x

Jansson, A., & Falkheimer, J. (2006). Towards a geography of communication. In Jansson, A., & Falkheimer, J. (Eds.), *Geographies of communication: The spatial turn in media studies* (pp. 9–25). Gothenburg, Sweden: Nordicom.

Jaschik, S. (2007, January 26). *A stand against Wikipedia*. Retrieved from http://www.insidehighered.com/news/2007/01/26/wiki

Java, A., Song, X., Finin, T., & Tseng, B. (2007). *Why we Twitter: Understanding the microblogging effect in user intentions and communities*. Paper presented at WebKDD, San Jose, CA.

Jenkins, H. (2006). *Convergence culture: Where old and new media collide*. New York, NY: New York University Press.

Jenkins, H. (1992). *Textual poachers: Television, fans and participatory culture*. London, UK: Chapman and Hall.

Jenkins, R. (2004). *Social identity*. London, UK: Routledge. doi:10.4324/9780203463352

Jenkins, H., Green, J., Xiaochang, L., & Domb Krauskopf, A. (2010). *If it doesn't spread is dead. Creating value in a spreadable marketplace. Convergence Culture Consortium*. MIT.

Jenkins, H. (2009). *Confronting the challenges of participatory culture. Media education for the 21st century*. Cambridge, MA: MIT Press.

Jenkins, H., Clinton, K., Purushotma, R., Robinson, A. J., & Weigel, M. (2006). *Confronting the challenges of participatory culture: Media education for the 21st century*, (pp. 1–72). Chicago, IL. Retrieved from http://digitallearning.macfound.org/atf/cf/%7B7E45C7E0-A3E0-4B89-AC9C-E807E1B0AE4E%7D/JENKINS_WHITE_PAPER.PDF

Jiang, J., Wilson, C., Wang, X., Huang, P., Sha, W., Dai, Y., & Zhao, B. Y. (2010). Understanding latent social interactions in online social networks. *Proceedings of the ACM Internet Measurement Conference (IMC'10)*, Melbourne, Australia.

Johnson, S. (2001). *Emergence: The connected lives of ants, brains, cities, and software*. New York, NY: Scribner.

Johnson, T. J., Bichard, S. L., & Zhang, W. (2009). Communication communities or cyberghettos? A path analysis model examining factors that explain selective exposure to blogs. *Journal of Computer-Mediated Communication*, *15*(1), 60–82. doi:10.1111/j.1083-6101.2009.01492.x

Johnson, T. J., & Kaye, B. K. (2004). Wag the blog: How reliance on traditional media and the Internet influence perceptions of credibility of Weblogs among blog users. *Journalism & Mass Communication Quarterly*, *81*(3), 622–642.

Johnson, T. J., Zhang, W., & Bichard, S. L. (in press). Voices of convergence or conflict? A path analysis investigation of selective exposure to political Web sites. *Social Science Computer Review*. doi:.doi:10.1177/0894439310379962

Johnson, T. J., & Kaye, B. K. (2009). In blog we trust: Deciphering credibility of components of the Internet among politically interested Internet users. *Computers in Human Communication*, *25*, 175–182.

Johnson, T. J., & Kaye, B. K. (2010). Choosing is believing? How web gratifications and reliance affect Internet credibility among politically interested users. *Atlantic Journal of Communication*, *18*(1), 1–21. doi:10.1080/15456870903340431

Johnson, T. J., Bichard, S. L., & Zhang, W. (2011). Revived and refreshed: Selective exposure to blogs and political Websites. In Comunello, F. (Ed.), *Networked sociability and individualism" Technology fo personal and professional relationships Hershey*. PA: IGI Global.

Johnson, B. (2010, January 11). Privacy no longer a social norm, says Facebook founder. *The Guardian*. Retrieved from http://www.guardian.co.uk/technology/2010/jan/11/facebook-privacy

Johnson, T. J., Kaye, B. K., Bichard, S. L., & Wong, W. J. (2007). Every blog has its day: Politically interested Internet users' perceptions of blog credibility. *Journal of Computer-Mediated Communication, 13*, article 6.

Joinson, A. N. (2008). Looking at, looking up, or keeping up with people? Motives and uses of Facebook. In *Proceedings of the 26th Annual SIGCHI Conference on Human Factors in Computing Systems* (Florence, Italy, April 05-10 2008), CHI '08, ACM, New York, (pp. 1027-1036).

Jonier, R., Gavin, J., & Duffield, J. (2005). Gender, Internet identification, and Internet anxiety: Correlates of Internet use. *Cyberpsychology & Behavior*, *8*, 371–376. doi:10.1089/cpb.2005.8.371

Junghee, L., & Hyunjoo, L. (2010). The computer-mediated communication network: Exploring the linkage between the online community and social capital. *New Media & Society*, *12*, 711–727.

Karaflogka, A. (2002). Religious discourse and cyberspace. *Religion*, *32*(4), 279–291.

Katz, E., Gurevitch, M., & Haas, H. (1973). On the use of the mass media for important things. *American Sociological Review*, *38*, 164–181. doi:10.2307/2094393

Katz, E., Blumler, J., & Gurevitch, M. (1974). Utilization of mass communication by the individual. In Blumler, J., & Katz, E. (Eds.), *The uses of mass communication: Current perspectives on gratifications research* (pp. 19–34). Beverly Hills, CA: Sage.

Katz, J. (1998). *Luring the lurkers*. Retrieved October 30, 2010, from http://slashdot.org/features/98/12/28/1745252.shtml

Kaye, B. K. (2005). It's a blog, blog, blog, blog world: Users and uses of weblogs. *Atlantic Journal of Communication, 13*(2), 73–95. doi:10.1207/s15456889ajc1302_2

Kaye, B. K. (2010b). Going to the blogs: Exploring the uses and gratifications of blogs. *Atlantic Journal of Communication, 18*(4), 194–206. doi:10.1080/15456870.2010.505904

Kaye, B. K., & Johnson, T. J. (2004). A Web for all reasons: Uses and gratifications of Internet resources for political information. *Telematics and Informatics, 21*(3), 197–223. doi:10.1016/S0736-5853(03)00037-6

Kaye, B. K., Johnson, T. J., & Muhlberger, P. (in press). I can speak freely now: Blogs as a source of democratic deliberation. In Dumova, T., & Fiordo, R. (Eds.), *Blogging the global society: Cultural, political and geographical aspects*. Hershey, PA: IGI Global.

Kaye, B. K. (2010a). Between Barack and a net place: Users and uses of social network sites and blogs for political information. In Papacharissi, Z. (Ed.), *The networked self: Identity, community and culture on social network sites* (pp. 208–231). New York, NY: Routledge.

Kaye, B. K. (2007). Blog use motivations: An exploratory study. In Tremayne, M. (Ed.), *Blogging, citizenship, and the future of media* (pp. 127–148). New York, NY: Routledge.

Kaye, B. K., & Johnson, T. J. (2006). The age of reasons: Motives for using different components of the Internet for political information. In Williams, A. P., & Tedesco, J. C. (Eds.), *The Internet election: Perspectives on the role of the Web in campaign 2004*.

Keen, A. (2007). *The cult of the amateur: How today's internet is killing our culture*. New York, NY: Doubleday/Currency.

Keep, C., McLaughlin, T., & Parmar, R. (2000). *The electronic labyrinth: Ted Nelson and Xanadu* (Vol. 2002). Keep, Christopher McLaughlin, Tim Parmar, Robin.

Kelly, K. (1995). *Out of control: The new biology of machines, social systems and the economic world*. Reading, MA: Addison-Wesley.

Kempe, D., Kleinberg, J. M., & Tardos, Ï. (2003). Maximizing the spread of influence through a social network. *Proceedings of the ACM Conference on Knowledge Discovery and Data Mining,* Washington, DC.

Kendall, L. (1999). Recontextualizing cyberspace: Methodological considerations for on-line research. In Jones, S. G. (Ed.), *Doing Internet research: Critical issues and methods for examining the Net* (pp. 57–74). Thousand Oaks, CA: Sage.

Kenny, D. A. (1994). *Interpersonal perception: A social relations analysis*. New York, NY: Guilford.

Kenski, K., Hardy, B. W., & Jamieson, K. H. (2010). *The Obama victory: How media, money, and message shaped the 2008 election*. Oxford: Oxford University Press.

Keum, H., Hillback, E. D., Rojas, H., de Zuniga, H. G., Shah, D. V., & McLeod, D. M. (2005). Personifying the radical: How news framing polarizes security concerns and tolerance judgments. *Human Communication Research, 21*, 337–364. doi:10.1093/hcr/31.3.337

Kim, J., & Rubin, A. M. (1997). The variable influence of audience activity on media effects. *Communication Research, 24*, 107–135. doi:10.1177/009365097024002001

Kim, Y. M. (2007). How intrinsic and extrinsic motivations interact in selectivity: Investigating the moderating effects of situational information processing goals in issue public's web behavior. *Communication Research, 34*, 185–211. doi:10.1177/0093650206298069

Kinder, D. R. (2003). Communication and politics in the age of information. In Sears, D. O., Huddy, L., & Jervis, R. (Eds.), *Oxford handbook of political psychology* (pp. 357–393). Oxford, UK: Oxford University Press.

Kirkpatrick, M. (2009). *Social networking now more popular than email, report finds*. Retrieved August 12, 2010, from http://www.readwriteweb.com/archives/social_networking_now_more_popular_than_email.php

Kittur, A., Chi, E., Pendelton, B., Suh, B., & Mytkowicz, T. (2007). *Power of the few vs. wisdom of the crowd: Wikipedia and the rise of the bourgeoisie*. Presented at the CHI 2007, San Jose, California. Retrieved from http://www.parc.com/research/publications/files/5904.pdf

Kittur, A., Lee, B., & Kraut, R. E. (2009). Coordination in collective intelligence: The role of team structure and task interdependence. In *Proceedings of the 27th International Conference on Human Factors in Computing Systems* (pp. 1495-1504). Boston, MA: ACM. doi:10.1145/1518701.1518928

Kittur, A., Suh, B., Pendleton, B. A., & Chi, E. (2007). He says, she says: Conflict and coordination in Wikipedia. *Proceedings of the SIGCHI Conference on Human Factors in Computing Systems*, 453-462.

Klobas, J. E., & Beesley, A. (2006). *Wikis: Tools for information work and collaboration*. Oxford, UK: Chandos Information Professional Series.

Kneidinger, B. (2010). *Facebook und Co. Eine soziologische Analyse von Interaktionsformen in Online Social Networks*. Wiesbaden, Germany: VS.

Knobloch-Westerwick, S., & Meng, J. (2009). Looking the other way: Selective exposure to attitude-consistent and counterattitudinal political information. *Communication Research*, *36*, 426–448. doi:10.1177/0093650209333030

Kollock, P., & Smith, M. (1996). Managing the virtual commons: Cooperation and conflict in computer communities. In Herring, S. (Ed.), *Computer-mediated communication: Linguistic, social, and cross-cultural perspectives* (pp. 109–128). Amsterdam, The Netherlands: John Benjamins.

Kollock, P. (1999). The economies of online cooperation: Gifts and public goods in cyberspace. In Smith, M., & Kollock, P. (Eds.), *Communities in cyberspace* (pp. 29–59). London, UK: Routledge.

Kopytoff, V. (2011, January 13). Wikipedia marks 10th anniversary - NYTimes.com. *New York Times Bits blog*. Retrieved February 21, 2011, from http://bits.blogs.nytimes.com/2011/01/13/wikipedia-marks-10-years-of-edit-it-yourself/

Koskela, H. (2004). Webcams, TV shows and mobile phones: Empowering exhibitionism. *Surveillance & Society*, *2*(2/3), 199–215. Retrieved from http://www.surveillance-and-society.org/articles2(2)/webcams.pdf.

Kozinets, R. V. (2010). *Netnography: Doing ethnographic research online*. London, UK: Sage.

Kramer, N. C., & Winter, S. (2008). Impression management 2.0. The relationship of self-esteem, extraversion, self-efficacy, and self-presentation within social networking sites. *Journal of Media Psychology*, *20*, 106–116. doi:10.1027/1864-1105.20.3.106

Krasnova, H., Spiekermann, S., Koroleva, K., & Hildebrand, T. (2010). Online social networks: Why we disclose. *Journal of Information Technology*, *25*(2), 109–125. doi:10.1057/jit.2010.6

Kraut, R., Patterson, M., Lumark, V., Kiesler, S., Mukhopadhyay, T., & Scherlis, W. (1998). The Internet paradox: A social technology that reduces social involvement and psychological well-being. *The American Psychologist*, *53*, 1017–1032. doi:10.1037/0003-066X.53.9.1017

Kriplean, T., Beschastnikh, I., McDonald, D. W., & Golder, S. A. (2007). Community, consensus, coercion, control: CS* w or how policy mediates mass participation. In *Proceedings of the 2007 International ACM Conference on Supporting Group Work* (pp. 167–176).

Kuk, G. (2006). Strategic interaction and knowledge sharing in the KDE developer mailing list. *Management Science*, *52*(7), 1031. doi:10.1287/mnsc.1060.0551

Kumar, R., Novak, J., Raghavan, P., & Tomkins, A. (2004). Structure and evolution of blogspace. *Communications of the ACM*, *47*(12), 39.

Kumru, A., & Thompson, R. A. (2003). Ego identity status and self-monitoring behavior in adolescents. *Journal of Adolescent Research*, *1*, 1–16.

Kushin, M. T., & Kitchener, K. (2009). Getting political on social network sites: Exploring online political discourse on Facebook. *First Monday*, *14*(11). Retrieved from http://firstmonday.org/ htbin/cgiwrap/bin/ojs/index.php/ fm/article/viewArticle/2645/2350.

Kuzma, J. (2010). Asian government usage of Web 2.0 Social Media. *European Journal of ePractice, 9,* 71-83, Retrieved March 11, 2011, from http://www.eupractice.eu

Kwak, H., Lee, C., Park, H., & Moon, S. (2010). What is Twitter, a social network or a news media? Proceedings of the *19th International Conference on World Wide Web (WWW'10),* Raleigh, North Carolina.

Lampe, C., Ellison, N., & Steinfield, C. (2006). A Face(book) in the crowd: Social searching vs. social browsing. *Proceedings of the Conference on Computer-Supported Cooperative Work* (CSCW'06), (pp. 167-170). Banff, Alberta.

Lampe, C., Ellison, N., & Steinfield, C. (2008). *Changes in use and perception of Facebook.* Paper presented at the CSCW, San Diego, CA.

Lange, P. (2008). Publicly private and privately public: Social networking on YouTube. *Journal of Computer-Mediated Communication, 13*(1), 361–380. doi:10.1111/j.1083-6101.2007.00400.x

Lanier, J. (2006, May 30). Digital Maoism: The hazards of the new online collectivism. *Edge webzine*. Retrieved March 11, 2008, from http://www.edge.org/3rd_culture/lanier06/lanier06_index.html

Lash, S. (2002). *Critique of information.* London, UK: Sage.

Lash, S. (2006). Dialectic of information? A response to Taylor. *Information Communication and Society, 9*(5), 572–582. doi:10.1080/13691180600965542

Lau, R. R. (1989). Construct accessibility and electoral choice. *Political Behavior, 11*(1), 5–32. doi:10.1007/BF00993365

Lazarsfeld, P. F., Berelson, B., & Gaudet, H. (1944). *The people's choice: How the voter makes up his mind in a presidential campaign.* New York, NY: Columbia University Press.

Leary, M., Kelly, K., Cottrell, C., & Schreindorfer, L. (2001). *Individual differences in the need to belong: Mapping the nomological network.* Unpublished Paper. Wake Forest University.

Lee, S. (2009). Online communication and adolescent social ties: Who benefits more from internet use? *Journal of Computer-Mediated Communication,* 14.

Lee, M., & Lee Elser, E. (2010). *The nine commandments of social media in public administration: A dual-generation perspective. PA Times, 33(3).* Washington, DC: American Society for Public Administration.

Lefebvre, H. (1991). *The production of space*. Oxford, UK: Blackwell.

Lefebvre, H. (1999). *The production of space*. Oxford, UK: Blackwell. (Original work published 1974)

Leighton, B., & Wellman, B. (1979). Networks, neighborhoods and communities. *Urban Affairs Quarterly, 14,* 363–390. doi:10.1177/107808747901400305

Lenhart, A., & Madden, M. (2007). *Teens, privacy & online social networks: How teens manage their online identities and personal information in the age of MySpace*. Retrieved December 8, 2010, from http://www.pewinternet.org/Reports/2007/Teens-Privacy-and-Online-Social-Networks.aspx?r=1

Lenhart, A., Madden, M., Macgill, A., & Smith, A. (2007, December 19). *Teens and social media.* Pew Internet & American Life Project. Retrieved October 28, 2010, from http://www.pewinternet.org/Reports/2007/Teens-Privacy-and-Online-Social-Networks.aspx

Leskovec, J., & Horvitz, E. (2008). Planetary-scale views on a large instant-messaging network. *Proceedings of the 17th International Conference on World Wide Web (WWW'08),* Beijing, China.

Leuf, B., & Cunningham, W. (2001). *The Wiki way. Quick collaboration on the Web.* Boston, MA: Addison-Wesley.

Levine, R., Locke, C., Searls, D., & Weinberger, D. (2000). *The cluetrain manifesto.* Cambridge, MA: Perseus Books.

Levy, S. (1985). *Hackers: Heroes of the computer revolution.* New York, NY: Dell.

Levy, M. R., & Windahl, S. (1985). The concept of audience activity. In K. E. Rosengren, L. A. Wenner, & P. Palmgreen (Eds.), *Media gratifications research: Current perspectives (pp.* 109-122). Beverly Hills, CA: Sage.

Lewis, K., Kaufman, J., & Christakis, N. (2008). The taste for privacy: An analysis of college student privacy settings in an online social network. *Journal of Computer-Mediated Communication, 14,* 79–100. doi:10.1111/j.1083-6101.2008.01432.x

Lewis, B. K. (2010). Social media and strategic communication: Attitudes and perceptions among college students. [from http://www.prsa.org/Intelligence/PRJournal]. *The Public Relations Journal*, *4*(3), 1–23. Retrieved January 27, 2011.

Li, C., & Bernoff, J. (2008). *Groundswell: Winning in a world transformed by social technologies*. Boston, UK: Harvard Business Press.

Libai, B., Bolton, R., Bügel, M. S., de Ruyter, K., Götz, O., Risselada, H., & Stephen, A. T. (2010). Customer-to-customer interactions: Broadening the scope of word of mouth research. *Journal of Service Research*, *13*, 267–282. doi:10.1177/1094670510375600

Licklider, J. C. R. (1960). Man-computer symbiosis. *IRE Transactions on Human Factors in Electronics*, *HFE-1*(March), 4–11. doi:10.1109/THFE2.1960.4503259

Licklider, J. C. R., & Taylor, R. W. (1968, April). The computer as a communication device. *Science and Technology*, 21-31.

Lievrouw, L., & Livingstone, S. (2006). *The handbook of new media (updated student edition)*. London, UK: Sage.

Light, J. S. (1999). From city space to cyberspace. In Crang, M., Crang, P., & May, J. (Eds.), *Virtual geographies: Bodies, spaces and relations* (pp. 109–130). London, UK: Routledge.

Lih, A. (2010). *The Wikipedia revolution: How a bunch of nobodies created the world's greatest encyclopedia*. Aurum Press, Limited.

Lindmark, S. (2009). *Web 2.0: Where does Europe stand?* JRC European Commission. Retrieved December 13, 2010, from http://ftp.jrc.es/EURdoc/JRC53035.pdf

Lipovetsky, G. (1983). *L'ère du vide. Essais sur l'individualisme contemporain*. Paris, France: Éditions Gallimard.

Liu, H. (2008). Social network profiles as taste performances. *Journal of Computer-Mediated Communication*, *13*, 252–275. doi:10.1111/j.1083-6101.2007.00395.x

Liu, B. (2010). Sentiment analysis and subjectivity. In Indurkhia, N., & Damerau, F. J. (Eds.), *Handbook of natural language processing* (2nd ed.). Boca Raton, FL: Chapman & Hall/CRC.

Livingstone, S. (2008). Taking risky opportunities in youthful content creation: Teenagers' use of social networking sites for intimacy, privacy and self-expression. *New Media & Society*, *10*(3). doi:10.1177/1461444808089415

Livingstone, S. (2004). The challenge of changing audiences: Or, what is the audience researcher to do in the age of the internet? *European Journal of Communication*, *19*(1), 75–86. doi:10.1177/0267323104040695

Livingstone, S. (2005). *Audience and publics: When cultural engagement matters for the public sphere*. Bristol, UK: Intellect Books.

Livingstone, S. (2006). Children's privacy online: experimenting with boundaries within and beyond the family. In Kraut, R., Brynin, M., & Kiesler, S. (Eds.), *Computers, phones, and the Internet: Domesticating Information Technology* (pp. 128–144). Oxford, UK: Oxford University Press.

Livingstone, S. (2003). The changing nature and uses of media literacy, *Media@lse Electronic Working Papers*, 4.

Lovari, A., & Parisi, L. (2009, November). *Amministrazioni pubbliche in ascolto. Prove di customer satisfaction attraverso la lente dei social network site*. Paper presented at the conference *Reti socievoli, convegno Pic AIS*, Urbino, Italy.

Lovari, A., & Parisi, L. (2010). *Pubbliche amministrazioni e cittadini 2.0, Esplorando forme di partecipazione civica e relazionalità*. Paper presented at AIS Conference, Milano, Italy.

Lovett, J., & Owyang, J. (2010, April 21). *Social marketing analytics. A new framework for measuring results in social media*. Web Analytics Demystified and Altimeter Group.

Lövheim, M. (2004). Young people, religious identity, and the internet. In Dawson, L. L., & Cowan, D. E. (Eds.), *Religion online: Finding faith on the Internet* (pp. 59–73). New York, NY: Routledge.

Lövheim, M., & Linderman, A. (2005). Constructing religious identity on the Internet. In Højsgaard, M. T., & Warburg, M. (Eds.), *Religion and cyberspace* (pp. 121–137). London, UK: Routledge.

Lövheim, M. (2008). *Finding and sharing religion online? Some new questions and challenges*. Presented at Association of Internet Researchers 9.0, Copenhagen.

Lowin, A. (1967). Approach and avoidance: Alternate modes of selective exposure to information. *Journal of Personality and Social Psychology*, *6*(1), 1–9. doi:10.1037/h0024531

Lucente, G. (1991). Modernism and postmodernism in Italian literature and philosophy. *Annali di Italianistica*, 9.

Luft, J., & Ingham, H. (1955). The Johari window, a graphic model of interpersonal awareness. In *Proceedings of the Western Training Laboratory in Group Development*. Los Angeles, CA: UCLA.

Lyon, D. (1994). *The electronic eye. The rise of surveillance society*. Minneapolis, MN: University of Minnesota Press.

Lyon, D. (2006). 9/11, synopticon and scopophilia: Watching and being watched. In Haggerty, K. D., & Ericson, R. V. (Eds.), *The new politics of surveillance and visibility* (pp. 35–54). Toronto, Canada: University of Toronto Press.

Machilek, F., Schütz, A., & Marcus, B. (2004). Selbstdarsteller oder Menschen wie du und ich? Intentionen und Persönlichkeitsmerkmale von Homepagebesitzer/inne/n [Self-promoters or ordinary people? Intention and personality of homepage owners]. *Zeitschrift für Medienpsychologie*, *16*, 88–98. doi:10.1026/1617-6383.16.3.88

Majchrzak, A., Wagner, C., & Yates, D. (2006). Corporate wiki users: Results of a survey. *Proceedings of the 2006 International Symposium on Wikis*, (pp. 99-104).

Malhotra, N. K., Kim, S. S., & Agarwal, J. (2004). Internet users' information privacy concerns (IUIPC): The construct, the scale, and a causal model. *Information Systems Research*, *15*(4), 336–355. doi:10.1287/isre.1040.0032

Manago, A., Graham, M., Greenfield, P., & Salimkhan, G. (2008). Self-presentation and gender on MySpace. *Journal of Applied Developmental Psychology*, *29*, 446–458. doi:10.1016/j.appdev.2008.07.001

Mann, S., Nolam, J., & Wellman, B. (2003). Sousveillance: Inventing and using wearable computing devices for data collection in surveillance environments. *Surveillance & Society*, *1*(3), 331–355. Retrieved from http://www.surveillance-and-society.org/articles1%283%29/sousveillance.pdf.

Mantovani, G., & Riva, G. (1999). Real presence: How different ontologies generate different criteria for presence, telepresence, and virtual presence. *Presence (Cambridge, Mass.)*, *8*(5), 540–550. doi:10.1162/105474699566459

Marinelli, A. (2004). *Connessioni. Nuovi media, nuove reti sociali*. Milano, Italy: Guerini.

Marwick, A. & boyd, d. (2010). I Tweet honestly, I Tweet passionately: Twitter users, context collapse, and the imagined audience. *New Media & Society*. Online.

Marzo, J. L. (2002). Cultura de registro. In Fundació Tàpies, et al. (Eds.), *Culturas de archivo*. Barcelona, Spain: Editor. English version retrieved from http://www.soymenos.net/registry_culture.pdf

Masini, M., Lovari, A., & Benenati, S. (Eds.). (2009). *Comunicazione pubblica digitale*. Acireale-Roma, Italy: Bonanno Editore.

Massey, D. (1994). *Space, place, and gender*. Minneapolis, MN: University of Minnesota Press.

Massey, D. (2005). *For space*. London, UK: Sage.

Massey, D. (2009). Concepts of space and power in theory and in political practice. *Documents d'Analisi Geografica*, *55*(55), 15–26.

Massey, D. (1999). Spaces of politics. In Massey, D., Allen, J., & Sarre, P. (Eds.), *Human geography today* (pp. 279–294). Cambridge, UK: Polity Press.

Massey, D. (2007). *Is the world getting larger or smaller?* Retrieved from http://www.opendemocracy.net/globalization-vision_reflections/world_small_4354.jsp

Matei, S. A. (2005). A sounding board for the self: Virtual community as ideology. *The Journal of Technical Writing and Communication*, *35*(4), 345–365. doi:10.2190/402T-KPLQ-V5QD-PCFX

Matei, S. A. (2005). From counterculture to cyberculture: Virtual community discourse and the dilemma of modernity. *Journal of Computer-Mediated Communication*, *10*(3). Retrieved from http://jcmc.indiana.edu/vol10/issue3/matei.html.

Matei, S. A., & Dobrescu, C. (2011). Wikipedia's "neutral point of view:"Settling conflict through ambiguity. *The Information Society*, *27*, 1–12. doi:.doi:10.1080/01972243.2011.534368

Matei, S. A., & Oh, K. (2005). *Collaboration and communication in online environments: A social entropy approach*. Presented at the National Communication Association Annual Conference, Austin, TX.

Matei, S. A., Bruno, R., & Morris, P. (2010). Visible effort: A social entropy methodology for managing computer-mediated collaborative learning. In *Proceedings of the Fourth Global Communication Forum*. Presented at the Global Communication Forum, Shanghai: Jiao Tong University. Retrieved from http://matei.org/ithink/?p=22040

Mathiesen, T. (1997). The viewer society: Michel Foucault's panopticon revisited. *Theoretical Criminology*, *1*(2), 215–234. doi:10.1177/1362480697001002003

Matsuo, H., McIntyre, K. P., Tomazic, T., & Katz, B. (2004). The online survey: Its contributions and potential problems. *Proceeding of the Survey Research Methods Section*, ASA 2004, (pp. 3998-4000).

Matzat, U. (2004). Cooperation and community on the Internet: Past issues and present perspectives for theoretical-empirical Internet research. *Analyse & Kritik*, *26*(1), 63–90.

Mayring, P. (2003). *Qualitative Inhaltsanalyse. Grundlagen und Techniken* (8th ed.). Weinheim, Germany: Beltz.

Mazer, J. P., Murphy, R. E., & Simonds, C. J. (2007). I'll see you on "Facebook": The effects of computer-mediated teacher self-disclosure on student motivation, affective learning, and classroom climate. *Communication Education*, *56*(1), 1–17. doi:10.1080/03634520601009710

McHenry, R. (2004). *The faith-based encyclopedia*.

McKenna, K. Y. A., Green, A. S., & Gleason, M. E. G. (2002). Relationship formation on the Internet: What is the big attraction? *The Journal of Social Issues*, *58*(1), 9–31. doi:10.1111/1540-4560.00246

McLeod, J. M., & Becker, L. B. (1981). The uses and gratifications approach. In Nimmo, D. D., & Sanders, K. R. (Eds.), *Handbook of political Communication* (pp. 67–100). Beverly Hills, CA: Sage.

McLuhan, M. (2001). *Understanding media: The extensions of man*. London, NY: Routledge. (Original work published 1964)

McPherson, M., Smith-Lovin, L., & Cook, J. (2001). Birds of a feather: Homophility in social networks. *Annual Review of Sociology*, *27*, 415–444. doi:10.1146/annurev.soc.27.1.415

Mead, G. H. (1934). *Mind, self, and society from the standpoint of a social behaviorist*. Chicago, IL: University of Chicago Press.

Mead, G. H. (1988). *Geist, Identität und Gesellschaft aus der Sicht des Sozialbehaviorismus*. Frankfurt am Main, Germany: Suhrkamp.

Medierådet. (2010). *Ungar & Medier 2010: Fakta om Barns och Ungas Anvandning och Upplevelser av Medier*. Stockholm, Sweden: Kulturdepartementet.

Meffert, M. F., Chung, S., Joiner, A. J., Waks, L., & Garst, J. (2006). The effects of negativity and motivated information processing during a political campaign. *The Journal of Communication*, *56*(1), 27–51. doi:10.1111/j.1460-2466.2006.00003.x

Mehdizadeh, S. (2010). Self-presentation 2.0: Narcissism and self-esteem on Facebook. *Cyberpsychology, Behavior, and Social Networking*, *13*(4), 357–364. doi:10.1089/cyber.2009.0257

Mellins, M. (2008). The female vampire community and online social networks: Virtual celebrity and mini communities: Initial thoughts. *International Journal of Media and Cultural Politics*, *4*(2), 254–258. doi:10.1386/macp.4.2.254_3

Melucci, A. (1989). *Nomads of the present. Social movements and individual needs in contemporary society*. London, UK: Hutchinson Radius.

Melucci, A. (1991). *Il gioco dell'io. Il cambiamento di sé in una società globale*. Milano, Italy: Feltrinelli.

Mergel, I. (2010). *Gov 2.0 revisited: Social media strategies in the public sector. PA Times, 33(3)*. Washington, DC: American Society for Public Administration.

Merleau-Ponty, M. (1962). *Phenomenology of perception* (Smith, C., Trans.). London, UK: Routledge. (Original work published 1945)

Mesch, G. S., & Beker, G. (2010). Are norms of disclosure of online and offline personal information associated with the disclosure of personal information online? *Human Communication Research, 36*(4), 570–592. doi:10.1111/j.1468-2958.2010.01389.x

Mesch, G. S., & Talmud, I. (2006). Online friendship formation, communication channels, and social closeness. *International Journal of Internet Science, 1*(1), 29–44.

Meyrowitz, J. (1985). *No sense of place: The impact of electronic media on social behaviour*. New York, NY: Oxford University Press.

Mikkola, H., Oinas, M.-M., & Kumpulainen, K. (2008). Net-based identity and body image among young IRC-gallery users. In K. McFerrin, R. Weber, R. Carlsen, & D. A. Willis (Eds.). *Proceedings of Society for Information Technology and Teacher Education International Conference 2008*, (pp. 3080-3085), Chesapeake, VA: AACE.

Miller, D., & Slater, D. (2000). *The Internet: An ethnographic approach*. Oxford, UK: Berg.

Miller, A. G., McHoskey, J. W., Bane, C. M., & Dowd, T. G. (1993). The attitude polarization phenomenon: Role of response measure, attitude extremity, and behavioral consequences of reported attitude change. *Journal of Personality and Social Psychology, 64*(4), 561–574. doi:10.1037/0022-3514.64.4.561

Milne, E. (2010). *Letters, postcards, email: Technologies of presence*. New York, NY: Routledge.

Minestroni, L. (2010). *Il manuale della marca. Consumatore, cultura, società*. Bologna, Italy: Fausto Lupetti editore.

Mislove, A., Marcon, M., Gummadi, P. K., Druschel, P., & Bhattacharjee, B. (2007). Measurement and analysis of online social networks. *Proceedings of the ACM Internet Measurement Conference (IMC'07)*, San Diego, CA.

Mitchell, W. J. (2000). *City of bits: Space, place, and the Infobahn*. Cambridge, MA: MIT Press. (Original work published 1995)

Mitchell, W. J. (2003). *Me++: The cyborg self and the networked city*. Cambridge, MA: MIT Press.

Mittel, J. (2007). *Constructing an older audience*. Retrieved from http://justtv.wordpress.com

Monte, L. (2009). *The social pulpit. Barack Obama, social media toolkit*. Retrieved March 15, 2011, from http://www.edelman.com

Moores, S. (1994). *Interpreting audiences: The ethnography of media consumption*. London, UK: Sage.

Moritz, J. M. (2008). Beyond strategy, towards the kingdom of God: The post-critical reconstructionist mission of the emerging church. *Dialog: A Journal of Theology, 47*(1), 27-36.

Muise, A., Christofides, E., & Desmarais, S. (2009). More information than you ever wanted: Does Facebook bring out the green-eyed monster of jealousy? *Cyberpsychology & Behavior, 12*(4), 441–444. doi:10.1089/cpb.2008.0263

Murray, C., Schroder, K., Drotner, K., & Kline, S. (2003). *Researching audiences: A practical guide to methods in media audience analysis*. USA: Bloomsbury.

Mutz, D. C. (2002). Cross-cutting social networks: Testing democratic theory in practice. *The American Political Science Review, 96*(1), 111–126. doi:10.1017/S0003055402004264

Mutz, D. C., & Martin, P. S. (2001). Facilitating communication across lines of political difference: The role of mass media. *The American Political Science Review, 95*(1), 97–114.

Nabatchi, T., & Mergel, I. (2010). Participation 2.0: Using Internet and social media: technologies to promote distributed democracy and create digital neighborhoods. In J. H. Svara, & J. Denhardt (Eds.), *Connected communities, local government as partners in citizens engagement and community building* (pp. 80-87). Retrieved March 10, 2011, from http://www.tlgconference.org/communityconnectionswhitepaper.pdf

Nielsen, (Ed.). (2009). *Global faces and network place. A Nielsen report on social networking's new global footprint*. Retrieved December 13, 2010, from http://blog.nielsen.com/nielsenwire/wp-content/uploads/2009/03/nielsen_globalfaces_mar09.pdf

Nimmo, D. (1990). Principles of information seeking in information processing: A preliminary political analysis. In Kraus, S. (Ed.), *Mass communication and political information processing* (pp. 3–17). Hillsdale, NJ: Lawrence Erlbaum Associates.

Norman, D. (1988). *The psychology of everyday things*. New York, NY: Basic Books.

Norris, P. A., & Jones, D. (1998). Virtual democracy. *The Harvard International Journal of Press/Politics*, *3*, 474–480. doi:10.1177/1081180X98003002001

Noveck, B. S. (2009). *Wiki government: How technology can make government better, democracy stronger, and citizens more powerful*. Washington, DC: Brookings Institution Press.

Nyland, R. (2007). *The gratification niches of Internet social networking, e-mail, and face-to-face communication*. (Unpublished master's thesis), Brigham Young University.

O'Reilly, T. (2005). What is Web 2.0? Design patterns and business models for the next generation of software. Retrieved December 13, 2010, from www.oreillynet.com

O'Leary, S. (2005). Utopian and dystopian possibilities of networked religion in the new millennium. In Højsgaard, M. T., & Warburg, M. (Eds.), *Religion and cyberspace* (pp. 38–49). London, UK: Routledge.

Orgad, S. (2009). How can researchers make sense of the issues involved in collecting and interpreting online and offline data? In Markham, A. N., & Baym, N. K. (Eds.), *Internet inquiry: Conversations about method* (pp. 33–53). Thousand Oaks, CA: Sage.

Ortega, F., Gonzalez-Barahona, J., & Robles, G. (2008). On the inequality of contributions to Wikipedia. In *Proceedings of the 41st Annual Hawaii International Conference on System Sciences*, (p. 304). doi:10.1109/HICSS.2008.333

Osimo, D. (2008). *Web 2.0 in government: Why and how?* European Commission, Joint Research Centre. Retrieved December 13, 2010, from http//ftp.jrc.es/EURdoc/JRC45269.pdf

Palmgreen, P. (1984). Uses and gratifications: A theoretical perspective. In Bostrom, R. N. (Ed.), *Communication yearbook 8* (pp. 61–72). Beverly Hills, CA: Sage Publications, Inc.

Pang, B., & Lee, L. (2008). Opinion mining and sentiment analysis. *Foundations and Trends in Information Retrieval*, *2*(1-2), 1–135. doi:10.1561/1500000011

Pang, B., & Lee, L. (2008). Opinion mining and sentiment analysis. *Foundations and Trends in Information Retrieval*, *2*(1-2), 1–135. doi:10.1561/1500000011

Papacharissi, Z. (2007). The blogger revolution? Audiences as media producers. M. Tremayne (Ed), *Blogging, citizenship, and the future of media* (pp. 21-39). New York: Routledge.

Parikh, R., & Movassate, M. (2009). *Sentiment analysis of user generated Twitter updates using various Classification techniques* (pp. 1–18). MOST.

Parikka, J. (2007). *Digital contagions: A media archaeology of computer viruses*. New York, NY: Peter Lang.

Park, N., Kee, K. F., & Valenzuela, S. (2009). Being immersed in social networking environment: Facebook groups, uses and gratifications, and social outcomes. *Cyberpsychology & Behavior*, *12*(10), 1–5.

Parks, M. R. (2008). *Characterizing the communicative affordances of MySpace: A place for friends or a friendless place?* Paper presented at the annual meeting of the International Communication Association, Montreal, Canada.

Parks, M. R. (2010). *Who are Facebook friends? Exploring the composition of Facebook friend networks*. Paper presented at the Annual Meeting of the International Communication Association, Singapore, Singapore.

Patchins, J., & Hinduja, S. (2010). Trends in online social networking: Adolescent use of MySpace over time. *New Media & Society*, *12*(2), 197–216. doi:10.1177/1461444809341857

Pempek, T. A., Yermolayeya, Y. A., & Calvert, S. L. (2009). College students' social networking experiences on Facebook. *Journal of Applied Developmental Psychology*, *30*(3), 227–238. doi:10.1016/j.appdev.2008.12.010

Perlmutter, D. D. (2008). *Blog wars*. New York, NY: Oxford University Press.

Peters, P. (2006). *Quitting Wikipedia and wanted you to know why* (Vol. 2006).

Petty, R., & Cacioppo, J. (1986). *Communication and persuasion: Central and peripheral routes to attitude change*. New York, NY: Springer-Verlag Pew Research Center. (2008a, December 15). *Internet now major source of campaign news: Continuing partisan divide in cable TV news audience*. Retrieved from http://people-press.org/report

Pew Research Center. (2008b, December 15). *Key news audiences now blend online and traditional sources: Audience segments in a changing news environment.* Retrieved from http://people-press/org/reports

Pew Research Center. (2010). *Americans spending more time following the news: Ideological news source: Who watches and why?* Retrieved from http://pewresearch.org/pubs/1725/where-people-get-news-print-online-readership-cable-news-viewers

Picciano, A. (2002). Beyond student perceptions: Issues of interaction, presence, and performance in an online course. *Journal of Asynchronous Learning Networks, 6*(1), 21–40.

Picó, J. (1999). *Cultura y modernidad. Seducciones y desengaños de la cultura moderna.* Madrid, Spain: Alianza Editorial.

Pieterson, W., & Ebbers, W. (2008). The use of service channel by citizens in the Netherlands: Implications for multi-channel management. *International Review of Administrative Sciences, 74*(1), 95–110. doi:10.1177/0020852307085736

Postill, J. (2009). *The weakness of weak ties: Personal media and social leadership in a Kuala Lumpur suburb.* Paper presented to the Anthropology Department, University of Vienna.

Postmes, T., Spears, R., & Lea, M. (1998). Breaching or building social boundaries? *Communication Research, 25*, 689–715. doi:10.1177/009365098025006006

Preece, J., Nonnecke, B., & Andrews, D. (2004). The top five reasons for lurking: Improving community experiences for everyone. *Computers in Human Behavior, 20*(2), 201–223. doi:10.1016/j.chb.2003.10.015

Prentice, D., Miller, D., & Lightdale, J. (1994). Asymmetries in attachments to groups and to their members: Distinguishing between common-identity and common-bond groups. *Personality and Social Psychology Bulletin, 20*(5), 484–493. doi:10.1177/0146167294205005

Prior, M. (2002). Liberated viewers, polarized voters - The implications of increased media choice for democratic politics. *The Good Society, 11*(3), 10–16. doi:10.1353/gso.2003.0016

Project for Excellence in Journalism. (2010). *How blogs and social media agendas relate and differ from the traditional press.* Retrieved from http://www.journalism.org/analysis_report/new_media_old_media

Purcell, K., Rainie, L., Mitchell, A., Rosenstiel, T., & Olmstead, K. (2010). *Understanding the participatory news consumer.* Retrieved from http://www.pewinternet.org/Reports/2010/Online-News.aspx?r=1

Puro, J.-P. (2002). Finland: A mobile culture. In Katz, J. E., & Aakhus, M. (Eds.), *Perpetual contact: Mobile communication, private talk, public performance* (pp. 19–29). Cambridge, MA: Cambridge University Press.

Putnam, R. (2001). *Bowling alone: The collapse and revival of American community.* New York, NY: Simon & Schuster Paperbacks.

Qualman, E. (2009). *Socialnomics: How social media transforms the way we live and do business.* Hoboken, NJ: Wiley.

Quan-Haase, A., & Young, A. L. (2010). Uses and gratifications of social media: A comparison of Facebook and instant messaging. *Bulletin of Science, Technology & Society, 30*, 350–361. doi:10.1177/0270467610380009

Quan-Haase, A., & Wellman, B. with Witte, J. & Hampton, K. (2002). Capitalizing on the net. In B. Wellman, C. Haythornwaite (Eds.), *The Internet in everyday life* (pp. 291-324). Oxford, UK: Blackwell.

Quocirca, (Ed.). (2007). Social networking and opportunities in the public sector. Retrieved December 13, 2010, from www.quocirca.com

Raacke, J., & Bonds-Raacke, J. (2008). MySpace and Facebook: Applying the uses and gratifications theory to exploring friend-networking sites. *Cyberpsychology & Behavior, 11*(2), 169–174. doi:10.1089/cpb.2007.0056

Radian6, 2010, Social media listening, measuring and engagement primer. Retrieved January 26, 2011, from http://www.radian6.com

Rainie, L. (2003). *Teenage life online: The rise of the networked generation.* Paper presented at the Youth.Net Conference. Singapore.

Rau, P.-L. P., Gao, Q., & Ding, Y. (2008). Relationship between the level of intimacy and lurking in online social network services. *Computers in Human Behavior*, *24*(6), 2757–2770. doi:10.1016/j.chb.2008.04.001

Raymond, E. S. (2001). *The cathedral and the bazaar: Musings on Linux and open source by an accidental revolutionary (Rev.)*. Cambridge, MA: O'Reilly.

Ren, Y., Kraut, R., & Kiesler, S. (2007). Applying common bond and identity theory to design of online communities. *Organization Studies*, *28*, 377–408. doi:10.1177/0170840607076007

Resnick, M. (1994). *Turtles, termites, and traffic jams: explorations in massively parallel microworlds. Complex adaptive systems*. Cambridge, MA: MIT Press.

Reynolds, G. (2006). *An army of Davids: How markets and technology empower ordinary people to beat big media, big government, and other Goliaths*. Thomas Nelson.

Rheingold, H. (2000). *The virtual community: Homesteading on the electronic frontier* (2nd ed.). Cambridge, MA: MIT Press.

Rheingold, H. (2003). *Smart mobs. The next social revolution*. Cambridge, MA: Perseus Book.

Rheingold, H. (2008). Using participatory media and public voice to encourage civic engagement. In Bennet, L. (Ed.), *Civic life online* (pp. 97–118). Cambridge, MA: McArthur Foundation.

Rice, R. E., & Love, G. (1987). Electronic emotion: Socio-emotional content in a computer mediated communication network. *Communication Research*, *14*, 85–108. doi:10.1177/009365087014001005

Ridings, C. M., & Gefen, D. (2004). Virtual community attraction: Why people hang out online. *Journal for Computer-Mediated Communication, 4*. Retrieved October 10, 2010, from http://jcmc.indiana.edu/vol10/issue1/ridings_gefen.html

Ritzer, G. (2004). *The McDonaldization of society*. London, UK: Pine Forge Press.

Ritzer, G., & Jurgenson, N. (2010). Production, consumption, prosumption: The Nature of capitalism in the age of the digital "prosumer". *Journal of Consumer Culture*, *10*(1), 13–36. doi:10.1177/1469540509354673

Roberti, G. (2006). Percorsi identitari giovanili. In Bovone, L., & Volontè, P. (Eds.), *Comunicare le identità. Percorsi della soggettività nell'età contemporanea*. Milano, Italy: FrancoAngeli.

Roberts, K. (2005). *Lovemarks. The future beyond brands*. New York, NY: powerHouse Book.

Roberts, K. (2006). The *lovemarks effects. Winning in the consumer revolution*. New York, NY: powerHouse books.

Roberts, N. C. (2010). Open-source, Web-based platforms for public engagement during disasters. In J. H. Svara, & J. Denhardt (Eds.), *Connected communities, local government as partners in citizens engagement and community building* (pp. 88-94), Retrieved March 10, 2011, from http://www.tlgconference.org/communityconnectionswhitepaper.pdf

Robins, K., & Webster, F. (1999). *Times of the technoculture: From the information society to the virtual life*. London, UK: Routledge.

Rosen, C. (2007). Virtual friendship and the new narcissism. *New Atlantis (Washington, D.C.)*, *17*(Summer), 15–31.

Rosen, J. (2010, July 21). The web means the end of forgetting. *New York Times*. Retrieved from http://www.nytimes.com/2010/07/25/magazine/25privacy-t2.html

Rosenberg, M. (1965). *Society and the adolescent self-image*. Princeton, NJ: Princeton University Press.

Ross, C., Orr, E. S., Sisic, M., Arseneault, J. M., Simmering, M. G., & Orr, R. R. (2009). Personality and motivations associated with Facebook use. *Computers in Human Behavior*, *25*(2), 578–586. doi:10.1016/j.chb.2008.12.024

Ross, C. (2008). *"What's up? LOL!" Optimism and gender differences in social support on Facebook.com*. Thesis, Ohio State University, Ohio.

Roszak, T. (1994). *The cult of information: A neo-Luddite treatise on high tech, artificial intelligence, and the true art of thinking* (2nd ed.). Berkley, CA: University of California Press.

Ruggiero, T. (2000). Uses and gratifications theory in the 21st century. *Mass Communication & Society*, *3*, 3–37. doi:10.1207/S15327825MCS0301_02

Sadeh, N., Hong, J., Cranor, L., Fette, I., Kelley, P., Prabaker, M., & Rao, J. (2009). Understanding and capturing people's privacy policies in a mobile social networking application. *Personal and Ubiquitous Computing*, *13*, 401–412. doi:10.1007/s00779-008-0214-3

Saffo, P. (2007). *Farewell information, it's a media age.* Retrieved from http://www.saffo.com/essays/essay_farewellinfo.pdf

Salimkhan, G., Manago, A. M., & Greenfield, P. M. (2010). The construction of the virtual self on MySpace. *Cyberpsychology: Journal of Psychosocial Research on Cyberspace, 4*(1), article 1.

Sandvoss, C. (2005). *Fans: The mirror of consumption.* Cambridge, UK: Polity Press.

Santor, D. A., Messervey, D., & Kusumakar, V. (2000). Measuring peer pressure, popularity, and conformity in adolescent boys and girls: Predicting school performance, sexual attitudes, and substance abuse. *Journal of Youth and Adolescence*, *29*(2), 163–182. doi:10.1023/A:1005152515264

Schneider, F., Feldmann, A., Krishnamurthy, B., & Willinger, W. (2009). Understanding online social network usage from a network perspective. *Proceedings of the ACM Internet Measurement Conference (IMC '09)*, Chicago, IL.

Schudson, M. (1995). *The power of news*. Cambridge, MA: Harvard University Press.

Schuler, D., & Day, P. (2004). *Shaping the network society: The new role of civil society in cyberspace*. Cambridge, MA: MIT Press.

Schutz, A. (1967). *The phenomenology of the social world.* Evanston, IL: Northwestern University Press.

Sciolla, L. (2007). Dimenticare l'identità o le concezioni riduzioniste dell'identità? Note sulle oscillazioni di un concetto. *La società degli individui, 29*, 33-45.

Sears, D. O., & Freedman, J. L. (1967). Selective exposure to information: A critical review. *Public Opinion Quarterly*, *31*, 194–213. doi:10.1086/267513

Seigenthaler, J. (2005, November 29). A false Wikipedia biography. *USA Today*. Retrieved from http://www.usatoday.com/news/opinion/editorials/2005-11-29-wikipedia-edit_x.htm

Serrat, O. (2010). *Social media and the public sector.* Asian Development Bank Report. Retrieved December 13, 2010, from http://www.adb.org/documents/information/knowledge-solutions/social-media-and-the-public-sector.pdf

Shah, D. V., Cho, J., Eveland, W. P. Jr, & Kwak, N. (2005). Information and expression in a digital age: Modeling Internet effects on civic participation. *Communication Research*, *32*, 531–565. doi:10.1177/0093650205279209

Shah, D. V., Kwak, N., & Holbert, R. L. (2001). Connecting and disconnecting with civic life: Patterns of Internet use and the production of social capital. *Political Communication*, *18*, 141–162. doi:10.1080/105846001750322952

Sheldon, P. (2008). Student favorite: Facebook and motives for its use. *Southwestern Mass Communication Journal*, *23*, 39–55.

Sheller, M. (2004). Mobile publics: Beyond the network perspective. *Environment and Planning. D, Society & Space*, *22*(1), 39–52. doi:10.1068/d324t

Sheller, M., & Urry, J. (2003). Mobile transformations of "public" and "private" life. *Theory, Culture & Society*, *20*(3), 107–125. doi:10.1177/02632764030203007

Shields, R. (2006). Flanerie for cyborgs. *Theory, Culture & Society*, *23*(7-8), 209–220. doi:10.1177/0263276406069233

Shim, J. (2008). Social networking sites: A brief comparison of usage in the US and Korea. *Decision Line*, *39*(5), 16–18.

Shirky, C. (2008). *Here comes everybody: The power of organizing without organizations*. The Penguin Press.

Shirky, C. (2010). *Cognitive surplus: Creativity and generosity in a connected age*. The Penguin Press HC.

Shorne. (2006, August 2). *User: Shorne*. Retrieved December 13, 2010, from http://en.wikipedia.org/w/index.php?title=User:Shorne&oldid=67292482

Sibilia, P. (2008). *La intimidad como espectáculo*. Buenos Aires, Argentina: Fondo de Cultura Económica.

Sifry, D. (2006). State of the blogosphere, October, 2006. *Technorati weblog.* Retrieved 19 November 2006, from http://technorati.com/weblog/2006/11/161.html

Siibak, A. (2010). Constructing masculinity on a social networking site. *Young: Nordic Journal of Youth Research, 18*(4), 403–425.

Siibak, A. (2009). Constructing the self through the photo selection – Visual impression management on social networking websites. *Cyberpsychology: Journal of Psychosocial Research on Cyberspace, 3*, article 1.

Sills, S. J., & Song, C. (2002). Innovations in survey research: An application of Web surveys. *Social Science Computer Review, 20*, 22–30. doi:10.1177/089443930202000103

Silverman, D. (2006). *Interpreting qualitative data*. London, UK: Sage.

Silverstone, R. (1999). *Why study the media?*London, UK: Sage Publications.

Simmel, G. (1969). *The sociology of Georg Simmel*. New York, NY: Free Press.

Simmel, G. (1950). The metropolis and mental life. In Wolff, K. H. (Ed.), *The sociology of Georg Simmel* (pp. 409–424). New York, NY: Free Press.

Sirianni, C. (2009). *Investing in democracy: Engaging citizens in collaborative governance*. Washington, DC: Brookings Press.

Smith, S. M., Fabrigar, L. R., & Norris, M. E. (2008). Reflecting on six decades of selective exposure research: Progress, challenges and opportunities. *Social and Personality Psychology Compass, 2*, 464–493. doi:10.1111/j.1751-9004.2007.00060.x

Smith, A. (2009). The Internet's role in campaign 2008. Retrieved from http://www.pewinternet.org/ Reports/2009/6--The-Internets-Role-in-Campaign-2008.aspx

Smith, A. (2010). *Governmento: The internet gives citizens new paths to government services and information.* Pew Internet & American Life Project. Retrieved December 13, 2010, from http://pewinternet.org/Reports/2010/Government-Online.aspx

Smith, A. D. (1999). Problems in conflict management in virtual communities. In M. Smith & P. Kollock (Eds.), *Communities in cyberspace*, 134-163. New York, NY: Routledge.

Smith, A., & Rainie, L. (2008, June 15). *The Internet and the 2008 election.* Pew Internet & American Life Project. Retrieved from http://www.pewinternet.org/Reports/2008/The-Internet-and-the-2008-Election.aspx

Soja, E. (1989). *Postmodern geographies*. London, UK: Verso.

Soja, E. W. (2009). Thirdspace: Toward a new consciousness of space and spatiality. In Ikas, K., & Wagner, G. (Eds.), *Communicating in the third space* (pp. 49–61). New York, NY: Routledge.

Solis, B., & Breakenridge, D. (2009). *Putting the public back in public relations*. Upper Saddle River, NJ: Pearson Education.

Solove, D. J. (2007b). "I've got nothing to hide" and other misunderstandings of privacy. *The San Diego Law Review, 44*, 745–772. http://ssrn.com/abstract=998565.

Solove, D. J. (2007a). Privacy in an overexposed world. In *The future of reputation*. New Haven, CT: Yale University Press. Retrieved from http://docs.law.gwu.edu/facweb/dsolove/Future-of-Reputation/text/futureofreputation-ch7.pdf

Sophos. (2007). *Facebook ID probe shows 41% of users happy to reveal all to potential identity thieves*. Retrieved October 15, 2010, from http://www.sophos.com/pressoffice/news/articles/2007/08/facebook.html/

Sorkin, A. R. (2010, July 22). Facebook tops 500 million users. *New York Times Blog*. Retrieved August 11, 2010, from http://dealbook.blogs.nytimes.com/2010/07/22/facebook-tops-500-million-users/

Soroka, V., & Rafaeli, S. (2006). Invisible participants: How cultural capital relates to lurking behavior. *Proceedings of the 15th International Conference on World Wide Web (WWW '06)*, Edinburgh, Scotland.

Spencer, H. (1885). *The principles of sociology*. London, UK: Williams and Norgate.

Sproul, L., & Kiesler, S. (1986). Reducing social context cues: Electronic mail in organizational communication. *Management Science, 32*(11), 1492–1512. doi:10.1287/mnsc.32.11.1492

Stafford, T. F., Stafford, M. R., & Schkade, L. L. (2004). Determining uses and gratifications for the Internet. *Decision Sciences*, *35*, 259–288. doi:10.1111/j.00117315.2004.02524.x

Stark, D., & Vedres, B. (2006). Social times of network spaces: Network sequences and foreign investment in Hungary. *American Journal of Sociology*, *111*(5), 1367–1411. doi:10.1086/499507

Steinfield, C., Ellison, N., & Lampe, C. (2008). Social capital, self-esteem, and use of online social network sites: A longitudinal analysis. *Journal of Applied Developmental Psychology*, *29*(6), 434–445. doi:10.1016/j.appdev.2008.07.002

Stephan, F. F., & Mishler, E. G. (1952). The distribution of participation in small groups: An exponential approximation. *American Sociological Review*, *17*(5), 598–608. doi:10.2307/2088227

Sterland, S., Powell, R., & Castle, K. (2006). *NCLS occasional paper 8: Inflow and outflow between denominations: 1991 to 2001*. Sydney, Australia: NCLS.

Stovall, J. G. (2004). *Web journalism: Practices and promise of a new medium*. New York, NY: Pearson.

Strano, M. M. (2008). User descriptions and interpretations of self-presentation through Facebook profile images. *Cyberpsychology: Journal of Psychological Research on Cyberspace*, *2*(2), article 5.

Streett, R. A. (2006). An interview with Brian McLaren. *Criswell Theological Review*, *3*(2), 5–14.

Stroud, N. J. (2008). Media use and political predispositions: Revisiting the concept of selective exposure. *Political Behavior*, *30*, 341–366. doi:10.1007/s11109-007-9050-9

Stroud, N. J. (2010). Polarization and partisan selective exposure. *The Journal of Communication*, *60*, 556–576. doi:10.1111/j.1460-2466.2010.01497.x

Stroud, N. J. (2006). *Selective exposure to partisan information.* Unpublished dissertation, University of Pennsylvania, Philadelphia, PA.

Stutzman, F. (2006). An evaluation of identity-sharing behavior in social network communities. International Digital and Media Arts Journal, 3(1).

Stvilia, B., Twidale, M. B., Gasser, L., & Smith, L. (2005). Information quality discussions in Wikipedia. In S. Hawamdeh (Ed.), *Knowledge Management: Nurturing Culture, Innovation, and Technology - Proceedings of the 2005 International Conference on Knowledge Management*, (pp. 101-113). Charlotte, NC: World Scientific Publishing.

Stvilia, B., Twidale, M. B., Smith, L., & Gasser, L. (2005). Assessing information quality of a community-based encyclopedia (pp. 442-454). Cambridge, MA.

Sunstein, C. R. (2001). *Republic.com*. Princeton, NJ: Princeton University Press.

Sunstein, C. R. (2006). *Infotopia: How many minds produce knowledge*. Oxford, UK: Oxford University Press.

Sunstein, C. R. (2007). *Republic.com 2.0*. Princeton, NJ: Princeton University Press.

Sveningsson, M. (2004). Ethics in Internet ethnography. In Buchanan, E. A. (Ed.), *Readings in virtual research ethics: Issues and controversies* (pp. 45–61). Hershey, PA: Information Science Pub.doi:10.4018/978-1-59140-152-0.ch003

Swindler, A. (1986). Culture in action: Symbols and strategies. *American Sociological Review*, *51*(2), 273–286. doi:10.2307/2095521

Taber, C. S., & Lodge, M. (2006). Motivated skepticism in the evaluation of political Beliefs. *American Journal of Political Science*, *50*(3), 755–769. doi:10.1111/j.1540-5907.2006.00214.x

Tapscott, D., & Williams, A. D. (2008). *Wikinomics: How mass collaboration changes everything*. London, UK: Atlantic Books.

Tapscott, D. (2009). *Grown up digital. How the Net generation is changing your world.* New York, NY: McGraw Hill.

Taylor, S. E. (1981). The interface of cognitive and social psychology. In Harvey, J. H. (Ed.), *Cognition, social behavior, and the environment* (pp. 189–211). Hillsdale, NJ: Lawrence Erlbaum Associates.

Technorati. (2008). *Technorati: About us*. Retrieved 6 May 2008, from http://technorati.com/about/

Technorati. (2010). *The state of the blogosphere 2010*. Retrieved 16 March 2011, from http://technorati.com/blogging/article/state-of-the-blogosphere-2010-introduction/

The Economist (Ed.). (2010). *A world of connections. A special report on social networking*. Retrieved December 13, 2010, from http://www.economist.com/node/15351002

Thelwall, M. (2008). Social networks, gender, and friending: An analysis of MySpace member profiles. *Journal of the American Society for Information Science and Technology*, *59*(8), 1321–1330. doi:10.1002/asi.20835

Thiedke, U. (2008). Die Gemeinschaften der Eigensinnigen. Interaktionsmediale Kommunikationsbedingungen und virtuelle Gemeinschaften. In Von Gross, F., Marotzki, W., & Sander, U. (Eds.), *Internet - Bildung - Gemeinschaft* (pp. 45–73). Wiesbaden, Germany: VS Verlag. doi:10.1007/978-3-531-90793-2_4

Thomas, S. (2006). The end of cyberspace and other surprises. *Convergence: The International Journal of Research into New Media Technologies*, *12*(4), 383–391.

Thompson, G. (2003). Weblogs, warblogs, the public sphere, and bubbles. *Transformations*, *7*, 1–12.

Thrift, N. (2005). *Knowing capitalism*. London, UK: Sage.

Tianxia, G. (2008). *Processing sentiments and opinions in text: A survey*. Department of Computer Science, School of Computing, National University of Singapore. Retrieved January 16, 2011, from http://www.comp.nus.edu.sg/~gongtian/CS6207/CS6207_Survey.pdf

Tidwell, L. C., & Walther, J. B. (2002). Computer-mediated communication effects on disclosure, impressions, and interpersonal evaluations: Getting to know one another a bit at a time. *Human Communication Research*, *28*(3), 317–348. doi:10.1111/j.1468-2958.2002.tb00811.x

Toennis, F. (1887). *Gemeinschaft und Gesellschaft. Abhandlung des Communismus und des Socialismus als empirische Culturformen*. Leipzig, Germany: Fues.

Toffler, A. (1981). *The third wave*. New York, NY: Bantam Books.

Tokunaga, R. S. (2011). Social networking site or social surveillance site? Understanding the use of interpersonal electronic surveillance in romantic relationships. *Computers in Human Behavior*, *27*(2), 705–713. doi:10.1016/j.chb.2010.08.014

Tong, S. T., van der Heide, B., Langwell, L., & Walther, J. B. (2008). Too much of a good thing? The relationship between number of friends and interpersonal impressions on Facebook. *Journal of Computer-Mediated Communication*, *13*(3), 531–549. doi:10.1111/j.1083-6101.2008.00409.x

Tönnies, F. (1979). *Gemeinschaft und Gesellschaft. Grundbegriffe der reinen Soziologie*. Darmstadt, Germany: Wissenschaftliche Buchgesellschaft.

Torkjazi, M., Rejaie, R., & Willinger, W. (2009). *Hot today, gone tomorrow: On the migration of MySpace users*. Paper presented at the 2nd ACM Workshop on Online Social Networks, Barcelona, Spain.

Touraine, A. (1997). *Pourrons-nous vivre ensemble? Egaux et différents*. Paris, France: Fayard.

Townsend, A. M. (2000). Life in the real-time city: Mobile telephones and urban metabolism. *Journal of Urban Technology*, *7*(2), 85–104. doi:10.1080/713684114

Trammell, K. D., Tarkowski, A., Hofmokl, J., & Sapp, A. M. (2006). Rzeczpospolita blogow [Republic of Blog]: Examining Polish bloggers through content analysis. *Journal of Computer-Mediated Communication, 11,* article 2. Retrieved from http://jcmc.indiana.edu/vol11/issue3.trammell.html

Tufekci, Z. (2008a). Can you see me now? Audience and disclosure regulation in online social network sites. *Bulletin of Science, Technology & Society*, *28*(1), 20–36. doi:10.1177/0270467607311484

Tufekci, Z. (2008b). Grooming, gossip, Facebook and Myspace. *Information Communication and Society*, *11*(4), 544–564. doi:10.1080/13691180801999050

Turkle, S. (1995). *Life on the screen: Identity in the age of the Internet*. New York, NY: Simon & Schuster.

Turner, B. S. (2008). Religious speech: The ineffable nature of religious communication in the information age. *Theory, Culture & Society*, *25*(7-8), 219–235.

Turoff, M. (1973). Human communication via data networks. In Blanc, R., & Cotton, I. (Eds.), *Computer networking* (pp. 241–245). IEEE Press.

Utz, S. (2007). Media use in long-distance friendships. *Information Communication and Society*, *10*(5), 694–713. doi:10.1080/13691180701658046

Utz, S. (2010). Show me your friends and I will tell you what type of person you are: How one's profile, number of friends, and type of friends influence impression formation on social network sites. *Journal of Computer-Mediated Communication, 15*(2), 314–335. doi:10.1111/j.1083-6101.2010.01522.x

Utz, S., & Beukeboom, C. (2011). The role of social network sites in romantic relationships: Effects on jealousy and relationship happiness. *Journal of Computer-Mediated Communication, 16*(4), 511–527. doi:10.1111/j.1083-6101.2011.01552.x

Utz, S., & Krämer, N. (2009). The privacy paradox on social network sites revisited: The role of individual characteristics and group norms. *Cyberpsychology: Journal of Psychosocial Research on Cyberspace, 3*(2). Retrieved from http://www.cyberpsychology.eu/view.php?cisloclanku=2009111001&article=1

Valenzuela, S., Park, N., & Kee, P. F. (2009). Is there social capital in a social network site? Facebook use and college students' life satisfaction, trust, and participation. *Journal of Computer-Mediated Communication, 14*, 875–901. doi:10.1111/j.1083-6101.2009.01474.x

Valkenburg, P. M., Peter, J., & Schouten, A. P. (2006). Friend networking sites and their relationship to adolescents' well-being and social self-esteem. *Cyberpsychology & Behavior, 9*(5), 584–590. doi:10.1089/cpb.2006.9.584

Van Buskirkr, E. (2008, June 9). Encyclopaedia Britannica to follow modified Wikipedia model. *Wired Magazine*. Retrieved December 13, 2010, from http://www.wired.com/epicenter/2008/06/ency/

Van Dijck, J., & Nieborg, D. (2009). Wikinomics and its discontents: A critical analysis of Web 2.0 business manifestos. *New Media & Society, 11*(5), 855–874. doi:10.1177/1461444809105356

Van Dijck, J. (2009). Users like you? Theorizing agency in user generated content. *Media Culture & Society, 31*(1), 41–58. doi:10.1177/0163443708098245

Van Dijck, J., & Nieborg, D. (2009). Wikinomics and its discontents: A critical analysis of Web 2.0 business manifestos. *New Media & Society, 11*(5), 855–874. doi:10.1177/1461444809105356

Van Dijk, J. (1999). *The network society. Social aspects of new media*. London, UK: Sage.

van Oenen, G. (2008). Interpassivity revisited: A critical and historical reappraisal of interpassive phenomena. *International Journal of Žižek Studies, 2*(2). http://zizekstudies.org/index.php/ijzs/article/view/96/230.

Varnelis, K. (Ed.). (2008). *Networked publics*. Cambridge, MA: MIT Press.

Vazire, S., & Gosling, S. D. (2004). E-perceptions: Personality impressions based on personal websites. *Journal of Personality and Social Psychology, 87*, 123–132. doi:10.1037/0022-3514.87.1.123

Veblen, T. (1899). *The theory of the leisure class*. London, UK: Macmillan.

Veenhof, B., Wellman, B., Quell, C., & Hogan, B. (2008). *How Canadians' use of the Internet affects social life and civic participation*. (Connectedness report series: F0004M-16, December 4.29).

Vergeer, M., & Pelzer, B. (2009). Consequences of media and Internet use for offline and online network capital and well-being. A causal model approach. *Journal of Computer-Mediated Communication, 15*(1), 189–210. doi:10.1111/j.1083-6101.2009.01499.x

Viegas, F., Wattenberg, M., & Kushal, D. (2004). Studying cooperation and conflict between authors with history flow visualizations. In *Proceedings of the SIGCHI Conference on Human Factors in Computing Systems* (pp. p. 575–582). Vienna, Austria: ACM. Retrieved from http://alumni.media.mit.edu/~fviegas/papers/history_flow.pdf

Viegas, F., Wattenberg, M., & van Ham, F. (2007, January 3). Talk before you type: Coordination in Wikipedia. *IBM Research*. Retrieved October 28, 2008, from http://www.research.ibm.com/visual/papers/wikipedia_coordination_final.pdf

Viswanath, B., Mislove, A., Cha, M., & Gummadi, K. P. (2009). On the evolution of user interaction in facebook. *Proceedings of the ACM Workshop on Online Social Networks (WOSN'09)*, Barcelona, Spain.

Vitkauskaite, E. (2010). Overview of research on cross-cultural impact on social networking sites. *Ekonomika ir vadyba, 15*, 844-848.

Von Kardorff, E. (2006). Virtuelle Netzwerke - eine neue Form der Vergesellschaftung? In Holstein, B., & Straus, F. (Eds.), *Qualitative Netzwerkanalyse. Konzepte, Methoden, Anwendungen* (pp. 61–97). Wiesbaden: VS Verlag.

Wall, M. (2006). Blogging Gulf War II. *Journalism Studies*, *7*(1), 111–126. doi:10.1080/14616700500450392

Waller, S. N. (2010). *Social media for public parks and recreation organizations: Bridging the communication gap. PA Times, 33(3)*. Washington, DC: American Society for Public Administration.

Walsh, K. C. (2003). *Talking about politics: Informal groups and social identity in American life*. Chicago, IL: University of Chicago Press.

Walther, J., Van Der Heide, B., Kim, S., Westerman, D., & Tong, S. (2008). The role of friends' appearance and behaviour on evaluations of individuals on Facebook: Are we known by the company we keep? *Human Communication Research*, *34*(1), 28–49. doi:10.1111/j.1468-2958.2007.00312.x

Walther, J. B. (1992). Interpersonal effects in computer-mediated interaction: A relational perspective. *Communication Research*, *19*, 52–90. doi:10.1177/009365092019001003

Walther, J. B., Van Der Heide, B., & Hamel, L., M., & Shulman, H. C. (2009). Self-generated versus other-generated statements and impressions in computer-mediated communication: A test of warranting theory using Facebook. *Communication Research*, *36*(2), 229–253. doi:10.1177/0093650208330251

Walther, J. B., Van Der Heide, B., Kim, S.-Y., Westerman, D., & Tong, S. T. (2008). The role of friends' appearance and behavior on evaluations of individuals on Facebook: Are we known by the company we keep? *Human Communication Research*, *34*(1), 28–49. doi:10.1111/j.1468-2958.2007.00312.x

Walther, J. B., & Parks, M. R. (2002). Cues filtered out, cues filtered in: Computer-mediated communication and relationships. In Knapp, M. L., & Daly, J. A. (Eds.), *Handbook of interpersonal communication* (3rd ed., pp. 529–563). Thousand Oaks, CA: Sage.

Wang, H., & Wellman, B. (2009). (forthcoming). Social connectivity in America. *The American Behavioral Scientist*, *52*.

Wang, H., & Wellman, B. (2010). Social connectivity in America: Changes in adult friendship network size from 2002 to 2007. *The American Behavioral Scientist*, *53*, 1148–1169. doi:10.1177/0002764209356247

Wardrop, M. (2010, August 18). Young will have to change names to escape cyber past, warns Google's Eric Schmidt. *The Telegraph*. Retrieved from http://www.telegraph.co.uk/technology/google/7951269/Young-will-have-to-change-names-to-escape-cyber-past-warns-Googles-Eric-Schmidt.html

Warf, B., & Arias, S. (Eds.). (2008). *The spatial turn: Interdisciplinary perspectives*. London, UK: Routledge.

Waters, R. D., Burnett, E., Lamm, A., & Lucas, J. (2009). Engaging stakeholders through social networking: How nonprofit organizations are using Facebook. *Public Relations Review*, *35*(2), 102–106. doi:10.1016/j.pubrev.2009.01.006

Watkins, C. S., & Lee, E. H. (2010). *Got Facebook? Investigating what's social about social media*. Retrieved December 9, 2010, from http://www.theyoungandthedigital.com/wp-content/uploads/2010/11/watkins_lee_facebookstudy-nov-18.pdf

Weber, M. (1922). *Wirtschaft und Gesellschaft*. Tubingen, Germany: Mohr.

Wehrli, S. (2008). *Personality on social network sites: An application of the five factor model*.

Weinberger, D. (2002). *Small pieces, loosely joined: A unified theory of the web*. Cambridge, MA: Perseus Pub.

Weinberger, D. (2007). *Everything is miscellaneous: The power of the new digital disorder*. New York, NY: Times Books.

Weinstein, D., & Weinstein, M. A. (1991). Georg Simmel: Sociological Flâneur Bricoleur. *Theory, Culture & Society*, *8*(3), 151–168. doi:10.1177/026327691008003011

Wellman, B. (2001). Physical place and cyber place: The rise of personalized networks. *International Journal of Urban and Regional Research*, *25*(2), 227–252. doi:10.1111/1468-2427.00309

Wellman, B. (2004). The three ages of internet studies: Ten, five and zero years ago. *New Media & Society*, *6*(1), 123–129. doi:10.1177/1461444804040633

Wellman, B., & Haythornthwaite, C. (Eds.). (2002). *The Internet in everyday life*. Oxford, UK: Blackwell. doi:10.1002/9780470774298

Wellman, B., Quan Haase, A., Boase, J., Chen, W., Hampton, K., & Díaz, I. (2003). The social affordances of the Internet for networked individualism. *Journal of Computer-Mediated Communication, 8*(3).

Wellman, B. (2001). Physical place and cyberPlace: The rise of personalized networking. *International Journal of Urban and Regional Research, 25*(2), 227–252. doi:10.1111/1468-2427.00309

Wellman, B. (2001b). Computer networks as social networks. *Science, 293*, 2031–2034. doi:10.1126/science.1065547

Wellman, B. (2001b). *The persistence and transformation of community: From neighbourhood groups to social networks*. Ottawa: Report to the Law Commission of Canada.

Wellman, B., Boase, J., Horrigan, J. B., & Rainie, L. (2006). *The strength of Internet ties*. Washington: Pew Internet & American Life Project.

Wellman, B., & Haythornthwaite, C. (Eds.). (2001). *The Internet in everyday life*. Oxford, UK: Blackwell Publishers.

Wellman, B., & Tindall, D. (1993). Reach out and touch some bodies. *Progress in Communication Science, 12*, 63–94.

Wellman, B. (2004). The three ages of Internet Studies: Ten, five and zero years ago. *New Media & Society, 6*(1), 123–129. doi:10.1177/1461444804040633

Wellman, B., Quan-Haase, A., Boase, J., Chen, W., Hampton, K., Isla de Diaz, I., & Miyata, K. (2003). The social affordances of the Internet for networked individualism. *Journal of Computer-Mediated Communication, 8*, ▪▪▪. Retrieved from http://jcmc.indiana.edu/vol8/issue3/wellman.html.

Wellman, B., Haase, A. Q., Witte, J., & Hampton, K. (2001). Does the Internet increase, decrease, or supplement social capital? Social networks, participation, and community commitment. *The American Behavioral Scientist, 45*, 436–455.

Wellman, B., & Hogan, B. (2004). The immanent Internet. In McKay, J. (Ed.), *Netting citizens* (pp. 54–80). Edinburgh, UK: Saint Andrew Press.

Wellman, B. (2002). Little boxes, glocalization, and networked individualism. In Tanabe, M., Van den Besselaar, P., & Ishida, T. (Eds.), *Digital cities* (pp. 10–25). Berlin, Germany: Springer Verlag.

Wellman, B., Quan-Haase, A., Boase, J., Chen, W., Hampton, K., Isla de Diaz, I., & Miyata, K. (2003). The social affordances of the Internet for networked individualism. *Journal of Computer Mediated Communication, 8*. Retrievedfrom http://jcmc.indiana.edu/vol8/issue3/wellman.html

Wesch, M. (2009). YouTube and you: Experiences of self-awareness in the context collapse of the recording webcam. *Explorations in Media Ecology, 8*(2), 19–34.

West, D. M. (2005). *Digital government. Technology and public sector performance*. Princeton, NJ: Princeton University Press.

White, H. (1992). *Identity and control: A structural theory of social action*. Princeton, NJ: Princeton Univ Press.

Wikipedia. the free encyclopedia. (2005, April 16). *Wikipedia talk: Neutral point of view/Archive 002*. Retrieved December 13, 2010, from http://en.wikipedia.org/wiki/Wikipedia_talk:Neutral_point_of_view/Archive_002

Wikipedia. the free encyclopedia. (2005, January 13). *Wikipedia talk: Neutral point of view/Archive 003*. Retrieved December 13, 2010, from http://en.wikipedia.org/wiki/Wikipedia_talk:Neutral_point_of_view/Archive_003

Wikipedia. the free encyclopedia. (2005, June 17). *Wikipedia talk: Neutral point of view/Archive 004*. Retrieved December 13, 2010, from http://en.wikipedia.org/wiki/Wikipedia_talk:Neutral_point_of_view/Archive_004

Wilken, R. (2008). Mobilizing place: Mobile media, peripatetics, and the renegotiation of urban places. *Journal of Urban Technology, 15*(3), 39–55. doi:10.1080/10630730802677939

Willems, H., & Pranz, S. (2008). Formationen und Transformationen der Selbstthematisierung. Von der unmittelbaren Interaktion zum Internet. In Willems, H. (Ed.), *Weltweite Welten. Internet-Figurationen aus wissenssoziologischer Perspektive* (pp. 189–222). Wiesbaden, Germany: VS Verlag.

Williams, A. D., & Tapscott, D. (2010). *Macrowikinomics: Rebooting business and the world*. Portfolio Hardcover.

Wilson, C., Boe, B., Sala, A., Puttaswamy, K. P. N., & Zhao, B. Y. (2009). User interactions in social networks and their implications. *Proceedings of the ACM SIGOPS Eurosys '09*, Nuremberg, Bavaria.

Wittel, A. (2001). Toward a network sociality. *Theory, Culture & Society*, *18*(6), 51–76.

Wolfradt, U., & Doll, J. (2001). Motives of adolescents to use the Internet as a function of personality traits, personal and social factors. *Journal of Educational Computing Research*, *24*(1), 13–27. doi:10.2190/ANPM-LN97-AUT2-D2EJ

Wollman, D. (2011, January 12). On 10th anniversary, Wikipedia aims for diversity. *MSNBC News*. Retrieved February 21, 2011, from http://www.msnbc.msn.com/id/41045439/ns/technology_and_science-tech_and_gadgets/

Woolley, J. A., Limperos, A. M., & Oliver, M. B. (2010). The 2008 presidential election, 2.0: A content analysis of user-generated political Facebook groups. *Mass Communication & Society*, *13*(5), 584–607. doi:10.1080/15205436.2010.516864

Workman, T. A. (2008, February). *Responding to the YouTube and MySpace generation: Thinking digitally about today's college student*. Paper presented at the 29th Annual National Conference on Law and Higher Education, Stetson University College of Law.

Wuthnow, R. (1976). *The consciousness reformation*. Berkeley, CA: University of California Press.

Yarow, J. (2010). *Facebook was more popular in the U.S. than Google last week*. Retrieved October 30, 2010, from http://www.businessinsider.com/facebook-was-more-popular-in-the-us-than-google-last-week-2010-3

Yoneki, E., & Crowcroft, J. (2009). GIS: Geographical information cascade in online social networks. *Proceedings of the International Conference on Network Science (NetSci)*, Venice, Italy.

Young, A. L., & Quan-Haase, A. (2009). *Information revelation and internet privacy concerns on social network sites: A case study of Facebook*. Paper presented at the Fourth International Conference on Communities and Technologies, University Park, PA.

Zaller, J. R. (1992). *The nature and origins of mass opinion*. Cambridge, UK: Cambridge University Press.

Zhao, S., Grasmuck, S., & Martin, J. (2008). Identity construction on Facebook: Digital empowerment in anchored relationships. *Computers in Human Behavior*, *24*(5), 1816–1836. doi:10.1016/j.chb.2008.02.012

Zhuang, L., Jing, F., & Zhu, X.-Y. (2006). Movie review mining and summarization. *Proceedings of the 15th ACM International Conference on Information and Knowledge Management*, (pp. 43-50). Arlington, VA, USA, November 05 - 11, 2006.

Ziemke, D. A. (1980). Selective exposure in a presidential campaign contingent on certainty and salience. In Nimmo, D. (Ed.), *Communication yearbook* (*Vol. 4*, pp. 497–511). New Brunswick, NJ: Transaction Books.

Žižek, S. (1999). Is it possible to traverse the fantasy in cyberspace? In Wright, E., & Wright, E. (Eds.), *The Žižek reader*. Oxford, UK: Blackwell.

Zook, M., Dodge, M., Aoyama, Y., & Townsend, A. (2004). New digital geographies: Information, communication, and place. In Brunn, S. D., Cutter, S. L., & Harrington, J. W. (Eds.), *Geography and technology* (pp. 155–176). Dordrecht, The Netherlands: Kluwer Academic Publishers.

Zywica, J., & Danowski, J. (2008). The faces of Facebookers: Investigating social enhancement and social compensation hypotheses; predicting Facebook and offline popularity from sociability and self-esteem, and mapping the meanings of popularity with semantic networks. *Journal of Computer-Mediated Communication*, *14*, 1–34. doi:10.1111/j.1083-6101.2008.01429.x

About the Contributors

Francesca Comunello (PhD, Sapienza University of Rome, Italy) is Assistant professor of Sociology of Culture and Communication at the Department of Communication and Social Research, Sapienza University of Rome (Italy), where she teaches Internet studies. She is also Member of the Teaching College Board for the PhD Course in Communication at the same Department. Her research focuses on the intersections between digital technology and society: namely, network theories, digitally-mediated social relations, social media and social network sites, digital interactive television, and the digital divide. Her work has been presented at national and international conferences. She has authored two books and several book chapters, and co-edited three books.

***

Romana Andò is Assistant Professor of Sociology of Culture and Communication at the Department of Communication and Social Research, Sapienza University of Rome (Italy), where she teaches Audience Studies. Her research focuses on media audiences, following the cultural studies approach, with a specific focus on: audiences' practices; media use and consumption; and the phenomenon of fandom, understood as a privileged point of view on new forms of engagement in the age of the convergence culture. Recently, she has examined the practices of the audiences in social media environments.

Martin Berg is a senior Lecturer in Sociology at Halmstad University but is currently appointed as senior Researcher at the strategic web agency Good Old, where he leads a three year research project investigating online sociability and social network sites with financial support from The Bank of Sweden Tercentenary Foundation. Martin Berg received his PhD from Lund University in 2008. His award winning doctoral thesis "*The fabricated self: self-reflexive gender play and queer social psychology*" established a theoretical framework based on the tensions between Judith Butler and George H. Mead, while using an analysis of self-presentations and diaries of cross-dressers on the web-community qruiser.com as an empirical foundation.

Shannon Bichard is an Associate Professor of Advertising in the College of Mass Communications at Texas Tech University. Her research interests focus on public opinion and consumer behavior with an emphasis on online communication and political engagement. Her research has appeared in journals such as *Journalism & Mass Communication Quarterly, Journal of Computer-Mediated Communication,* and *Health Communication*. She teaches courses in media planning, advertising campaigns, as well as graduate level classes on integrated campaigns and public opinion.

Robert Bruno (PhD, Purdue University) is a Lecturer of Communication at Purdue University. His research examines the social and cognitive effects of emerging communication technologies.

Paul Emerson Teusner is a recent PhD graduate from the School of Media and Communication at RMIT University in Melbourne, Australia. The title of his thesis is *Emerging church bloggers in Australia: Prophets, priests and rulers in God's virtual world*. At present he is teaching in RMIT's Master's of Communication program on Media Technologies, and is conducting research on young people's relationships with mobile media devices and how they influence how young people talk about friendships, family, work and career, and spirituality. He lives in the countryside with his two children, where he also works as a social worker, managing youth programs for child offenders in the justice system.

Thomas J. Johnson (PhD University of Washington, 1989) is the Amon G. Carter Jr. Centennial Professor in the School of Journalism at University of Texas at Austin. Johnson has studied the role of the media in each election since 1984. Beginning with the 1992 election he began studying the role of new media (and how people used such media). Much of Johnson's work has focused on the credibility of the Internet and its components, but he has also examined uses and gratifications of the Internet and its components, selective exposure and the Internet, the degree to which the Internet has served as a substitute for traditional media, the agenda-building role of the media, and how factors influence journalistic frames. Johnson has authored or co-edited three books. Johnson has 50 refereed journal articles published or in press, 19 book chapters, and more than 100 papers at international, national, and regional conferences.

Barbara K. Kaye (PhD, Florida State University, 1994) is Professor in the School of Journalism & Electronic Media, University of Tennessee at Knoxville. Research interests include media effects, consumer uses of new communication technologies, and the influence of the Web, blogs, and social media on political attitudes and media use. She also studies the uses and effects of profanity on television programs. She has co-authored three textbooks: *Electronic Media: Then, Now, and Later; Just A Click Away: Advertising on the Internet;* and *The World Wide Web: A Mass Communication Perspective.* She has published over 30 articles in such journals as *Journalism & Mass Communication Quarterly, Journal of Broadcasting & Electronic Media,* and *Harvard International Journal of Press/Politics.* Additionally, she has written 11 scholarly books chapters and more than 50 conference papers. She as taught abroad in Italy and Austria, and was named a NATPE (National Association of Television Program Executives) fellow in 2000.

Jenny Kennedy is a PhD candidate in the Media Studies Department of the Humanities, Arts and Social Sciences Faculty at Swinburne University of Technology, Melbourne, Australia. Her research considers the intersection of online and offline, both in topic focus and methodological approach. Specifically, she analyses identity performance in spaces of converged social interactions, which she terms as networked spaces. Her work addresses the tensions of online/offline distinctions across three tiers - individuals, interface, and industry - to identify the relationship between the specificities of communication technologies, the embodied social experience, and the socio/economic framework in which they are situated.

Bernadette Kneidinger has been working since 2008 as a Scientific Assistant in the Department of Communication at the University of Vienna and wrote her dissertation about "national identity construction in the network society," She graduated in communication science and sociology and specialized in media sociology. Her research activities are focused on empirical communication research in the fields of national identity construction, online communication, and the social web. In addition to her research activities, she teaches communication research courses at the Department of Communication of the University of Vienna. She has published a book and several papers about social interaction forms in social network sites.

Alessandro Lovari studies the relationships between public administrations, media and citizens, in particular focusing on the role of communication and digital technologies. His research interests embrace the characteristics of Web 2.0 and social media and their impact on organizations and citizens' communication behaviours; he also studies public and university communication. In 2011, he received a PhD in Communication Studies from the Department of Communication and Social Research at Sapienza University of Rome, Italy. Previously he has been a visiting scholar at Purdue University, Department of Communication (USA) and an intern at Stony Brook University Office for Technology Licensing and Industrial Relations (USA). Currently he works at the University of Siena Department of Communication (Italy) where he collaborates in the teaching activities of undergraduate and graduate programs. He is on the board of the Italian University Communicators Association (AICUN).

Alberto Marinelli is Full Professor, Sociology of Cultural and Communicative Processes, in the Department of Communication and Social Research at Sapienza University of Rome. He is Course Coordinator for the MS in Cultural Industries and Digital Communication and Member of the Teaching College Board for the PhD Course in Communication. He is Scientist responsible for the Laboratory of Multimedia Communication and member of the Scientific Committee of the CATTID Research Center (Sapienza University of Rome); his research activities are focused on the technological and relational dimensions of interactive communication systems. He is the author and/or editor of several books and papers, including Le reti della comunicazione politica: Tra televisioni e social network (with E. Cioni), Connessioni: Nuovi media, nuove relazioni sociali.

Sorin Adam Matei (PhD, University of Southern California) is Associate Professor of Communication at Purdue University. His research focuses on the social effects of collaborative communication technologies and in designing and studying communication technologies that facilitate the interaction between geographic and virtual spaces. He is the creator of Visible Effort (http://veffort.us), a visualization and self-moderation tool for Mediawiki, and of the ubiquitous publishing platforms Visible Past (http://visiblepast.net), and Ubimark (http://ubimark.com).

Miriam J. Metzger (PhD, Annenberg School for Communication, University of Southern California) is Associate Professor in the Department of Communication at the University of California, Santa Barbara. Her most recent work has examined how information technology alters our understandings of trust in the new media environment, with a specific focus on the credibility of information available on the Internet; and on how trust intersects with privacy and disclosure in online social networks. Prior work has examined media effects generally, the impact of media on public opinion, and the theoretical and regulatory changes brought about by new media technologies.

Mario Morcellini is Full Professor of Sociology of Communication. He is the Dean of the Department of Communication and Social Research, Sapienza University of Rome (Italy), and he has formerly served as the Dean of the Faculty of Communication at the same university. He has also been the Director of several Master's Degrees. He is also the President of the National Conference of the Deans of the Faculties of Communication (Italy) and a Council member of CUN (National University Council, Italian Ministry of University). He is the President of the Teaching College Board for the PhD Course in Communication, Sapienza University of Rome. He has obtained research grants from several public and private institutions. He has authored, edited, or co-edited several books and journal articles. His research has examined the mass media system (with a special focus on television and journalism) and its intersections with digital media; the process of socialization in the age of mass- and digital media; young people's cultural consumptions; the Italian school and university system; media education processes.

Lorenza Parisi studies the interactions between social relations and digital technologies. In her PhD thesis ("Where 2.0"), she explores the impact of digital media on place experience and urban space. She also studies the new trends of political participation based on digital media. In 2011, she received a PhD in Communication Studies from the Department of Communication and social research at the University of Rome La Sapienza. Previously she was a visiting student at HIIT (Helsinki Institute for Information Technology) and at MIT Media Lab (Boston, Mass.). She currently has a research grant from the "Polo Universitario di Colle Val d'Elsa (Italy)," where she is working at the development of the social network "Panmind" (https://panmind.org/).

Rebekah A. Pure is a PhD candidate in the Department of Communication at the University of California, Santa Barbara. She works under Professor Miriam J. Metzger, studying issues of social interaction, privacy, reputation, aggression, and credibility in the digital age. She earned her BA in Speech Communication from the University of Illinois at Urbana-Champaign in 2007, and her MA in Communication from the University of California, Santa Barbara in 2010.

Geraldina Roberti, since 2008, has been Assistant Professor of General Sociology at the Department of History and Comparative Methodologies at the University of L'Aquila, where she teaches Sociology of Ethical Consumption. In 2003, she obtained her PhD in Communication at the Department of Sociology and Communication, Sapienza University of Rome, with a dissertation on: "Young people after 2000: cultures, styles, and media consumptions." Her research is focused on the study of young people identity; cultural consumptions; media audiences; TV and movie language analysis; mass communications theory and application. Among her works are *Multigiornalismi. La nuova informazione nell'età di Internet*, Milano, Guerini e associati, 2001 (with M. Morcellini) and *Mediamente giovani. Percorsi, stili e consumi culturali*, Bulzoni, Roma, 2005.

Anna Lisa Tota is Full Professor of Sociology of Culture and Communication at the University of Rome III, where she teaches Sociology of Communication, Artistic Communication, and Public Communication. Since 2000 she is Invited Professor at the Faculty of Communication Sciences at the University of Lugano (Switzerland). Since 2008 she has been a Guest Professor at the University of St. Gallen (Switzerland). Since 2000 she is an expert evaluator for the European Commission. She is member of the International Advisory Board of the journal *Cultural Sociology* (SAGE) and member of the

Editorial Board of the *European Journal of Cultural Studies* (SAGE). She was Vice-Chair (1999-2001) and Chair (2001-2003) of the Research Network "Sociology of the Arts" of the European Sociological Association. She was Vice-Chair (2005-2007) and is now Chair of the Research Network Sociology of Culture (2009-2011) of the European Sociological Association.

Sonja Utz is an Assistant Professor at the Communication Science Department at VU University Amsterdam. She received her PhD in psychology 1999 from Catholic University of Eichstaett, Germany. Her research focuses on impression formation on social network sites, the effects of social network site use on interpersonal relationships, privacy and trust in Web 2.0, online reputation management, and crisis communication via social media. Her work has been published in major scientific journals, among others in *Journal of Computer Mediated Communication, New media & Society,* and *Communication Research.* She also co-edited the book "*Mediated interpersonal communication.*"

Christo Wilson is currently a third year PhD student in the Computer Science Department, U. C. Santa Barbara working under Professor Ben Y. Zhao. He completed his M.S. ('06-'07) and B.S. ('02-'06) in Computer Science at UCSB. He is currently supported by a Dean's Fellowship from UCSB, and was the previous recipient of a Distinguished Graduate Researcher Fellowship from UCSB. His research focuses on emergent topics pertaining to online social networks, including measurement studies, systems engineering, security, and privacy.

José María Zavala Pérez holds a Bachelor's degree in Sociology (2004, Universidad del País Vasco) with a specialization in politics and society in the contemporary world and a Diploma of Advanced Studies (DEA) with a focus on contemporary problems in the information society (2008, Instituto Universitario Ortega y Gasset – UCM). He is currently PhD candidate at the Universidad Complutense de Madrid and expert at the Living in Surveillance Societies (LiSS) COST research programme.

Ben Y. Zhao is currently an Associate Professor at the Computer Science Department, U. C. Santa Barbara, and a visiting Professor at KAIST. He completed his M.S. and PhD degrees in Computer Science at U.C. Berkeley (2000, 2004), and his B.S. from Yale University (1997). He is a recipient of the National Science Foundation's CAREER award, MIT Technology Review's TR-35 Award (Young Innovators Under 35), and ComputerWorld Magazine's Top 40 Technology Innovators award. His research spans areas of security and privacy, networked and distributed systems, wireless networks, and data-intensive computing. Most recently, he has spent most of his time measuring, analyzing, and modeling online social networks, as well as studying systems issues in dynamic spectrum access networks.

Weiwu Zhang is an Assistant Professor of Public Relations in the College of Mass Communications at Texas Tech University. He is past President of the Midwest Association for Public Opinion Research (MAPOR) (2011). He has published in diverse areas of public opinion, mass communication, and public relations. His current research interests include new media and politics, framing and public relations, media relations, and strategic political communication.

Index

E

F

G

H

I

K

L

M

N

O

P

R

S

T

U

V

W

CPSIA information can be obtained at www.ICGtesting.com
Printed in the USA
BVOW051458071211

277460BV00008BA/3/P

9 781613 503386